Relaxing reefs, exhilarating drift dives and some seriously diverse marine life. From the tiniest critters to massive wrecks... Dive Bequia has got it all.

Opening Hours:

Mon - Sat 8am to 4.30pm.

Sun - By Appointment.

We offer schedule[d] dives departing the[...] 9am, 11.30am and [...]

Private charters available on request

Snorkel Tours to Devil's Table or Moonhole

at 2.30pm

Not a Diver? Want to try?

Come and try a Discover

[...]ffered

[...]e and [...]y FREE!

Spaces are limited, please reserve

Using the PADI system beginners sessions can be counted towards Open Water certification

SPECIAL 10% OFF GUIDED DIVING FOR VISITING YACHTS - JUST MENTION IT!

© www.teup.co.uk

DIVE BEQUIA

TEAM

DIVERSE MARINE LIFE

FRIENDLY DIVE CENTER

BEST DIVE BOATS

SAILORS GUIDE TO THE

Chris Doyle	Text, charts, layout
Lexi Fisher	Assistant
Sally Erdle	Illustrations
Chris Doyle	Photos
Polly Philipson	
Ben Farnham	
Lexi Fisher	
Shaid Rambally	
Marian Cawley	Editor

DISTRIBUTION

USA AND WORLDWIDE
Cruising Guide Publications
P.O. Box 1017
Dunedin, Florida 34697-1017
Tel: 727-733-5322
Fax: 727-734-8179
info@cruisingguides.com

ST. VINCENT & THE GRENADINES
Heather Grant, Erika's, Union Island,
St. Vincent and the Grenadines
Tel: 784-485-8335,
vip@erikamarine.com

ST. LUCIA
Ted Bull, P.O. Box 125
Castries, St. Lucia
Tel/Fax: 758-452-8177
windshift@candw.lc

GRENADA
Alan Hooper, Box 308
St. George's, Grenada
Tel: 473-409-9451
sark@spiceisle.com

Cover photos:
Bequia Regatta, Pitons
Tobago Cays

AUTHOR'S NOTES

In the text we give a very rough price guide to the restaurants. This is an estimate of what you might spend to eat out and have a drink:

$A is $60 U.S. or more
$B is $30 to $60 U.S.
$C is $15 to $30 U.S.
$D is under $15 U.S.

We are happy to include advertising. It gives extra information and keeps the price of the book reasonable. If you wish to help us keep it that way, tell all the restaurateurs and shopkeepers, "I read about it in the Sailors Guide." It helps us no end.

If you like, tell us about your experiences, good or bad. We will consider your comments when writing the next edition.

Chris Doyle
email: sailorsguide@hotmail.com
or: c/o Cruising Guide Publications
P. O. Box 1017, Dunedin
FL 34697-1017
Fax: 727-734-8179

ACKNOWLEDGEMENTS

To everyone who helped; those who sat me down in their bars and shops to explain what they are trying to achieve; those who tapped me on the shoulder and said "know what you should say…"; to all those who have emailed me in suggestions and information – a big thank you to all of you! A special thanks to Jacques-Yves Imbert for his input on St. Pierre, and Jacques and Ciarla Decker, for their help in Martinique.

This book would not be the same without your input. Chris Doyle

WINDWARD ISLANDS

Published by
CHRIS DOYLE PUBLISHING
in association with
CRUISING GUIDE PUBLICATIONS

ISBN_978-0-9914550-9-6

First edition published.............1980
Second edition published 1982
Third edition published...........1984
Third edition revised 1985
Third edition revised 1986
Fourth edition published 1988
Fifth edition published 1990
Sixth edition published 1992
Seventh edition published 1994
Eighth edition published 1996
Ninth edition published............1998
Tenth edition published...........2000
Eleventh edition published......2002
Twelth edition published.........2004
Thirteenth edition published ...2006
Fourteenth edition published...2008
Fifteenth edition published 2010
Sixteenth edition published.....2012
Seventeenth edition published ...2014
Eighteenth edition published...2016

Please check for updates at
www.doyleguides.com

SKETCH CHART INFORMATION

Our sketch charts are interpretive and made for yachts drawing 6.5 feet or less. Deeper yachts should refer to the depths on their charts.
ALL DEPTHS ARE IN FEET

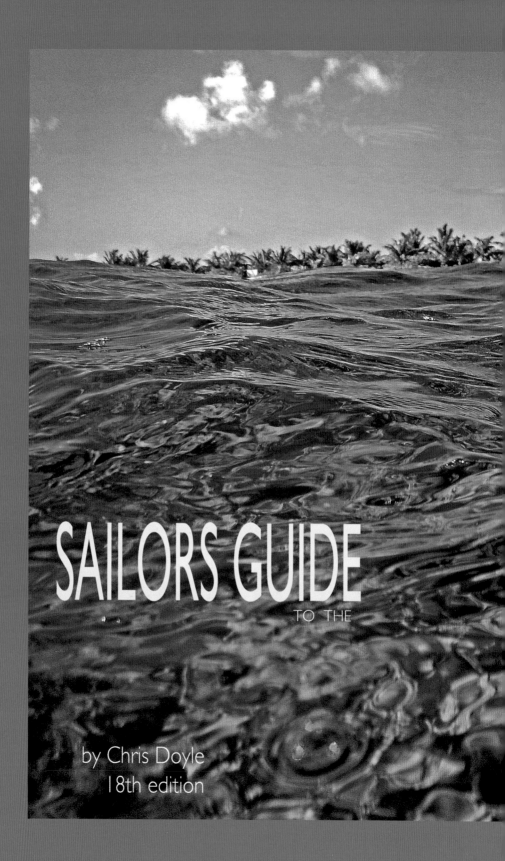

SAILORS GUIDE
TO THE

by Chris Doyle
18th edition

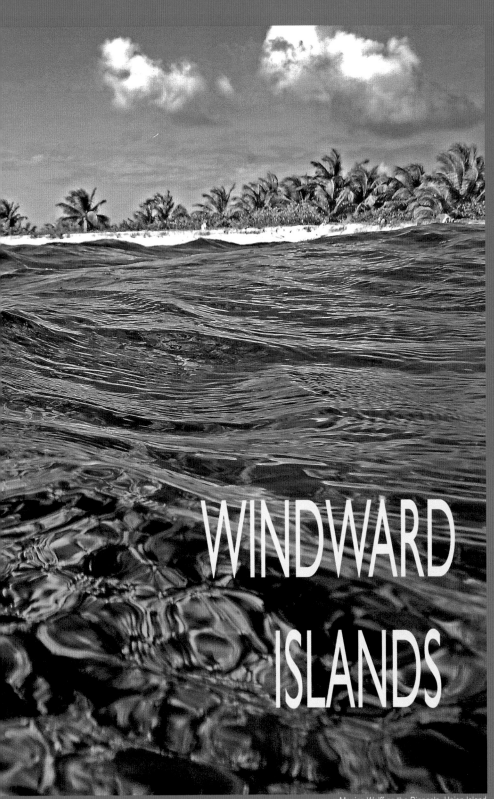

WINDWARD

ISLANDS

Monica Wolff on the Pinnacle, Union Island

TABLE OF CONTENTS

PLANNING AND CRUISING 10

Star Charts 12
Introduction 14
Local Lore 18

Currency 18
Language 18
Tourist Season 18
What to bring 18
Drugs 18
Communications 19
Local etiquette 20
Water skiing 20
Suntanning 20
Local food products 22
Transport 22

Bugs, Beasts, Plants & People 23
Don't let the cockroaches bug you 23
Dangers 24
Taxi Drivers 25
Boat vendors 25
"Tiefs" 28

Photography, Fishing & Medical 29
Entertainment & Special Events 32
Protecting the Environment 34
Cruising Information 39

Weather 39
Local radio 40
Buoyage 42
Tides and currents 42
Charts 42
Distance table 43
GPS 44
Customs & immigration 44
Anchoring 45
Mooring 46
GPS TABLE 48

Chartering 51
Professional Yachts 54
Scuba Diving 57

ANCHORAGES IN THE WINDWARD ISLANDS...................... 60

▌MARTINIQUE 62

Martinique at a glance............................63
St. Pierre 71
Le Carbet...79
Case Pilote...79
Schoelcher..82
Fort de France 83
The Industrial Zones 93
Trois Ilets 98
Trou Etienne 100
Anse Mitan 100
Anse a L'Ane 104
Anse Noir & Anse Dufour 105
Grand Anse D'Arlet 107
Les Anses D'Arlet 109
South Coast of Martinique 111
Baie du Marigot 111
Point Bourgesse to Anse Figiers 113
Ste. Anne 114
Marin...118
East Coast of Martinique 137
Baie des Anglais 137

Passages between Martinique & St. Lucia......................... 139

▌ST. LUCIA 140

St. Lucia at a glance.................................141
Rodney Bay 145
From Cap Estate to Vigie 165
Castries and Vigie 167
Castries Town.......................................167
Vigie...170
Marigot Bay...172
Marigot to Anse La Raye 179
Anse Cochon to Anse La Vedure 181
Anse de Canaries....................................184
Soufriere and the Pitons 185
Anse Chastanet 188
Trou au Diable......................................188
Hummingbird Anchorage...............................189
Soufriere Town......................................192

CONTINUED ON NEXT PAGE

SKETCH CHARTS

Windwards.....................................15

MARTINIQUE
Martinique....................................69
St. Pierre 72
Le Carbet.....................................78
Case Pilote...................................80
Schoelcher....................................82
Approaches to Fort de France 84
Fort de France Anchorage 87
Fort de France Plan 91
The Industrial Zones 96-97
Rivière Salée.................................97
Pte. du Bout to Trois Ilets 99
Anse Mitan...................................103
Anse a L'Ane 104
Anse Noir & Anse Dufour 106
Grand Anse & Anses D'Arlet...................108
Baie du Marigot..............................112
Ste. Luce to Marin Entrance 113
Ste. Anne & Cul de Sac Marin 115
Anchorages south of Ste. Ann 116
Marin..126
Baie des Anglais 137
Passages Martinique/St. Lucia 139

ST. LUCIA
St. Lucia....................................144
Rodney Bay 146
Rodney Bay Lagoon 158
Castries town 168
Port of Castries 170
Marigot Bay..................................174
Anse Pilori to Canaries......................180
Canaries to Anse Chastanet...................183
Soufriere and the Pitons 187
Laborie......................................201
Vieux Fort...................................203
Vieux Fort (plan)............................204
Passages St. Lucia/St. Vincent...............207

ST. VINCENT & THE GRENADINES
St. Vincent..................................211
Chateaubelair................................214
Troumakar Bay................................215
Cumberland Bay...............................215
Wallilabou...................................219
Barrouallie 221
Buccament Bay................................222

CONTINUED PAGE 9

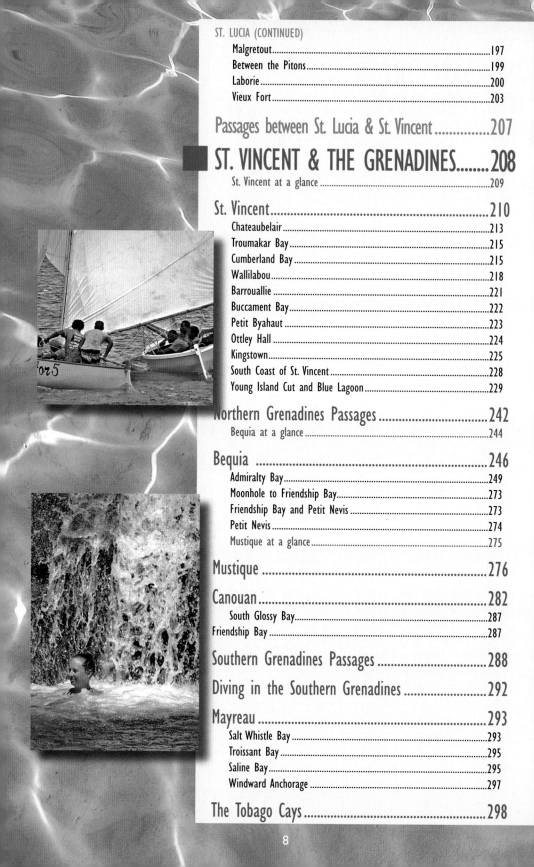

ST. LUCIA (CONTINUED)
Malgretout..197
Between the Pitons......................................199
Laborie..200
Vieux Fort...203

Passages between St. Lucia & St. Vincent...............207

ST. VINCENT & THE GRENADINES........208
St. Vincent at a glance.................................209

St. Vincent...210
Chateaubelair...213
Troumakar Bay...215
Cumberland Bay...215
Wallilabou...218
Barrouallie..221
Buccament Bay...222
Petit Byahaut...223
Ottley Hall..224
Kingstown...225
South Coast of St. Vincent............................228
Young Island Cut and Blue Lagoon.................229

Northern Grenadines Passages....................242
Bequia at a glance.......................................244

Bequia 246
Admiralty Bay..249
Moonhole to Friendship Bay..........................273
Friendship Bay and Petit Nevis.......................273
Petit Nevis..274
Mustique at a glance...................................275

Mustique 276

Canouan...282
South Glossy Bay..287
Friendship Bay 287

Southern Grenadines Passages...................288

Diving in the Southern Grenadines.........292

Mayreau 293
Salt Whistle Bay...293
Troissant Bay...295
Saline Bay...295
Windward Anchorage...................................297

The Tobago Cays...............................298

Palm Island 302

Union Island 303

Clifton 304
Frigate Island 317
Chatham Bay 318

PSV & Petite Martinique 320

PSV 320
Petite Martinique 323

GRENADA & CARRIACOU 326

Carriacou at a glance 327

Carriacou 328

Hillsborough 329
Sandy Island & L'Esterre Bay 334
Tyrrel Bay 337

Passages between Carriacou & Grenada 346

Grenada at a Glance 347

Grenada 348

Halifax Harbour 354
Happy Hill 356
Dragon Bay 356
Grand Mal 356
St. George's 357
Grand Anse 370
Pt. Saline to Prickly Bay 374
True Blue 376
Prickly Bay 381
South Coast beyond Prickly Bay 392
Mount Hartman Bay 393
Hog Island 394
Clarkes Court Bay 395
Phare Bleu Bay 404
Port Egmont 406
Calivigny Harbour 406
Westerhall Point 407
Petit Bacaye 407
St. David's Harbour 408
Grenville 412

WINDWARDS DIRECTORY 414

General Index 428

Advertisers Index 432

SKETCH CHARTS

ST. VINCENT & THE GRENADINES (continued)

Petit Byahaut 223
Ottley Hall 224
Kingstown 226
Young Island to Blue Lagoon 229
Northern Grenadines Routes 241
St. Vincent to Bequia & Mustique .. 242
Bequia 247
Admiralty Bay 248
Port Elizabeth 256
Lower Bay 267
Friendship Bay & Petit Nevis 273
Mustique 277
Canouan 283
Suggested routes to Tobago Cays .. 288
Suggested routes 289
Southern Grenadines 291
Salt Whistle Bay 293
Mayreau and the Tobago Cays 295
Tobago Cays 299
Union Island 305
Clifton Harbour 310
PSV and Petite Martinique 320
PSV anchorage 320

GRENADA & CARRIACOU

Petite Martinique Plan 323
Northwest Carriacou 329
Carriacou 330
Hillsborough 331
Hillsborough to Tyrrel Bay 334
Tyrrel Bay 338
Carriacou to Grenada 345
Grenada 350
Halifax Hbr. to Black Bay Pt. 354
Beausejour to Grand Mal 355
St. George's 358
St. George's Town 367
Southwest Grenada 374
True Blue 376
Prickly Bay to Hog Island 384
Hog Island to Westerhall 397
Westerhall Point to
St. David's Point 408
Grenville 412

PLANNING &

CRUISING

Anse La Roche, Carriacou

STAR

Polaris · CEPHEUS

URSA MINOR · CASSIOPEIA

URSA MAJOR · Capella

LEO · PERSEUS

Denebola · AURIGA

Regulus · Pleiades

FEB · TAURUS

VIRGO · ORION

HYDRA · Betelgeuse

CANCER · GEMINI

CANIS MINOR

ARGO NAVIS · Sirius

CANIS MAJOR

13°N 61°W

N

E ◁◁◀

S

CEPHEUS · Polaris · BOÖTES

URSA MINOR · URSA MAJOR

DRACO · Arcturus

CYGNUS · LEO

Vega · GEMINI

HERCULES · CANCER

· VIRGO

MAY · HYDRA

LIBRA · Spica

SAGITTARIUS · SOUTHERN CROSS

SCORPIO

Antares · ARGO NAVIS

ARA · Hadar

TRIANGULUM AUSTRALIS · Rigil Kent

Times for which our star charts are good:

FEBRUARY		MAY	
January 1st	2400	April 1st	2400
January 15th	2300	April 15th	2300
February 1st	2200	May 1st	2200
February 15th	2100	May 15th	2100
March 1st	2000	June 1st	2000
March 15th	1900	June 15th	1900

CHARTS

CEPHEUS
Polaris
URSA MINOR
CASSIOPEIA
DRACO
PERSEUS
Vega
Deneb
HERCULES
ANDROMEDA
BOÖTES
PISCES
CYGNUS
PEGASUS
DELPHINUS
AUG
AQUARIUS
Altair
CAPRICORN
LIBRA
Fomalhaut
Antares
GRUS
SCORPIO
Al Na'ir
ARA
SAGITTARIUS
TRIANGULUM AUSTRALIS

N
W
S

CASSIOPEIA
Polaris
URSA MINOR
PERSEUS
DRACO
AURIGA
CEPHEUS
Capella
CYGNUS
Pleiades
ANDROMEDA
GEMINI
DELPHINUS
TAURUS
ORION
NOV
Rigel
PEGASUS
Sirius
CAPRICORN
CANIS MAJOR
AQUARIUS
ARIES
Fomalhaut
PISCES
GRUS
CETUS
PHOENIX

Note: Hold this book over your head with the east arrow pointing to the east (normally your bow).

AUGUST		NOVEMBER	
July 1st	2400	October 1st	2400
July 15th	2300	October 15th	2300
August 1st	2200	November 1st	2200
August 15th	2100	November 15th	2100
September 1st	2000	December 1st	2000
September 15th	1900	December 15th	1900

Sailing into the Tobago Cays

Introduction

The islands of the Caribbean sweep southward in a huge arc, like a string of giant-sized stepping stones from Florida to Venezuela. On the eastern, or windward, side, the Atlantic Ocean pounds the shore. On the leeward side, the calmer Caribbean Sea lies tranquil, sparkling in the sun.

The Windward Islands are at the southern end of this chain, the last links before Trinidad and South America. The British called them the Windwards, because you had to beat to windward to get there from many of their other possessions.

They lie almost across the easterly trade winds, which makes for easy passages north or south, and they are just far enough apart to allow for some wild romps in the open ocean before tucking into the calm of the next lee shore.

The four main Windward Islands ~ Martinique, St. Lucia, St. Vincent, and Grenada ~ are lush and richly tropical, with high mountains that trap the clouds and produce dense green vegetation. Here you can find excellent examples of tropical rainforest, easily accessible to those who hike.

Between St. Vincent and Grenada lie the Grenadines ~ a host of smaller islands, some with hills of a thousand feet, others no more than a reef-enclosed sand cay sprouting a few palms. Drier than the large islands, they all have perfect white beaches, crystal clear waters, and colorful reefs.

Over 2000 years ago, the islands were colonized by the Arawaks, an oriental-looking people who were great navigators, artists, and sportsmen. They were somewhat peaceful. Those in residence when Columbus arrived were a more warlike tribe called the Kalinargo, renamed Caribs by Columbus. The Kalinargo resisted the Europeans and refused to be slaves. In Grenada, the northern town of Sauteurs marks the spot where the last of the Grenada Kalinargo leapt to their deaths rather than be taken captive. They held out the longest in St. Vincent, where the steep terrain made colonization harder. Even here the European colonists

THE WINDWARD ISLANDS

N
NW NE
W — E
SW SE
S

MARTINIQUE
ST. PIERRE
FORT DE FRANCE
CAP SALOMON
ANSE D'ARLET
MARIN
ST. ANNE

ST. LUCIA
RODNEY BAY
CASTRIES
MARIGOT
CANARIES
PITONS
VIEUX FORT

ST. VINCENT
CHATEAUBELAIR
GEORGETOWN
WALLILABOU BAY
KINGSTOWN
YOUNG I.
BLUE LAGOON
20

BEQUIA
I. DE QUATRE
BATTOWIA
BALICEAUX
MUSTIQUE
P. CANOUAN
SAVAN I

CANOUAN
MAYREAU
CAYS
UNION I.
HILLSBOROUGH
PSV
P. MARTINIQUE
CARRIACOU
TYRREL BAY

I. DE RONDE
BIRD I.
GRENVILLE
ST. GEORGE'S
GRENADA
PRICKLY B.

14° 30'
14°
13° 30'
13°
12° 30'
12°

62°
61° 30'
61°
60° 30'

Sandy I. Carriacou

Case Pilote house

Upper Concorde Falls

eventually drove them out. Today, just a handful of Kalinargo remain in the Windwards, on the north end of St. Vincent in a village called Fancy.

Years of colonization followed, and the Windward Islands were fought over by the British and French. Plantation owners became rich from the production of sugar, and slaves were brought from Africa to work in the fields. After slavery was abolished, many former slaves showed a healthy disinclination to work for their previous masters, preferring to eke out a living fishing and farming. The planters imported East Indian laborers to take over the fieldwork.

Today, the intermingling of the races has produced an interesting blend of people who live in harmony together.

During its colonial history, Martinique, the northernmost Windward Island, was nearly always in French hands. Today, it is still part of France and therefore a member of the European Community. The language and ambience are French, and while not essential, it certainly helps to speak the language.

St. Lucia, St. Vincent, and Grenada are now all independent nations with a British tradition. Each has its own laws and customs.

The main industries throughout this area are tourism, farming, fishing, and, more recently, international company services and yacht registration. While all the islands produce some rum, Martinique has a large industry producing their own specially flavored product, "Rhum Agricole." Farmers in Martinique also grow excellent pineapples. Grenada has traditionally grown nutmeg and cocoa. St. Lucia and St. Vincent have been heavily involved in bananas. Both Grenada and St. Lucia have artisan chocolate factories that make delicious chocolate.

Tourism is probably responsible for much of the rise in the standard of living that has been visible over the last 30 years. We had a boom in selling land to visitors which tapered off with the last recession. Yachting tourism is a significant factor in the economy of many of these islands, and has encouraged the growth of restaurants, shops, handicraft artisans, and support services. The dollars you spend in the islands really do help the local economy.

The Windwards are a joy for the sailor. Good trade winds ensure exhilarating passages, and delightful anchorages abound. The weather is pleasant year round, the people are friendly, and there are not too many annoying regulations. You are free to sail and enjoy some of the most beautiful islands on earth.

Welcome to the Windwards!

Tobago Cays

Local Lore

Currency

In Martinique the currency is the Euro, currently worth more than the US dollar. Change bureaus give better rates than banks.

In the other islands, the currency is the Eastern Caribbean (EC) dollar, at a fixed bank rate of 2.67 to one US dollar. This is usually a slightly better rate than that offered by shops or taxi drivers, though most people are willing to take US dollars. You get a lot of EC dollars for the US ones, but they are much more quickly spent. Oh well, "EC come, EC go," or, as Jimmy Buffet said: "It's much more fun to spend money with pictures of flowers and palm trees on it than money with pictures of green old men." Spend it all or change it back locally. Bankers just laugh if you try to change it back home.

Credit cards, especially the Visa/MasterCard group, are widely accepted and they are much safer and more convenient than sporting big wads of cash. Let your credit card company know you are traveling so they do not block your card.

Language

In Martinique the language is French, and though an increasing number of people speak English, it is by no means a bilingual society. Some knowledge of French is very helpful. *French for Cruisers*, by Kathy Parsons, is a good aid and, unlike most phrase books, includes boat and engine parts.

In the other Windwards, the official language is English, though the dialect can be hard to understand when locals talk fast among themselves. In St. Lucia, nearly everyone is bilingual. When you sit on a bus or hear people talking in the streets they are usually speaking in Patois, a dialect of French, influenced by English and African, which is the most commonly spoken language. However, English is used when writing or talking to visitors.

Tourist season

Charter and hotel rates vary with the time of year. Most people want to visit when it is cold up north, so the winter

months (November to April) are the high (expensive) season; the rest of the year is low season. Restaurant and bar prices are generally the same year round. During the quietest months (September and October), some small hotels close down and the staff go on holiday.

What to bring

Nearly all visitors bring too much luggage and do not realize that it is almost impossible to stow hard cases on a yacht. Only soft bags should be used. One of my charterers once arrived without luggage, the airline having spirited it away. Rather than wait, he bought a bathing suit, two pairs of shorts, and a shirt and wondered why he had ever bothered packing anything else.

If you need prescription drugs, bring an ample supply and make sure they stay in your carry-on bag.

Life is very informal here, and even in the best of eating places men can get by with a pair of slacks and a sports shirt, women with a simple dress.

Drugs

Marijuana grows in the Windwards and is part of the local Rasta religion. It is, how-

OVERSEAS CALLS
From local private, public, and GSM phones.
This is what you dial from the following islands:

Martinique: 00 + country & area code + number for Zone A & B*

St. Lucia/Grenada/St, Vincent: country & area code + number for Zone A

St. Lucia/Grenada: 011 + country & area code + number for Zone B

St. Vincent: 0 + country & area code + number for Zone B

* Except within French territories, where you just dial the area code
and number.
When dialing overseas, if the first digit of an area code is 0, leave it off.
When dialing Martinique from overseas, the number is +596 596 + 6 digits
(regular phones) or +596 696 + 6 digits (mobile phones)

SATELLITE PHONES
For each phone we give the same example for calling
Grenada, 444-4266

GLOBALSTAR

If you use a Globalstar phone set up for the Americas, it works just like a USA phone: For USA and NANP countries, dial 1 + the country & area code, + 7 digits. To call overseas dial 011 + country & area code + number. Example: dial 1-473-444-4266

IRIDIUM

Dial 00 + the country & area code - e.g. for the USA dial 001 then the area code + 7 digits. Example: dial 00-1-473-444-4266.

INMARSAT

Dial 00 + the country & area code - e.g. for the USA dial 001 then area code + 7 digits + #. The # key is used after all numbers are entered to initiate the call. Example: dial 00-1-473-444-4266-#

Country Codes
Zone A NANP
(North American Numbering Plan)

USA 1-(area code)
Anguilla 1-(264)
Antigua 1-(268)
Barbados 1-(246)
Dominica 1-(767)
Grenada 1-(473)
Montserrat 1-(664)
St. Lucia 1-(758)
St. Vincent 1-(784)
St. Kitts 1-(869)
Trinidad 1-(868)

Zone B
UK 44
Australia 61
New Zealand 64
Austria 43
Germany 49
Guadeloupe 590
Martinique 596
Denmark 45
France 33
Italy 39
Sweden 46
Switzerland 41

Planning & Cruising

ever, illegal, as are most other mind-bending substances except alcohol and tobacco. Laws are very strict, and those caught can expect yacht confiscation and up to life imprisonment (a longer vacation than you may have intended).

Communications

The Windwards have excellent communications with the rest of the world, and even in quite small islands you will find internet cafes. For both general calls and emergencies, have a phone on the boat. From a yachting point of view, the most convenient are the phones that use prepaid cards, so there is no billing. You can buy a GSM phone locally, or bring your own and get a local SIM card ($25-50 EC).

Both Digicel and Lime (Cable and Wireless) are fairly seamless through all the islands from Grenada to St. Lucia (Barbados included). Take your phone with you when you want a recharge. They work well for local and regional calls. Calls outside the region from an island other than the one where you bought your SIM are prohibitive, so it is best to buy another SIM. If you use your phone a lot, then Lime's "anywhere minutes" are a good deal; ask for details. Martinique is on a different system: Digicel will work in Martinique, but for more than a few calls it may be worth getting a Martinique SIM. To make a call in Martinique on a SIM from the other islands, you have to enter a + in front of the phone number. Orange Martinique have a worthwhile deal: for a few Euros you can buy a three-week Caribbean pass, which makes calls to the USA and the Caribbean the same price as the local calls.

If you have a smart phone and cable to your computer, the phone companies all have digital packages. (Turn off automatic updating.) Another solution is wifi, which is widely available; a few stations are free. Unless you want to take your computer ashore, you will need to buy a booster wifi aerial to plug into your USB port. At anchor, turn on your computer and try connecting to likely stations. Once you are connected, just try to open any internet page. If it is an appropriate station, that should initiate the registration.

Satellite phones work everywhere and

Mt. Carmel Falls

some can also handle email. Some cruisers also use an SSB-based service.

Local etiquette

Clothing. Unlike many other western seaside towns, people in the Caribbean will look somewhat askance at you if you wander away from the beach in a bathing suit or, perish the thought, a bikini. Away from the beach, even in that tiny waterfront village, people generally wear at least a shirt and pair of shorts or skirt. In the major towns, people dress much as you would if you were going to your local town.

For women, toplessness, for a while fashionable in Martinique, seems to have died owing to increasing awareness of skin cancer. It is illegal in most other islands. Complete nudity is best confined to anchorages where you can be sure of not being seen.

Greetings. Great store is set on greetings: "good morning" or "good afternoon" (or in Martinique "bonjour" or "bonne nuit"). It is considered rude to approach people with a question or to transact business without beginning with the appropriate greeting.

Tipping. Everyone likes to be tipped, but it is not always expected. In restaurants where no service charge is added, a 10% tip is normal. If service has already been included (as it is by law in Martinique), a little extra is appreciated, but not essential. Taxi driv-

ers do not normally expect to be tipped, but if they go out of their way to help you, you can add a few dollars to the fare to show your appreciation. If you get help from kids carrying your suitcases, they will expect an EC dollar or two.

Water skiing, jet-skis

Local laws require that a water-ski vessel have at least two people on board. Water skiing or jet-skiing within 100 yards of a beach or in harbors where yachts are anchored is strictly forbidden. St. Vincent and the Grenadines have some enlightened environmental laws, and jet-skiing is completely forbidden throughout the country. Jet-skis are also forbidden in the Soufriere Marine Management Area in St. Lucia. Legislation is being considered in other islands.

Suntanning

Whatever the season, the sun is intense and adequate protection is essential. It is advisable to bring down plenty of sunscreen (30+) and use it from the start, building up exposure slowly. The tops of your feet are vulnerable and light cotton socks can help. Loose, long-sleeved, cotton clothing, hats, and sunglasses are essential. Heavy burning can still take place on cloudy days and in shade.

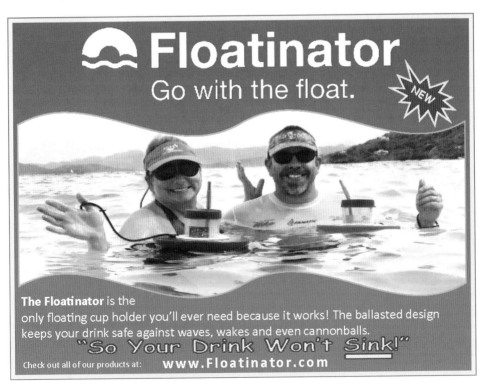
Planning & Cruising

21

Local food products

Many local products, some unavailable anywhere else, are sold in the islands. Some make great presents. Locally bottled peanuts and cashews taste much fresher and better than imported ones. Grenada has two chocolate factories and St. Lucia one. Most islands have local rums, and on every island you will find a big variety of hot sauces. Local cocoa sticks can be grated into hot milk to make a rich cocoa. (Commercial cocoa has had most fat removed.)

Coconut water is sold in bottles in some islands and is delicious. Unfortunately, it has a short shelf life, so is not good to take back home. Many islands offer locally smoked fish.

All the main islands have great fruit and vegetable markets. These are always colorful, but Saturday morning is the best and busiest time, with the greatest selection (Friday in St. Lucia). Never be afraid to ask about things you do not recognize. The market ladies are helpful and will tell you how to cook different vegetables. Some things are not what they appear to be. For example, many fruits that look like bananas have to be cooked.

Transport

If you don't like to hoof it, you have a choice between taxis, buses, communal taxis, and rental cars.

Taxis are plentiful and come in all shapes and sizes. For long trips, some bargaining is usually possible. In any case, always ask for the fare in EC dollars (or, in Martinique, Euros) before you start. If you think you are being quoted too high a figure, try another driver.

Colorful, noisy, and cheerful, the buses in the English speaking islands are the mainstay of the transport system. They often bear such names as "Trust No Man," "De Bad Ride," "In God We Trust," and similar reflections. Not only is this an inexpensive way to travel, but you get to experience some local life. Most nowadays are minibuses. They are not for the claustrophobic, for there is always room for one more on a local bus. Just when you think the whole thing is packed to bursting, the driver's assistant manages to

IATA (FAA) Airport Codes

IATA (FAA) Airport Codes

For on-line booking, or finding out if your travel agent has booked you the right airport

Martinique
FDF - Fort de France

Grenada
GND - Point Saline
CRU - Carriacou

Barbados
BGI - Bridgetown

St. Lucia
SLU - Vigie, Castries
UVF - Vieux Fort, Hewanorra

Trinidad
POS - Port of Spain (Piarco)

St. Vincent Grenadines
UNI - Union Island
MQS - Mustique
CIW - Canouan
BQU - Bequia
SVD - Arnos Vale (Kingstown)

create a tiny square of spare air and, like a conjuror, he whips out yet another seat ~ a pullout piece of wood that is jammed in to take the extra person. Most buses have stereo systems and the drivers like to run them, like their buses, at full bore. The buses are a wonderful example of the kind of service you can get with free enterprise. If you are carrying heavy shopping and wish to go off the normal route, this can be negotiated. In some islands, buses will stop to pick you up anywhere[in others (including St. Lucia), they are only allowed to pick up at designated stops. Buses do get rather few and far between after dark, and may be very limited when going to a distant spot. Before taking off to the other end of an island, make sure there will be a bus coming back.

If you arrive by air at a reasonable hour, without too much luggage, and can make it to the nearest main road, St. Lucia's Hewanorra Airport and the airport in St. Vincent are on bus routes, and Martinique's airport is on a communal taxi route.

Bugs, Beasts, Plants, and People

Don't let the cockroaches bug you

The unmentionable, indomitable cockroach thrives. If you are on a yacht, the odds are that eventually you will find yourself face to face with one of these miniature, armor-plated monstrosities. No need to panic. Despite their off-putting appearance, they are quite harmless, make good pets, and in reasonable quantities are not a reflection of the cleanliness of the boat. A good dose of spray will keep them out of sight for a couple of days. (This will be done automatically on a skippered yacht.) If you are on a boat with a bad infestation, the permanent cure is as follows: First, give a good spray to reduce the numbers (not necessary if you only have one or two). Then, using a mortar and pestle, grind equal quantities of boric acid and white sugar together and distribute freely under drawers, in bottoms of lockers, etc. This will normally give at least six months of cockroach-free living. Some people prefer to mix the boric acid into a gooey mess with condensed milk because they can then stick it on walls and ceilings. I also find some large versions of the "Sticky Box" (usually found in Martinique) to be very

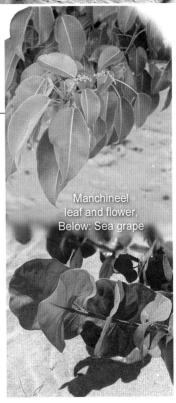

Manchineel leaf and flower, Below: Sea grape

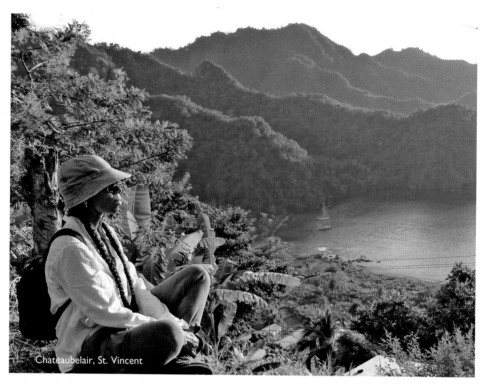
Chateaubelair, St. Vincent

effective. Cockroaches generally arrive on board as stowaways in cardboard cartons or amid fruits and vegetables. It helps to keep "cockroach free" crates and boxes on board and transfer all incoming supplies into them. Examine fruits and vegetables before you stow them. So much for the bad news. The good news is that the boat variety, known as the German cockroach, is relatively small, quite unlike the huge shoreside monsters that grow up to two inches long and are aptly called "mahogany birds."

Aedes aegypti, a mosquito that thrives in the Caribbean, has stripy legs, most often bites by day, and can carry both the dengue zika and chikungunya viruses. Boating folk are less often affected than dirt dwellers, and mosquitoes breed more in the rainy summer months than in the winter. A little repellent spray now and again will help keep you safe.

Mosquitoes are not usually a problem on board because of the breeze, but jungly anchorages or enclosed lagoons on the lee of the large islands are occasionally buggy. If you find yourself in such a bay, you can always resort to the mosquito coil. This is not a contraceptive device for mosquitoes, but a spiral of incense-like material that burns slowly and puts the mosquitoes to sleep. It is effective, but you should be warned that it does not usually kill the bugs and, should the coil go out before you awake, they will be up first and you will be breakfast.

In the evening, beaches can be buggy, especially on a still night in the rainy season, July to November. Worse than mosquitoes are the minute sand flies known as no-see-ums. Any brand of bug repellent will help prevent your sunset barbecue from becoming a free-for-all slapping match.

Dangers

Perhaps we should start with the rum punch. This delicious concoction, a mixture of rum and fruit juice, is available in any waterside bar. It can be positively euphoric in small doses and lethal in large. Strongly recommended at sunset, but be warned that the potency is often stronger than the flavor would suggest.

There are poisonous scorpions and centipedes on the islands, but luckily they are rare and not generally deadly. Still, take a good look at that old pile of twigs and leaves before you sit and take care when picking up coconut husks to burn for your barbecue.

A real danger is the manchineel tree (*Hippomane mancinella*), which grows abundantly along some beaches. This pretty tree with yellow-green apples is toxic. The leaves can produce a rash like poison ivy. It is all right to take shade under the tree, but never stand under a manchineel in the rain, and avoid using the branches for firewood, or that song "Smoke Gets in Your Eyes" may take on new meaning. If you eat the apples, they will cause blisters from stem to stern.

Martinique and St. Lucia are also home to a deadly snake, the fer de lance, which is thankfully quite rare. Various parasites can live in fresh water. Usually they need entry via a break in the skin. It is safest to stick to clear, fast-flowing streams. Swimming in murky, swollen rivers in the rainy season increases the risk.

The main dangers in swimming and snorkeling are negligent and speeding fishermen, yacht-tender drivers, and water taxis. There have been some serious accidents over the years, so swimmers and snorkelers should be aware of small craft movement at all times. Lesser dangers include sea urchins. These are spiny creatures whose prickles penetrate the skin and break off on contact. This is quite painful, especially for the first few hours. They are virtually impossible to pull out once embedded, as they break into little pieces. It is best to leave them in and treat them with hot lime juice, as the acid helps dissolve them.

There are sharks and barracudas, but unlike their cousins in the movies, they have yet to attack anyone in these waters unless harassed and so are not considered dangerous here. There is no question that spearfishing can excite these fish. I have dived and snorkeled at night with no problem, but since so few people swim at night, it is impossible to assess how safe it is. Despite their reputation, moray eels are short-sighted and timid, but it would be pushing your luck to stick your hand into holes in rock or coral.

Corals eat by stinging their prey, and many can sting you, so look and do not touch. This is also better for the coral. Coral scratches can become infected. If you get one, scrub it well with soap and fresh water. Stinging jellyfish are not frequent but do exist, and occasionally the swimmer may feel a mild tingling from minute animals known as sea ants. If you do get a jellyfish sting, soaking with vinegar can help

A good book on dangerous marine animals would certainly list some more horrors, but the truth is that harm from any of these is extremely rare and, provided you watch where you put your hands and feet and keep an eye on the sea conditions and current, snorkeling is safer than doing the weekly ironing and a lot more fun.

Taxi drivers

Taxi drivers are often colorful characters, owners of highly individualized cars, and they have a fund of local knowledge. The ambitious ones, who used to act as commission agents as well, running around shopping, tracing lost luggage, and obtaining hard to find parts, have morphed into yacht agents. In Martinique, only a few of the drivers speak English, though they will bear with your French.

Unfortunately, among the good ones there are an overenthusiastic few who will bully or confuse the unwary passenger into going on a tour he or she really does not want. There are two basic rules: always discuss and agree on a price before you embark on a taxi ride and make sure you are both talking the same kind of dollars (EC or US) or, in Martinique, Euros.

Boat vendors

At some point, there will be a thump on your topsides and a voice shouting "Hey skip, want some limes? How about a nice T-shirt? Or a coconut boat? It sails very good." You are in islands with a great spirit of free enterprise ~ better get used to it. From the skipper's point of view, the most harrowing thing is that these vendor's boats are often built of several hundred pounds of rough wood and exposed nail heads, which bang your topsides as they hawk their wares. Their cheerful cry of "no problem, skip" does nothing to remove the scratch.

Planning & Cruising

25

The problem is exacerbated in some areas where the competition is so keen that you may be approached two miles from port. This most often occurs with line handlers in the Soufriere/Pitons area in St. Lucia and the Cumberland/Wallilabou area in St. Vincent. In these places, line handlers offer a useful service, because the water is so deep it is necessary to drop an anchor and tie stern to a palm tree, and they help you tie up. However, some vendors you meet way out will want you to tow them in. It is unwise to tow these heavy boats a long way and there are always line handlers close to the shore, so refuse these offers. You can tell them your insurance does not allow for towing. When you get closer to shore, come to a standstill and negotiate the price before handing over any lines. (I offer a set fee of $10-20 EC on a "take it or leave it" basis.) When finally at anchor, put out at least two big fenders and make sure any local boats coming alongside stay on them.

You will probably be offered, at various times, t-shirts, jewelry, fruit, scrimshaw, model boats, ice, and bread. It is worthwhile to consider what is offered.

Vendors are part of the local scene and endemic to undeveloped countries with struggling economies. Some visitors enjoy the interactions and the opportunity to do business in this way; most vendors are friendly and helpful. However, those who have no prior experience with vendors can find them irritating, and I have had letters from people saying they would not revisit some anchorages because of their experiences with vendors.

Dealing with vendors is easier once you know to expect them. Be straightforward, look them in the eye, always demand professional behavior, and keep your sense of humor and you will be okay. If you imagine yourself in their position, it is not hard to figure out how they operate and why.

You will find vendors in the Grenadines, St. Vincent, and St. Lucia. In the Grenadines, most are very professional. If you say no, they will leave you in peace. On the other hand, the situation on the west coast of St. Vincent reminds me of the airport in Grenada back in the early '70s, when it was very amusing to watch the hapless and unsuspecting passenger stagger forth into the daylight with his three or four suitcases. Within seconds, three or four taxi drivers would rush up and each grab a bag and head in a different direction, entreating the passenger to follow as loudly as they could. He would stand confused and sweating in his traveling suit, wondering if this was the start of a trip to hell. Clearly, things could not go on that way, and a taxi-driver union was formed to prevent the chaos of competition. Such an organization would be helpful for boat vendors in Wallilabou, St. Vincent, where people sometimes find themselves surrounded by vendors all shouting at once. They have now formed an association, and we will see how it goes. In St. Lucia, where it used to be like that, some strides have been made in the Soufriere Marine Management Area, and some vendors and taxis are now licensed and are helpful.

People sometimes complain that while vendors are fine, there are just too many of them. If I were a charterer (prime customers for vendors; cruising folk don't have as many problems), I would make a couple of clearly visible signs I could hang from the lifelines near the cockpit saying "I am not buying now, leave me in peace ~ visit again when this sign is down."

You may also get vendors you should clearly not do business with. Sometimes someone will come out to your boat touting a local restaurant. This is fair enough, but when he or she tells you not to visit the other restaurant because the food is bad and the cockroaches in the kitchen are the size of small rats, common sense should tell you this is not an unbiased judgment. Some visitors are naive enough to heed such advice, and end up with the worst meal in the harbor as a result. (There is logic to this: restaurateurs who encourage such unscrupulous behavior are likely to be equally dastardly in the kitchen and in dealing with customers.) People have sometimes paid youths to watch their dinghy, which has resulted in the creation of an unnecessary service by dinghy watchers who are often rude. Lock your dinghy on with a cable and refuse such service, unless you really want it. Make sure

PROTECT YOURSELF AGAINST PETTY THEFT
If you take the following precautions, you are unlikely to have a problem

✔ Lock up when you leave the boat, and leave someone on board at night in main towns like St. George's, Castries, and Kingstown.

✔ Lock your outboard onto your boat at night.

✔ Lock your dinghy to the dock by day and onto your yacht by night.

✔ Be cautious about inviting strangers on board.

✔ Do not bring big wads of cash; use credit cards instead. Do not leave cash on the boat. Insure valuables such as cameras.

✔ Don't leave things unattended on the beach or in the dinghy in public places.

✔ Bring copies of CDs rather than your orginals.

your locking line is at least 16 feet long so that you do not block others approaching the dock. Never leave your outboard raised, as it is likely to damage other boats.

Some kids beg. "It's my birthday, what are you going to give me?" is a favorite line. It is important to bear in mind that wages for an unskilled adult may only be $50-100 EC a day. If young kids end up getting twice that much liming around the docks, begging from tourists, or getting grossly overpaid for watching dinghies, they skip school and it is hard for them to adjust later when they need to go out to work. By all means, employ kids and find something useful for them to do; that helps the economy. But just throwing money around can be harmful. For those who like to give away money, there are a few beggars who have handicaps. Local associations for the handicapped are also happy to accept donations.

"Tiefs"

Most islanders and yachtspeople are very honest, but obviously there are shady characters, too: thieves, con men, and extortionists. Dinghies and outboards are sometimes stolen at night. It is hard to say how many, because no one wants to admit that his dinghy disappeared after that final rum punch because the "rabbit" lost its way while going through the "hole" to make the bowline. There have been cases where a dinghy was returned the next day and the finders demanded huge sums for the "rescue."

Boats occasionally get robbed when

people are ashore. The thieves are mainly looking for cash and easily saleable items. Instead of cash, use credit cards (Visa, and MasterCard are most widely accepted). Insure valuables such as cameras and binoculars. This way, if you do get a break in, the results will not be as bad.

There are a few locals who will provide a service and then demand outrageous sums, so always ask the price before accepting any service, including taxis. Make sure you are both referring to EC dollars.

Violent crimes, like armed robbery, assault, and rape, are rare but not unknown on yachts. Cruisers tend to be more worried than charterers, as they stay a lot longer. If you sleep with all hatches open, a portable chime alarm will help wake you if someone boards. An air fog horn and very bright light are my second line of defence. After 40 years of cruising I have not had to deploy them yet.

If you are planning to walk or hike into remote places, it doesn't hurt to ask around first, especially if you are alone or with just one other person. Daytime is generally safer than night. Keep in mind that while the islands are generally safe, there are isolated incidents, as there are anywhere in the world. For current information on where there are problems, ask in any charter company office and check my website (www. doyleguides.com), read the updates, and go to the security links on the advisories page. Also, read the free waterfront newspaper, *Caribbean Compass*, which often highlights areas where there are problems.

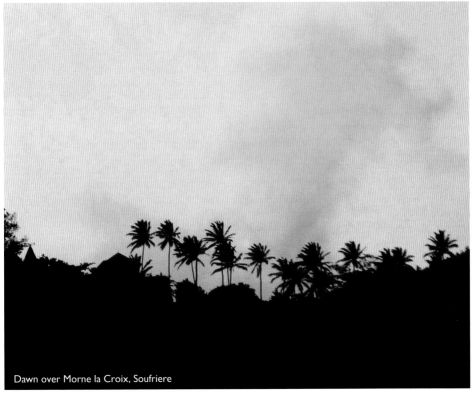

Dawn over Morne la Croix, Soufriere

Photography, Medical & Fishing

Photography

These days we are all using digital cameras, which makes photography much easier: instant results and no more running around looking for film.

The light in the Windwards is so bright that colors often photograph better in the early morning or late afternoon. This changes radically when you venture into the rainforest, where light levels are so low that a tripod is useful for long exposures.

Learn enough about the setup of your camera that when you venture into the forest you can take pictures with the camera set at an equivalent of 400 ASA.

A polarizing filter can really enhance sea shots, giving dramatic results. You can watch the colors change as you twist the filter. Keep an eye on the sky as well as the sea, as it will turn gray at some angles.

It is polite to ask when you want to photograph someone. Local attitudes can be a little strange. People with cameras sometimes become a focal point for frustrations and feelings of being exploited. If you try to take a crowd scene, someone will often object, and funnily enough, that person might not even be in the picture. Vendors who deal with tourists are usually happy to say "yes," especially if you are buying something. Digital cameras help, as you can show the subject their image on the screen after you have taken it.

Medical care

There is adequate medical care for most ailments in all the larger islands, and any hotel or charter company will help you get in touch with a doctor. In emergencies, remember that all cruise ships stand by on VHF: 16 and have doctors on board. If you

29

have a life-threatening situation or a serious head injury, plan on immediate transport to Martinique or Barbados. SVG Air (784-457-5124) do medical flights; the big hospitals may be able to organize a helicopter ambulance.

For diving accidents where decompression is needed, call Martinique's main hospital or Tapion, St. Lucia, or Barbados, (246) 436-6185, for immediate evacuation.

Martinique: For advice on facilities and to help with arrangements, call Douglas Yacht Services: 0696 45 89 75. The main hospital is Hôpital Pierre Zobda-Quimann (0596) 55 20 00. For lesser ailments, try Dr. Monique Roussi, (0596) 58 90 16, in Marin Marina, or Dr. Jean Louis Deloge and Dr. Veronique Claisse (office 0596 74 98 24) in Marin.

St. Lucia: For most problems, the Rodney Bay Medical, (758) 452-8621, or the M-Car Medical Clinic, (758) 453-2552/452-9032, both within walking distace of the JQ supermaket dinghy dock in Rodney Bay, will suffice.

Tapion Hospital, (758) 459-2000, is a kind of medical mall with all kinds of doctors. Dr. Andrew Richardson, the general surgeon (also a sailing man), is good, and may also be consulted as a regular doctor. Tapion has a hyperbaric chamber for divers.

For dental care, Dr. Glace, in Rodney Bay, can handle everything from fillings to implants, (758) 458-0167.

St. Vincent: Maryfield Hospital, Kingstown: (784) 457-8991 (highly recommended by some of our readers).

In the **Grenadines**, Mustique is a good place to get sick. There is an excellent small clinic, (784) 458-4621 (ask for the clinic), situated next to the airport, in case you need to be flown out for further treatment. Bequia (784) 458-3294, VHF: 74 (24 hours), has a doctor and a little clinic in Port Elizabeth that responds to emergency calls. For dental care, Profamdental: (784) 529-2480/ 529-0745 run by Johanna Osborne, a dental and maxillofacial surgeon, has a surgery in St. Vincent weekdays and one in Bequia on Saturday mornings.

Grenada: If you need hospitalization, try the St. Augustine's Medical Clinic, (473) 440-6173/5. It is quite complete, with a lot of modern equipment.

For a doctor, Dr. Michael Radix, (473) 444-4850/440-4379 surgery or (473) 443-5330 home, is a good old-school doctor, who is pleasant to visit and makes house calls. If you need surgery, Dr. Yearwood is a general surgeon and urologist (also a competitive yachtsman): Ocean House, Grand Anse, (473) 444-1178. Dr. Jenny Isaacs is a good dermatogolist, (473) 440-3963

Good dentists includeDr. Roxanne Nedd, (473) 444-2273, in the Excel Mall in Grand Anse, and Island Dental Care (Dr. Tara Baksh and Dr. Victor Samaan), Wall Street, Grand Anse, (473) 437-4000.

Fishing

In some islands, dive shops organize hunts for the invasive lion fish, which can be good eating. They use special three prong spears. Otherwise, forget spearfishing, Hawaiian slings, pots, nets, and diving down to pick up conch or sea urchins; it is illegal for visitors to engage in these activities. Fishing regulations are very strict. Even though trolling and handlining may not be strictly legal unless you have a license, most islands have agreed to turn a blind eye to these activities, unless you are in a marine park or protected area. This courtesy does not extend to sports-fishing boats, which usually need a license. So, leave the rest, but get out your rod and enjoy.

Trolling for fish is fun, and fish you catch yourself taste better. If you are on a short holiday, you can just walk into any fishing-tackle shop and buy a couple of ready-to-go lines, complete with lures. Shell out extra for (or create) a good device that will let you know you have caught a fish. If you do not know a fish is there, it will likely break the line and you will lose both lure and fish. Setting two lines, one from each side of the boat doubles your chance of catching a fish. Set the lee long (about 50 yards) and keep the other short (about 25 yards); a little skipping does not hurt). Haul in for a weed check every 40 minutes or so. Remove any weeds.

When you catch a fish, you may need to slow the boat. If you have two lines out, have someone reel in the empty one so it doesn't get tangled. One easy way to slow down is to furl the jib. Luff also, if necessary,

skipjack tuna
not shown:
blue fin tuna
yellow fin tuna
big eye tuna

yellow tail snapper

rainbow runner

tuna is thon
in French

great barracuda

Spanish mackerel

black fin tuna

albacore

wahoo (thazar in French)

kingfish

unmistakable
shape of the
dolphin fish
or dorado
(dorade in
French)

tuny fish
(ti thon in French)

Planning & Cruising

but not until the spare line is in. Gloves are a big plus when you heave your catch out of the water and into the cockpit, or at least on deck where someone can hold it. I put mine in an ice box, as this cuts down on the mess.

Proper reels are best. Not only will you instantly know when you have a fish, but the give of the reel will stop you losing the occasional fish when it strikes.

If you are making your own rig, you need a swivel on the end of your line, and a wire leader helps. Have the wire leader at about 10 lb lower breaking strain than the line so that a monster does not break the line. A test line of around 80 lb should bring in most of the fish you will catch. The lighter the line and gear, the more strikes you will get, but the more fish you will loose.

Any fish you catch out in open water will almost certainly be good to eat. Ciguatera fish poisoning, common farther north, is a rarity here. One might be suspicious of a really large barracuda that could be down from up north visiting relatives, but smaller barracuda (around 5 lb) are delicious. Dorado, the tuna family (including tuny fish), albacore, and wahoo are not considered risky even in bad areas up north.

The photos of the most common catches are to help with identification.

They were taken after the fish had been caught, so most of the subjects have lost a lot of color. The dorado (or dolphin fish; no relation to flipper) is the most dramatic at this ~ it gives a brilliant display of bright color, then fades to nothing. Most fish will change color significantly before your eyes, so shape and markings need to be taken even more seriously than color when making an identification. If you get a fish with a really large eye, it is probably a horse-eye jack. They are not choice, and are very bony, but some people eat them.

Fish can have worm-like parasites. Both cooking and deep-freezing will kill them. However, if you do the sushi thing, observe the flesh closely; the worst parasites are visible to the eye.

Lobster season is usually from the first of October to the end of April. During this time, lobsters can be bought from local fishermen, and the most likely places to find them are Mustique, Union, the Tobago Cays, and P.S.V.

It is against the law to buy lobster out of season, lobsters less than 9 inches long, or lobsters bearing eggs at any time, and the fines are steep. You may be offered one, but please refuse.

Entertainment & Special Events

Green flash

In the evenings, sunset brings an opportunity to look for the elusive "green flash." This happens as the sun disappears below the horizon. For about a second (blink and you've missed it), the very last bit of the sun to disappear turns bright green. To see this you need a clear horizon and the right atmospheric conditions. Some say rum punch helps. Binoculars make it a lot clearer. Photographers will need a telephoto lens and an auto drive.

Entertainment

The most popular form of evening en-

tertainment is the "jump up." This usually happens in one of the bars or hotels and takes the form of a dance, most often to a live band. If enough rum flows, everyone does indeed "jump up." Both Martinique and St. Vincent have casinos, but these are very low-key. Most of the larger hotels offer evening dancing with a floorshow. Some hotels serve Sunday lunch to the accompaniment of a steel band. You can dance, swim, or just enjoy the music.

Special events

There are a variety of local festivals

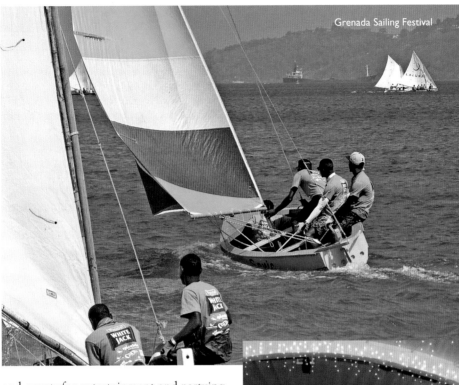

Grenada Sailing Festival

and events for entertainment and partying. If you happen to be here at the right time, they are worth investigating; some are worth a special trip.

Carnival started as a riotous bacchanal before Lent. Carnivals feature costumed parades, calypso contests, steel bands, and days of dancing in the street. Martinique still has their carnival before Lent, but St. Vincent, St. Lucia, and Grenada have switched. Check our information on holidays at the beginning of each island section.

St. Lucia has a jazz festival that lasts about a week in early May. Some of the events are on Pigeon Island, and you can anchor your yacht below. Basil, in Mustique, runs a small but good blues festival in both Mustique and Bequia sometime during late January or early February. Carriacou has a Maroon and String Band Festival around the end of April/beginning of May. Carriacou has a Parang Festival before Christmas.

You can join in sailing events. Martinique has a fun week in early June, with races from port to port around the island and plenty of good food and entertainment. If you are here on July 14th, the French na-

tional holiday, you may see yole (pirogue) races around Fort de France. Yole races also feature in each coastal village during celebrations for the village's patron saint. Anyone interested can get a list from the local tourist office. Martinique has a series of races that tour the island over several days in January and a sailing week at Schoelcher in February.

St. Lucia has many events, including the big Mango Bowl Regatta, usually held in late November or early December.

Bequia's Easter Regatta is well worth attending. It includes yacht races, local "two-bow" fishing boat races, model boat races, and cultural shows.

The Grenada Sailing Festival is held in January. It is a program of race events backed by a well-organized social program. All entrants are welcome, from serious racing boats to live-aboards. The Round Grenada race, a two day event with a stop in Carriacou, is arranged by the Petit Calivigny Yacht Club (PCYC) and normally takes place in August. The Carriacou Regatta, in late July or early August, is a local event featuring races for small fishing boats and the larger cargo-carrying sloops. These are some of the finest sailing vessels made in the islands. Ashore there is plenty of fun.

People lose more dinghies in regattas and big parties than at any other time. Some drunks take the wrong dinghy and then fail to secure it. Other drunks untie your dinghy while trying to untie their own and let it go adrift. Many dinghies tied together tempt theives. Lock it up for security, especially during regatta time!

Protecting the Environment

Most visitors are courteous and well behaved. With the increasing volume of yachts in the area, it definitely helps to be considerate. Anchorages here have been reasonably free of loud noises, including drunken raucous laughter, stereo equipment, endlessly running generators, and loudly clanking halyards. Luckily, there is plenty of room in most anchorages, so those who want to make noise or need to run generators for much of the time can just stay well away from everyone else. Most of us have to run our engines at some time during the day, but let us at least leave the hour around sunset free, so everyone can enjoy it in peace.

One or two inconsiderate people still blast the anchorage with the sound of a noisy windmill. Most makes are quiet and unobtrusive, yet a few can be heard well over a hundred yards away. They destroy the natural peace of many a quiet anchorage. Plus, some people who own them seem to think that because they are not using fossil fuels, they are on the side of the angels and can do no wrong. They run them 24 hours a day without giving any consideration to others who find the noise irritating. These windmills do not have to be obnoxious; quiet blades are available for most brands. If you have not yet bought a windmill, make sure the one you buy is quiet or, if you want to be sure, use solar panels. If you already own a noisy one, and cannot be bothered to get the quiet blades, try to anchor to the back of the fleet, and when your batteries are charged up, stop the blades.

Right now you can don a mask and snorkel and dive in the water anywhere in the Windwards and find the seabed pretty clean. Let's keep it that way.

Fishing and hunting

The days have gone when we could jump over the side, bristling with knives and festooned with spearguns long enough to be sold by the yard, to decimate the local fish population. Spearfishing has proved too damaging and new laws have been passed to control it. It is now illegal for visitors to spearfish (or Hawaiian sling) anywhere from St. Lucia to Grenada. It should be mentioned that spearfishing, apart from being completely illegal, is very harmful to the environment; spears that miss their target can damage coral and allow infection to take hold. Gloved hands grabbing coral, can also stress the reef. Most speared fish are reef cleaners, so fishing them can affect the whole ecosystem. Lobsters, when caught this way, cannot be sized and checked for eggs. For this reason, even locals are not allowed to spearfish lobsters; they must use a snare. Try not to give moral support to other cruisers who boast about their spearfishing exploits.

34

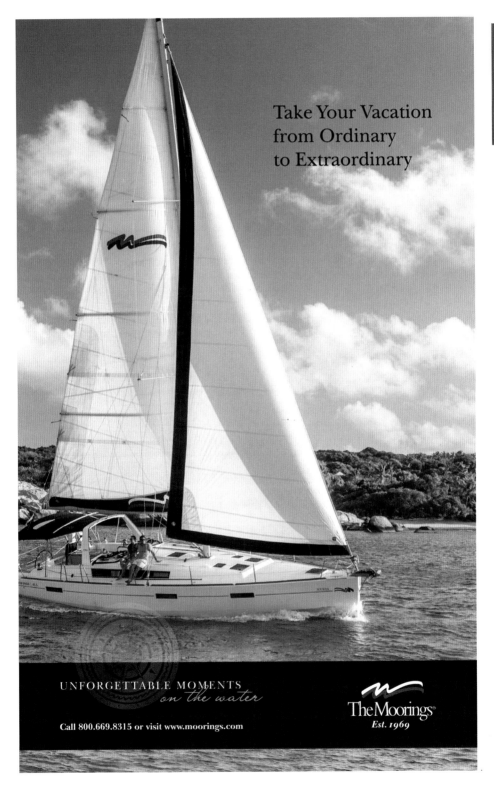

It is a bad thing to do, especially now, when reefs are already degraded, at least in part because of us.

Hunters should note that all cows, goats, and sheep, even on remote uninhabited islands, are privately owned. They are often put out to graze and left for months on end. They should not be harmed.

Garbage

Yacht garbage can be a problem in the Grenadine Islands, where it can totally overwhelm the available facilities. We need to cut down on what we bring ashore, and we have to be careful what we bring ashore. Food waste of all kinds should be stored in a separate container and dumped, far from reefs, when you are out at sea in deep water. Carrying organic matter from one island to another as garbage is a dangerous practice. Island agriculture is very sensitive, as we saw some years ago when an introduced pink mealy bug spread rapidly through some of the Windward Islands, costing millions of dollars in lost produce. More recently, a mango worm was introduced to Grenada, causing greeat harm. Organic matter may contain fruit flies, cockroaches, fungi, and other potentially dangerous pests, so take care when transporting and disposing of fresh fruit and vegetable matter. In addition, it is unwise to transport things like woven palm hats and baskets between islands.

Most harbors are open to the west, and if you are stuck in such a harbor too long, dinghy the food waste as far out of the harbor as you can and dump it there, preferably at dusk. Never do this in places like the Tobago Cays, where there are islands and reef downwind. Rinse all your empty cans and containers in seawater before putting them in the trash.

It is best to buy things with as little packing as possible and use returnable bottles. Take along your own shopping bags and avoid those plastic ones.

In addition, yachtspeople have caused considerable degradation by letting locals dispose of their garbage for a fee. Never give garbage to vendors. Some will offer to take your garbage for a couple of dollars. However, these people have no proper means of disposing of it. The good ones try to burn it, but combustion is never complete and the remains are left strewn around. Others dump your garbage in holes in the bushes, and the worst take it to the nearest beach, rummage through for items of interest, and abandon it. You are responsible for your own garbage. If you give it to someone else for a fee, they are considered your employee, and if they litter with your garbage, you are responsible.

Never throw plastics, including bags and bottled water containers, at sea. Leatherback turtles eat jellyfish, and many have been found dead, their stomachs filled with plastic bags. Smelly bags can be rinsed in the ocean before storing. Other items that should never be thrown out at sea include string and fishing line, which might form a tangle trap somewhere or be eaten, or plastic-lined cardboard cartons (juice cartons, etc.) and tin foil. These can be rinsed in seawater before stowing. Similarly, anything that could be the least bit toxic, including aerosol sprays and chemicals, should not be dumped at sea.

Most garbage consists of paper, cardboard, cans, and bottles. Should we throw these at sea? Ideally, no. The ocean is not a dumping ground, and if we are not very careful where we dump such garbage, we can damage reef structures. On the other hand, we should not take these items ashore and dump them in the Grenadines, where the facilities are totally inadequate. So what to do? As far as possible, keep such garbage for an adequate refuse facility in one of the larger islands. Martinique has plenty of places to put garbage, and you will find adequate facilities in Rodney Bay and Marigot Bay in St. Lucia, and in The Yacht Club and Spice Island Marine in Grenada.

If you are unable to do this, then it is probably marginally better to dump non-returnable bottles, cans, shredded paper, and cardboard far from land, with no islands or reefs in the lee, in water over 600 feet deep, than it is to pile them in a heap on land where they are not being collected. Paper and cardboard will eventually dissolve (though we do not know about the toxicity of the inks printed on them). Cans and bottles will sink and sit on the seabed, which, in deep water, is mainly sand or mud;

Grenada's Interior, Rosemount Estate

they provide homes for baby fish. Nothing should ever be dumped near a reef or in an anchorage.

Holding tanks

I have not yet seen a convincing study showing that pumping toilets into our anchorages has a measurable ecological impact. However, it can have an aesthetic one, and it is reassuring to know you are swimming in water that someone has not just dumped in. Some marine parks are now asking people to use holding tanks. If you do not have one, you can make a temporary one using a bucket (and a lid for when not in use), and carrying a bag of sawdust. Sprinkle the sawdust before and after each use. Empty and rinse the bucket after you have left the anchorage. Use the regular head for pee.

Save our reefs

In minutes, anchors can destroy what nature has taken generations to build. A coral structure is a colony of millions of minute animals called polyps. They are fragile, and reefs grow very slowly. Always anchor on sand, never on coral. If there is any doubt, have someone snorkeling when you drop your anchor. Dinghy anchors also do harm, so use a sand anchor for your dinghy and anchor on the sand beside the coral, rather than on the coral itself.

When snorkeling or diving, be careful of coral structures. Avoid standing, bumping into, getting swept onto, or grabbing coral. Even a small amount of damage can open a coral to being taken over by sponges and algae. Don't wear gloves when diving and snorkeling, and never take anything from the reef.

Eco-purchasing

Few people realize how powerfully their dollars speak, and one of the very best things you can do for the environment is to spend wisely.

Dollars spent on wood carvings, jewelry made from decorative local seeds, banana crafts, straw goods, woven grasses, art, and anything made from coconut shells will really help the economy and the environment. Jewelry made from conch shells is also okay, as these are caught for their meat and the shell is otherwise thrown away. (However, check importation regulations in your home country.) T-shirts and other locally manufactured items are fine, too.

Avoid buying coral and turtleshell products. Considerable damage to reef structures is done by youths who take corals to sell to

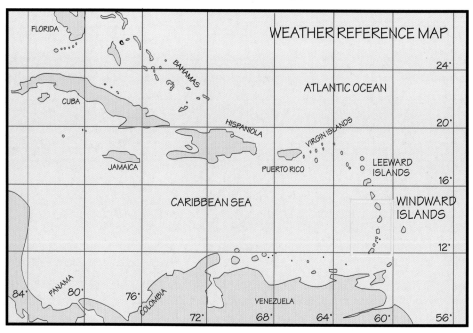

jewelry makers. The hawksbill turtle, most often killed for its shell, is an endangered species, as are all Caribbean sea turtles, and importation of turtle shell is forbidden in most countries. These items are sold mainly to yachts, so let us say "no" to these vendors and support the turtles and reefs. If you visit during the lobster season and are buying lobsters, always turn them over to see if they have eggs underneath (easily seen as red caviar). If they do, refuse to buy them.

I am happy to say that in the years since I included this paragraph, the amount of coral and turtle shell products offered to yachtspeople has diminished significantly. Thank you!

One purchase that might significantly affect the environment is your choice of antifouling. TBT paints have been banned nearly everywhere in the world for their damage to the environment. In the Caribbean they are still legal. Make sure you know what your paint has in it, and choose wisely.

Cruising Information

Weather

Continuous sunshine and balmy trade breezes, right? Well, not too far wrong.

There are two seasons, the dry and the wet, but they are not always well differentiated. During the dry season (February to June), there will often be weeks of clear, sunny weather broken only by an occasional small rain shower. In the wet season (July until January), there will still be plenty of sunshine, but with more frequent showers and occasional rainy days with no sun. There is very little temperature difference between the seasons; you can expect 78° to 87°F (25° to 31°C) year round.

The winds nearly always blow from between northeast and southeast at 10 to 25 knots; calms are rare. The wind tends to strengthen around the northern ends of islands. Rain usually arrives in intense squalls that can be seen coming from afar. Sometimes these squalls have a lot of wind in them (40 knots or more); often they do not. There is no way to tell before they arrive. Infrequently, a squall or cold front produces westerly winds, making the usual anchorages uncomfortable to untenable.

During the winter months, storms and cold fronts farther north sometimes produce swells that reach the Windwards. These northerly swells can make anchorages that are open to the north or west rolly and occasionally untenable. Few swells are really bad, but when they are, you have to be prepared to move to a calmer spot, even in the middle of the night. Swells have caused the demise of quite a few unattended yachts. Hurricanes also cause swells during the hurricane season. These swells may come from any direction, depending on the position of the storm.

In the winter a big high-pressure area to our northeast is a dominant feature. When the isobars get tight, the wind increases and is sometimes very fresh (25-30 knots). We call these Christmas winds. This high pressure is offset by cold fronts that come down from the northwest. They almost never make it as far as the Windwards, but as they approach, we often get very calm and sunny weather followed by wind and rain, as their tail ends affect this area.

Visibility varies from an exceptional low of 5 miles to a high of over 50 miles. Extremely hazy days are caused by dust from Africa. Sometimes, reddish traces may be found on the cabin and decks. On hazy days, avoid dust stains when doing the laundry by wiping off the lifelines before hanging out the washing.

The hurricane season is from June to October. People now talk of "named storms," only about half of which will reach hurricane strength. Hurricane frequency for the months of June, July, and October is about one hurricane every three years for the whole western Atlantic, including the Caribbean

LOCAL RADIO

For news, views, and weather

FM
Grenada Broadcasting Network, Hott FM
98.5, 1055,
also 540 AM
St. Vincent Radio ------------------705
Waves (St. Lucia) ----------------94.5, 93.7
   weather daily at 0730 & 1630
Sound of the Nation
(St. Vincent)-----------------------90.7, 107.5
   weather at 0700 after news and ads
St. Vincent -------------------------100.5,
   weather 0745
Radio Caraibes (French)---------89.9

HAM & SSB (local times)
East Caribbean weather, 8137 kHz USB
   @0700
East Caribbean weather, 8137, 1235
   kHz USB @0830
Caribbean emergency /weather net,
   3815 kHz LSB @ 0630
NMN Offshore forecast 4426, 6501 &
   8764 kHz USB @ 0530, 1130, 1730 &
   2330
For information on weather fax check:
http://weather.noaa.gov/fax/gulf.shtml

For more updated info on HAM and SSB
weather forecasts, visit:
www.CaribbeanCompass.com

VHF
Cruisers nets (not Sunday)
Grenada, Channel 66 at 0730,
Bequia, Channel 68 at 0800
St. Lucia, Channel 68 at 0830
In Martinique, COSMA gives forecasts in
   French at 0730 and 1830 on VHF: 11.

Sea and the Gulf of Mexico. During August and September, the number is around five each per year. Hurricanes frequently start well out in the Atlantic Ocean, often at the latitude of the Windwards, but then they usually swing north and pass through the Caribbean farther north. Very few hit the Windwards and sometimes years go by without one in this area, but it is essential to check the forecasts, especially in these days of rather active hurricane seasons. You can get weather on the radio, but it is hard to find consistently good forecasts.

It is probably easiest to go into an internet cafe and get the weather on the web. (We give links to several forecasts on doyleguides.com.) Cruisers nets are good for weather. Local cruisers nets are Monday to Saturday. Grenada is on VHF: 66 at 0730, Bequia is on VHF: 68 at 0800, St. Lucia (Rodney Bay) is on VHF: 68 at 0830.

Here are some terms you will hear on the radio and what they mean: "Intertropical convergence zone" affecting the area: this is not any kind of low, but you may get some rain squalls or cloudy weather. "Tropical disturbance," "tropical wave," and "upper-level trough": poorly organized weather systems associated with rain squalls of varying intensity. A "tropical depression" is an organized weather system with sustained winds of up to 35 knots and rain. Sometimes these can be very nasty and other times they turn out to be nothing. A "tropical storm," on the other hand, is definitely something to be avoided, as it has lots of rain and sustained winds of 35-63 knots. When the sustained winds become more than 64 knots, it is called a hurricane.

Hurricane winds can come from any direction, so be prepared to get out of the way or run for one of the hurricane holes: Cohe du Lamentin, Trois Ilets, or, better still, Cul de Sac Marin in Martinique; Rodney Bay Lagoon or Marigot Bay in St. Lucia; the mangrove swamp in Tyrrel Bay, Carriacou; and in Grenada, Port Egmont. Drive your boat aground bow first into the mangroves. Tie off to the biggest mangrove trees with all available lines (use at least ten). Put out two anchors astern, turn off all seacocks, remove all sails, awnings, and biminis, leave

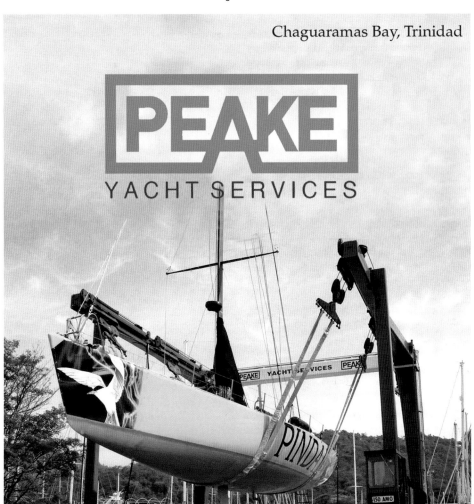

the boat, and find somewhere safe ashore.

During one of the few hurricanes that we did get, a charter party was advised by their company to make at once for a safe harbor to ride it out. "Oh no," they said "we have confirmed flights out and don't want to miss them. We will make it in time." They sailed north from St. Vincent to St. Lucia, but by the time they reached Soufriere, it was raining cats and dogs, and the wind was howling, so they anchored and went ashore. The boat soon began to drag and the skipper, aided by a local fisherman, tried to re-anchor. They managed to get their anchor line caught in the prop so they could not use power, and it was blowing too hard to make sail. In the end they drifted all night through the hurricane, and were rescued, after the winds fell, by a French coastguard boat off Martinique. I suppose the moral of the tale is that it is amazing what you can get away with, but better not to try.

Buoyage

All the islands now use the IALA B buoyage system. Main channels are marked with red and green buoys or beacons with red to starboard when entering: in other words "Red Right Returning." Other shoals and channels are indicated by black and yellow buoys or beacons coded with respect to both color and triangulation (using cones), as shown in the diagram.

Lights and buoys in the Windwards are unreliable. Lights do not always work, buoys go adrift, and beacons lose color and cones. Treat navigational aids with great caution.

Tides and currents

The tidal range is around two feet, not enough to be critical except in a few places. The lowest tides are in the summer. An equatorial current sets to the west-northwest. This current is affected by the tide when you are within a few miles of land. A counter-current begins about one hour before low water, offsets the equatorial current, and can run up to one knot to the east. This continues for about five hours, until about four hours after low water. Skippers of boats that are very slow to windward can make use of this to help them when sailing between islands. However, it is a mixed blessing because the counter-current usually sets up much rougher seas.

Charts

You have a choice between British Admiralty (B.A.), U.S. Defense Mapping Agency (D.M.A) and yachting charts. U.K. charts are much more expensive in the U.S. and vice versa. New charts should be based on WG 84 data so they can be used with GPS.

Nautical Publications supply their charts in kits, each kit covering several islands. They are in color, and the format is relatively small (23.5 by 16.5 inches), so you never need to fold them. Each kit comes in a handy plastic see-through envelope that you

CHANNEL BUOYS & BEACONS

PORT HAND

STARBOARD HAND

THE COLORS OF THE BUOYS OR BEACONS AND THE POSITIONS OF THE TRIANGLES

IALA SYSTEM B BUOYAGE
RED RIGHT RETURNING RULE HOLDS FOR CHANNEL BUOYS; SHAPES MAY VARY.

N

W   SHOAL   E

S

DIVIDED CHANNEL: PREFERRED CHANNEL TO

PORT   STARBOARD

ISOLATED SHOAL

INDICATE THE POSITION OF THE SHOAL SHOWN IN THE DIAGRAM

MILEAGE CHART

This table is approximate and offered as a guide to planning. Distances sailed are often in excess of those shown due to wind and current.

From \ To	Ft. de France	Anse Mitan	G. Anse D'Arlet	Ste. Anne	Rodney Bay	Castries	Marigot	Pitons	Vieux Fort	Wallilabou	Kingstown	Young Island	Admiralty B.	Friendship B.	Mustique	Canouan	Mayreau	Tobago Cays	Union I.	P.S.V.	Hillsborough	Tyrrel Bay	St. George's	Prickly Bay	Mt. Hartman B.
St. Pierre	12	14	16	30	42	45	47	56	67	90	97	99	105	109	115	122	127	130	133	136	139		166	172	173
Fort de France		3	7	21	33	37	39	47	57	83	90	98	102	108	115	120	123	126	129	132			159	165	166
Anse Mitan			6	20	32	36	38	46	57	82	89	97	101	107	114	119	120	123	126	129			158	164	165
Gd Anse D'Arlet				15	26	30	32	41	52	77	84	86	91	96	102	109	114	113	114	117	120		152	158	159
St. Anne					21	26	30	32	39	50	76	83	85	91	95	101	108	113	113	116	119		156	161	162
Rodney Bay						5	8	18	29	55	62	64	70	74	80	87	92	113	113	116	117	123	135	140	141
Castries							4	13	24	50	57	59	65	69	75	82	87	90	108	113	120	123	130	135	136
Marigot								10	21	46	53	55	61	65	71	78	83	86	104	109	114	126	126	131	132
Pitons									11	36	43	45	51	55	61	68	73	76	86	90	93	116	116	121	122
Vieux Fort										34	41	43	49	53	59	66	71	74	77	90	93	114	114	119	120
Wallilabou											7	9	15	19	25	32	37	40	43	77	81	83	84	85	85
Kingstown												2	9	11	16	27	32	35	38	42	77	83	80	80	81
Young Island													8	10	15	20	27	32	35	42	45	80	75	80	81
Admiralty Bay														7	12	24	26	29	33	35	38	45	68	73	74
Friendship Bay															7	19	24	26	31	33	36	45	66	71	72
Mustique																14	19	19	25	28	31	50	61	66	67
Canouan																	7	6	10	14	16	31	49	54	55
Mayreau Saline Bay																		4	3	7	9	12	44	49	50
Tobago Cays																			4	6	11	14	42	47	48
Union (Clifton)																				4	7	9	40	45	46
Hillsborough																					7	4	39	44	45
P.S.V.																						4	39	44	45
Tyrrel Bay																							30	35	36
St. George's																								7	8
Prickly Bay																									2

can take into the cockpit with the current chart on top. This also ensures that rather than losing one chart over the side, the whole kit will blow over, so make a little hole in the plastic and tie the envelope down. Hasko Scheidt of Nautical Publication has done several surveys in the Caribbean, and in those areas he has surveyed, including the east coast of Antigua and the south coast of Barbuda, their charts are particularly good. His charts include very detailed land information as well as nautical information; the kit includes both paper and a digital DVD.

Imray Iolaire also does yachting charts, and these are printed on plastic so they almost last forever and you can get them wet. However, vigorous rubbing will take the color right off them, so experiment a little before you cover them with temporary pencil lines. These charts are sold individually, so you can tailor your collection to your needs, and while they are large-format, like the hydrographic charts, you need fewer of them, as most include detailed harbor plans. They also come in digital format, but these are sold separately.

I have found the Garmin Blue Map series of electronic charts, which works on my little Garmin mapreader, to be exceptionally good at placing you in the right place with respect to land. These charts are somewhat simple and sometimes lack adequate depth data.

GPS

GPS is the biggest leap in navigational science since the invention of the chronometer. Now we can always know our position anywhere in the world. Accurate though this system is, there are limitations. I have noticed occasional inaccuracies, up to a tenth of a mile, even when the GPS suggested better accuracy. Therefore, I would not advise using a GPS to navigate reef-strewn passages at night or in poor visibility. Older charts were created on unspecified formats, and inaccuracies of up to half a mile may occur. Newer charts are based on WG 84 data and work with GPS. The charts in this book are on GPS grids created by using a Garmin on WG 84 data, using much interpolation. No guarantee is offered about their accuracy. We include a table of GPS positions for route planning. You can download them from www.doyleguides.com. Remember, land and shoals may be on your line of approach, depending on your route.

Customs and immigration

The Windwards contain four separate countries: Martinique, St. Lucia, St. Vincent (including the Grenadines to Petit St. Vincent), and Grenada (which includes Carriacou and Petite Martinique). Each has its own customs regulations, and it is necessary to clear in and out of each country. On arrival, you should hoist a yellow flag and anchor in a port of entry. After that, you can go ashore in search of customs and immigration officers. Take passports, ship's papers, and the clearance from your last port with you. All the Windwards now have simple one-page forms.

In Martinique, you do your own entry on a customs computer. Elsewhere, a pre-clearance system called sailclear (www.sailclear.com) can greatly ease formalities. You can preclear from any internet connection, and it saves you filling in all the forms. All your data are stored on the site making it easy the next time. It currently works in most ports in St. Lucia, in some Grenada ports (Prickly Bay is excellent), and in Carriacou when the itnernet works (occasionally). With luck, it will soon work everywhere.

Customs and immigration officers will refuse to deal with anyone not wearing a shirt and looking reasonably presentable. Charges and other details are given under island and harbor headings.

Officers are often late to the office, so if you need to get going, clear the night before.

Dogs

So you've brought your pet all the way over the ocean and now you want to take it for a walk. Well, here is what you can expect from the local authorities. In Martinique and Grenada, if you have a rabies vaccination certificate handy when you clear in, you can walk your dog ashore. St. Vincent and St. Lucia are both rabies-free, and animals are not allowed ashore without significant paper work and a vet visit.

Some people do not realize that dogs in the Caribbean are subject to a deadly heart worm. Check with a vet for appropriate counter-measures before leaving, or as soon as you get here.

Anchoring

It amazes me that you can safely keep a yacht in place with an anchor. Many yachts weigh from six to twenty tons and provide a stack of windage, yet we hold them in place with a tiny (35-60 lb) anchor. This does work, most of the time. Anchoring can be simple or fraught with dangers to your yacht, your relationship with your crew (especially your spouse), and other yachts.

The first critical decision is where to drop the anchor. Check your chart for no-anchoring channels and for depths, then look at the boats and harbor for possible anchoring spots, and for places best avoided (like fish pots and moorings). Clear the foredeck for action, and shorten the dinghy painter so it does not end up in the prop.

In normal conditions, the wind in the Windwards will be blowing somewhere from the east, and you can expect to end up as the other anchored yachts are lying. It is safest to anchor behind the other yachts so there is no one for you to drag into. You can drop anchor as close as 50 feet behind another boat in most conditions. If you go in front of another yacht, you need to drop the anchor at least a hundred yards in front of them, or you will end up on top of them.

The wind often shifts 20 or 30 degrees: Will that put your boat over someone's anchor, or you over theirs? In rare calm conditions with boats facing all directions, you have no idea which way chains are laid out. All you can do is anchor well clear of all other boats. Even if the wind is constant,

boats swing from side to side, and each does it differently, so you do not want to end up close beside anyone.

It is best to anchor when the sun is high, so you can choose a light-colored sandy patch where the holding will be good, rather than a dark-colored weedy patch where you may drag. Always approach your spot into the wind.

To give the anchor a chance to hold, you need to let out at least five times as much chain or rope as the depth of water you anchor in, plus the height of your bow. (Let out more if bad weather is expected.) If you are anchoring on chain, the chain needs to be marked so you know how much you are letting out. This is imperative. Chandleries sell clever plastic chain markers in different colors, which sit inside the chain and do not interfere with the windlass. Cruisers can use these or paint their chain. Charterers should ask the company how they have marked the chain (and they should have). If they have not, you will need to flake it out on deck while you are still on the dock and mark it yourself. Good temporary markers are plastic electrical ties in different colors; use two or three for each mark, in case one breaks. Put the bulky bit inside the chain where it will not get crunched by the windlass. If these are not available, you could try whipping twine. You are never going to use less than 50 feet of chain, so this can be your first mark, then mark every 20 feet up to about 150 feet.

If you have a chain/rope combination, it is much easier to estimate how much you are letting out and also to see whether you have let out enough by the angle of the rode after it is set (see diagram below). While rope alone, or rope and 12 feet of chain, will work in sand and some other seabeds, you will need at least 50 feet of chain for beds of

angle of 5 to 1 scope

Tobago Cays

dead coral. If you use mostly rope, you will wander around more should the wind drop, and you need to allow for this.

To look good while anchoring, always bring the boat to a complete stop before dropping the anchor. Let out enough chain for the anchor to reach the bottom; then, as the boat swings back with the wind, keep letting out more, bit by bit, till you have let out the right amount. Never dump the chain or rope all at once. When the boat has settled down, facing the same way as all the others, nudge the engine into reverse at low revs till the rode becomes tight. If the boat does not drag, keep increasing the revs (take bearings ashore), and make sure you are holding. If the anchor holds at high revs in reverse you are probably okay, but it is always good to dive on your anchor and make sure it is well dug in. If you do drag, the spot you are in is poor holding, so move to a different place and try again. Do not try the hard reverse if you are anchoring on soft mud; in that case, the anchor may need a very long time to settle.

The crew on the bow cannot hear the helmsman with the engine running, and the helmsman certainly cannot hear the crew. Hand signals look more professional and work better than screaming, but only if you figure out a signal system in advance.

If you do end up a little too close to someone else, you can often solve this by putting out a second anchor, at about 30 degrees to your first, which will pull you clear and restrict your swinging room.

Make sure the rope is cleated properly or the chain secure (the windlass does not secure it). Leave the foredeck clear of clutter, so that if you have to move in the middle of the night, you are not fighting surf boards and hammocks. Check your bearings periodically to make sure you have not dragged.

Mooring

Moorings are rapidly becoming much more widespread in the islands, which is a mixed blessing. Moorings do sometimes help protect the seagrass, which encourages turtles, echinoderms, and many kinds of fish.

Owners of rentable moorings include

towns (especially Martinique), marinas, marine parks, charter companies (St. Vincent), and private individuals. The technology to properly design, place, and maintain moorings at a level where they will not fail has existed for years. Where I grew up in the UK, hundreds of boats were on town moorings. These were hauled and inspected annually, and they had to withstand major storms; I do not remember a single failure.

Unfortunately, moorings in the Caribbean are not well maintained, and as nearly every bad consequence of failure (and there have been many), has landed on the yacht owner, not the mooring owner, there has been no incentive for improvement. Official moorings are generally correctly put down, but there is often little or no maintenance. In some places, mooring use is compulsory. I avoid using moorings where possible, and snorkel on them if there is no alternative. Never run a line from one side of your boat through the mooring to the other, because as the boat swings the rope will chafe through. Use a separate line on each side.

In the Grenadines, outside official marine park moorings, locals view moorings as a personal parking meter to gather income. Most of these are poorly designed and constructed, and the guiding philosophy for most mooring owners is to rent it till it breaks, and then fix it. I would not trust any of them without a very close underwater inspection. They are almost never properly installed, and often not a single shackle has been wired, so they can fall apart. Lines can often catch on the concrete block and chafe right through, and the size of the block or the means of attachment is frequently inadequate. They have no legal status; there is even a warning about them in the Bequia customs office. You can anchor right beside one; the owner has absolutely no rights over the seabed and cannot make you move, though he is quite likely to act like a jerk. If you take one, and it is too close to a boat that is already anchored, you must move; such moorings carry no rights. If you decide to take one of these moorings, you are taking substantial risk, so make sure your insurance covers it.

If moorings are okay, we will mention that in the text.

GPS WAYPOINTS

For planning purposes only. These waypoints may be downloaded from
www.doyleguides.com along with links to help you put them on your GPS.

All miles are nautical miles.

ID	Latitude	Longitude	Comment
MARTINIQUE			
WMTQ01	N14°26.00'	W061°05.00'	Approach to Martinique's SW coast
WMTQ02	N14°44.50'	W061°10.70'	Off main dock St. Pierre
WMTQ03	N14°38.40'	W061°08.50'	0.1 miles W of harbor wall, Case Pilote
WMTQ04	N14°37.80'	W061°09.20'	Approach to Case Pilote
WMTQ05	N14°36.80'	W061°06.40'	Schoelcher
WMTQ06	N14°35.00'	W061°05.00'	Approach to Fort de France
WMTQ07	N14°35.70'	W061°04.50'	Approach Fort de France anchorage
WMTQ08	N14°32.90'	W061°02.10'	Approach to Trois Ilets
WMTQ09	N14°33.60'	W061°02.80'	Approach to Trou Etienne
WMTQ10	N14°33.70'	W061°03.40'	Pointe du Bout
WMTQ11	N14°33.00'	W061°04.00'	Approach for Anse A L'Ane
WMTQ12	N14°31.80'	W061°05.40'	Anse Noir
WMTQ13	N14°30.00'	W061°06.00'	Grand Anse D'Arlet
WMTQ14	N14°29.20'	W061°05.20'	Anses D'Arlet (middle of bay)
WMTQ15	N14°27.70'	W061°00.50'	Approach for Baie du Marigot
WMTQ16	N14°25.00'	W060°55.00'	Approach to St. Anne & Marin
WMTQ17	N14°26.70'	W060°54.00'	Cul de Sac Marin (entrance)
WMTQ18	N14°26.20'	W060°53.20'	Ste. Anne (western part of anchorage)
WMTQ19	N14°24.90'	W060°49.80'	Baie des Anglais (entrance)
WMTQ20	N14°24.00'	W060°53.80'	Approach to Grande Anse des Saline
ST. LUCIA			
WSLU01	N14°05.50'	W060°58.20'	0.1 miles west of Pigeon Island
WSLU02	N14°04.73'	W060°57.40'	Rodney Bay Lagoon (entrance)
WSLU03	N14°04.10'	W060°58.70'	Southern approach, inside Barrel of Beef
WSLU04	N14°01.20'	W061°00.50'	Castries (entrance)
WSLU05	N13°58.05'	W061°01.90'	Marigot (entrance)
WSLU06	N13°56.40'	W061°03.20'	Anse La Raye (entrance)
WSLU07	N13°55.60'	W061°03.70'	Anse Cochon
WSLU08	N13°54.70'	W061°04.30'	Anse de Canaries
WSLU09	N13°51.50'	W061°05.20'	0.4 miles SW of Anse Chastanet reef
WSLU10	N13°51.20'	W061°03.80'	Soufriere
WSLU11	N13°48.50'	W061°05.00'	0.2 miles west of Gros Piton
WSLU12	N13°43.00'	W060°58.00'	0.75 miles WSW of dock Vieux Fort
WSLU13	N13°46.00'	W061°05.00'	2.3 miles south of Gros Piton
WSLU14	N13°44.50'	W061°00.00'	Entrance to Laborie
ST. VINCENT			
WSTV01	N13°20.00'	W061°15.00'	2 miles northwest of Chateaubelair
WSTV02	N13°16.00'	W061°15.80'	Cumberland Bay (center of entrance)
WSTV03	N13°14.90'	W061°16.50'	Wallilabou (center of entrance)
WSTV04	N13°14.40'	W061°16.90'	0.1 miles W of Bottle & Glass
WSTV05	N13°11.40'	W061°16.20'	Buccament Bay (center)
WSTV06	N13°10.90'	W061°16.20'	Petit Byahaut

ST VINCENT (cont.)

WSTV07	N13°09.50'	W061°14.90'	Ottley Hall (entrance)
WSTV08	N13°09.00'	W061°14.00'	Kingstown (center of bay)
WSTV09	N13°07.60'	W061°12.40'	0.1 miles SW of Fort Duvernette
WSTV10	N13°07.50'	W061°11.90'	Approach to Blue Lagoon

GRENADINES

WGNS01	N13°00.70'	W061°15.10'	0.1 miles west of Devil's Table, Bequia
WGNS02	N12°59.50'	W061°17.60'	Bequia, West Cay (just off W end)
WGNS03	N12°59.10'	W061°14.00'	Bequia, Friendship Bay
WGNS04	N12°53.50'	W061°12.00'	Mustique approach, north of Montezuma
WGNS05	N12°52.50'	W061°12.00'	Mustique approach, south of Montezuma
WGNS06	N12°52.80'	W061°11.50'	Mustique, Britannia Bay
WGNS07	N12°44.40'	W061°20.00'	Canouan, northwest point
WGNS08	N12°42.70'	W061°20.20'	Canouan, Charlestown Bay (center of)
WGNS09	N12°42.40'	W061°21.40'	Just northwest of Glossy Hill, Canouan
WGNS10	N12°39.50'	W061°23.00'	0.5 miles west of Baline Rocks
WGNS11	N12°38.20'	W061°21.80'	0.1 miles W of Petit Rameau, Tobago Cays
WGNS12	N12°39.00'	W061°23.70'	Mayreau, Salt Whistle Bay
WGNS13	N12°38.00'	W061°24.50'	Mayreau, Saline Bay
WGNS14	N12°36.00'	W061°28.00'	0.25 miles W of Chatham Bay, Union
WGNS15	N12°36.00'	W061°24.20'	Union, northen approach to Union/Palm
WGNS16	N12°35.00'	W061°25.00'	0.25 miles W of Grand de Coi, Union
WGNS17	N12°32.90'	W061°24.10'	0.2 miles N of Mopion Channel, PSV
WGNS18	N12°32.00'	W061°23.50'	0.5 miles west of PSV dock
WGNS19	N12°32.00'	W061°27.00'	0.7 miles WNW of north end of Carriacou
WGNS20	N12°30.00'	W061°30.80'	2.8 miles west of Jack a Dan, Carriacou
WGNS21	N12°29.70'	W061°28.20'	Just west of Jack a Dan, Carriacou
WGNS22	N12°27.00'	W061°30.00'	Tyrrel Bay (entrance)
WGNS23	N12°19.00'	W061°36.00'	Isle de Ronde

GRENADA

WGDA01	N12°15.00'	W061°40.00'	1 mile N of David Point
WGDA02	N12°06.70'	W061°45.00'	Halifax Harbour (entrance)
WGDA03	N12°05.20'	W061°45.90'	Dragon Bay (entrance)
WGDA3A	N12°05.50'	W061°45.90'	Happy Hill (approach)
WGDA3B	N12°04.40'	W061°45.70'	Grand Mal Bay (approach)
WGDA04	N12°02.70'	W061°45.50'	0.25 miles W of entrance to St. George's
WGDA05	N12°00.20'	W061°48.40'	Point Saline (just off tip of land)
WGDA06	N11°59.60'	W061°46.20'	True Blue (entrance)
WGDA07	N11°59.30'	W061°46.00'	Prickly Bay (entrance)
WGDA08	N11°58.60'	W061°45.90'	0.25 miles W of Porpoises rocks
WGDA09	N11°59.00'	W061°45.10'	Approach for Mt. Hartman Bay
WGDA10	N11°59.00'	W061°44.20'	Approach for Hog Island
WGDA11	N11°59.10'	W061°43.50'	Approach for Clarkes Court Bay
WGDAPB	N11°59.30'	W061°42.90'	Approach for Phare Bleu Marina
WGDA12	N11°59.30'	W061°42.70'	Approach for Port Egmont
WGDA13	N12°00.00'	W061°42.10'	Approach for Calivigny harbour
WGDA14	N12°00.60'	W061°41.30'	Approach P. Bacaye/Bacelot Bay
WGDA15	N12°00.60'	W061°40.70'	St. David's Harbour (entrance)

Hiking the Pinnacle, Union I

Chartering

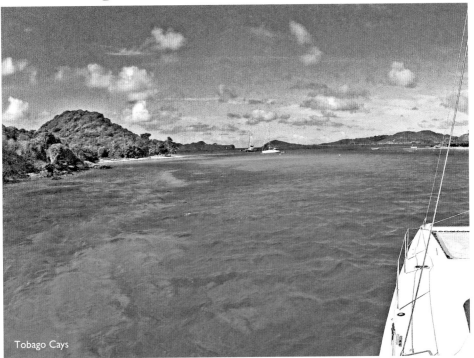
Tobago Cays

Whether you want to go bareboat, fully crewed, one way, multihull, or monohull, you can find something to suit in the Windwards. I give a list of charter companies in the directory, and links to them on doyleguides.com.

For bareboaters without much experience, the easiest sail is from St. Vincent to Union or Grenada. Most charter companies will be happy to arrange one-way charters for an extra fee, and most skippered yachts will pick up and drop off at ports of your choice for no extra charge.

The sail from St. Lucia to St. Vincent is a long, hard day's sail. The return trip is often worse. If you are starting a charter in St. Lucia or Martinique, it makes a lot of sense to sail one way and finish in Union Island or Grenada. This is especially true if you only have a week or so.

Bareboating

I had the pleasure of running one of the first Caribbean bareboats ~ a little 31-footer called Rustler. When we said "bareboat," we meant it. Rustler came with a hand-start diesel that would barely push her out of the anchorage, a small icebox full of ice, and 40 gallons of water, which were pumped up by hand. Mechanical complexities consisted of a massive British marine toilet, with endless valves and pumps. This antiquity was almost impossible to clog, but at the same time, however much you worked on the packing gland, within a couple of days it tended to squirt you in the eye. The outboard was a close relative ~ all chrome and stainless, with no cover. You had to wind the cord round the flywheel for every start and go through an elaborate system of switching valves and vents and bleeding for exactly the right number of seconds. The only thing to be said in its favor was that even the roughest of mechanics could do a major overhaul with a screwdriver, a big hammer, and a pair of pliers.

When I look at some of the bareboat ads these days, it seems that people want to take it all with them when they get away from it all. Freezers, fridges, hair dryers, microwave

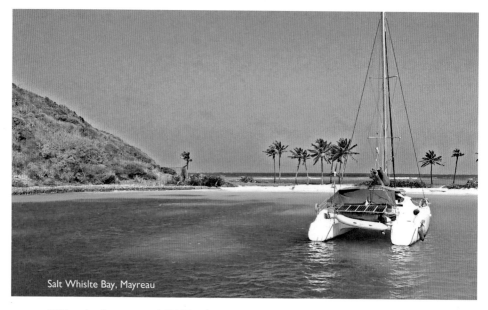

Salt Whislte Bay, Mayreau

ovens, TV, telephones, and DVD players are all available.

One thing that years of sailing has taught me is that anything mechanical, electrical, or electronic, when installed on a well-used yacht, will eventually go wrong. Bareboats are particularly susceptible because of all the different people using the gear. In practical terms, this means that breakdowns are part and parcel of a modern sophisticated yacht, and not necessarily a reflection on the efficiency and ability of the charter company. The charter people realize this, so they all help each other's yachts and do their best to have a breakdown and backup service, despite the problems posed by the Windwards, which are well spread out. But it is important that bareboaters appreciate the essentially adventurous nature of a bareboat holiday and not let it be ruined by a malfunctioning hair dryer.

I still have the log book from Rustler, and there is an entry I am especially fond of. At the beginning, it is written in the hand of the group's self-appointed leader, Dr. Smith, who was not the least bit happy. Each day was another disaster. He couldn't make the outboard start, he couldn't find the boat hook, one of the navigation lights malfunctioned, he was "very disappointed" in the condition of the boat. Then the handwriting changed and the new entry said:

"Dr. Smith had to return home for pressing personal reasons. Rustler is now a fine yacht, the weather is perfect, the sailing fantastic. We are having a marvelous time."

A good thing about chartering is that those occasions that are terrible at the time make great stories later. Some years ago, a bareboat was on a reef in the middle of nowhere and the skipper was on the radio to the company's local representative, who was trying to assess the situation.

"We are hard aground, the rudder is broken, and we cannot steer," lamented the charterer.

"Ok. I've got that," said the rep. "Now tell me, are you taking on water?"

There was a pause of a few seconds, then back came a very definite answer, "Oh no, we did that yesterday in St. Vincent."

Crewed charters

Having spent years both running bareboats and skippering charters, I can attest without any question that skippered charters produce more glowing praise. A crewed charter is also a real holiday for everyone, with no galley and cleaning chores.

Many agents talk a lot about matching charterers to crew. In fact, most charterers are happy, easy to please, and good company, and good professional skippers can adapt themselves to all kinds of people. Cooks

Planning & Cruising

develop a sensitivity to produce the right kind of food.

The modern large charter yachts that now make up the bulk of the fleet have enough crew, and separation of guests from the crew, that it is a bit like having your own mini-cruiseship, but with much better food and service.

Tipping is a big item for most crews, as this makes up a large part of their income. Unless otherwise stated, 10 percent of the total charter fee is the norm and an appropriate figure for good service.

On smaller yachts, with only a captain and cook, it is worth keeping in mind that although yacht crews really enjoy what they are doing and genuinely like their guests, there is some strain to always being on one's best behavior and there are a few things that can make life a lot easier. It is a huge help if all the charterers go ashore for a couple of hours each day, either to shop, walk, or go to the beach. At this point, the crew can put on their favorite music full blast and clean the boat with much banging and gay abandon.

The charterers will return to a clean boat and a much-refreshed crew.

Cooks hate to be watched while they work. It makes them nervous and upsets their concentration. There is no way you would know this, because they are trained to smile and answer a string of questions; much better to leave them alone in the galley, and give them the attention they deserve when they produce that final work of art.

The cook usually works much harder than the skipper, so it is a great break if the guests decide to eat out, even if it is just a matter of having a sandwich ashore instead of returning for lunch. Unfairly, the best cooks get the fewest breaks, as no one can bear to miss a single meal.

It is a tradition on smaller yachts that at some point, the guests take their crew out for dinner. For the crew, the break is more important than the dinner, and if you are on a budget, they don't mind if it is somewhere quite simple.

We list charter companies in the directory and on doyleguides.com.

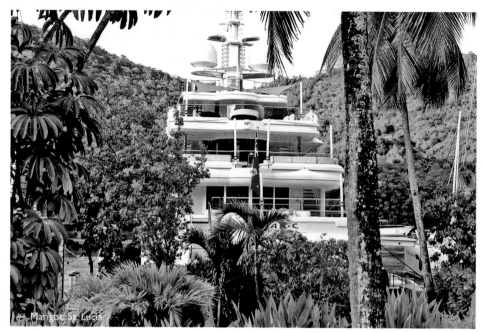

Marigot St. Lucia

Professional Yachts

Most cruisers quickly adjust to island time. If it doesn't get done today, tomorrow will suffice. This does not work for professional charter and superyachts on strict timetables, with guests arriving, chores to get done, and breakdowns to be coped with. I remember once many years ago arriving in Grenada with a charter turnaround on the eve of some holiday and not being able to get laundry done at any price.

Happily, things are much better today. There are a number of good businesses that cater to professional yachts, and they will do what it takes to make things happen. I list these below.

Many of these agents have reasonable standard fees for things like clearing customs, and it would pay bareboaters or cruisers with short stops (one day to clear in and out and tour the island, for example) to take advantage of these services.

AGENTS

Martinique

Note: when dialing Martinique from over-seas, dial + 596 596 + 6 digits, unless it is a mobile phone, in which case it is, + 596 696 + 6 digits

You can base a superyacht in Martinique. It has all necessary support services, and you will find Douglas Rapier (he is available 24/7) of Douglas Yacht Services to offer the very highest standard of professional service in everything a superyacht may want, from full provisioning and technical help to overseeing travel, private plane arrivals, restaurant reservations and personal arrangements. English is his native tongue, so you will have no communications problems. His office is in Marin Marina, but he keeps his mobile with him.

Douglas Yacht Services, (0696) 45 89 75, (0596) 52 14 28, F: (0596) 52 07 36, VHF: 09, douglas@yachtservices.fr

St. Lucia

St. Lucia has dedicated agents to work with the large yachts. They can deal with customs, clear parts, and arrange fuel, local provisions, and anything else. They will all work in any of St. Lucia's ports.

With the IGY Rodney Bay Marina, and the Cappella Marina and Resort in Marigot Bay, St. Lucia has become a good place to base a superyacht.

Ben Saltibus in Soufriere has been at it forever and is very professional. You will be in good hands with him. He works quite closely with Sam Taxi Service in St. Vincent and Henry Safari Tours in Grenada.

Benny Adjouda is the other accredited yacht agent.

CJ Taxi Service in Rodney Bay Marina will also help with most things locally.

Ben's Taxi Service, (758) 459-5457, F:(758) 459-5719, Cell: (758) 484-0708, saltibus@slucia.com

Harmony Yacht Services (Benny), (758) 559 5050, cell: (758) 287 4261, F: (758) 458-5033, VHF: 16, harmonyiii@hotmail.com

CJ Taxi, (758) 584-3530, (758) 450-5981/458-4283, F: (758) 452-0185, VHF: 16

See also Rodney Bay Marina and Capella Marina & Resort under *Marinas and fueling*. Both can arrange most things.

St. Vincent & the Grenadines

This archipelago offers ample support for a visiting superyacht. Sam, of Sam Taxi Tours, is an official ship agent and works with large yachts and some cruise ships. He has sub-agencies in Bequia and Union Island. He can clear your yacht in or out from most anchorages and handle all other needs. He has a good office up on a hill where he and his team keep an eye on arriving yachts.

Erika's Marine Services can handle yachts anywhere in St. Vincent and the Grenadines. They have agents in Union Island, their main base, and St. Vincent, Bequia, and Canouan. They are efficient and friendly and have a plane.

Sam Taxi Tours, (784) 456-4338, F: (784) 456-4233, cell: (784) 528-2240, VHF:68/16, sam-taxi-tours@vincysurf.com.

Erika's Marine Services, (784) 458-8335, Cell: (784) 494-1212, VHF: 68, VIP@erikamarine.com

Grenada

Grenada makes a good superyacht base and has superyacht agents. They will handle anything you need, from checking in through customs to finding dock space, provisioning, and dealing with problems, and they will visit all Grenada's ports.

Roger and Claire Spronk run Spronk Ltd., a company based in True Blue. In addition to helping superyachts, they own both a gourmet store and a wholesale provisioning business, which handles a considerable quantity of the island's seafood, so they are particularly good at provisioning. Their base is at their restaurant, Bananas, in True Blue. They have started work on a waterfront base in Benji Bay.

Dennis Henry, of Henry's Safari Tours, has been at it the longest and he is professional, imaginative, and reliable, with a good back-up team. He owns four laundries, a large fleet of taxis and a cooking gas depot. Henry rather likes to be challenged on the odd occasion when he is thrown a problem he has not had to cope with before.

Henry's Safari Tours, (473) 444-5313, Cell: (473) 405 6313/407 0522, F: (473) 444-4460, VHF: 68, safari@spiceisle.com,

Spronk Mega Yacht Services, (473) 407-3688/439-4369/443-5663, Fax: (473) 444-4677, claire@spronksprovisioning.com

MARINAS AND FUELING

In Martinique, large yachts can fuel and dock in Marin Marina.

Marin Marina, (0596) 74 83 83, F: (0596) 74 92 20, VHF: 09, port.marin@wanadoo.fr

In St. Lucia, IGY Rodney Bay Marina has fueling, but check the current depth into the lagoon.

IGY Rodney Bay Marina, (758) 452-0324, F: (758) 452-0185, VHF: 16, rbm@igymarinas.com

Capella Marigot Resort & Marina has fueling on their large yacht docks.

Capella Marigot Resort and Marina, (758) 451-4275/1, 728-9900, VHF: 16/12, marigotbay@capellahotels.com, manager@marigotbaymarina.com

Other fueling options include St. Lucia Yacht Services in Vigie and Cool Breeze fuel station by the main town dock in Soufriere. Contact the agents to arrange tanker truck fueling in the main dock in Castries or Vieux Fort.

Cool Breeze Gas Station, (758) 459-7729, F: 459-5309

St. Lucia Yacht Services (758) 452-5057, VHF: 16

In St. Vincent, call Sam Taxi Tours. He will usually arrange for a tanker truck alongside the main docks in Kingstown.

Sam Taxi Tours, (784) 456-4338, F: (784) 456-4233, VHF: 68/16, sam-taxi-tours@vincysurf.com

An easy and good fuel dock in the Grenadines is B & C Fuels in Petit Martinique.

B&C Fuels, (473) 443-9110, F: (473) 443-9075, BabdCfuels@gmail.com

Carriacou Marine sells fuel, including duty-free, but draft is limited to about 8 feet. You can also arrange fueling on the main dock in Tyrrel Bay through Bullens in Hillsborough.

Bullen's, (473) 443-7468/7469, F: (473) 443 8194, vbs@spiceisle.com

In St. George's, Grenada you can arrange fuel at the Grenada Yacht Club in St. George's. They can take boats about 160 feet long on their dock. You can also get fuel at the new Port Louis Marina, taking it from one of the superyacht berths, or you can arrange fuel on the main St. George's wharf through an agent.

Grenada Yacht Club, (473) 440-3050, F: (473) 440-6826, VHF: 16, gyc@spiceisle.com

Port Louis Marina, (473) 435-7431, dockmaster: (473) 415-0820, VHF: 14, reservations@cnportlouismarina. com

Docking and fuel can be found at Prickly Bay Marina in Prickly Bay and Secret Harbour Marina in Mt. Hartman Bay. Take care to choose a channel suitable to your depth. Either marina can take almost any size of yacht that can make it into the bay.

Secret Harbour Marina, (473) 444-4449, F: (473) 444-2090, VHF: 16 &71, secretharbour@spiceisle.com

Prickly Bay Marina, (473) 439-5265, VHF: 16, pricklybaymarina@spiceisle.com

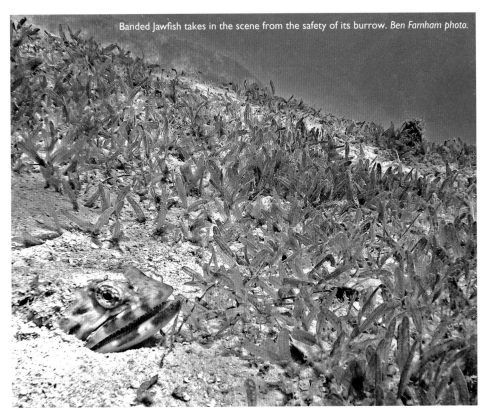

Banded Jawfish takes in the scene from the safety of its burrow. *Ben Farnham photo.*

Scuba Diving

"It's fantastic. I could breathe under-water just like a fish, and fish swam up and looked at me. What an incredible feeling."

"It's the greatest sensation I've ever felt. When we swam back with the current it was just like gliding through a beautiful garden!"

These are typical comments from first-time divers who find that diving is the most exciting thing they have ever done. No wonder ~ it is the closest most of us will ever come to visiting a strange planet. Not only that, under water we are weightless and seem to fly. Like birds, we can soar, hover, and dive down to see anything of interest.

The underwater world is full of wonders: tall, soft, waving "plants" that are really colonies of tiny animals, sponges that look like ancient urns in colors ranging from yellow to a psychedelic luminous blue. Huge schools of fish swim by, unconcerned about our presence. Little squids move by jet propulsion,

turtles and giant rays glide with elegant ease.

Yet many people are put off diving because they are under the impression it is complicated and difficult. Nothing could be farther from the truth. With modern equipment, diving is very simple, and with one of the popular "resort courses," you can be diving in half a day. In fact, the problem most divers have is boring their non-diving friends to distraction with tales of undersea adventure. The minimum age for most courses is 10.

Equipment

Experienced divers will want to bring their own masks, fins, and regulators. A really good comfortable B.C. (buoyancy compensator) is worth bringing, too. As for the rest, forget it. There is no point in humping tanks and weight belts; far better to rent them here. Those without any

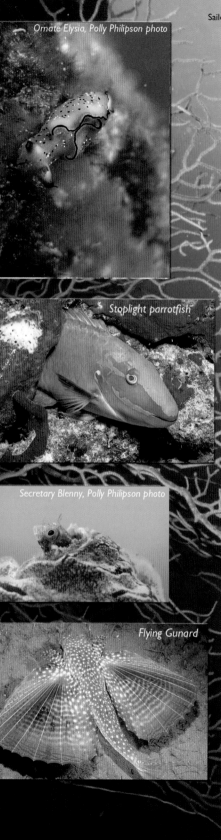

Ornate Elysia, Polly Philipson photo

Stoplight parrotfish

Secretary Blenny, Polly Philipson photo

Flying Gunard

equipment don't need to worry. The dive shops will supply everything, and it is usually excellent up-to-date gear. In many parts of the world, you have to wear a protective wet suit against the cold, but in the Windwards the water is warm enough that for most of us this isn't necessary.

Courses for beginners

Anyone who just wants to give diving a go can do so very quickly with a "resort course." It will take one whole morning or afternoon. First you get a one-hour talk that tells you in simple language what diving is all about. Then you try out the equipment in shallow water, and lastly, you go for your first dive. A resort course only qualifies you to dive under the close supervision of an instructor at the same dive shop.

First dive

Wherever you take a resort course, the instructors will choose a site that is easy, but interesting enough to attract aficionados. A typical example is Devil's Table in Bequia. The rocks and coral start at 12 feet and slope down to about 35 feet deep. You enter the water and feel a bit nervous, but you breathe out and gently sink. Soon your attention turns outwards. Large pillar corals rise from among the rocks. They look fuzzy, but if you swish your hand really close to them, the tentacles withdraw, leaving them looking like rocks. You stop to examine some pretty shells clinging to a waving sea fan, and to your surprise a tiny damsel fish shoots up and tries to chase you away. He's protecting his patch, and you don't scare him; it's then you learn that you can even laugh through your regulator. There is a great deal more to see: brightly colored parrotfish and angelfish, moray eels staring from their holes, strange-looking arrow crabs, and brightly banded coral shrimp. You enjoyed it? Good! Time to go to the next level.

Certification

If you've ever thought about getting certified, or if you try a dive and like it, then it makes sense to get certified on your holiday. If you get certified at home, chances are that it will be in a swimming pool, with nothing more interesting to look at than tiled walls. Your open-water dives are likely to be in some frigid, grey lake. Furthermore, you will probably have to buy or rent equipment that is normally included in the course price down island. In the Caribbean, you can train at a cost not much greater than the dives alone. The course includes all equipment, you do everything in open water, the dives are fantastic, and you can take home a diving certificate as well as your memories. There are several diving associations that have accredited diving instructors who can train you and give you a certificate. These include Padi and Naui, which are equally good. The next step from the resort course is the new Padi Scuba Diver. This two-and-a-half-day course certifies you to dive with any dive master at any shop to a depth of 40 feet. It is a good introduction and, being short, it is easy to do on holiday. You can complete your training on your next holiday, as this course counts as credit towards being an independent open-water diver.

A full diving course in the islands takes about four or five days and includes a couple of hours of instruction each day, followed by a dive, during which you increase your practical skills.

For qualified divers

Some people, especially those chartering yachts, prefer to rent gear and go off diving by themselves. Others prefer to join a dive with professional instructors. At least for your first dives, I recommend going with the dive instructors. They know all the good sites: the hidden caves, the special ledge where angelfish live, and maybe where there is a tame octopus, seahorse, or frogfish. A good instructor is also a good guide and can point out many things that would otherwise be missed, which adds interest to your dive. Perhaps the most important reason is that many good dive sites are in places that can only be reached with a powerful dive boat rather than a dinghy. I have worked with many charterers who have tried it both ways and noticed that those who went with dive instructors had a much better time than those who went on their own.

The diving in the Windwards varies markedly from island to island and from one dive site to the next, so enthusiasts will want to try diving in several different spots. Since the introduction of the predatory and invasive lionfish, many dive shops organize occasional lionfish hunts, to keep at least some reefs clear of them. They teach you how to avoid the poisonous spines.

We will mention the good sites and their accessibility in the text under each anchorage section. Dive shops are listed in our directory.

Look for easy-to-visit dive and snorkel sites on our sketch charts. They are marked by flags.

Diving   Snorkeling

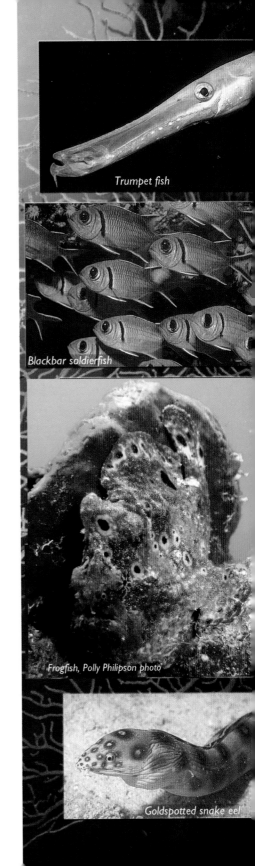

Trumpet fish

Blackbar soldierfish

Frogfish, Polly Philipson photo

Goldspotted snake eel

59

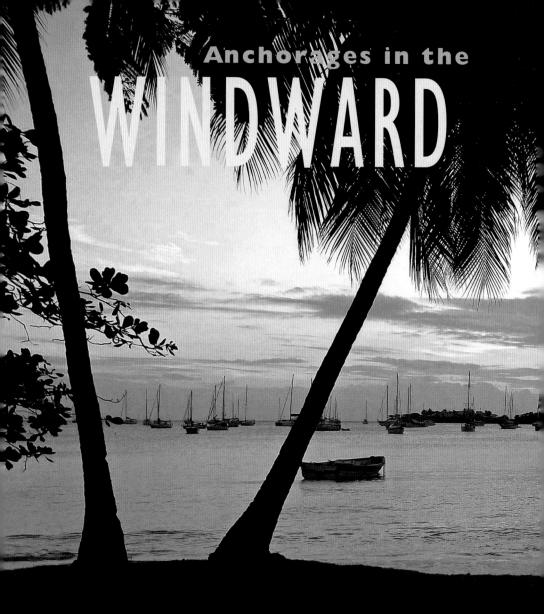

Anchorages in the
WINDWARD

**Martinique, St. Lucia, St. Vincent &
the Grenadines, Grenada,
Carriacou, & Petite
Martinique**

ISLANDS

Sunset, Prickly Bay, Grenada

Martinique

Flamingo pond, Zoo du Martinique

Regulations

Clear customs in Fort de France, Marin, Anse Mitan, Les Anses D'Arlet, Ste. Anne, or St. Pierre. Yachts in Martinique waters over six months in one year are liable to import duty, with exemptions for storing your yacht while you fly abroad. Visas are not necessary for EU or US citizens. Other nationals should check. For places and time to clear, see our anchorage sections. Yachts pay no overtime fees or charges. Foreign yachts over 5 tons need national registration. (US state registration is not accepted.)

A 5-knot speed limit is in effect within 300 meters of all coastline.

Shopping hours

Shops often open 0800-1200 and 1500-1730, Monday through Saturday. Many offices close on Saturday. Supermarkets often stay open till 1900 and open on Sunday mornings.

Holidays

Jan 1 & 2, New Year's Day & Recovery
Carnival Monday to Wednesday, 40 days before Easter, Feb 27-28, 2017, Feb, 12-13, 2018
Feb 22, Independence Day
Easter Friday, Sunday & Monday, April 14-17, 2017, and March 29-April 2, 2018
May 1, Labor Day
May 8, Victory Day (1945)
Ascension Day, ,May 25 2017, May 10 2018
Whit Monday, June 5, 2017,May 21, 2018
May 22, Abolition of Slavery
Corpus Christi, June 15, 2017; May 31, 2018
July 14, Bastille Day
August 15, Virgin Mary Day
Nov 1, All Saints Day
Nov 11, Victory Day (1918)

Dec 25, Christmas Day

Telephones

The simplest thing is to use a mobile phone and get a local sim; Carte Orange or Digicel. They cost around 15 Eu with 5 Eu credit. If you are calling the USA on Orange dial #141# to buy a pass Caraibes which will give you calls to the US and other Caribbean islands at the same rate as local calls.

Dial + or 00 to get out of the country and then the country code and number you want. Martinique numbers are 10 digits, starting 0596, except cell phones, which are 0696. To call from the US, dial 011 596 then the whole number, excluding the first 0. It will start:

011 596 596... or 011 596 696....

If you are roaming on a mobile phone, you will have to add + to the beginning of the number. Local sims are available from Cart Orange and Digicel, as are prepaid USB ports for internet.

If you are not into mobile phones, an internet cage may be able to make a skype call for you.

Transport

Martinique has a good system of buses or communal taxis (TC). These are reasonably priced, are found on most town squares, and run on fixed routes, mainly to and from Fort de France. There are also taxis. Typical taxi rates in Euros for up to 4 are:

Airport to Fort de France 25
Airport to Anse Mitan/Marin ...60
Anse Mitan to golf course 10
Fort de France to Carrefour 10
St. Pierre to Fort de France........55
St. Pierre to Airport...................75
Short ride 10
Shopping/tours per hour for 4....40
Over 4, pp, per hour 10
Rental cars are available. You can use your own license. Drive on the right.

ville SAINT-PIERRE
de charme et d'émotions

VILLE DE SAINT-PIERRE
MARTINIQUE

Avant 1902, date de l'éruption de la Montagne Pelée, Capitale économique et culturelle de la Martinique appelée " **Le Petit Paris des Antilles** "...

Aujourd'hui, Saint-Pierre, **ville incontournable,** attractive et culturelle riche en **vestiges et survivances** du passé.

Entre mer et montagne, située sur la côte nord caraïbe entre le Carbet et le Prêcheur, c'est la seule ville de Martinique à bénéficier du label "**Ville d'Art et d'Histoire**" et non sans raison.

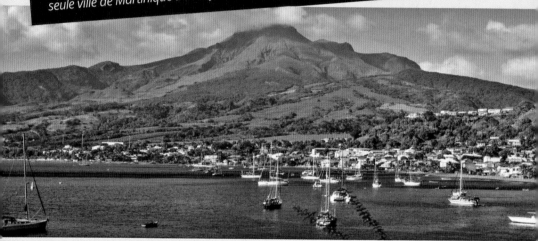

ATTRAITS PATRIMONIAUX, CULTURELS & NATURELS,

Considérée comme l'un des plus **beaux sites de la Caraïbe,** la magnifique **baie** de Saint Pierre offre des **spots de plongée exceptionnels** dont une douzaine d'épaves devenues des **récifs artificiels**. Des clubs de plongée avec un encadrement très professionnel et sécurisant, du matériel de très bonne qualité et parfaitement entretenu. Vous voilà à la découverte de fonds marins d'une pure merveille.

Sur le bord de mer, la **Place BERTIN** avec

son **marché couvert,** lieu de rencontres et d'échanges par excellence...

Tout le long de ce bord de mer, de bonnes tables pour se régaler au gré des pêches et

passer un agréable moment. Mais aussi des petits bars sympathiques d'où l'on peut admirer le coucher du soleil.

D'autres restaurants en périphérie sont une invitation pour le palais de tous fins gourmets... entre **gastronomie et tradition.**

Au centre-ville se côtoient les constructions récentes et les vieilles pierres.

Nombre de **sites historiques**, une fois foulés, vous rappelle à la fois la richesse disparue, l'ampleur et la violence de la catastrophe de 1902. Véritable témoignage du passé, ils vous offrent **des promenades pleines de charme et d'émotion.**

ENTRE MER ET TERRE DES RUINES QUI VALENT LE DETOUR...

Au centre, celles des maisons de commerce dont une partie des murs est encore visible tels les **ruines du Figuier.**

L'**escalier du théâtre,** témoin de la richesse de la vie culturelle de la ville.

Le **« cachot de Cyparis »,** le plus célèbre des survivants après la catastrophe.

Le **Pont de Pierre** également appelé **Pont Roches,** unique édifice rescapé de l'éruption, qui permet en traversant la rivière Roxelane d'accéder au **quartier du Fort** où se trouvent les ruines de **l'ancienne église** et les vestiges de **la rue Monte au Ciel,** ancienne ruelle connue à l'époque pour être un lieu particulièrement animé qui témoigne avec la rue Levassor du niveau de vie et de confort des pierrotins de l'époque. A quelques centaines de mètre, les ruines de la Maison Coloniale de Santé, premier hôpital psychiatrique des Antilles et des **Bureaux du Génie.**

SAINT-PIERRE C'EST AUSSI...

Le **quartier du mouillage** où se trouvent, **l'hôtel de ville,** d'une architecture « moderniste » datant de 1934, la Maison de la bourse, véritable archétype de l'architecture créole, témoin du raffinement et de la prospérité de la ville à la fin du XIXe siècle. la cathédrale Notre Dame de l'Assomption, **le cimetière du Mouillage et son ossuaire.**

...MAIS C'EST SURTOUT

Le point de départ d'une **liaison Inter-îles** vers la Dominique et la Guadeloupe.

Un **Centre de Découverte des sciences de la Terre** à faire impérativement avec les enfants pour une meilleure connaissance des volcans.

Un **petit train, Cyparis** pour mieux appréhender Saint-Pierre et son histoire. Et la **Maison Relais du Parc Naturel Régional de Martinique** où film artistique et historique et produits artisanaux se côtoient.

La **distillerie DEPAZ,** dans un cadre magnifique, féérique pour nous permettre de comprendre les étapes de fabrication du Rhum. Visite qui lie tourisme et dégustation.

Le **musée** volcanologique et historique, **Franck A. PERRET** pour revivre un moment historique émouvant. Guide bilingue.

Le Caribbean Open Tour pour découvrir Saint-Pierre et la côte Caraïbe autrement. Sans oublier **IGWA Tours** pour des circuits **éco-touristique.**

Des commerçants accueillants, pharmacies, boulangeries, médecins, dentistes, institut de beauté, podologue ...location de voiture... **à proximité en cœur de ville.**

Contacts pratiques

Municipalité : 35 rue Caylus - Tél. : 0596 78 10 32
Ouverture le lundi et jeudi : 07h30 – 17h00 ; Mardi, Mercredi et Vendredi : 07h30 – 13h00

Musée Franck A. PERRET : Rue Victor Hugo - Tél. : 0596 78 15 16
Ouverture du lundi au samedi de 09h00 - 17h00. Fermé le dimanche et jours fériés sauf les 08 et 22 mai.

Office de Tourisme : Rue Victor Hugo - Tél. : 0596 67 75 83.
Ouverture du lundi au vendredi - 09h00 - 15h00. Fermé le samedi et le dimanche

The town of SAINT-PIERRE
Gracious charm and strong emotions

Before 1902 and the eruption of Montagne Pelée, Saint Pierre, the capital of Martinique was known as "The Little Paris of the West Indies".

Today, Saint Pierre has earned the label "Ville d'Art et d'Histoire" "Town of Art and History" in recognition of it's cultural and historical richness.

SAINT-PIERRE: CULTURE AND NATURE

Considered one of **the most beautiful in the West Indies, the Bay of Saint Pierre** offers exceptional diving sites with a **dozen shipwrecks turned artificial reefs**. Professional diving clubs will welcome you on an **underwater visit of this unusual site**.

In the near future, a dedicated anchoring site will be established, making your nautical visit to Saint-Pierre easy and safe.

On the seafront, **Place**

Bertin has been the center of social activity since the founding of Saint-Pierre. Restaurants and small bars line the boardwalk, waiting to serve you the day's catch or simply offering you a rum punch and a glorious sunset.

Gourmet and traditional cuisine stand side by side in the many dining establishments dotted around the town.

In the town centre, **old stones remind you of what Saint-Pierre once was.** Imagine the violence of the explosion and the terror of the population on that fateful day. As you walk slowly around town you become **a witness to a living history full of strong emotions.**

SAINT-PIERRE... THE RUINS

◊ Business houses like **Figier**
◊ The **Staircase to the old Theatre**
◊ The **prison cell of Cyparis**
◊ The **"Pont de Pierre"** also called the **"Pont Roches"**, the only structure to escape destruction bridges the Roxelane River into the area of the old fort.

◊ The old church, the street called **Monte au Ciel** or go to Heaven Street and **"Levassor Street"**
◊ The first psychiatric hospital in the West Indies known as the **"Maison Colonial de Santé"**
◊ The **"Bureaux du Génie"**

More recent architecture is reflected in the creole style of the **"Maison de la Bourse"** on Place Bertin dating from 1934. The **"Notre Dame de l'Assomption"** Cathedral, the **Anchorage Cemetery** with it's ossuary and the façade of the Town Hall are portraits of the prosperity and refinement of Saint Pierre during the nineteenth century.

SAINT-PIERRE... TODAY

Offers her visitors **an inter-island connection to Dominica and Guadeloupe;** the geology museum at the **"Centre de Découverte des Sciences de la Terre";** the little train **"Cyparis";** a must ride for children as well as adults; the Kiosk Shop of the **Parc Naturel** to see its film on old Saint-Pierre and enjoy it's locally made treats; the **Depaz Distillery** visit and tasting; the **Franck A. Perret Volcano Museum; the Caribbean Open Tour bus** and **the IGWA eco-tours...**

Saint-Pierre...like no other place...much to see, much to learn, much to enjoy.

Practical contacts

Municipality: 35 rue Caylus – 97250 Saint– Pierre – Tél. : 0596 78 10 32
Open Monday and Thursday: 7:30 – 17:00 ; Tuesday, Wednesday and Friday: 7:30 – 13:00

Museum Franck Arnold PERRET: Rue Victor Hugo - Tél.: 0596 78 15 16
Open Monday to Saturday: 9:00 –17:00. Closed Sundays and public holidays except may 8 th and 22 th

Tourist Office : Rue Victor Hugo - Tél. : 0596 67 75 83.
Open Monday to Friday: 9:00 - 15:00. Closed Saturdays and Sundays.

Crédit photos : Gaspard le RoiMage

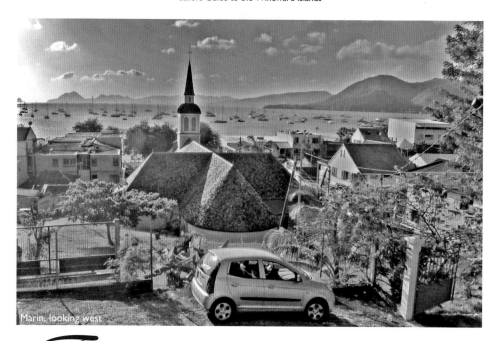
Marin, looking west

*T*he Caribs called Martinique *Madinina* ~ Island of Flowers. It is the largest of the Windwards and, apart from a few short spells under the British, has been French since it was colonized. It is a part of France and feels it, with excellent roads and a thriving economy. Nearly every bay has a wonderful government-built dock, ideal for leaving your dinghy. Fort de France is a busy city, bustling with shoppers and cars. The smaller towns are quieter and some look so clean they could have just been scrubbed. You will notice the smells of wonderful coffee and delicious cooking.

You can get almost anything done in Martinique ~ from galvanizing your boat to having stainless steel tanks made. The sailmakers are first rate, the chandleries magnificently stocked, and restaurants and boutiques abound. In short, when you have had enough deserted beaches and raw nature, Martinique is the place for a breath of civilization. And the island has enough excellent and varied anchorages for a week or two of exploring. Choose bays with fashionable resorts, sleepy waterfront villages, or visit deserted bays with excellent snorkeling. Well-marked trails make hiking a delight.

The Martinique Yachting Association aims to ensure you will have a wonderful visit. They are the voice of yachting in Martinique. They try to keep officialdom yacht friendly and see that there are adequate facilities. They speak good English, so call them if you have any questions about Martinique. If you need to get something done, or need help in dealings with authorities, they will put you in touch with a good professional service. They cannot help in trade disputes, as this is the realm of the tourist office, which you can visit in Marin Marina. They want your input as to what is good and bad and have a survey for this purpose on their web page. Let your feelings be known at: martiniqueyachtingassociation.fr

Empress Josephine grew up in Martinique on a 200-acre, 150-slave estate near Trois Ilets. A strange quirk of fate links Josephine and Martinique to the Battle of Trafalgar. In 1804, Napoleon was master of Europe, but the British still had naval supremacy and largely controlled Caribbean waters. However, ships were always scarce and some bright spark noticed that Diamond Rock on the south coast of Martinique was just about where the British would station another ves-

MARTINIQUE

sel if they had one, so they commissioned the rock as a ship. It was quite a feat to climb this steep, barren, snake-infested pinnacle and to equip it with cannons and enough supplies and water for a full crew of men. But they succeeded and for some 18 months H.M.S. Diamond Rock was a highly unpleasant surprise for unsuspecting ships sailing into Martinique. Napoleon was incensed; this was, after all, the birthplace of his beloved Josephine. Brilliant as he was on land, Napoleon never really understood his navy or its problems and considered his men to be shirkers. Consequently, he ordered them to sea under Admiral Villeneuve, to free the rock and destroy the British admiral Horatio Nelson while they were about it. Villeneuve slipped out under the British blockade of France and headed straight for Martinique. Lord Nelson smelled blood and bounty and hurtled off from England in hot pursuit. Poor information sent him on a wild goose chase to Trinidad, so Villeneuve was able to liberate the rock and return to France, prudently keeping well clear of Nelson.

Napoleon was none too pleased with Villeneuve because the British fleet was still in control of the high seas, so he was ordered to report in disgrace. Villeneuve preferred death to dishonor, so he put his ill-prepared fleet to sea to fight Nelson at the Battle of Trafalgar. Ironically, Villeneuve, who wished to die, survived the battle, and Nelson died.

Today Martinique is very civilized, and while it helps to speak French, it is not absolutely necessary. Many more locals now speak English.

Numerous ATM machines will keep you in cash, and most restaurants and businesses accept Visa and MasterCard. However, one or two only accept French cards. Ask before that seven-course meal or you may spend many hours washing dishes.

Navigation

The west coast (excluding the Bay of Fort de France) up to St. Pierre is mainly steep-to, and a quarter of a mile offshore clears any natural dangers.

Fish farms pop up off the coast from time to time. These are not dangerous by day but can be at night. They usually have flashing lights marking the outer limits. Currently, there is one off Bellefontaine with a clear passage inside or outside, approximate position 14° 40.2, 61° 10.2

The Bay of Fort de France has many shoals, especially at its eastern end. Check the charts and instructions given under the appropriate section.

The south coast of Martinique between Ste. Anne and Diamond Rock has several shoals extending up to a half mile offshore. Fish traps are plentiful and two or three are often tied together. It is best to stay in several hundred feet of water, outside the heavily fished area. The beat to Marin, usually against the current, is in protected water and can be exhilarating. It generally pays to tack fairly close to shore. On the rising tide, when the current sets east, the south coast can occasionally turn into a washing machine.

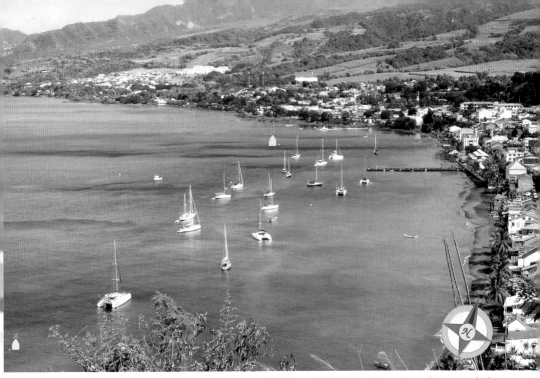

St. Pierre with visible anchorage zone buoys overlaid

ST. PIERRE

St. Pierre lies at the foot of the Mt. Pelée volcano, not far from where European settlers wiped out the last of the Carib residents in 1658. It is said that before the last ones died they uttered horrible curses, invoking the mountain to take its revenge. Mt. Pelée, in true Caribbean fashion, took its own sweet time, until Ascension Day, the 8th of May, in 1902.

At that time, St. Pierre, with a population of 30,000, was known as the Paris of the Caribbean and was the commercial, cultural, and social center of Martinique. The wealth of the island lay in the plantations and the richest of these surrounded St. Pierre. Ships would take on rum, sugar, coffee, and cocoa, and enough was sold to make several of the plantation owners multi-millionaires. There were also enough cheap bars, brothels, and dancing girls to satisfy the sailors.

The volcano gave some warning. Minor rumblings began early in April, and on April 23 a sizeable eruption covered the town in ash. Refugees from outlying villages started pouring in. On the 2nd of May a major eruption covered the city with enough ash to kill some birds and animals. Later the same day,

Pierre Laveniere, a planter with an estate to the south of St. Pierre, went to inspect his crops with a party of workers and they were swept away by a vast avalanche of boiling volcanic mud. On the 5th of May, it was the turn of the Guerin Estate, just a couple of miles north of St. Pierre and one of the richest in the area. A torrent of volcanic effluent, including mud, lava, boiling gasses, and rocks, estimated to be a quarter of a mile wide and 100 feet high, completely buried the estate, much of the family and many workers.

Even before Ascension Day, many people had been killed in and around St. Pierre. So why did people stay? Evacuation posed huge problems, the roads were primitive and rough, and the ferries, the main form of transport, did not have the capacity.

Governor Mouttet, on the island for less than a year, desperately wanted the problem to go away and was encouraged to sit tight by most of the planters and business leaders who would have suffered financial losses if the city were evacuated. If he had gone against them, and the volcano had not gone off, his career would have been over. He formed a

CENTER DE DECOUVERTE DE SCIENCES DE LA TERRE

TO DEPAZ

STADIUM

14° 45.0'

MILITARY
CHURCH
RUINS

JEAN-BAPTISTE CAR RENT

ECOMAX

CITE ARTISANALE
PROTO MECA
LAUNDERETTE   PATH TO WATERFALL

GAS
STATION

shoals

BLEU DES ILES
THEATRE RUINS

RELAIS DU PARC R.N.
MUSEUM

PELEE REST

TOURIST OFF

MARINA
PIZZA

LE FIGUIER

LAUNDERETTE

PAPA D'LO
DIVE SHOP

R. DE PETIT VERSAILLE

LE CERCLE DE ST PIERRE

TOWN HALL

BUSES
TO MORNE
ROUGE   CAR RENTAL

MARKET

No Anchor
zone

POST

BAKERY   CYBER BAS

WMTQ02
14° 44.5'N
61° 10.7'W

8 À HUIT   R. GEN. DE GAULLE

44.5'

R. CLAVIUS MARIUS

LA
VAGUE

BUSES
TO
LE CARBET
FORT
DE FRANCE

TAMAYA

L'ALSACE A KAY

R. VICTOR HUGO

RESERVOIR

GAS
STATION

MAMAN D'LO
YEMAYA   ANTONIO RESTAURANT

STATUE (CONSPIC)

ST. PIERRE

14° 44.0'

ANSE LATOUCHE
ZOO DE MARTINIQUE

61° 11.0'   61° 10.5'

committee to assess the risk, led by the science teacher at the school, Professor Landes, and they concluded there was no danger, a premature conclusion, given the scant knowledge of volcanoes at the time.

Evacuation would also have affected the coming elections, in which black voters were seriously challenging the status quo for the first time. The local paper, *Les Colonies*, also did its best to persuade people that there was no danger, despite the deaths. Several hundred individuals had the sense to leave, but for the rest the destruction of such an important city was unimaginable.

Many were eyewitnesses to the disaster. People were approaching from Fort de France for the Ascension Day church service when they saw heavy, red smoke from the volcano descend on St. Pierre. Rather than continue, they climbed the surrounding hills to see what would happen next. The end came at two minutes past eight in the morning. The side of the volcano facing St. Pierre glowed red and burst open, releasing a giant fireball of superheated gas that flowed down over the city, releasing more energy than an atomic bomb. All that remained were smoking ruins. An estimated 29,933 people burned to death, leaving only two survivors in the center of town: Leon Compere-Leandre, a cobbler, and the famous Louis-Auguste Cyparis, imprisoned for murder in a stone cell. Twelve ships in the bay were destroyed at anchor. One managed to limp away with a few survivors.

Part of Planatation Depaz

Many ruins still remain. Post-disaster buildings have been built onto old structures, so many new buildings share at least one wall with the past. Ruins also form garden walls, and some have been tidied up as historical icons. A museum in a modern building depicts that era and the tragedy. It stands on top of old walls that are artistically lit up at night, making an enchanting backdrop for those anchored below. (You can read a more detailed history on doyleguides.com)

Navigation

St. Pierre makes a good overnight anchorage except when there are heavy northerly swells. There is an adequate shelf on which to anchor, about 25 feet deep, the drop-off is very steep, so make sure you are well hooked. Occasionally, you have to move for local fishermen.

A series of yellow buoys with a cross on top designate a no-anchoring area to protect the dive-site wrecks. The wrecks are also buoyed. The anchoring shelf gets a little wide round at Anse Latouche, so there is plenty of room.

A conspicuous statue on the hill at the southern end of town is lit at night.

Regulations/communication

St. Pierre is a port of entry. L'Alsace A Kay is the closest place to clear with a customs computer. Closed Thursday they otherwise open at 1030 till 1700, and on Mondays, Tuesdays, Fridays and Saturdays they are open till 2200. Most restaurants have wifi, but L'Alsace A Kay is choice with a fabulous upstairs dining room overlooking the harbor. Go mid-morning or afternoon between meals. They are also a restaurant and shop (see *Provisioning and Restaurants*).

You can also check in at the tourist office, on the east side of the road just south of the museum. They open weekdays 0800-1600 except Wednesday 0800-1500. On Saturday they open 0900-1200. If you are leaving on a weekend, clear out in advance to be safe.

Cyber Base (closed Mondays) is a big internet station, open 0900-1300.

General yacht services

If you get permission from the town hall, you may be able to come alongside the town dock to take on water. Tie your dinghy towards the inner end. (A giant ferry comes once a week to the outer end and charter yachts use it.) Do your wash at one of two laundromats, the smaller waterfront one or the larger one near the river mouth.

Technical yacht services

Proto Meca is in the Cité Artisanale on the edge of town. Proto Meca is owned and run by Jean-Michel Trébeau, who trained as an aviation machinist in France and now has a first-rate shop. Anything you can break, he can fix, be it in stainless, aluminum, or bronze. He welds these metals and does all kinds of machining. He can rebuild your engine and resurface the block.

In the same compound you will find a carpenter and, if you are having a really bad day, a coffin maker.

Provisioning/shopping

The waterfront area has been renovated and includes an elegant replica of the old financial center. There are a couple of banks, several ATMs (the one at the post office is reliable), pharmacies, and a convenient 8 à Huit supermarket that closes for lunch and half an hour earlier than its name suggests. It also opens Sunday mornings. This is a good and quite large supermarket, but half of it is upstairs, so make sure you visit both floors.

The morning market offers a great variety of reasonably priced produce and is best on Saturdays. The fish market is just below and sometimes open. Good bread and pâtisseries can be found at three bakeries on

the back street. L'Alsace A Kay, a gourmet store, has lots of specialty foods mainly from Alsace, including St. Pierre beer, which comes from St. Pierre in Alsace in man-sized bottles. They are also a restaurant.

Ecomax supermarket is inexpensive with a limited range. Clothing boutiques, souvenir shops, and places selling local fabrics abound.

Restaurants

St. Pierre has lots of restaurants, several open for both lunch and dinner. Le Tamaya [$C] is an excellent little French restaurant, smart and clean, with nautical decor, and both the food and presentation rank considerably higher than the very reasonable prices charged (a good two-course menu starts at about 15 Eu), making it one of the best restaurants to visit in Martinique. It opens daily for lunch and dinner except Wednesday when it closes for dinner. It is owned by Peggy and Jean-Luc who are very welcoming and themselves yachtspeople who sailed the Atlantic and cruised the Caribbean. They post the windguru forecast outside their door. Seafood is always available, as are delicious desserts. Peggy speaks excellent English as well as German, French and some Italian. They open for lunch and reopen for dinner at 1830. While they have wifi, this is not an internet cafe (see *Communications*).

Philippe Mehn's L'Alsace A Kay [$A-B] has a lovely upstairs dining room overlooking the bay. They have a fairly large and sophisticated menu, specializing in recipes from Alsace, with some French and Créole dishes. They are closed Thursdays but otherwise open daily for lunch, when in addition to the regular menu, they often have an inexpensive special. They open for dinner on Mondays, Tuesdays, Fridays, and Saturdays. Take a look at the menu outside and if you like the choice make a reservation.

Bleu des Iles [$C-D] is right next to the old theater ruins; you climb a few steps to get to the door, which is above the road. They have a terrace with a good view of Mt. Pelée and a glimpse of the sea. This is a simple, but very nice French-Créole restaurant that offers a tasty local lunch menu every day except Thursday, when they close.

Their fish and Christophene au gratin is very good. They stay open for dinner on Monday, Tuesday, Friday and Saturday.

Two restaurants opened in 2016 on the new waterfront promenade. Le Cercle de Sainte-Pierre [closed Tuesday, $C-D] is an authentic Breton crêperie and glacier. Le Figuier [$D] is a pizzeria.

Caraibes is popular come sunset, with its tables right out on the street. They serve meals and sometimes have entertainment. Next door is Tai Loong, a Chinese snack bar. On the west side of the road, La Vague [$B-C] has an impressive waterfront location and you can enjoy a Créole meal here.

Heading south are two restaurants with doors on the road and dining rooms on the beach; both offer a perfect view. Le Reservoir [$C-D] is a little grill and crêperie. The owners are very welcoming; the open about 1130 and stay open in the evening. They work hard and serve up good food in the little kitchen. Antonio Restaurant is further down, near the gas station. They close Thursdays but are otherwise open every day 1130-1530. On Monday, Wednesday,

Friday and Saturday they open for dinner 1900-2130. They are reasonably priced and serve traditional Créole food.

Marina Pizza [$C-D] is a pizza/pasta place and an ice cream parlor. Le Coulibri Cyber Snack serves fast food including takeaway.

More restaurants open just for lunch. Chez Marie-Claire [$C] and Le Guerin [$C] are upstairs in the restored market and both serve good local Créole food. Up on the hill by the museum at Pelée [$D] you eat out under awnings overlooking the harbor. Owner Herve spent some years in the East End of London and speaks English. He serves very tasty and inexpensive Créole food.

Ashore

Pet lovers can find a recommended vet, Dr. Patrick Arien, at 159 Rue Bouille (not far from the dock) (0596) 78 10 03.

St. Pierre sits amid the most magnificent scenery in Martinique, so if you are thinking of sightseeing, this is an excellent place to begin. Rental cars are available from Jean Baptiste Garage and Bethel-Loc.

Relais de Parc Regional Naturel de la Martinique, just north of the museum, is the place to visit for information on parks and trails for St. Pierre and the rest of the island. You can pick up maps, ask questions and buy locally made goodies like jams, honey, woven articles, and souvenirs. They show a movie (free) about the history of St. Pierre and you can book from a variety of guided tours in the town and surrounding countryside. They open Tuesday to Saturday 0930-1400.

Visit the tourist office as well. Ask for maps of St. Pierre that show most of the historical monuments; you can make your own walking tour. Get a hiking map for Martinique and ask for details of particular hikes you plan. The tourist map will get you to the start of the hiking trails, and more detailed maps of the trails are posted by the trail parking areas.

The museum on the hill is dedicated to the 1902 eruption. It opens daily 0900-1200 and 1500-1700. There is an admission charge. It was started by Le Clerk, one of the

players in the event, and is now somewhat dated. The much newer Centre de Decouverte des Sciences de la Terre gives a much better idea of 1902 and is about a 20-minute walk. Go to Economax and take a curious lane that runs from its north side. You see a big rock overhanging the lane at the top. Follow this past the old military church ruins (it turns to dirt) and keep going till you get to a major road. Turn right and the Museum is right ahead just past the Stadium. It is closed Monday but otherwise opens at 0930. The entry fee is about 5 Eu. Pick up an English speaking player which will describe everything to you. Upstairs ask them to add English subtitles to the next movie, and take a seat, you will feel you were there. You are now half-way to Distillerie Depaz (see below), so you can keep going.

Two of the most interesting places to visit in town are the theater ruins beyond the museum and the prison where Cyparis was jailed, which is just below the theater (no charge).

For the energetic, there is a great walk

Visiting Zoo de Martinique

(about an hour round trip) up to the statue of the Virgin Mary, which has the best view of St. Pierre. Our map shows the way.

It is a 45-minute walk to Distillerie Depaz, and those used to hiking can make it. As an incentive, visiting is free and they give you rum to taste. The distillery is in lovely grounds set against Mt. Pelée as a backdrop. Make sure to visit the big old plantation house. The machinery is run by a steam engine and this is a perfect place to learn why that French white rum makes such distinctive petit punch. You can spend a long time wandering around and stay for lunch [$B-C] at the restaurant, perfectly situated on a hill overlooking cane fields to the sea beyond.

Zoo de Martinique in Habitation Latouche started as a garden among the ruins of a big estate that was built in 1650 and destroyed by the volcano in 1902. They added a zoo (and pirate house) to increase the appeal. It is very close, about a 10-minute walk on a busy road. When you leave the town heading south, the road follows one headland then comes to a beach. The garden is behind this beach. You could dinghy there. It is a wonderful excursion, designed by Jean Philippe Those, who created Jardin de Balata. You walk one-way, mainly on a raised wooden path, that takes you through lovely gardens amid ruins. They have a variety of animals, though the huge walk-in aviaries are best, with some great birds including rosy flamingos and scarlet ibis in one and a giant aviary of very tame Australian lorikeets that will likely land on your hat. It takes an hour or two, so you are happy to end at a good inexpensive restaurant. They open every day 0900-1700.

St. Pierre has a lovely little waterfall, with a small pool just deep enough to sit and cool off. A new easy path starts just beyond the Cite Artizanale and should be finished soon. But if not, you can make it as long as the path builders are not working.

In the mountains to the south of St. Pierre, there is an extraordinary walk along the Canal de Beauregard. Built by slaves in 1760, this canal brought water around a steep mountain to supply the distilleries of St. Pierre. It is most interesting to start at the bottom end of the canal and walk towards the source. The canal is fairly level, often shady, and easy, but you must have a head for heights, for you walk along the outer canal wall, which is about 18 inches wide, and the panoramic views are often dizzyingly precipitous.

If you drive past Precheur till the road ends, a footpath continues to Grand Rivière on the north coast.

If the weather is clear, ambitious hikers can head up Mt. Pelée. A road takes you within a mile and a half of the summit. Turn right just at the entrance to Precheur on the Chameuse Road. Non-hikers can enjoy the view from the top of the road.

For a scenic drive, the rainforest starts behind St. Pierre and the road up to the conspicuous volcanic observatory is impressive.

Gorges de la Falaise are dramatic waterfalls in a narrow canyon on the east side of Mt. Pelée. The hike takes about an hour and a half from the entrance and it is closed in heavy rains.

Water sports

Snorkeling is surprisingly interesting on the grass in the anchorage and off the pier. Baby reef fish hang out in the grass as do snake eels and trumpet fish.

Snorkel, too, on Maman d'Lo, an underwater sculpture in about 15 feet of water, about 50 yards off the beach in front of Antionio Beach restaurant, and marked by a yellow buoy. It is a Siren lying in the sand, partly submerged, made by Laurent

Valere in 2004. A little sister called Yemaya (several tons, in 3 parts; head, buttocks and tail), belted, with a conch crown, just joined her in 2015 in her mission to protect the sanctuary of the Bay of Saint-Pierre.

Twelve wrecks of ships that sank in the tragedy of 1902 are nearby, most within dinghy range of the anchorage, and at depths from 30 to 150 feet. The best way to find them is to dive with a local dive shop. Otherwise, watch the local dive boats, which visit them frequently (most of them are now buoyed). In addition, the north coast has the best diving in Martinique, with dramatic walls, canyons, and reefs, and many more fish than you find farther south.

If you are diving on your own, there is an easy dive right off the beach in front of the big wall under the museum. It is a good reef, dropping from 40 to 90 feet, decorated with old anchors, a huge old chain draped over the coral, and plenty of fish.

Papa D'Lo is a good dive shop, on the front street north of the main dock. Owner Serge Rueff will take you on a good wreck dive. Surcouf, is another dive shop at the south end of town, just past the gas station. They will fill tanks.

Amphitrite, 0696 80 38 62, is good at finding dolphins and also does fishing tours.

Case-Pilote

LE CARBET

Carbet is a small town on the headland just south of the bay of St. Pierre. You do not want to be here in northerly swells, but otherwise it makes a reasonable lunch stop, and in suitable conditions you could overnight. Edge quite close to the beach south of the dock ~ some people like to anchor all the way down off the hotel in the south. Use the dock for your dinghy with a stern anchor to keep you clear, or beach it.

The attraction is a lovely beach on which there are several restaurants. Two of these are worth special mention.

Just north of the dock, Beach Grill [$B-C] is right on the beach (the floor is sand) and open to the sea. The food is good, and the generous portions are artistically presented. They open for lunch Tuesday to Sunday and for dinner Wednesday to Saturday.

Right down at the south end, Le Petibonum [$B] is famous for excellent food, more gourmet style, served right on the beach, and they open every day for lunch and dinner. Either can be crowded, so reservations are a good idea.

Art lovers should see the museum about Gauguin on the road towards St. Pierre. It includes letters, documents, artifacts, and reproductions of Gauguin paintings. It is soon to be renovated.

CASE-PILOTE

Case-Pilote is a picturesque fishing port, both charming and unspoiled, with Martinique's oldest church. An extension to the port in the form of a sturdy, big ferry dock and other waterfront renovations have been completed. No ferry service is planned, so you can tie up on the outside, as the inside is usually full. Some swells reach the dock, which has big rubber fenders that will mark your topsides; a fender-board would help.

Anchorage outside the port is limited by the needs of the active fishing fleet, and when the fishermen put out seine nets at about 0600 hours, they will wake anyone they feel is in their way and ask them to move. It is not every day, but please do move willingly and right away, if asked. To avoid this, spend the night in Petit Fourneau in about 25 feet of water, though they sometimes seine net there, too.

Regulations/Services

There are no customs in Case-Pilote; clear elsewhere. You can leave your dinghy in the port. You will find garbage bins around the port or the village. A small gas station in the marina sells fishing gear and ice, but they cannot supply yachts with fuel. For that and for diesel, you will have to jug it from the gas station.

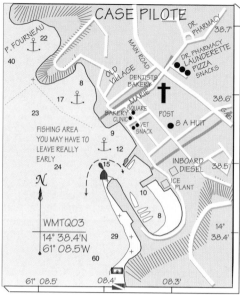

People come here to visit Frank Ågren's Inboard Diesel Service, which is right at the entrance to the port. Frank is the regional headquarters for Volvo Penta for much of the Eastern Caribbean and does Volvo surveys and diagnostics up and down the islands. He also does warranty work. His big shop has a whole floor devoted to spares and he has the largest stock in the Windwards. He can supply spares at somewhat lower prices than you might pay elsewhere and shipping parts to other Caribbean islands is no problem. Beatrice, in his office, takes care of this. Frank has a hotline to the factory and, being Swedish, he speaks the same language as the engine, so anyone having Volvo Penta problems should give him a call. Frank and his team are now also a fully qualified sales and service agency for Northern Lights Generators and MTU engines, which should help the large yachts. Those visiting Frank can come inside the port, where he has about three reserved spaces with free wifi. Frank speaks perfect English. A large supply of new and secondhand spares is kept in stock, as are new engines and generators. Inboard Diesel Service has a fast service boat and can, if necessary, visit other ports and islands. Frank has a shop in Marin and Volvo associates in most other islands.

Ashore

Case-Pilote is one of the oldest villages

CASE-PILOTE
Where the Future is Now

CULTURAL and NATURAL ATTRACTIONS await your visit : our charming town square with it's fountain and statue, the oldest church in Martinique with it's historical cemetery, the Town Hall. Shops and services, bakeries, covered market, doctors, dentists, post office, veterinarian at your fingertips.

in Martinique, founded around 1640 when the church was built. Now a historical monument, the exterior of the building is particularly beautiful with its brand new tiled roof and the newly renovated Presbytery beside it. Inside, you will notice that the architecture of the church leaves you no doubt that Case-Pilote has always been turned toward the sea. In the cemetery behind the old church is the final resting place of Victor Severe, born in Case-Pilote in 1867 and the deputy for Martinique who led the cause for liberation in the French Assembly. He participated in the French resistance and died in 1957 at the age of 90.

While fishing is the major economic activity, market gardening takes place on level areas. Lettuce, tomatoes and herbs as well as cabbages and local root vegetables thrive, and everyone owns chickens. (There is even a memorial to a favorite cock in one of the tombs.)

The fruit and vegetable market opens on Fridays from 1600 and on Saturdays from 0700-1200. They also sell flavored liquors and syrups like coco punch. Sometimes an accras truck will be selling hot, fresh accras

and doughnuts. The Town Hall Cultural attaché sometimes organizes an art exposition and fair for local artists.

For topping up provisions, visit 8 à Huit, whose name gives you their Monday-Saturday hours. They also open Sundays and holidays in the morning.

Across the main road from the church is a small shopping centre. Here you will find a pharmacy, a doctor upstairs from the pharmacy (no appointment necessary: just wait your turn), a laundromat, an excellent snack bar, Chez Colette, for local foods and, to the delight of all aboard, but especially the cook, Remy Pizza. The terrace in front of Remy Pizza is a good place to stop for a lunch with the kids while the laundry spins around. All of Remy's employees speak English, so you can be sure you will get the right toppings. Enjoy the two bakeries. The one by the market has a splendid little Parisian-style terrace for that morning coffee and croissant

The new Kay DADA [$D] restaurant on the seafront is the Friday and Saturday night hotspot. For a more down to earth venue, look for the new restaurant on the boardwalk named Shell Beach [$D]. Snack Bar de La

Ville de CASE-PILOTE
Authentique et dynamique

Attraits culturels et naturels Petite place centrale avec sa statue et sa fontaine, son église, la plus ancienne de l'île, entourée de son cimetière et des commerces, boulangerie-pâtisserie, marché couvert, médecin, dentiste, vétérinaire, mairie, la Poste... à portée de main

SCHOELCHER

Plage [$D] is also on the waterfront

Opposite the shopping center is another small collection of buildings in which a second pharmacy and doctor are located.

This is a convenient place for pet owners to come for a vet. You will find Dr. Fournier at 2, Rue Schoelcher, (0596) 69 38 91, emergency: (0696) 01 84 48. A new health services building opposite the veterinarian is occupied by a physical therapist, a nurse who also gives blood testing procedures. Three dentists work out of the same building on Rue Allegre, up from the Town Hall

Water sports

Diving and snorkeling off the headland just south of the marina are very good. Huge rocks rise from 70 feet and the whole area is filled with brightly colored sponges, corals, and fish. If you don't have your own gear, contact the Case-Pilote Diving Club. For those interested in wildlife, there is a bat cave in the cliffs behind the snorkeling area.

If you want to do some sport fishing or see dolphins from a local yole, call Goadou at (0696) 07 82 65 or Tilo Sicot at (0696) 22 11 88.

Originally Case Navire, this town was famous for the water provided by its two rivers, making it a vital rest stop for ships of old. It was renamed after Victor Schoelcher, the anti-slavery advocate, and now covers a large area, bisected by the west coast highway. The waterfront part is easily accessible to yachts and has the atmosphere of a tiny town on its own. It is a less urban anchorage than Fort de France, with pleasant beaches. Buses run to Fort de France frequently; it takes 15 minutes. It is easier here than in Fort de France to rent a car and organize shopping runs or trips to the mountains. The tourist office will help you (in French).

The official anchoring area, off Anse Madam, is marked and good. People still anchor off the renovated waterfront and beach south of the dock. If you do that, be prepared to move if fishermen or officials ask you to. You can tie your dinghy to the town dock, though you will need a dinghy anchor. The waterfront adjoining the dock is a park area. Anse Madam has a long beach and is home to one of the largest and best sailing schools in the area.

Ashore

Chan's is a good little supermarket

within easy walking distance of the dock. Zen Cafe [$D] is an ice creamery and crêperie. The beachside Balade de Neige [$D], opens early for coffee and sells ice creams, crepes and sandwiches from 1100 right through into the evening. Fan de Pizza [$D] next door is a good pizza place that also sells grilled foods in the evening. Apicius [$B-C] is a nice-looking Italian restaurant.

The Madiana Center is also within walking distance for the reasonably energetic. This entertainment center has the best cinema in Martinique. (On Thursdays they show movies in their original language.) One of the restaurants here will delight pub aficionados, as it has a microbrewery on site with good beer and serves a variety of food. Other small businesses include a hair stylist.

For a major provisioning, you will need a cab or a car to visit the huge malls on the road to Fort de France. There is also the Leader Price at Terreville. Go out of town and straight up the hill on the road to L'Enclos.

L'Ajoupa Deux Gros lies in a bay halfway between the town of Shoelcher and Case-Pilote. There is no problem anchoring there, but forget landing on the little concrete wall or the beach if there are any swells. However, if you do make it (a big tender can do so from either port), it is one of the fancier restaurants in Martinique.

Pet owners can find a recommended vet, Dr. Veto-Dom, at 12 Ave Anse Madam (0596) 61 05 08, emergency (0696) 27 17 47.

Fort de France

FORT DE FRANCE

Fort de France, the capital of Martinique, is the largest and liveliest city in the Windwards. It is a great place for shops, restaurants, and people-watching. It has one of the nicest city anchorages in a pleasant area under Fort St. Louis, opposite the park and close by the public beach, which is well used in the early mornings. The new waterfront is a huge boardwalk where bouncing waves whistle below. This is also the dinghy dock and it leads onto a great kids' playground. In the late afternoon kids come to play, people hang out, and vendors set up on the roadside with snack foods and drinks. If you are puzzled by the turnstiles to get out, they

are to keep obnoxious kids from zooming up and down the boardwalk on scooters.

Occasionally kids can play in dinghies and damage them. On my last visit they had some security officers around, which was a comfort. If worried, the higher dock to the west of the dinghy dock is probably safer.

In town, the central Rue de la République has been converted into a delightful pedestrian street and the large Cours Perrinon Mall is right in town. Those wanting to explore Martinique can take advantage of the many buses that use the capital as their hub. You are close to chandleries and many yacht services.

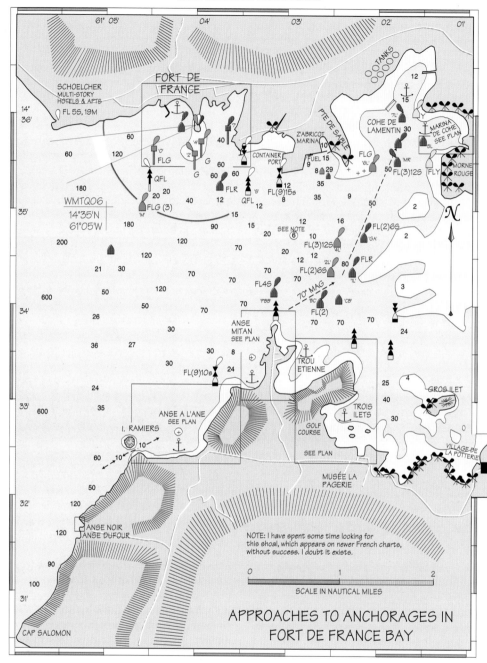

APPROACHES TO ANCHORAGES IN
FORT DE FRANCE BAY

NOTE: I have spent some time looking for this shoal, which appears on newer French charts, without success. I doubt it exists.

SCALE IN NAUTICAL MILES

Navigation

When approaching Fort de France from Cap Salomon, it is hard to see at a glance exactly where the harbor is, as the surrounding area is built up, including a huge hotel and some apartment blocks at Schoelcher, a couple of miles west of Fort de France. As you approach, you can identify the main yacht

anchorage by the prominent slab-sided fort wall, the big new circular apartment block that from afar looks like a giant water tank, and the yachts at anchor.

The yacht anchorage is on the east side of the bay, between Fort St. Louis and a line between the red and yellow buoys in the center of the bay. Leave the red buoy to

Fort de France

starboard to avoid the isolated rocky shoal to its southeast. Charts show only about 5 feet on this shoal. I could not find any depths much less than 7 feet, but there may be shallower rocks (see chart page 87).

The water is shallow and rocky if you get close to Fort St. Louis, but level in many areas once the depth reaches about nine feet. The anchorage is deeper (25-40 feet) towards the center of the bay for deep-draft yachts. Holding in the bay is good when you hit clay-like sand, variable in soft mud. Fort de France is connected to Anse Mitan, Anse à L'Ane, and Trois Ilets by frequent ferries, which make the anchorage rolly from time to time.

If you need work done, you can find a work berth in the Baie des Tourelles. (Make arrangements in advance and give cruise ships wide clearance.) If you are heading

east to get there or southeast toward Anse Mitan, keep well clear of the shoals off the fort. It is possible to cut somewhat inside the green buoys, but to be on the safe side, go around them.

A good new Marina Z'Abricots serving Fort de France is by Pte. du Sable. See our section on *The Industrial Zones*. If you visit Fort de France by car, the easiest pay parking is one of the many Vinci-parkings. There is one in the block next to Sea Services.

Regulations

Clearing in and out is easy in Sea Services. Fill the form out on the customs computer, print your clearance, and have one of the staff stamp it. You can peruse the chandlery at the same time (open weekdays 0830-1715; Saturdays 0830-1230). Or you can dinghy to the DCML fuel dock, open

0800-1800, Sundays and holidays 0800-1230.

Communications

The Marie has a Cyber Base in the lovely old Pavillon Bougenot building on Rue Victor Severe. Closed Monday, they open 1900-1700 on Tuesday and Wednesday, 1300-1700 on Thursday, and 0900-1200 on Friday and Saturday. Turn left at the Schoelcher Library and look opposite the police station. It can be crowded. You can call 0596 55 68 48 for reservations. Lina's cafe has comfy seating, air-conditioning, and great coffee and is perfect for wifi. Quick, an inexpensive fast food restaurant upstairs in Cours Perrinon, has wifi. Ask for the code.

General yacht services

A good dinghy dock lies all along La Savanne. Small litter bins line the dock. Bigger tips are on Rue Déproge, but since they have wheels, check out the location before carting in garbage.

DCML is a good fuel dock in Baie des Tourelles. It is a low floating dock so you may need to deploy a ladder to get down. They offer fuel, water, oils, beer, coffee, and both cube and chipped ice, lunch sandwiches, and sundry items. This is the easiest place to get ice in Fort de France. They open 0800-1815 daily except Sundays and holidays 0800-1245. They may close earlier in the summer. Charter yachts qualify for duty-free when they have cleared out. Take the boat down or, for small things, dinghy down.

Marina Z'Abricots has a fuel dock on the outer marina wall. It is a low floating dock, substantially built with 9 feet of water alongside. They sell diesel, gasoline and ice, but no duty free.

La Laverie de la Pointe, a new launderette is open from 0645 to 2200 seven days a week. Washers for 7, 11 or 14 kilos of laundry and dryers vary in price from 7 to 10 euros. Quick Pressing laundry and dry cleaning can also do your laundry on Blvd Allegre.

You cannot get gas tanks filled in Martinique. In an emergency, buy a small new French butane tank at a snack store beside the fire station on Blvd Admiral Gueydon. Continue along the canal to see Fontaine Gueydon, once part of the water system and now a monument.

Barnacles bugging you? Need a new stainless fuel tank? The yacht services compound in Baie des Tourelles should solve your problems. You can dinghy there, bring the yacht, or check it out on foot. The walk to Quai des Tourelles is about 15 minutes from town. Head past Quai Ouest on the main road out of town heading east. Turn right immediately after the big, new buildings on the right side of the road. Follow the road and turn left when you come to a junction. This leads you to the new basin. At the heart of this compound is a haul-out run by Carenantilles, who have a larger facility in Marin. The shallow parts of the canal on the southeast side have been dredged to about 11 feet. The haul-out has a 35-ton marine hoist that can haul boats about 2 meters deep. Artisans and engineers can do everything you need. Small boats can be stored on racks. Language is not a problem, as most people speak some English.

If you are too long, wide, heavy, or ugly to haul elsewhere, you can arrange to be slipped alongside a ship in the huge Martinique dry dock, which will take anything up to a cruise ship (see also *Marin Services*).

Chandlery

Sea Services, on Rue Déproge, is one of Martinique's largest chandleries. It is owned by Christophe Sirodot who worked for some years in the US. Valerie, the manager, has been here the longest and speaks English, as do most of the other staff, and all are attentive.

Sea Services is really two adjoin-ing stores. The western store sells yacht gear, including International Paints, 3-M products, 316 stainless fasteners, tenders, liferafts, stoves, anchors, barbecues, charts, and guides. Their rope stock includes the new ropes that replace wire for rigging. They stock a good range of electrical equipment, from wire and connectors to solar panels, windlasses, and Aerogen wind generators, as well as a good stock of yacht electronics. This includes waterproof cell phones and tablets. They are big on Matt Chem clean-ers in both yacht and commercial sizes, also Aquasale biodegradable products, includ-ing soaps. They have a full rigging service

FORT DE FRANCE
ANCHORAGE

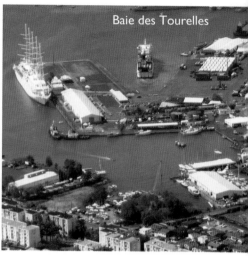

Baie des Tourelles

from a dinghy locking line upwards. Their on-the-spot swaging works for up to 12mm wire and they do larger diameters by order. They sell and service inflatable life jackets. Sea Services regularly delivers antifouling paint to all Martinique haul-out facilities, and can arrange haul-out quantities duty-free for visiting yachts for use in Martinique or to take away.

The eastern part of Sea Services features decorative nautical objets d'art, tableware, and linens, but most of all a wide selection of good nautical casual and sportswear, including St. James, and TBS. Many superyachts come by here to outfit the crew with shorts and shirts. They also have goodies for kids, microfibre products, elegant soft towels, non-skid molded shoes with removable soles, and all kinds of carriers, from backpacks to wallets.

You will find other chandleries in the Baie de Tourelles Carenantilles, an easy dinghy ride away. Max and Cedric's Polymar is a big chandlery, and very strong on construction materials. It has a stock of ropes,

fittings, lots of fishing gear, yacht hardware and general accessories. Polymar sells many products for projects, including marine and teak ply, which can be bought cut to size (they often have a box of off cuts for sale that may be perfect for a project), resins, gel coat, cores, foams, cloths, and paints (including the International line). They sell and service Lacomble Schmitt hydraulics. They have a good selection of hinges and other fittings, also steering seats and pedestals. This is a good place to look at electrics and electronics, gauges and bilge pumps. Polymar is also the place to get your scuba tanks filled. You can talk to them about glass repair. They have a second store in Robert.

M. Josepha's Coopemar is a fishing store, but it also has electronics, jerry jugs, some hardware and paints, as well as oilskins and shoes.

The famous fishing store Littoral closed, but a new one Jessypeche has just opened. I have put it in the same place as Littoral, but it may be up or down the road.

Anyone need personal protection? Visit Levalois Racing on Rue Déproge for CS gas or foam and stun guns.

Technical yacht services

Most yacht services are to be found at the Carenantilles compound in Baie des Tourelles.

Jean Pierre and François Chalmessin can work wonders with titanium (one of the few places that can weld it), stainless and aluminum, including welding, bending, building, and machining. Whether you have a broken winch or want a new pulpit or water tank, they can do it. They can fix most marine cooking stoves, and it is worth talking to them if you have a simple refrigeration problem. They can replace most parts and recharge systems.

Emanuel Plisson's Sarl A2M is another large metal shop a few doors down with TIG and MIG welders, and they can fabricate anything in aluminum and stainless.

Manu Voile is a sailmaking shop owned by Emmanuel Resin, who has sewn sails as long as I have written guides. He has help and can tackle anything from new sails (any size) to repairs, biminis, and cushions. Their location right on the waterfront is very convenient for unloading sails. They also make lazy bags for the mainsail. They open weekdays 0800-1300 and 1430-1800 and can collect and deliver.

Bellance at Debrouilla Marine specializes in household and marine electronic and electric work

Maxi Marine has a magnificent and very clean showroom and workshop. They are the agent for Mercury outboards, which they sell, install, and repair. They are also sales and repair agents for Cummins Diesel. Upstairs they have a chandlery aimed at power boats with quite a lot of gear including safety equipment, fasteners and interesting accessories.

S.A.V. des Moteurs, run by Joseph Féré, is on the road as you approach the compound. He services OMC outboards.

Marc Eugene at Renovboats does good fiberglass repair and spray painting, as well as electrical work. He can repair your starter or alternator or fix your electrics to European standards and bring in electrical things fast from Florida. It is easiest to contact him by phone (0696-25-01-92).

Propeller out of whack or spinning? Propeller Caraibe Service (PCS) is at 177 Avenue Maurice Bishop. Maybe give them a call before you walk out that far.

Injectors or injection pumps need servicing? Check out our section on the *Industrial Zones.*

Provisioning

(See plans pages 91 and 96-97)

Changing money in Fort de France is now easy at the best rates, thanks to efficient

Approaches to Baie des Tourelles

little change places like Change Caraibes, which is at the Savanne end of Rue Ernest Déproge and opens weekdays 0800-1730, Saturdays 0800-1230. Another money-changing shop, Martinique Change, is at the Blvd. Allègre end of Rue Victor Hugo, and yet another is at the La Savanne end of the same road. Cash machines are everywhere, most intimidatingly public. Just beyond Sea Services, outside the car park, is an enclosed room where you can get your cash without being right on the street. The bank in the Cours Perrinon is also somewhat discreet.

Provisioning in Fort de France is a pleasure, but when shopping always remember to take bags. The Carrefour Market in the Cours Perrinon is large and good, the best in town. Leader Price, opposite Sea Services, is a popular market, with bargain prices on canned and dry goods, beer, and more. They have reasonable frozen and produce sections. It can be crowded and slow. Neither of these stores currently delivers.

The place for fresh produce and spices is the main market, best in the mornings and especially on Saturday.

Friandises des Isles, on Rue République, is a great little bakery with a good variety of bread, including whole wheat, and baked delights. You can buy a coffee here, and salad to go with your bread.

For the fun of shopping in a really big supermarket, you need to visit the out-of-town malls, where small shops surround gargantuan modern supermarkets, called hyper-marchés. Buses go to all these places from the big bus and TC station in Point Simon, right beside the dinghy dock. Two of the best supermarkets, Carrefour and La Galleria, are described in *The Industrial Zones*.

The others are towards Schoelcher and the closest is HyperU at Le Rond Point. It can be reached via the Schoelcher communal taxi, which leaves from the big taxi stand in front of the anchorage. The energetic may prefer to walk. It is rather uphill, but half an hour will get you there at an easy pace. En route, you may want to check out Weldom, a really giant hardware store with a vast range of household and project-related stock. Villa Verde is a garden store with lots of hose fittings and Christmas lights, and Sport 2000 is a giant sports store that includes kayaks

and water sports. Farther along (next round-about, we are no longer walking) is a Casino Géant, which has good frozen fish and many Chinese fixings.

For duty-free supplies, Martinique customs deem that you must be a charter boat. The definition of a charter boat is rather left up to the business. You must mark charter yacht on your customs form, and a brochure helps. But even if you do not qualify, the duty-free purveyors offer good wholesale prices on cases of beer and wine. Go down to Quai de Tourelles and check Vatier, mainly drinks, and TCS, another wholesaler, who also has a retail jewelry store.

Fun shopping

Visit the tourist office in La Savanne or the one on Rue Lazare Carnot. They will give you a good Fort de France map as well as a Martinique one, and they will answer your questions. Ask for their dining guide.

Cours Perrinon is a big mall right in the middle of town, open 0800-1900. With two floors, it has glass-fronted elevators, escalators, and lots of shops, restaurants, and a really large bookshop (opposite the supermarket) with computers, stationery, and more.

If you need printer inks or special paper, check Encre Pour Tous, a block down Rue Perrinon.

Right opposite Sea Services, Diamond Distribution is a good hardware shop with lots of tools and household stuff. Upstairs in Cours Perrinon La Foire Fouille is a giant household store, generally cheap and junky, but it always has something you need. Another, even cheaper, is Bazar Pas Cher on Rue de la Republique.

Fort de France is the place for both fashionable shopping and souvenir hunting. The biggest handicraft market is on Boulevard Alfassa and another is near the fish market. You will find everything from jewelry to handbags, paintings, and varnished palm fruits. Half the artists and carvers in Haiti must be kept busy whipping out an overwhelming number of coconut trees, banana plants, fruits, and models in balsa wood. These are available all over town. The biggest congregation of souvenir shops is on Rue Déproge towards La Savanne.

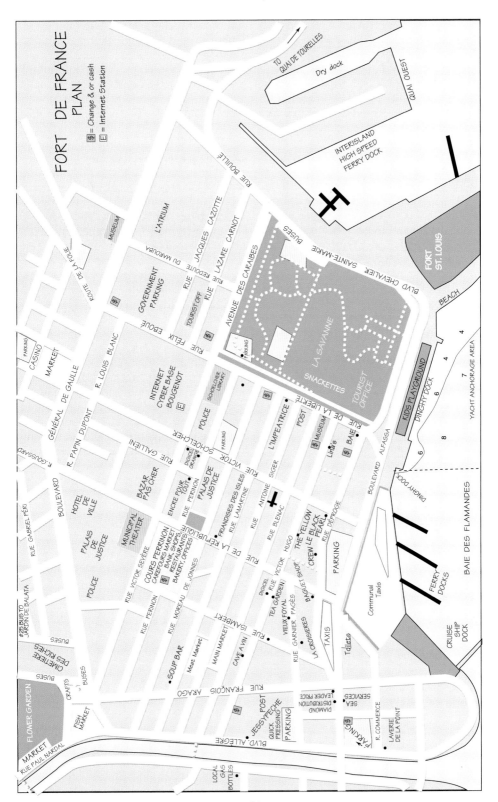

FORT DE FRANCE PLAN

$ = Change & or cash
E = Internet Station

Fort de France is the only place in the Windwards for Paris fashions and stylish clothing shops. Make a beeline for Cours Perrinon, which has tons of stores, and enjoy Rue de La République, which is mainly pedestrian. Otherwise just wander around all the town's little streets and enjoy. When you need a break, you can have a coffee at Lina's. Don't forget to check out the St. James line of clothing at Sea Services (see *Chandlery*) or visit the local market.

Restaurants

Restaurants are plentiful, geared to the local market, and for the most part, prices are moderate and the food is straightforward and correctly prepared. Lunch is the best value for money, as restaurants compete to attract the workers. Fort de France also has a pleasant atmosphere in the evening, with outside seating in several places, not many peple are around, it is very quiet.

For a Continental breakfast or coffee, try L'Impeatrice [$D]. They have wicker chairs and outside seating, and it is inexpensive.

A pleasant place to take lunch is in the main market, between Rue Victor Hugo and Rue Antoine Siger, amid the bustle of people selling fruits, tropical flowers, exotic alcoholic drinks, souvenirs of all kinds, and straw goods. Tables are set out both at one end of the market and upstairs. About half a dozen small restaurateurs [$D] offer typical Créole meals at bargain prices. There is a fresh fruit juice stand where you choose your fruit and watch it being juiced.

The Crew [$B-C, closed Saturday and Sunday evenings] is reliable and moderately priced. They serve good French food. It is easy to find room at dinner, though it is packed with businessmen for lunch.

Le Black Pearl [$A-C] is new, modern, efficient, and open daily from 0700 to 0130, you can eat any time. Their present outside seating area on Rue Schoelcher is unusable till the building shades the area (mid afternoon), but it should move back to the front soon.

The food is good and the portions generous, with local fresh fish, meat, and salads including an excellent Créole salad plate

with boudin, crab back, fritters and more. The have an upstairs bar with simple food called Le Triangle.

I have not been to The Yellow [$A-B] upstairs at 51 Rue Victor Hugo, but it is the new restaurant everyone raves about. It opens Monday to Friday from 1200-1430 and Monday to Saturday in the evening from 1900-2300. I am told that it has great food, nicely decorated with a menu that changes all the time, and that it is specially charming at night. It is apparently not easy to find, and the map location we give may be slightly off.

La Baie [$B-C], owned by Jocelyne Guiout, is a pleasant upstairs restaurant overlooking the anchorage and park. You can sit inside in air conditioning or outside on the balcony. They serve Créole dishes, and the food is generally good. Down below Hasta La Pizza for pizza, crepes and Hagendaz ice cream.

In the evening, for something cheap, try the Soup Bar [$D, opens at 1700]. It has an old-fashioned atmosphere, with seats inside and out on the street. The food is good and reasonably priced as they concentrate on soups, salads, lasagnas, and a few other things. Neujo Mejico [$C] (opposite Sea Services) is upstairs and good, with reasonable lunch time specials, and while you can eat Mexican, you don't have to.

La Croisière [$B-C, closed Sunday], is a pleasant upstairs restaurant with a great balcony for watching life on the street below. It is informal, relatively inexpensive, and serves both French and Créole dishes for lunch or dinner. Owner Alex Zizi has good local jazz groups on Friday and Saturday nights.

Fancy a smoked salmon sandwich? Then Lina's [$D] on Rue Victor Hugo is just the ticket, with elegant sandwiches and salads and wine by the glass, all in a pleasant air-conditioned building with seating on two floors. Leave some room for dessert and excellent coffee. Lina is open till 2200. If you are in Carenantilles, Le Grand Voile is open for lunch.

If you are on one of those big yachts, the chef has left in a huff, and the owner is finding everything too down market, try La Cave a Vin [$A], owned by M. Grouvel, It is both an upmarket restaurant and a gourmet food and wine store. They expect you to dress well.

Wherever you eat, beware of those little green peppers. They are often put beside the food as decoration, and they are the hottest of hot.

Transport

Fort de France is a convenient starting point to see the island, as there are buses and communal taxis that go to all major towns and villages. Currently, many of them start right outside the new ferry docks. If you are going to the airport, take the "Ducos" car. The charge is just a few Euros. Most of the suburban buses go from the west end of Blvd. Général de Gaulle. These include buses to Dillon, Balata, and Didier. Buses to Lamentin go from the east side of La Savanne.

A trip to Jardin de Balata is easy from Fort de France. The gardens are set in the rain forest, beautifully maintained, and include a canopy walk, a pond, and lots of flowers and hummingbirds. It is best when there are not too many cruise ships in port. Entrance is around 13 Eu. Take bus no. 25 from the east side of the cemetery (just a little north of where we show it on our plan), which takes you right there and costs about 3 Euros round trip.

Taxis are available. Tours and shopping trips work out at about 40 Eu an hour for up to 4 people, 10 Eu per person per hour for more than 4. Some drivers speak good English. Vincent Thomas has three sizes of car, works with his wife Elodie. He is easy to contact by mobile phone 0696-07-54-37 and he speaks excellent English. He is based in Rivière Salée, so knows the industrial area well. For all day tours he will also pick up in Marin.

Marc Pharose is also a good English-speaking taxi driver who knows where everything is (0696 45 09 56). He does not work on Sundays.

Ashore

History buffs should visit the little pre-Columbian museum on Rue de la Liberté [closed Sunday] and the Ethnic History Museum on Blvd. Général de Gaule. Architecture buffs should see the Schoelcher Library,

a very elaborate metal building designed by Gustav Eiffel, made in France and shipped here. La Cimetière des Riches is also of interest, as until recently, only the rich and famous could be buried there.

THE INDUSTRIAL ZONES

With coastal regions collecting top dollar for rentals, it is not surprising that more and more businesses are now found in the industrial zones, which run from Fort de France, past the airport, to Rivière Salée. If you are renting a car, drive to Carrefour and take the airport road. Most businesses are reached from one of the following major exits: the first is Rivière Roche, the second Jambette, the third Californie, and the fourth, which is easily identifiable by La Galleria, is Les Mangles. Note also the turnoff to Le Lamentin or La Lezarde. Lareinty is a zone right opposite the airport. Continue on for Rivière Salée, using the same exit as for Trois Ilets. Taxis can be of help. Buses go to Carrefour from the western end of Blvd. Général de Gaulle, by the cemetery.

Marina Z'Abricots

There is an excellent new community-

CACEM
Communauté d'Agglomération du Centre de la Martinique

LE PORT DE PLAISANCE COMMUNAUTAIRE DE L'ETANG Z'ABRICOTS, UN OUTIL FONDÉ SUR LES ATTENTES DES PLAISANCIERS

PORT DE PLAISANCE COMMUNAUTAIRE
ETANG Z'ABRICOTS.
MARTINIQUE F.W.I.

Le Port de Plaisance Communautaire de l'Etang Z'Abricots répond à plusieurs enjeux :

• **Offrir un espace de plaisance** aux nombreux bateaux basés ou de passage à la Martinique ;
• **Doter l'île d'un équipement nautique moderne qui respecte l'environnement** ;
• **Renforcer la position de l'île dans le marché caribéen** de la plaisance ;
• **Développer les activités et les emplois inhérents** au secteur de la plaisance et du nautisme.

Situé dans le prolongement de la Pointe des Grives sur une superficie de 12 ha, le projet du Port de plaisance a été initié en 1988 par la Ville de Fort-de-France.

Par la suite, en 2003, la CACEM, dans le cadre de sa compétence Développement Economique, a déclaré d'intérêt communautaire la construction et la gestion du Port de plaisance.

L'ensemble de l'opération a coûté 40 millions d'euros.

Le Port de Plaisance Communautaire de l'Etang Z'Abricots a ouvert ses portes en janvier 2015.

DESCRIPTIF
• Un **plan d'eau** (bassin Z'Abricots) d'une profondeur maximale de 4m comptant **340 anneaux** ;
• Un **bureau du port** ;
• Un **parc à bateaux** de 150 places (terre-plein Grives).

SERVICES & EQUIPEMENTS

BUREAU DU PORT
• Clearance
• Point Rafraîchissement
• Douches/Sanitaires
• Point Météo
• Point Touristique
• Laverie automatique
• Vente de produits annexes (huile, liquide de refroidissement...)
• Vente de produits de consommation courante (eau, gaz, glaçons...)
• Prestations bureautiques

SERVICES
• Réseau WIFI
• Cale de mise à l'eau
• Eau/Electricité
• Parc à bateaux
• Station d'avitaillement
• Tri sélectif en carburant (gasoil et sans plomb)
• Collecte des eaux usées

Un protocole de protection et de suivi de la mangrove a été bâti en vue de préserver, au mieux, les qualités environnementales du Port de Plaisance Communautaire de l'Etang Z'Abricots.

Un plan de récupération, de traitement et d'élimination des déchets a été formalisé par la CACEM.

HORAIRES

ACCUEIL DU PUBLIC
Lundi au vendredi : 7H - 17H
Samedi : 7H - 14H
(excepté les jours fériés)

PERMANENCE
Samedi après-midi, dimanche et jours fériés

BUREAU DU PORT
Etang Z'Abricots
Tél. : 0596 75 11 57
contact.zabricots@marinov.fr

CACEM
Direction Gestion des Equipements et Aménagements Nautiques
Tél. : 0596 75 82 72 - www.cacem.fr

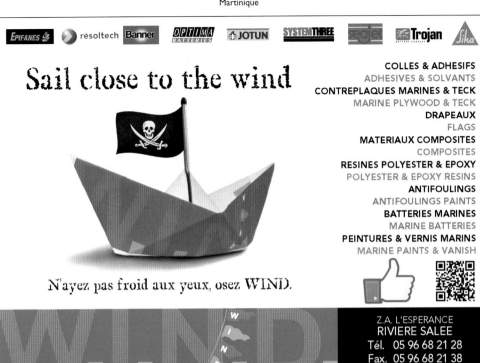
owned marina in this area called Port de Plaisance de L'Etang Z'Abricots (Marina Z'Abricots). It is peaceful and quiet and is an excellent place to leave your boat safely while you rent a car to shop or explore. It is not hurricane proof, so not suitable for hurricane storage.

For the deepest approach, come from the south and pass between the red and green buoys. The entrance between the outer floating docks is marked with red and green beacons. You can ask for assistance coming in (0596 75 11 57). On the larger yacht docks (the ones nearest the bay) each berth has a mooring line attached to a cleat. You have to pull it up and take it to the bow (a dinghy could help)

The Marina offers security, free wifi, water and electricity. They have a separate fuel dock outside to the west where you can buy diesel, water, gasoline and ice. The dock is very low, so you may need ladders to get down. There is nine feet of water on the dock. They also have a haulout area for small craft. Washing machines are planned, and they hope to attract a restaurant and many

more services soon. There is anchoring room outside if you want to anchor while you arrange a berth.

Provisioning

Carrefour at Dillon is the first large and well-laid-out supermarket you come to on the airport road and it is excellent for a major provisioning. Some prefer to go a little farther, to the giant La Galleria, with over a hundred shops, lots of restaurants, and glass-fronted lifts and escalators, making it a favorite hangout for the young. Their Hyper U supermarket has everything. Price differences exist between this market and Carrefour, but neither is consistently higher.

If you are coming from Marin, Euromarché at Genipa is the market of choice, between Rivière Salée and the airport, or there is the Hyper U at Place D'Arms; both of these will keep you out of the heavy traffic nearer town.

Eden Bio is a good and reasonably priced organic food store with many interesting products.

Chandlery and services

Inter Sport is across the major highway from Carrefour. It is a vast general sports shop that includes fishing, boating, kayaking, windsurfing and surf-kiting gear. You might not find what you are looking for, but you will certainly find something you want. Mer et Sport in La Jambette is a large general sports store. Decathlon is a large super sports store not too far from Galleria, they cover all sports, and the prices are reasonable.

Turn off at Californie for Atelier Sylvestre, the hydraulic hose specialists. They can remake any hose. They also stock many special hoses and you can buy fuel-resistant hoses or very heavy-duty hoses. Fittings are available in stainless or aluminum, and the owners speak English.

Of interest at La Lezarde is Antilles Miroiterrie. They stock glass, mirrors, acrylic sheet in various thicknesses and quality, and PVC. They will cut all materials to shape.

The Fedex office is near the airport, in the original airport block. Continental Ma-

rine in Lamentin is the Yamaha agent. It has spares and can sort out Yamaha problems.

Rivière Salée is the home of West Indies Nautic Distribution (WIND), run by Bruno and Marty. This is a big store with a good showroom. They specialize in everything you need for any kind of boat job, as well as selling marine batteries, and they sell wholesale and retail. Their technical knowledge about all their products is more than excellent, and they know about compatibility between paints, how to make a two-part polyurethane flexible, which resins to use, and more. The base of their paint system is Lechler. This paint system can be supplied in one- or two- part polyurethane, binder for brush or spray application, from glossy to matt effect, tailored for paint coating project and even as gel coat. This is perfect for a big two-part paint job, because you can take some extra paint as a single-coat enamel, which is perfect for touch up.

They sell epoxy and polyester resins, fiberglass materials, and the latest cores, in-

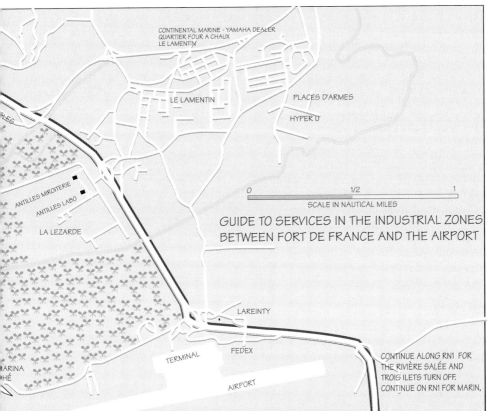

CONTINENTAL MARINE - YAMAHA DEALER
QUARTIER FOUR A CHAUX
LE LAMENTIN

PLACES D'ARMES

HYPER U

LE LAMENTIN

ANTILLES MIROITERIE
ANTILLES LABO

LA LEZARDE

0   1/2   1
SCALE IN NAUTICAL MILES

GUIDE TO SERVICES IN THE INDUSTRIAL ZONES BETWEEN FORT DE FRANCE AND THE AIRPORT

LAREINTY

MARINA
HÉ

TERMINAL   FEDEX

AIRPORT

CONTINUE ALONG RN1 FOR
THE RIVIÈRE SALÉE AND
TROIS ILETS TURN OFF.
CONTINUE ON RN1 FOR MARIN,

cluding the ultra-light hollow polypropylene cores, as well as the best structural foams. They have high-quality ply, including teak and holly flooring ply. They sell sandpaper, masks, gloves, brushes, and all the application tools. On big jobs you can negotiate wholesale prices. They also sell Jotun and Epifanes and Stoppani varnishes and top coats, and Seajet and Jotun antifouling. Bruno is mindful of the environment and been trying for 25 years to get a really sustainable solution to the fouling problem. He is now offering the new Seajet 038, which tests show to be very effective, while being biodegradable and eco-friendly. I, for one, wish to try it on my boat next year.

If you need new batteries, chat with Bruno. I learn something new on every visit. Like many cruisers I use the Trojan golf cart batteries. I found out that for a little more money, Trojan makes a much higher quality and slightly taller and heavier renewable-energy battery of the same capacity that is likely to last twice as long. WIND stocks lead

N1 TO
FORT DE FRANCE

RIVIÈRE SALÉE
SHOWING W.I.N.D

W.I.N.D.

CARREFOUR
SUPERMARKET

LEADER PRICE
SUPERMARKET

TO
TROIS ILETS

N1 TO
MARIN

acid, gel, absorbed glass mat (AGM) gel, and now lithium batteries for starting and deep cycle applications, and they are always fresh.

WIND is also the best flag outlet in the Eastern Caribbean. They have or can quickly get any kind of courtesy flag or ensign. They also wholesale flags. You can check out flags of all nations on their web page (www.wind-flag.com), plus meet the staff and see some products.

It is worth visiting the store, but if you cannot make it personally, email or call Bruno (he speaks excellent English) and he will happily deliver to your boat.

Madinina Diesel is also here, near

Leader Price. This is the place to service injectors and pumps

While here and with a car, and if you are in too much of a hurry to make the giant stores, you can shop at Leader Price, which has easy parking.

TROIS ILETS

Trois Ilets is a photogenic town, not overrun with visitors. Most of the old houses are built of wood or stone and capped with fish-scale tile roofs. A handsome square lies between the church and the town hall. This pleasant area offers several scenic, quiet, and secure places to anchor, some of which are protected enough to ride out a hurricane. You land on the fancy new waterfront walk-way and head towards the church.

Approach from Anse Mitan by leaving the black and yellow buoys off Pte. du Bout, Pte. de la Rose, and Pte. Angboeuf to starboard. The easiest anchorage is found by following the coast in from Pte. Angboeuf

and anchoring off the golf course. There is one 4-foot shoal, but otherwise the approach is easy. The approach to town is between the islands: Steer for the eastern island till you see the green buoy and leave it to port. After rounding the buoy, turn a little east again to avoid the shoals off the island to the west. Do not anchor in the main channel marked by yellow buoys. Holding is variable.

Communications

For internet, visit Cyber Base des Trois Ilets above the library. Open Tuesday 1000-1400, Wednesday and Friday 0830-1300 and 1400-1700, Thursday and Saturday 0800-1300.

Restaurants

For dinner try Damien Pele's fine old Fleur de Sel [$A], open daily from 1900 and maybe for Sunday brunch. The atmosphere is artistic, with many cozy eating spaces. The service is attentive, the food inventive and beautifully served. The menu challenged

POINTE DU BOUT

channel no anchoring

Trois Ilets

my French vocabulary, but don't worry, whatever you end up with will be good. It gets busy, people come here from afar, and reservations are essential on the weekend.

Opposite Fleur de Sel, Il Gallo Rosso is Italian and it too only opens for dinner. Several other restaurants are on the same road and they also serve lunch. Green [$C-D] has Créole food and occasional entertainment. Beyond that is an inexpensive snack bar that serves Créole lunch and farther down on the other side of the road a Pizzeria and a grill. On the waterfront, some small snack bars offer a great location for a drink.

Ashore

A ferry to Fort de France runs about every half hour. Garbage bins are at either end of the waterfront.

In town you will find a local market (open every day), a post office, a butcher, a wonderful boulangerie/patisserie/ice creamery, a pharmacy, a couple of general stores, and a hospital. A tourist office is stationed in the market square, and should you wish to rent a car, they will help.

Plenty of attractions are a fair walk away. You can play golf overlooking your yacht in the bay below. Opposite the 18-

POINTE DU BOUT TO TROIS ILETS

Trois Ilets church

TROU ETIENNE

Swells have occasionally driven me to anchor in Trou Etienne when I had things to do in Pointe du Bout, though without a pressing need to be there, Trois Ilets would be a better option. As you come from the west, leave both yellow and black buoys to starboard and as you enter the bay, do not go too close to shore. There are many private moorings and the water is either rather deep or too shallow for easy anchoring. Docks and roads are private, but there is a small public access path just north of the hotel. The hotel is quite conspicuous.

ANSE MITAN

Anse Mitan is part of the Trois Ilets district, and the head of the peninsula is called Pte. du Bout. It is attractive and popular, and there is always space to anchor.

Originally a super-chic tourist area, it has a couple of seedy edges, with the abandonment of the giant hotel (originally the Meridien), and the destruction of the Ponton du Bakoua. But it is still great and has a lot to offer, including beaches, boutiques, and restaurants, and it is fun for people-watching. Two ferry services run to Fort de France and Anse à L'Ane: one out of the marina at Pte. du Bout, the other from the Langouste Dock at Anse Mitan. Ferries start at around 0600 and finish at about 2300. Check times on the notice boards on the docks.

When approaching Anse Mitan, the main danger is the reef lying 200 yards west of Le Ponton, which is marked by a red and black buoy. Anchor anywhere among the other yachts. Holding is good in sand, but poor on patches of dead coral. Leave a couple of hundred feet in front of the beach clear for swimmers and leave the channel clear for the ferry. The various areas are often marked by yellow buoys.

On those very rare occasions when there is a bad northwesterly swell, go to Trou Etienne, on the other side of Pte. du Bout, or better, to Trois Ilets.

hole golf course is La Pagerie Museum, the original home of Empress Josephine. Our guide explained that most of the old estate house burned down when Josephine was three years old, and her father was such a gambler and womanizer that he could not afford to rebuild. They lived in part of the factory, where she stayed until she left for France for an arranged marriage at the age of 16. Her first husband was killed in the French revolution, but she escaped thanks to a lover (of which our guide emphasized she had plenty). When she married Napoleon he was 27 and she was 33. Since this was an unthinkable age difference, it was published that they were both 28.

About one and a half nautical miles to the east are some potteries, one of which produces the lovely fish-scale roof tiles used both in Trois Ilets and in St. George's, Grenada. Around these is the Village de la Potterie, a visitor attraction with numerous boutiques, restaurants, and a place to rent kayaks for mucking in the mangroves. The adventurous can dinghy there, tide permitting. It is opposite Gros Ilet and obvious because of the big industrial-looking brick warehouse and red roofs. Head east from Trois Ilets, follow the coast till you get past the first shoal on your port, then head towards Gros Ilet about half way before heading into the pottery. Tie up amid the bricks before you come to the tiny kayak dock. You might be able to make use of a couple of makeshift wooden landing platforms. Take care in the shallows.

Pointe du Bout

Regulations

You can clear customs via a computer in Somatras Marina office. Opening hours are 0900-1230 and 1500-1800 weekdays, 0900-1200 Saturday.

Communications

Most bars and restaurants offer free wifi.

General yacht services

You can tie your dinghy on the inside of the ferry dock. A good small floating dinghy dock has been added at the north end of the beach. It is convenient for everything and I hope it stays. Many people use one of the old docks from the abandoned hotel (see our sketch chart), but there are no guarantees this will continue. You can find garbage dumpsters all through town.

Somatras Marina (Marina Pte. du Bout) [VHF: 9] is a small marina offering stern-to berthing with water and electricity (no fuel). Short- and long-term berths are occasionally available for yachts up to 50 feet long and with less than 8-foot draft.

Laverie Prolavnet by Village Créole is a fast laundry, open 0830-1200, 1630-1830, closed Sundays. Owner Mme. Lamarthee, from Mauritius, speaks excellent English. She will iron if you wish, as well as arrange dry cleaning. Your laundry is done the same day; she stays till the work is finished.

Provisioning

Kdmax is a compact and good small supermaket with most things. They open 0830-1930 Monday to Saturday, 0830-1230 Sundays and holidays. Stock up on baked goodies in La Baguet. Vegetable sellers sometimes set up on the roadside.

In the marina block behind La Marine is Il Gallo D'Oro, gastronomia Italiana. It is a delicatessen which belongs to the fancy Il Gallo Rosso Restaurant on the main read near Trois Ilets. You can buy cut meats or get a great coffee, sandwich or dessert.

For more, rent a car and drive to the giant Carrefour at Genipa. Turn left towards Fort de France, pass two roundabouts,

LE KANO

Anse Mitan Beach - Trois Ilets
Martinique F.W.I.

contact.lekano@orange.fr
(+596) 596 78 40 33

then take the tiny turnoff with a very small Genipa sign. Go under the highway and it is on your left.

Fun shopping

Like ice-cream? Well, you will find lots of it here, and all of it good. Italian Cocco Bello is on the outer part of Créole Village; more glaceries are inside, and Ice'n Coffee is on the road to the marina.

Pointe du Bout is a shopper's dream of trendy little boutiques. Try starting at the Créole Village, beside the entrance to the Bakoua. It is built in Caribbean style, just Disneyfied enough to make it theatrically enticing. It is chock-a-block with shops that sell elegant clothing, kids clothes, jewelry, handicrafts, and objets d'art. Continue down the street towards the marina for more of the same, plus more casual clothing, souvenirs, magazines, and books. There are several hairdressers, a pharmacy, and a massage parlor/beauty salon.

Restaurants

One of the delights of Anse Mitan is to stroll over to La Baguet and have a breakfast of French coffee, fresh croissants, and pain au chocolat. Dozens of restaurants line the streets. I mention a few.

There are a couple of restaurants I would make a beeline for. Cristophe Luon's Kano [$A-C] is closed Tuesday but is otherwise open in the evening from 1700 for drinks and starters, serving main meals about 1930. On Sundays it opens at 1200. It is in a pleasant Créole house that rambles seaward from the road until it opens right out onto the sea. It has several rooms and garden areas. The little floating dinghy dock is a few steps away. There are some lounging areas and nice old pieces of furniture. The walls are covered in good art, which is for sale, with a revolving exhibit that changes every couple of months. The food is good traditional Créole and nicely presented. The coconut flan with mango sauce is wonderful. They have typical Créole music such as Zouk at least once a week. They stay open quite late should you be out on the town. If you come early you will probably get in most days but booking is essential on Saturday evening or Sunday lunch or if you are part of a group. Arrive in time for happy hour, 1700-1800.

For fine French food, try Oz [$A, closed Tuesday and Wednesday midday]. It was very good when it was called La Manureva and it looks like the new owners are trying to keep up the standard. On non-holiday weekdays they offer a very good fixed lunch menu, well worth trying.

For something cheap and cheerful, Al Dente is an Italian take-away, next to Kano, but they do have a few seats.

For the pleasure of sitting on the beach and watching scantily clad beautiful people, check out Au Soleil Couchant or Barracuda [$C-D]. If you prefer to watch people clad in designer clothes, try one of the restaurants by the marina. The most reliable is La Marine [$B]. Here you get to sit out in the open, facing the marina, the surroundings are pleasant, and the food fair value.

There are seven restaurants in La Village Créole. Havana Café is the place to sip a drink and watch people pass, and Le Bistrot d'en Face [$B] has a nice pub-like

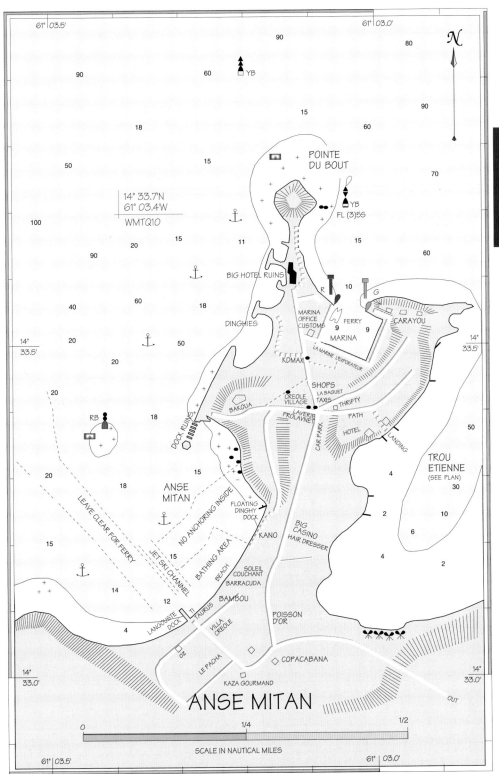

POINTE DU BOUT

90
80
60
90
15
18
60
15
70
50
90
100

14° 33.7'N
61° 03.4'W
WMTQ10

YB
YB
FL (3)5S

20
15
11
15
60

90
40
60
18
R 10
G

20
50
DINGHIES
MARINA OFFICE CUSTOMS
FERRY
9
9
MARINA
CARAYOU

BIG HOTEL RUINS

20
KDMAX
LA MARINE L'EXPLORATEUR

SHOPS
LA BAGUET
CREOLE VILLAGE
TAXIS
THRIFTY
BAKOUA
LAVERIE
PROLAVNET
PATH
HOTEL
LANDING
50
CAR PARK

RB
18
DOCK RUINS

15
ANSE MITAN
NO ANCHORING INSIDE
TROU ETIENNE
(SEE PLAN)
30
4
20
18
FLOATING DINGHY DOCK
2
10
15
KANO
BIG CASINO HAIR DRESSER
6
LEAVE CLEAR FOR FERRY
JET SKI CHANNEL
BATHING AREA
4
2
15
BEACH
SOLEIL COUCHANT
BARRACUDA
14
BAMBOU
12
LANGOUSTE DOCK
TI
TAURUS
VILLA CREOLE
POISSON D'OR
4
OZ
LE PACHA
COPACABANA
KAZA GOURMAND
OUT

ANSE MITAN

0   1/4   1/2

SCALE IN NAUTICAL MILES

61° 03.5'   61° 03.0'

Martinique

atmosphere and includes a traiteur, patisserie, and wine store. Infinity Restaurant is new, looks modern and is worth trying.

Copacabana [$A-C] is both a Brazilian restaurant and a pizzeria. Go when you feel in need of stoking up on some really good meat, prepared the Brazilian way.

La Villa Créole [$B] is touristy but fine if you want entertainment along with a Créole meal. Le Bambou on the beach has entertainment most nights; wander in and have a drink. They also have a courtyard open to the beach with some colorful chairs and small fast food places.

Ti Taurus right on the Langouste dock,

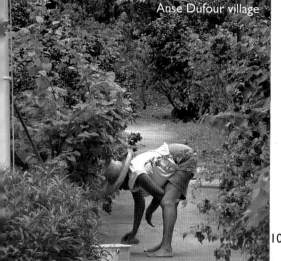
Anse Dufour village

is cheap, cheerful and has a great location.

Ashore

Anse Mitan has many car rentals and it is a good place from which to explore the island. The taxi stand is on the main road opposite Somatras Marina.

Water sports

If you want to go diving, check out the Attitude Plongée in Somatras Marina; they have people who speak English.

ANSE A L'ANE

Just around the corner from Anse Mitan is Anse à l'Ane, a sweet little bay with a charming beach. It is a pleasant anchorage in good conditions, though you may roll each time the regular Fort de France ferry runs.

Right in the middle of the bay, about one-third of a mile offshore, is a hard-to-spot reef about four feet deep. You can pass on either side to anchor in about 12 feet on a sand bottom. Make sure your anchor is well dug in and leave the ferry channel clear (it is sometimes buoyed). Anse à l'Ane is open to the northwest and should be avoided in times of heavy ground swells. When ap-

Anse a L'Ane

proaching from Anse Mitan, give the first headland a wide clearance as it is all rocky and shoals stick out 270 yards at Pte. Alet (see chart). When heading toward Cap Salomon from Anse à L'Ane, you have about 9 feet of water between Ilet à Ramiers and the mainland, enough for most yachts to pass.

Services/shopping

Anse à l'Ane is a holiday area, though much less built up than Anse Mitan. The beach has some shade, provided by seagrapes and palm trees. Leave your dinghy on the dinghy dock (swells permitting) or on the very inner end of the ferry dock.

Garbage bins are at either end of the car park and a gas station that sells ice can be found on the main road. A good 8 à Huit supermarket is open 0800-2000 except Sunday when it closes at 1300. Opposite is a hair stylist and to the side is Blu Coco, a big gift/beach shop. You can find places to rent cars here.

Restaurants

Ready for a meal out? Restaurants line the beach, Le Little Bay on the east side of the bridge, La Case a Glace [$D], Nid Tropical [$B-D] and Kreol K fe just the other side.

Pignon sur Mer [$A-B closed Monday] and Pignon Nouvelle Vague are rather more upmarket, Les 3 V is a snack bar restaurant and ice cream shop near the main dock.

The restaurant at the Club Trois Ilets [$A-B] offers both lunch and dinner, with entertainment many nights. Les Saveurs le Ti Calabesse is across the street.

Water sports

Dive with the dive shop Corail Club Caraibes at Club Trois Ilets, or Calypso Plongée behind the dinghy dock. David Dauphin takes people dolphin watching.

ANSE NOIRE & ANSE DUFOUR

Anse Noire and Anse Dufour lie about halfway between Ilet à Ramiers and Cap Salomon; two bays, one white sand, the other black, both with good snorkeling. They should be avoided in northerly swells but are otherwise well protected. Anse Noire is a lovely hideaway and there is an excellent dinghy dock. Small, colorful cliffs rise on the southern headland and there is a steep hill on the northern one. Palms line the black sand beach at the head of the bay and a large fancy dock juts out from the beach. Behind the beach, a steep jungly valley rises into the mountains. Popular as a daytime anchorage, Anse Noire is usually deserted and peaceful at night. The wind swings in all directions.

Anse Dufour is a picturesque small fishing village with a white sand beach, and lots of bougainvillea. It is popular with visitors because of the beach and snorkeling. You will find good anchorage in 20 feet off the beach or on the south side behind moored fishing boats. Be prepared to move for the fishermen if they ask.

Ashore

It is pleasant just to sit in Anse Noire and watch the kingfishers and other birds on the cliffs. An interesting trail follows the shady strip of riverine forest up the seasonal river behind the beach to the main road or right over to Anse A L'Ane. Domaine de Robinson, behind the beach, sometimes has rooms to rent.

You probably won't get dinner, but for lunch climb the steps up the cliff, and follow the road. On your left, Desir's Sable D'Or [$C-D, closed Tuesday], specializes in fresh seafood and Créole meat dishes at reasonable prices.

Or, in Anse Dufour, you can choose between Chez Marie Jo [$C-D, closed Sunday], Maga Most [$D], and Snack Chez Nini [$D], on the beach.

Water sports

The snorkeling around the headland into Anse Dufour is superb: walls, crevices, and rocks decorated with sponges, tubeworms, and anemones, which attract a large variety of small fish. A particularly lovely deep grotto is halfway in Anse Dufour (you can see it in the aerial photo).

The snorkeling is even better on the south side of Anse Dufour, with rocks and lots of fish. It is worth trying a dive here, off the point.

Grand Anse D'Arlet

GRANDE ANSE D'ARLET

Grande Anse d'Arlet is a little village set on a white sand beach with magnificent mountains towering behind. In the right light, when the hills are lush green, it has the feel of some exotic Pacific hideaway. Once a fishing village, a few dugout fishing pirogues remain, though for the most part it is now geared to tourism and the northern corner has a touch of the Riviera, with brightly colored beach umbrellas. A fancy new walkway runs behind the beach. Avoid sailing too close to the center of the village, as a shoal area extends seaward several hundred feet. The holding is variable, with weed and some broken coral, as well as good sand.

Regulations

Le P'Ti Bateau is trying to get a customs computer, but in the meantime you can walk 20 minutes to customs over in Les Anses D'Arlet. Yacht moorings have been placed on either side of the harbour. (See our sketch chart for details.) There was a plan to maintain and charge for them, but things seem chaotic for the moment, and only a fraction remain. Pick one up (check in carefully) or anchor.

General yacht services

Le P'Ti Bateau can provide water via a long hose that reaches down the dock.

Le P'Ti Bateau, Coco Delice, and Ti Sable offer wifi; Bidjoul's sometimes works.

Isabel's Kay Zaza is a boutique and laundry. Isabel does wash, or wash, dry, and fold by the 5 kg load, normally ready the next day. Kay Zaza is an artistic shop with gifts, ornaments, casual clothing, hats, art, and jewelry. They sell stamps and postcards and will mail them for you.

Ashore

Grand Anse d'Arlet wakes late and is fully ready for the day by about 1100. Earlier risers wander down to L'Abre Pain for coffee at their beach bar in the form of a boat, which can be quite a gathering place from 0900.

Two small food stores sell groceries and ice. When you get to the dock, go up

Grand Anse D'Arlet

Moorings system
Grand Anse D'Arlet
North side moorings 1-3 are
for boats less than 8 meters.
Moorings 4-51 for boats
8-15 meters, and
moorings 52-59 for
boats 15-20 meters.
The middle moorings
are for local fishing boats.
South side moorings 1-23
(first 3 rows) are for boats
less than 8 meters, the rest
take boats 8-15 meters.
Les Anses D'Arlet,
moorings 11-12 and 17-34
are for boats between
8-15 meters. The rest are for
boats less than 8 meters.

to the main road, and whichever direction you turn, you will come to one. These open at 0800. For more, you will have to visit Les Anses D'Arlet.

Le P'Ti Bateau [$B-C], right at the head of the dock, is a pleasant, reasonably priced restaurant open for lunch and dinner every day, with free wifi. The owners are enthusiastic. You can sit in the building, but most gravitate to the tables right on the beach.

At the northern end of the beach, behind all the fancy Mediterranean-style sunshades, is Ti Sable [$A-C], a slightly fancier establishment for good Créole food. You occasionally need to book for lunch, though not for dinner.

Otherwise, Bidjoul [$B-C], Les Arcades [$B-C], L'Abre Pain [$B-C], and Ti Payot [$B-C] are all Créole restaurants along the pathway behind the beach. They set tables and chairs on the beach to create an enchanting spot for a waterfront meal. The location is lovely, food and service variable.

Just beyond Ti Payot is a restaurant owned by Plongée Passion. They do a very

FISH FARM

KEEP CLEAR

ANSE CHAUDIERE

Les Anses D'Arlet

good local lunch on the beach. Chez Evelyne and Chez Nita are also open for lunch only at the southern end of the beach.

Cars can be rented from the beach area, and the coast road from Anse d'Arlet, which winds over the hills to Diamant, offers spectacular views. Anse d'Arlet is within easy walking distance.

An excellent trail follows the headland round to Anse d'Arlet. From the dinghy dock, turn right on the road and look for the sign on your righthand side, or head south along the beach and look for a red arrow on your left. Another trail at the north end of the bay takes you out to Cap Solomon and includes a mangrove walkway. You can also hike from here over to Anse Dufours. More details are available from doyleguides.com.

Water sports

Snorkeling is excellent when the water is clear. The main grassy anchorage is often full of turtles and starfish. A marine park on the south shore has lovely snorkeling, and the north shore and all round to Anses D'Arlet is also good. Divers can join Plongée Passion, Alpha Dive, or Bubbles.

LES ANSES D'ARLET

The photogenic small town of Les Anses D'Arlet has some lovely old houses and a picturesque church. Everything is well painted and maintained. A handsome promenade follows the waterfront. Les Anses D'Arlet makes a good overnight anchorage unless the wind is too far in the south.

When approaching town, look out for the rocks to the west of the dock. Some are visible, but others extend some yards seaward. Take a mooring or anchor (see regulations). A fish farm is in the southern part of the bay. Parts of it are marked by unlit green buoys; other parts are unmarked. Avoid this area at night and keep a good lookout by day.

Anchorage may also be found at Anse Chaudière in the southeastern corner of the bay, which is a great hideaway with good snorkeling. Approach with caution, as isolated rocks extend about 100 feet offshore. Anchor on the sand bottom in 10 to 12 feet.

Les Anses D'Arlet

Regulations

The Customs computer is in Cyber Base, just a couple of doors towards the church from L'Oasis boutique; the sign is small and easy to miss. They open Monday to Friday 0800-1300 and 1400-1700. This is also a major internet station.

Use the moorings that remain or anchor. Charges were planned, but given that most moorings have failed, this seems unlikely.

Services/ashore

The market has crafts, some produce, and an ATM by the entrance. Fresh fish is sold opposite, and a few steps further on, Fournil Arlesien has good bread, pain au chocolat and more. Some kind of shopping center is planned just as you head towards Grand Anse d'Arlet. Alain's L'Oasis boutique is connected to Zaza's in Grand Anse d'Arlet, and Alain should be able to arrange to take laundry there for you. He also sells casual clothing, hammocks, pareos, and many colorful gifts.

For lunch, gravitate to the plastic chairs set out on the beach northwest of the river. Sandwiches and local meals are available from many small restaurants. This area has been carefully renovated, with a pleasant walkway along the waterfront. Some of these restaurants also open in the evening.

Otherwise, Le Littoral [$B-C] is a pleasant little Créole restaurant a short walk away on the road leading south out of town. They have a great view overlooking the bay and open every day 1100-1500 and 1900-2200.

You can hike from here over the headland to Grand Anse d'Arlet and return by the road, which is shorter.

Water sports

Mada Plongée will be happy to take you diving, and David, the owner, speaks English. They sometimes have exhibitions of local art next to the dive shop. Snorkeling is good in Anse Chaudière. It may be worth giving scuba a go here as well. If you are anchored in town, try the rocks off the dock. Everyone else does.

THE SOUTH COAST OF MARTINIQUE

There are no good anchorages along Martinique's south coast until you get to the eastern end. Several shoals along this coast extend up to half a mile offshore. There is deep water (over 100 feet) outside these shoals. It is best to stay in this deep water to avoid the numerous fish traps at lesser depths.

As long as you don't get too far offshore, the sail east to Ste. Anne is usually a brisk beat to windward in protected water, and can be a great sail. Sometimes on a rising tide, when the current reverses to the east, it can become a bit like being in a washing machine. If it gets really rough, you can head well offshore till you are away from the tidal influence.

BAIE DU MARIGOT

Having said there are no good anchorages along this coast, there *is* an anchorage. It is not good, in that it often rolls (though this should be no problem for multihulls), and entry is extremely tricky and should only be attempted by those with years of Caribbean and reef navigation experience. The reefs are not at all easy to see and they are very dangerous, with swells often building as you go in. Once inside, it is a delightful bay with the large Novotel on one side and a deserted headland on the other. The view is great.

Navigation

Baie du Marigot lies to the east of the town of Diamant. When coming from the west, you see a conspicuous peaky hill behind. A building with a red roof stands on the western headland, and the Novotel buildings are to the west of this, though partially hidden by trees. A reef, Caye de Obian, lies almost on a direct line between Pte. du Diamant and the entrance. It is about a mile offshore.

The approach is down a very narrow channel, 30 feet deep, with shallow banks and reefs on either side, up to half a mile offshore. While there is just enough water to stray onto the banks in some places, you want to stay in the deep water. Swells usually roll into the shore, making the approach dangerous if you make a mistake. The channel includes a curve. The approach should only be made in calm, sunny conditions, with good light for spotting the shallows, which are often hard to pick out. It is strictly a matter of eyeball navigation.

Once inside, there is ample room for anchoring. The prettiest area is towards the eastern headland. If you are on a monohull, you will probably need to use a stern anchor to make life bearable.

Ashore

The large Novotel on the western shore has boutiques and restaurants.

BAIE DU MARIGOT

N

14° 28.5'

HOTEL

LA TETE DE SINGE

HOUSE WITH
A RED ROOF

PTE DU MARIGOT

CAYE DE OBIAN
14

14° 28'

14° 27.7'
61° 00.5'
WMTQ15

61° 00.5'

61° 00'

Baie du Marigot
Note the long passage between shoals
that are hard to see.

CAYE DE OBIAN

PTE. BORGNESSE TO ANSE FIGUIERS

Pte. Borgnesse is the western headland as you enter Cul de Sac Marin. A couple of pleasant anchoring areas lie between this headland and Anse Figuiers, with some quiet hidden beaches. This is a protected area and strictly no fishing.

Navigation

A wide shelf, about 9-14 feet deep, follows this coast. Off the shelf, the depth drops rapidly to 200 feet. There are some large shallow areas on the shelf that must be avoided. You can find your way inside them to anchor. A mile to the northwest, Anse Figuiers is a delightful bay and a popular holiday beach, behind which you can see the eco-museum building with its conspicuous chimney. To get into Anse Figuiers, pass outside the shelf in deep water and approach Anse Figuiers from the southwest. There is a good shelf off the beach in 10-25 feet of water. If you have a fast dinghy, you can visit that way from Ste. Anne.

Ashore

Snorkeling is fair all around the headlands.

There is ample water to dinghy up the Rivière Pilote for a couple miles to the town of Rivière Pilote. This is an entertaining exercise and the scenery is quite pretty. Along the eastern shore is an area with numerous junked railway cars from the days when sugar cane was moved by rail. Entry to the river is close to shore between the coast and a man-made causeway. You will see many fishing boats and even a mini-marina along the first part of the trip.

STE. LUCE TO THE ENTRANCE OF
CUL DE SAC MARIN

SCALE IN NAUTICAL MILES

STE. ANNE

STE. ANNE

The white buildings of Ste. Anne stand out clearly against the surrounding green hills. Above the lovely historic church, a walled path zigzags up a small hill to a shrine. At each turn of the path an agony of Christ is depicted.

Ste. Anne is a delightful seaside town, with a sleepy holiday atmosphere. The town is tiny, but it has an adjoining beach that is magnificent and popular. The surrounding countryside is attractive, with shore walks to even better beaches.

Navigation

Yellow buoys delineate a no-anchoring area off the beach and town. Some years they drift away, so yachts anchor back in town. The anchoring area in any case is huge. You can also eyeball your way south and anchor off the Caritan Hotel. The water depth is 10 to 20 feet, sand bottom. Most is good holding, though there are some patches where

the sand is too hard to get the anchor down. Shoals lie close to shore between Ste. Anne and Anse Caritan and off the southern part of Anse Caritan.

Weather permitting, you can visit pretty daytime anchorages south of Ste. Anne off Anse Meunier and Grande Anse des Salines. Approach Anse Meunier with caution, as the bay is quite shallow. Avoid the rocky shallows between Pointe Catherine and Pointe Pie. Grande Anse des Salines is spectacular and popular.

Regulations/communications

You can clear customs at Snack Boubou (closed Wednesdays). It is next to Les Tamariniers. It also has an internet cafe with computers and wifi. The computers and the customs computer are open 0800-1900 (the bar is open longer). Call them at 0596 76 28 46 for more details.

Cyber Base is a government-run internet center in the tourist office. It is upstairs at the back of the building (take the side

STE. ANNE AND CUL-DE-SAC DU MARIN

street). Opening hours are Monday and Thursday 0730-1630, other weekdays 0730-1330, subject to frequent change.

La Dunette and Paille Coco, among others have wifi. Take your computer in and have a coffee to get the password. It might work from anchor.

Services

The town dock is good for dinghies, though sometimes overcrowded. Garbage bins are just beyond the dock. If they go, look down towards the market. Ice is available at the Rendezvous Restaurant and the supermarket adjoining the market. Down by the old Caritan, you can tie to the dinghy dock and walk uphill a few hundred feet to a laundromat. Abrilav laundromat is close to the

Club Med behind all the beach restaurants (see the sketch chart). Maya Beach water sports (by the Aqua park at Caritan) will sell you water if you bring jugs (no boat fill).

Provisioning/shopping

Get cash at one of the two ATMs; one is at the post office. Step off the dock and turn right, walk down the street, and you will find an 8 à Huit supermarket adequate for topping up your stores.

Cherie Doudou, the boulangerie/patisserie, has room on the beach side for coffee, pain au chocolat, or sandwiches. The market is farther down the street on the right, fish market first, then the general market, with fresh meat, fruits, vegetables, and handicrafts.

You will find a pharmacy in the main square and another up the hill heading north.

Casual shoppers will enjoy the little craft stores and boutiques on every street. Ozar, by the market, is the most interesting, with work of many local artists and craftsmen.

Restaurants

Restaurants abound, both in town and on the beach that stretches from Ste. Anne to the Club Med.

Chez La Martine, a shop on the little street opposite La Dunette, is the place to be at 1800. They put tables on the street and serve delicious accras, beer, and other drinks at bargain prices ~ the best deal in town.

Two of the cheapest eateries are Snack Boubou, where you clear customs, and La Dorade, which is opposite the market. If you come in for breakfast, Snack Boubou, La Dunette, and the boulangerie are the places to try.

Le Coco Neg is a tiny back street res-

Sainte Anne

taurant with a pleasant atmosphere that serves traditional Créole meals. La Dunette [$B] has a perfect location and a dinghy dock. This is the happening place, with live music, and it is a perfect place to stop for a beer or ice cream. Otantic, on the hill by the cemetery has a great sunset view.

Les Tamariniers [$B-C] has a cute exterior, and Le Rendezvous, which is inexpensive, has a good waterfront location. Paille Coco, in front of Epi Soleil, also grabbed a great location. It is a little touristy but usually open and okay. Isabella's Al Casanova, has a good reputation for first-rate Italian food.

The whole of the long beach is lined with restaurants mostly open only at lunch. For a great and relaxing meal in Ste. Anne, go to Madi's Delices Caraibe. It is excellent value, with good seafood and daily specials, and you can get a giant mixed-seafood plate. The service is first rate and they all spoke English this year. It has an adjoining snackbar called Ti Kano.

Le Filet Bleu has been around forever and is quite popular. This is the only one that might be open for dinner.

Grand Anse des Salines

Ashore

The church square leads to two main streets, one along the waterfront and a parallel one at the back. From the dock, turn left along the front street to climb over the hill, past the cemetery, and down to the popular beach that stretches all the way to Club Med. (A coastal walkway avoids the hill.)

The coastal area from Ste. Anne right round the south and back up the east coast to Anse Trabaud is a park with a trail. Hikers and bikers should take the road toward Anse Caritan and then follow the trail that goes all the way along, or just behind, the shore to Anse des Salines. Anse des Salines is one of Martinique's finest palm-backed beaches, and very popular, ideal for people watching. Those who prefer a more private setting will pass several smaller beaches along the way. Bikers can continue on to Anse Trabaud and back over the middle. (The trail is such that you will push a lot.) It takes about three and a half hours at a leisurely pace. You can rent bikes from Herve at Velo Club Aosa Cap 110 [closed Monday]. He also organizes cycling tours around the island. He is near Club Med next to the laundromat. Give him a call: (0696) 25 34 18. Communal taxis run to Fort de France.

Water sports

A good place to start snorkeling or diving is at the second red buoy in the channel toward Marin. Snorkelers can follow the shallow part of the reef and divers can head south into deeper water, where they will find a large collection of sponges, including some unusual shapes. This is a good place to see corallimorphs, pencil urchins, and small, colorful reef fish.

Kalinargo, the local dive shop, is at the Ste. Anne end of the beach that leads to Club Med. They dive twice daily, at 0830 and 1330. They will also fill tanks.

Another dive shop, Natiyabel, is at the fishing port and rents kayaks.

Small sailing catamarans and sailboards are available for rent on the beach.

Cul-de-sac du Marin

MARIN

Marin, a pleasant small town, is one of the Caribbean's largest yacht centers, with the huge Marin Marina, a big haul-out facility, and a vast array of yacht services and technicians. Where else in the Windwards can you walk into a mechanic's shop and view a row of marine engines on show and ready to install? You can find technicians of all stripes and they are generally helpful and good at what they do ~ and there is not much that cannot be done. This is the main base for the Martinique charter industry: Star Voyage, Outremer Concept, Dream Yacht Caribbean, Punch Croisieres, Azur Spirit, VPM Dufour, Corail Caraibes, Regis Guillemot Charter, and MerMer Location all have bases here.

June 21 is the French national music

day, a good day to visit when you can be sure of some free concerts in town. Ask the marina for details.

Navigation

Cul-de-Sac du Marin is a vast, deeply indented bay, surrounded by hills and lined with mangroves. It is full of shoals that are visible in good light. It is a gunkholer's dream and the best place to be in Martinique during a hurricane. The entrance channel is well marked by buoys and beacons. After you pass Club Med, head for the apartment buildings behind the forest of masts until you see the big red and green buoys in the middle of the bay. Pass between them, leaving the red one to starboard and the green one to port. Follow the channel in, leaving the red buoys to starboard. Shoals lie in the "no anchoring" area off Marin Beach, so avoid it.

Small yachts going between Marin and Ste. Anne can take a short cut between the outer two red buoys. Avoid the 6-foot shoal that lies east of the outer red buoy (see our sketch chart, page 115).

Regulations

Marin is a port of entry. Do-it-yourself customs computers are in the capitainerie in the marina mall. Clear 0800-1730 Monday to Saturday and 0800-1230 Sundays. There is a charge of 5 Eu. Add half an hour, and these are also the marina office hours.

It is possible for non-European yachts to bring things in VAT-Free; Douglas Rapier can handle clearance for you. He can also pre-clear large yachts via the internet.

European-registered yachts that have been exported tax-free will likely be charged tax on entry.

Anchoring is forbidden in the swimming area marked by yellow buoys in front of the beach.

Communications

Both Carte Orange and Digicel sell USB wifi ports (3-G) that use prepaid cards. These are good for all the French islands. For SIMS and phone time, there is an Orange/Digicel store in Artimer and a main Digicel in the Annette Mall. Time for both is available in the Marin Bay Commercial Center (a short walk from Leader Price), or across the road from the new Marina Mall. The mini mart next to the market sells Orange time.

Many people take their computers into Mango Bay, which has free wifi for customers. Those on the hard can use the email over in the Carenantilles main office.

Captain has a good bay-wide wifi system which also works in St. Anne. Marin Marina has wifi, currently under upgrade.

General yacht services

Services, shops, and restaurants in Marin are in several locations, easy to reach by dinghy. Some are close around the marina; others are over by Carenantilles, the large slipway, or at Artimer. All have dinghy docks.

Artimer is a big development, designed to include the boating trade. It has been cleverly designed to use the river and you can dinghy right up; the dinghy ride is novel. You pass the anchored yachts off Carenantilles, staying quite well inshore until you see the

Sea Services
SHIPCHANDLER

109 rue Ernest DEPROGE
97200 FORT-DE-FRANCE - MARTINIQUE
Tél +596 596 70 26 69 - Fax +596 596 71 60 53
E-mail: seaservices972@orange.fr

CHANDLERY
RIGGING
PAINT
ANTIFOULING
International.

channel, which is marked by buoys. Pass down the channel, leaving red right returning, then enter the river. For a short while you get a river ride among the mangroves in the middle of nowhere. Suddenly you arrive in a giant shopping mall with dinghy tie up in a little basin. You need to be able to climb one of the ladders, which are very large and secure. Carenantilles and Artimer are also close to each other for easy walking.

You will find garbage disposal at both the marina and the haul-out, with glass, paper and plastic, and oil and battery recycling. You can get water and fuel at both.

Marin Marina [VHF: 09] (Marina du Marin) is the only giant marina in Martinique. Owned by the Jean-Joseph family and managed by Eric, it is good, friendly, and inexpensive, and most people in the office speak English. They have been awarded the blue flag as an environmentally friendly marina. Dinghy docks are in front of the nautical block (by Mango Bay) and down at the marina mall (Capitainerie). With 830 berths, there is normally plenty of room for visitors who are placed on the most accessible berths (see sketch chart). Two docks have finger docks for alongside berthing, suitable for cats. The fuel dock takes three or four yachts (or one superyacht)and you can get diesel, gasoline, and water daily: 0730-1730. Superyacht fueling is at 12,000 liters an hour. Dockage is available with 220-volt/50-cycle electricity; 110-volt transformers are also available. (The 220-volt does not work with two lines of 110.) Four hundred volts is available for superyachts. They have 100 moorings, but most are on permanent rental. You can often get one for a few nights. Call on the VHF: 09 to get help coming in. Docks 3 and 4 have holding-tank pump out. C and H docks have finger piers rather than stern-to berthing. The marina is huge, but most of it is connected with a waterfront walkway. The marina facilities are in two blocks. The original nautical block is where you have chandleries and many services. The Capitainerie (Port Office) is in the huge marina mall at the head of the bay. This big block has restaurants, charter companies, shops, and nautical services. The Capitainerie can change $US/EC/pounds.

Some berths are suitable for mega yachts of any length and up to 4.5 meters draft. At Douglas Yacht Services, Douglas Rapier and his team, including Eugenie and Natalie and Virginie will help you in every way. Douglas is perfect for those that want utterly dependable, top quality service and are willing to pay for it. Douglas has some berths with dedicated wifi service for his customers.

Douglas and his team are there to ensure that big yachts have everything they need. They can pre-clear yachts before arrival and do full provisioning and refueling, as well as providing technical support, and arranging travel, private jet arrival, and medical, and other personal arrangements. Douglas is available 24/7 and keeps his phone at his side. For smaller yachts, he does project management (see *Technical yacht services*).

If you are doing a large maintenance project, it is now possible to get all the hauling and work VAT free and all parts shipped in duty and VAT-free. You do need to set this up in advance, and Douglas is the man to speak to about this.

He is agent for Axxess Marine, a high-end internet service for the Caribbean. It gives you 50 gigabytes of service per month for $590 US, and you only pay for months you want to use it. To have it working properly, giving you wifi throughout your boat, you will need to buy the right gear, not only to ensure sufficient bandwidth, but to allow Axxess to help you if you have any problems. For a heavy user this turns out to be less expensive per gigabyte than the Eu 20 that I pay Orange for one.

Douglas also represents Sevenstar Yacht Transport, and you can make all arrangements with him for shipping your yacht most places in the world.

Kathy, who is with Kashmir of Equinox Welding, will be starting a help and shore base support office aimed at helping cruisers who need to do a shopping trip, get some local help, find some part or product or whatever. Kathy speaks English, Dutch, Spanish and French, has a car, and when you need help she will be there.

Carenantilles [VHF: 16/73] is a large haul-out facility, newly renovated, with many support services. We show their location on our sketch chart. You can easily visit by dinghy, but it is gated, so it is not as easy as it was to use it as access to the land. However, if you are a customer of Carene Shop, it has doors on both sides.

Carenantilles is for hauling and working on boats. They have plenty of work docks for going stern-to with moorings and some alongside. They have two for superyachts, with side pillars. It is a little pricier than the marina, as they want to reserve it for work.

Carenantilles holds about 230 boats ashore, and they have two marine hoists. The small one is 80 tons and takes about 32 foot beam, the larger is 440 tons and takes about 46 foot beam.

For the most part, there is plenty of water in the bay for the approach. If you start at the outer buoy and head towards the dock, you should have 14 feet. The shallowest part is out by the buoy. While Carenantilles are happy to store boats, they concentrate more on boats undergoing work. Rates depend on how long you need to be ashore and the

Martinique

current exchange rate for the euro. Fax them for a rate sheet. You can do your own work on the slip, or many good workshops can do it for you (see *Technical yacht services*). Facilities include toilets, showers, and a restaurant. The yard is run by Arthur De Lucey; Jocelyne, who speaks good English, manages the reception.

Dock Cleaner Ecologique is an ecologically friendly floating dry dock run by Dream Yachts. It can take anything up to 70 tons, 13 meters wide, and 1.8 meters deep. Call Alain Rollet: 0696 92-62-47.

Blanc Marine is a convenient modern launderette in the marina mall. It has a central computerized system that takes both coins and notes. If you have a big load, they have a 14 kilo machine, as well as several at 7 kilos, and the driers are large. Soap is available, and for those big party nights, there is a dishwasher. It is open daily 0600-2200. They are also the only laundry in the marina that can collect and deliver your laundry, also ironed if you want. E-mail them for a quote.

If they are full, you can cross the road to Ecolavarie just outside the marina.

Bichik, the fuel and water dock at Carenantilles, is a good establishment run by Line and Guy. They open 0800 ~1900 Monday to Saturday. If you bring your laundry, you can have it washed, washed and dried, or washed, dried, and carefully folded, which works well if you have 5 kilos or less. They put the laundry right in the machines, so bring it before 1600. They refill and sell Camping Gas, and can send faxes. This is also an active social spot. People come to the Bichik store to drink a beer or coffee, have a lunchtime sandwich, watch some sports on TV, and use the book swap, which includes an English section.

Other laundries include Lav@net in the Annette Mall, and Laverie Marie before Ti Toque, from the marina mall.

Martinique has boat brokers in every corner. Azur Spirit in the nautical block is run by Jimy, who has a big listing. He also charters yachts and looks after and repairs boats (see *Technical yacht services: Project management*).

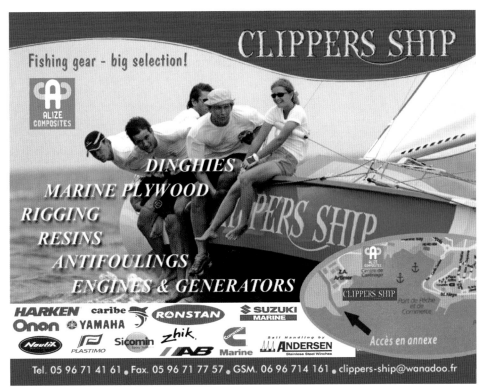

Corail Caraibes Charter sells new Lagoons and Beneteaus.

Eva Yachting and Antilles Nautism are in the same office and between them sell both sail and power yachts. Try also Eric Vasse at Punch Croisieres charter company, Veronique at Petit Breton, or A&C brokers. All are in the original nautical block. Other charter companies also sometimes sell used yachts. Caribbean Yachts, managed by Stephanie, is part of a larger company, with offices in Guadeloupe, St. Martin, the Dominican Republic, and Panama. They are in the marina mall.

If you need a survey, Jacques Scharwatt is a surveyor and his office is upstairs next to Diginav.

Medical problems can be fixed according to severity and need. Dr. Monique Roussi is good and easy to find upstairs in the marina mall. She is there Monday-Thursday and till 1230 on Saturday. Walk in, 0730-1330, or make an appointment, 1530-1830. Stephanie Eustache is a nurse next door. Dr. Grossen is a dentist in the same block. If you walk up the hill from the market you will find Dr. Jean Louis Deloge and Dr. Veronique Claisse. Dr. Claisse specializes in sports medicine, perfect for tortured muscles and joints. Behind Leader Price is the big Alizes Medical Center. You can walk in, but will probably have to wait quite a while.

If you need serious and immediate attention, get Douglas at Douglas Yacht Services to help you. Otherwise, the emergency number is 115.

For glasses, La Lunetterie is modern, big and in the Artimer Mall.

Chandlery

Marin has wonderful chandleries; the best collection in the Windwards. In the marina nautical block Le Ship, owned by Patrice Caillot, is a great chandlery with a big stock. You will find stoves, heads, anchors, including the new Rocna, chain, rope, charts, pumps, stoves, a great collection of LED bulbs, electronics, cruising guides, charts, Lofrans winches and all kinds of yacht hardware. They have some good buys on aluminum-hulled PVC inflatable dinghies. This is also the place for good acrylic wine glasses, linens, and some fun and fancy nautical decorations.

Caraibe Marine, which is combined with numerous technical services, is the largest chandlery with multiple areas and departments. Owner Philippe Leconte started as a rigger, he then expanded into electrics and built a chandlery. He now has workshops that cover rigging (Caraibes Gréement), electrics and water makers (Caraibes Energie), electronics, (Caraibes Electronique), refrigeration (Caraibes Refrigeration), and woodworking (Caraibes Menuiserie). For details see *Technical yacht services*. This expansion is reflected in the chandlery, which is the largest in Martinique on the technical side. It also means if you buy something that needs installation, they can do it for you, and if it later needs service, they can do that, too. Need some new hatches? Caraibe Marine will have them in all shapes and sizes, as well as all the seals when you need a replacement. I am impressed, because they stock things like the little plastic inserts for track cars that wear out and are hard to come by. You will find a wide range of general chandlery, including safety gear and general hardware, as well as cooking stoves, charts, ropes, paints, and electronics ~ everything down to a kettle.

Caraibe Marine also has a large electrical showroom. Ask Philippe about solar panels. He advises 24-volt panels for a 12-volt system with a converter, because this gives a higher input over a longer time. Upstairs is a complete nautical boutique with elegant casual, sailing, and beachwear with labels from Musto, Sebaco, Sun Valley, and many more. They have bathing costumes in all sizes. Caraibe Marine is the Caribbean service center for Fountaine Pajot, Jeanneau, CBN (the larger Lagoons) and Catana.

Dinghy over to Artimer to visit Clippers Ship, another giant chandlery that takes up two floors. It is owned by Jocelyne and her son Emmanuel, sometimes helped by Nicolas. They are all helpful and speak good English. They have a broad selection of materials and fittings, including sheets of marine ply, resins, cloth, Andersen winches and spares, electrical panels, solar panels, electronics, anchor winches, Morse cables, hatches, and portlights. They have an excellent selection of pumps and light fittings, with all the latest LED bulbs. They stock stainless and aluminum pipe, icemakers, windmills, Lewmar and Harken hardware, AB, Caribe and Apex inflatable dinghies, Onan generators, and Suzuki and Yamaha outboards, which they also repair and service. They carry Zhik racing clothes and nautical shoes. This is a good place to buy fishing and snorkeling gear: they have a great selection. Clippers Ship carries a big range of fasteners, sold in convenient packages, which makes building a collection easy. They also sell rivets, which can be hard to find. Emmanuel and Nicolas also own Alizes Composites. They do all kinds of fiberglass repairs and construction. See *Technical yacht services: Glass and paintwork*.

Over in Carenantilles, Carene Shop, owned by Hervé Ferrari, is in the Carenantilles compound, it has two floors with two names. Downstairs, Carene Shop is a good technical chandlery for everything you might need on the slip or for a job. Paints, antifoulings, epoxies, polyesters, and cloths are carried, as well as zincs, through-hulls, plumbing, cleaning and polishing products, and a huge stock of marine batteries. You can buy marine ply, acrylic sheet, PVC and Starboard cut to size, and sometimes offcuts.

Upstairs (Le Grenier du Marin), is a fascinating place to visit, offering both new and second-hand gear, and you can bring

PLAN
ARTIMER &
CARENANTILLES

GAS ST
BANK
ECONOMAX
BAKERY
BRICO SOLEIL
BANK
BIKE PHONE BRICO
STORE STORE SOLEIL

ARTIMER
VOILERIE CARAIBES
YES
EQUINOX
DINGHY

CLIPPERS SHIP
RESTAURANT
BAR HOTEL
SMS

CHAMPION ANNETTE
LA SURVY
CARENE SHOP
YARD OFFICE
NAUTIC SERVICES
INBOARD DIESEL SERVICES
MARTNIK VOILERIE
MECANIQUE PLAISANCE
SEXTANT

ALTEC MARINE
CARAIBE
MENUISIERE
ALIZES
COMPOSITES
BICHIK FUEL
FUEL
DINGHY
TONY CRATER
EM COMPOSITES

LES ALIZES
MEDICAL
CENTER
COTRELL
BUILDERS
STORE
MARINE
BAY
COMMERCIAL
CENTER
DOMIA
LEADER PRICE

MARIN MARINA
NAUTICAL BLOCK

UPSTAIRS
DIGINAV
CARAIBES
REFRIGERATION
SURVEYOR
BALADE SUR MER
A&C BROKERS
BOUTIQUES
DYT YACHT TRANSPORT
CHARTER COMPANIES

OVER ROAD
VOILERIE
DU MARIN
MARIN
MOUILLAGE

DOWNSTAIRS
MANGO BAY RESTAURANT
MECANIQE PLAISANCE ET LE SHIP
CARAIBES MARINE
DOUGLAS YACHT SERVICES
MARTINIQUE YACHTING ASSOCIATION
LE MELLISIME
CHARTER COMPANIES
JUMBO CAR
EVA YACHTING

28.5'
14° 28.0'
52.5'
60° 52.0'

LA SURVY
LEADER PRICE
TC'S TO FORT
DE FRANCE
ISLE AUX PAIN
SUPERMARCHE
ANNETTE

MARIN

ARTIMER
CARREFOUR
CARENANTILLES
RESTAURANT BICHIK FUEL
TONY CRATER
EM COMPOSITES
HOLDING AREA
FOR DREDGING
LEAVE CLEAR

DOCTORS
CALEBASSE CAFE
CHURCH
ZANZIBAR
EAU DE TIARE
MARKET
STORE
FISHING BOATS
FISHING DOCK

BANK
STADIUM
MARIN YACHT
HARBOUR NAUTICAL
BLOCK
TONY BOAT
DIVE SHOP
TI TOQUES
LAUNDRY
SHOPS
CAFES
SIMPLY

DINKS VISITORS
FUEL
VISITORS
MARIN MARINA
MALL & PORT
OFFICE CUSTOMS

DINGHY
RED FLAGS
NO ANCHORING AREA
KEEP CLEAR
(POSSIBLE MOORING AREA)
MOORINGS

DRY DOCK

N

FL R
FLR(2) 6S
RB
FLG(2) 6S
FL(2) 6S

your treasures of the bilge to sell. It has a lot of general chandlery including inflatables, fasteners, and safety gear, with some great bargains. Last time I visited they had a selection of good second-hand folding bikes.

YES has a technical chandlery mainly devoted to electricity and plumbing. Their stock includes Echotech water makers and Sinemaster portable generators. They usually have a good collection of led bulbs and lights, solar panels, and there are fastenings and other items worth checking out. Thierry, the owner, also does electrical and water-maker repairs (see *Technical yacht services*).

Maxi Marine in the Marina Mall has a general chandlery with some useful items including lots of safety gear, fastenings, anchors and a big well-laid-out rope selection. They are somewhat geared toward power yachts so have plenty of rollers. They sell and service Mercury and Mercruiser motors.

Regis Guillemot are a charter company in the new marina mall. They are also the Martinique agent for Highfield inflatable dinghies and keep a good stock, including the ultralight aluminum ribs. They stock both the PVC and hypalon models. I had not realized until I looked at their price list how much cheaper the PVC range is, enough difference that you could have protective chaps made for the PVC and still come out ahead.

For general hardware, Brico Soliel is a good small hardware store in Artimer, and for more than that, Cotrell is a building supplier.

Technical yacht services
Sailmakers/Canvas/Cushions

Technical yacht services are found in Marin Marina, in Carenantilles and in Artimer.

North Sails has a loft in the marina mall. This excellent, small, personal, and friendly operation is run by Gavin Dove. Gavin is the son of Andrew Dove, who started the big North Sails Caribbean, now based in Antigua, and being half-English, he is bilingual. Some of the staff also speak Spanish. They can get you an instant quote for a new sail and repair your old one, however technically

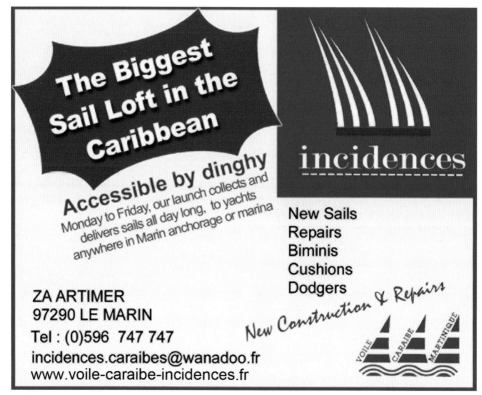
sophisticated. They also do straightforward canvas work, but not cushions or biminis. This small loft is part of a group with representatives in nearly every country in the Eastern Caribbean. They can arrange collection of your sail and delivery. If you need a little dacron, tape, or other sewing supplies for your own project, Gavin will be happy to sell them to you.

In Artimer, the Incidences (Voilerie Caraibes) sail loft, some 6000 square feet of state-of-the-art design, is the largest and most capable in the Caribbean, a giant by international standards. Hervé Lepault, the owner, speaks perfect English and he and his team can tackle any job from windsurfer to superyacht. Sails may be brought in by launch or truck and hoisted straight up into the loft on a giant traveler system. Their launch collects and delivers sails on board anywhere in the Marin anchorage or Marin Marina at any time during working hours from Monday to Friday, with no extra charge; call on VHF: 16.

This is a huge, efficient loft that does excellent work, so turn-around time on repairs is fast. Hervé also has an upholstery department for boat cushions and will bring in any color fabric to suit your job. New sails are by Incidence, the well-known French sailmaker, and carry their guarantee. They are computer-designed in France and sewn here. If you want a better sail at about 40% higher cost, they make many cruising sails in woven Spectra, which has a life and weight similar to Dacron but is more resistant to abrasion and will hold its shape significantly better. With this giant loft, there is plenty of capacity for making new sails fast. Hervé also has a loft in St. Martin in Marigot.

Voilerie du Marin, run by Daniel Karner, is opposite the nautical block. Dan is the agent for Doyle Sails. He can measure your boat for a new set and get a quote. He also repairs lots of sails, whatever the make. He also does all kinds of canvas work.

Upstairs in the nautical block, Charlotte Jardin's Sellerie Marine has small but well-organized space to do any kind of canvas work, including biminis, awnings and covers, and dinghy chaps, or interior cushions, curtains and blinds. If custom hardware is needed, like a bimini frame, she works with Equinox.

Jean Luke's Martnik Voilerie is upstairs in Carenantilles, though the access is outside round the back of the building. This is a small friendly shop. Jean Luke repairs sails, does all kinds of canvas work, including biminis and lazy bags, and also makes cushions.

Technical yacht services
Electrics, Electronics & Watermakers

Upstairs in the marina nautical block is Jacques Fauquet's Diginav electronics showroom and workshop. Jacques has been in this business for over 30 years. He knows more about marine electronics than anyone else in Martinique and is one of the few who can go in and change components on a board. He works on all makes and knows what goes wrong with many of them, so when a repair becomes due, he can work efficiently, repairing if possible, only replacing when necessary. Jacques speaks English and is pleasant to deal with.

Diginav's showroom has a good display of Raymarine, Furuno, Brookes and Gatehouse, Simrad, and Garmin electronics in stock, as well as many spares for them. Jacques is environmentally conscious and would prefer to sell you a unit that will work for many years and can be repaired than to deal with designed obsolescence.

They can set you up with a satellite communication system or a wifi bullet, as well as safety gear like Epirbs. They do a lot of sales and installation work for American and European yachts, and are agents for the well-built Silentwind generators.

Jacques is technically excellent, and can handle the most complex systems, including superyacht electronics. It is helpful if you contact him in advance (email is fine).

Caraibe Energie, part of Caraibe Marine, sells, installs, and repairs electrics and water-makers. They are agents for Sea Recovery, HRO, and Aquabase watermakers, for Kohler, Fischer-Panda and Onan generators. They stock batteries, solar panels, and wind generators, including the cost-effective LE300, and you will find all kinds of electrical components, including Link and Blue

Sea, as well as electrical parts, water filters, and more.

Caraibe Electronique, also in the Caraibe Marine stable, sell, install, and service Raymarine, NKE, Furuno, Icom, MC technologies, and Nexus. Since they are together with Caraibe Gréement, it is a convenience, when you are getting a new mast or taking the old one out for service, that they can install most of the electronics at the same time without having to deal with a third party. (See them at Caraibe Marine; see *Chandlery*.)

Frederic, of Tilikum, in the marina mall is a first rate electrical man and the Caribbean main station for Victron energy, so you can buy all that gear here and get any warranty work done. Fred is good at all charging systems, inverters, and problem solving, and he does a lot of solar panel installations. He is the French Caribbean agent for Marine LED and keeps an excellent selection of the latest led bulbs. He also does refrigeration (see *Refrigeration*).

Pochon Marine, in the marina mall,

MARIN ANCHORAGE & MARINA

NO ANCHORING

DINGHY CHANNEL TO ARTIMER

is a branch of a large French electronics company. They sell Furuno, Icom, Garmin, Lowrance, Simrad, Magellen, B&G, MC Technologies, Raymarine, Cobra, NKE, Sharp, and Hummingbird, and they are agents for Kannad and other Epirbs. They have Thrane and Thrane Sailor communications, and Schenker water makers. They also carry televisions for yachts, windmills, and hydro-generators and are agents for torqueedo electric outboards. Ponchon Marine is run by Eric Dejour.

Artimer is the home base of Thierry's Yachting Engineering Services (YES). This is a technical shop (see *Chandlery*) and a service point. They fix all electrical problems and install any kind of electrical equipment. They sell, service, and install solar panels and watermakers, and fix all makes. They have a van and can make visits to other harbors.

Technical yacht services
Rigging

In the marina, Caraibe Gréement (part of Caraibe Marine) is a full rigging service run by Philippe Leconte. Philippe can handle any rigging problem you may have, from replacing stays to a complete re-rig of your yacht, even including a new mast. This is probably the best rigging shop in the Windwards. They can swage up to 26 mm and have equipment for some rod rigging and hydraulic hoses. Difficult splices, including rope to wire, are a breeze. Caraibe Gréement are agents for Profurl, Facnor, Lewmar, Navtec, Gioit, Z-spar, Spectra, Selden Harken, and many other brands. They always keep spare booms, poles, and all kinds of battens in stock. Anything they do not have can be shipped in on short order by Carole, the special-order specialist. They are happy to work on your yacht and make repairs aloft. They fix and sell hydraulics, including Le Comble. They will also reglaze and seal your worn-out, leaky hatches.

Their new website allows you to estimate the cost and order rigging and other items online. Visit them at Caraibe Marine (see *Chandlery*).

Bernard Blaineau and his son Sylvan

run Antilles Gréement, a general rigging shop. They work cheerfully and well on all kinds of masts, including carbon fiber and all kinds of rigging except rod. They can swage up to 16mm wire. They will make visits anywhere in Martinique and are happy to climb up the mast. They do smaller work such as lifelines and do their own aluminum and stainless welding for rigging parts. Sylvan speaks good English, and you can call him at (0696) 40 91 07.

Technical yacht services
Refrigeration
Frederic Moser at Tilikum has an office in the marina mall. He is an excellent man for refrigeration and air conditioning, and also electrics. He speaks English and does new installations as well as repairs on either air- or water-cooled units, and he can figure out the best system for you. He is agent for Danfoss and Coldex compressors. Fred also does electrics (see *Electrics*).

Patrice Fougerouse, at Caraibes Refrigeration (formerly Fraicheur Service), is part of the Caraibe Marine group. Patrice

is another first-rate refrigeration man, the shop is agent for Webasto, Danfoss, Cruisair, Climma, and Frigoboat, Dometic, Frigonautica, Vitrifrigo, and Air Marine air conditioning. He will fix any make of refrigeration and air-conditioning and he can sell you a new unit and do full installation. You will find him upstairs in the marina nautical block, above Douglas Yacht Services.

Nautic Froid is a small refrigeration shop. The owner works out of his boat in the marina, so it is easiest to call.

Technical yacht services
Mechanics/Welding/Fabrication
Patrice Caillot's Mecanique Plaisance is in the marina. Their shop stocks a good range of Perkins, Volvo, Westerbeke, and Yanmar engines and generators, as well as Honda outboards at competitive prices. The diesel engines can be sold to overseas yachts tax-free. The shop also sells a full range of spares for most things mechanical, including all kinds of filters for fuel and oil. They have inverters, batteries, fasteners, and isotherm fridge units (no service on these). They have

a big repair shop over in Carenantilles and are the main repair shop for all the brands of motors they sell. They also help out with other makes of engine when they have time. They guarantee their work. There is easy access to come alongside to remove an engine.

For welding and machining (all metals) see Laurent Dubois (Kashmir). He has an office in the marina block which he shares with Caraibes Yachts. He has a workshop in Artimer and a larger plant where he plans to build aluminum dinghies. Kashmir started as an artist in France, but when the market ran dry for giant interactive mobile installations he turned to fixing and fabrication in Martinique. He also has a launch and mobile welding unit with a generator so he can come weld on board in St. Anne or at anchor. He has a machine shop and can make most parts that are not too large. He can fix broken winches and other mechanical bits and he speaks excellent English .

Inboard Diesel Service, Frank Agren's big Volvo shop in Case Pilote has a shop with a mechanic in the Carenantilles compound, and offers full service and support for all Volvos, MTUs and Northern Lights. See *Case Pilote* for a full description.

Maxi Marine the chandlery in the Marina Mall, offers full sales and support for Mercury and Mercruiser.

Meca Boats is in the nautical block of the marina. It is run by Rubin Martial who used to be a BMW mechanic, and he fixes both inboards and outboards. He is very good, but he is also a one-man show, so try to give him a little notice, especially for a big job.

Tony Boat is an outboard shop in a container near Sparkling Charter. Owner Tony Cavalier can fix your outboard, whatever the brand and whatever the size.

As you come off the dock in Carenantilles, Altec Marine is in a big building in the corner of the yard, ahead and to the right. This is a big machine and fabrication shop, with a huge amount of equipment for any kind of fabrication or repair, including turning shafts up to 80 mm. They are normally busy, so now-for-now may not be possible.

Crater Tony works in a container in back of EM Composites outside Carenantilles. He does tig and plasma welding and fabricates, welds, and polishes stainless and aluminum and makes many bimini frames.

See Clippers Ship for sales and service of Suzuki outboards.

Technical yacht services
Glass and Paintwork

Alizes Composites is owned and run by Gillet and Emmanuel. They have a big paint shed in Carenantilles and their young and energetic team has a mobile workshop in a large van and can work on site. They do all kinds of fiberglass repairs and construction, including composites; they match gel coat, spray topsides, and treat osmosis. They can also construct and repair wood-epoxy. You can ask at Clippers Ship, with which they are closely associated. (See *Chandlery*.)

Talba Gaston's Nautic Services in the Carenantilles compound is a good place to get your boat's antifouling, epoxy, or coal tar priming done. He is a specialist at various coatings and has over 20 years of experience. He is an authorized antifouling applicator for International, Sea Hawk, and many other brands, and he works with brush, roller or spray. Gaston has a giant sandblaster, and one of his major specialties is removing old antifouling by judicious and careful wet sandblasting. He is the man for dry sandblasting, which he does on steel, aluminum, and polyester. He can polish your topsides so you are ready for the season. If you prefer to do things yourself, he rents some equipment, including a high-pressure washer. Gaston builds professional moorings and makes cradles for shipping yachts long-distance.

EM Composites is on the other side of the river from Carenantilles; just walk out of the gate and keep turning right. Etienne Maran does fiberglass construction: fishing boats, dinghies, tanks, and two-part polyurethane spray painting. He has waterside access for large runabouts or very small yachts.

Technical yacht services
Woodwork

Serge Pivan runs a woodworking shop in Carenantilles called Caraibe Menuiserie, which is part of Caraibe Marine. He is a good man to see for all your woodwork, from planks to joinery. His shop is just north of Bichik. Otherwise, there is a house carpenter, Menuiserie Ebenisterie, near Leader Price.

Technical yacht services
Liferafts & Inflatables

La Survy (outside the Carenantilles gates) is run by the Phillias family who have been working with inflatables forever. They will fix any kind of inflatable and repair and are warranty agents for Zodiac, Avon, Bombard, BFA, and Plastimo. They stock inflatables, liferafts, and safety gear.

Technical yacht services
Project Management and Other Services

If you are going to leave your boat in Martinique and have work done while you are away, it makes a lot of sense to have a project manager. Several people can do this; they are all pleasant to deal with, and work well.

Douglas Rapier of Douglas Yacht Services will act for you in this capacity. English is his first language, he has all the right contacts and will make sure you get a top class job on time, with great attention to detail. He has an excellent team, and is the person to go to when you want the best, and don't mind paying a little extra for it.

If you have a big project in mind, he can arrange the hauling and work to be VAT-free and any imported parts to be duty-free, but paper work is involved and this does need to be set up in advance. If you are in a hurry and need some work done quickly, he can organize it for you.

Azur Spirit in the Marina Mall is run by Jimy. Jimy looks after boats when the owners are away and does any repairs and maintenance that might be needed. He also sells boats and has some for charter.

Roberto Maxera at R M, is half Italian and half Argentinian and he once lived in England, so is fluent in English, Spanish, Portugese, Italian, and French. He is an excellent generalist who can take care of maintenance and most boat problems, and you can leave your boat in his care and he will have it ready when you return.

Frank has a lovely computer shop called Infogeek in the marina mall. He has fair prices on laptops and accessories and he can fix your laptop and sort out computer problems. He works on integrated marine computer systems of the kind found on fancy yachts. He does much of this work in association with Douglas Yacht Services.

If you need a new name on your boat, check out Jean Luc Neugnat at SMS in Artimer next to Clippers Ship. He designs all kinds of graphics, numbers and names and then make the transfers to put them on you your boat. He can also put them on for you. He can also make t-shirts, so if you want your favorite photo a t-shirt, go talk to him.

If you have a Lagoon that needs help, Corail Caraibes Charter is the Caribbean agent (unless it is a big one, in which case it is Caraibe Marine). If you have a Jeanneau, Catana, or Fountaine Pajot, contact Caraibe Gréement. If you have an Amel that needs help, Jean Collin is the agent in the marina mall.

Transport

We give the location of the TC stop on our map, and it is easy to get to Fort de France. Your bike can get you a lot of places. Car rental agencies include Jumbo, in the nautical block, and GD location, in the marina mall.

Taxis stand by just outside the marina on the town side. If you want to call one, try

Thierry Belon. He is personable and reliable, and he speaks a little English (0696 25 88 52). If you need someone more fluent in English, call Max Lamon (0696 26 03 94). If you are going on a long jaunt, consider Vincent Thomas (0696 07 54 37) from Rivière Salée, who is highly recommended. Don't want to sail home? Check Douglas Yacht Services or Dockwise Yacht Transport.

Provisioning

Appro Zagaya is an excellent provisioning service run by Cathy and Pascal. Contact them by phone, fax, or email, or go onto their web site (www.appro-zagaya.fr) and shop or download their lists. This is a professional and friendly operation where they enjoy their work, provisioning many hundreds of bareboats every year. They deliver right to your dock, or if you are chartering a bareboat, they load it on board. They need three days' notice, and this is a full provisioning service, so your order needs to be over 200 Eu. This is perfect for people coming down on charter, those short of time, or those who hate shopping. They have a wifi system you can get in most of the bay and even over to Ste. Anne with the right aerial. From this, you can access their web to order. If you are one of their charter customers, they may be able to arrange some wifi time for emailing or uploading your holiday picks on Facebook.

Douglas Yacht Services does full provisioning for the superyachts. This is a fully professional service, and items not available in Martinique are flown in from France.

If you prefer to shop yourself, remember to take your own shopping bags and you have a choice of supermarkets and shops.

Leader Price has the best location, with its own dinghy dock. This is a reasonably priced market that is popular with locals and often has good fresh produce, frozen meats, fish, and shrimp. Many things they sell, like Real Cola, are their own brand. Mix it with enough rum and lime, and no one will ever know.

The Carrefour Supermarket in the Centre Commercial Annette, just behind Carenantilles, is in a mall that includes a mobile store, beauty shops, gift shops, a boulangerie/patisserie, and rotisserie. It is not too far from the Leader Price or Artimer dinghy docks.

Simply is the most spacious market, very modern with big, wide aisles. You will not feel claustrophobic here. They have a pretty good selection and are just behind the marina mall, within easy walking distance through the car park. They open 0800-1930 except Sunday, when they close at 1300. The Economax, at Artimer, is inexpensive but very limited.

Port Apporte in the marina mall sells wine, beer, beverages, and tobacco products, as well as a fair selection of groceries. If you are in the marina, they will deliver right to your boat.

In the marina nautical block, Le Millesime is a fancy wine liquor and tobacco store. You can sit down with them and sort out your wine collection.

None of the local supermarkets are really complete. For a giant, modern, really good supermarket, Carrefour at Genipa is the closest and avoids the heavy traffic near Fort de France. Drive past the Rivière Salée exit, pass two roundabouts, and look for a tiny right turn with a small Genipa sign (blink and you've missed it). Pass under the highway; it is right ahead.

The local market is good for produce, spices, local drinks, and souvenirs, especially on Saturday mornings.

Douceurs Mainoises is a great boulangerie/patisserie in the marina mall, and there is another just across the road. You can find a health food store in the Annette Mall.

Fun shopping

The marina mall has lots of levels, corners, steps, and even a spiral staircase. It is a natural for kids, and in the afternoon parents let their kids explore while they check out all the boutiques. These include Made for Marin, Cargot, Madras design, and Les Comptois du Cotton. Look for Frank's computer shop called Infogeek. One Sunday morning every two months the whole marina turns into a big open air market.

Fishing enthusiasts can get their hooks into shopping at Akwaba, in the marina mall. This is a giant fishing store, with rows of rods and hooks, lines, and sinkers. They have nautical clothing, snorkeling gear, lots of good tackle boxes, and any kind of fishing gadget you might want.

Clippers Ship in Artimer Mall (see *Chandlery*) also has excellent fishing gear and also nautical clothing.

The giant Domia household store is fun to visit in the Marine Bay Commercial Center, where you will also find a fair stationery store. If all this coincides with lunch, check out Le Midi du Marin. If they serve you the best meal you have ever had, you clearly need to get out more, but it is cheap, quiet, not bad, and, being cafeteria style, instant. They also sell good bread.

Oye Oye is a mixed-bag store near Leader Price ~ from power tools to household and exercise machines. If you need a bike or music store, Artimer has both.

Marin market has many souvenirs.

Restaurants

There are many restaurants to choose from. I mention a few. Mango Bay [$B-D] is right in the marina nautical block, hanging out over the water with a great view of the boats. It is casual enough that you will be welcome in shorts. This is an excellent place to come for breakfast, lunch, or dinner. They have a deli with good sandwiches, croissants, pain au chocolat, and ice cream. Their bar is a gathering place in the evenings for many yacht crews. They have free wifi and there is a section where you see people busy on their computers. But don't be fooled by all this casual bustle. Mango Bay is also a very good restaurant, with excellent food, and one of the most reliable restaurants in Marin for a good meal right on the water's edge. Daily specials, pizza and pasta, and a menu that changes every few months are available for both lunch and dinner. They cook both French and Italian specialties, and their daily special is usually a bargain. On Thursday nights they have karaoke.

The Marina Mall has become a popular restaurant area. From breakfast to dinner people congregate to hang out or eat, enlivened many times a week by live music. Kokoarum [$B-C] is cheerful, open to the view, and serves burgers, barbecued foods, and a good lunch special. They offer a big variety of tasty ice creams and sorbets. Their

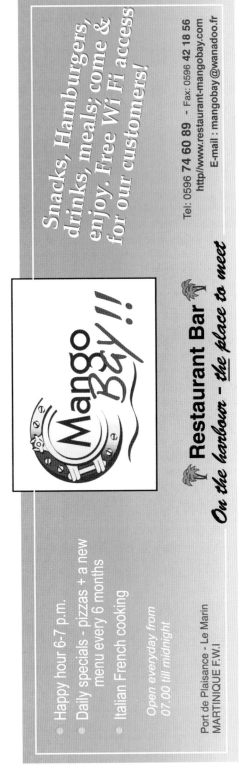

bar specializes in Caribbean rums. They open every day from 1030 to 2400 and have live music on Fridays and Wednesdays.

Numero20 [$B-C] sprawls across the top floor and you pretty much bump into it on your way to the Capitainerie. They open every day for lunch and dinner, except Sunday, when they do not open for lunch. They have a tapas and regular menu, a separate bar, and live music on Tuesdays

On hot days L'Annexe [$B-D] has an interesting cooling system; cold water is shot out as a vapor. This is helpful when you select their "pierrades". You choose your meat or fish and they bring it to you raw, accompanied by an incredibly hot stone. They also have generous pasta dishes, wraps and salads. They have live music on Saturdays.

O Ble Noir [$D, closed Mondays] is a crêperie and ice cream place with ample space for hanging out. Pizza Amis is a popular pizza place where many come to hang out when work is over. Across the road is a whole row of even cheaper little bistros.

Marin Mouillage [$D] is cute and upstairs right behind the marina. They do a brisk lunch trade, with tasty local specials, and are open Friday and Saturday evenings for a barbecue. The food is good and reasonably priced.

Ti Toques [$B-C] is a smart, modern, street-side establishment open to the breeze, with fast, snappy service. Their food is generally good. They post old favorites and daily specials on a blackboard. While they serve mainly French cuisine, they also do pizza and ice cream. Eat there or take away. Zanzibar [$B] is fancy, upstairs and open to the breeze. Their food is very good, and their fondant chocolat and creme brulée are delicious. Indigo [$B-C] is the floating restaurant, just outside the marina mall. It serves Créole food.

Le Sextant (closed Sunday and Monday) is the Carenantilles restaurant in the new block at the back. They serve generous daily lunch specials, which are great value and geared to hungry workers. In the evening it is a bar and hangout with live music, usually a couple of times a week.

Restaurant La Paillote Cayali [$C-D] is for those who want to eat right on the beach.

Sit out next to the waves and eat a variety of local specialties at reasonable prices. Open all day every day. Calebasse Café, has interesting musical groups some evenings.

Artimer has a little hotel by the dinghy dock. Its restaurant is sometimes open.

Ashore

One of the better shore treats is to visit Eau de Tiaré, a complete beauty and health spa run by two delightful women, Kathy and Carina. Kathy is a Vincentian who grew up in Mustique, so English is her first language. She is full of fun and will make you feel immediately at home. They created a splendid new facility out of part of the upstairs of the historic building next to the market that houses the big pharmacy. The door is on the road leading up the hill. You have to climb to the top, but the view is great when you get here, and they have a sauna, massage, rooms, hairdressing salon, treatment rooms, and showers. They offer all kinds of beauty treatments, including manicure, pedicure, facials, waxing, and more, as well as a variety of massages, and every kind of hair styling. Prices vary from about 40 to 80 Eu.

Marin is a good area to shake the rust off your old bike and give it a run. The road up to Le Cap and over to Macouba is pleasant, and from here, trails lead south along the coast. If you like parasailing you will find a lot of it in the area of Cap Chevalier.

If you rent a car or hike, make an effort to climb the hill on the west side of Marin for the spectacular view, not only across the bay but all the way to Baie des Anglais. As you leave Marin and head for Fort de France, there is a roundabout just opposite Ilet Dupres. Follow the signposts for Morne Glommier and enjoy the ridge.

Water sports

Nautica Antilles is a diving-equipment rental shop in the marina nautical block. They are linked to a larger retail outlet near the airport, so if you need gear, ask ~ they can bring it in.

If you want to go diving, check out Christophe at Immersion Caraibe. He speaks English and will make it easy. You will find him in a little house near Tony Boat.

EAST COAST OF MARTINIQUE
BAIE DES ANGLAIS

ILET HARDY TO I. TOIS ROUX AND ALL
ASSOCIATED ISLANDS AND ROCKS ARE A NATURE
RESERVE FOR BIRDS. LANDING IS NOT
PERMITTED

THE EAST COAST OF MARTINIQUE

This guide covers all the most frequently used anchorages, but does not include most of Martinique's east coast. This area is pleasant and interesting, but it is also tricky, with many reefs and shoals in water that is often difficult to read. The charts that are available are short on details where it matters, and over the years it has claimed more than its fair share of hulls. Adventurous cruisers who wish to visit should buy the Trois Rivières guide to Martinique by Jerome Nouel. It is now only in French but it has color photographs, and is the only guide that covers this area well. We do include Baie des Anglais, the closest east coast anchorage.

BAIE DES ANGLAIS

The wine locker is full, you are stuffed on restaurant meals, you have seen enough elegant boutiques to last a lifetime. What next? Consider a few days of quiet recovery in Baie des Anglais. Baie des Anglais is less than three miles up Martinique's east coast. It is a large mangrove-lined bay, with some small beaches and several little islands for dinghy exploration. There are no restaurants, no shops, and while there may be another boat or two, you are likely to have it to yourself.

Regulations

The islands at the entrance to Baie des Anglais, including Ilet Hardy, Ilet Perce, Ilet Burgaux, and Ilet Tois Roux, are bird sanctuaries, and going ashore is not permitted.

Navigation

The navigation is tricky and Baie des Anglais should only be visited in relatively light trade winds (<15 knots). The entrance is downwind and down sea. Enter between Ilet Hardy and the group of islands that include Ilet Perce, Ilet Burgaux, and Ilet Tois Roux. Ilet Hardy has a distinctive rock knoll on its southeastern shore. Once past Ilet Hardy, look for the two reefs to the northwest of Ilet Perce and pass fairly close to them. (You will see Fond Blanc to starboard.) Note that there are quite a few isolated rocks just to the east of Ilet Aigrettes. By now the seas should be relatively calm, and you will find a large daytime anchoring area about 20 feet deep to the west of Fond Blanc, between Ilet Aigrettes and the visible reef on the other side of the channel.

Your strategy from here on in depends on your draft, the size of your engine, the strength of the wind, and whether your insurance premium is up to date. You have to cross a bar of soft mud in unreadable water with the wind right behind you. For boats of less than 6-foot draft, there will probably be little problem. For boats of 6.5-foot or 7-foot draft, the width of the deepest channel is very narrow, and at low tide sounds out at about 7 feet. The seamanlike thing to do is to anchor in the deep water and sound out the channel with a lead line in your dinghy. As you look at Ilet des Parletuviers, you will see an old mill tower just behind it, a little to its left. A range I found helpful is to be on a line between the northern edge of Ilet Burgaux and this old mill tower. The deepest water is probably a hair to the southwest of this line. Once over the bar, you have plenty of water and many perfectly protected anchoring spots; inside, Ilet des Parletuviers is the most popular. If you dinghy over to the shore near Ilet Aigrettes, you can find a way through to Anse Trabaud, a lovely but fairly popular beach. Dinghy exploration is also good up to Ilet Chevalier.

Go to Baie des Anglais well provisioned, because should the wind and sea get up while you are there, seas break across the entrance and you may have to wait a while to get out.

For an adventure, dinghy up behind Ilet Chevalier, carry on to the beach with the

Baie des Anglais

MT. PIMARD MT. FLAMBEAU

PIGEON ISLAND

kite-surfing, and land the dinghy.

A coastal footpath takes you round to Ste. Anne in the south and Anses Macabou in the north.

PASSAGE BETWEEN MARTINIQUE AND ST. LUCIA

Northbound

The passage from St. Lucia to Fort de France is usually a fast reach. A course of due north from Rodney Bay gets you close to the lee coast. It doesn't hurt to be a little offshore when you arrive, as the wind tends to follow along the coast and is fluky close in. If Martinique is visible at the outset, it will appear as two islands, because the low-lying land in the center is not visible from St. Lucia. As you approach Martinique, Diamond Rock stands out as a clear landmark.

If you are heading for Ste. Anne, you can often make it in one tack, but be sure to head up a bit to allow for current as you cross.

Southbound

The southerly passage from Grande Anse d'Arlet is sometimes a pleasant reach. At other times it can be hard on the wind. As the wind flows round the land, you will be pointing high as you follow the coast. It often pays to motor sail to stay reasonably close to shore before setting off across the channel. If sailing, it may pay to sail fast on the southerly

tack and hope to play lifts later. When you see St. Lucia, head for the highest (rather rounded) mountain in the north end of the island until you make out the distinctive shape of Pigeon Island, a clear double peak joined by a slope. The higher twin mounds of Mt. Pimard and Mt. Flambeau (see Rodney Bay chart) also sometimes stand out.

The sail from Ste. Anne to St. Lucia is usually an easy reach.

St. Lucia

Marigot Bay

Regulations

Ports of entry are Rodney Bay, Castries, Marigot Bay, Soufriere, and Vieux Fort. Entry charges in $EC are: $15 navigational aids, $10 practique (up to 100 tons), and clearance fees of $5 under 40 feet and $15 over 40 feet. In addition, charter yachts less than 40 feet pay $20; between 40 and 70 feet, $30; and over 70 feet, $40. Charter yachts also pay $15 per passenger. Three day in-and-out clearance is available with the same crew and you can save paperwork and pre-clear on sailclear.com. Immigration insists everyone fill in an immigration form (download from Doyleguides.com). They usually give six months on entry.

Normal office hours are weekdays 0800-1200 and 1330-1615. Those clearing outside these hours pay $100 overtime fee. One or two customs officers may ask you where you want to visit. If you list Rodney Bay, Marigot, Soufriere, and Vieux Fort, and go where you want, you should be okay. If you list anywhere else, a few officers may charge you a permit fee.

Spearfishing, damaging corals, and buying coral, turtle shell, or out-of-season lobsters (lobster season changes annually; it is usually August to February or later) are forbidden. Sailing yachts are generally allowed to troll a single line or handline for pleasure, others need a fishing license. No scuba diving (except for underwater work on your yacht) may be done without a qualified guide. To take a pet ashore involves considerable advance planning and paperwork . Personal watercraft need a license from the ministry of tourism.

Holidays

Jan 1 and 2
Easter Friday, Sunday & Monday, April 14-17, 2017, and March 29-April 2, 2018
Feb 22, Independence Day
May 1, Labor Day
Whit Monday, June 5, 2017, May 21, 2018
Corpus Christi, June 15 2017, May 31 2018
Carnival (varies) – Monday and Tuesday, around the middle of July
First Friday in August, Emancipation Day
Thanksgiving, October (variable)
All Saints' Day, 1-2 November
St. Cecilia Day, 22 November
December 13, National Day
December 25 and 26, Christmas

Shopping hours

Most shops open 0830-1230, then 1330-1600. Saturday is a half-day. Banks close by 1500 except Fridays, when they are open till 1700. Supermarkets open longer.

Telephones

Lime or Digicel cell phones are the easiest way to go. For the USA & NANP countries, dial 1 + 10 digits (see p.19). For other overseas calls, dial 011 + country code + number. When dialing from overseas, the area code is 758 followed by a 7-digit number.

Transport

Buses ($1.50-$7 EC) run to most towns and villages. If you are going a long way, check on the time of the last returning bus. Taxis are plentiful. The sample taxi rates below (for 1-3 people) may increase soon:

	$EC
Rodney Bay to Vigie	66
Rodney Bay to Castries	66
Rodney Bay to Hewanorra	220
Castries to Hewanorra	180
Rodney Bay to Marigot	130
Short ride	20
Day tour	500

Extra charges after 2200, before 0600, and for more than three people.

There are plenty of rental cars. You need to get a temporary local license at $54 EC.

The airport departure tax is $68 EC, usually included in your ticket.

Mud Bath, Sapphire Falls, Soufriere

*S*t. Lucia, the largest of the English speaking Windwards, is mountainous and lush, with many beautiful white sand beaches. Tropical rainforest covers the steep slopes of the center and gives way to cultivated agricultural land around the more moderately sloping coastal fringe. Bananas are still a major crop. For sheer physical beauty, the area around Soufriere and the Pitons is outstanding.

St. Lucia offers excellent sightseeing and hiking. You can see most of it by taxi, bus, or rental car. Adventurous travelers willing to combine driving with hiking will want to rent a four-wheel drive vehicle and explore some faraway corners such as Grand Anse or Anse Louvet on the windward shore. Any taxi driver will be delighted to take you on a tour. St. Lucia has several ziplines on which you can fly through the countryside. If that is too energetic, you can take an aerial rainforest canopy tram.

Those interested in nature should contact the National Trust, which runs tours to Frigate Island and the Maria Islands as well as turtle-watching tours. It is worth calling the forestry department about rainforest tours. They can supply knowledgeable guides.

There are many marked trails in St. Lucia that you can follow on your own, including rainforest hikes at the height of land as you drive across the island on the main road to the airport.

Cocoa Sainte Lucie is a new, small (one woman for now), organic chocolate factory based in Canaries. It is run by Maria Jackson, and her chocolate is excellent; the local "spice" chocolate special. By the time this book comes out, she may have a visitor center, which would be easily visited from Soufriere or on a tour. You can call her and ask, 459-4401. Otherwise, look for her chocolate in Zaka in Soufriere or Hallmark in the JQ Mall in Rodney Bay.

St. Lucia offers an excellent, full-service marina with a haul-out in Rodney Bay and a smaller marina in Marigot. The choice of restaurants is the best in the Windwards. St. Lucia is a charter center, with several charter companies in Rodney Bay.

ST. LUCIA

14° 07'N
60° 58'W
WSLU00

0 1 2 3 4
SCALE IN NAUTICAL MILES

N
NW   NE
W   E
SW   SE
S

PT. DU CAP
50
240
600

PIGEON I.
HOTEL
HOTEL
PT. HARDY
90
FOUS IS.
600

RODNEY BAY

BARREL OF BEEF
600
ESPERANCE

600
PLAN
CAP MARQUIS
FL (2) 20 S 5M
50

18
HOTEL
75
HOTEL
RAT I.
HOTEL
9
18
90
P. DAUPHIN
ANSE MARQUIS
600

FL (2) 10S, 22M
AIRPORT
PLAN
120

600
10
HOTEL
CASTRIES
GRAND ANSE
120
14° 00'

BUOY
30
CUL DE SAC BAY
PITON FLORE 1850'
TORTUE PT.

OIL DEPOT
120
LOUVET PT.
ANSE LOUVET
BOUCHE I.

TANKS
600
MARIGOT
30
PLAN
50
600

PLAN
ANSE LA RAYE
FOND D'OR BAY
120

PT. DE LA VILLE
120
ANSE COCHON
DENNERY
60

JAMBETTE PT.
600
55'

CANARIES
MT. BEAUJOLAIS 1158'
PORT PRASLIN
60

120
600
MAMIKU GARDENS
120

600
120
ANSE CHASTANET
FOX GROVE INN
ANSE CHAPEAU
600

GD CAILLE PT.
SOUFRIERE
600
RAIN FOREST
90
50'

PETIT PITON (2500')
PLAN
WALK
110

GROS PITON (2600')
MT. GD. MAGASIN 2117'
MICOUD
90

1800
360
90
DES CANELLES PT.

120
CHOISEUL
DOREE
30

50
LABORIE
30
GAUTIER PT.

WSLU13
13° 46'N
61° 05'W
65
90
30
PLAN
40
14
40

13° 45'
600
36
AIRPORT
30
90
120
13° 45'

36
100
MARIA ISLANDS
600

GEORGIE PT.
VIEUX FORT
80
120
MOULE A CHIC (FL 5S, 22M)

600
PLAN
70

05'
61° 00'
80
40
55'
50'

144

Navigation, west coast

Between the northern tip of St. Lucia and Rodney Bay, there are several shoals and no anchorages, so it is best to keep clear.

Rodney Bay offers several anchorages that are dealt with in detail below.

Barrel of Beef is a low-lying rock about a quarter of a mile off the southern side of the entrance to Rodney Bay. It is marked by a white light that flashes every five seconds. The water is deep enough (about 18 feet) for most yachts to pass inside it.

Between Barrel of Beef and Castries, the coast sweeps back in a large bay containing Rat Island. The northern part of this bay is full of reefs and is best avoided. On leaving Rodney Bay, the normal route is to pass either side of Barrel of Beef and head directly toward Castries Harbor.

Tapion Rock forms the southern entrance to Castries Harbor. There are some rocks close by, so give it a reasonable clearance. Two miles south of Castries, Cul de Sac Bay is a huge depot for Hess Oil. It is well lit and makes an obvious landmark by day or night. There is a flashing buoy in the middle of the entrance to this bay.

From Cul de Sac Bay to the Pitons, St. Lucia is mainly steep-to, and keeping a quarter of a mile offshore clears all dangers. There are a few rock hazards lying up to 100 yards or more offshore. The worst is a sizable rock patch off the southern end of Anse Chastanet that should be given wide clearance.

RODNEY BAY

Rodney Bay is over a mile long. On the northern shore, an artificial causeway connects Pigeon Island to the mainland, providing the bay with protection. In the old days, when Europeans entertained themselves by sailing around in wooden boats taking potshots at each other, Pigeon Island was the main base for the British navy in this area. It was ideally situated, being in sight (on most days) of Martinique, the main French base. There used to be a fort, hospital buildings, barracks, and storerooms. Now the St. Lucia National Trust conserves it as a delightful park. There are shady gardens, and the fort

has been partly restored. The climb to the top of both peaks is well rewarded by the views. Strategically placed signboards tell you about the history.

There is an entry charge to the park (about $6 US). This helps finance the National Trust, which works to preserve the environment as well as historic sites. The anchorage off Pigeon Island is scenic and breezy. If you are staying here a long time and wish to use the park often, become a member of the National Trust, as the entry fees can add up.

Near the Pigeon Island Park dinghy dock, you will find Jambe de Bois [$C-D], a delightful restaurant/bar and art gallery run by Barbara Tipson, an active member of the local animal-welfare organization, which often helps place unwanted animals. Jambe de Bois is slightly offbeat, with an arty atmosphere. You can relax in an easy chair, catch up on email on their wifi, check the bookswap, and enjoy local art. It makes a great hangout, with comfy corners inside and breezy spots on the Hobbit furniture outside. Jambe de Bois opens daily 0900-2100,

RODNEY BAY

N

14° 05.5'N
60° 58.2'W
WSLU01

14° 05.0'N
60° 58.5'W

0   1/2   1
SCALE IN NAUTICAL MILES

THERE ARE SOME FISH TRAPS IN
RODNEY BAY

BARREL OF BEEF FL (2) 5S. 2M

14° 04.1'N
60° 58.7'W
WSLU03

BURGOT RKS.   BECUNE PT.   CAP ESTATE
PIGEON ISLAND   NATIONAL PARK   CLUB ST. LUCIA
OLD FORT   JAMBE DE BOIS   GREAT HOUSE &DEREK WALCOTT THEATER
HOTEL (CONSPIC)   CAUSEWAY (LOW)   TO GOLF CLUB
THE LANDINGS
GROS ISLET   RADIO MAST
BREAK WATER
ELLIOTS GAS CAR RENT STORE
POSTS   SEE PLAN   RODNEY BAY MARINA
REDUIT BEACH   HOUSES
HOTELS   RODNEY BAY VILLAGE
MT. PIMARD 639'
MT. FLAMBEAU 533'
CUTI COVE
GAS
BAY WALK MALL   SUPER J MALL   HOTELS CLUB   JULIAN'S   NIGHT CLUB   IL PAPPA
WINDJAMMER LANDINGS
PT. LAMBRELOTTE

except Mondays, when they close at 1700. On Sunday nights, they feature good jazz groups, and on Saturdays, they often have a group playing oldies. You have to pay the park entry fee until 1700. The restaurant does a late breakfast, as well as lunch and dinner. Fresh fruit juice is available, along with many daily specials and snacks.

On the causeway, Sandals, a conspicuous, all-inclusive hotel with bright red roofs, makes a good landmark.

A little farther down, The Landings Beach Club is a large condo development built around canals where owners keep their yachts. You can dinghy up to their Beach Club [$B-C], an informal restaurant set between the beach and the canal. It is open all day, offering everything from sandwiches and burgers to full meals and daily specials. A fancier dinner is to be had at Palms [$A], a gourmet restaurant near reception, and they also have a beach bar open for lunch called the Callaloo [$B-C].

Outside the lagoon, on the north side is Gros Islet Village, which is occasionally a hotbed of crime. Marine patrols have made things way better and there have been few problems recently, but take care if anchored close to the village.

To the south of the channel entrance is Reduit Beach, one of St. Lucia's finest beaches and the home of many hotels and the St. Lucia Yacht Club. This is a popular anchorage with mainly good holding.

Navigation

Rodney Bay Lagoon is a large and completely protected inner lagoon that is entered via a dredged channel between Reduit Beach and Gros Islet village. This is lit by port and starboard lights at the entrance and at the inner end of the channel. Approach the channel in the center. IGY Rodney Bay Marina has dredged the entrance and marina area, so there is sufficient depth for yachts of 13 feet draft to come in and tie up. Yachts of 15 feet draft have made it with care and attention to tides. The shallowest water is just outside the entrance, so if you can make it into the channel, you should be good to the big boat dock.

Many yachts tie up at the marina. It is also possible to take an IGY marina mooring in the inner lagoon, where depths are 7-9 feet. You may anchor in the outer bay to the southeast of Pigeon Island, anywhere off the causeway to Gros Islet, and off Reduit Beach.

The outside beach anchorages occasionally become untenable in extreme northerly swells. Anywhere within acoustic range of Gros Islet beach can be noisy (more so out in Rodney Bay than in the lagoon).

Rodney Bay is a major hub of tourist activities, with many hotels, malls, restaurants, and an 18-hole golf course nearby.

IGY Marina has 24-hour security. You can always call them, 720-4139 or VHF:16. They will come directly if you are in the marina, or pass it on to marine police and coastguard if you are at anchor.

Regulations

IGY Rodney Bay Marina is a good place to clear in. If you plan to stay in the marina, go into a berth (see below) and walk to the customs office, or anchor and dinghy in.

Customs open daily 0800-1200 and 1330-1630. On Thursdays and Fridays they often stay open till 1800. Overtime charges ($100 EC) apply on weekends, holidays, during lunch, or after 1615. Entry charges are $30-40 EC, depending on the size of the boat, with extra fees if you are on charter. Details of fees are given at the beginning of this chapter. Only the skipper should come ashore to clear; other crew should stay on the

Pigeon island

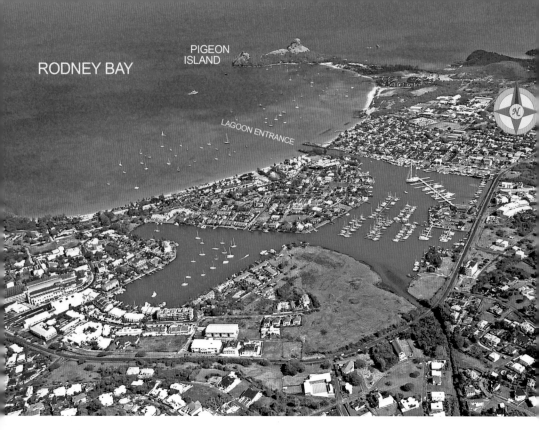

RODNEY BAY

PIGEON ISLAND

LAGOON ENTRANCE

yacht till clearance is complete. If you have internet access, you can save time and effort by pre-clearing the entry on sailclear.com. St. Lucia has more paperwork than other islands as they insist everyone fills in an immigration form. To save time, download it at doyleguides.com

If you need clearance when everything is closed, ask Ben's Yacht Services to help, or try the customs guardroom in Castries, (758) 468-4859.

Do not exceed the 4-knot speed limit in Rodney Bay Lagoon or close by other anchored yachts in the bay. This applies to all vessels, including inflatables and dinghies. Anchoring is not allowed in the lagoon, but IGY moorings are available.

Shipping in parts? Invoices and shipping papers must be marked "for transshipment." Many items are duty-free. There are charges for documentation, and you need to use one of the two excellent agents. Ian Duzauzay (Reliant Brokerage) will clear your package in and can also rent you a car. Lisa Kessel, the wife of Chris, the surveyor, does a lot of shipments for yachts.

Communications

Bernard Logan runs a cruisers net on VHF: 68 at 0830, Monday to Saturday. He gives weather, upcoming events, and cruiser get-togethers.

You can use Rodney Bay Marina as a postal drop and for sending faxes. If you have a marina berth or mooring, the marina wifi should cover you.

Other internet and office services can be found behind Harmony apartments and in Rodney Bay Village near Home Services. Digicel and Lime have sales outlets in the Baywalk Mall. Nearly all restaurants and bars have free wifi.

General yacht services

IGY Rodney Bay Marina [VHF: 16] is an attractive marina with a large, solid dock that can take 32 superyachts up to 285 feet long. Fancy floating docks accommodate 221 regular yachts. They have 30 convenient and well-maintained moorings in the inner lagoon (daily rate $0.45 US per foot).

Rodney Bay Marina is a pleasant place to stay, well protected from the elements

Rodney Bay Marina during ARC

St. Lucia

amid lawns and coconut palms, dockside restaurants, and cafes. It is home to a business community that includes a bank, marine services, a food store, boutiques, massage therapists, and many taxi drivers, as well as a well-stocked, duty-free chandlery. A few charter companies are based here. The businesses are friendly, and for many yachting folk, Rodney Bay Marina has become a home away from home in the Caribbean, creating a sense of community.

The manager, Paul Ash, is open, accessible, helpful, and popular with his customers. He is assisted by Sean Deveau You will usually get a spot in the Marina, though it can be packed when the Arc arrives in mid-December. Call for a dock space and the staff will help you in.

Dock I, the big, new concrete dock, is available for yachts up to 250 feet long and has 110, 220, and 380 volts up to three phase and both 50- and 60-cycle electricity. This dock also has high-speed fueling.

Docks A through E have 220-volt, 50-cycle electricity. Docks F, G and J have 110-volt, 60-cycle electricity. All docks have water and wifi and, if you have a suitable aerial, wifi is available on the moorings.

Hot showers are a pleasant feature, and they use Greening the Caribbean for garbage disposal so you can recycle by separating into cardboard and paper, tins and glass, tech stuff (computers/batteries/etc) and general rubbish. There is a place for used engine oil.

The management sometimes offers double docks for safer berthing for the hurricane season: ask in the office.

If you need a technician, or help with varnishing, the main desk will have a list of registered independent contractors and day workers. You can get your laundry done and fill all kinds of LPG gas tanks at Suds Laundry. If you need to get boat parts cleared in, ask at the front desk.

A convenient bus runs from outside the marina to town, and some of the best restaurants in the Windwards and a golf course are close by. Within the marina, day trips to Martinique or along the coast are available.

Rodney Bay Marina Boatyard [VHF: 16] is part of the marina and is St. Lucia's only haul-out facility. It is well organized. Yard supervisor Milton McKenzie or Juliatta will answer your questions in the yard. The travel lift is 75 tons and can take up to a 28-foot beam. For most boats it will not be necessary to remove a stay. They have room for about 120 yachts in long-term storage and another 20 undergoing work. You may live aboard. If you are leaving your yacht here in the summer months, the yard has cradles and tie-downs.

You can work yourself or the marina boatyard can organize subcontractors to get your work done. A gelcoat stripper is available for osmosis work, and they have two big under-cover paint sheds.

The fuel and work dock (open daily

0800-1600) is alongside, to the east of the travel lift, making lifting and working on engines and masts easy. High-speed fueling is also available on Dock I. Anyone who has cleared out can buy fuel duty-free. The fuel dock also sells water, ice, and lubricants. If there is a problem getting water on the fuel dock you can ask a dockmaster about the possibility of a space on a regular dock for buying water.

A little fuel dock stands on the northern side of the Rodney Bay entrance canal, where the fishing boats tie up; they sell diesel, gasoline, and engine oils. You can tie your dinghy there, but the dock is not suitable for most yachts. It has often saved my bacon when the marina is closed.

Island-wide superyacht services are offered by Ben Taxi, who has self-contained rooms to rent overlooking Rodney Bay and offers jeep rentals. He lives in Soufriere but has people in Rodney Bay. CJ Taxi is always in the north and also provides yacht services for all sizes of yachts (see *Transport*).

You won't find a better place for dental work in the Caribbean (and beyond) than

Kent Glace and Associates, just a few steps from the dinghy dock by Baywalk Mall. Pass the Baywalk Mall towards the main road and look on your right behind Caribbean Smiles. Kent Glace is excellent, and, in addition to regular dentistry, he does all the surgical work: implants, complex extractions, crowns, cosmetics, root canals, and fixing root canals that have gone bad. He is aided by two other dentists, Dr. Barnard and Dr. Michel, and two qualified hygienists, a rarity in the Caribbean. You will get top-quality care here at less expense than in the USA. If you happen to have kids, Desma, at Caribbean Smiles next door, is an orthodontist. Kent Glace and Associates is open weekdays 0800-1700 and Saturdays 0900-1200. Kent himself works in town on Thursdays, but the other staff are still there.

For medical problems, I have been getting excellent reports about M-Care walk-in Medical Clinic, open Monday to Saturday 0800-1800, with two good GPs, both women. It is a few hundred yards beyond the Rodney Bay Medical Center, which is a block east from the JQ Mall. Rodney Bay Medical Center is also good to walk in, and they have several GPs, as well as a dermatologist, an ear, nose and throat specialist, a pediatrician, and testing services. Nearer the dinghy dock is a pain clinic with an orthopedic surgeon and physiotherapist. Prices vary, so ask. Tapion Hospital in Castries has many medical services including an excellent dermatologist, a heart specialist, surgeons, and lab facilities. Call for details and appointments.

Chandlery

Island Water World is a large, duty-free chandlery managed by Ian Cowan, one of St. Lucia's most knowledgeable yachtsmen, and his wife, Rosemary. They have an excellent team, including Sophie, who has been answering questions from those on yachts for many years. This store is part of the Caribbean-wide chain, which has its 50th anniversary this year, and draws yachts into Rodney Bay. You can get just about anything here, from electronics to toilets and fridge units, plus cores, ply, and Burma teak. If you don't see what you want, ask Ian. If it cannot be had in St. Lucia, he can order, ship, clear, and deliver anything from a main engine to a small part directly to your boat. Island Water World stocks Johnson and Mercury outboards and is an agent for Yamaha. They sell Caribe and Walker Bay inflatables. Ian is the person to source your Yanmar parts.

Johnsons Hardware is a large marine and general hardware store on two floors opposite Rodney Bay Marina. They keep a good stock of basic marine equipment at reasonable prices. This includes deck gear, rope, chain, anchors, fenders, fastenings, electrical fittings, lights, wiring and fuses, paint and sandpaper, fishing and snorkeling gear, fuel and oil filters, and outboard accessories. They can special-order any marine hardware you might want, duty-free. In addition, they keep a big selection of plumbing, and electrical supplies, wood, gardening and household goods, and hardware, including power tools. In the building over the road they have appliances.

See also Mac's Marine and Liferaft and International Inflatable under *Technical yacht services.*

Technical yacht services
Project Management & Maintenance

Ulrich, at Destination St. Lucia (DSL), is very helpful, straightforward, and knowledgeable about boats and local technicians. His crew can get your boat repaired, your refrigeration cooling, and your engine back working. If there is something they cannot handle, they will recommend the right technician. DSL will look after your yacht while you go away and will undertake all kinds of yacht management. They will put suitable yachts in their large charter fleet. If you are looking for a boat they sometimes have one for sale. This is a long-established company you can rely on.

Technical yacht services
Sails/Rigging/Cushions

Rodney Bay Sails is the sail loft and rigging shop in the marina. Kenny Abernaty is the man to see. He has worked as a sailmaker for over 30 years, is very good, and owns the loft. Rodney Bay Sails do any form of sail or canvas repair and will create new biminis, awnings, and covers. They build many bimini and awning frames and are set up to work and bend 1-inch stainless tube. You can order new sails from Doyle Sails in Barbados.

When Kenny has time, Rodney Bay Sails are also riggers and can handle anything from replacing a shroud to ordering and installing a complete new rig. (They do not do swaging, however.) In this, they work closely with Ian Cowan, who is the agent for Selden masts, Furlex, and Profurl.

For cushions, see *Inflatable Repair*.

Technical yacht services
Electrics/Electronics/Watermakers

You will be in good hands at MarinTek, run by Egbert Charles, who speaks French and Spanish as well as English and has many years of experience working with yachts. Egbert is the Volvo dealer, and this is a good place to buy an engine, as he keeps a stock of engines and sail drives from 30 hp to 55 hp, including those in the Volvo Compact Collection. He also custom orders. He does Volvo warranty work and is factory-qualified for all Volvo engines, including electronic diagnosis.

Marine Tech is the dealer for Northern Lights and Kohler generators. They may be able to help with other generators if they have time. They are excellent at electrical installations or fixing electrical problems, and they have a department for rewiring starters and alternators.

MarinTek are the agent for Dessalator watermakers, and the company repairs and services all watermaker brands. In addition they polish fuel and clean tanks. It is easiest to call them, but if you want to visit the shop, it is north of the boatyard on our map of Rodney Bay Lagoon.

Regis Electronics is the St. Lucian branch of the UK Greenham Regis chain. Jon White, the owner, offers sales, installation, and service for all marine electronics, air conditioning, charging systems, refrigeration, and watermakers. He is the agent for most brands of electronics and keeps both new equipment and many spare parts in stock, which makes Regis the best place for your electronic requirements, whether you are buying a whole new system or upgrading or repairing your present one.

Regis is the factory-authorized dealer for all the major manufacturers, including Amptech, Balmar, B&G, Cruisair, Furuno, Fischer Panda, Garmin, HRO, Icom, Marine Air, Mastervolt, Onan, Raymarine, Spectra Watermakers, Seafresh, Simrad, Schenker, Victron, Waeco and Westerbeke. You can also start from scratch here and order new gear from the catalogue. Jon and his team will have some good ideas on what to buy, have it shipped duty-free, and install it on your boat.

Technical yacht services
Mechanical/Metalwork

Quick and Reliable Mechanical Services is run by Alwin Augustin, who lives up to the company's name. He works on all diesel engines, from Caterpillars on super-yachts to Yanmars on cruisers. He does mechanical work on generators, including Onan, Fischer Panda, and Northern Lights, and he has an excellent reputation for efficiency, service, and skill. It is easiest to contact him via his mobile, (758) 520-5544/584-6544. For parts, he works with Ian Cowan at Island Water World, who can bring in all parts fast and is hooked into the Yanmar computerized system.

Tony's Engineering is run by Tony George, a good, careful general mechanic who can weld and repair diesel engines of all makes including Caterpillar, Detroit, and Perkins. He can come to the yard to sort out your alignment and shaft problems. It is easiest to call him (715-8719/520-1612).

In the boatyard compound, Lawrence (Chinaman) runs the metalworking shop. He can weld and fabricate in any metal.

Heading down the channel, Rory MacNamara's Mac's Marine sells Evinrude Ecotech and the smaller Mapi outboards (which seem very similar to Yamaha), and fixes all brands. They have a dock where you can unload your engine for repair. KL Marine, the local Yamaha Agent, is a separate company in the same compound in the waterfront office.

Island Marine Supplies, run by Pinkley, is next to Mac's Marine. It is the sales and service agent for Mariner, Mercury, and Mercruiser. They keep a good range of engines in stock for all sizes of boats, fix all makes of outboard, and sometimes have Zodiacs for sale.

Roger is a mechanic who often works in the marina. He can get your outboard up and running again and also works on inboards. You would have to call him (284-6050).

For Volvo diesels, Northern Lights, and Kohler, see MarineTek under *Electrics*.

Technical yacht services
Glass/woodwork/paint

On the marina docks, Ismael "Friend" and Jeremiah "Nucky" (718-3888, 520-6400) often work together to do first-rate brush and roller painting, both two-part polyurethane and regular, cleaning, polishing, servicing winches, and general care and maintenance. They take care of yachts when the owners go away. They are good and have had years of experience here in the US, with owners who have flown them up to help in the summer. They are also happy to work in Marigot Bay.

In the boatyard compound, Elvis (Mermaid Repair) does a good job on all glass repairs, painting, and general on-the-slip work.

Fiber (721-0272) is another contractor who does fiberglass repairs of all types, gel-coat matching, spray painting, and anti-fouling. Kelly Charles is another good paint-and-glass man, as well as a varnisher (715-3369).

Richard Cox of Cox Enterprises has years of fiberglass, woodworking, and other maintenance experience. He can sometimes be found around Mac's Marine, where he helps build boats.

Several good guys can handle your carpentry, including decking, joinery, and planking. You generally have to call them, as their shops are not close to the marina. They include: Pride (284-7948), Tyson (719-3394), Robin Unwin (485-1101), and Simon Edwards (458-0213).

Sean Kessel is kept busy by Regis Electronics most of the winter months, where he works on watermakers and climbs up masts. In the summer, if things are slow, he works independently on general boat maintenance, including plumbing, electrics, simple rigging, and just about anything a first-rate yacht maintenance man can do (720-3394).

Technical yacht services
Inflatable Repair

Francis's Liferaft and Inflatable Center is on the left side of the channel as you enter the lagoon. They have an 80-foot customer dock with about 10 feet alongside, making it easy to drop off and collect dinghies. They

are happy to help out their clients with water. They should be IRSA approved by the time you read this.

The business has two sides, the Liferaft and Inflatable center for repair and International Inflatable Ltd. for duty-free sales of dinghies, outboards, and other gear.

At Francis and Debra's Liferaft and Inflatable Center, they test, fix, and vacuum-bag all makes of liferafts; they are certified for Zodiac, Plastimo, Avon, Ocean Safety, and SOLAS. You are invited to watch them unpack and examine the contents and decide what gear should go back in. They have one of the few Caribbean stations that can test and fill liferaft cylinders. They repair all makes of inflatables, do some of the best work in the islands, and guarantee their work for a year. If you have an expensive aging RIB, they can retube it. They can apply dinghy names along the fabric on both sides. They also offer repair and renovation for solid fiberglass and RIB boats up to 30 feet.

When you take an inflatable in for repair, be there when they give it a good check over, so you can decide if it is better to replace it; they take old dinghies and dinghy/outboards in trade. This makes buying the new one more affordable and means they often have guaranteed, beautifully restored secondhand inflatables for sale. Apart from liferafts, you can bring your fire extinguishers, lifejackets, and M.O.B modules for testing and servicing.

International Inflatable are agents for Budget Marine. You can go in and order anything you need out of the catalogue and they bring it fast by DHL duty-free.

St. Lucia

They have a nice showroom for inflatables and outboards and stock duty-free AB and Zodiac dinghies, Tohatsu and Yamaha outboards. They do a fine job of restoring old inflatables of any make and usually have some for sale. They also keep a stock of inflatable accessories.

If you need a cover (chaps) for your dinghy they will make them, and since their upholstery shop is general, they will also do cushion covers and other yacht upholstery.

Technical yacht services
Refrigeration

Check with Regis Electronics and if that does not help, try Prudent Repairs or Wayne of Quick Fix refrigeration.

Technical yacht services
Other Services

Chris Kessell (Kessel Marine) is the local yacht surveyor; his prices are reasonable, and you can arrange for him to come and visit anywhere in St. Lucia.

John and Verniel Leo can give a helping hand. They have a modern, air-conditioned mini-bus taxi, and are happy to run you around. Verniel does laundry (she collects and delivers, and it is done well), as well as interior boat cleaning. John does detailed cleaning or polishing inside or out and can generally lend a hand. Call 486-9481/520 5747/486-7872. You might also see Sparkle, another laundry.

Jo Boxall has Scribble, a design studio in her home. She will design boat names and signs and arrange for the transfers to be cut and placed. She can also design fancy yacht brochures, and she has a contact for helicopter photos.

If you need a new yacht mattress or sheets to fit your triangular bunk, try Lubeco bedding factory, which has an outlet in American Dry Wall on the road to Castries. They supply both fitted and flat sheets for any size bunk (take a pattern) and have nice fabrics, including cotton and organic cotton. Regular sheet sizes are kept in stock. They also produce good-quality, high-density foam mattresses, properly finished with a quilted cover. You really need to make sure they understand the size and shape.

Windward Island Gases, just beyond Glace Motors, tests scuba tanks and can fill most kinds of gas bottles, including CO_2, argon, helium, and nitrogen.

Ask Tony George, MarinTek, or one of the project managers about hydraulics. Some hydraulics can be fixed, but if the job is complex and requires high pressure, Martinique is probably the nearest place to get complex issues solved.

Transport

When you want to get out and about, you will find a taxi stand by the gate and buses on the main road. All the registered Marina taxi drivers (452-9957) wear uniforms and are reliable and good. They are used to dealing with yachts, and if, when you return to your yacht and find that you forgot your camera or handbag on their seat, you know where to find them. JQ Mall has another stand.

Chris Joseph (C.J. Taxi, VHF: 16) is a good and reliable driver who usually listens to his VHF radio. He also rents cars and jeeps, can arrange limousines, and owns some rental apartments. Chris runs good tours and is always on time for that early airport departure. In addition to cruisers, He connects well with the superyachts, and he has the know-how to arrange fuel bunkering, clear in parts, and bring customs to your yacht. He will help with flowers and provisioning and any arrangements you need.

Many water taxis are around.

If you want to join a tour, you can check out Tropical Discoveries opposite the Flower Shack.

Provisioning

In the marina, Flower Shack, a great little flower shop, is close by the dinghy dock. Deirdre, the owner, cuts flowers either the day they sell or the day before, so they are really fresh and long lasting. Her business has its own greenhouses for anthuriums and orchids, and she also sells potted plants. Deirdre does flower arrangements and can handle all the demands of the superyachts. She sells great little herb plants like basil, dill, and parsley hat you can keep and grow on your boat; with just a little water you will always have a few fresh leaves to add to your salad or flavor your fish. She will deliver anywhere in St. Lucia. Deirdre also has an apartment to rent on airBnB.

Kevin White's Crown Foods is a fancy delicatessen and provisioner in Rodney Bay Marina great for both cruisers and big charter yachts. For the cruisers you can walk in and select from a fine range of meats, seafoods, and cheeses and the prices are listed on the blackboard. They also have a wonderful selection of elegant preserves, oils, and wines. Charter yachts can arrange full provisioning with Crown Foods. Almost everything is available, but for some more exotic products that might need to be brought in from overseas, some days notice may be necessary. This small store is backed by a much larger operation with big warehouses, and the staff are friendly and helpful. They open weekdays 100-1700, Saturdays 0900-1600,

G's Marina Mart is a good minimart where you can top up your stores, especially liquor and beer. They open 0700-2100 except Sundays, when they open 0800-1400. It is part of the bigger Glace Supermarket, which is across the road beyond Johnson's Hardware. They also sell phone top-up cards.

The Bread Basket (BB's) sells fresh bread, croissants, cakes, Danishes, and other baked goods. For really large quantities, contact them in advance.

A local farmer's market sets up on the marina lawn on Saturdays. They have lots of produce, coconut water by the bottle, and locally processed coconut oil. Morning is best.

For large supermarkets and more shopping, dinghy over to the malls in the southern part of Rodney Bay, in the general area known as Rodney Bay Village. There is a dinghy dock close by. Super J is in the JQ Mall, and Food Market is in the Baywalk Mall. Neither has a big variety of local produce but both are otherwise excellent. Food Market is fancier, more spacious, with more upmarket items. Both open 0700-2200 Monday to Saturday, 0700-1800 Sundays and holidays.

Fun shopping

Right in the marina, Drop Anchor is a branch of the famous Sea Island Cotton

Shop, with a wide range of casual wear and attractive handicrafts.

Rodney Bay has giant malls with cash machines, pharmacies, clothes shops, household goods, computers, and more. The JQ Mall has 60 stores and businesses, including a stationery store and a bookstore. The inside shops in JQ are generally quite small and adjoining, which makes for easy browsing. Across the road, the even bigger Baywalk Mall has endless shops, banks, restaurants, and vendors' stands. The shops here tend to be larger, with lots of clothing.

Walk out of the JQ Mall and turn left and you will find a big new pharmacy that sells a lot of household things. If you cannot find the perfect gift in the marina or Rodney Bay Village, check out the boutiques in the big beach hotels. You can also check out Caribbean Perfumes, where local tropical aromas from trees, plants, and flowers are made into perfumes and colognes ~ an unusual gift or souvenir. You will find this inside Jacques Waterfont Dining (see *Restaurants*)

Restaurants

Rodney Bay has the best collection of restaurants in the Windwards, with many of St. Lucia's top chefs in attendance. Restaurants are excellent and plentiful, with five in the marina alone. Nowhere else has such a choice of really fine places to eat out.

One place to start the day in the marina is the Taylor family's BB's [$B-D] any time after 0730 for coffee with a full cooked breakfast or a plate of fresh croissants. Nick, Carmen, and family have turned this into a delightful marina restaurant. The inexpensive local lunch specials are as good a bargain as you will find, and locals come here to eat or take away. Their snack menu, which includes rotis and sandwiches, is available morning to evening.

In the evening, BB's changes character; the bar comes alive, the decorative lights turn on, and it becomes a pleasant place for a reasonably priced dinner [$C] or pizza in an informal atmosphere. Come in shorts if you want. The food is straightforward, carefully cooked, and very tasty. The menu includes lots of fish and shrimp dishes, as well as steak and ribs. Arrive in time for happy hour, 1700-1900, with two-for-one beers, wines, and rum punches; sit at the long bar or in

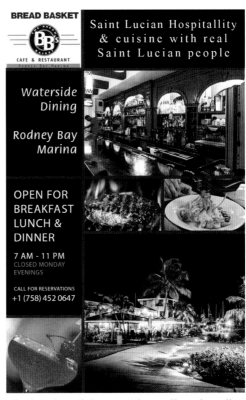
the outside seats. They do an opulent Sunday lunch with roast beef, turkey, or fish, and have a big TV for important games.

Café Olé is a charming cafe with a delightful eating space outside facing the marina. They serve good coffee and always have a selection of delicious baked goodies to choose from. This is a great place for lunchtime sandwiches and salads. To ensure a seat for lunch, go early. Charlotte (Charlie) and Ben, who own it, are welcoming and helpful. Café Olé opens at 0700 for breakfast and stays open through the evening. Meals and snacks are always available. Ben and Charlie also have the adjoining Boardwalk Bar, which is the marina's most popular meeting spot. It opens about 1230, has a popular happy hour from 1700 to 1800, and keeps going till midnight. You can get food from Café Olé.

Zaika [$B-C] is new and owned by Sachin Nahari and Ashok Vaswani who have created an fancy authentic Indian interior full of intricate delights. It has the best location in the marina, near the dinghy dock with a swimming pool. Zaika is open daily for lunch and dinner. The staff are friendly and efficient and the food excellent, not too heavy, with each dish tasting quite different. The chef, Devendra Kathayal, has worked in the best restaurants in India and has fed many celebrities, including the Prime Minister. Try Zaika (the Taste) Thali Platter which will give you a great sampling in one order, or even better, try the Royal Thali for dinner, a meal fit for a king. To have a broad appeal at lunch they serve both Indian and a full international menu. When I was there they had a stack of menus you could pick up offering a 10% discount.

Next door, Rituals Sushi (closed Mondays) opens at 1100, serves lunch till 1600 and stays open for dinner. They have excellent sushi, individual dishes or platters, and lots of other dishes like beef and chicken teriyaki, a variety of salads and some great appetizers, including a big plate of spicy calamari, or deep-fried shrimp. It is a fun place to visit and very popular, especially in the evenings. They also offer takeout.

Close by is Elena's [$C-D]. Elena, who is Italian, runs a great coffee shop with all very good food. Being upstairs, it has a quiet atmosphere, and during the ARC you can often get service here when the others are forming queues.

Other restaurants are all around the lagoon, in Rodney Bay Village, opposite the St. Lucian, and on the small roads near Super J. Dinghy tie-up is available at Super J and Harmony Apartments.

Razmataz [$B-C, evening only, closed Tuesdays] is a first-rate traditional Indian restaurant, and has been around way longer than the others. The old wooden building and decor could have been dreamed up by Somerset Maugham. Try to make the 1700-1900 happy hour, which is very popular, and look for any specials. Razmataz is owned by Suzie Wright, who has Indian connections, and her chef, Dependra Bahadur, from Nepal, has been with her for years and cooks like an angel.

Since many fruits and vegetables from India were introduced to the Caribbean long ago, fresh ingredients are no problem. A tandoori oven is kept going 24 hours a day, and the food is reasonably priced and excellent. Nepalese, Tibetan, or Chinese specialties are often added to the menu. It is best to reserve in advance. Ask for a table on the patio.

kinds of coffee, an ice creamery, and a giant pizza oven. The shop is open for breakfast (cooked or continental) and stays open till dinner. The pizza oven (closed Mondays) is fired up from 1200 to 1500 and from 1800 on. The thin-crust genuine Italian pizzas are delicious. They make fresh fruit juices, crepes, sandwiches, and salads that are available any time during the day.

Upstairs, Bosun's [$C-D] has a comfy, pub-like atmosphere where tables are set out on the balcony with a view of the marina. They open every day till late at night and have a wide-ranging menu with generally

Walk into Big Chef Steak House [$A] on any night of the week and you'll find the appetizing aroma of steaks on the grill and the cheerful buzz of happy patrons, many of them regulars, combined with music from the new piano bar which provides nightly piano, jazz and vocals. On Saturday nights from 2030 to 2230, Bo Hinkson and Jab alternate playing music. Owners Rose and Marc serve excellent seafood. Rose has been both a teacher at the English Cordon

Razmataz, shades of Somerset Maugham

St. Lucia

Bleu and a yachtswoman who completed the Sydney-Hobart Race. They run a super operation, with first-rate service and top-quality ingredients. You will not get better steaks. They start with the best certified Angus beef, cook it exactly the way you want and present it artistically. (If you eat one of their largest [32 oz.] steaks, you can return for a free steak another night.) But leave room for dessert; their crème brulée is divine. The Big Chef Steak House opens every night at 1800.

Rosie and Marc, from Big Chef, own the adjoining Tapas on the Bay set on a breezy deck overlooking the lagoon right next to the dinghy dock for the JQ Mall. Until 1700 the menu is from Lil Chef with all-day breakfasts and Mediterranean lunches, great for a big hearty fry-up or a healthy spread, with all sorts of tasty options in between. From 1700 the menu turns to tapas, which are authentic and delicious, with a little Caribbean flair thrown in with seasonal platters and specials. St. Lucia Yacht Club Members can get a 10% discount at both places. Big Chef also has the Big Chef Bakery and produces a wonderful variety of breads that are sold in most of the local supermarkets or at Tapas. They also run Chef-2-U, which sells frozen cooked meals vacuum-bagged for your boat's freezer. Ask at Tapas.

The dinghy dock makes for easy access from Rodney Bay Marina for Tapas on the Bay and Big Chef.

Delirius [$B-D] is a bar and restaurant, that opens from 1100 to late at night weekdays, and from 1700 Saturdays (closed Sundays). It is owned and run by Duncan and Michelle, who are popular enough that it has quickly become not only a great restaurant, but also the happening bar. The atmosphere is informal and open, and it is among the most popular drinking spots in the area, from a dedicated early crowd to a late-night hangout crowd. On the deck, you can get an excellent meal at a reasonable price. Delirius serves good coffee, snacks, lunch, and dinner.

If you would like to meet some of the local yachting community, the best place to do so is at the St. Lucia Yacht Club [$D]. They have an upstairs bar right on the beach, which opens in the season Monday to Friday from 1500. Weekends and holidays are special, when they open from 1000 and serve inexpensive, simple, and good lunches. Although it is a members' club, visiting yachtspeople are always very welcome, and the atmosphere is pleasant and friendly. The club has an interesting bookswap, a TV for sports events, wifi, and world-class squash courts. You can pull your dinghy up on the beach outside or walk from one of the dinghy docks. This is the place to find out about local sailing events and they run a first-rate program to teach children how to sail. Consider becoming a member. Overseas membership is very reasonable, supports local youth sailing, and gives you discounts in the club, at Jacques (as well as use of his dinghy dock), Big Chef, Tapas on the Bay, Garden Gate Flowers, and, for picture framing, the Inner Gallery. (These can change, so ask.)

Another of St. Lucia's top restaurants

for fine dining and simple elegance is Jacques [$A-B, open for lunch and dinner]. They have a superb location on the waterfront overlooking the lagoon and marina, next to the channel. You can tie your dinghy right outside. St. Lucia Yacht Club members can use this dock to tie up and walk to the club and they get a 10% discount on meals.

You will be charmed by owner Jacques and his wife, Kathy. Jacques has worked in the best hotels, and Kathy is a professional restaurant manager. Jacques brings his training and experience as a skilled chef from the Loire Valley. He has adapted this to local ingredients to produce what Kathy calls "an exciting blend of flavors, herbs, and spices of France and the Caribbean." Jacques provides a lot of different flavors that will delight and surprise. His cooking is inventive, and he is very much into seafood. Try his excellent Mediterranean fish and seafood soup. You will eat well here and enjoy the ambience. Come relax on Sundays when they offer a wonderful jazz brunch from 1130 to1500. This is also the home of Caribbean perfumes (see *Fun shopping*).

Spice of India [$B-C, closed Mondays] is in Baywalk Mall. Owner Adil Pervez Shwerwani is from Deli and spent some years as executive chef in some of Grenada's best hotels. He brings his chefs from north India and keeps people happy. Cool out for lunch in their air-conditioned dining room, when they offer a big tasting menu with a large selection of dishes that changes every day. This will satisfy the hungriest sailor, or, for lesser mortals, two can share. Dinner starts at 1800, when Adil presents his food decoratively. It is not a bad idea to book, especially if you have a big group.

Pat Bowden has a golden touch when it comes to restaurants, and she has done well with Buzz [$A-B], located opposite the Royal St. Lucian. The garden setting is pleasant, and the cuisine inventive. Vegetarians will find they get equal treatment here in their choice of dishes. The menu has a wide selection of seafood, meat, and vegetarian dishes. Pat may retire soon, but I expect Buzz will keep buzzing.

There are a couple of restaurants offering good food at great prices. Renato's [$C-

D], off the main road behind the malls, offers fast, fresh, and tasty Italian food, Cheap for breakfast and lunch, it is reasonably priced for dinner.

Bottle and Spoon [$C-D] is a Trinidadian restaurant on the road side of the haul out yard. Trini's are great cooks, so give it a try. For a quick snack, Sefano's is a pizza joint that serves pizzas whole or by the slice.

Il Papa is a fancier Italian Trattoria, offering good thin-crust Italian pizzas and gelato ice cream,

Blue Olive [$A-B] is on the water in the lagoon: you can tie up right outside. It is more upmarket, and the owner, Bruno, is a wine specialist.

Fire Grill and Lounge Bar [$A-B], is a big, open building with a massive kitchen, which leads into a coffee area and then a bar, which together make up the central hub. This leads out to numerous areas and corners. You can get perfectly barbecued meat and fish cooked right in front of you and artistically garnished.

Bay Gardens Beach Resort {$B-C] is open and very friendly. They have wifi, a great pool and jacuzzi, and a first-rate restaurant. They sometimes host the regular, open get-together women's lunch on Wednesdays (listen to the morning net VHF: 68, 0830 for details, or call Marsha on the same chan-

nel). They have an excellent beach buffet with live music and other entertainment on Saturday nights.

Memories of Hong Kong [$C-D] offers fine Chinese food. The Cockpit [$C-D], open all day every day, is a simple restaurant for the Harmony apartments on the road side. The best bargain for a cheap lunch is one of the restaurants outside or up on the top floor of the JQ Mall.

Ashore

Face to Face takes up two floors, with balconies and comfortable places to relax while waiting. It is upstairs near the marine office. Owner Tracy Farrin has been in the business 30 years and her parlor is up to top international standards, with several employees. They have a big shower room, so yachties can get really cleaned up. They offer all kinds of massage and cosmetic work, including waxing, pedicure and manicure. They are happy to make boat visits.

Cas-en-bas is a lovely beach on the east coast, a couple of miles from Rodney Bay (main road north, turn right at the Gros Islet turn-off). The road is rough but walkable, with good hiking north or south from Cas-en-bas. Marjorie's offers a reasonable local lunch on the beach. Marjorie recently retired, but the restaurant still keeps going.

Taking in the view from Pigeon Island

You will also find Aquaholics kite surfing here (726-0600). If horse riding is more your style, call Trimm's (758-8273)

If you have a mountain bike, this east coast area, from Cap Estate to Esperance Harbour, is perfect.

It is not unusual for yachtspeople to sail into Rodney Bay, check out the protected anchorage, and say, "This is it, I am going to buy property." If having your boat close to your house is important, then look at some of the available properties in Rodney Bay lagoon. The new Admiral Quay, with waterfront and garden apartments, all with docking facilities, and the similar Rodney Quay both have enough units that some are usually on the market.

An agent who handles these and properties all over the island is fellow yachtsman Jonathan Everett. He is very straightforward and will give you the honest low-down on local ownership. You will find him at Home Services, an office in Rodney Bay Village.

The small town of Gros Islet is picturesque and very local, with lots of small restaurants. On Friday night the village is closed to traffic and everyone dances in the streets or wanders from bar to bar. All along the street, stalls sell such goodies as barbecued conch on a skewer and barbecued fish and chicken. If you would prefer to eat sitting down a bit away from the noise, Breadfruit Corner does an excellent buffet on Fridays and Tuesdays. Security was a problem here for a while. It seems better now, but to be safe, go in a group or by cab or bus and return the same way. Stay in well-lit areas.

Water sports

The water in front of the St. Lucian Hotel is completely flat and is good for beginner windsurfing. Boards are available for rent at the hotel.

There is passable snorkeling around Pigeon Island. New scuba sites are being found in the north. If there is not too much surge, Burgot Rocks is a place you often see eagle rays. Barrel of Beef has boulders, sponges, and colorful reef fish, including sergeant majors. Fisheries regulations require that visiting scuba divers go with an approved dive shop.

Dive Saint Lucia is way in advance of most Caribbean dive shops with its own on-

St. Lucia

site purpose-built pool and state-of-the-art classroom facilities. Couple this with great retail facilities and top-class staff, and this a dive shop to love.

Their dive boats match the shop; spacious cabin cruisers that take up to 30 divers, with fully stocked fridges for refreshments before and after dives. The Boats are immaculately maintained and stored dry on lifts after the day's work.

Dive Saint Lucia is a PADI 5 star IDC center offering all PADI courses from beginner to instructor together with guided dives and snorkel tours of all the best dive sites in St. Lucia. It is run by Marcel Buechler and Dawn Shewan who, with a team of highly trained St. Lucian instructors, also participate in education, community involvement and environmental projects.

Dive Saint Lucia generally dives every day, often starting about 0900 and returning about 1500 for a two-dive excursion. They are open to locals and tourists alike. For diving, snorkeling or learning, give them a call.

Next to Dive Saint Lucia, Daniel Buechler, also a yachtsman, is completing a 115 room hotel called The Harbor Club

Scuba Steve's Diving is a Padi 5-star Golden Palm Resort owned by Stephen and Shirley Smith. They are highly qualified and can do nitrox, as Steve is a gas blender and EFR instructor. They will be happy to teach you or take you on a dive in their fast boats with bimini protection. You will find them in the entrance to the lagoon, next to the inflatable workshop.

FROM CAP ESTATE TO VIGIE

Outside Rodney Bay, from Cap Estate to Vigie, are more attractions just a walk, bus ride, or taxi-hop away.

Transport

Travel World is owned by Jocelyn and run out of her home. Just call her on the phone and tell her what you want ~ tickets, car rentals, or tours ~ and she will arrange everything and deliver your tickets (or car) to you. Jocelyn is more than a regular travel agent; she will help you find a house rental, can source things on the island for you, or turn her hand to anything else that would save you time and effort.

Jocelyn works hard to get you the best airline ticket rates, which has earned her many dedicated customers. The business has a service charge of $20 US, but it is well worth it, because the service is good.

Ashore

If you cannot find what you want at Johnson's, Fleva, next to Renato's behind the Baywalk Mall, has power tools, radios and other hardware and electronics. You could walk to S and S, on the road to Castries, but it is not pleasant, with too much traffic. S and S is a big cheap store selling everything from kitchen wear to clothing.

Sunbilt is another big hardware store about a mile and a half towards Castries. A little farther is Computer World, a giant computer store where you can buy computers or get yours fixed. Another mile or so brings you to the first roundabout and Mega J, a gi-

ant store selling everything from foods (bulk or retail) to plumbing, with auto accessories, electrical, household, and pharmacy items thrown in.

The Gablewoods Shopping Center is about halfway between Rodney Bay Marina and Castries. As you approach Vigie, American Drywall is on your left (includes a bike shop and Lubeco bedding factory), and opposite is Home Depot, a good household store. At the next roundabout is Fedex.

Cap Estate, a luxury development, is set in green, rolling hills to the north of Gros Islet. Golfers will be happy to know that this is the place to play golf. The National Trust has a nice little park at Pt. du Cap (Morne Pavillon), which makes a good walk from Rodney Bay (see doyleguides.com).

Windjammer Landings is an upmarket villa development just south of Rodney Bay. The anchorage is tricky, so those who want to go there by boat should contact the managers and they will provide a guide. They have restaurants and boutiques.

Cas-en-Bas

166

VIGIE CREEK

VIGIE

TAPION ROCK

CASTRIES HARBOUR

CASTRIES AND VIGIE

Orchids Pink Plantation

Castries is a reasonable anchorage, so when you are ready to visit town, by yacht is a fine way to do it. Half a mile away is the quiet Vigie Cove, also a good, if small, anchorage. When cruise ships are in town, these two are linked by numerous little ferries that tour around the harbor, stopping at the Coal Pot, Pointe Seraphine, and the craft market.

CASTRIES TOWN

Castries lacks a unifying architectural style but has plenty of variety. Some effort has been made to retain the Caribbean character of the buildings that face Derek Walcott Square along Brazil Street. The area between Peynier Street and Chausee Road, along Brazil, Micoud, Chisel, and Coral Streets has an interesting Creole atmosphere, with balconies, gingerbread, and old and new buildings. Happily, many smaller new buildings are now being designed in keeping with the old architecture.

The new buildings on the north side of the waterfront are of a more recent style, and these, plus other new blocks in town, look modern and clean. The big market, with food, handicrafts, and clothes, is fascinating. For fresh food, Fridays and Saturdays are better than earlier in the week.

Regulations

Castries is a port of entry, though it is much easier to clear

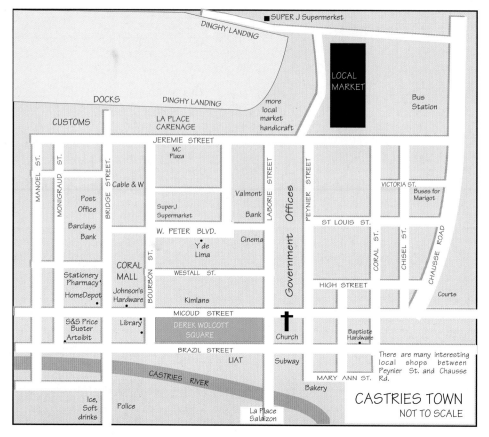

Castries Town map: SUPER J Supermerket, DINGHY LANDING, LOCAL MARKET, DOCKS, DINGHY LANDING, CUSTOMS, LA PLACE CARENAGE, more local market handicraft, Bus Station, JEREMIE STREET, MANOEL ST., MONIGRAUD ST., Cable & W, MC Plaza, Valmont, LABORIE STREET, PEYNIER STREET, VICTORIA ST., Buses for Marigot, Post Office, SuperJ Supermarket, Bank, Government Offices, ST LOUIS ST., Barclays Bank, W. PETER BLVD., Cinema, CORAL ST., CHISEL ST., CHAUSSE ROAD, CORAL MALL, Y de Lima, BOURBON ST., BRIDGE STREET, Stationery, Pharmacy, WESTALL ST., HIGH STREET, Courts, HomeDepot, Johnson's Hardware, Kimlans, MICOUD STREET, S&S Price Buster, Library, DEREK WOLCOTT SQUARE, Church, Baptiste Hardware, Artsibit, BRAZIL STREET, LIAT, Subway, There are many interesting local shops between Peynier St. and Chausse Rd., CASTRIES RIVER, MARY ANN ST., Bakery, Ice, Soft drinks, Police, La Place Salaizon, **CASTRIES TOWN** NOT TO SCALE

in Rodney Bay or Marigot. The officials insist that entering yachts come straight to the customs dock, or if there is no room, to the anchorage right beside it.

Give the cruise ships a wide berth when entering and leaving so you don't make the port police anxious.

Communications

Restaurants and bars have wifi.

Transport/Services

The big bus station is behind the local produce market. All routes are numbered: 1A is Gros Islet, 2H is Vieux Fort, 3D is Soufriere. The Marigot and Canaries buses go from Victoria Street.

You can find somewhere to leave your dinghy between the craft market and La Place Carenage, although you need to make sure it does not interfere with the ferries. Entry is through La Place Carenage, which

makes it pretty safe, but it closes at night, so ask what time. You can also leave it on the north shore, which is always open and unguarded. You can find a sign or tree to lock to.

Provisioning

The easiest supermarket is Super J, close to the market. You can tie your dinghy close by. Pharmacy and stationery stores are on Bridge Street.

You will find general and household hardware at Home Depot or Valmont. If you need acrylic sheet or synthetic canvas, then J. N. Baptiste is the specialist. For auto, electrical, and other household items, try Johnson's. Bandag sells auto parts.

La Place Carenage has duty-free liquor stores, well situated for stocking up on small or large quantities of wine, liquor, and Cuban cigars. It is right on the main wharf in town, so you can load up your dinghy.

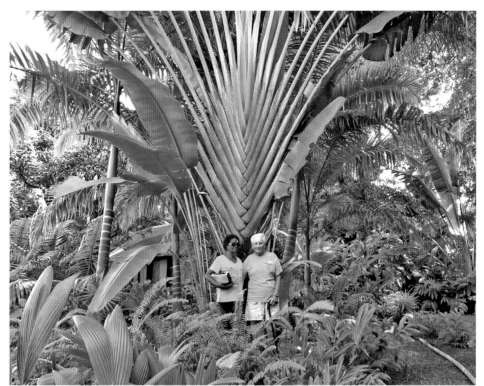

Many thanks to Ted and Maryann Bull, retiring from Sailors guide after his issue, in the Pink Plantation garden

St. Lucia

Fun shopping

St. Lucia's local market ranks among the best in the islands. It occupies several buildings, as well as outdoor areas, and spreads to both sides of the road. It is a riot of color and excitement as hundreds of local vendors sell their wares. Spend an hour or two here enjoying the scene and take the opportunity to stock up on local foods, t-shirts, coal pots, straw work, and handicrafts. The market includes a street of tiny food stalls, each owning a single outside table. Here you will find the cheapest and tastiest local food on the island. A ferry links the market with Pointe Seraphine, the duty-free shopping mall where you will find about 50 pleasantly laid out tourist shops. Take your passport for the duty free.

Just down the road, La Place Carenage is another place for tourist shops ~ lots of them, all pleasantly laid out with everything from international jewelry to handicrafts in a cool air-conditioned atmosphere. They have a theater where they run Our Planet, an interactive light and sound production.

Coral Mall has a good selection of local shops.

Restaurants

The Pink Plantation House [$B-C] is a special restaurant that I highly recommend for lunch, whether you are anchored in Castries or in Rodney Bay. It is on Chef Harry Drive, just outside Castries (a short taxi ride), set high on the Morne with a spectacular view over Castries. It belongs to Michelle, one of St. Lucia's best local artists and potters. She has shops in Pointe Seraphine, Marigot and JQ Mall and also owns the Coal Pot (see Vigie). Michelle has taken this historic estate house with beautiful gardens and created a super restaurant on the generous balcony. The food is traditional Caribbean and excellent. You can wander in the garden, which has an extensive collection of orchids, and you can see Michelle's work in the house, both pottery and paintings. While doing so you will soak in the atmosphere

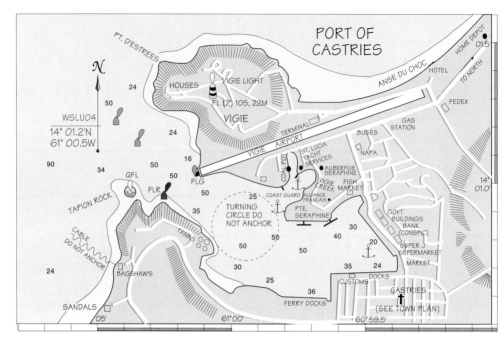

of the lovely old Caribbean estate house, which will give you a feeling of the Caribbean from years ago. The Plantation house is open for lunch Mondays to Fridays They will do special functions at night and open for dinner occasionally.

If you need something right in town, probably your best bet is Rituals [$D] in Coral Mall.

VIGIE

A light on Vigie Hill (flashing twice every 10 seconds) is helpful in identifying Castries Harbor at night.

Vigie is a good overnight stop on your way up or down; take dinner at the Coal Pot and maybe a quick trip to town. It is handy for Vigie Airport as well. You can anchor either inside or outside Vigie Creek. Although generally well protected, Vigie Cove does suffer from a surge in a really bad northwesterly swell.

Anchoring in the creek can be tight but there is more room outside. Carnival Cruises have several moorings; the outer two are white and used when swells come in. If there are no swells, you can often use them for a small fee if you talk to the crew on

their catamarans. On cruise ship days, Vigie bustles with ferries and day-charter boats. There is easy access to Pointe Seraphine.

Services/provisioning

St. Lucia Yacht Services (SLYS) has a fuel dock and they sell water and fuel weekdays 0800-1600, weekends 0800-1400.

There is no public dinghy dock, but you can use the SLYS dock after hours, and some of the surrounding waterfront at other times. If you are visiting the Coal Pot, you can tie your dinghy up by their waterfront shed, or dock your yacht on their big dock just beyond the restaurant. Pointe Seraphine has its own dock, but you must stay clear of the ferries and be off when day-charter cats come in.

A short walk on the road to town gets you to a big NAPA agency, which stocks filters, parts, sprays, seals, polishes, and tools. They are agents for OMC outboards, with full sales and service. In addition, they stock inflatables, ropes, and some marine hardware.

If you need a taxi, give Theresa a call. She is good and reliable and stationed in Vigie Airport (384-9197/458-4444). The main Fedex office is a mile away, opposite

S A I N T   L U C I A

the bottom of the runway.

Also in Vigie (in the white pyramid opposite the Pointe Seraphine entrance) is the Alliance Francais. They offer French lessons and an internet cafe, and it is worth checking out their coming cultural events. Dinghy to town to provision.

Restaurants

A good reason to come to Vigie is to eat at the Coal Pot [$B, closed Saturday lunch and all Sunday]. It has a romantic setting right on the waterfront. Many years ago, Bob Elliot sailed across the Atlantic and into this cove. He fell in love and married Sonia, whose family owned the land, and they built this as their house. Michelle, their daughter, spent her first few years growing up here. Later, Bob converted the house to a storehouse for his beloved day-charter brig, Unicorn, and then into a restaurant, keeping the suitably nautical decor. Michelle now runs the restaurant, and the food is very good. Mango Moon, a gym, is on the Coal Pot grounds.

While in Vigie, check out the amazing colony of egrets and other birds around the colorful lily pond in front of Auberge Seraphine. Auberge Seraphine is also a fine place for coffee or a meal and they have wifi and an internet station.

Navigation
Castries to Marigot Bay

As you leave Castries, give a reasonable clearance to Tapion Rock.

Marigot lies about a mile south of Hess Oil's huge tanker depot at Cul de Sac Bay. In the old days, it was so well tucked away that a British admiral is reputed to have hidden his fleet here, disguising the masts by tying coconut fronds in the rigging. Today you cannot miss it, with the prominent buildings of the Marina Village and all the yachts inside. Once you pass the Hess Oil depot, the wind tends to become light and contrary, not a bad place to start powering.

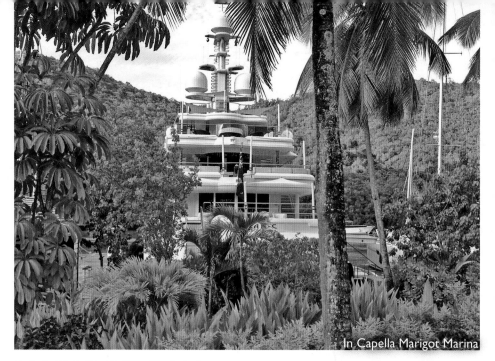
In Capella Marigot Marina

MARIGOT BAY

Marigot Bay is a completely sheltered, mangrove-lined bay, famous as a hurricane harbor. From inside, it affords a perfect backdrop for that sunset photo and rum punch, as you look across the beach spit with its lacy palms. Over ther years it has grown from a sleepy backwater, where nothing happened, to being a pleasant place to shop, eat out, take a stroll, or hike, and admire any superyachts that may be in.

Navigation

Enter down the channel, which favors the southern shore and avoids a shoal that extends way out from Marigot Beach Resort. Most channel buoys, which were placed and maintained by the marina, are missing under the Capella management, and their replacement uncertain. The minimum depth in the channel and inner bay is 5 meters (16.5 feet). Costly and delicate underwater electric cables and water pipes cross right at the entrance to the inner harbor. Do not anchor!

You can anchor on either side of the channel where there is adequate depth, or inside if you can find room among the moorings, where the holding is passable in soft mud. The Marina at Marigot Bay has 20 reliable moorings in the inner harbor, which are white with a blue stripe. They cost $30 US a night ($20 in the summer), but you may raft up to three boats (combined maximum 70 tons) for this. If you call the marina they will send a dinghy to help you tie up. Otherwise, many locals will be happy to tie you up for a tip. But do not pay them for the mooring ~ go into the marina office and pay.

Many will greet you, offering unofficial moorings (all the outside ones, and one or two inside) that look just like the official moorings. Some of these moorings are poor and go adrift, so you are taking a chance. Just say "no" to anyone who becomes persistent, pushy, or in any way objectionable. Check doyleguides.com for any updates. Outside is a lovely anchorage, but you get more vendors and speeding dinghies than in the lagoon, also more thefts (unfortunately you get some thefts in both parts, so lock up well). If you are eating at Chateau Mygo you can tie to their dock at no charge if they have room.

Regulations

There is a 4-knot speed limit in the harbor. Marigot Bay is an official port of entry, with customs, immigration and SLASPA (port authority), which collects the entry fees. They are usually open 0800-1200 and 1330-1615. The offices adjoin the marina office on the dock. Sailclear works well. If

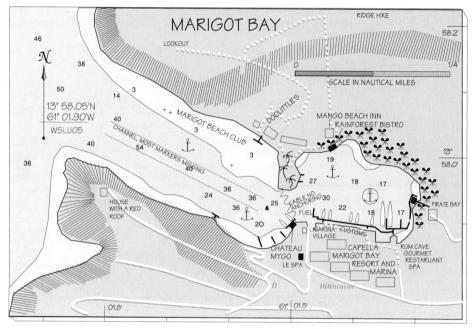

MARIGOT BAY

RIDGE HIKE

LOOKOUT

58.2'

46

38

N

50

13° 58.05'N
61° 01.90'W
WSLU05

14

3

40

40

40
54

36

++ MARIGOT BEACH CLUB

CHANNEL, MOST MARKERS MISSING

3

DOOLITTLES

MANGO BEACH INN
RAINFOREST BISTRO

O   1/4
SCALE IN NAUTICAL MILES

13°
58.0'

3

19

27   18   17

24

36   36

36

20

25   CABLE NO
ANCHORING 30

FUEL

22

18   17

PIRATE BAY

HOUSE
WITH A RED
ROOF

MARINA   CUSTOMS
VILLAGE

CHATEAU
MYGO
LE SPA

CAPELLA
MARIGOT BAY
RESORT AND
MARINA

RUM CAVE
GOURMET
RESTARUANT
SPA

01.8'   61° 01.5'

you know you will arrive after closing, and someone is leaving early the next morning, contact one of the agents for help.

Yachts in Capella should use the garbage bins in the Marina (look for the signs). Others should take it to the public dump in the car park straight back down the road.

Communications

Capella has a variable wifi for their customers. Chateau Mygo also has wifi, as does Doolittle's.

General yacht services

Dinghy docks are at Chateau Mygo, in the Marina Village, by the Rum Cave, at Doolittle's Restaurant, or over at JJ's. Dinghies must not be tied to the yacht docks.

Capella Marigot Bay Resort and Marina has moorings and alongside and stern-to berths for yachts up to 250 feet. Contact the marina team (451-4275/728-9948/9, VHF: 16/12). The marina and the hotel are integrated, and if you use the docks you can get room service on board. Their lower pool, above the Rum Cave, is open to marina visitors. You can also put meals on your marina tab. The emphasis is on exceptional customer service, and you can expect the marina staff will make sure you have every-

thing you need for berthing. If you require concierge services, the marina will assign you a personal assistant. Some big yachts have St. Lucia agents that they already use, and skippers are welcome to continue using these while in the marina. Agents like Ben Yacht Services come on a regular basis (see *Soufriere*).

The superyacht berths have high-speed, sealed fueling, and smaller yachts can get diesel at their berth. For visitors, diesel and gasoline are available on the fuel dock next to the ferry dock. Duty free is available. Electricity, 110- and 220-volt, 50- and 60-cycle, is available, as is 410-volt, 3-phase for superyachts. They provide holding-tank pump-out. Ask the marina about special rates on hotel nights ashore; they can also arrange laundry (5 kg is about $20 US).

The marina can help organize day labor, and Saltwater in the marina village sells phone cards, has local information, arranges taxis or reservations, and does all manner of tours.

Chateau Mygo [VHF: 16] offers laundry services ($50-$150 EC depending on the load); ironing is extra. They have berths and moorings for their charter company. They do not rent these, but if you are having dinner, they will be happy to give you a free berth, or mooring, when there is room.

Chandlery/technical yacht services

Chateau Mygo has a small surf/chandlery shop, with boating accessories, cleaners, safety gear, and fishing equipment. They have an arrangement with Island Water World and can bring anything from that store quickly.

Shaid has a team to repair and fix his charter fleet, and he offers this service to visiting yachts. If anything goes wrong, from the motor to the mast, this is a good place to start. For larger yachts, the Marina staff will organize what they need.

On the other side of the bay, Complete Marine Services has a work barge with a crane. Their main line of work is marine construction. They also do yacht surveys, and excellent underwater and salvage work. They watch boats when people are away, undertake project management, install new equipment, and fix things. If it is not something they like to do, they will point you in the right direction.

Provisioning/fun shopping

Mari Gourmet, behind the Marina Village, is a good, small supermarket. They are open 0800-1900, except Sundays and holidays, 0800-1300. They can sell duty-free

Marigot Bay,
Shaid Rambally Chateau Mygo photo

cigarettes and liquor. Next door is an ATM machine.

Chateau Mygo have many suppliers for their restaurant and are happy to provision for yachts, either a full provisioning, or getting some things you cannot source in Marigot.

A local market often takes place in the Village Marina square, 0800-1400.

In the marina village, the Rowley's Caribbean Cafe sells good bread and baked goodies and is a pleasant hangout for lunch.

You will also find a collection of souvenir, jewelry, and art shops. One of these, Clear Blue is owned by local artist Michelle, who sells some of her own pottery and paintings, as well as those of other local artists.

Transport

Numerous ferries and water taxis are available to go anywhere in the bay or to and from your yacht. Chateau Mygo [VHF: 16] has several water taxis and land taxis and offers all kinds of tours or will run you where you need to go.

Taxi Service Marigot [451-4406, VHF: 16] are the local taxi drivers who wait near the public dock at the end of the road.

Restaurants/ashore

In the marina village, the Baguette Shop has pleasant seating and sells wonderful sandwiches, coffee, pizza, soups, salads and burgers; great for breakfast or lunch. It may change name with the rebuild.

Chateau Mygo [$B-D, VHF: 16] is a large enterprise run by the Rambally family. Years ago, Mama Sheila started it as a no-frills food shack. Now, a waterfront restaurant, guest houses, Le Spa, and boutiques, are set in tropical gardens that go from the road to the beach.

The Ramballys are a Caribbean/East Indian family who have many ties to yachting. Doreen runs it with her son Shaid, and they both like cruising, so whichever one is not off sailing runs the restaurant. Shaid speaks English like a Californian and Spanish like a Costa Rican, which is where Andrea, his wife, is from. Among them, the family speaks English, Spanish, Italian, French, Norwegian, Patois, and Hindu. Chateau Mygo restaurant stands on legs out over the water and has both a main menu and a variety of thin-crust Italian pizzas.

Their food is essentially Caribbean from fresh local sources, spiced by ideas garnered from around the world. Local seafood is their specialty, including lobster, shrimp, lambi, scallops and a variety of fish. Their grilled fish in a mango and passion fruit sauce offers delicious local flavors.. Baby-back ribs and USDA black Angus steaks are popular with many sailors.

In season, they have live music on Tuesday and Wednesday nights and fire up their open-air barbecue for a special menu on Wednesdays and Fridays. For lunch try their delicious fish Taco with local salsa or their wonderful shrimp burrito.

Shaid hosts a local TV cooking show (Stir it Up) combining sailing, surfing, and cooking, He is known as the Adventure chef. Once a fortnight or so he offers a fun and reasonably priced group morning cooking program. He takes the group to the market, to meet his suppliers and buy the food, then you return and learn to cook the dishes before enjoying them.

Their little "Hurricane Hole" beach bar, named after the first hotel in the bay is fun in the evening, and sometimes the liveliest spot in the harbor. On the road they have a gelato ice cream shop. Chateau Mygo opens for breakfast and is a great place to start the day.

Gloria, another Rambally, runs Le Spa Marigot here. She has you covered head to toe with the best barber in St. Lucia, a good hair stylist, manicures, pedicures, nails, massages, and even make up. She is popular locally for doing complete make-overs for brides, and will even arrange the wedding. Her team will do on-boat treatments. Her prices are reasonable, and customers say it is great. If you want a quickie, they offer massage for $1 US per minute.

Shaid runs a charter company (Bateau Mygo) with both day- and term-charters available from his dock as well as reasonably priced bare-boat charters to qualified people. He uses locally trained crew. In addition, the Ramballys have very nice villas to rent and a small real-estate office.

Ready for a special night out? You have

a delightful surprise awaiting you at the Rainforest Hideaway [$A]. It is open every night in the winter, but closed Sunday and Tuesday nights in the summer. The hideaway location and wonderful food make it one of my favorites for a special night out. It has been listed by Trip Advisor as one of the top ten fine-dining Restaurants in the Caribbean and by Fodors as a choice restaurant in St. Lucia. Approachable only by sea, it combines brilliant food with an absurdly romantic atmosphere in an intimate dining area where you eat amid the mangroves, perched out over the water. Brightly lit fish in the enclosed dinghy dock are the before-dinner cabaret. This restaurant was built by hand by Jim Verity and Myron. Jean Rene DuBoulay is the general manager, Wilson Rosedale the Maitre'D, Asa Johansson the chef.

It is a magical experience, so you want to don at least long pants and a sports shirt, and you need to reserve as long in advance as you can. The menu changes frequently. You choose between a two- and three-course menu. (Couples often go for the two-course and split a starter and dessert.) There is always fresh fish, shrimp, and meat on hand,. The flavors are Caribbean, cooked with flair and imagination and served with great artistry. A full moon makes for perfection. Four nights a week they have excellent jazz at a volume where you can still enjoy a conversation. If you have a party of six or more adults wanting to come for dinner from Rodney Bay, call and they will arrange complementary transportation for you.

Above, and connected, is the Marigot Beach Inn, bright and sunny with a lovely bay view, perfect for shore time. It is run by Judith Verity, and if you love it here, ask about future plans to build some houses.

Cappella has three restaurants amid beautifully gardened walkways. Service in all three is excellent. You dinghy to the Rum Cave [$B-C] dock, which is under the bridge. It is casual, with a big selection of rums and offers finger foods, salads, sandwiches and both a lunch and dinner menu. Up one level is the Grill 14°61 [$A], which opens for breakfast and dinner, and the dinner is fine and fancy French cuisine

on a lovely deck overlooking the bay. Good for a special night out. One level up again at the upper pool is Brut [$B-D], a lovely pool bar that serves light and healthy food; sushi, sushimi, seafood and some meat. They have lunch specials, but are not open at night. To reserve, you call the general Capella -line (458-5300).

On the north shore, by the entrance, is Marigot Beach Club, owned by Dave, from England. This is a delightful area, magnificently gardened and leading onto the beach. His Doolittle's restaurant [VHF: 16, $B] is comfortable and right on the waterfront. Nightly happy hour, two-for-one, is 1700-1900. Live entertainment is frequent in season, and it is a great hangout. They offer a wide variety of food and have specials every night. Marigot Beach Club has rooms for nights ashore.

Ulrich Augustin has Pirate Bay, a French-style Bistro, built on the dock. It opens every day for lunch and dinner, and specializes in a wide variety of seafood, including the big "Seafood Feast". The food is good, fresh and served with flair, which has made them popular with visitors and locals. They do Hibachi grills so you can cook food yourself right at the table. They have their own special ales on tap, Pale Mutiny and Golden Buccaneer. Ulrich, who has managed several fine Caribbean restaurants, has also taken over the old JJ buildings behind the mangroves (a lovely wooden walkway takes you there). Here he has renovated the pool, and is putting in a pizzeria, sports bar and night club.

Upstairs in the marina village, Massala Bay ($B-C) is a very pleasant Indian restaurant, run by Chef Govind Joshi. The service is wonderful and they serve both Indian and Hakka (from the Chinese/Indian border) cuisine.

If you walk up the hill behind JJ's, you come to Marigot village, which is local, friendly, and enjoyed by locals and visitors. JJ has a restaurant right at the bottom of the road that opens when he has room guests. At the top of the hill you can enjoy the view, buy souvenirs and get a drink. Julietta's Restaurant [$B] is high on stilts with a magnificent view of Marigot. Do not come when you are rushed, but do come and enjoy; the food is good. Opening hours are variable.

The top of the hill on the north side of Marigot Bay is a national park with a wonderful short hike (about an hour and a quarter). Dock at Rainforest Hideaway, walk up to Mango Beach Inn, and ask them to show you the trail. It is a very steep straight climb to the ridge. Hike down along the ridge till you come to the crossroads to either the Lookout or Oasis. Go to the Lookout, then back a short way and take the trail down to Oasis and thus to Doolittles. From here a path runs behind the mangroves back to Rainforest Hideaway. This whole area is a favorite with birders.

Walk about a mile to the main road to catch a bus to Castries. On the return journey, most bus drivers are willing to bring you all the way to the customs dock for a little extra.

Water sports

Dive Fair Helen's office is in Doolittle's. They will be delighted to take you on one of several excellent dives just south of Marigot in the area of Anse Cochon, or down to Soufriere.

Marigot to Soufriere regulations

The Soufriere Marine Management Association (SMMA) manages two marine management areas, from Marigot to Caribe Pointe, Choiseul. The northern part is the Canaries and Anse la Raye Marine Management Area (CAMMA), and the southern part is the SMMA [VHF: 16]. They regulate all anchoring, snorkeling, diving, and fishing. They have placed many yacht moorings, which are white (some with a blue stripe) for yachts up to 70 feet. (Red or orange moorings are for dive boats or snorkeling dinghies.) Five moorings are available for yachts up to 120 feet. In some places you may also anchor (see section descriptions).

There are charges for taking a yacht into the Marine Management Areas, which includes use of the moorings. They are as follows (check doyleguides.com for updates, lower off-season rates are under consideration):

Boats up to 70 ft. 1 Night = $20 US/$54 EC/18 Eu. 1 week = $120 US/$324 EC/108 Eu

Boats 70-120 ft 1 Night = $100 US/$270 EC/89 Eu

Boats over 120 ft 1 Night = $200 US/$540 EC/180 Eu

As in the rest of St. Lucia, spearfishing and damaging, taking, or buying coral or sponges are strictly forbidden, as is dumping garbage, oil, etc. Fishing is forbidden in the marine reserves. You can pick up any available mooring. Always put your mooring line through the loop on the mooring rope; do not put the loop on the mooring rope on your cleat. An SMMA ranger will come by to collect the fees, or fees can be paid at the SMMA offices in Soufriere if you clear customs, as they are in the same building. SMMA rangers carry identification and give official receipts. The SMMA staff are very helpful with finding taxis, giving weather alerts, and making yachters feel welcome.

MARIGOT TO ANSE LA RAYE

Trou l'Oranger is a small white sand beach occasionally used by day-charter boats. Anchoring off this beach is only permissible 0900-1700. In calm, pleasant weather, it can be worth a stop for a swim and a snorkel.

Anse La Raye is a picturesque fishing village and a fair overnight anchorage. It is good in settled conditions with no northerly swells (no fees currently collected). There is plenty of swinging room off the town in 15 to 20 feet of water. The northern part of the bay shoals quite rapidly. The night to go is Friday, when they have a fish fest. Tables and chairs are put right down the center of the front street, and vendors set up stalls on both sides of the road and cook seafood: fish, lobster, lambi, and floats to go with them. It is very popular locally and currently has an atmosphere of peace, good will, and good food. You can use the big new dock or pull your dinghy up on the beach, swells permitting.

River Rock Falls is a good 2-mile hike

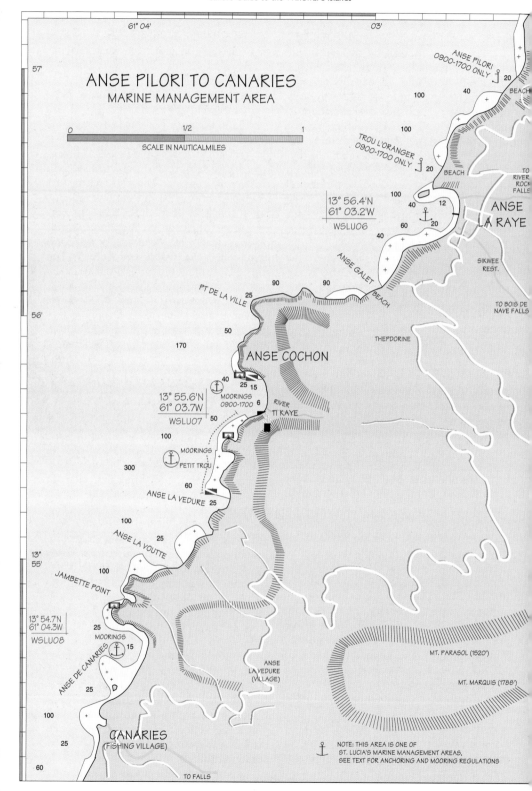

ANSE PILORI TO CANARIES
MARINE MANAGEMENT AREA

57'

61° 04'   03'

0   1/2   1
SCALE IN NAUTICAL MILES

ANSE PILORI
0900-1700 ONLY   20

BEACH

100   40   100

TROU L'ORANGER
0900-1700 ONLY   20

BEACH

TO
RIVER
ROCK
FALLS

13° 56.4'N
61° 03.2'W
WSLU06

100   40   12

ANSE
LA RAYE

60   20

40

SIKWEE
REST.

PT DE LA VILLE   25

ANSE GALET BEACH

TO BOIS DE
NAVE FALLS

56'

90   90

50

THEPDORINE

170

ANSE COCHON

40
25   15
13° 55.6'N
61° 03.7W
WSLU07   50

MOORINGS
0900-1700   6

RIVER
TI KAYE

100

MOORINGS
PETIT TROU

300

60

ANSE LA VEDURE   25

100

ANSE LA VOUTTE   25

13°
55'

100

JAMBETTE POINT

13° 54.7'N
61° 04.3W
WSLU08   25

MOORINGS   15

ANSE
LA VEDURE
(VILLAGE)

MT. PARASOL (1520')

ANSE DE CANARIES   25   D

MT. MARQUIS (1788')

100

CANARIES
(FISHING VILLAGE)

25

NOTE: THIS AREA IS ONE OF
ST. LUCIA'S MARINE MANAGEMENT AREAS,
SEE TEXT FOR ANCHORING AND MOORING REGULATIONS

60

TO FALLS

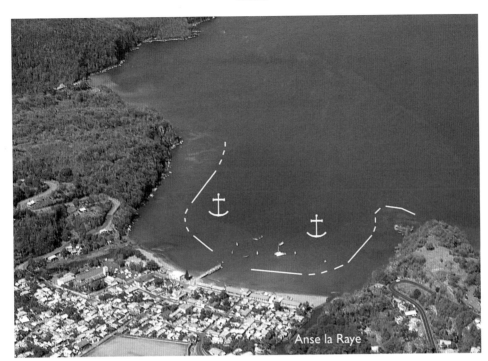

Anse la Raye

up a pretty road that starts on the northern edge of the village. It is well signposted, Robberies on the way up are not unknown, though once there you should be okay, as workers are often around. Do not expect a wild, tropical falls; this is a gardened area where the fall and rock pool have been partially created with concrete. What you lose in immediate visual satisfaction you gain by the convenience of seats, tables, changing rooms, and a generous balcony overlooking the falls. Currently there is no fee because of security. You may have it to yourself.

The much wilder and more beautiful Bois de Nave fall is in the hills to the southeast of the village. You will probably need to hire a guide to show you the way. The hiking in this area is excellent, with trails laid out by Jungle Tours. However, swimming in the falls is not encouraged, as it is a drinking-water source. After hiking, you can cool off in the big pool to the left of the road on your way back to the village. This large pool by a cleft in the rocks is the most popular bathing place for locals.

Anse La Ray has a few bars, Albi's looks like it would serve you a good and reasonably priced meal.

ANSE COCHON TO ANSE LA VEDURE

Anse Cochon is a beautiful little bay with an attractive beach and Ti Kaye, an enchanting little hotel on one headland. It lies about 3 miles south of Marigot. You pass Anse La Raye, after which is a rocky headland. Anse Cochon is tucked up in the corner just past this headland. SMMA has Moorings in Anse Cochon. They are white with a blue stripe. There are also specific moorings for local tourism charter boats, but they are easily distinguishable from the rest. Moorings continue about half a mile south to Anse La Vedure. There may also be moorings located at the northern end of Canaries in a picturesque bay just before the village. The coastline is attractive all the way along and usually comfortable enough for overnighting. If no moorings are available, anchor on sand.

Ti Kaye has a small dock, which is used by the dive boat. If the dive boat leaves for the night you can use the dock for your

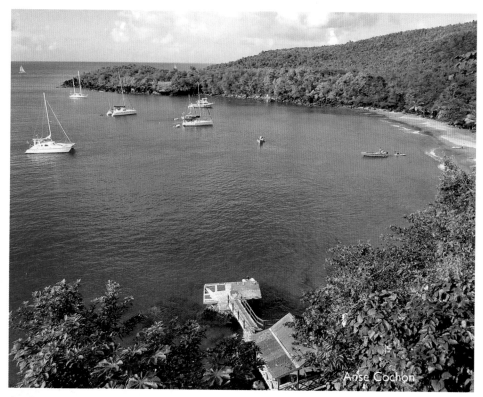

Anse Cochon

dinghy. You may need a stern anchor. Other times, beach your dinghy; take great care in swells. Ti Kaye has wifi, which you can probably get from your yacht.

Ashore

Ti Kaye [VHF: 16] is a charming cottage hotel perched on the southern headland of Anse Cochon. Up at the hotel, the gardens, the view, and the exceptionally friendly staff, make you feel like you have arrived in a little Garden of Eden. Whatever you decide to do here, you do need to make reservations as they have a lot of their own guests and want to be sure you are not disappointed. On the beach, Ti Manje [$B-C], set on a big deck over the rocks, makes a perfect lunch stop; the view is perfect, the food good and reason-

ANSE LA RAYE

ANSE COCHON

ably priced. You can call Ti Manje at 718-1122 and they may be able to deliver lunch right to your boat. On Mondays they often stay open for a five-course seafood dinner.

Climb the scenic staircase up to the top of the hill and into a whole new world with lovely gardens, a pool, and fabulous views over the bay. Plan a trip to Kai Koko Spa, which is spectacularly beautiful, perched on the edge of the cliff, the precipitous view of the bay filling one side of each room. Allow some relaxing time in the welcome room, with a hot tub right by the open view (bring a bathing costume). Enjoy many kinds of massage and beauty treatments. If you arrange it for late afternoon, it will allow time for a relaxing drink after, followed by dinner, which starts at 1830.

Kai Manje [$A-B], with its panoramic view, is the main restaurant. You get a perfect photo of your yacht below and the very best platform for viewing the green flash. Dinner is an imaginative blend of local, oriental, and other dishes, artistically presented with a daily changing menu that usually includes lots of fresh seafood and meat. Vegetarians are catered to and the food is excellent. They serve lunch if you want a break from the beach. For your pre-dinner drink, Kai Manje's bar (open from 1500) is air-conditioned and built on the edge of the cliff, with the whole of the west wall in glass looking over the bay. A happy hour with two-for-one on selected drinks is 1800-1900 every day except Wednesday, when they have the manager's cocktail party and a band up in the restaurant. Ti Cave is their famous wine cellar under the main restaurant. They have a huge collection, including some at the very top of the line, and they do sell these by the bottle. Managers Chris and Sarah usually organize a wine tasting three times a week at about 1600. The Cellar can also be booked for private wine dinners. Call for details.

Water sports

Island Divers make diving here really easy; the diving is in small groups and fun. They are a full Padi shop. Talk with Curtis, 456-8110. They keep their fast, comfortable dive boat in Castries, so can easily pick up dive groups from yachts in Marigot and meet up with yachts in Soufriere. Snorkeling and land/sea trips are available.

The diving is excellent. The water is 25-60 feet deep, with a coral and rock slope descending onto sand. Isolated rock outcrop-

CANARIES TO ANSE CHASTANET

CANARIES

25

0   1/2
SCALE IN NAUTICALMILES

13° 54.0'
61° 04.9'

60   25

ANSE LA LIBERTE

30

200   60

ANSE MAHAUT

30

MAHAUT

30

60

13° 53.0' 12
61° 04.9'

BLANCHE POINT

30

BOUTON

ANSE JAMBON

60

30

ANSE MAMIN
BEACH

15

60
CHAMIN COVE
MOORINGS 15

RINGS IN CLIFF

60

15   ANSE CHASTANET

183

CANARIES courtesy SMMA

pings out on the sand are covered in corals and sponges. These underwater fairy castles teem with small fish. Though there are not many large fish, the abundance and variety of small fish and reef creatures more than compensates. The wreck of the Lesleen-M is in the middle of the bay. It is a 165-foot freighter and lies in 67 feet of water. It was deliberately sunk in 1986 to make a dive site. The wreck has attracted an exceptional collection of invertebrates, many of which are uncommon elsewhere. Rosamond's Trench is another delightful dive in this area. It starts between two small canyon walls. There are many sponges, invertebrates, and colorful reef fish.

The snorkeling on the south side ranges from interesting to excellent, especially for more experienced snorkelers. Snorkeling off the rocky headland at the north end of Anse Cochon is fair, with brightly colored sponges, corals, and parrotfish.

ANSE DE CANARIES

Anse de Canaries is supposed to have several moorings about a third of a mile north of the village. They keep getting stolen, but you can anchor in the same spot in about 20 feet of water. Cliffs surround this pleasant, quiet area, and overnighting is permitted. The snorkeling is good, but move for fishermen if asked.

Canaries has great hiking, interesting bars, restaurants, a night club, and a famous street party. Unfortunately, the dock is pretty useless for a dinghy. You can beach it if swells permit.

Margaret Edwards (459-4402/4701) has the beautiful La Maison Estate, with lovely gardens, about a 10-minute walk on the road to Soufriere. She has another establishment called Moon River, which is on the road along the river (turn left after the bridge). Moon River often has events on a Friday night open to the public, and both places are open for private functions.

Enjoy excellent hiking to two waterfalls in the area. To find them, go to the main road and head south across the bridge. Take the road on your left just over the bridge. This soon leaves civilization as it winds back into the forest. After a couple of miles, you look at an amazingly verdant and broad valley surrounded by hills. Follow the well-marked road till it becomes a path and continue for another half-hour till you come to an old bridge crossing the river. Keep straight (do not cross the bridge) and you come to the first falls, small and dramatically set in a grotto, with the water pouring through a hole in the rock. The lighting can be spectacular mid- to late morning, when the sun shines through the hole. A good pool for swimming lies below. If you have the energy, return to the bridge and continue another hour for the second, even prettier falls. Take $5 EC each to pay the owners of the land. You can get a trained guide who knows the history and the plants. Ask anyone for Dave Julien.

Cocoa Sainte Lucie, an excellent one-woman chocolate factory is planning a roadside outlet within walking distance up the hill heading for Soufriere. You can call Maria Jackson, the chocolatier, and ask: 459-4401.

SOUFRIERE AND THE PITONS

Soufriere is a small, picturesque town set amidst a scenic wonderland dominated by the towering twin Pitons. Its exceptional beauty will enthrall hikers and photographers. The surrounding water is a magnificent marine park. There are many great things to see and do, the coastline is wonderful, there are lots of small restaurants, and those who like snorkeling, hiking, and diving could easily spend a week in the area.

Soufriere has some rough edges, and while serious harassment is a thing of the past, a few waterfront youths pester yachts, take drugs, and are best avoided.

Many young, untrained vendors will meet you way out or get between you and the mooring to help you attach, whether you want them to or not. I let them do this and give them a few dollars ($5-10 EC). If they demand more, tell them that is the rate printed in the book. Pay more if you ask them to speed ahead and secure a particular mooring for you. It is also different if you are using them to take a line ashore, which is more complicated and probably worth $20 EC if it goes very smoothly.

However, a word of caution for those who do not know the area. Some vendors, especially those in dinghies, like to put boats on private moorings in the Baron's Drive area, and then take a mooring fee. The SMMA moorings are included in your fee, so you want to be on an official SMMA mooring. The private fishing boat moorings are of unknown quality and sometimes placed so close together that yachts collide. Bottom line: if a guy ties you up for a small tip, fine. If he wants to charge you a mooring fee, and he is not wearing an official uniform in an official boat giving an official receipt, leave and find an official mooring. SMMA plan to clearly mark their moorings. Until then the ones closer to the fishing boats are likely to be fishing boat moorings.

What these guys really want is to organize a tour for you. The prices can be highly variable. (See *Transport*)

The paid guards and security officers on the town dock let kids run riot to try and make a buck off the yachts by "watching the dinghy". If they ask me, I tell them security is going to watch it for me and they generally disappear, but do bring a stern anchor or some other way of stopping your dinghy going under the dock in any kind of swell.

If vendors "bad mouth" a restaurant, avoid them; they plan to get you to go to some bad restaurant where you can be overcharged so they can get a kick-back.

St. Lucia

Moorings

ANSE CHASTANET courtesy SMMA

Security in the park is generally very good except in the area of the bat cave moorings, and even these have been fine for some months. However, it is most unwise to invite strangers onto your yacht; some will check out the yacht with an eye to returning when you are out.

Do ask the rangers about security, they know what is going on. If you have trouble, take a description of the person and the name of their craft, and give Peter Butcher, the head ranger, a call (718-1196, or call Jackie, 724-6333, another ranger).

When approaching Soufriere from the north, beware of the shoal that extends from the south side of Anse Chastanet, off Grand Caille Point. If you run aground, you will be fined for damaging the reef.

The biggest danger is speeding pirogues and other craft. Stay alert, especially when swimming and snorkeling.

Regulations

The whole area shown on our sketch chart is part of the SMMA. Regulations and fees for using the management areas are given on page 177 (see *Marigot to Soufriere, Regulations*). The SMMA has an office in Soufriere on the waterfront where you can check up on the latest weather. The current manager, Michael Bobb, comes from Soufriere, he is working to solve the prob-

lems of the park.

If you need any assistance the SMMA staff are very friendly and welcoming.

The SMMA provides moorings, and anchoring is only allowed in a few places. SMMA check their moorings, which are generally reliable, though they occasionally fail in big swells. If there are no moorings available, an SMMA ranger will show you to a permitted anchoring place. Please call them. There are five large yacht moorings for yachts up to 120 feet.

Soufriere is a port of clearance for pleasure yachts. Customs is in the SMMA building and immigration is at the end of the police station block. Customs hours are Monday-Thursday 0800-1630, Friday 0800-1800, Saturday and Sunday 0800-1630. You will pay $10-$15 EC overtime after 1630 on Fridays and on weekends. Sailclear sometimes works. There are also port fees to pay, not currently collected in Soufriere; we give these in *St. Lucia at a glance*, page 139.

Don't give garbage to vendors, as they will dump it in the sea. Take smallish bags into town and ask the SMMA where to put it. If you are using Ben's yacht services, he can send a water taxi to collect it.

Anyone scuba diving must be accompanied by an official dive guide. An SMMA diving fee applies to all dives within the SMMA and CAMMA. It is $5.00 US/

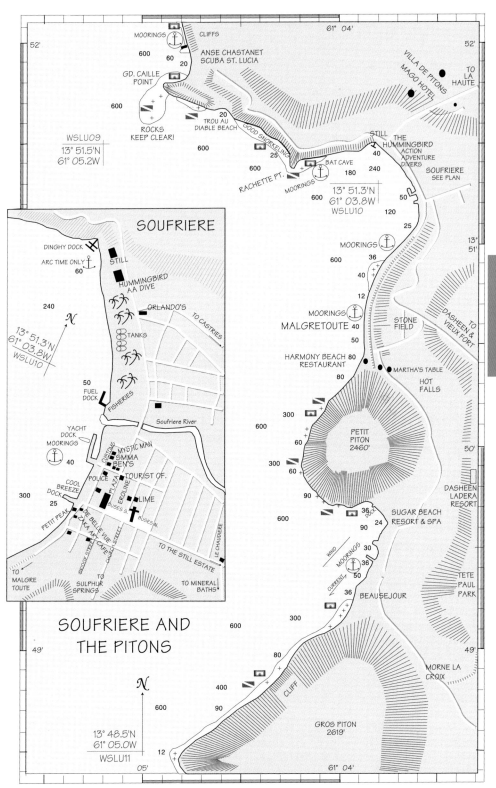

$13.00 EC for one day, or $15 US for the season. Pay an SMMA ranger or the dive shop. If you are an accredited diver and have your own equipment, the SMMA may be able to put you in contact with an official guide, or visit one of the yacht-friendly dive shops. Action Adventure Divers provide all levels of service, including guides and yacht pick-ups, (see *Hummingbird Anchorage*). Island Divers do rendezvous pickups (See *Anse Cochon*).

If you have a problem, Tapion Hospital has a hyperbaric chamber.

Services

Many people with boats will offer to help run you to town or take you for a tour or longer ride to Castries or Vigie (it is faster by boat than by car). The best are members of the Soufriere Taxi Association or the Watercraft Association [VHF: 16], professional groups of properly equipped and insured water taxis, and the only ones to use for longer trips. Mystic Man Tours is one (see *Soufriere, Services*).

Some registered Soufriere water taxis are too busy for small trips, like a run ashore, but there are pirogue owners (not always registered) who are happy to do such short runs. These include Malcolm's Water taxi (722-5048/286-2277), Livity (488-7820/717-2019), Justice (384-4087). They are nearly always on the water.

ANSE CHASTANET

Anse Chastanet is an attractive cottage hotel built on a hill that slopes to the sea. Several yacht moorings are usually available off the cliffs north of the beach in Chamin Cove. Underwater rocks lie just south and north of the moorings, so approach with caution. While often reasonably peaceful, this area can be untenable in times of a northerly swell. The snorkeling right from your boat is superb.

The Anse Chastanet beach bar is a congenial lunch spot, with two boutiques in the same area. For dinner, they have a very fancy restaurant called Jade up the hill.

Water sports

Scuba St. Lucia at Anse Chastanet [VHF: 16] is one of the largest dive operations in the Windwards, with two resort courses and four dives daily. They do not fill tanks. Scuba St. Lucia takes divers on the Anse Chastanet Reef for their first dive at 1100. It is best to turn up half an hour early and remember to bring your diving card. If you are not certified, resort courses are available, and these usually start at around 0900.

Anse Chastanet reef extends seaward from the beach and is still in reasonably good condition. The shallower parts are fair for snorkeling, but avoid cruise ship days. Diving is excellent along the length of the reef, which slopes from about 30 to 80 feet. Sheet corals, solitary corals, and brain corals are abundant, as are a delightful variety of sponges, from the azure vase sponge to large barrel sponges. The water is clear and reef fish abound, with clouds of brown and blue chromis, along with sergeant majors, brilliantly colored parrotfish, and goatfish. All kinds of jacks and snappers cruise just off the reef. Currents are fierce on the outer part of the reef.

Snorkeling is excellent along much of this coast.

Navigation

When you go from Anse Chastanet toward Soufriere, be very careful of the reef off Grand Caille Point. Not only might you damage your boat, but you will also be liable for hefty fines (up to $5,000 US) for damaging the reef.

TROU AU DIABLE

This beach lies between Gd. Caille Point and Rachette Point. Sand covers the middle of the bay, but there are lovely coral gardens, ideal for snorkeling and diving, to both the east and west. The snorkeling is better to the east, the diving to the west. It is a reasonable dinghy ride from Soufriere or the Hummingbird, and you can tie to an orange dive buoy, if available, or to one of the SMMA marker buoys if not.

HUMMINGBIRD ANCHORAGE

You can anchor stern-to at the Hummingird Restaurant 1800-0600. This is a fishing priority area so you must move promptly at 0600 if asked to do so by fishermen. This does not happen every day and sometimes not every week, but you must not leave the boat here unattended by day, as it may need to be moved for fishing.

Otherwise use one of the seven yacht moorings in the area of the bat cave. It has an attractive, remote feel, and the snorkeling is good right off your boat. Ask the rangers about security here (it has been okay recently). For greater security at dinner ask Malcolm (722-5048/286-2277) to take you ashore and keep an eye on your boat. A dinghy dock in the corner of the bay makes getting ashore easy by day. But I would not use this at night, as at least one violent robbery has been reported here. It is safer to use the beach right outside the Hummingbird. Use a stern anchor for swells, or tie bow and stern between docks. Be prepared to deal with unneeded dinghy watchers. If you are using the Hummingbird, ask them to watch it for you.

Communications/services

The Hummingbird offers free customer

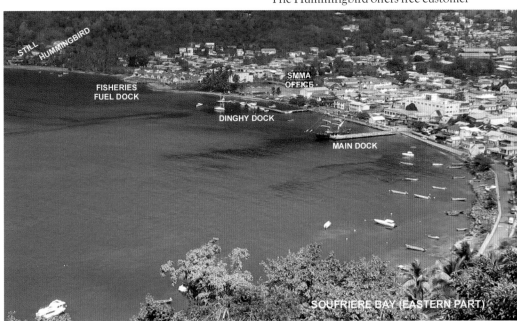

SOUFRIERE BAY (EASTERN PART)

wifi and the staff will help customers with telephone calls or faxes during normal office hours. You can check your email here. Wifi from other sources may reach the moorings.

Owner Joyce has run the Hummingbird for over 30 years, now with her son David as chef, and recently was awarded an M.B.E for her services to St. Lucia's tourism, she gets much of her business from yachts and welcomes them warmly. Dinner guests from yachts are welcome to a free shower, 12 gallons of fresh water if they bring containers, and a bag or two of free ice to take back on board.

Ashore

The Hummingbird Restaurant [VHF: 16, $A-B] is the most elegant and charming of Soufriere's waterfront restaurants, featuring wonderful hand carvings and an exquisite view across the pool to the Pitons beyond. The food is excellent ~ a blend of French and Creole cuisine, with seafood a specialty and generous portions.

A skipper bringing in a party of five or more gets a meal selected by the house for free. Meal guests are also welcome to use the pool. They have live music most Wednesday nights in season. If you are leaving your dinghy on the dock by day, tell one of the security guys and they will keep an eye on it for you (a tip after is appreciated).

Joyce also has the Hummingbird's Bamboo Beach Bar, which is popular for sunset or moonlight cocktails. Happy hour is 1700-1800 and the bar keeps going till the last person leaves. If there is no one there you may have to ask for a barman to come down.

Hummingbird is a great daytime hangout with soups, salads, and sandwiches or full meals for lunch

The office is very helpful with advice and will answer any questions you may have. They will arrange taxis and tours at a fair local rate. Batiks, handmade on the premises, are featured in their boutique, and Joyce offers a 10% discount on batiks (but not other items). Rooms are available, with a 15% discount to yachts in the summer, 20% in winter.

Orlando's [$A-B] is close to Hummingbird on the road to Soufriere. Orlando is one of St. Lucia's most famous chefs. Like some good chefs, he is part showman and is at home giving cooking demonstrations and teaching. He was one of the first to create an exciting new artfully presented Caribbean cuisine from all fresh local ingredients. His restaurant has attracted some famous chefs and other celebrities, including John Major (former British Prime Minister), as guests.

The restaurant has a pleasant courtyard atmosphere and includes a bar with wifi where you can hang out and eat "Ti Manje" (little eats). The food ranks among the best in St. Lucia, is elegantly served, and will please the most demanding gourmet. Orlando has a knack for mixing local fruits into many dishes, providing a light and delicious touch, and his desserts are excellent. For a real feast, try his five-course taster menu. He is open every day for dinner and every day except Monday and Tuesday for lunch. Lunches are lighter and less expensive, but very good. Orlando is available as an onboard guest chef or for demonstrations. He likes the challenge of a small galley.

The Still Beach Restaurant [$B-C] is next to the Hummingbird and, with the associated Ruby Estate, which lies just out of town, is run by David Dubolais. This restaurant has a big balcony overlooking the anchorage and serves good local food. The staff are welcoming and friendly, and you can ask them about Ruby Estate and the tours that are available there.

Water sports

Snorkeling is good all the way between the anchorage and Trou au Diable Beach. If you snorkel in shallow water off the beach in front of the Still Beach Restaurant, you are likely to see streams of bubbles rising to the surface. They are from a minor underwater volcanic vent.

Action Adventure Divers, in the Hummingbird, work with yachtspeople wanting to dive in the SMMA. It is run by two brothers from a fishing family in the area: Chester (an advanced Padi instructor) and Vincent (a dive master). They know all the good spots. You can contact them through VHF: 16 or phone. They will be happy to come by your yacht and pick you up. They offer a variety of

services, from resort courses to full certification, and if you have all your own gear and boat, their charges can be as low as $25 US per person, the standard rate for a guide. They use a pirogue with a bimini for sun cover, are flexible and helpful, and are delighted to work with those on yachts, who they see as their main customer base. You can ask them about underwater hull cleaning.

SOUFRIERE TOWN

The town of Soufriere was the set of the movie *Water*, starring Michael Caine, and it has many charming old Creole buildings with balconies and gingerbread. Much has been done recently to upgrade the town and waterfront. Unfortunately, two of the loveliest and most historic buildings were recently lost to fire.

There is a yacht and general-purpose dock just off the SMMA. You can use this for your dinghy. Guards on duty (0800-1600) do not seem to try to prevent would-be dinghy watchers, but if you tell the watchers that the guards are going to watch it for you, they lose interest and disappear.

Moorings start to the south of town and continue right round into Malgretoute. You swing on these moorings, so do not need a stern line. Security in the SMMA has been generally good except in the bat cave area, and even that has been good recently. Make sure you go on an SMMA mooring, not a private one (see page185).

Communications

Ben Yacht Services and Pier 28 Bistro and Lounge have the big building next to the SMMA office. Both have wifi and Ben has a computer for his customers. Many other places have wifi. You might pick up a wifi signal on a mooring.

Services

Water, fuel (gas and diesel), and chipped ice are available alongside the fishing port dock, open 0630-1800 every day. You can also buy fish here.

St. Lucia's two main yacht agencies are based in Soufriere. They have very similar names which can cause confusion.

Ben's Yacht Services is in the big building next to SMMA right opposite the dinghy dock. Enter through his niece's Pier 28 Bistro downstairs; his office is upstairs. Ben offers fueling, provisioning, taxis, car rentals, customs clearance, and laundry. He can book and save you a mooring. In addition, they will source parts, find technicians, and organize crew visas. Pier 28 has wifi, and Ben keeps a computer for customers who need to get on the internet. If you have any problems in the bay or approaches, or need a water taxi, you can call Ben. He has Yannick in the Bay. (See also *Transport*)

If you are trying to use Ben by VHF, know that there can be confusion, as Benny [VHF: 16: Harmony Yacht Services] also offers all superyacht services and may pick up, as might his son, who has Ben Taxi and Tours.

Charles Richards (Mystic Man Tours) can organize water for you on the town dock outside the SMMA. He is easy to reach, with an office next to the SMMA. The dock is in constant use, so make arrangements with him in advance. He also operates a profes-

Dasheen at Ladera

sional water taxi service, has a good success rate if you want to go sports fishing, runs great whale-watching tours, and is good for longer trips (getting to Castries, for example). In addition, he fixes most of the local outboards in the area (his workshop is in the fishing complex) and he can get yours running again if you have a problem.

Transport

Ben's Yacht Services stands by on VHF: 16. and has an office right opposite the dinghy dock. Ben has a fleet of taxis and will happily take you on a tour of the area, help you provision, find fresh flowers or fruits, get your guests to the airport, make restaurant reservations, take you there, and be your general help in Soufriere. He has a fleet of taxis and good drivers, and also rents cars and jeeps. Call him on the phone. For a half day tour Ben generally charges $20 US per person, minimum four. For a whole day it is likely to be around $70 US depending

on what is involved. His one way rates (for four) to La Haute or Morne Coubaril are about $10 US, for Dasheen $20 US. Ben also offers full superyacht services (see *Services*).

This gives you some idea, as many guys tying you up to a mooring will want to organize tours for you. Many places you may want to see have entry charges. These are included in some tours, not in others. You need to ask a lot of questions before making a decision. Unforunately, there are no set rates for short one way taxi trips so everything is negotiation. Ben is fair.

However it is also easy to take a bus, and most things that you want to see are on a bus route. The buses all line up on the main square; one lot heads north to Castries and the other south towards Vieux Fort. Everything is uphill from Soufriere, so riding one way then walking back downhill is a good option. La Haute is to the north, Morne Coubaril, the drive-in volcano and Ladera Resort are to the south.

Provisioning/fun shopping

In town, Eroline's Foods is a fair little supermarket, with a reasonable array of foods. It is connected to Fond Doux Estate, which supplies much of their produce. It opens 0800-2000 Monday to Saturday, and 0900-2100 on Sundays and holidays. If you buy more than you can carry, ask them about delivery to your nearest dock. Soufriere has a couple of banks and pharmacies.

A couple of good guys may come buy in boats to sell you fruits and vegetables, Distant Thunder is most often around and you can always call him, 718-8592.

Zaka Art Cafe, on Bridge Street, is a wonderful cacophony of bright colors and interesting characters. The walls are covered in Zaka masks found throughout the Caribbean decorating restaurants and homes. They pick their own coffee in the surrounding hills and process it in-house. It has a wonderful flavor while being non-acidic. You will want to buy a bag to take with you. Fresh fruit smoothies are made on the spot. Breakfast is from 0900, and, if you give Leah a little notice, she will produce a fine local lunch or dinner. This is a good place to buy the Cocoa Sainte Lucie organic chocolate. Stop by for a drink and take a look at the masks, maybe see some being created.

Restaurants

There is lots of very tasty, inexpensive local food available in town, probably cheaper than cooking for yourself. Lisa William's Pier 28 [$D] is air-conditioned and right opposite the main dinghy dock, along with Ben's Yacht Services. If you prefer to be outside, she also has the two beach bars with outside tables across the road. All have wifi. She makes good coffee, has local lunch specials that are generous and delicious and also a general menu. I am that told when available, the hamburgers are top class.

Skipper's and Archie's [$D], side by side next door, are also excellent cheap-and-cheerful joints. The cooking is local and good, and they serve food all day long. Archie's has a big TV and shows the latest sports events. Skipper's is open to the street and has some outside tables.

De Belle Vue Restaurant [$C-D] is in a cute room upstairs looking out over the water, and they cook good local food. Opposite, Petit Peak [$C-D] is in the building that served as the town courthouse back in 1898.

The more exciting and memorable restaurants are outside town (see also Hummingbird Anchorage, just a short walk away). Some you can hike to, others are a short taxi or bus ride away (see *Transport*) The Dasheen Restaurant at Ladera Resort [$A] has the most awesome view of any bar in the Caribbean; just to walk in is unforgettable. The original owner/designer made the most of the location, keeping the buildings small and interesting and completely open to the view. He was called back as architect when they expanded, and under his hand, the restaurant and bar are exotically designed as a series of three completely open rooms climbing the ridge line. They are perched on the edge of a giant precipice looking straight down the valley between the Pitons. It is hard not to exclaim "Wow!" when you first see it. From the top room you can look down through both the second room and the bar to the bright blue swimming pool set in a flower garden below. It gives a spectacular 3-D effect within the hotel and beyond to a dramatic Pitons view. Ladera Resort is managed by the owner, assisted by Daly. The staff will welcome you for lunch or dinner and are attentive and friendly.

Lunch is, of course, a great time for the view, though if you arrive for an early cocktail, dinner offers you both a day and night perspective, with the chance of a dramatic sunset. Nights are spectacular when the moon is full. Gourmets will prefer evenings, when the gold-medal-winning chef creates a dinner that is a fitting accompaniment to the view. In addition to the restaurant, ample snacks and sandwiches are available in the bar for lunch (make sure you try the chocolate mousse). Sunday buffet brunch is an excellent choice, but come reasonably early. If you are just walking in to look at the view (rather than using the bar and restaurant), there is a charge of $25 US per person. While there, do not miss their new boutique, which stocks local crafts, pottery, books, and essentials.

By day, the energetic can walk up to

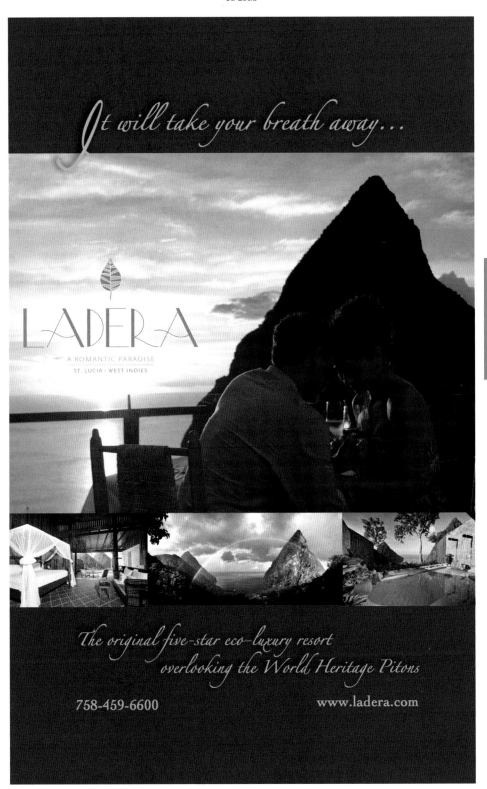

St. Lucia

Dasheen from Malgretoute. Walk up the Jalousie road away from Petit Piton, turn right on the main road, and keep going; it is a fair hike.

Opposite Dasheen is Hotel Chocolat, originally Rabot Estate, owned by the English chocolate maker. They cultivate cocoa for their chocolate (made in England), have pricy plantation tours and rooms for rent, along with a tall spidery restaurant [$A]. Happily, over the last few years, vegetation has covered much of the lackluster architecture. The restaurant is pleasant inside, and the food is good. To me, their buildings don't fit the beautiful countryside and are a stark contrast to their gorgeous old estate house, which is still standing and lovely.

Much more pleasant in appearance is Morne Fond Doux, another old estate with a nice restaurant. It has some lovely, authentic Caribbean buildings. They have added rooms by buying pretty traditional buildings from various parts of the island and rebuilding them on the estate. Their restaurant is open for both lunch and dinner [$B], and you can take a half-hour estate tour on delightful trails.

In the other direction, the road from Soufriere to Castries climbs a steep hill, and several restaurants lie along this road. All have great views over Soufriere.

La Haut Resort [$B-D] has a spectacular panoramic view of the Pitons, which is greatly enhanced by a brilliant display of bougainvillea planted in the foreground, making a perfect photograph. The grounds have been artfully gardened and include little fishponds, and many people find them rewarding for bird-watching. Owner Stephanie Allain, from Canada, offers a variety of dishes using local ingredients enhanced by ideas from the outside. Come for lunch or dinner. If you come for dinner, arrive before sunset, and in any case bring your swim suit and plan to spend some time hanging out in the pool with its spectacular Pitons view. La Haut is a mile and a half uphill from Soufriere. Get a bus or taxi up (see *Transport*). Walk back down: just keep sticking one foot in front of the other and gravity takes care of the rest.

Villa de Pitons [$B-D] has a rather quaint atmosphere, with lots of rooms linked by many steps around a central swimming pool with a fountain, and murals and batiks all over the walls. They open from breakfast to dinner, with a lighter lunch menu.

The Beacon is even farther uphill than La Haut. They have a big open platform restaurant with a good view over Soufriere, and they host special functions.

Water sports

Snorkeling and diving are good throughout the area. Action Adventure Divers will arrange whatever kind of dives you want (see *Hummingbird Anchorage*).

Ashore

The naturally hot Diamond Baths are scenic and pleasant, built by Louis the 16th. They are a 20 minute walk out the back of town. Pass the Soufriere Estate and look for a road on your right. It is posted, but only if you look back. The baths are combined with a beautiful tropical garden.

Take a few dollars and your towel, and you can luxuriate in these baths set amid a well-tended tropical garden. My favorite are the big private baths at the top, where piping hot water comes straight from the volcano into two huge tubs. Pay the person in charge as you go in: $10 EC per person to enter the gardens, $15 EC per person for the private baths, or $10 EC for the tepid outdoor pools. They have a snack bar and shop on the river.

As you head uphill to the south, Morne Coubaril is right opposite the road that goes to Jalousie (about a mile). It is a delightful old estate with a restaurant, and they offer half-hour estate tours, ziplining and horse riding. Their zipline trail is pleasant and scenic. Many of the lines start on platforms up big old banyan and mango trees. The guides are entertaining and knowledgeable about the area, as well as very safety conscious.

The turnoff to the Drive in Volcano (sulphur-springs) is a little further down the road, it is less than a mile from the main road and looks like a scene straight from hell, with barren, brightly colored earth, bubbling pools, and huge spurts of steam. They have an area here where you can take a mud bath.

In this area, the lovely little Sapphire

Sapphire Falls

water falls is set amid lush tropical vegetation. The river comes from the volcano, tepid and a little grey. It reaches a high rock promontory and falls down in two streams. Just below the falls is an area of volcanic mud, perfect to use for a face or body pack. There is no swim hole, but standing under the falls is wonderfully refreshing and delivers a whole body massage. Come late morning or early afternoon when the falls are in full sun, stand in them, look down, and a beautiful rainbow forms right round you. It is a blissful place, on the land of Jahrod, who charges $12 US pp for a visit. The path is changing, so my recommendation is to call Jahrod (617-8396), and arrange to meet him at the beginning of the road to the Sulphur Springs (a short bus ride, or $10 US taxi if you use Ben). For $20 US pp he will hike in with you (about 20 minutes), give you as much time as you need to enjoy the falls and then walk you down to the road that eventually takes you to Diamond baths and gardens and thus back to Soufriere. Jahrod is the hiking and waterfall man, he can hike with you to many beautiful falls in the area.

The rainforest area near Morne Fond St. Jacques has exquisite views for walking or hiking. You are required to have a guide and pay a fee when hiking in the rainforest reserve ($10 US per person), but walking on the road leading to it, amid the lush vegetation with hidden glimpses of the Pitons below, is also beautiful. For hikes in the rainforest, ask the Soufriere Foundation to call the forestry department. They have knowledgeable guides in the Soufriere area who can arrange to take you on a rainforest tour. One of the most interesting is a 2.5-hour loop tour to the Maho waterfalls. Take your bathing things for a shower in the falls, and a swim in the pool above it.

On the road to Fond St. Jacques New Jerusalem and Toraille (in a lovely little garden), are pleasant little waterfalls; take your swim things.

The Cocoa Sainte Lucie chocolate factory may have opened its little roadside attraction (see the beginning of the St. Lucia section), and if they have, you can easily visit by taking the bus towards Castries.

See also *Between the Pitons*.

MALGRETOUTE

This is a lovely place to moor, along a beautiful beach. The Marine Park has put in moorings, including at least two that take yachts up to 120 feet. One is right in front of Benny's, one is farther north. Small yachts can use them if no big boats are booked in.

A pretty old road (now a trail) runs from the waterfront in Soufriere to the far end of Malgretoute beach, which makes walking to town easy. A big new hotel is being very slowly built here. Since this road is on their property, I am not sure of its future, though

St. Lucia

197

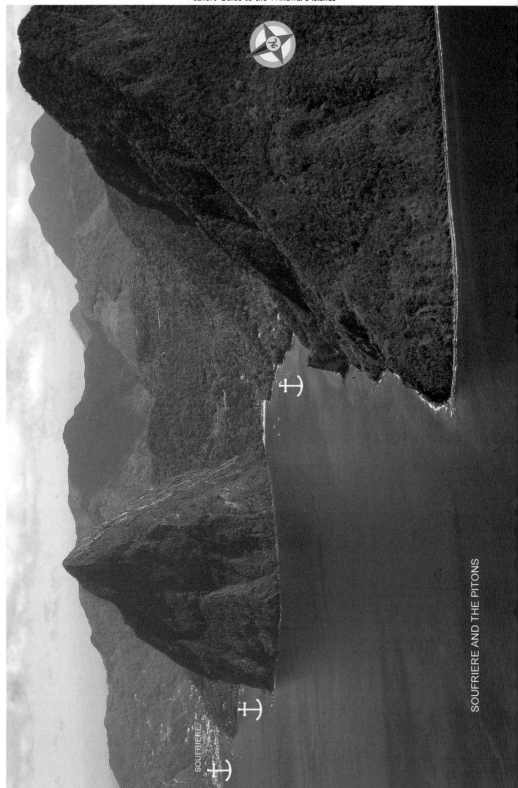

SOUFRIERE AND THE PITONS

SOUFRIERE

it has been a right of way for generations, so should stay.

Restaurants/Ashore

This is an area in transition, as a big hotel group has bought most of the shore and many locals were told to sell out to them. On the other hand, having emptied out the old people's home, and put up a fence, the project seems to keep stalling. One of the affected properties is Harmony Beach Restaurant, run by Marcelene, who cooks excellent Creole fish. Everything is cooked from scratch, they use all fresh ingredients and have a great view of Malgretoute and Soufriere Bay. She is not always open, but if you want to visit give her a call.

Just above the anchorage you can see Stonefield Estate [$B-C]. This elegant family hotel has a lovely restaurant area with a swimming pool and a view over the yachts. Trails lead to some excellent examples of Carib petroglyphs. If you walk uphill to the concrete Jalousie road and keep going uphill (away from the Pitons), the estate is to the left and is marked. They serve elegant Creole food.

If you turn left on the upper concrete road, you can head to the main road. Hikers can turn right on the main road and walk to the sulfur springs and Ladera.

If you head towards Sugar Beach, there is a trail to a cute little gardened water fall you can visit for a fee.

Diving and snorkeling are excellent around Petit Piton, though there is current. Drift-snorkel with your dinghy from Malgretoute.

BETWEEN THE PITONS

Moorings are available in the area shown from Sugar Beach Resort south along the shore. Local boat vendors will probably reach your mooring before you, to help with your lines. The wind and current can be strong in this area, and the current is sometimes against the wind. This area is sometimes calm, sometimes rolly, and it can change with the tides. It is also popular, and

sometimes full. The three outer moorings are suitable for yachts up to 120 feet.

The beach between the Pitons is part of Sugar Beach, a Viceroy Resort, which has a spectacular setting, though they are beginning to spoil it by overbuilding. To access the beach and restaurants, you can tie your dinghy to the end of the jetty off the beach, but do not lock it, and leave the sides clear. If you are hiking you can leave it onshore south of the other huge, shiny white sand beach on the south side of the bay.

Ashore

Sugar Beach Resort [$A] is open to the public, with two restaurants and the Cane Bar, which opens around 1800 and serves sushi and light dishes.

The Bayside Bar and Restaurant is on the beach and serves both lunch and dinner, and at other times you can get snacks and sandwiches from the bar next door. The Great Room, for fine dining, is in the main building. Walk into Bayside for lunch, book for dinner in either restaurant. They have an excellent spa, with a massage center, facials, hairdressers, saunas, and hot tubs.

There is a lovely hike from this anchorage up to Tete Paul which has a really spectacular precipice view of Petit Piton and the anchorage (2-3 hours). You go through the villages of Morne La Croix and Chateaubelair. The easiest way to do this is to contact Anthony (488-7820/717-2019), who runs water-taxi Livity. He is a great guide and will collect you from your boat, drive you up to Morne La Croix, hike with you, and bring you back through farmland and a beautiful private estate for about $30 US a head (minimum four people or $120 US). There is a also Tete Morne trail fee of about $5 US per person. You can also ask him about climbing Gros Piton and any other hikes. He is also good at arranging beach barbecues or picnics.

Lesser mortals might want to at least walk from the anchorage up to the village of Morne La Croix; it has to be one of the steepest roads in the world.

Water sports

You can talk to the dive shop here, or

199

Laborie anchorage

call Action Divers. The dive around the base of Petit Piton is excellent. Start from close to the beach and explore at whatever depth you feel comfortable. There are wonderful sponges, good coral formations, and an extraordinary variety of fish. Sometimes huge schools of fish make magical patterns in the sunlight. Apart from reef fish, such as angelfish, blue chromis, parrotfish, scorpionfish, and damselfish, there are lots of hunters out there: jacks and snappers swim in fair-sized schools, and occasionally one sees a monster fish. Another good site for both snorkeling and scuba is under Gros Piton, just below the prominent cliff. A sloping dropoff with plenty of fish and coral goes down to great depths. There are sometimes currents in this area.

Navigation
South coast: Pitons
to Vieux Fort

The trip from the Pitons to Vieux Fort is against both wind and current, but it is only about 11 miles and is usually somewhat protected. Keep clear of the reefs that extend about half a mile offshore between Choiseul and Laborie. Laborie, about three miles before Vieux Fort, is a delightful little harbor.

LABORIE

Laborie is an authentic small fishing village on the south coast, about three miles west of Vieux Fort. It is easily identified by the big quarry just to its west. If you are tired of tourist spots, visit Laborie: The locals are friendly and not intrusive, the pace of life is easy-going and it is easy to feel right at home.

Navigation

Some old charts and map readers show a big reef north of Petit Trou extending west, and no reef west of the dock. If yours looks like that, ignore it and use ours or your eyes.

Approach from the south or southeast to avoid Laborie Reef, which lies up to half a mile offshore on the west side of the bay. The entrance is now buoyed, but this seems to confuse some, who go between the first red and green markers, ignore the "reef to the north" Iala marker, and go aground on it.

The approach is easy in good light, and if the sun is in your eyes, you can anchor in Petit Trou. The best anchorage is right off the town dock in about 15 feet of water.

Or you can find your way in towards the beach on the other side of the center reef, and you might even explore the broken reef farther up the beach for an anchoring spot. (Best to do this with a dinghy first, as it is tricky.)

Laborie is exposed to the south, reasonably well protected in most conditions, and often a little rolly.

LABORIE

Services

You may be able to pick up wifi from your yacht, but if not, Bamboo has wifi. A fuel station is at the head of the dock; water and fuel on the dock are planned. Rene (488-5433) is the local taxi driver. Or you can call Winson (584-1183) in Vieux Fort.

Ashore

Turn left on high Street. A big community center and post office is conspicuous, and then comes a small local market, a basic supermarket, and an active fish market. Listen for the conch shell horn as the boats arrive. Bars abound from First Stop at one end to Smoking Monkey at the other.

The restaurants in town are inexpensive, locally owned and good. Take a few steps along the beach from dock and have coffee, snack, or lunch in the great new Salt Rush Cafe right on the beach (closed Thursdays and Sunday morning, otherwise 0900-2100). This is the gathering place for enthusiastic kayakers and you can ask them about trips. They serve great fresh bread, sandwiches, baked goodies and more. Caroline will be happy to tell you about the town.

Captain Kent and Jeanie's Big Bamboo Cafe [$C-D, closed Tuesday] opens from about 1600 until late. It has an outside bar and barbecue at the back, tables out on the pavement, and inside is a VIP lounge. You can get delicious fresh fish, fried plantains, breadfruit balls, and much more.

Mama Rose (Market Place) Restaurant [$C-D] is almost opposite and was one of the first Laborie restaurants, opened by Mama

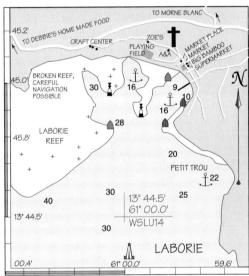

Rose and now run by grandchildren Adon, Quill, and Minel. They open Monday to Saturday 0900-2300, serve good local food, as well as tasty fish 'n chips, and always offer an inexpensive local lunch plate.

Walk down to the water to two shady beach tables on the other side of the fish market. Look back up a little road at the big green building and you will see Dolphin's Hideaway [$D], owned by Shads and Ace, They open every day except Monday. They prepare lunch daily and will do dinner if asked.

A few steps further down the beach is a little hole in the wall called Anna's Place, where you can get a good local lunch plate for $10-12 EC. She opens every day for lunch only, and you sit on the beach.

Farther west, over the bridge, you can

201

Vieux Fort

get a great roti at Ann Marie's A & A. It is a tiny building marked only by a Piton sign. Farther west on the left, clean and modern with its balcony overlooking the playing field, is Zoe's [$C-D, closed Mondays]. You can walk in about noon for local food on Saturday or come Sunday evening for pizza. Other times, give Zoe a little notice for a good local meal.

Further down the road is the Papel Craft Center with a spa, shops, and Miranda's great

Big Bamboo, Laborie

little cafe [$C-D]. She opens daily 1100-2000, and serves good and very inexpensive local food, with seats out in the open.

Gibbon Holder's Smoky Monkey is a bar on the beach below. He is the son of Linda, who owns the Sea Breeze, once an active restaurant, above. It is currently just a bar, but he does beach barbecues. You can call him (723-0073) and ask about the next one.

If you take any bus heading to Soufriere, you can get off a mile or two down the road at Debbie's Home Cooking [$B-D]. This is a large restaurant quite well known for its local food and Sunday buffet.

Walk the spectacular long beach. Way up in the hills behind Laborie is Morne le Blanc (aka The Top of the South). The GSM aerials on the hill will show you where it is. They have a picnic spot and a viewing platform with a panoramic view towards Vieux Fort.

Water Sports

Iyanola Dive Adventures is on the waterfront a bit north of the dock. It is owned by master instructor Laurent John, who will be happy to take you diving, probably down in the SMMA.

VIEUX FORT

Vieux Fort is convenient for Hewanorra airport. It does not have a tourist bone in its body and is a thriving local town with some great old wooden houses and two active ports: commercial and fishing. The people are generally friendly and welcoming, and you will find supermarkets and hardware stores in shopping malls. The fishing port makes it amenable for visiting yachts, though if you are used to the tourist scene, you may suffer from culture shock. There are also some rough edges and, with a brief intermission when the marine police patrolled, there were a string of thefts over some years culminating in the murder of a yachtsman. The murderers were caught by the locals so that is not a problem, but theft still could be. No problem if someone is onboard. Laborie is an alternative.

The anchorage is well protected and a long walk (or short ride) away is one of the Caribbean's most magnificent windward beaches, a beach so long that you are guaranteed half a mile or so to yourself.

Navigation

The sail to Vieux Fort from the Pitons is 11 miles, usually to windward. It is somewhat protected, but if the current is running to the east, it can be rough. Keep well clear of the reef that extends about half a mile offshore between Choiseul and Laborie.

The most convenient anchorage for getting ashore is west of the new fishing port. Leave the green marker to port as you approach. Anchor between the marker and the western wall in 10-20 feet of water, or outside the green marker in 25 feet of water. Avoid the shoal along the northern wall of the fishing harbor that extends both north

203

and west. Here you are close to town and can leave your dinghy in the fishing port. The holding varies between good and poor, so make sure you are well dug in before going ashore.

You can also anchor in either of the bays southwest of the large ship harbor marked on our chart. Anchor south of all the beacons. Shoals extend from the shore, so approach cautiously. To enter the first bay, pass to the west of the big, rusty post just outside the bay, as there is a shoal inside this post toward the shore. The second bay is far more scenic, with some passable snorkeling. A shoal comes out from the middle of the bay but you can anchor either side of it, or outside it. Several wrecks in both bays manage to snag anchors. If you are worried, have someone snorkel to help pick the spot.

The large ship port is run by St. Lucia Marine Terminals. They are not geared for yachts but have been quite helpful. You can often leave your dinghy alongside the roll-on dock to the north of the main pier. You cannot leave it here when the dock is in use. For town, use the fishing port.

Regulations

Vieux Fort is a port of entry, and customs and immigration are at the head of the large ship dock (not the fishing port). If they are closed, you can try the airport. Sailclear does not work here yet.

Yachts may not anchor by the Maria Islands, it is a protected area.

Communications

The Document Center, an office store with internet and Fedex, is in the big building where Clarke St. joins the highway. Most bars have wifi.

Services

Ice and outboard fuel are available in the fishing port on the eastern dock. You could stay overnight in the fishing port stern-to on the northwest wall if there is room. You may be charged $20 EC. There are no dockside services; ask first. Depths in the fishing port are about 6 feet close to the eastern dock, and about 7-8 feet farther out, where you can stay the night.

Winson Edward (584-1183, 520-5231) is an excellent taxi driver. He is knowledgeable, reliable and likes to hike. Bayne (720-8425) has another taxi.

Filling with water is possible alongside the roll-on dock in the commercial port (when free). Talk to someone in the operations department, as you will have to arrange it with the water department. Big yachts can have fuel trucked to the commercial port. There is no water for filling a yacht in the fishing port, but you can probably arrange to fill a couple of jerry jugs in the port for a small fee if you ask security. Cooking gas is available at the gas depot just outside the commercial port.

Fletcher's Laundry and Dry Cleaning is on New Dock Road. Virginia Fletcher charges $30 EC for a load to wash and dry and can turn it round in a day if you get it in early enough, otherwise 24 hours. Open approximately 0900 to 1700.

The fishing port is the obvious place to

leave your dinghy. Put it in the northwest corner on the dock. Lock it up and, if leaving it at night, ask the security guard to keep an eye on it for you and tip him when you come back. On holidays and weekends, school kids can be pestiferous. Bribing one to guard the dinghy works, but it would still be smart to take the red kill switch with you. If you have a problem, there is a good chance you can leave it on the roll-on dock at the secure Commercial Port, where they are very helpful, though ingenuity is necessary for tying up, as there are no rings.

Hippolyte, right outside the dock area, is the DHL agent and can clear parts through customs. Francis Raymond, of St. Lucia Refrigeration on New Dock Drive, has lots of refrigeration and stove parts, but he does not make repairs.

Lubeco bedding factory is owned by Stephanie Allain, who also has La Haute in Soufriere. They supply both fitted and flat sheets for any size bunk (take a pattern) and have really nice fabrics in many designs, including cotton and organic cotton. They also sell towels and they produce good-quality, high-density foam mattresses cut to any shape. You get a mattress properly finished with a quilted cover, which adds comfort. Lubeco is in the industrial estate, just off the road to Laborie. They also have a store in American Dry Wall near Castries.

Provisioning

Shopping is good, and most banks have ATMs. One large supermarket is in the mall by the roundabout. The even bigger Gablewoods South is a few miles down the main road heading towards Laborie. Fruits and vegetables in town are good and are less expensive than in Castries. The fish market in the fishing port has great buys on fresh fish.

Napa has batteries and tools, and there are other hardware stores.

Restaurants

Kimatrai [$C] stands on the hill overlooking the yacht anchorage. It is an old-fashioned hotel, cool and breezy, with a marvelous view of the harbor. It is open all day and is a great place to hang out, relax, write postcards, play pool, use the wifi, catch up on your diary, or watch cable TV. It has the perfect location for sunset, and they serve food.

Old Plantation Yard [$D], owned by Conrad Simon on Commercial Street, is a wonderful lunch place full of character. You eat in a courtyard shaded by breadfruit trees and decorated with an old pirogue. They serve local stews and dishes and it is inexpensive and fun. You can see some historical artifacts in the main room.

When you are ready for some beach time, hang out at The Reef [$C-D, closed Monday evenings], on the eastern shore. The owner, Cecile Wiltshire, is a software engineer and runs slucia.com (not stlucia) and has wifi. The Reef is open for breakfast, lunch, and dinner, serving local dishes. Seamoss and coconut water, saltfish bakes, lambi, and squid are on the menu, as are pizzas. The Reef collects interesting people, makes a great hangout, and is an excellent place to spend a few hours. It has four simple rooms for an overnight.

Cecile is also a windsurfing instructor, and her Reef Kite 'n Surf Center has international instructors and all the latest kitesurfing and sailboard gear. It normally opens from November to June. Secondhand gear is often for sale.

Next door, Island Breeze [$C-D] is a good cheap and cheerful bar/restaurant right on the beach, open every day for lunch and dinner, serving beach bites, burgers and grilled food, and the food is good.

East of Vieux Fort, the Maria Islands are a nature reserve and home to a species of lizard and a snake unknown anywhere else in the world. The National Trust building is right beside The Reef, and you can arrange for a guided trip. (You are not allowed to anchor there.) The energetic should hike up to the Moule a Chic lighthouse for the view.

PASSAGES BETWEEN ST. LUCIA & ST. VINCENT

Northbound

The northbound passage between St. Vincent and St. Lucia can be hard on the wind and hard on the body. The north end of St. Vincent is unbelievably gusty on occasion and more than a little bumpy. It is not unusual to have gusts of 30 to 40 knots for a few miles, so it pays to be prepared. I often do this trip single-handed and am not overly fond of it, but find the easiest way to do it is as follows: motor-sail close to the coast under reefed main and engine and wait until the full force of the wind hits before deciding what to do. If you are comfortable under main and engine, keep going that way until the wind steadies down. Otherwise, if you have roller furling, just unroll a little of the jib until it gets calmer. The main thing is not to arrive at the north end with too much canvas, where reducing sail can degenerate into hanging onto flailing Dacron as the boat bucks about and tries to throw you over. Once you get about five miles north of St. Vincent, wind and seas generally become more constant and you can adjust sail accordingly. The current will set you to the west, so head up if possible. It is going to be a long day, so plan to leave early from Cumberland Bay or Wallilabou, as that will make it seem shorter.

You may be able to avoid some wind and sea by heading offshore from Wallilabou, but in that case you are likely to have a hard beat to St. Lucia.

If heading north from Blue Lagoon in reasonable weather, the passage up the windward side of St. Vincent is shorter and you get the windward part over early, leaving a good sail to the Pitons. The trick is to tack about 4 miles to the east of St. Vincent to stay well off any bad seas close to shore. If the wind is in the north, you may have to make more than one tack. There is a windward lee under the Soufriere volcano (back pressure). When you reach this, if you tack out a few miles, you will get better wind and a better angle for crossing the channel.

Southbound

The southbound trip is usually a lovely broad reach. If you cannot see St. Vincent from St. Lucia, a course of 208° magnetic should start you in the right direction. If you plan to stop in St. Vincent, nature lovers will favor Cumberland or Wallilabou (you can clear in Chateaubelair) and those who like waterfront bars can clear customs in Blue Lagoon. If you plan to go all the way to Bequia, make sure you allow plenty of time.

In reasonable conditions, you may prefer to go windward of St. Vincent when sailing from Vieux Fort or Soufriere to Bequia.

Map: PASSAGES BETWEEN ST. LUCIA AND ST. VINCENT

PITONS AT 13° 48'N 61° 05'W · SOUFRIERE · ST. LUCIA · 600 VIEUX FORT, 13° 43.'N 60° 58'W · 211° (31°) MAG, 30 MILES · 230°(50°) MAG, 24 MILES · 13° 23'N 61° 13'W · SOUFRIERE VOLCANO · CHATEAUBELAIR · ST. VINCENT

St. Vincent &
the Grenadines

Montreal Gardens

Regulations

St. Vincent and the Grenadines together make up one country. The customs stations are in Chateaubelair, Wallilabou, Kingstown, Blue Lagoon, Bequia, Union Island, Mustique and Canouan.

The entry charge is $35 EC per person per month, unless you leave within that month, in which case you pay again when you reenter. In addition, charter yachts based outside St. Vincent are charged $5 EC per foot per month, with a $125 occasional license fee. You can cruise here as long as you wish. You will normally be stamped in for a month and then return for extensions, which are in the same office and easy to obtain. Those clearing outside normal office hours (weekdays 0800-1200, 1300-1600) will pay overtime.

Overtime fees on Sundays/holidays are: customs $63 EC, immigration $50 EC. On other days: customs $45 EC, immigration $35 EC.

No jet skis or similar craft are allowed anywhere in St. Vincent and the Grenadines. Spearfishing is strictly forbidden to all visitors.

You are welcome to fish, but only for your own consumption. You can troll when sailing, or hand-line at anchor or from the shore, except in any marine park, where no fishing is allowed. Buying lobster out of season (the lobstering season is October 1 to April 30) is illegal, as is buying a female lobster with eggs (easily seen as red "caviar" under the tail), or any lobster less than 9" in length. Corals must not be damaged. Fines run at around $5,000 EC.

Holidays

Jan. 1, New Year's Day

Jan. 2, Recovery Day

Jan. 22, Discovery Day

Easter Friday, Sunday & Monday, April 14-17, 2017, and March 29-April 2, 2018

First Monday in May, Labor Day

Whit Monday, June 5, 2017 and May 21, 2018

Carnival, 2nd Monday and Tuesday in July

August bank holiday; 1st Monday in August

October 27, Independence Day

Dec. 25, Christmas

Dec. 26, Boxing Day

Shopping hours

Most shops open 0800-1200 and 1300-1600. Saturday is a half day and most places are closed by noon. Banks normally open Monday through Thursday 0800-1200 and 1300-1500, and Fridays 0800-1200 and 1500-1700.

Telephones

It is simplest to get a cell phone and use a local sim card. For calls to USA and other NANP countries, dial 1 plus the full number. For other overseas calls, dial 0 + country code + number. When dialing from overseas, the area code is 784, followed by a 7-digit number.

Transport

There are inexpensive ($1.50-$6 EC) buses running to most villages. If you are going a long way, check on the time of the last returning bus. Taxis are plentiful. Sample taxi rates for up to four are:

	$EC
Blue Lagoon to Airport	40
Kingstown to Young Island	40
Airport to Young Island	30
Kingstown to Blue Lagoon	50
Short ride	25
By the hour	80
Arnos Vale shopping run	80

Rental cars and motorbikes are available (see our directory). You will need to buy a local license, which costs $65 EC.

Airport departure tax is $40 EC, usually included in you ticket.

Welcoming kids in Coull's Hill on St. Vincent's west coast

St. Vincent

St. Vincent is an island of towering mountains, craggy peaks, and dramatic precipices. Everything is dressed in a tangle of dense green forest. St. Vincent's steep and wild terrain was among the last to be settled by Europeans. At the time Columbus sailed through the islands, St. Vincent was inhabited by the Kalinargo, who had migrated from South America and had a more poetic name for the island, Hairoun, which means "home of the blessed." They were a fierce tribe and had wrested the land from the Arawak people who preceded them. Columbus called them Caribs.

While the newly arrived Europeans exploited nearby islands, a slave ship was wrecked off Bequia and the Caribs took the slaves as their own. However, these slaves were fierce and warlike and proved to be a problem. To control this, the Caribs decided to kill all the young male black children.

This caused a revolt among the slaves, who killed all the Caribs they could, stole their women, and ran into the hills. They kept the names the Caribs had given them, followed some Carib customs, and became known as the Black Caribs. Over the years they took control of much of the land from the original Caribs and put up intense resistance to British settlement. Finally, in the late 18th century, the Black Caribs were defeated by a superior British force and shipped en masse to Honduras.

The northern end of the island is dominated by Soufriere, a 3,000-foot volcano. A friend of mine was anchored under the volcano in April 1979 with an amateur geologist on board. Together they scaled the volcano and peered into the depths. The geologist declared it safely dormant. That night, which happened to be both Friday the 13th and Good Friday, there was a rumbling

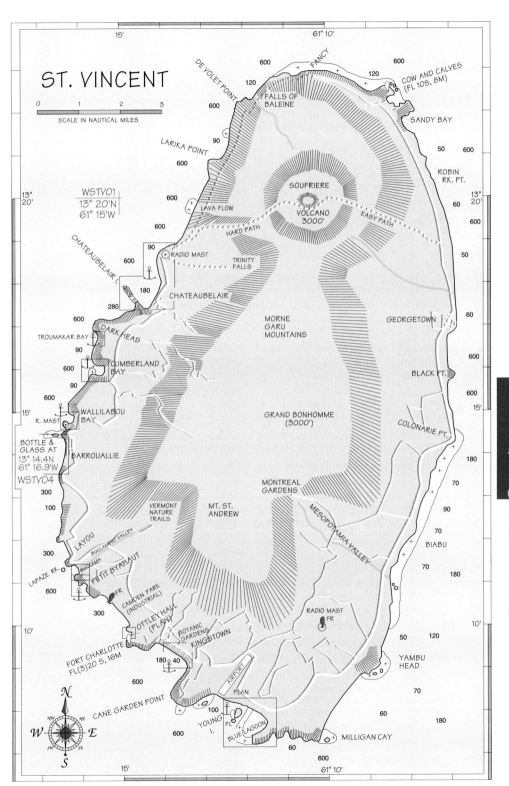

from the very bowels of the earth and the volcano erupted with a massive cloud that landed dust hundreds of miles away. It created murk in the area so thick they couldn't see to the bow of the boat and had to leave completely blind, steering by compass to get away. The eruptions, which lasted for some days, were Soufriere's second since 1902. The other was in 1973. As you sail by, you can see some rivers of dark volcanic matter that flowed down from the summit. Despite the absence of any warning, everyone left soon after the first eruption and there were no casualties.

The enthusiastic should hike up Soufriere, as it is unquestionably one of the Windwards' best and most exciting hikes. Starting on the windward side, there is a clear trail that begins in farmland and goes through rainforest, montane forest, and then into an area where only tiny plants can survive. The mountain top is often in cloud, and you need a little luck to see down into the crater or get the views over the island. The wind often blows hard, and it is cool and damp, so take a rain jacket. Be careful not to get blown into the crater, which is a sheer 1,000-foot drop with no guardrail. Take lunch with you and eat it near the top, as the longer you spend there, the more likely you are to get windows in the clouds and be able to see into the crater. The crater is an impressive cone, with a huge, growing, smoking volcanic dome in the middle. The crater rim is at 3,000 feet; the mountains to the north attain 3,800 feet. The volcano can be approached from the leeward side, but it is a much longer hike (about four hours each way) and a reliable guide is essential.

It seems that neither nature nor man was sure they wanted tourism in St. Vincent, for it lacks the acres of white sand beach, and the convenient, easy anchorages of the Grenadines. In compensation, this very beautiful island remains unspoiled, and you can drive or hike amid exotic, almost theatrical, scenery. Its fierce, rugged terrain is the perfect scenic complement to the appealing and gentle Grenadines farther south. Those doing a round trip from St. Lucia who only wish to stop one way are better off visiting St. Vincent on the way north, as this makes the northbound trip shorter.

Try to see some of St. Vincent's interior, which is totally wild. Roads run up both of St. Vincent's coasts, but none goes all the way round or crosses the middle. I love Montreal Gardens in the Mesopotamia Valley. Perched upon the very threshold of the mountains, they are at the end of the road. Tim Vaughn and his team maintain these gardens as a work of art. Little paths, dense vegetation, a river, and broad views make the gardens a perfect place to spend an hour or two away from it all.

Those who like things closer to town can tour the Botanical Gardens and Fort Charlotte. The Botanical Gardens are the oldest in the western hemisphere, and it was here that Captain Bligh brought the breadfruit tree after the mutiny on the Bounty fiasco. A direct descendant from his original tree is on display. You will find many youths to guide you through the gardens. One or two are good and entertaining, but negotiate fees in advance.

While many places are good for wandering off on your own, a guide is essential for some hikes, especially the western approach to the volcano. Bad robberies have occurred in this area, which has also become the smokebasket of the ganga generation.

Good guides are available who will cover everything mentioned above. Clint and Millie Hazel, who run Hazeco Tours, come from Vincentian families dating back to the 1700s, and they have an exceptional and intimate view of the island's history, politics, and society. They are willing to arrange tours from Cumberland and Wallilabou, but you will need to contact them in advance, as their radio does not reach these little bays. Many people also contact them from Bequia and get met on the ferry. We also mention other guides under various anchorages.

Chateaubelair: Chateaubelair Island is in the foreground

Navigation, west coast: north to south

Navigation along this section of the coast is straightforward, as the land is steep-to except for the clearly visible Bottle and Glass rocks near Barrouallie. A quarter of a mile offshore clears all other dangers.

One yachtsman was murdered and another injured in a robbery in Wallilabou in March 2016. They came by boat and the murder is not yet solved. This has led some to avoid the west coast. Others continue to visit, and so far they have not struck again.

CHATEAUBELAIR

Chateaubelair lies at the southern foot of Soufriere, St. Vincent's volcano. The coast here is rugged and photogenic, with dramatic hill and mountain outlines, cliffs, and beach. In settled weather it can be a dream. However, in times of really bad northerly swells, Chateaubelair can be untenable, so use caution during the winter months. A steep cliffy slope covered in palm trees lies along the eastern half of the bay. This is the calmest and most scenic place to anchor. There is an ample anchoring shelf, 20-40 feet deep. Don't anchor too close to shore, as rocky patches extend in places. The bottom is sand, but some of the boulders you see tumbling into the sea along the water's edge have made it onto the sand, so if you anchor on rope, snorkel on your anchor.

There is also a good sandy anchoring shelf with excellent holding in front of the Beach Front Restaurant, though just to the north-east of the restaurant is a deep hole. Anchoring south of the dock along the shore is the closest for just clearing customs.

A rock lies in the middle of the channel between Chateaubelair Island and the mainland. A navigable passage, some 35 feet deep, runs just south of this rock (between the rock and the mainland). There are rocks around, so only attempt this in good light.

Be prepared to move for fishermen if they ask. Getting ashore may be hard to impossible in any swell. The best place is the stub of the old dock remains.

There were serious security concerns here for some years. The bad guys were put away and plenty of people have been anchoring here without any problem for the last couple of years. Always check our Windwards updates on doyleguides.com. The local police number is 458-2229.

Regulations

Chateaubelair is a port of clearance and you can clear in here. Turn right and walk along the beach a couple of hundred feet from the dock. Look for a path leading to the left beside a house. Customs is in this house. Immigration is in the police station. Head up the road from the dock, take the uphill left turn, and it is on your right. Whenever

I have cleared in here, it has been a friendly experience. Customs is usually open weekdays 0800-1600, and Saturdays 0800-1200. When leaving, it may be wise to clear out before you sail here, in case customs are away.

Ashore

Most people in the north of St. Vincent are naturally friendly in the nicest way. Try to keep it that way. Treat people with friendly respect. It is good to buy produce if vendors come out and offer it to you, but beware of giving anyone money to go buy fruits or run errands in the village. Don't give to beggars unless they have real handicaps.

Esron Thompson's Beach Front Restaurant [$D] is a conspicuous building on the beach. He and his wife Gail will cook you the most wonderful fresh fish at very reasonable prices that are geared to the local market. For preference, eat upstairs under a shelter with a panoramic view of the bay. But watch out as you get towards the top of the stairs ~ the third one from the top is a little higher than the rest and tries to trip you up. If you are not overnighting, this makes a great lunch spot when heading south; anchor right off the restaurant. They do sometimes have very loud, late-night music on weekends.

Chateaubelair lies in the heart of some of St. Vincent's best hiking. The volcano is a full day's hike. Trinity Falls is a four-hour round trip, but you can get a taxi some of the way. The Darkview Falls are a pleasant 40-minute hike, with a second falls higher up. Take your bathing things, for you can swim at Trinity Falls and take a good shower at the Darkview Falls. Ask about the ancient carved stones. Wherever you go, it will be in beautiful scenery. Taxi tours and walking guides are available through the Beach Front Restaurant.

Water sports

The whole of Chateaubelair Bay is an invitation to snorkel. Interesting boulders and rocks abound. For divers,

Chateaubelair Island is magnificent and you can find a good dive almost anywhere around it. On the west side, a steep wall has been sculpted by the sea into ravines, hollows, and tiny caves that are home to eels, soapfish, and other creatures. It is decorated by a variety of black corals, including wire coral. Giant gray angelfish often gather over the sand at about 90 feet. You will find a reef 40 feet deep where huge structures covered with a colorful mixture of corals rise from the sand like fairy castles. Pufferfish swim by with what look like broad smiles on their faces. Huge schools of tiny silver fish catch the sun in a brilliant display. You will see a good variety of brightly colored reef fish and creatures such as Christmas tree worms, snake eels, and maybe an octopus. On the north end of the eastern side, a dramatic wall plunges to about 130 feet, with elegant soft coral formations. Farther south, diving is not as deep but is equally pretty.

You might be lucky and find the dive mooring just off-island in the passage between the island and the mainland.

TROUMAKAR BAY

This small, isolated bay has room for only a handful of yachts. It is well protected, except in bad northerly swells. Steep hills ashore afford panoramic views for energetic walkers. There is good snorkeling all along the northern shore. The water here is deep ~ you begin to think the bottom does not exist as you approach the beach. Anchor bow or stern to the old block plant ruins at the northern end of the beach, or tie to a palm tree.

Ashore

Troumakar is at the end of the road, but a good end. Perched on the slope near some massive ruined foundations is Marsy's Bar and Restaurant [$C-D, VHF:16], owned by Alstar Mars and Yvonne, who also own much of the hillside. You can drink here all day long at regular prices, which are lower than most happy hours, and Yvonne will be delighted to cook you a local meal at a very reasonable price, given an hour or two notice. There have been few boats and no security problems here, but just in case you need it, their number is 458-2879.

CUMBERLAND BAY

This deep and enchanting bay is part of an estate in the heart of St. Vincent's wildest and richest land. A forest of coconut trees and bananas flows down the valley to the beach. At dusk, cattle egrets roost together in nearby trees, and at night, the tree frogs set up a rich chorus. Sometimes the bay becomes a boiling mass of jumping tuna and fishermen can often be seen with their seine nets, waiting patiently. Cumberland is unspoiled by tourism. There are many here happy to take you on a tour or feed you, but it is all so unsophisticated that it has the charm of an untouched settlement. This is a very friendly little bay. The land around is steep and dramatic, with excellent hiking. Enter toward the north of the bay to avoid the large rocky shoal that extends from the southwestern headland. Cumberland is very deep and you will need to anchor bow or stern to a palm tree. Many will be eager to help. Do not tow any helpers into the bay; wait till you get right in and choose one of the people inside the bay itself. You can anchor to the north or south of Bay Central. The water on the north side is shallower.

Regulations/services

Cumberland Bay has no customs; clear in or out at Wallilabou or Chateaubelair.

St Vincent & the Grenadines

215

Cumberland Bay

Bay Central (Cumberland Beach and Recreation Park) is a government-built facility with free open wifi (good signal for most of the bay), a dock selling water ($50 EC up to 200 gallons), ice, a launderette ($35 EC wash and dry), showers (for $5 EC they even supply a towel), bar and restaurant, and a welcome center. They also have surveillance cameras that take in their dock and much of the bay. You can come alongside for water (up to about 2 meters draft), and deeper boats can come stern-to; the depth drops off fast. The staff, including Matthew and Althea, are very helpful. Many of the people who have businesses sleep on the beach, so there are generally people about.

Restaurants

Five local and one French restaurant line the bay, all dependent on visiting yachts, all reasonably priced and fun. So plan to eat out for lunch or dinner.

Two cousins, Julian and Lloyd, have Mojito [$C-D] at the north end of the beach. It has a great view over the rest of the bay. No need to get your feet wet; dinghy to Bay Central and walk. Someone may well dinghy or swim you a menu, which includes pineapple and lemon grass seafood curry and rack of lamb with coffee mint sauce. The captain eats free with five or more guests.

Venetia, who serves you, is lovely, and the food is excellent.

Bay Central [$D] has a little restaurant open from 0800 until the last customer leaves. This is the cheapest place to eat and you get good local Creole fish or chicken, and they have a dinghy dock. They have karaoke on alternative Saturday nights.

Joseph is a fisherman who has been here for as long as I can remember. He has a restaurant right on the beach, DJ-20 or Joseph's Place [$C], now run by his son Gregory and his wife. They cook local-style barbecue of fresh fish or chicken and are into music, so entertainment can be arranged. Joseph is also out and about in the bay fishing, taking yacht lines, selling a little handicraft, and helping however he can.

Bennett [$C-D] has the bar/restaurant called Beni in the middle of the beach. He has been here for a long time. It is an amusing place to hang out. Beni can cook a good local meal, especially seafood, and serve fresh local juice. But he needs advance notice so give him a call (434-9328). Bennett is also a good man to talk to about hiking. The new Cumberland Nature Trail (about three hours) is in the rain forest high above Spring Village near the water source for the hydro-electric piping, which carries water to a series of several small generators. You need a taxi

Calabash artist, Coull's Hill

to take you there. Beni can also take you to other hikes, including Darkview Falls. Beni has a great package, which includes a tour and full dinner with a drink afterwards. If you are eating in his restaurant, he will give you free water and ice.

Mama Elma [$C] is near Joseph and open for lunch and dinner every day. You can get everything from goat water to lobster, with plenty of fish and chicken. She sometimes has local provisions for sale.

The Black Baron [$B-C], a tavern run by Jean-Louis and Corinne from France, has the most character, with a pirate's den complete with a treasure chest. They open every day in season and serve French and Creole food made with fresh local ingredients. This was the first to offer, on two day's notice, a whole roasted suckling pig for dinner; now several restaurants offer it. They have a good-sized menu, and for lunch you can get lighter soups and salads. Being French, they attract many French boats. They also own a couple of moorings that dinner customers may use for free.

Ashore

Although some of the locals look like bad guys in a spaghetti western, for the most part they couldn't be nicer and more helpful. Joseph can sell you fish, and Ricky or Charles will bring round a crate of fruits on his windsurfer. Wesley Roy Mason, also sells produce out of his boat.

Carlos, Brother, Billy, Marlin, and Blackman all have water taxis and arrange coastal trips. Suzanne Stapleton often hangs out in Bay Central and sells her crochet handicrafts, occasionally acting as a guide. Kenny takes lines and guides. Rasta Joseph helps with lines and takes around Juniel who makes her own handicrafts. James sells handicrafts, and Carolyn sells jewelry next to Thelma. Others will take your lines and be generally helpful. You will have to be their judge. Try not to do business with anyone you find aggressive or objectionable in any way. A young man called William sometimes comes out in a borrowed inflatable to take lines. If you use him, agree on price in advance He seems to get angry and cuss rather easily, not the most desirable trait for someone in tourism.

Shamara braids hair and does manicure and pedicure under a palm tree and will give you an artistic nail-art job. Give her a call (531-3336) or ask for her at Mojito's.

Walking here is fun. An easy walk is up Coull's Hill to the north, which rewards you with a great view of the anchorage. Walk back to the road, turn left and keep going. (If you land on the south side of the bay, you must ford a small river, but that is part of the fun.) There is a rum shop on Coull's Hill, just at the point when you are dying for a drink.

Better yet, arrange for someone to take you on the Cumberland Nature Trail in the rain forest. You need transport to get you to the start, which is up above Spring Village.

St. Vincent & the Grenadines

217

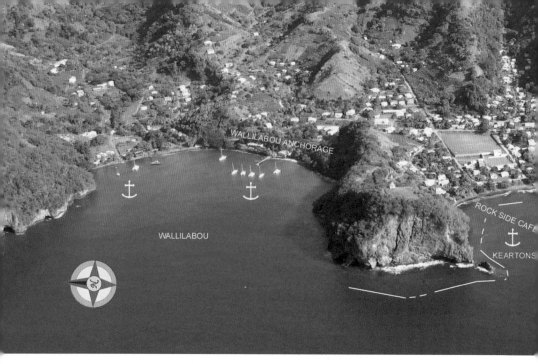

WALLILABOU

Wallilabou, a picturesque bay surrounded by dramatic hills, is about a mile south of Cumberland. Here you are in the heart of St. Vincent, among charming and delightful people. A picturesque tropical waterfall lies just a mile down the road. In 2003, Wallilabou became famous as the main location for the movie "Pirates of the Caribbean," starring Johnny Depp. Wallilabou Anchorage, a pleasant restaurant/hotel, makes part of the waterfront. They maintain a room full of artifacts from the movie, and have some of the props for you to see.

Enter in the middle of the bay and pick up the moorings put down by the Wallilabou Anchorage Restaurant, or anchor where there are no moorings, and tie bow or stern to the wall, or to a tree. In times of northerly swells, the northern corner of the bay is more protected. The bay has long had a reputation for occasional thievery, I was told there were video cameras monitored by the coast guard and security guards with flashlights at the Wallilabou Anchorage Hotel; this did not seem to help, as they had a murder in 2016 currently unsolved. It seems likely the murderers arrived by boat.

Men in rowing boats occasionally approach you from as far as three miles away, asking to take your stern line ashore. Refuse all such offers; there are always plenty of line helpers in Wallilabou itself. The good guys have now organized themselves as an association, and I recommend only using members who carry ID tags. They include Lyndon Davis, Yellowman (Moorings agent), Donald, Joel (Sunsail/Moorings agent), Speed, and Ron Jordan (one of two twin brothers known as the twins).

The going rate for someone to help you with your lines is $20 EC.

You may enjoy buying fruits and vegetables on display by vendors, but beware of the offer to "go fetch you nice produce." The quality of the product rarely matches the description, and if you give money in advance, you may never see the vendor again.

You can also stop in Keartons Bay, one bay south. Rock Side Cafe has five well-maintained bow and stern moorings, which they keep for lunch or dinner guests. Call them before you come in and they will arrange for someone to help you.

Regulations

Customs clearance is available daily between 1700 and 1800. Overtime is charged. It is only customs clearance, and if you are entering you will need to check with immigration at the next port. If you are leaving you will probably get away with customs only.

Communications

Wallilabou Anchorage Restaurant has wifi, for which you need a password. This is good for a year and costs about $5 US. You can get it in the bar, and it may reach your yacht.

Services

Steve and Jane Russell, who run the Wallilabou Anchorage Restaurant [VHF: 68], are keen to attract yachting customers. They have a good dinghy dock and offer moorings ($20 EC, refundable when you eat ashore), free showers, and inexpensive water via a long hose from the dock. Phone, fax, and email communications are available, as are cube ice and overnight accommodation. Do not give garbage to the boat vendors. Most stick it in the rocks. Wrap it well and take it ashore to the restaurant and they will show you where to put it (no charge).

In Keartons, Rock Side Cafe has internet, wifi, laundry, and showers and can provide water to the moorings via a long hose. These are mainly provided for their dinner guests.

If you need a mechanic, Yellowman

is your best bet and can fix most things. If you want to go hiking, talk to Association members Lynden, Donald, Speed, Cedric, or Ron, or set it up with Rock Side Cafe. Local hikes of interest include Soufriere Volcano, Darkview Falls, and Vermont Nature Trails. If you have any problem with any vendor, call the coast guard: 457-5445.

Restaurants

Rock Side Cafe [VHF: 16/68, $A-B] in Keartons, away from the bustle of Wallilabou, is a magical tiny garden oasis overlooking the bay. Orlando, from St. Vincent, and Rosi, from Germany, are the owners. They are the Trans-Ocean Support base and if you need to clear customs they can tell you the way or take you over. They keep moorings for their dinner guests; call and book so they can arrange for someone to help you tie up. You can also walk over from Wallilabou, or ask them to fetch you by car. The small size of this place is part of its charm. You eat outside under a thatched roof. You need to call them to get ashore (they will bring you in or show you the way), as a reef lies along much of the

St. Vincent & the Grenadines

beach. Rosi and Orlando are wonderfully welcoming and treat you as friends. They can also provide water, internet, wifi, showers, fresh produce, and laundry. The food is usually fresh fish and really excellent; visiting is a special experience. Give them at least a couple of hour's notice, if possible.

Orlando has Orlando Adventure Tours, based at Rock Side Cafe. He is a scuba diver and can take qualified people diving and anyone snorkeling. He can also arrange hiking, driving, and boat tours, and for German guests, Rosi often guides.

The Wallilabou Anchorage Hotel, Restaurant and Boutique [VHF: 68, $B-C] has a delightful location where you can eat looking out over your yacht, in a "Pirates of the Caribbean" ambience. Owners Steve, who is from St. Vincent, and his wife Jane, from England, are very pleasant and sometimes are in the bar in the evenings. The restaurant is great for seafood. It serves generous portions of very well-prepared local food, particularly fish, shrimp, and lobster in season. Happy hour, with cheaper drinks, is 1700-1800. They have a small museum, with some magnificent Carib stone head carvings, plus ancient telephones, whalebones, a room of "Pirates" movie artifacts, and lots of tortoises. They will provide a lively little band by special request.

Ron and Ronnie, the twins, have the Golden Spoon Bar in the village, a short walk away, an interesting place for a drink if you want a local experience.

Behind the ruins of the big dock in the north of the bay is the Pirates Retreat. This is a rough-and-ready bar. Come here and have a good rum punch hand-made by the owner Anthony (The Shadow) Edwards, aka Captain Jack Spanner. Anthony is probably the most entertaining character in the bay, and he likes music.

Joel Francois has Pirates Grill [$D] out by the road. It is open every day as a bar and he will fire up the grill given a few hours notice for either a lunch or dinner of chicken, fish and local vegetables. Expect plenty of music and a lively Friday night.

Ashore

A little waterfall garden lies about a

Wallilabou Falls

mile up the road from Wallilabou, with a perfect swimming hole. It is a mini park with a bar, changing rooms, and toilets. Gardens with pretty walkways surround the falls and show the old dam ruins at their best. Bring a towel for a beautiful and refreshing swim; you will feel far from the sea, and it is worth going just to see the magnificent old fig tree that has become part of the wall on the far side of the old dam. Entry is $5 EC per person, and while the park officially closes at 1700, the guard will usually let you in later. The walk here, through lush countryside, is delightful. Go to the main road and turn left; look for the falls on your right. Along the road you will pass Morna's Craft Shop. Here, Berthold does impressive machinery sculptures and weaves great baskets and bowls. He also sells brightly colored t-shirts and his own guava liqueur, from the guava tree outside.

Wallilabou also makes a good base for exploring St. Vincent. The Soufriere volcano, the rainforest, Trinity Falls, and the Vermont Nature Trails are not too far away. The approach to the volcano from this side passes rather close to the center of the Marijuana Growers Association land. This is not a smart place to venture on your own. Arrange for a guide and stay with him.

Water sports

The diving in this area is excellent. For those who like to go on their own, a fair dive can be made right off the rock arch on the northern side of the bay (the snorkeling is good here also). You will find a pleasant reef at 30-40 feet, with lots of colorful sponges and soft corals inhabited by many reef fish, including angelfish.

For other dives you will need a seaworthy dinghy or local pirogue and guide. Castle Cove is off the headland just north

WALLILABOU

KEARTONS

BOTTLE AND GLASS

⚓

BARROUALLIE

of Troumakar Bay. This dive has a fabulous terrain of steep slopes and cliffs full of crevices, holes, and tunnels. The sponges are brightly colored and plenty of hiding places usually harbor lots of fish. The return trip along the top of the cliff makes for some great views, with schools of brown chromis hovering on the edge. We saw spotted drums, angelfish, and slipper lobsters. Seahorses and frogfish are not uncommon here.

Rock Pile is off Mount Wayne (the second long black sand beach south of Barrouallie). This unusual dive is along a massive pile of rocks about 20-30 feet deep. The outer edge of the rocks is shaped much like the bow of a boat, and the presence of an old anchor here makes one wonder whether there may be a wreck buried among the rocks. Rock Pile is very colorful, with many sponges and soft corals. Schools of barracudas are the norm, and lots of moray eels live here. You have a good chance of seeing frogfish.

Peter's Hope is off the old factory south of Barrouallie. This is a colorful shallow reef, from 20 to 60 feet, where you find a lot of king crabs and have a good chance of seeing turtles.

BARROUALLIE

You can easily identify Barrouallie by the conspicuous Bottle and Glass rocks. It is a picturesque local town with a few quaint buildings. People used to stop here to clear customs. That no longer happens,

but if you want to experience a laid-back local village. this is it.

Navigation

If you are coming from the north, give a reasonable clearance to the last visible rock in Bottle and Glass, as there is an underwater rock that extends seaward a few hundred feet. Anchor between the town dock and Pint Rock. There is an adequate anchoring shelf for a quick stop in about 25 feet of water. For overnighting, it is advisable to get one anchor hooked in the shallow water, drop back, and set another in the deeper water, holding the boat bow to the beach. You can tie your dinghy to the town dock. You do not need any line handlers here.

Buccament Bay

Bat Ca...

BUCCAMENT BAY

Buccament Bay lies at the base of the Buccament Valley, one of the longest, deepest and most scenic valleys on the leeward coast. The hills attract showers that often hang there without reaching the coast; in the afternoon, it is not unusual to see an ever-changing rainbow over the valley for up to half an hour at a time.

The bay is well-protected and very calm,

though like any west coast anchorage, it is susceptible to exceptionally bad northerly swells. It is well protected from the southerly surge that can affect other south coast anchorages farther east. The easiest place to anchor is close to the beach from the north corner to the river. The water is very deep off the shelf, so make sure you are well hooked.

Ashore

Buccament Bay Beach Resort is a high-density waterfront resort. As you sail by, it sticks out like a badly fitting toupee: a glowing white beach of imported sand for tourists along this coast of black sand beaches. This does not stop it being a very pleasant place to stop ashore for a meal, though there is rather too much security to make it yacht friendly. You will be stopped and questioned. You can go to one of the restaurants but you will probably have to contact them and have them come escort you in. The Bay is the main beach bar overlooking the pools and the bay. They also offer the Safran, the Bamboo, and a sushi bar. They may not always be open. Some big yachts use the town dock at Layou to the north to drop off paperwork. It is not tender friendly.

Water sports

The snorkeling from this bay round to Petit Byahaut is exceptionally good, with lots of brightly colored sponges, small healthy corals, many reef fish, octopuses, and more.

Bat Cave

Petit Byahaut

Tow your dinghy; anchor it here and there in spots you like, and use it to return when you are tired.

PETIT BYAHAUT

This small and beautiful bay has a little beach backed by hills, with several conspicuous peaky outcroppings of rock. It is a perfect hideaway anchorage with excellent snorkeling. Usually a good overnight anchorage, it is occasionally uncomfortable in southerly swells, when a stern anchor will help cut the roll.

If you are coming from the north, you pass the village of Layou, then Buccament Bay with the big new development. The next major bay is Petit Byahaut. Byahaut Point is a distinctive rounded headland. Pass the headland, head into the bay, and anchor. The seabed is mainly weed ,so make sure you are holding. If you are coming from Kingstown, Byahaut Point is the farthest headland you see after you leave Kingstown Bay, after Camden Park, Questelles, and Clare Valley. Ashore, Petit Byahaut looks private; you may see a small green roof poking out of the vegetation.

Ashore

Petit Byahaut, approachable only by sea, is a charming, edge-of-the-world spot. It used to be a mini tent hotel, which is now ruins, and the bay is for sale.

Water sports

Snorkeling is super in Petit Byahaut Bay and there is excellent snorkeling and diving easily accessible by dinghy right along the coast to Buccament Bay. However, currents can be strong. The bat cave is a short dinghy ride away and can be done as a dive or a snorkel in calm conditions. There is about three feet of water at the cave entrance. You can find somewhere to anchor your dinghy outside, and there is good snorkeling in this area. Inside the cave, it is quite dark, but you can see the bats, which cling by the hundreds to the cave walls and roof. Crabs climb up among the bats. You can just glimpse a tunnel that leads off to the left by the hint of light at the end of it. This tunnel is about 30 feet long and about 4 feet wide. You rise and fall on the swells and if the swells are large, it can be dangerous. The tunnel leads out into a fissure about 30 feet high and 40 feet deep. Below, the water is a brilliant blue. You swim out through the fissure, and divers can dive to two huge rocks at 80 and 130 feet that are covered in sponges and corals and teeming with all kinds of fish. The ascent is up a wall textured with nooks and crannies. If you do the bat cave, it is most important not to disturb the bats. Two species live here: fishing bats (*Noctilio leporinus*), which eat fish and insects, and the St. Vincent fruit-eating bat (*Brachyphylia cavernarum*), which was thought to be extirpated and is in any case endangered. So swim quietly through the cave, without talking or splashing, and don't use flashlights or take flash photographs.

Dinosaur Head is the face of Byahaut Point that faces the anchorage. Below is a 120-foot wall covered in coral, sponges, and seafans. You swim through large schools of tangs and see queen angelfish, eels, snappers, and spotted drums.

OTTLEY HALL

Ottley Hall yachting facility lies just to the west of Kingstown, on the far side of Fort Charlotte.

Services

This yard has a 35-ton travel lift, a 200-

OTTLEY HALL

SCALE IN NAUTICAL MILES

Ottley Hall

ton ship lift, and a dry-dock for anything up to 65 meters long, 15 meters wide, and 6 meters deep. Special covered sheds on rails can be rolled over yachts on the hard or in the dry-dock so that respraying and repainting can be done out of the rain. There is a fuel dock and long-term storage for smaller yachts. A marina area in front of the work space is passable under many conditions, but when swells come in it can be untenable.

Ashore

Ottley Hall has been taken over by a private company, part Vincentian, part Venezuelan. Check it out for yourself and see if it suits.

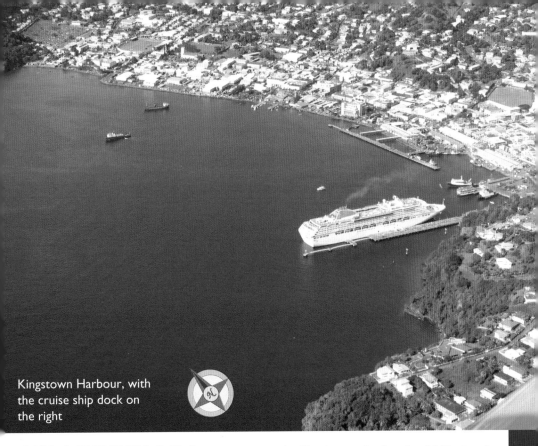

Kingstown Harbour, with the cruise ship dock on the right

KINGSTOWN

Kingstown, St. Vincent's capital, is an interesting local town, for those who want to see the authentic, rough edges and all. It has some charming corners with old stone buildings, cobblestone sidewalks, and handsome arches. The older buildings date back to the late 1700s. An unusual feature of the architecture is that many buildings have pillars on the outside of the pavement supporting floors above, leaving a covered walkway underneath. The new market is a fascinating place to shop, despite the building being architecturally challenged, with a gloomy interior. (Designed by a foreigner, it seems to me a strong argument for governments to have more faith in their own people.) It has several floors of stalls and small shops with excellent fresh fruits and vegetables on the ground floor, clothing and handicrafts upstairs.

Attractions in Kingstown include the botanical gardens (you can walk there) and Fort Charlotte for the great views (take a taxi). Check out the lovely old National Trust building, which has a permanent exhibit of Kalinargo pottery.

The new cruise ship facility has a yacht dock at its inner end where superyachts can tie up to clear customs and provision. Facilities for smaller yachts are poor. You can anchor west of the bus station and may find a space to tie up your dinghy at the cruise ship facility. Keep yacht and dinghy guarded. Most yachtspeople currently visit Kingstown by road or ferry. Taxis and buses are readily available from both Young Island Cut and Blue Lagoon, and ferries connect Kingstown with Bequia.

Regulations

Entry here can be long-winded. Customs are in the baggage hall and are normally fast, but immigration, down the road at the police station, often has long lines of passport applicants. The system is not designed for yachts. It is much better to clear in Blue lagoon. Sam Taxi Service can do it all for you from any anchorage.

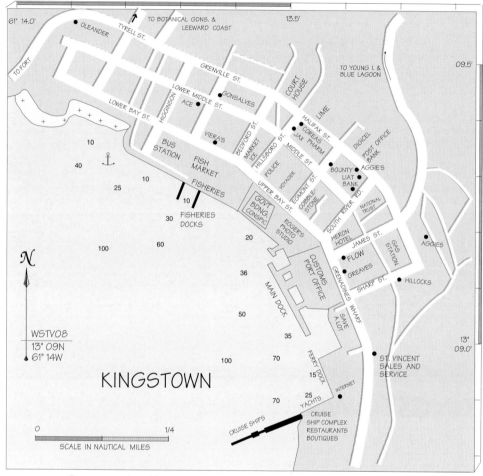

Communications

Internet stations are fast, air-conditioned, and inexpensive. Try the Port Authority Internet cafe, just outside the cruise ship dock, and Computec, on Egmont Street.

Chandlery

For yacht chandlery, look at our section on Young Island Cut and Blue Lagoon. Of interest in Kingstown is St. Vincent Sales and Services, a modern shop conveniently placed opposite the ferry dock. They are a NAPA jobber, have excellent buys on filters, and make hydraulic hoses while you wait.

For more general hardware, visit Ace or Viera, opposite the bus station. They have good buys on silicone seal, 5200, sandpaper, and tools. Trottman's has a good range of electrical supplies, and you can find several lumber yards, as well as plumbing and hardware stores.

Provisioning

The biggest and best downtown supermarket is C.K. Greaves, which is open 0800-1700 Monday to Thursday, 0800-1900 on Fridays, and 0700-1300 on Saturdays. Its subsidiary by the airport is open till 2000 nightly, except Thursdays and Fridays, when it opens till 2100, and Sundays, when it opens 0800-1100. The Greaves, in town, gives a charter yacht discount (just tell the cashier), and delivery to Young Island Cut is negotiable (talk to a supervisor). Products include delicatessen meats, smoked fish, French cheeses, whipping cream, and a good selection of wines and liquors. You can contact them in advance for a full provisioning service, and if you need anything they do not

226

have, they will buy it for you.

Opposite Greaves, Massy's is another big supermarket with excellent buys on some items.

The local market and surrounding area is overflowing with fresh produce at prices generally much more reasonable than on the other windwards.

Gonsalves is a state-of-the-art wine and liquor shop set in a historic building with a climate-controlled wine cellar in a lovely old brick room, one of the nicest wine stores of its type in the Windwards. It is a pleasure to visit. They sell wholesale as well as retail and have a huge selection from all over the world. You can contact them in advance for a list of products. They will deliver to the nearest dock, and their staff can give good advice on their wines. They are open Monday to Friday 0800-1700, and Saturday 0800-1300.

Fun shopping

Shopping in Kingstown can be fun ~ the stores are all interesting and local. You sometimes find car batteries rubbing shoulders with fabrics. Department stores include Laynes and Jax. Middle Street is quaint and like a local clothing market, with stalls down much of one side.

For boutiques geared to tourists, wander down to the cruise ship complex.

Restaurants

Andrew and Jolene's Flow wine bar is excellent and a great choice. It opens weekdays at 1100 and Saturdays at 1800. The entrance, which is poorly signposted, is upstairs over Subway. Walk up a flight of stairs away from the bustle of town into Flow's casually elegant ambience. They offer a good selection of wines, as well as Krew beers that they brew themselves, including Isle IPA, Duppy brown, and Snapper red ale. For food, they offer many delightful tapas-sized dishes, sandwiches, salads and pizzas. It is all freshly made and artistically served.

You can climb up the stairs to Flyt where a couple of tables are amid the rooftops. Pleasant at night it has views over Kingstown and the hills around and is popular with smokers.

Basil's, in the Cobblestone Inn [$C], is cool, spacious, and sociable. Here you can get a first-rate lunch buffet, and this is where everyone meets. Or head round the back and upstairs to the roof garden, where you can get a meal with a good view.

Several small lunch places [$D] are on

St. Vincent & the Grenadines

WILKIE'S

YOUNG ISLAND

YOUNG ISLAND CU

the cruise ship pier area. You can sit in the open overlooking the bay and take your choice. Mona's is usually open and good for local food.

To get to Sid and Michelle's Oleander [$A-B], walk right down Grenville Street to just past the cemetery and it is on your left in a lovely old Caribbean house. It is not only a restaurant, but also a fancy little boutique and flower shop. They open for lunch only Monday to Saturday, and serve dinner on Friday. The daily menu is posted on a blackboard and always contains both seafood and meat. Sid has run many excellent restaurants, and the food is very good. It is small, so reservations are a good idea. .

Grenadine House [$A-C] is a really nice upmarket restaurant with excellent food. It is in a hotel and part of the same group as Bequia Beach Hotel in Bequia. Take a short taxi ride there. You can walk back.

Fort Duvenette

THE SOUTH COAST OF ST. VINCENT

Navigation

The current along this coast is predominantly westward, up to two knots. It reverses weakly to the east for a few hours on the rising tide, which can create choppy seas.

When leaving Kingstown for Young Island, give the headland good clearance, as there is a submerged rock about 200 feet south of its eastern end.

Two good anchorages, Young Island Cut and Blue Lagoon, lie close together. Both are well served by buses to Kingstown, and are well placed for exploring St. Vincent. These anchorages are within dinghy reach of each other, and we treat them as one area.

Several bareboat companies have bases here, including Barefoot Yacht Charters, Dream Yachts, and Horizon.

The closest supermarkets and shopping area are near to the airport, a short taxi ride away. Cooking gas is in this area, at the filling station just before the airport.

YOUNG ISLAND TO
BLUE LAGOON

0   1/4

SCALE IN N.M.
NOTE: BLUE LAGOON IS FULL OF MOORINGS
WITH VERY LITTLE ROOM TO ANCHOR.
THEY ARE AVAILABLE FOR RENT

YOUNG ISLAND CUT & BLUE LAGOON

The coast from Young island to Blue Lagoon is St. Vincent's main yachting center, with several charter companies and plenty of services. It is a lovely area, with the first-rate Blue lagoon Marina and Hotel and several places to anchor, as well as a big choice of restaurants and bars. This is a marine park area; the water is clear, with plenty of reefs and good snorkeling. You can climb the historic Fort Duvernette. This is an excellent spot to use as a base to explore St. Vincent and hike the volcano.

Blue Lagoon is a pleasant reef-enclosed bay with a beach backed by palm trees. You can lie comfortably, protected by land and reef. Large beacons mark the main shoals between Blue Lagoon and Young Island (see sketch chart). These are in fairly shallow water, so do not cut them too fine.

Two large beacons (red and green) mark the entrance channel. Pass between them.

The water is deeper a shade north of the center. After that, head straight across the reef into deep water. Depths in the channel vary with the tide, from about five feet nine inches to about seven-and-a-half feet. Call Blue Lagoon Marina on VHF: 68, or Desmond the dockmaster (528-2416) for the state of the tide. Kelly, who owns Blue Lagoon Marina, plans to deepen this channel and mark the deeper one on the south. Until that happens, do not use the south one, as it is dangerous and has gotten many a yacht in trouble. If you are really in a hurry, the marina or one of the charter companies can have Ras Mike pilot you in for $20 US.

Once inside, you can tie up at the marina or pick up one of the many moorings, which have a good record for reliability. Fourteen of the most comfortable ones belong to the marina, and the fee of $25 US per night includes free wifi. About 20 belong to Barefoot Yacht Charters, $15 US (some are a little rolly). Three belong to Ras Mike who charges $20 US a night and is negotiable

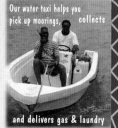
for stays of several days. You can try and call him to arrange one: 496-7783, but cell phone number management is not his strong suit.

Young Island Cut lies in clear water between Young Island and the mainland. Young Island Cut is open and easily entered from the west. The channel to the east of Young Island curves, is narrow, and is best given a miss, even with the beacons. At night, the lights of Young Island take on a fairy-tale look.

You have to anchor with care. The current sweeps through both ways and the center of the cut goes as deep as 60 feet. There is good holding in the northern or western parts of the anchorage, but it occasionally rolls. Anchoring bow and stern is essential or your boat will swing with the change of current and bang into someone else. Holding is poor close to Young Island. Young Island's electrical cable carries 11,000 volts, enough to make your whole boat glow, so anchor well clear or use a mooring.

Moorings are available in Young Island Cut and are a great help, as anchoring is not

easy. The present system of unauthorized moorings is managed by Sam Taxi Tours and Charlie Tango, who both feel that if you rent one of their moorings, you should also take their taxi. To avoid two boats competing for your business when you arrive, call on the VHF and book your mooring in advance. Mooring rates for boats up to 80 feet are $20 US. Charlie charges the same for bigger boats. Sam charges $29 for larger boats. As with all private moorings, do your best to check them for yourself. Charlie is a diver and does check.

You can also anchor outside the lagoon off the St. Vincent Yacht Club dock and Barefoot. This tends to be more rolly than tucked well up in the Lagoon.

Regulations

Blue Lagoon Marina has customs open daily from about 0800 to 1800. The office is just to the west of the main building, in the same area as Flowt. Clearance here is simple, fast and good.

Communications

Blue Lagoon Marina has good wifi, as does nearly every bar and restaurant. Sam Taxi Tours has a wifi system that works both in Young Island Cut and Bequia. Beachcombers has an internet computer during normal business hours.

General yacht services

The Blue Lagoon Marina and Hotel [VHF: 68] is a pleasant marina with wide floating docks. Electricity (110/220-volt, 50 cycles) can be arranged at the dock. If you prefer, you can take one of their moorings ($25 US per night). Top up on water, fuel (both diesel and gasoline), and ice. Other services include showers, a laundry ($82 EC for a big machine load), and free wifi. Desmond the dockmaster (528-2416) will help you in, and the main desk will find you anything you need, like taxis and rental cars. Mark Solomon, the manager, is welcoming, friendly and helpful, as are all the staff. Kelly and Janke Glass, who own the marina, have done a wonderful job of converting a very basic boatel into a lovely and elegant little boutique hotel and marina which is a real pleasure to visit.

A wide board-walk carries you round the marina and to the beach. The cafe, beach bar and a restaurant are all delightful. Should you want a night ashore, they have lovely rooms with balconies looking out over the lagoon. Several charter companies, includ-

ing Horizon and Dreamyachts, use this as a base. It is home to Indigo Dive shop.

Phillip Barnard, his mother Mary, and Seth run Barefoot Charters and Marine Center [VHF: 68]. They are the only charter company here that has an ASA-accredited sailing school. Their dock is on the outside of the reef, with about 6.5 feet at the end at low tide, and they have about six moorings outside and 20 moorings inside. They offer diesel, laundry, water and ice, full communications, a travel agency, and air charter service. They rent reliable moorings ($15 US a night). Barefoot has five lovely balconied rooms with views available for nights ashore, and their center includes a shop, restaurant, sail loft, and other services. They can often fill cooking gas bottles.

The St. Vincent Yacht Club is a yacht dock outside the reef. Reg and Reggie Adams have built a basic docking facility along the foreshore to the east of Barefoot. The depth off the dock is about 6 feet on the eastern end and 7 feet on the western end, but the water gets deeper rapidly and deeper-draft boats can come in stern-to on the western part. Multihulls can easily make it on the eastern end, but check out the depths first. The docks have water and electricity. The building includes a restaurant and seven rooms for a night ashore, each with a big balcony overlooking the bay.

Sam, of Sam Taxi Tours [VHF: 68], is one of those who rents moorings in Young

Island Cut. Sam is an agent for large yachts and even cruise ships. With agents in Mustique, Bequia, Canouan, and Union, Sam can handle big yacht needs right through the islands. His customs clearance is very popular, and he can arrange it anywhere, even the Tobago Cays through his agent in Union. Sam charges $80 US for yachts up 80 feet, and up to $400 US for really large yachts with many people. (Extra transportation charges are applicable in some anchorages.)

His crew does laundry and fills gas bottles. Sam Taxi Service handles communications (including email), and many skippers get their spares sent here, which Sam will clear through customs. Sam Taxi Tours also rents cars and has a fleet of taxis for scenic or shopping trips, and he arranges duty-free fuel bunkering for larger yachts. He will collect and dispose of well-wrapped garbage in Young Island ($5 EC a bag).

Charlie Tango [VHF: 68] is the other moorings man; Charlie runs a full taxi and tour service, has apartments to rent, and will help in any way he can. He is also a diver so works on his own moorings.

Erika's Marine Services is another superyacht agency based in Union Island. They, too, have agents in St. Vincent, Bequia, Mustique, and Canouan. (See *Union Island* for a full description.)

Chandlery

Barefoot Charters and Marine Center keep a good stock of spares for their boats and will help cruisers if they need a part, or they will order parts from the catalogs. They work with Budget Marine and Lewis Marine and will bring in anything at catalog price plus freight; they are good and efficient, and can often get parts not in the catalogs.

KP Marine, owned by Keith Howard, is the sales and service agent for Yamaha outboards, which in St. Vincent are duty-free. His prices are among the best. Between KP and Howard Marine (same owner) across the street, you can buy Yamaha and Johnson outboards and Yanmar inboards. KP Marine also stocks general chandlery, with chain,

St. Vincent & the Grenadines

Enjoy the comfort of trade-wind sailing with a one-way charter

St. Vincent to Grenada

Horizon Yacht Charters | +1 784 456 9395 • info@horizonstvincent.com • www.horizonyachtcharters.com

anchors, rope, antifouling paint, resins, West system epoxy, some electronics, and more. Two-stroke outboard oils are available wholesale for those with large engines. They sell to both local fishermen and powerboat enthusiasts. They are in Calliaqua opposite Howard Marine.

Technical yacht services

Barefoot Charters and Marine Center is your best bet for sorting out any boat problems; they have an excellent services center. This includes a large new sail loft run by Phillip Barnard, a top racing sailor, who knows about racing sails as well as cruising ones. They sell and service both Doyle and North Sails and will take care of the measurement and fitting. They repair sails, do cushions and canvas, and can make bimini frames. They weld Weblon and True Tarp, so you can get a stitch-free top that does not leak. They can do small onboard weld repairs. They are agents for Harken and can help out with rigging.

Barefoot repairs and maintains all kinds of diesel engine; they run diesel engine repair courses, and can help you with your engine. They do good gel-coat matching and cosmetic repairs. In addition, they sell Raymarine and Tacktic and can help install it. You can also talk to them if you have an electronics problem.

Horizon Yachts is a charter company that has found that the team that keeps their boats can help maintain and fix yours. They offer help with all repairs and maintenance, and if you wish to leave your boat in their care or have a full refit, you can arrange it here, though they will want to do most work in Grenada.

Howard Marine [VHF: 68] fixes all makes of outboard and they are agents for Johnson. They are happy to fix all diesels, and are agents for Yanmar.

Verrol, at Nichols Marine, has an efficient mechanized workshop where he repairs and reconditions alternators and starter motors in a few hours. They come back looking and working like new. Call him on the telephone and he will come and sort out your problem, wherever you are in St. Vincent. (In Bequia, you can leave things for him with

GYE.) Verrol's workshop is in Belaire, just behind the airport, which is closer to the south coast than to town. Oscar's Machine Center is a few houses down from Verrol. Oscar is good and can do all manner of jobs on all kinds of metals, resurface engine blocks, or fix your old winches.

Provisioning

In Blue Lagoon Marina Gold Doubloon is a food store, open every day from 1000-1800. Convenient for picking up heavy items like bottled water as you can bring your dinghy very close.

In Calliaqua, you can sometimes buy fish from the fish market in the afternoon when the boats come in ~ try around 1600.

The road around the airport is becoming a major shopping area. It is easy and cheap, though occasionally terrifying, to catch a bus to this area or to town. Bus drivers usually have music at full blast and handle their vehicles like racing cars. There are plenty of buses, but in the mornings quite a few are full.

Sunrise Supermarket, opposite the airport terminal, is one of the biggest and best markets, part of C.K. Greaves.

From Greaves, Massy's supermarket is on the left heading toward Calliaqua. Nearby is a large Ace hardware store.

Several more supermarkets are on the Young Island side of the airport. Delco has not only food but quite a selection of hardware. Another new supermarket lies just round the corner. Trotmans has a branch of their electrical store a little farther toward the airport on the right side of the road.

Fun Shopping

Wander up to the top of Barefoot and check out their Surf Shop and Boutique. They stock good-quality foul-weather gear essentials, casual wear, hats, jewelry, souvenirs, and even sandals. Ask here about snorkeling gear; it may not be in the shop, but Barefoot rents snorkeling gear and has some new stock for sale.

Blue Lagoon Marina has two boutiques, Caribbean Lifestyles and the marina boutique at the entrance.

Café Soleil

Life just got a little bit sweeter!

BREAKFAST   LUNCH   DINNER

BLUE LAGOON MARINA | ST. VINCENT & THE GRENADINES | WEST INDIES | TEL (784) 456 8550

/CAFESOLEIL1

Restaurants

There are many restaurants. Some are on a boardwalk that runs from The French Verandah to the beach. Along the beach are more, and others are in Blue Lagoon Marina and Barefoot Yachts.

In the marina, the popular Cafe Soleil [$B-C] adds a touch of continental elegance with its outside seating under shades on two sides of the Marina board walk; open to the bay and beach, it is a perfect setting, as long as it is not raining (they have a little inside room in case it is). It a great place to start the day with breakfast, and it stays open all day, with a big variety of tasty food which includes, starters and snacks, a collections of fresh salads, soups and sandwiches, seafood and meat dishes, and ice creams and desserts.

The Loft [$A-B], upstairs in Lagoon Marina, has a sweeping panoramic view of the marina, the bay and the beach. The bar is a great hangout, and the restaurant is open from breakfast through dinner. The service is attentive and friendly. It is a tad more upmarket than the other marina restaurants, and you will enjoy the food, which is more

St. Vincent & the Grenadines

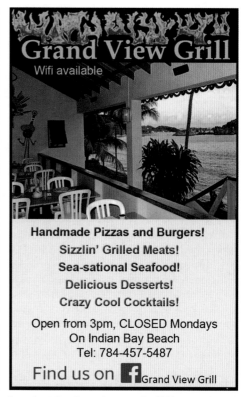
elaborate and artistically served, with well thought out combinations of flavors, using fresh local ingredients.

Also in Blue Lagoon, Flowt Beach Bar [$D, closed Tuesdays] is an ideal cruiser's bar; a shack on the beach, with seats on a deck. They open at noon and keep going till the last person leaves. You can get inexpensive local grilled fish, burgers, and chicken, along with chips or vegetables. The food is simple but beautifully cooked, making it a prime choice when you cannot be bothered to cook for yourself. If you see a sailing yacht enter the lagoon (under sail or power), call it out to the barman and you will get your next drink half-price.

If you look west from Young island Cut, you will see a large building at the end of the beach, to the west of Young Island Cut, in Indian Bay. This is the Grand View Beach Hotel, one of St. Vincent's treasured hotels, opened in 1964, and owned by the Sardine family. By day the adventurous can walk there by going up the road at the end of the Young Island Cut beach, down the other side to the next beach, then follow the

beach. The Grand View Grill [$B-D, closed Mondays], on the beach, opens at 1500 and the kitchen stays open until 2200. This is a great place to relax. They serve pizzas, grilled meats, crazy cocktails and everything in between.

Up the hill, the hotel pool has one of St. Vincent's most panoramic views from atop a cactus knoll, and Wilkie's Restaurant [$A-D] is open for breakfast and lunch daily, with dinner by reservation. Grand View has squash and tennis courts, and a gym with yoga and pilates classes available to the public.

Some of the most pleasant restaurants here are up a few steps, on broad verandas overlooking the sea. One of them is Barefoot's Driftwood Restaurant and Lounge [VHF: 68, $B-C]. It is very comfortable, with a touch of elegance and a great open view south to Bequia. They have a big choice of good food, including fresh seafood, burgers, baby back ribs, pastas, pizzas and salads. It is sometimes packed in the evening, so to be sure of a table for dinner, make a reservation. If you blow it, you can always eat at the bar.

236

Young Island

Back in Young island Cut, Beachcombers [VHF: 68, $B-D] is at the western end of the beach. You can leave your dinghy at one of the docks in Young Island Cut and walk down the boardwalk to the beach. Depending on the tide, you may need to time waves or risk getting your feet wet. Steps lead up from the beach to their large wooden sunning/pool deck with the adjoining restaurant open to the view. It is airy and pleasant, with a view of the sea framed by almond trees. Delightful flower gardens are in back. Seafood, local specialties, snacks, wraps, burgers, and more are available. They are open all day every day. Beachcombers has rooms for rent and a popular health spa and a gymnasium.

The Mariners Hotel and its French Verandah restaurant [$A-B] is owned and run by Vidal Browne, who also has a big share in Young Island Hotel and has been in the hotel business for years. They have their own dinghy dock. They serve fine French food and, on the lighter side, milk shakes and ice creams.

High Tide [$B-D, closed Monday] is another lovely restaurant which looks towards Young island and has a good dinghy dock. It is owned by the Greaves family and managed by Desiree. They can supply water on the dock, but the depth at the end of the dock is only 4-5 feet. They open most days at 1600, Sundays at noon. They have a huge menu, with everything from salads and snacks (including good rotis) to a full shrimp, steak, or fresh fish meal. They also offer showers, which are free if you are eating.

On the beach, Paradise Beach Hotel [$B] is run by Earl and Kim Halbich, who also own the Fantasea tour operation. It is large and open, serving good local food, and it is a very pleasant place to eat. They have a very popular captain's barbecue on Fridays from 1900. They have rooms for a night or two ashore.

Sunset Shores is a slightly formal hotel with a pool, just behind the beach. The cooking is international.

Boat Club [$C-D] is an informal local hangout with music. They open daily from about 0700 till late at night and serve local food, occasionally hosting karaoke and other parties. Their pool table is often in use.

Across the water, with a good dinghy dock, Young Island Resort [VHF: 68, $A] is a wonderful place of tropical flowers and trees, and well worth a visit for a sundowner. They have a steel band and other entertainment on a weekly basis (call for details). If you wish to dine at Young Island Resort, make reservations in advance.

Take a stroll into Calliaqua, just a few steps from the St. Vincent Yacht Club, and check out Maryna Bar and Grill [$C-D] in the green building. It is owned by Don Martin, who was doing chart checkouts when I first came here and told me what to put in the guides. They open Monday to Saturday from 1000 and serve good snacks and meals, including rotis, seafood chowder, and grilled fresh fish.

Sue's Surfside Restaurant [$B-C] is also in Calliaqua, but it has its own dinghy dock (look for the small thatched shelter). She runs a good restaurant, that serves pizzas and snacks, along with grilled fish and chicken.

The Yacht Club have their own (Mrs Seappy's) bar and restaurant, good for beers and local snacks.

Ashore

Fort Duvernette stands behind Young Island, a monument to the ingenuity of the soldiers of a bygone age, who managed to get cannons up to the top. Fort Duvernette was used in the late 18th century, when the settlers were fighting off the Black Caribs

St. Vincent & the Grenadines

237

inland and the French at sea. Cannons face in both directions. There is a small place to tie a dinghy. About 250 concrete steps take you up. After being abandoned for some years, these were rebuilt in 2011 with the help of a grant from Finland to the National Trust. The views from the top are splendid, and if you take lunch up, you can enjoy it at a shaded table.

Blue Lagoon and Young Island are ideally situated to visit St. Vincent's interior. Make every effort to spend a few hours at Montreal Gardens in the Mesopotamia Valley. The drive through this rich agricultural valley is reward enough in itself, with spectacular views in every direction. Montreal Gardens, tucked in right at the head of the valley against the steep mountains, is the most spectacular garden in the Eastern Caribbean. Owner Tim Vaughn and his team have taken seven acres and created a totally crazy and beautiful space. Their art has been planning and planting and then letting nature run riot with the plants, so rather than being well ordered and neat, it is wild and jungly and brilliantly colorful. There are winding paths, bridges, steps, and a river, all among brilliant tropical flowers. The only sounds are running water and bird song. You feel like you are in a fantasy world. He charges a very nominal fee for entry. You can see the gardens in an hour, but much better, spend several and really soak up the atmosphere. Bring lunch and enjoy it in one of the garden shelters. (Montreal Gardens is open December to August, Monday to Friday, 0900-1600 only.) You can sometimes get Tim on his cell: 432-6840. The taxi fare is high enough that you might want to have four to share. You can also take buses. First, take one to the roundabout at Arnos Vale at the top of the current (not new) airport. Take the next bus to Richland Park Junction. Get the driver to show you the road; it is a two-mile walk from there. You can also ask if he would take you there for an extra fee. (If you start in Kingstown, just get the bus to Richland Park Junction.)

Another world-class hike that is easy to do from here is the St. Vincent volcano. It takes a whole day, but it is a day you will always remember.

Transport

Blue Lagoon is a good place to leave your boat while you explore ashore. The marina can arrange a car rental or call you one of their taxi drivers, Ivan Oliver (529-1222) or Harold (493-3779).

If you are down in Young Island, Sam Taxi Tours and Charlie Tango are the main taxi men.

Water sports

Diving in St. Vincent is really wonderful. The rugged shoreline is equally dramatic below the surface. Walls and reefs that drop far deeper than any sane person can dive are common, and fish are everywhere ~ feeding in schools, tucked under rocks, and hiding in sponges. The long coastline and the presence of only a few divers has kept this environment pristine.

Right in the Marina, Indigo Dive is run by David and Luiz Fery. David is American, ex-air force, who previously taught in Curacao. He speaks English and Spanish and his wife is Spanish. It is a PADI shop and they have the hotel pool for teaching purposes. They have a very fast 25-foot boat and take a maximum of eight divers. They normally go diving at 0930 and 1430.

You will also enjoy diving or snorkeling with Vaughn Martin at Serenity Dive. He used to run the Canouan dive shop and has now opened his own. You will find him helpful, friendly and enthusiastic. The dive shop is in the yacht club complex.

Dive St. Vincent [VHF: 68], facing the main Young Island dock, is owned by Padi/Naui instructor Bill Tewes and run by Jackie, DJ, and Cally. They usually head out for a one- or two-tank dive around 0900 in the morning. They also rent both diving and snorkeling gear to yachts heading out on charter.

Barefoot Yachts has a snorkeling shop where you can rent snorkeling gear when going on charter.

Fantasea Tours has four excellent boats for tours and a water taxi service and is run by Earl and Kim Halbich. They do coastal and whale-watching trips and often take charter guests to and from their boats in other islands. They are based in Young Island Cut,

St. Vincent & the Grenadines

at the Paradise Beach Hotel, where Fantasea also has a cute boutique.

Those diving on their own will find the base of Fort Duvernette easily accessible, though you do have to be mindful of the current that tries to sweep you out to sea. Anchor your dinghy to the west of the Fort Duvernette dinghy dock. Follow the base of Fort Duvernette down. Almost as soon as you begin you will be surrounded by large schools of brown chromis. At 40 feet you find yourself in a pleasant area of house-sized boulders, with nooks and crannies where eels, shrimps, and angelfish hide out. Large schools of sergeant majors hug the rocks, while jacks, mackerels, and schools of margates patrol a little farther out.

Other, even better dives are best done with a local dive shop, as the anchorages are dangerous for yachts and local knowledge about the currents is essential. Bottle Reef, under Fort Charlotte, starts at 25 feet. You descend along the foot of an underwater rock headland. On your right is a gentle slope of coral, decorated by sponges and many smaller soft corals. On the left, the headland turns into a sheer wall adorned by deep-water sea fans. There are small bushes of black coral in several colors. At the bottom we found several cherub fish. These little critters, the smallest of the angelfish, are only a couple of inches long. You round the bottom of the headland at 100 feet and ascend through huge schools of grunts and even larger schools of brown chromis that seem to explode into a variety of patterns all around. There is always a chance of finding ancient bottles. A curious current pattern here makes it possible to have the current with you the whole way.

Kingstown South is on the south side of Kingstown Harbor. You can see by looking at the sheer cliffs above and the schooling chromis below that this will be an interesting dive. The descent is down a steep slope, and this is the place to look for the unusual red-banded lobster. This colorful little crustacean is clearly marked in bands and spots of red, white, and gold. Unlike other Caribbean lobsters, it has claws, though they are tiny. We saw one when we finished our descent and three more later, as well as a slipper lobster and the more normal spiny lobster. We circled slowly counter-clockwise up the slope, looking at sponges, corals, and big rocks. You often see large pelagic fish swimming out toward the sea. Among the many reef fish you will meet are spotted drums and filefish. There are also three wreck dives in the harbor. One is an ancient French sailing frigate. There is not much left but you might get lucky and find a bottle.

There is a good advanced wreck dive in Camden Park. The Romark, a 160-foot freighter, sits upright on the bottom in excellent condition. It is deep (mast at 55 feet, bottom at 135 feet).

New Guinea Reef is on the east side of Petit Byahaut. This spectacular dive takes you down a wall to 90 feet, where large black corals occur in bushes of white, pink, dark green, light green, brown, and red. Fish include black jacks, parrotfish, French angelfish, and occasional sightings of the rather rare frilled goby, frogfish, and seahorses. An overhang near the bottom makes this dive visually spectacular.

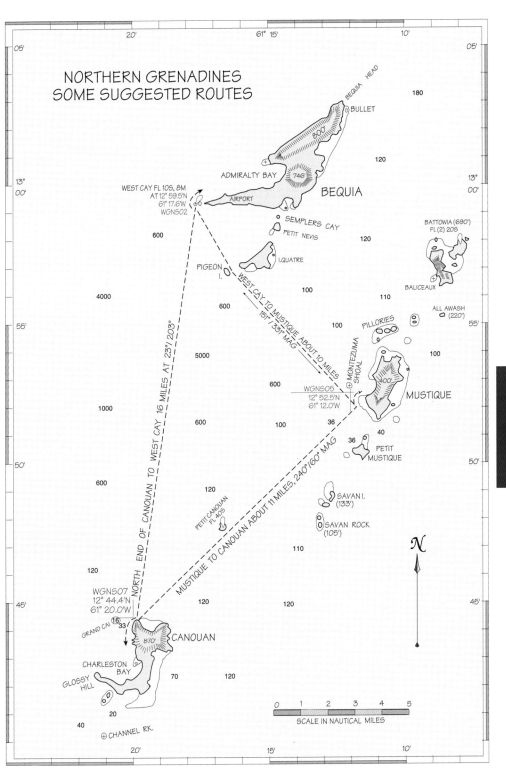

NORTHERN GRENADINES
SOME SUGGESTED ROUTES

BEQUIA HEAD

BULLET

180

800

120

746

+

ADMIRALTY BAY

BEQUIA

WEST CAY FL 10S, 8M
AT 12° 59.5'N
61° 17.6'W
WGNS02

AIRPORT

SEMPLERS CAY

PETIT NEVIS

120

BATTOWIA (690')
FL (2) 20S

600

PIGEON
I.

I.QUATRE

100

BALICEAUX

4000

600

110

ALL AWASH
(220')

55'

5000

PILLORIES

100

MONTEZUMA
SHOAL

100

WGNS05
12° 52.5'N
61° 12.0'W

400

MUSTIQUE

1000

600

100

36

40

600

36

PETIT
MUSTIQUE

600

120

SAVAN I.
(133')

PETIT CANOUAN
FL 40S

SAVAN ROCK
(105')

110

N

120

WGNS07
12° 44.4'N
61° 20.0'W

120

120

GRAND CAI 16 33

CANOUAN

870'

CHARLESTON
BAY

70

120

GLOSSY
HILL

20

40

CHANNEL RK.

WEST CAY TO MUSTIQUE ABOUT 10 MILES
151° / 331° MAG.

NORTH END OF CANOUAN TO WEST CAY 16 MILES AT 23°/ 203°

MUSTIQUE TO CANOUAN ABOUT 11 MILES, 240°/60° MAG.

0   1   2   3   4   5
SCALE IN NAUTICAL MILES

St Vincent & the Grenadines

NORTHERN GRENADINES PASSAGES

Bequia and Mustique, in the northern Grenadines, are both frequently visited by yachtspeople. Although only about eight miles apart geographically at their closest points, they are very different from each other.

Navigation

A strong current sets to the west throughout the Grenadines. Its effect is particularly noticeable in the Bequia and Canouan channels, so whether you head north or south, it is advisable to point east of your destination and check your bearings periodically to see how much you are being set. There is least set when the tidal stream runs counter to the regular current, but this is a mixed blessing, since the seas become rougher and sometimes positively uncomfortable. The roughest seas are to be found just north of Canouan and off the Bequia side of the Bequia Channel, especially up by Bequia Head. It is not unusual for the current to be going in two different directions on opposite sides of the channel.

St. Vincent to Bequia

The passage from Young Island Cut and Blue Lagoon in St. Vincent to Bequia is usually pleasant, off-the-wind sailing. It is closer to the wind if you are coming from St. Vincent's west coast, but usually still easily done on one tack.

Although Admiralty Bay is hidden till you get quite close, you can usually see the headland that you have to round, because it stands out against the more distant land behind. Look behind you to see which way you are being set by the current, and make adjustments so you stay on course. Big seas can lead to a little exciting surfing, and one often covers the eight or nine miles in about an hour and a half. Be prepared for the Bequia Blast after the lee of Devil's Table. Many drop their sails here, but if you fancy an exhilarating

ST. VINCENT TO BEQUIA AND MUSTIQUE

short beat, keep going. When approaching Devil's Table, you might notice what appears to be a madman zooming around your yacht, standing up in a tiny inflatable and being badly bounced by the waves. Fear not ~ it is just Kenmore Henville, who makes his living taking photographs of arriving yachts. If he takes your yacht's picture, he will bring a proof for you to see. There is no obligation to buy. If you want to be sure of a picture, call him in advance.

Sailing the other way is a different matter. To make Young Island or Blue Lagoon from Admiralty Bay, you normally have to tack to windward against a foul current. It usually takes two hours and can take three or more. It is generally quicker to tack or motor sail up the Bequia coast and then shoot across from Anse Chemin, the bay just southwest of Bequia Head. This is fine in calm weather, but on rough days you can sail straight into a range of liquid mountains near Bequia Head. If the seas are rough, head straight over to St. Vincent and then work back up the coast.

Sailing to the west coast of St. Vincent is usually a fine reach.

St. Vincent to Mustique

The trip between Blue Lagoon and Mustique is about 15 miles, and in good going it takes two-and-a-half to three hours. The seas around the north end of Bequia can be very rough, but one often gets an exhilarating reach. Whether you are sailing north or south, keep well off Bequia Head and the Bullet, as the current pulls you down that way. Otherwise, just strap everything down, hang on tight, and ride 'em!

Bequia to Mustique

Most people approach Mustique from Admiralty Bay. The easiest way is to round West Cay and sail out between Pigeon Island and Isle de Quatre. As you approach Mustique, Montezuma Shoal is a real danger, more so now since the big beacon washed away and has been replaced by a buoy. Keep well clear.

There are passages between Semplers Cay and Petit Nevis, and between Petit Nevis and Isle de Quatre, but they can be very rough and the current extremely rapid. Furthermore, there is a reef extending well south of Petit Nevis, so serious thought should be given to prevailing conditions before choosing either of these routes. It is an easy seven-mile reach from Friendship Bay to Mustique or back.

Bequia to Canouan

As you round West Cay (Bequia) and head south, it will be possible to see Petit Canouan. If the visibility is good, Canouan itself will be in sight. Glossy (Glass) Hill, the southwestern point of Canouan, is joined to the rest of the land by a low isthmus that stays below the horizon till you get quite close, so from a distance, Glossy Hill looks like a separate island.

Mustique to Canouan

This trip can be a rolly run, with the wind right behind. I often tack downwind to make it a reach.

Canouan

Deep draft vessels (over 12 feet) should avoid Grand Cai, a small, isolated 16-foot shoal about 0.75 miles west of Jupiter Point at 12° 44.490'N, 61° 20.645'W. Seas in this area are often 6-8 feet high.

| BATTOWIA | BALICEAUX | The Bullet | *BEQUIA HEAD* | Anse Chemin | | Devil's Table **ADMIRALTY BAY** round the corner | West Cay |

Approaching Bequia from St. Vincent

Regulations

Port Elizabeth is a port of entry for St. Vincent and the Grenadines. The procedure is simple.

The entry charge is $35 EC per person per month, unless you leave within that month, in which case you pay again when you reenter. In addition, charter yachts based outside St. Vincent are charged $5 EC per foot per month plus a $125 occasional license fee. You can cruise here as long as you wish. You will normally be stamped in for a month, and then return for extensions, which are in the same office and easy to obtain. Forms may cost a few dollars.

Customs is open weekdays 0830-1800 (overtime after 1600). On Saturdays, they open 0830-1200 and (overtime) 1500-1800. Sundays and holidays, they open (overtime) 0900-1200 and 1500-1800.

Overtime fees are Sundays/holidays, customs $63 EC, immigration $50 EC, other days, customs $45 EC, immigration $35 EC.

Jet skis and the like are strictly forbidden throughout the Grenadines, as is spearfishing by visitors (see also *St. Vincent*).

Garbage must be taken to the facility by the market, or you can pay Daffodil to take it. Do not give it to other vendors.

Shopping Hours

Office and bank hours are as for St. Vincent. Most stores open 0800-1200 and 1400-1700.

Telephones

Card and coin phones may be found near the tourist office. You can buy cell phone cards in lots of stores. See also *St. Vincent*.

Holidays

See *St. Vincent*.

Transport

Inexpensive buses run to many parts of the island. (Ask in the little tourist office on the quay.) Taxis are plentiful and reasonable. Sample taxi rates for up to four people are:

	$EC
Most rides	20
Longer rides	25-40
Tours	81 per hour

(for 5+ $6 US per person per hour)

Rental jeeps and motorbikes are available. You need to buy a local license, which costs $65 EC. Drive on the left.

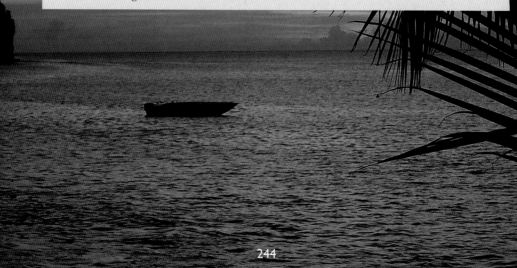

THE YACHT CLUB
Bequia Marina

MARINA
dockage / power / fuel / ice / water

RESTAURANT & BAR
good food / tasty drinks / live music

HOTEL
4 luxury rooms / en-suite baths / ac / water views

FULL SERVICE SPA
massages / facials / manicures / pedicures

HOME OF TRADEWINDS
crewed luxury yacht charter

The Yacht Club Inc.
Bequia Marina
Port Elizabeth
+1 784 457 3361
info@bequiamarina.com
www.bequiamarina.com
VHF 68

TRADEWINDS

TradeWinds
Bequia Marina
Port Elizabeth
phone +1 784 457 3407
USA toll free 888 401 1430
info@trade-winds.com
www.trade-winds.com

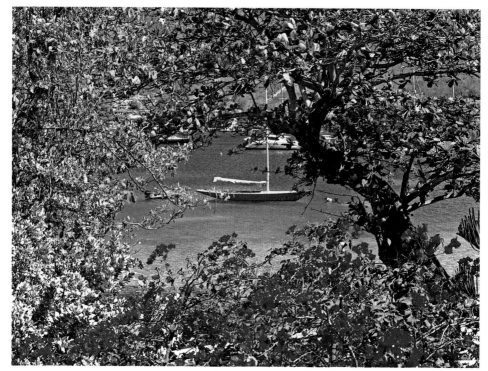

Admiralty Bay

Bequia

equia has long been a favorite of yachtspeople. Isolated enough to remain relatively unspoiled, yet lively enough to be stimulating and entertaining, it provides a blend of the old and new that many find perfect. It is well connected with St. Vincent and the other Grenadines, both by a small airport and by the cheaper and more traditional ferries. Some yachtspeople leave their boats anchored in Bequia and take a ferry to visit St. Vincent.

Bequia is an island of sailors and boats, linked to the outside world mainly by the sea. The old traditions continue. Boats are built on the beach in the shade of palm trees, though these days the building methods are a lot more high tech and the traditional fishing boats have morphed into sports boats capable of speeds well over 10 knots. Bequians travel all over the world on cargo vessels, and

quite a few have ended up owning their own. Some are intrepid fishermen who venture all over the Grenadines in little open boats.

The island has an active whaling station in a low-key and traditional way. By IWC agreement, local whalers can take four whales a year, but in some years they do not get any. The whaling season is from February to April. At this time of year, humpback whales leave their northern feeding grounds and head south to mate and bear young. Few people are left in Bequia with the skills necessary to hunt them ~ a daring feat in an open sailing boat, using hand-thrown harpoons. On the rare occasions that they make a kill, the hunters tow the whale to Semplers Cay for butchering.

Much of Bequia's tourist industry is based on visiting yachts, so you will find good yacht services, restaurants, shops, and

BEQUIA

SCALE IN NAUTICAL MILES

0 1 2 3

handicrafts, many made only here. Best of all, Bequia people understand yachting.

Bequians are a proud people, descendants of settlers who came from North America on whaling boats, from farms in Scotland, from France as freebooters, and as slaves from Africa.

Bequia's main harbor is Admiralty Bay. Friendship Bay is a harbor on the south coast and there is a daytime anchorage at Petit Nevis.

Friendship Rose in Admiralty Bay

ADMIRALTY BAY

Admiralty Bay is a huge, well-protected bay with Bequia's only town, Port Elizabeth, at its head. Small hotels, bars, restaurants, and shops spread from town along both shores, strung together in the south by the popular Belmont walkway. This delightful coastal path, renovated and extended by Action Bequia, meanders along the shore skirting a few trees to Plantation House. Here it climbs the hill before bringing you back to the sea via a lovely wooden staircase. Here it turns into a causeway that takes you to Princess Margaret beach.

Several yacht services are grouped together in Ocar on the northern shore. Others are in Port Elizabeth. Good dinghy docks are spaced around the bay.

Navigation

The entrance to Admiralty Bay is straightforward. As you approach from the north, the bay begins to open up, and you can see two fine beaches, Lower Bay and Princess Margaret, separated by a distinct headland. East of Princess Margaret Beach, from the Plantaton House to town, it becomes more built up.

When approaching, allow plenty of room for Devil's Table, which extends a good way from shore; it is marked by a yellow and black beacon. Once in the harbor, take care not to hit the shoals that lie offshore between the eastern end of Princess Margaret Beach and the Green Boley. Yachts anchor

inside some of these shoals, so it looks like tempting empty space. If entering at night, avoid the unlit, heavy metal buoys near Bequia Marina. These are used for big ship tie-ups. A line of smaller yellow cone buoys are lit and mark hoses running underwater to the shore. Keep clear!

Anchor well clear of the local ferry channel to the main dock. The ferries are large and need plenty of turning room. Keep out of their way at all times. Yachts may not tie up to the ferry dock or the dinghy dock.

There are many places to anchor. Some choose a spot up in town, off the Frangipani Hotel. The water is deep, and it takes lots of anchor line and sometimes a couple of tries to get hooked in the muddy sand.

The area by Bequia Marina is calm. Avoid anchoring on the wreck that is at 13° 00.67'N, 61° 14.47'W and another (Tail Wagger) a few hundred feet farther east. They both have at least 12 feet of water over them, but have tied up many an anchor. Some yachts anchor off the Fig Tree and the Plantation House. This area is mainly 8 to 10 feet deep, shoaling toward the shore, shoaling outwards from the western headland and from the Gingerbread. Shallow draft boats can go practically anywhere here, but those with deeper draft need to use caution.

Sometimes this is a beautiful spot, calm as a lake, the water decorated with floating pink blossoms from the white cedar trees that line the shore. Yet in times of bad northerly swells, it is untenable. The banks on both sides of the harbor (8-20 feet) con-

St. Vincent & the Grenadines

DEVIL'S
TABLE

ADMIRALITY BAY

TONY GIBBONS BEACH

tain patches of hard sand and dead coral, which make for poor holding. You need to let out ample chain and make sure you are well hooked.

Princess Margaret Beach is one of the easiest and prettiest anchorages, and is within a reasonable dinghy ride to town. Holding is good in sand close to the beach. It occasionally becomes rolly in northerly swells, when landing a dinghy on the beach can be hazardous. The new dinghy dock at Jack's helps. Lower Bay is also easy and picturesque, though a little farther away and more subject to swells.

Moorings are available and the usual charge is $60 EC per night. They are uncontrolled and (except Daffodil's) without legal standing. The customs office posts a warning about them. Some are better than others. Some people know Bequia well and trust a particular mooring owner. For a stranger, it is a problem. I have dived on many of them and have found most to be poorly designed and executed, and they break free quite

often. In general, I do not trust them. On the other hand they sometimes hold better than the way some bareboats anchor. If you take one, snorkel on it to make sure it is okay. Ask for a receipt, or at least know to whom you are paying money. The moorings on the south side, on the bank off the Fig Tree, are occasionally untenable in bad northerly swells, which usually arrive in the middle of the night. If you anchor close to an empty illegal mooring, you cannot be made to move. Similarly, if you take a mooring and an anchored boat swings too close, you must move if they were there first. Rely on your judgment: the vendors are *only* interested in collecting the fee. Keep this in mind when they give you advice about shore services. Daffodil, Phat Shag, and African probably check their moorings more often than most.

Regulations

Port Elizabeth is a port of entry. Customs and immigration, along with the post office, are in a comfortable office right be-

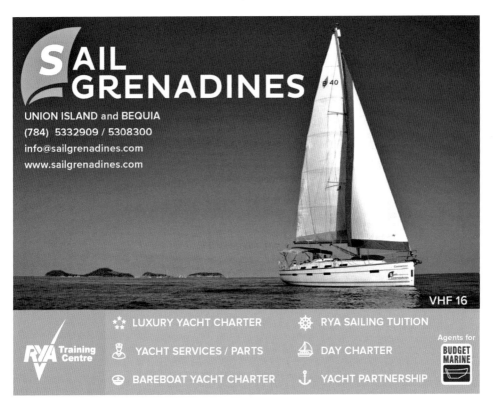

hind the ferry dock. Formalities are simple ~ just one single-sheet form, or better still, check sailclear.com to see if they have joined the sailclear program yet. If they have, you can pre-clear online (not in 2016). Customs opens weekdays 0830-1800 (overtime after 1600). On Saturdays, they open 0830-1200 and (overtime) 1500-1800. Sundays and holidays (all overtime) they open 0900-1200 and 1500-1800. Fees are given in *Bequia at a Glance* (page 244).

There is a five-knot speed limit in the harbor. This applies to dinghies, tenders, and water taxis, as well as to yachts and ships. If you need to speed into town, do so only in the main shipping channel in the center of the harbor. Currently, small, fast boats are the most serious danger to life and limb in this harbor. There has already been one death and several bad accidents. Is five minutes worth it?

Communications

In many cases you can email from your yacht with wifi. But if you go to an internet place, most are air-conditioned, and many will help you with overseas calls, either net-to-phone or via the operator, at rates that are better than the public phones.

Turn on your computer to access bay wide wifi. Mega network and Pirate Wifi are normally there, Hothothotspot is meant to be.

The Fig Tree, Maria's French Terrace, Whaleboner, Gingerbread, Coco's, and Sail Relax Explore have free wifi for customers.

When you need a computer, RMS, run by Ros, is conveniently placed just opposite the market and very close to the market dinghy dock. Ros has several computers and has a digital photo center where you can download and print digital pictures, as well as make posters and burn CDs. Ros does customs brokerage, photocopying, phone and fax, typing, laminating, and creating cards and flyers. She rents Digicel phones and sells the cards to go with them.

Campbell's Bequia Technology Center (look for the Digicel signs), next to Andy's, has a savvy owner and has a bank of com-

St. Vincent & the Grenadines

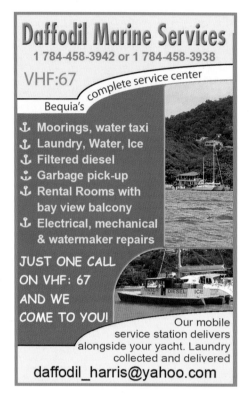
puters. They also do phone, fax, software engineering, CD creation, and photo work, and will top up your phone.

Antoinette runs the Hothothot Spot wifi system, but it seems more off than on.

For computers, electronics, accessories, USB keys or SD cards, Andrew is the man to see at ACS Computer Services, above Grenadines Yacht Equipment (GYE). He is also the Bequia DHL agent.

General yacht services

The Yacht Club aka Bequia Marina (VHF: 68) belongs to Tradewinds Yacht Charters and is open to the general public for docking, water, ice, and diesel. They can take yachts up to 150 feet long and 12 feet draft (stern to). Electricity is 220-volt/50-amp, 3-phase/100-amp, 50 Hz. They may be able to offer a 120 volt transformer. They are open 0800-1600, every day. Space may be a

little tight on weekends when Tradewinds do their turn arounds, but it is a fairly big dock.

The marina has pleasant rooms available, a Spa (see *Ashore*) and their Yacht Club at the Marina (see *Restaurants*). Sail Grenadines base boats here (see *Water Sports*).

Daffo at Daffodil's Marine Services has made a name for herself with a great alongside water, fuel, ice and laundry delivery system. Nowhere in the Caribbean is this easier. Just give her a call [VHF: 67] and a service boat arrives right alongside. For laundry and ice delivery or garbage pick-up, they will send a smaller boat. Daffodil usually carries block ice as well as cubes. Her laundry is excellent; fast, efficient, and properly washed and dried.

Miranda also collects and delivers laundry. She does a good job and can be reached at Miranda's Laundry [VHF: 68].

Lighthouse Laundry [VHF: 68] has a big laundry by the power station and have showers for a fee. Below Maria's Cafe, Andy has machines where you can do laundry yourself.

GYE fills cooking gas bottles, including French ones. It takes overnight. Cube ice may be found at the Porthole, Gingerbread Cafe, and the Frangipani.

When it comes to garbage in Bequia, please continue to observe the following: put your garbage in the big dumpsters near the head of the market dinghy dock (no charge). Or call Daffodil Marine any time and they will collect it from you at a charge of $5 EC a bag. They take it to the main dump, not to town. Never accept offers from anyone else to "take your garbage!"

African (Winston Simmons) looks after boats when people go away and can organize work to be done on them. He will also help with provisioning or anything else. He does deliveries, has a 41 foot lagoon charter cat, and rents moorings (593-3986, VHF: 68).

Local water taxis are painted brightly and bear such names as Outernet, African, McCarthy, and Radio. Their charges vary, depending on the destination and time of day. Didi (455-5681), on Blessings, with her little sun awning, is very popular because she drives carefully and will take up to four people almost anywhere in the bay during the day for $20 EC (more than four and night trips are more). Others who drive carefully are African (593-3986), and McCarthy (495-3425). McCarthy provides an excellent service every morning by delivering bread around the anchorage from around 0700. He is a low-key salesman, so you will have to watch out for him and give him a shout, or call him on VHF: 68. In season, vendors sell lobster.

Superyachts requiring help can check with Sam Taxi Service (St. Vincent), or Erika's Marine Services (Union). Verna May, Erika's Bequia representative, is very helpful and easy to deal with.

Bequia is the home of *Caribbean Compass*, the Caribbean's best waterfront paper. Pick up your free copy practically anywhere around town.

Chandlery

With three chandleries in town, you will usually find what you need. They have completely different suppliers, so each stocks different things. Dockside Marine (ex Wallace & Co.), right in town, is both a good marine hardware and a fishing store. They are the Icom agent and carry a full range, including waterproof, hand-held VHF radios. They also sell rope, blocks, shackles, stainless yacht hardware, stainless chain, Delta anchors, fenders, flags, West System epoxy, and first-rate safety gear. There is often new and interesting stock. This is an excellent fishing store, with many lures, rods, and both Penn and Shimano reels (sales and service). In addition, they stock snorkeling gear and some diving equipment.

Piper Marine store, under Alick's sail loft, is another interesting chandlery. Piper has an excellent stock of cleaning products and consumables, plus lots of general chandlery, including cloth and West System epoxy, pumps, lights, good blocks, safety gear, and much more. Piper is a rigger (see *Technical yacht services*). and he may have a bike to rent.

GYE [VHF: 16] has a chandlery that

Piper Marine
Chandlery & rigging shop
Back Street, Bequia, Tel: (784) 457-3856/495-2272
VHF 68
A treasure trove of marine hardware

RIGGING

Marine Hardware
Paints, Resins, Polishing
Electrical, Plumbing
Fastenings, Safety
things you need...
Ask about bike rentals

We do boat visits and take care of all your rigging problems. We stock all lifeline wire and fittings, plus regular rigging wire, turnbuckles and ropes

is good on technical things, including an excellent stock of brass pipe fittings, stainless steel fastenings, resins, electrical bits, and a huge stock of batteries, Danforth anchors, marine accessories, and parts. This is a good place to get your gas bottles filled. It is connected with Oscar's Machine Shop in St. Vincent and they will accept work for him (see *Technical yacht services*). They also have a bookswap.

Lulley's Tackle Shop is upstairs in the big building that has Island life Boutique. Wander up here and take a look. This is the oldest fishing shop in Bequia and it is still used by many of the island's professional fishermen. It has a wide range of fishing gear, snorkeling gear, and knives. They carry heavy commercial gear, as well as sporting equipment. They have a vast variety of lures and you can get ready-made tackle that is very easy to use, as well as rods.

Caribbean Woods sells South American hardwoods and has a good woodworking shop as well. They can put you in touch with Cliff, who will cut that special bit of

St. Vincent & the Grenadines

253

wood to size or make you a fancy book shelf. Upstairs is an excellent paint shop with paints, fillers, sandpaper, and resins, as well as good tools, including power sanders, bits, and cutting blades.

For general hardware, check out Bequia Venture, Knights (upstairs), and J's Outlets Tools, which also has household things

Technical yacht services
Sails/Canvas/Cushions

Several places do sail and canvas work and all are good. Bequia Canvas, near GYE, does just about everything but sails: interior and exterior cushions, awnings, boat covers, dinghy covers, and biminis. It is an efficient operation run by Chris Lochner from Germany and Norrell from Bequia. They keep a wide range of materials, including closed-cell foam. Wander by and you might find just the tote bag or ditty hanger you have been looking for. You can call them on the phone and arrange for Chris to come to your yacht to discuss a job.

Grenadines Sails is owned by Avell Davis, a Bequian who has spent years mak-

ing sails in Bequia and Canada. His shop is close by Bequia Marina. Avell is the North Sails representative and works with Andrew Dove out of Guadeloupe to get you a fast quote for a new North Sail. Avell has the widest range of experience, from traditional, handmade sails to modern, high-tech ones. New awnings, covers, and alterations can easily be done in the loft. Avell does excellent biminis and bimini frames.

Alick [VHF: 68] is in Port Elizabeth, on a back street, not too far from the town dinghy dock. Alick is low key, personable, thorough, and reasonably priced. You can ask him about new sails, awnings, cushions, and covers. Alick (who trained under Lincoln Simmons) is an excellent man to tackle that devilish splice in one of those new ropes. He will even show you how to do it. At his store he keeps a stock of fabrics, foams, and webbing that you can buy for your own project.

Technical yacht services
Other Services

Don Lewis at the chandlery Piper Marine [VHF: 68] is the man to fix your rigging problems. He carries rigging wire, a full range of life-line wire, and press fittings. He will be happy to come to your yacht, where he will get his nephew, Jason, to go up the mast to do whatever is needed. He lives on a sailboat himself. Give him a call or drop by the shop.

KMS Marine Services [VHF: 68] is run by Kerry Olliviere from Mount Pleasant. Kerry worked for many years for various charter companies, where he learned to fix everything that usually goes wrong: diesel engines, starters, alternators, outboards, refrigerators, watermakers, electrical gadgets, and, of course, heads, macerator pumps and plumbing. Kerry can weld and is often asked to install solar panels. He works closely with GYE and can arrange high-tech welding and machining through them in St. Vincent.

Tyrone Caesar, at Caribbean Diesel [VHF: 68], spent nine years as an engineer on cargo carriers and several more working for large organizations such as Cummins. He is a very well-trained diesel mechanic, especially with Perkins, Northern Lights,

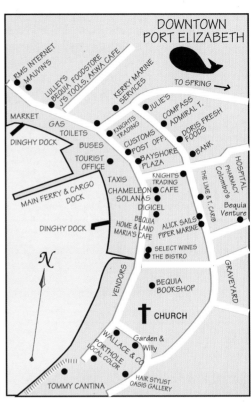

Detroit Diesels, GMs, and Yanmars.

Tyrone has a complete mobile fuel polishing system (diesel or gas) for cleaning fuel tanks, which can handle any size of tank. It comes with bendable rods that can fit into tight spaces. He can also sample your tank and access the state of the fuel at the bottom. His shop is in the church yard, but it is probably easiest to call. If you cannot find him, ask in Piper Marine Chandlery.

Just down the road from Bequia Marina you will find Robin, of Simpson Engineering, aka Fixman 2 [VHF: 68]. Robin came into mechanics from working on racing cars in England. He is a generalist, so you see washing machines, outboard motors, shiny engine innards, and more in his workshop. He is the man in Bequia for stainless and aluminum welding and for machining. He is an excellent choice for almost any problem except refrigeration. Robin works Tuesday to Friday and be may be cutting back further.

Sam Saville of Knock Refrigeration provides excellent service for both refrigeration and air-conditioning. You will find him two doors east from GYE, or call him on his cell: 529-1682.

Oscar has an excellent machine shop in St. Vincent, with full machining, milling, and turning gear, and he can fix just about anything, as well as welding stainless and aluminum. He owns GYE in Bequia. Oscar is near Verrol Nichols of Nichols Marine, the starter and alternator magician (Verrol will fix anything and send it back looking like new). You can arrange to leave work for either of these specialists at GYE, or get KMS Marine Services to come and deal with it for you.

Winfield Sargeant and his team come well recommended for varnishing, hand-painting, cleaning, and polishing. Winfield comes by in his own launch. It is easiest to contact him on VHF: 68 or by phone.

Handy Andy is a good, two-part polyurethane spray painter who can still occasionally be persuaded to tackle a job. Bequia also has many shipwrights and carpenters.

Provisioning

Bequia is quite a good place to stock

Quality meats, smoked fish, shrimp, wines, cheeses, gourmet foods

VHF:68, Phone:(784) 458-3625, Fax:(784) 457-3134

Now on Back Street, behind Customs

For yacht provisioning

The place to shop

French Bread (baguettes) daily Dieter's special whole wheat bread with yogurt (keeps wonderfully). Fresh croissants daily in season.

MasterCard and Visa welcome

wir sprechen Deutsch

up on provisions. Doris Fresh Foods [VHF: 68/16] is almost legendary in Bequia. It is a great, air-conditioned supermarket on the back street where you will find excellent cheeses and deli foods, good wines, local chutney, gourmet items, and good, fresh produce. You will not find a better selection of frozen meats. Baked goodies include 8-grain bread, which tastes good and keeps well, making it popular with those setting out to sea. Fresh French bread is baked daily in season, as are croissants and fancy pastries. Among my favorites here are the packets of delicious frozen conch and callaloo soup. So far, Doris has been unmatched for variety and availability of harder-to-find foods.

Another place for fancy pastries, including quiches, is Stelton Bakery at the Plantation House. He cooks for their restaurant, so for provisioning quantities you need to order in advance.

Noeline Taylor's Shoreline Mini-Market is associated with her Porthole restaurant, so you can shop from early in the morning to late at night. If you see it closed, just ask in the restaurant and Noeline will

open. You can pull your dinghy up on the beach just outside, making it convenient for carrying cases of beer. It is well stocked with most things, including wine, French baguettes, and whole-wheat bread baked daily. Shoreline closes on Sundays, out of season.

On the north side of the harbor, O. King, the beer wholesaler, has the best buys in cases of beer.

Knight's Trading is one of the older and larger of the Bequia supermarkets. They stock almost everything except fresh produce, and their prices are often good. They will deliver to the dinghy dock. You can do one-stop shopping here, as upstairs they have a lumber/hardware/electrical store. Knight's has a smaller outlet on Front Street.

Select Wines, next to the Bistro, has a well-organized and large selection of wine, soft drinks, beer, cheese, meat, French bread, and lots of specialty items, like chocolate-covered hazelnuts. In addition, they have a fair selection of regular canned and dried foods. They open from about 0800 to 2200, so it is almost never too late to shop.

Bequia Foodstore offers a good selection

St. Vincent & the Grenadines

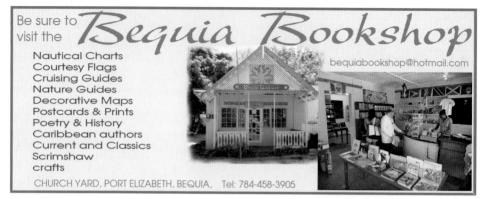
of canned and dry goods. It is open daily 0800-2000, making it convenient for late shopping.

In the Shoreline Plaza, Lina's is a great little bakery/delicatessen. When they bake they have a whole selection of good bread, both yeast and sourdough. They sell Danish, pain au chocolat, and more. Get a cup of excellent coffee here in the morning and sit outside under the umbrellas. Return for a lunchtime sandwich. Lina's also offers specialty foods, including the Caribbean's widest selection of pepper (the spice).

You can buy fruits and vegetables in the market. The selection is good, but high-pressure Rasta salesmanship has driven many locals and regulars to Doris, or to the quieter stalls dotted around the main street. (Check out the notice painted on the wall of the market.)

The Gingerbread Cafe has baked goods, coffee, and a few other items. Maranne's has yogurt and homemade ice cream.

In Lower Bay, Nature Zone is a one-room shop attached to a small organic garden run by Jacqueline McLean. You can find great fresh items here, straight from the garden. Jacqueline also bakes bread and banana bread, makes chutneys, pickles, fresh juices and all kinds of good things. If you need something special, give her a call, 458-3793

Fun shopping

The waterfront in Port Elizabeth is colorful, with vendors selling t-shirts, model boats, and handicrafts along the street and in the market. Bequia produces excellent handicrafts, of very high quality that are unique to the island. Add in the clothing

store in the Chameleon Cafe and you have an interesting selection of shops.

The Chameleon Cafe's clothing department offers the smartest and most elegant lines of swim, beach and casual wear, with fashion brands like Huley, Reef and Nike. It is hard to know it is there, but just walk into the cafe and you will see it.

The building of model boats has been a Bequia specialty for generations. Craftsmen will build any design to order, but all-time favorites are the model whaling boats, both full and half models. They are artfully built and beautifully painted. Check out Mauvin's, near the market, or Sargeant's, closer to Bequia Marina.

Kingsley has taken the coconut boat tradition to the level of real artistry with his glossy coconut boats. You can see some at the Oasis Art Gallery, which also features the wonderful art of L.D. Lucy, as well as having special exhibits of visiting artists and local craftspeople. They open Tuesday to Friday after about 1000.

Hand-painted calabashes and coconuts by Pinky, who is based in Bequia, are lovely and deservedly popular. You will find some in Solanas.

Jurgen from Wallace and Co., has become a potter. He bases his designs on those of the skilled Arawak potters who inhabited the Caribbean starting about two thousand years ago. Most are built up the old way, by laying down strip after strip of clay, rather than using a wheel, and he has mastered polishing the ancient way with a piece of conch shell. They are real works of art, featuring, as the did the originals, frogs, bats, and lizards. You may find some at the Oasis

Gallery. Jurgen also likes to grow orchids, so you may be able to buy a pot with an orchid growing in it.

Scrimshaw is another Bequia tradition and you can find it in the Bequia Bookstore and along the waterfront.

Bequia has a wide range of small, pleasant boutiques. The market has its own dinghy dock. Many shops here sell t-shirts, souvenirs, and gifts. Others are scattered through town.

Solana's, run by Carmette and Solana, is packed with hand-painted t-shirts, shorts, and batik work, as well as handicrafts, jewelry, books, videos, flags, phone cards, and maps. Solana's is the Fed Ex agent, and they sell Digicel cards. Buy second-hand books here, and the money will go to help local children. They also have a lovely house for rent overlooking Princess Margaret Beach.

The Bequia Bookshop, in the church compound, is spread through two rooms, with an excellent range of nautical books, charts, local books, videos, and novels. They sell postcards, souvenirs, games, and art by local artists, including the popular Caron Nichols. Scrimshaw, locally hand-crafted by Sam McDowell, is on display, as are sailors' valentines, made by Sam's wife, Donna.

Manager Cheryl also runs Sweety Bird, a garden cafe down the road with elegant teas, coffee, fresh juices, and a great lunch at local prices. A good place to read the novel you have just bought, or wait for the ferry. Cheryl also runs The Fig Tree and has a reading club for kids every other Saturday and always needs volunteers to help the kids. If you are interested, ask her about it.

Silk screening has long been a Bequia tradition and is carried along today by Angela Hinkson, whose factory, shop, and bar is on the road to Spring (on the way to the turtle sanctuary). Here you can see the fabric being silk-screened upstairs and buy fabric and clothing in the shop. You can also find some of these items in the Whaleboner Boutique on the waterfront.

In the Bayshore Mall you can find boutiques, a barber, and a travel agent.

Sail Relax Explore has hammocks, great canvas bags, cushions, sail bags, and underwater cameras.

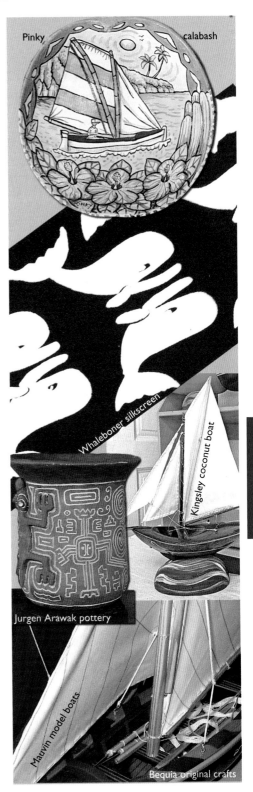

Pinky calabash

Whaleboner silkscreen

Kingsley coconut boat

Jurgen Arawak pottery

Mauvin model boats

Bequia original crafts

St. Vincent & the Grenadines

It's Back!

Better than ever

BEQUIA PLANTATION HOTEL

Bequia . West Indies

Phone: 1 784-534-9444
or 1 784-534-9333
info@bequiaplantationhotel.com
www.bequiaplantationhotel.com

Traditional, elegant old-style Caribbean Hospitality at affordable prices

▶ Stelton's bakery eat or takeaway wholesale and retail
▶ Waterfront bar/ pizza and dining - happy hour daily 1700-1900 open breakfast to dinner
▶ Entertainment three times a week   Fine dining on the Verandah for a special night out
▶ Beautiful rooms with a sea view - Caricom rates for yachtmen on short notice
▶ Accommodation/event/special packages. Check us out!

In a spacious upstairs location, Local Color has both a good collection of clothing and a selection of handicrafts.

Restaurants

The waterfront has a wonderful mixture of bars and restaurants. Those on the south side of the harbour are all linked together by the Bequia walkway, recently completed by Action Bequia and others, that runs from Port Elizabeth down to Plantation House, then over the hill to Princess Margaret Beach.

The Gingerbread Hotel is in an impressive Caribbean-style building with an adjoining hotel managed by Gretel Mitchell. It has delightful rooms with big balconies, looking right over the harbor and the Gingerbread coffee shop under the trees at the head of their dinghy dock. This popular gathering place sells coffee, fresh local juice and baked goodies. In the same compound, check out Maranne's and try her famous gourmet ice cream, frozen yogurt, or sorbet. Everything is homemade from fresh ingredients.

Upstairs is the Black Pearl [VHF: 68, $A-C] in a big room with intricate gingerbread trim and a tall wooden roof supported by mast-like poles. This restaurant is graced by a piano on a stage and a grand harbor view. It is run by Laurel Joseph, aided by Simon Carey, who some may remember from Sunsail. They open every day at 0730 and serve a full Caribbean or American breakfast. If you are on a yacht, this comes with a free bag of ice on request. 1730-1930 is happy hour, two for one. The cuisine is

Caribbean fusion, featuring fresh fish and lobster, top quality meat, chicken and more. The cooking is very good, the fish and lobster delicious. Save some room for cinnamon ginger creme brulee. Lunch is lighter, with soups, salads, rotis and sandwiches (including fresh fish).

The atmosphere is enlivened on Sunday nights by local musician J Gould. From time to time, they have barbecues outside with a steel pan band. Simon Carey also works in the World Pediatric Project, bringing medi-

St. Vincent & the Grenadines

cal care, and sending kids away for high-tech treatment.

I am delighted to see the Plantation House back in action. Built as a hotel, it was originally called the Sunny Caribbee. Many years ago it was bought by an Italian offshore banker, who had aspirations and renamed it Plantation House, filled the garden with statues, and the rooms with clients he wished to impress. He had to suddenly flee various authorities and the property declined and became derelict. Kelly (who also has Blue Lagoon Marina and Hotel) has done a magnificent job of renovating and improving the property, creating an elegant but affordable boutique hotel.

At the head of their dinghy dock is their beachfront bar and restaurant. This is open to the bay on one side and the pool on the other. People wander in for breakfast or mid-morning for coffee and some fine pâtisseries created by their pastry chef, Stelton Levy, who trained under Ali in Mustique making fancy pastries for the rich and famous. (If there are leftovers at happy hour, sometimes they sell them off at a discount.) They have a traditional pizza oven, which is fired up at noon and keeps going for lunch and dinner. They cook thin-crust pizzas with your choice of three toppings, generously applied, and you can add more if you wish. They also offer quiches and other dishes, and in the evenings you can opt for a full three-course meal. Happy hour is 1700-1900, and they have entertainment about three times a week. By the time this book comes out your choice will be expanded by the main-house verandah, where they plan to serve fine cuisine. If you want a night ashore, elegant rooms are available both in the main building and in cottages. All have balconies.

Papa's [$B-D], up on the hill above Bequia Marina, and managed by Gert, overlooks the bay and is well worth the walk. It has an informal clubby atmosphere with comfy lounging seats as well as a giant, half-roofed deck looking over the harbor. This is the place to come for a big sports event like the Superbowl, as they can project TV right on the wall. They open every day for lunch and dinner, with both a menu and daily specials. The food is good, straightforward in style, and includes burgers, chicken, lobster in season, and sandwiches. On Saturday nights they have live music.

Cheryl's Fig Tree [$B-D] is along the waterfront close to Mac's Pizzeria; just follow the coastal path. This restaurant is right on the water. The food is local and delicious for lunch or dinner. You get a nice array of local vegetables and they do a chocolate samosa, which while not exactly Caribbean, is totally scrumptious. Cheryl, who is always around and welcoming, also organizes the cruisers' VHF net in the morning at 0800, and she runs a children's reading group here every other Saturday (cruisers' children welcome) and always needs volunteers from yachts to help children read. If anyone is looking for a place for a meeting, scrabble competition, or other event, it is likely they will come here. In season, every Friday is "Fish Friday", with seafood specials, and live music. This is very popular in season, so book. Wednesday is curry Wednesday, also with live music.

Cheryl occasionally runs poetry clubs.

The Chameleon Cafe and clothing store is on main street in Port Elizabeth. With a broad balcony, brightly colored cushions, and the wonderful aroma of freshly brewed coffee, it adds a touch of casual sophistication to town. They open at 0800 for breakfast, Continental or full, and stay open till the last person leaves, or till 1900 if no one is around. All day long you can get delightful salads (including fresh tuna), quiches, sandwiches and starters, with baked goodies and their famous lime cheese cake. They serve beer, wine, fruit smoothies (you can add a little rum), cocktails and coconut water. The space is intimate, and sometimes quite a few people are there using the free wifi, so if you want to be sure of a table for lunch come early, or if it is a big group, call. In the evening they serve tasty tapas; share a few and make a meal of it. While there, take a look in their clothing store (see *Fun shopping*).

The Yacht Club at Bequia Marina, run by the Tradewinds Charter company, is

St. Vincent & the Grenadines

open daily for casual dining, with a happy hour, 1600-1800, many days. They offer gastro-pub cuisine featuring soups, salads, sandwiches and fresh fish and lobster with local vegetables. Try their lobster quesadilla. They have musical entertainment about three times a week, and rooms are available for a night ashore.

There are plenty of first-rate places to get good local food. Noeline Taylor's Port-hole [VHF: 68, $C-D] is a popular meeting place for breakfast, morning coffee, lunch rotis, an afternoon beer, or a relaxing dinner. Noeline has local fresh juices and a large menu, with everything from snacks to freshly caught fish. Check out the menu posted outside showing the daily specials. Entertainment is usually on Wednesdays and Sundays. Noeline has the biggest bookswap in Bequia, so you often see people browsing through the shelves. There is a very nominal charge that enables Noeline to keep the books in good order. Let Noeline know before you do your swap.

Maria's Cafe is upstairs on Front Street. This is a gathering place where people come and use the internet computers and wifi, to meet and chat, while looking out from the magnificent balcony that overlooks life below and the harbor. It brings in people of all nationalities and types, and the atmosphere is casual. Their menu has something for everyone, from burgers to lobster, with some good conch and other seafood. Everything is cooked from scratch, so it is fresh and tasty, but depending on what you order, it can take a little time.

Andy, the owner, is often around. He runs the Bequia Youth Sailing Program and has an office which sells property downstairs.

The Frangipani Hotel [$A-B, VHF: 68, closed September] is owned by Son Mitchell, former Prime minister of St. Vincent and the Grenadines, and has been in his family since the turn of the last century. The upper floor of the main building used to be the family home and downstairs was the storehouse for the Gloria Colita, which, at 131 feet long, was the largest schooner ever built in Bequia. In 1940, she disappeared at sea and was later found drifting empty in the Bermuda Triangle. Today Son's daughter, Sabrina, ably manages the Frangipani. By day, it is a good place to meet people and enjoy a great fresh tuna sandwich for lunch. By night, they offer romantic candlelit dinners of Caribbean specialties. Everyone comes by on Thursday nights when they have a barbecue and jump up to a steel band. They also have music on Mondays in season.

Jacques is a Frenchman who, with Eileen, has spent 22 years in the restaurant business. Auberge des Grenadines [$B-C] is on the waterfront on the northwest shore of the harbor, with a good dinghy dock, and is very popular.

During the lobster season, Jacques and Eileen keep a large, live lobster tank full in their restaurant. The lobsters go from tank to plate in a matter of a few minutes; it does not get fresher. Jacques has specialized in lobster for over 20 years, and you can expect them to be done perfectly. You can get gourmet style French and Creole food, and while the emphasis is on seafood, tenderloin in crushed black pepper and old rum sauce should keep the carnivore happy.

It is also excellent and reasonably priced

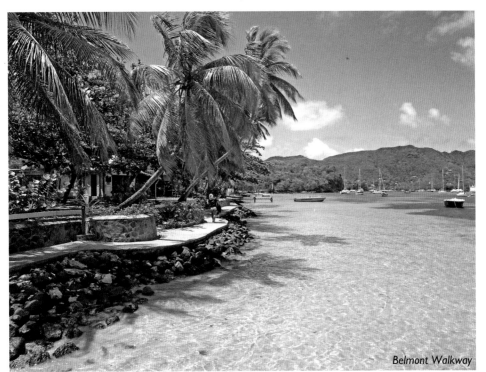

Belmont Walkway

for lunch. Their salad Nicoise with lightly seared fresh tuna is the best I know in the Eastern Caribbean. If a captain brings in six or more guests, he dines for free.

The Hinkson family own and run the Whaleboner [$C-D]. It is conveniently situated next to the Frangipani. Much of the food comes from their farm, so you know it is fresh. True to its name, the bar, stools, and entrance have all been built of whalebone from the old whaling days. Angela and her daughter Ruth cook good snacks, pizzas, chicken, and fish. They also do full evening meals at a reasonable price, including curried and roast pork. The meat comes from their hand-raised animals. Chicken and fish are always available, as is lobster in season. Come for the daily happy hour (1700-1800) and enjoy entertainment on Monday nights, in season, and on other special occasions.

Akwa Cafe is upstairs, opposite the market. It is local, cheap and cheerful and has a great harbor view. Their bar is built like a local trading boat.

Coco's [VHF: 68, $C-D] is upstairs in the first building on the road behind Bequia Marina. They have an excellent view of the yachts at anchor and Caribbean decoration. Coco is famous for good, local cooking, especially seafood. In season, they do a fabulous Sunday buffet lunch, and they generally have music on Tuesdays and Fridays.

When you get tired of local food, Tommy Cantina specializes not only in your favorite Mexican dishes, such as tacos, enchiladas, and burritos, but also in seafood. They have a perfect sunset view and open Monday to Saturday.

Mac's Pizzeria's [$C-D] tasty pizzas are legendary among yachtspeople, with many choices, including lobster. You can also get quiches, salads, soups, and goodies from their bakeshop, along with daily specials. The atmosphere is congenial, and it is popular. In season, it is essential to make a reservation. They also do take out.

The Bistro [$C-D] is open to the main street. They have hearty meals, pizzas, and hamburgers, as well as local fish, shrimp, and lobster. It is a great place to enjoy a few drinks or a cup of coffee and watch the world pass by.

For a cheap and cheerful lunch, consider Colombo's [$D]. They cook excellent pizza

St. Vincent & the Grenadines

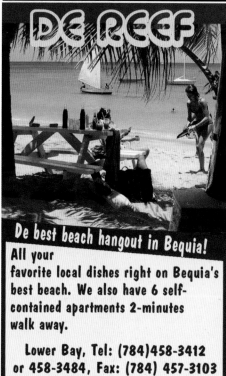

and pasta, and their lasagna is great. (You can buy it by the tray for a party.).

On Back Street, the Lime Garden has a cheap bar where you can sit and relax, and they often fire up the grill for a bargain meal.

Other local restaurants include Lyston Williams's Green Boley [$D], a popular bar; Isola McIntosh's Julie's Guest House [VHF: 68, $C], where advance booking is necessary; and the Pizza Hut, which is self-explanatory, but which also sells French bread.

Tantie Pearl's [VHF: 68, $B-C] is an aerobic 7-minute walk up a steep hill behind the cemetery. The restaurant is perched on the edge of a steep slope with a bird's-eye view of the harbor. Tantie Pearl offers good, local food, but book before you go.

Behind the slipway is the Sailor's Cafe [VHF: 68, $C-D]. Owner Elfic Grant, aka The Singing Chef, is entertaining and runs a good, clean establishment. You can drop in for soup and some good Chinese fried rice or chow mein. For more elaborate fare, you need to book in advance. The bar makes a pleasant hangout; ask about happy hour.

These are just the restaurants in Admiralty Bay. There are also good restaurants in other places, and taxi fares are reasonable ($12-20 EC). (See also *Restaurants* in *Friendship Bay*, later in this chapter; it is a long walk or short drive away.)

For a lovely get-away, go to Industry. Here you will you will find Sugar Reef set in a big stone building on the waterfront. It is a big, light open space, looking through palms and seagrapes to the beach where the water is protected by a reef.

This is part of a big estate owned by Emmet and it is managed by Judith. The food is local and fresh; much of it is from the estate. You can even feel good about drinking piña coladas here, as they make the coconut milk from fresh coconuts. They offer great salads and rotis (including lobster roti) as well as delights such as callaloo lasagna. They have a fine dinner menu, much of it seafood, but they also serve meat, vegetarian, and vegan meals. They have a full-moon party when they feature a special menu often exploring a particular cuisine, such as Thai, Indian, or Japanese, with a string band. For anyone who wants a real retreat, rooms are available.

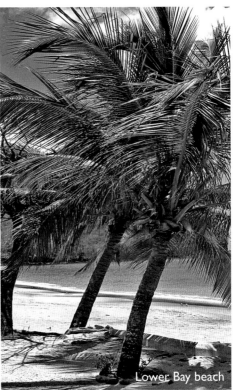

Lower Bay beach

A mile or so back towards town, Firefly Hotel [$A-C] at Spring is owned by Stan and Elizabeth who also have the Firefly in Mustique. It looks across a swimming pool over a field of palm trees towards the east coast, with the feel of being in the country. The manager, Rodney, and his staff are welcoming and friendly. Much of the food comes from the estate. Their Sunday curry lunch and Wednesday Creole lunch are both popular. They have a daily happy hour 1730-1900. On Friday nights they have Caribbean night with Caribbean food and music, and on Saturday nights, they continue the Caribbean theme with jerk food and reggae.

They offer an estate tour for $10 EC a person; Keith shows you all around and tells you about the local plants and their uses.

While in this area, visit the Whaleboner silk-screen factory (see *Fun shopping*).

Jack's Bar, on Princess Margaret Beach is big and open, built of wood and canvas. The location is fabulous, right on the beach. You can dinghy over and tie up on their dock. The people who have been running it for years are about to move out, but I am sure someone will take over. Take a look.

Lower Bay has one of Bequia's best beaches, set in a low-key, rural atmosphere of fishing boats and drying nets. While here check out Nature Zone, a tiny fresh food store, (see *Provisioning*). Great for swimming by day and romantic on a full-moon night, it is a popular place to hang out, especially on Sundays. Recently, people have begun to gravitate there for an evening of inexpen-

sive seafood dinners. Lower Bay makes an acceptable anchorage in settled conditions and is within dinghy reach of Admiralty Bay. However, there is usually enough swell to make landing on the beach a damp affair, so it is better to take a cab or water taxi ($15-25 EC). By day, it is interesting to follow the walkway to Princess Margaret Beach, and then go over the next bluff to Lower Bay.

Once you arrive, there are several local restaurants to choose from. De Reef [VHF: 68, $C-D], right on the beach, is the most famous, popular for lunch, and is a major gathering place for locals on Sundays. You can get chicken, fish, conch, or sandwiches any day of the week. By night they serve dinners by reservation, and from time to time, they throw a wild fete.

La Plage [$B-C] is a good restaurant with seating inside the building and over the road hanging over the beach. It is run by Cecile, who is an excellent French cook. Her menu runs from burgers to steak and seafood. While she is open most days in season, as soon as the crowd dies, it is weekends only.

St. Vincent & the Grenadines

Keegan's [VHF: 68, $C-D], opposite the beach, with on-the-beach seating, offers inexpensive meals featuring chicken, shrimp, fish, or conch. By day, they do fish or chicken 'n chips and snacks.

B's Cafe [$D, closed Monday] is a simple cafe with baked goodies, desserts and sandwiches. It was closed in 2016.

Further down, Dawn's Cafe [$D} is a real jewel. It is in a simple but attractive open building behind the beach in a pleasant garden. Dawn serves breakfast, soups, sandwiches, burgers, and often a daily special. Prices are very inexpensive; her food is delicious and she is open quite late, so you can also eat a simple evening meal here.

Fernando's Hideaway [$C], run by Fernando, is simple, low-key, and serves very good meals of local fish and meat. Fernando is a fisherman and catches the fish himself. Advance reservations are pretty much essential. It is down a back road. Take a taxi so you can find it.

While you are in Lower Bay, consider seeing if you can visit the home of French artist Claude Victorine (now in her nineties and going strong). Claude's main medium is painting on silk. She creates superb cushion covers, wall hangings, and fabrics that are guaranteed to add a touch of class to any boat or home. Paintings are also on show. Claude accepts the occasional visitor by appointment only (458-3150).

On Princess Margaret Beach, you can find Willie among the jewelry salesmen. Willie does a beach barbecue to order, which was highly recommended to me.

Transport

Two different companies run ferries to St. Vincent: Admiralty Transport and Bequia Express. The Admiral makes four trips on weekdays and two or three on weekends. The first ferry normally leaves Bequia at 0630, and the last returns at 1900. You can get details on the times of all ferries in the Bequia Tourist Office by the main dock.

You can rent mountain bikes at Handy Andy's or at Piper Marine store.

Local buses can be useful for getting around the island, especially if you are going to La Pompe or Paget Farm, both of which can seem like a never-ending walk. Just watch for one and stick out your hand.

Taxis are fairly inexpensive in Bequia, and sightseeing is highly recommended. (Check out some of the attractions under *Ashore*.) If you call a taxi in advance, they can meet you outside the Gingerbread or Frangipani. Most of the taxi drivers are good. There may be one or two who hustle a bit too much. Those I mention are pleasant, punctual, reliable, and always straightforward and informative about the island and its people. Gideon has three taxis, works well with the yachts, and listens to VHF: 68. His rates are reasonable and he also has four-wheel-drive rentals.

The Ollivierre family has been involved in Bequia boatbuilding from way back. Lubin Ollivierre (De Best) was one of the first taxi drivers and will be happy to tell you about what changes he has seen and what he knows of the history. He also has jeep rentals. Sandra and Curtis Ollivierre have a couple of bright yellow taxis and some four-wheel-drive cars for rent. They listen to VHF: 68.

Sightseeing cab fares for four people are only about $30 US an hour, plus $6 US per person for over five. You can see a lot in an hour, and the whole island in four hours. If you just want to visit Spring, Friendship, or Lower Bay, or want to try some different place for dinner, hop in a taxi; the island is small, so the fares are reasonable.

Ashore

If the hair on your head is beginning to resemble the stringy weed growing under your hull, then both men and women can contact Gillian's Hair Salon (457-3600), well down the road and up the hill past

Bequia Venture.

Johanna Osborne, a dentist and maxillofacial surgeon, now runs a clinic on Saturdays. Her office is on the road towards Spring, near the high school. Call for an appointment: 529-0745.

Bequia has good walks. If you follow the coastal path along the waterfront to Princess Margaret beach, you can walk from there along the beach and over the next headland to Lower Bay. If you laze on the beach and swim, keep an eye on your handbags and cameras.

Watch a sunset from Mount Pleasant, or walk to Friendship Bay, Spring, or Industry for lunch or dinner and enjoy the great variety of views along the way.

If you want to go on an adventurous hike, then Brent "Bushman" Gooding will be happy to guide you. He knows all the trails. Call him at 495-2524.

You will find that Bequia is far more than the waterfront. The hills of Mount Pleasant are almost like another world. If you are not inclined to walk, take a cab one way or both. You can see all the best and most scenic spots in a leisurely three-hour tour. Each place you visit seems so different that sometimes Bequia feels like several islands in one. Highlights include an old fort looking over the harbor, Bequia's summit, Mount Pleasant, the beautiful windward beach of Spring, and the new Maritime Museum in Friendship Bay. The taxi drivers are proud of their island and are knowledgeable guides.

The Old Hegg Turtle Sanctuary at Industry is a great destination. Brother King takes turtle eggs and rears turtles till they are old enough to have a better chance of survival. The establishment of the sanctuary has done much to raise environmental consciousness in Bequia. There is a small charge ($5 US) to visit, which goes toward the cost of feeding and housing the turtles.

On the way back, stop at the new

St. Vincent & the Grenadines

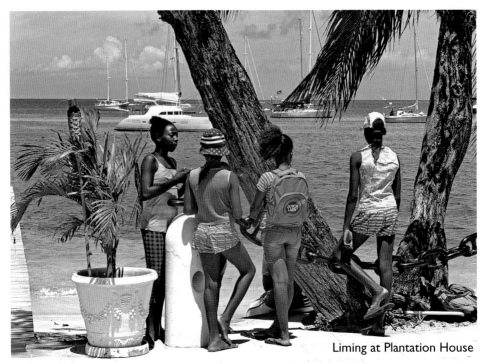

Liming at Plantation House

Whaleboner Silk Screen factory, shop, and bar right along the road.

You can hike to Hope, a lovely, remote beach where the shallow water sets up long lines of breakers often suitable for bodysurfing (but watch the undertow).

There is an exceptionally pleasant hike (about 40 minutes each way) to Peggy's Rock, right on a ridge line, with a spectacular view of Admiralty Bay. You start by the Bequia Whaling and Maritime Museum. Take a taxi or bus there; it is on the road to the airport. Hike details may be found on doyleguides.com

You can visit the other Bequia Maritime Museum in town in exchange for a contribution ($5 US suggested). Lawson Sargeant, the original model boat builder, runs it. Inside are some awesome, historically correct, giant models of whaling boats and schooners, along with photos of historic Bequia boats and the harbor from about 50 years ago. It is best to call for an appointment (495-8559/457-3685). Tennis courts are available at Spring, Friendship Bay, and Gingerbread.

If you come at Easter, you can get involved in the Bequia Regatta, a four-day extravaganza of local boat races, yacht races, and lots of partying. This may be the best, friendliest, and most successful of the Caribbean's medium-sized regattas. Everyone is made to feel welcome.

Christmas is also a popular time in Bequia, but "Nine Mornings," which starts some two weeks before Christmas, can make the town anchorage throb with disco music through the night.

You can also get off-island. Bequia has a special day-charter boat, the Friendship Rose, a sailing schooner, which for years was the island's only ferry. Given the price of mooring in Mustique, some yachties figure it is worth taking a day tour on the Rose instead. Friendship Rose does diving, waterfall, and other tours that are not as easy on your own boat. Their Sail Relax and Explore office is by the Frangipani and you can check out their itinerary. The same group run Grenadine Island Villas, which rents and sells villas, so if the whole family comes to visit, you can house them ashore.

Bequia has a very active youth sailing program to get the youngsters learning. They have a fleet of small sailing boats, plus one or two J 24s. The boats are kept opposite the

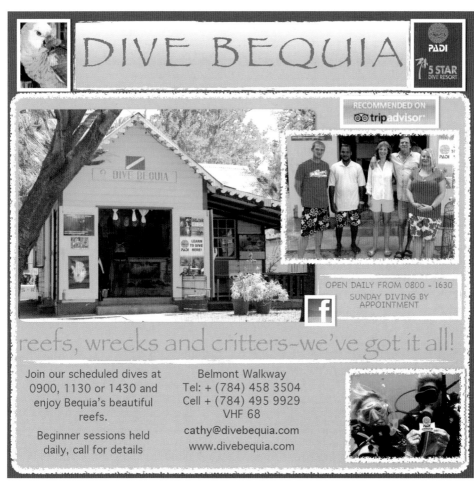

St. Vincent & the Grenadines

Bistro. If you feel like getting involved by contributing some time or money, Handy Andy is the man to talk to.

If a Spa is more your kind of activity, check out Serenity Day Spa run by Darcel John in The Yacht Club (Bequia Marina). She does it all, from Swedish massage to waxing and nails. Her prices are quite reasonable. Drop by and pick up a flier.

Water sports

Katie Bingham runs Sail Grenadines out of Bequia Marina. Katie is very friendly and helpful and they offer fully crewed, semi-bareboat, and bareboat charters. They do short-term charters to pick you up in one island and drop you off in another. Those who want to advance their skills should ask about their full gamut of practical RYA courses, which one can join as an individual.

Diving in Bequia is excellent and not to be missed by scuba fans. For the uninitiated, it is an ideal place for a resort course. There are two dive shops in Admiralty Bay.

Dive Bequia's Charlie

Dive Bequia is the dive shop near the Gingerbread, owned by Bob Sachs. Sachs is one of scuba's greatest enthusiasts and Bequia's most experienced diver. His wife, Cathy, is charming and an excellent teacher, especially for kids, or for those who are nervous (a view endorsed by quite a few reader emails). Call Dive Bequia [VHF: 68/16], and Bob or one of his staff will arrange to collect you from your yacht. Return to the bar later to socialize with them and other divers. Their seaworthy dive boats make getting in and out easy and allow for occasional diving and exploring trips to St. Vincent or the other Grenadines.

Bequia Dive Adventures [VHF: 68] is on the waterfront next to Mac's Pizzeria. It is run by Ron, an instructor from Bequia. He is experienced and operates with small groups and does all levels of training, from resort courses through assistant instructor training. He is happy to do boat pickups and drop-offs.

Both dive shops have retail sections with snorkeling and diving gear for sale. Both will help with equipment service or rental and tank fills.

For those diving on their own, the most accessible good dives are around Devil's Table. A reef extends from the shore to the black and yellow beacon. There are moorings, so you can tie up your dinghy. (The moorings belong to the dive shops, so leave plenty of line so they can tie up alongside you.) From the shallow inshore end you can dive out along one side of the rocky shoal and back on the other. The depth at the outer end of the reef is about 65 feet. There are plenty of different corals and reef fish. Sergeant majors can often be seen guarding their eggs. An even prettier dive is along the stretch of coast from inside this reef northwards to Northwest Point. There is a sloping reef all along this shore. The maximum depth is about 60 feet at Northwest Point. Coral formations include lots of pillar corals, and there are usually large schools of blue chromis. Garden eels pop their heads out over the sand. On both dives you must mind the current.

More exciting dives are far from the anchorage, and the current makes them drift dives. Flat Rock Drift Dive is on Bequia's northwest coast, starting at the western end of Anse Chemin. This is a gentle, easy dive where you hardly have to use your fins, and there is time to examine all the little creatures. You swim along a captivating reef that slopes gently into sand at 60 feet. You will see an excellent selection of soft and hard corals, lots of fish, arrow crabs, lobsters, tubeworms, and anemones. A couple of spotted snake eels hang out here, and you will often see a ray.

The Boulders is a pleasant drift dive about two-thirds of the way between Admiralty Bay and Moonhole. A gentle descent 60 feet down a coral slope takes you into an area where hundreds of fish, including huge schools of blue chromis and sennets, make ever-changing patterns as you drift with the current. Barracudas patrol up and down; moray eels, lobsters, crabs, and shrimps can be found. The reef gets deeper till you come to the boulders, which are tall rock formations, each about 20 feet high, starting from a bottom depth of 93 feet. There are tunnels to pass through and holes and caverns that provide hiding places for nurse sharks, groupers, angelfish, and jacks. As you return to the dive boat, you may see a frogfish or seahorse.

Pigeon Island, to the west of Isle de Quatre, has beautiful dives. The island slopes off steeply to around 100 feet. There are walls, overhangs, rifts, and hollows decorated by deepwater lace coral. The visibility is generally excellent, and you will see huge schools of blue and brown chromis, big groupers, passing pelagic fish, and sometimes rays and turtles.

The Wall (West Cay, northern side) is an adventure dive down to 114 feet, with dramatic vistas, the odd large pelagic, and lots of great stuff to examine along the wall on your way up. Moonhole (outside the Moonhole complex) offers temporary anchorage, though I would leave a crew member on board. Make sure you are anchored in sand and do not tie to the dive moorings. The easiest dive starts right in the bay and follows the reef around the point to the east, but watch for currents. This is a gentle dive to 60 feet, with hard and soft corals and a variety of smaller fish.

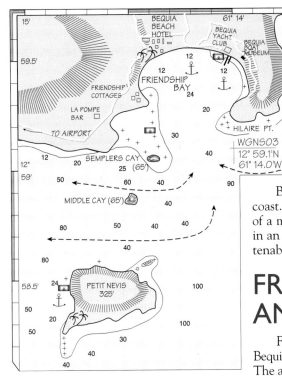

Snorkeling is good around Devil's Table and along the coast to Northwest Point. The dive shops also offer snorkeling trips.

MOONHOLE TO FRIENDSHIP BAY

If you are sailing from Admiralty Bay to West Cay, you will undoubtedly catch sight of Moonhole. This rather isolated community, founded by the late American architect Tom Johnson, is not easily accessible by either land or sea, there being no road or good anchorage. Moonhole houses are certainly different; the original was built under a natural arch known as "Moonhole." It was abandoned when a huge boulder fell from the ceiling and crushed the empty bed. The other houses grow out of the rocks without straight lines or right angles. They have huge arches, fantastic views, and lovely patios. There is seldom glass in the windows and the breeze is constant. There is no electricity. Moonhole is a special kind of vacation home for the right people. The architecture is worth marveling at you sail by.

Bequia's airport is built along the south coast. There is a fishing dock about a third of a mile to its east, off Paget Farm, where in an emergency you can get ashore from a tenable, if rolly, anchorage.

FRIENDSHIP BAY AND PETIT NEVIS

Friendship Bay, on the south side of Bequia, is gorgeous, with a lovely white beach. The anchorage is secure, with good holding, and in times of northerly swells, it provides better protection than Admiralty Bay. A small swell often creeps in from the southeast, but you can cut the roll with a second anchor from the stern to keep yourself into the swells.

Navigation

A reef extends from the shore to Semplers Cay and beyond. Don't try to sail in or out that way, as some have. On the opposite side of the harbor, a reef extends out a fair way from Hilaire Point (locally called "Hillary"). Keep in the center of the channel. Once inside, anchor in the east of the bay or off the Bequia Yacht Club dock. Note that a reef extends from the west side of the Friendship Bay Resort dock down to the beach.

Communications

Bequia Beach Hotel has wifi in the bar, and you can carry your computer there.

Ashore

On the western half of the beach is Bengt's hotel, the Bequia Beach Hotel, one of Bequia's largest and run well. It starts on

273

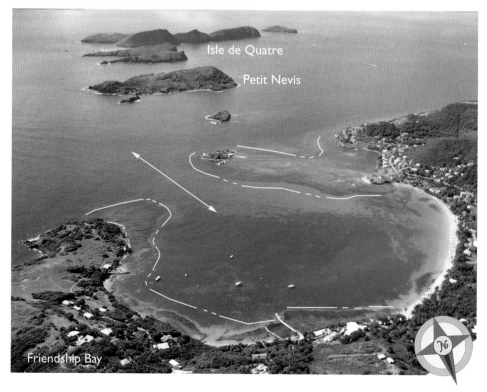

Isle de Quatre

Petit Nevis

Friendship Bay

the beach and flows uphill to the road.

Their Bagatelle Restaurant [$A-B] is delightfully open and right on the beach, with waves lapping just outside. The food is a fusion of local and European cuisine, beautifully cooked and served, making this a very popular destination, not only for people anchored in Friendship Bay but also as a "getaway" from Admiralty Bay. Their Blue Tropic Restaurant is up the hill, open weekday evenings only, for fine Italian food, reservations essential.

If you are making a day of it over here, ask about their day passes and spa treatments.

For yachts, their Bequia Yacht Club down at the east end of the bay is at the moment just one long refurbished dock. They plan to rebuild the dinghy dock to its east and extend the main dock, then link the two to make suitable stern-to docking for superyachts up to 50 meters in length. Water and electricity should be available, and they are building mansions behind.

To the east of the Friendship Bay Hotel, progress has been made on the Bequia

Heritage Foundation's Bequia Boat Museum. Some of Bequia's traditional whaling and fishing boats are here, along with a dug-out canoe. A walk-around platform, always open, will ensure that you can see the exhibits. Take the road that goes around the back of Friendship Bay Hotel and the museum will be on your right.

Water sports

The best snorkeling in Friendship Bay is between Semplers Cay and the shore. You can also try the reef along the shore to the west of the old Friendship Bay Resort dock.

PETIT NEVIS

Petit Nevis was the original whale-rendering island. It makes an interesting daytime anchorage with good exploring. The snorkeling along the shore is good, although the current can be strong out of the lee. If passing southward, note the long, southerly reef.

Mustique at a glance

Regulations

Mustique is a private island. Anchorage is only allowed in Britannia Bay, and there are fees. Access to shore is sometimes restricted. See Mustique text for details.

If you need clearance, customs and immigration are at the airport, normally 0800-1600, but the island is so small that they cannot be too far away out of hours.

Jet skis and the like are strictly forbidden, as are spearfishing and anchoring without supervision. Water-skiing is not permitted in the yacht anchorage area.

Vessels carrying more than 25 passengers are not allowed in Mustique.

Shopping Hours

Corea's food store: Mon-Sat, 0800-1200, 1500-1800. Boutiques: 0900-1200 and 1400-1800. Some boutiques, Ali's and Corea's, open Sunday mornings.

Holidays

See *St. Vincent*.

Telephones

Most Mustique numbers start (784) 488 + four digits. If you are using a private phone in Mustique, you just dial the last four digits of 488 numbers. The most used such phone is in Basil's Bar.

Basil's, 8350
Coreas, 8479
Firefly, 8414
Dive shop, 8486
Mustique Moorings, 8363
Security, 8848/8342
Horse riding, 8316
MMS (bike, mule rental), 8555
Mustique Company, 8424,
Airport, 8336; Customs, 8410
Immigration, 8348
Police, 8339
Medical clinic, 8353
Cotton House, (784) 456-4777 or
    8215

Transport

Ask Mustique Moorings or call:
Johnny P, (784) 530-6285
Pecky, (784) 433-8074
Eddie Boom, (784) 532-1834

Basil's Bar

ST. VINCENT

BEQUIA

BALICEA

PILLORIES

MONTEZUMA SHOAL

BRITANNIA BAY
MUSTIQUE

Mustique

ustique, a privately owned island, was developed by Colin Tennant as a playground for the colorful, rich, and famous. The house owners bought the island from him and have restricted further development. House prices soared from about a million to way over ten times that much and ownership has transitioned from the exotic to business people who value their privacy and don't want nautical yahoos with cameras hiding behind hedges, mistaking them for aging rock stars and models.

Mustique, although private and exclusive, has been kept as friendly and open to yachting visitors as possible. However, some restrictions apply (see *Regulations*). Please help keep it open. Use common courtesy: stick to the roads, do not walk up people's driveways or onto private property. Use the beach south of the anchorage for beach time, or the Cotton House beach if you are hanging out at the beach bar there. Take scenic photos for your own use, but do not photograph residents.

Mustique has about 90 large houses, one hotel, a guesthouse, a beach bar, a few boutiques, a small local village, and a fishing camp. About half the houses are available for rent when the owners are not in residence. As you would expect for an island of this type, prices are geared to the well-heeled. It also has an excellent small medical clinic run by Dr. Michael Bunbury, with good equipment for its size. Call 488-8353 for surgery hours.

What is wonderful about Mustique is that much of the island has been left wild and there are some great trails and not much traffic. As other islands sprout buildings like some invasive weed, much of Mustique remains beautiful and unspoiled, an island where you can often hike or bike in peace on one of the best preserved Grenadine islands, with fabulous beaches and shady pathways.

Navigation

Montezuma Shoal is about half to three-quarters of a mile west of Britannia Bay. It presents a real hazard and has ground pieces off the hulls of a cruise ship, a large charter yacht, and many a bareboat. It is marked by a red and black buoy. Stay at least a quarter of a mile away. If you come from the south, do not follow the coast too closely, as there is quite a reef extending seaward from the southern point of Britannia Bay.

The only permissible anchorage is in Britannia Bay. Anchoring is not allowed anywhere else. If you see a yacht moored in Endeavour Bay, it belongs to one of the house owners. Britannia Bay has sparkling clear water and is a lovely area for swimming and snorkeling, though it is generally rather rolly. The north side of the harbour has loud music Wednesday nights.

Regulations

The Mustique Company controls the coastal waters of Mustique and provides 30 well-maintained moorings for yachts up to 60 feet, and legally they cannot take yachts even one inch longer. Yachts over 60 feet must anchor outside the moorings under the direction of Berris Little, the harbormaster (Mustique Moorings, VHF: 16/68, (784) 488-8363/533-0216). They are around most of the day from 0800-1800, but sometimes away 1230-1430.

There is a conservation fee that entitles you to a three-consecutive-night stay. This fee in $EC is: up to 70 feet, $200; 71-85 feet, $300; 76-100 feet, $400; over 100 feet, $500. Berris or Shean Snagg collects the fees and gives you an official receipt. Their hut is at the end of the jetty. The moorings do not lift, so can be hard to reach. Call Berris and he will come out and help you. Otherwise put a dinghy in the water, or, if you have a stern platform, come stern-to so you are low enough to tie onto the mooring. There is no extra charge for the moorings.

Each buoy has a swivel on top. Attach your lines through the swivel. Use two lines, one to each side of your bow. Allow plenty of line to increase the scope (20 feet minimum, more if your bow is high off the water). Never use a single line from one side of the boat through the mooring to the other side. Yachts of up to 45 feet and 6- to 7-foot draft can use any mooring. Longer and deeper yachts should use the outer moorings which are more widely spaced over sand. If you are over 60 feet or all the moorings are taken, contact Berris for anchoring instructions.

Day-charter yachts visiting Mustique pay a landing fee of $30 EC per head. This is also charged to those on yachts taking day trips and tours; ask Berris for details.

Tenders should only be used to drop people ashore in Britannia Bayn or go to the beach in the same bay. They should not be used to visit other parts of the island.

Drones and press photography are banned unless express permission has been given by the Mustique Company.

Mustique is a private island, with owners who are concerned about privacy and security. Unfortunately, a few guests from yachts have trespassed in private houses. Captains are responsible for their crew and guests, and the Mustique Company has the right to permanently ban any captain and yacht whose passengers or crew misbehave.

Regulations may be changed by the Mustique Company at any time. Here is how things stand:

The designated visitor area is open. This goes all the way from the local village past the anchorage, and south along the western shore as far as the salt pond, and you can walk the salt pond trail. If you wish to go outside this area, please talk to Berris or Sean at the moorings office, and let them know what you wish to do. This way they will know who is wandering about the island and what they are doing.

Sometimes (normally three weeks over Christmas and the new year, two weeks in August, and two weeks over Easter), land access is restricted and you cannot go outside the visitors area unless you have a confirmed reservation for the Cotton House or Firefly in which case, you must ask them to send

Stanley's Market

transport for you. If at these times you need to visit customs or the clinic, arrange it with Berris or Sean.

There is some flexibility, and during these times, you can call Berris before you come to discuss what you want to do. You may even be able to hike, though you may have to take a local guide.

Beach picnic tables have been set up for the use of residents. People on yachts may sometimes be able to use the ones in the visitor area at no charge; ask Berris for details.

Communications

Mustique has an excellent library, where you can catch up on the internet (six computers) or read the latest magazines and peruse their books. You can send faxes or make photocopies. Contributions of good books are always welcome. They open Monday to Saturday 0900-1300, 1500-1800.

There is wifi around Basil's and Sweetie Pie, and you might be able to get it at anchor.

Services

Garbage disposal is at the head of the dock. Transport within the island is provided by a Mustique bus service, and these can sometimes take you on an island tour. They can be found outside Mustique Moorings and Berris can help you make arrangements.

When you realize the roll is so bad you will never be able to sleep a wink, contact The View, Firefly House or The Cotton House to see if they have available rooms. (Basil's Bar can put you in touch.)

Provisioning and shopping

Corea's supermarket has a good selection. Augment this with fresh fruit and vegetables from Stanley's photogenic little stall, where prices are reasonable and the service unbeatable. Go to Basil's Gourmet store for wines, cheeses, fine coffees, and specialty foods (also for local/nature books and music CDs). For fish, try the fish market, where you can buy fresh fish and lobster in season. Glendina sometimes sells fresh produce at a stand on the road to the local village.

In the morning, head down to Sweetie Pie Bakery, Cafe and Boulangerie between the pink and purple houses to stock up on fresh croissants, pain au chocolat, and Danish, along with many other pastries. French owner Ali bakes these, plus many kinds of excellent bread. Ali will be happy to discuss charter boat requirements. They also sell coffee, ice cream, lunch-time sandwiches, and over 150 daily and weekly newspapers in many languages. They have comfortable outdoor seating and open 0700-1800.

The Purple House is an excellent boutique run by Susie, who has a collection of swimwear, casual and not-so casual clothing, hand-crafted gifts and souvenirs, games, hats, pareos, hand-painted calabash art, costume jewelry, and more. The Pink House has a more complete range of elegant clothing, plus some casual clothing and kids' togs, and a big selection of jewelry.

Basil has two shops: Basil's Boutique is in Basil's Bar, and Across Forever, which is an antique and collectibles shop, is on the other side of the road. Basil travels to far eastern ports and brings back his favorite items for the shops, plus the famous Basil's t-shirts and bags.

The Cotton House has a boutique on the left, just before Endeavour Bay, in the same building as the Gym. If you need household hardware, get a taxi to take you to the Mustique Depot.

Restaurants

Basil's Bar [VHF: 68, $A-B] is built of wood and bamboo and is perched on stilts over the water, with waves lapping underneath. Informal, and the most popular establishment with the yachting community, this is the Caribbean's most famous beach bar and is the place to meet people, to contact other establishments on the island, to relax and look at the sunset, or just to get off your rolling boat for dinner (seafood and lobster are specialties). Many come for the popular Wednesday night barbecue buffet, which is followed by a jump-up. They usually have light jazz/blues music from 1730 to 1930 on Sundays, often featuring Jan and Louis. Basil organizes a superb two-week blues festival towards the end of January to early February, which also visits Bequia. Proceeds from the sale of CDs from this go to Basil Charles Eduction Foundation, supporting

St. Vincent & the Grenadines

local students and schools throughout the country. If you are interested in helping, pick up a flyer in Basil's.

The local village is always open to yachts and here Lisa Lewis has a restaurant with an incredible view of Britannia Bay, naturally called The View [$C-D]. Take the short cut up the hill: take the little path at the side of the boutiques, bear left at the bird cage, turn right on the road, and then left up the steps shortly after. At the top, turn left, walk to the end, and you are there.

Lisa opens from breakfast to dinner every day. For lunch, Lisa does a big trade in take-out for both locals and residents. You can walk in for lunch, but calling in advance is much better and will give you a choice of food. If you are coming to dinner, you have to give her a little warning. She is personable, hardworking, and will cook you a delicious meal with good fresh vegetables for a reasonable price. Her fish is fresh, and her sautéed conch delightful. You can also get beef, mutton, and chicken. Saturday night she does a popular barbecue. If you need a night ashore, Lisa has some rooms.

Other village restaurants include Brockie's, owned by Becky, and Selwyn's Embassy Bar [both $D], both of which serve good lunch specials most days. Brockie's sometimes has chicken and chips in the evenings and both will cook a good dinner to order. If you want to just hang out for a drink, try Piccadilly Sports Bar or Hill Top Bar.

Stan and Elizabeth, from England, own a guesthouse and bar/restaurant called Firefly [$A]. It has a dramatic view over the flood-lit swimming pool to Britannia Bay. The atmosphere is elegant and a touch formal, yet friendly, making it popular with those who spend time on the island. Regulars gather round the bar in the evening, and a piano occasionally inspires one of them to play for a while. Their food is an inventive blend of Caribbean and European cuisine, using fresh ingredients. You will love the desserts. Wander up for lunch or dinner. The short walk will whet your appetite, but for those who prefer to ride, a staff member will come and collect dinner guests from the dock. Reservations are advisable.

For superb cuisine in lavish elegance,

don your best evening pants or a dress (it is somewhat formal) and call the Cotton House [$A]. It is about a 15-minute walk, but if you make dinner reservations, they are happy to come and get you. Cotton House, owned and run by the Mustique Company, is one of the fanciest hotels in the Caribbean. Originally an 18th century coral warehouse and sugar mill, it was artfully rebuilt by the late British designer, Oliver Messel.

They usually have top chefs and, when on form, their dinner restaurant, the Veranda, produces the best cuisine on the island. The Beach Cafe, right on the beach in Endeavour Bay, is perfect for a morning coffee and pastry, ice cream, or lunch of fresh fish or lobster (1230-1500). The Beach Cafe sometimes opens in the evening (ask reception for a program) and is available in the evening for private functions.

For a real treat, renovate your body with a visit to the Cotton House Spa, featuring ILA treatments and a gym. Cotton House has a museum in the sugar mill with some good pre-Columbian pottery and stone work. It is usually open, just walk in and take look.

Ashore

For a quick view of the island, you can see if a Mustique bus can do a tour (this is sometimes restricted). To really enjoy the beauty of this island, go hiking. Basil's Gourmet store has great books on the natural history of Mustique. If you turn right at the main dock and follow the road south, staying on the path that follows the shore, you will have a delightful walk. It joins a trail that goes around the salt pond, and brings you to a perfect beach at Lagoon Bay.

If you get more ambitious, (and there are no restrictions) follow our map taking the roads that lead to Obsidian Bay. Head south from the dock, staying on the road. After about 20 minutes you will pass a couple of roads on your right and see gate posts on the road; continue through the gate posts. Turn left at a junction where there is a concrete shed on the left corner and a grate across the road, and a sign saying "Penthouse" opposite. Go up the hill, and where you have a choice of concrete (left fork) and dirt track (right fork), take the dirt. This brings you to

Obsidian Bay, and from there you can follow wonderful trails around South Point and up the east coast to Pasture Bay. From here you can walk back to Britannia Bay (total hike 3-4 hours).

Another excellent hike is around North Point, from the north around to the east, till you can see Macaroni and Pasture Bays. For this one, you need to get a taxi to drop you off at the trail head right by L'Ansecou House. The trail starts down what looks like a nameless private drive, but just before the "private" sign, the trail leads off to the right. It follows the coast, sometimes along open cliffs, sometimes bounded by dry scrub trees. By the time you have walked back to Britannia Bay it will take about three hours, though you can bail out halfway at Rutland Bay. Keep your eye open on all hikes for the pretty land tortoises.

Horseback riding is done in the cool of the day, at 0800, 0900, 1500 or 1600. Mountain bikes are sometimes available through Mustique Mechanical Services or Mustique Moorings.

Water sports

You can go sailboarding or diving at Mustique Water Sports [VHF: 68]. Brian Richards, the dive instructor and manager, is very good and will pick divers up from their yachts when space is available. The water is generally very clear, and diving is pleasant.

Walk-in Reef is just off the dive shop dock and ideal for beginners. At South Britannia Drift Dive, you let the current carry you through a delightful garden of soft corals as you watch large schools of Bermuda chubs and Creole wrasses. The occasional sight of an eagle ray makes it perfect. The wreck of the Jonas, a 90-foot dredge, lies in 40 feet of water on the east side of Montezuma Shoal. Beautiful coral formations there are home to barracudas and nurse sharks. At Southeast Pillory Drift Dive, the current sweeps you along a steep slope, which drops from 20 feet to 90 feet. The scenery is ever changing as you go along, with lots of reef fish and large soft corals. Dry Rock (on the south side of Petit Mustique) is the place for the big fish: schools of barracudas, nurse sharks, and rays. You often see turtles.

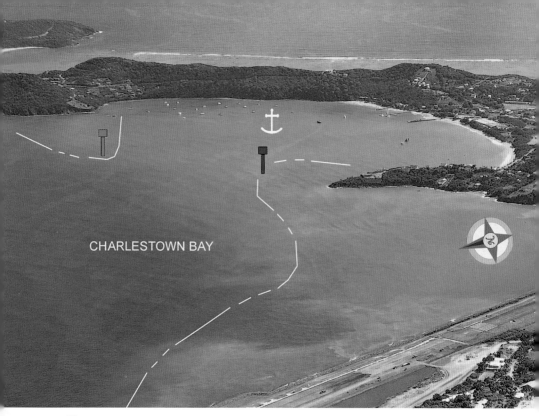

CHARLESTOWN BAY

Canouan (For information on holidays, customs, etc., see *St. Vincent*)

Canouan is a lovely island with spectacular beaches, pleasant walks, and great views almost anywhere. Walk up the hill to the east and see the fabulous windward lagoon, where an outer reef protects the island.

It is also an island of three parts. The southern (local) part has moved from a sleepy backwater of small wooden houses and fields of pigeon peas to a prosperous settlement of big solid houses. This local part, with the main anchorage is warm and welcoming; the locals are friendly, love visiting yachts, and provide services for them.

The Canouan Resort Development Company (CRD) owns, has developed, and manages the north of the island. This, the largest part, is gated, with guards at the entry points, and locals and visitors alike need permission to enter. CRD built a hotel of about 180 rooms with a giant beach restaurant and pool. Now they have torn it all down and built

a boutique hotel of about 25 rooms farther down the shore.

To the southeast, Dermot Desmond has the big new "Marina of the Grenadines" project well under way. It will take boats up to 110 meters with 5.3 meters draft. I hope access to that end of the island and South Glossy beach will remain open to the public and not be gated against the 1500 local residents who live in the middle, as the north is.

The airport is excellent, with plenty of room for the largest private jet, and maybe the cutest thatched-roof airport building in the world.

Navigation

Deep-draft vessels should avoid Grand Cai, about 0.75 miles west of Jupiter Point. While this shoal is generally about 36 feet deep, it has a small isolated 16-foot shoal at 12° 44.490'N, 61° 20.645'W. Seas in this general area are often 6-8 feet high, further reducing the depth. It badly damaged the keel of a sailing super-yacht. It is too small to cause a noticeable difference in the sea state and is normally of no consequence to yachts with less than 10-foot draft.

Planes approaching the airport come in low over the sea, so give the western end of the runway good clearance.

Rameau Bay is a pleasant spot, far from the village. You may have to try a couple of times to get the anchor dug in, and the wind shifts around, so two anchors are advisable.

Make sure you do not damage the coral. L'Anse Guyac (aka Corbay) is one of the most protected anchorages on the island. Mr. Pignataro, one of the developers, built a private eating house here, imported many tons of white sand and persuaded the government to ban anchoring in the bay. You can anchor just outside in about 20 feet of water. Watch out for the reefs off both headlands. Whether you anchor here, in Rameau Bay, or in town, you should dinghy to this beach and enjoy all that imported sand, and also the good snorkeling around the headlands.

St. Vincent & the Grenadines

SOUTH GLOSSY BAY

FRIENDSHIP BAY

Charlestown Bay is the main anchorage and the entrance is marked by a red and green beacon on either side. Pass between them. You can anchor anywhere in the bay except close to Tamarind Hotel Beach, where you must anchor outside any moorings. The anchorage can be pleasant, but northeasterly winds with northerly swells will make it uncomfortable and, in extreme conditions, untenable. The holding is fairly good in sand, poor in weed. Leave a large, clear channel into the big dock for ferries.

On windy days, the wind gets held up in the hills and then shoots down from the north in intense gusts. Boats swing every which way.

Regulations

Customs and immigration are in the big Government revenue office building in town, 0800-1600 on weekdays. They are also at the airport almost any time of day and on weekends.

Communications

You can check email at Tamarind Beach Hotel in reception, they also have wifi. With a smart phone/computer hook up you wifi in the bay is good using either digicel or Lime. Both of which have offices in town, which tend to open around 1030.

General yacht services

A large ferry dock and roll on platform is on the beach, and two docks are just north at the Tamarind Beach Hotel. In big swells they are all dangerous. The big ferry dock is high and difficult. You may use the Tamarind Beach Hotel docks as long as the swells are not too big. The other hotel dock is abandoned.

Two marine services run by cousins Marcus and John provide most things you need. They offer good, frequently inspected moorings at $50 EC a night. They sell ice and water (currently desal water at $1 EC a gallon delivered alongside making Canouan the best Grenadines top up). They will also take your garbage for a small fee. Either can take you ashore, and help arrange any kind of tour or anything else you need.

Call John's Marine Services or Marcus Marine Services on [VHF: 16]. Many of their moorings are in front of the Tamarind

NEW MARINA UNDER CONSTRUCTION

St. Vincent & the Grenadines

Beach Hotel. (If you anchor inside these, you are too close to the hotel.) Marcus's son Mark, aided by Sharka, normally runs his boat. John is often on his boat, or his assistant, who wears a company t-shirt. You will be happy with either service; both are professional.

Gazimo plans to bring in a fuel barge which will deliver diesel and gasoline alongside. In the meantime, John and Marcus can help you out with fuel.

Tamarind Beach Hotel [VHF: 16] sells freshly made bread at Gastronomy Deli and the Palapa Restaurant. Ice is also available. They have a massage and body-care center, and a taxi service. Hotel day pass rates are available; ask at reception.

There are some garbage bins ashore: two are often close to the big government building, and a couple others are on the main street. Try not to bring in too much.

The coastguard station and dock are in the north end of the bay. Diesel and gas are sold at the gas station behind the southern end of the beach and will be in the marina when it is completed.

Technical yacht services

Gazimo Marine Services [VHF:16] is owned and run by Gazimo (Earl) who worked for years as head mechanic in a Toronto marina repair shop. He is competent, easy to work with, and can deal with any problem you have, from a clogged head to a jammed winch. He is an excellent diesel mechanic and can fix outboards. He has tons of experience fixing broken charter yachts in Canada, and his ex-boss, Robert, who has a holiday house here, occasionally likes to help out. Gazimo is also the man to see if you have a torn sail - he does not sew himself, but there is a woman on the island with a big heavy machine and he can arrange it. Gazimo also rents golf-carts and mules. See *Transport*. He is also bringing in a fuel barge for alongside delivery of gas and diesel (see *general yacht services*)

Provisioning and shopping

Tamarind Beach Hotel's Italian deli, Buon Appetito, is a fancy delicatessen selling the finest Italian cold cuts and cheeses, and Bar opens at 1600. You are welcome in shorts/casual wear. Comfortable seating in a garden setting overlooking the bay makes this an ideal hangout. Meals are available and include seafood and meat dishes as well as pasta. They also prepare great pizzas in a wooden pizza oven from 1900.

Their Beach Bar opens from 1000 to 1800. You can get lunch or a light snack between 1200 and 1800.

Andre's Sea Grape is just south of the main dock. He has done a great job renovating this building, which is on the beach. It is open every day 0900-2200. You can get lunch and dinner, but you need to make reservations for dinner, They offer good local food, specializing in fresh local seafood, but also offering meat dishes.

Mangrove [$C-D] is a good local restaurant owned by Albert, who also owns Canouan Food Limited. It is quite far down the road, just where the airport road turns up the hill. The beach location is perfect, the prices and food are local, with very inexpensive lunches and moderately priced dinners, including fresh fish and lobster. They open for lunch and dinner every day.

Marcus's sister, Phyllis, has a restaurant called DQ's [$D] on the main street opposite the road that comes from the town dock and a few steps to the left. It opens for lunch and dinner and she cooks good and inexpensive barbecue foods. Frontline [$C-D] is a cute little restaurant on main street

The Pink Sands Club [$A] is a very fancy boutique hotel in the gated northern part of the island, with tennis courts, villas, and a golf course. They may offer day passes, golf passes, and you may be able to visit for a meal.

Other restaurants include Pompoy's Bar and Restaurant, Tip Top Bar (opens at 1900; for a meal call Chester Deroche in advance, 458-8021), Honey Chrome, and Glimpses Bar.

Transport

Gazimo and his partner Deborah at Gazimo Marine Services [VHF:16], rent various sized mules and golf carts, which are ideal for anything you need to do on the island, be it a fun tour, leaving from the

preserves, pastas, cookies and sauces, along with a wide selection of Italian wines, French champagne, and liqueurs. They are open 1000-1400 and 1800-2000, closed Mondays.

Panini and freshly baked bread are available daily. You will be able to find all kind of specialty food like pate, truffles and buffalo mozzarella. They can prepare gift baskets. If you come for lunch, you can use the seats in the Pirates Cove Bar.

Canouan Food Limited is on the main street and opens 0800-2000, except Sunday, 0800-1200. They have a good selection for a small market, including quite a few local and imported vegetables. If you are buying cases of beer and more than you can carry, they will deliver to the dock. Some other shops are okay, check out Rock Steady bakery next to Gazimo. The bank has an ATM.

Market stalls on the street leading to the ferry dock have local produce.

Restaurants

The Tamarind Beach Hotel [VHF: 16, $A] has an ideal beach location with a good dinghy dock, and yachts are welcome. This elegant hotel has two waterfront restaurants under the picturesque thatched roofs that have been built in the traditional Southern American style.

La Palapa is the most formal restaurant and is open for breakfast, lunch and dinner. You are asked to wear long trousers, shirt and closed shoes for dinner. It is advised to make reservations in advance to be sure of seating.

The informal Pirate's Cove Restaurant

airport, or provisioning. These carts have a roof but are otherwise open to the breeze and view. The golf carts are easy to drive, can do a U-turn on any road, and are perfect for this small island. They are not expensive, there is no paperwork, and they will rent them by the half-day which is great for an island tour.

You can also arrange a regular taxi with Tamarind Beach Hotel.

Ashore

Rent one of Gazimo's mules or golf carts and take a tour; there are many spectacular views. Or at least walk up to the ridge to see the wonderful, reef-protected lagoon.

Mount Royal is the highest hill in Canouan, with great views. It is in the gated part of the island so you will have to call up and arrange a guide to take you (about $20 US per head).

The Tamarind Hotel can also arrange island tours or picnics on secluded beaches.

SOUTH GLOSSY BAY

You can anchor off this lovely beach. The water here is gorgeous, but it can be rolly. The best shore access will be via the marina.

The new Marina of the Grenadines is under construction here, a joint project between Dermont Desmond (IIU) and the government. They hope to open the marina about the time this guide comes out.

FRIENDSHIP BAY

Keen snorkelers might be interested in a daytime stop at Friendship Bay on Canouan's south coast. Approach past Glossy Bay, pass inside or outside Dove Cay and associated rocks, and follow the coast, keeping a good lookout for coral heads. Friendship Bay is usually a bit rolly, but is the best anchorage in large northerly swells. You can use the fishing dock for your dinghy. In settled conditions you can dinghy up the windward side of Canouan inside the reefs, where the snorkeling is good and some yachts would anchor and kitesurf. The government has currently banned this but a few yachts still go.

Water sports

At least 10 good dives can be found in Canouan. There are walls with giant boulders and sloping reefs, and sharks, turtles, and rays are often spotted. For those diving on their own, the easiest spot to anchor for a dive is in Corbay. Dive to seaward of the rocky headland on the northern side of the bay. You can dinghy north up the coast and look for your own spot. Snorkeling is good around the rocks in Rameau Bay.

Canouan Scuba Center, a Padi dive shop, is in the Tamarind Beach Hotel, at the head of the longer dock, south of the dinghy dock. Jean and Steve are well qualified and helpful. They are happy to pick people up off the yachts here and farther south in the Grenadines. It is a Padi operation.

St. Vincent & the Grenadines

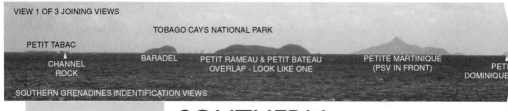

TOBAGO CAYS NATIONAL PARK

PETIT TABAC

CHANNEL
ROCK

BARADEL

PETIT RAMEAU & PETIT BATEAU
OVERLAP - LOOK LIKE ONE

PETITE MARTINIQUE
(PSV IN FRONT)

PETIT
DOMINIQUE

SOUTHERN GRENADINES IDENTIFICATION VIEWS

SOUTHERN GRENADINES PASSAGES

From Canouan to Carriacou, the Grenadines huddle together, each just a short hop from the next. The islands are generally small and quiet.

Any island with a few inhabitants will also have a rum shop where you can meet people and learn to drink Jack Iron ~ a powerful, rough, white rum, sometimes distilled far from government inspectors. A small shot is poured into a glass, and the idea is to down it all in one gulp, preferably without tasting. Then you reach for a large glass of water to put out the fire.

Navigation

The current sets to the west most of the time, so head east of your destination until you have got the feel of its strength. The southern Grenadines are strewn with keel-hungry reefs. This is the area where people make the most mistakes, and several yachts have been lost. Usually this is because people misidentify islands. If you approach this area with just a shade of apprehension and self-questioning, you should be okay.

Several navigational beacons help. Most of them are on the edges of shoals, so keep well clear.

Sailing south

When you round Glossy (Glass) Hill at Canouan, you must be sure you know which island is which. Mayreau lies in front of Union, and some people see the two as one island and then mistake the Tobago Cays for Mayreau. If you are heading for the lee of Mayreau, your compass heading should be around

VIEW 2 (REPEAT)

SALT WHISTLE
BAY

CARRIACOU

MAYREAU

PALM ISLAND

PETIT
DOMINIQUE

BALEINE
ROCKS

VIEW 2
SALT WHISTLE BAY
CARRIACOU
MAYREAU
PALM ISLAND
PETIT DOMINIQUE
BALEINE ROCKS
VIEWS TAKEN WHILE ROUNDING GLOSSY HILL

225-230° magnetic. If you find yourself sailing between south and 200°, you are probably heading for the Tobago Cays ~ and trouble.

Tobago Cays. (See also sketch charts, page 295 and 299), If you approach the Tobago Cays from the north, the easiest and best route is as follows: after you round Glossy Hill, head for the middle of Mayreau (about 228° magnetic). As you approach Mayreau, you can see Baleine Rocks. Leave these to port, giving them reasonable clearance, and sail on until you are over halfway between them and Mayreau, before heading up into the Tobago Cays. Line up the day markers in the Cays if you can see them. (Note: Petit Rameau and Petit Bateau look like one island for much of the approach.)

An alternative, and much trickier approach is to head a bit to the east of Mayreau from Glossy Hill, and then sail 100 yards to the east of Baleine Rocks, between the rocks and the northwest end of Horseshoe Reef. This entrance channel is about a quarter-of-a-mile wide, and Horseshoe Reef is often not visible, so caution is advised. The current can be strong, so make sure you are not being set down onto the rocks. Once past the rocks, hold course until the day markers line up, then head up into the islands.

Mayreau. When approaching Mayreau, you have to avoid Dry Shingle, which only has a stump of a marker. Pass close to Salt Whistle Bay. When sailing round the lee of Mayreau, watch out for the reef off Grand Col Point, which is usually marked by a red buoy, but the color and even the buoy itself are not reliable. Pass well outside this reef. When heading to Palm or Union, you need to head well up, at least to the middle of Palm Island, until you figure out how much you are being set down, as the current can be

St. Vincent & the Grenadines

VIEW 3
SALT WHISTLE BAY
THE PINNACLE
UNION ISLAND
CATHOLIC ISLAND
CATHOLIC ROCKS
MAYREAU

Carriacou   Mayreau   Union Island   Glossy Hill   Catholic Island

North Canouan affords an ideal spot from which to identify some of the islands to the south

very strong. Watching the airport on Union against Carriacou gives an idea of current set. Union's deadly windward reef (Newlands Reef) extends halfway to Palm Island, so you have to sail almost to Palm before heading west into Clifton Harbour. Note that there are three red beacons on Newlands Reef. You leave these to starboard as you head into Clifton. Swing in a curve well outside them.

Grand de Coi, between Union and Palm, is a dangerous reef. It is not quite as bad as it used to be, as the center part of it is now usually above water and visible. There is a yellow and black beacon on its western side. You must always pass to the west (Union Island side) of this beacon, keeping well clear. Numerous yachts have run aground here, and several have been destroyed, usually coming from Petit St. Vincent (PSV) to Palm or Union. The following pointers may also be helpful in gauging your position.

All directions: When there is a gap between PSV and Petite Martinique, you are too far south to hit Grand de Coi. When this gap is closed, keep clear of Grand de Coi by watching the western side of Mayreau against the Union Island airport. If you keep the west side of Mayreau behind the airport you will be west of Grand de Coi. A gap between the two stands you in danger.

For all directions south: Sail to the entrance of Clifton Harbor, then pass west of the Grand de Coi beacon.

To Carriacou: Head toward the northwest coast. When you approach Hillsborough, it is safest to pass to the west of Jack a Dan before rounding up into town.

To PSV: When you have passed Grand de Coi, steer for the east side of Carriacou until PSV bears due east, then head on in, passing well to the south of Mopion, Pinese,

and all their surrounding reefs. Keep an eye on current set and compensate if necessary.

A trickier and more dangerous way is to pass between the two little sand cays, Mopion and Pinese. The course from the lee side of Grand de Coi is around 165-170° magnetic, though with current you may have to head considerably more to the east. A bearing of 160° magnetic on the highest peak of Petite Martinique takes you close enough to eyeball your way in. Mopion usually has a small thatch shelter on it. Always sail through the center of the passage, and do not round up too soon, as the reef extends about a quarter of a mile southwest of Mopion. Recently, this has been easier because another small sandbar formed closer to the edge of the reef (see our PSV and Petite Martinique chart). Treat this passage with caution.

Sailing north

From Carriacou to Clifton and Palm:
The safest route is to pass to the west of Jack a Dan, and then follow the coast up to Rapid Point. From Rapid Point, aim for the east side of Union, checking on the current set by watching Frigate Island against Union. As you near Union, you should be able to see the reefs between Frigate and Clifton. Do not get too close to these, as the current and wind are setting you down on them. On the other hand, keep a good eye out for the Grand de Coi reef to the east. Stay to the west of the beacon that marks this reef (see also Grand de Coi notes, above, under Mayreau).

From PSV to Union:
Sail due west till you are on a line between the east coasts of Carriacou and Union before changing course to Clifton. Before the gap closes between PSV and Petite Martinique, edge westward till the finger of land on the western side of

61° 30'   25'   16

100

SOUTHERN GRENADINES
SOME SUGGESTED ROUTES

*THE CHANNEL EAST OF BALEINE ROCKSAND THE CHAN-
NEL BETWEEN PINESE AND MOPION CAN BE TRICKY DUE
TO STRONG CURRENTS AND SHOULD BE USED WITH
CAUTION.

CANOUAN

GLOSSY HILL

12° 42.4'N
61° 21.4'W
WGNS09

20

40

100

110

12°
40'

CATHOLIC I.

(230'/150'm)

BALEINE RKS.

211° / 31° M*

⊕ CHANNEL RK.

⊕ BREAK RK.

⊕

90

40'

TOBAGO
CAYS

600

90

MAYREAU

90

P. TABAC

60

UNION I.

120

12° 36.0'
61° 28.0'
WGNS14

CHATHAM
BAY

CLIFTON

60

PALM I.

60

35'

FRIGATE I.

⊕ GRAND DE COI

80

35'

130

90

177° / 357° M*

MOPION

70

PINESE ⊙

195° / 15° M

226° / 46° M

PETIT ST.
VINCENT
(PSV)

RAPID PT.

600

90

FOTA ⊕

PETITE
MARTINIQUE

12° 30.0'N
61° 30.8'W
WGNS20

JACKADAN ⊙

P. DOMINIQUE

50

30'

MABOUYA I.

4

SANDY I.

40

25

70

24

SISTERS

N

HILLSBOROUGH

RADIO
MAST

NW   NE

W   E

SW   SE

70

TYRREL
BAY

S

CARRIACOU

90

0   1   2   3   4   5

WHITE I.   SALINE I.

120

SCALE IN NAUTICAL MILES

61° 30'   25'   20'

St. Vincent & the Grenadines

Mayreau disappears behind Union Island airport. Pass to the west of the Grand de Coi beacon. Experienced sailors could head out between Mopion and Pinese and then head for the Pinnacle until the finger of land on the western side of Mayreau disappears behind the new Union Island airport, or until the Grand de Coi beacon is identified. Always pass well to the west of the Grand de Coi beacon.

From Palm northwards: Always sail round the lee of Mayreau. Pass to the west of Grand Col Point, staying well clear of the reef. Then, as you get to the north of Mayreau, stay well east of Dry Shingle (marked by a black and yellow beacon), which extends eastward from Catholic Island.

Approaching the Tobago Cays from the south: Sail round the lee of Mayreau, then head straight up toward the middle of the Cays. If you are tacking under sail, favor the Mayreau side of the channel when passing Baleine Rocks to avoid the one-fathom shoal to their south. There is a southern entrance to the Cays, but it is tricky and should not be attempted without local knowledge. Many charter yachts have run aground here. However, if you are in the Cays on a quiet day with good reef visibility, you could try leaving by this route to go south.

When leaving the Cays to go north: The safest route is to sail from the anchorage to the north end of Mayreau, then head north after you have passed Baleine Rocks. There is also a channel to the east of Baleine Rocks about a quarter of a mile wide. From the Cays, you have to head just south of the rocks until you reach the channel and then turn north, or you are in danger of hitting the western edge of Horseshoe Reef.

DIVING IN THE SOUTHERN GRENADINES

The normally clear water makes diving in the southern Grenadines wonderful, though currents can be strong, and many dives have to be done as drift dives.

Diving within the Tobago Cays marine park (the area from well to the west of Mayreau through to the outside of World's End Reef). must be with a local dive shop.

One call and a dive boat will come by and pick you up from your yacht in the Tobago Cays, Mayreau, or Union.

Grenadines Dive [VHF: 16/68] is a pleasant, relaxed, dive operation in Union Island run by Glenroy Adams from Bequia. Glenroy has incredible experience in this area, knows the sites better than anyone else, and has done much for environmental education in Union, and for the conservation of the Tobago Cays. Glenroy will collect you from your yacht in Union, Mayreau, PSV, or the Tobago Cays. If you are on a big yacht with a large tender and own your own dive gear, Glenroy can supply a really knowledgeable dive guide. He will also do private dives. If you are short of ice or have run out of bread, he will happily bring some along on his way out.

Jean-Michel Cousteau Diving is based in PSV. This upmarket operation, where everything is top class, is primarily for PSV guests. They may occasionally have room for additional guests. See also Canouan Dive Center under *Canouan*.

You can still dive on your own in Canouan, Union, and PSV. In Union, you can dive on the outer edge of Newlands Reef, which is very easy from your yacht. In Chatham, you can dive on the northern headland and the coast farther north, and in PSV you can dive on the north side of the reef around Mopion.

Dives within the park include the wreck of the World War I gunboat Purina. It is marked on our chart (page 291). While you can certainly get some elegant views of large schools of fish, framed by pieces of wreckage, this dive does not compare in scenic beauty with the reef dives. As it is only 140 feet long, it is a dive where you don't move much ~ you are already there. Take it easy and get on more intimate terms with the fish and sea creatures, of which there are a great abundance. Since the fish are very tame, it is ideal for underwater photography.

Surface current over the wreck can be strong, but down on the wreck it is not usually a problem. I start with a slow exploration to see the layout to get a feel for the kinds of fish present. Then I examine each part of the wreck, concentrating on the invertebrates and letting the fish come to me as they will.

Diving outside Horseshoe Reef on either side of the small boat passage is pretty, but watch for current, though in this area it is mostly on the surface. Farther north, the current can be very strong, and it is more suitable as a drift dive. Diving is also good on the reef outside Petit Tabac.

Diving in some of the cuts among the reefs between Mayreau and the Cays is spectacular. Discovered by Glenroy, this area is called Mayreau Gardens. If you manage to dive one of these in clear visibility, it could turn out to be the dive of your holiday. There is usually a lot of current, so we are talking drift dives, sometimes so rapid that you come to the surface over a mile from where you

went down. You hardly need to fin. The current does all the work while you get wafted through a delightful garden of hard and soft corals, sponges, and fish. My favorite part is on the southern side of the gardens. A sloping reef drops to a sand bottom in 40-60 feet. The reef has a wonderful texture made up of all kinds of corals. Boulder, pillar, and plate corals rise in a variety of intricate shapes. Some areas of huge sea fans are so large you can play hide-and-seek behind them. The special luminous quality of the light, typical in the Grenadines, seems to extend below the waves. Massive schools of brown and blue chromis engulf you from time to time, swimming inches from your mask. A few yards away, schools of snapper and jack swim by purposefully creating a flurry of nervousness in the chromis. Angelfish, trumpetfish, large boxfish, and brightly colored parrotfish are there as well.

Mayreau

Mayreau is rimmed with pristine beaches and offers spectacular views from up on the hill. It is one of the smaller locally inhabited Grenadines with a just one village. Originally the whole island was owned by the Eustace family of St. Vincent, and inhabitants owned no land. Then land in the village was made available to them and now much of the island has been sold.

For generations the Roman Catholics were the only religious show in town with their picturesque little church on the hill. Now, a big new church faces it on the other side of the road, courtesy of one of the Eustace family, offering a livelier approach to the almighty. Apart from this the island is relatively unchanged. Most islanders are happy to see you, and indeed yachts are a mainstay of the economy. You can and should walk around the island, up to the village and down the other side and explore

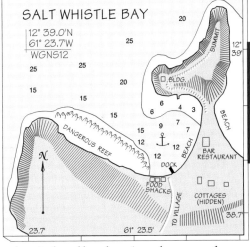

the windward beaches. A road now runs from Saline Bay to Salt Whistle Bay, with many side roads. All the waters around Mayreau are part of the Tobago Cays Marine Park. Park visitation fees are not being collected, but there is no diving on your own.

SALT WHISTLE BAY

This spectacular bay has a beautiful, sweeping half-moon beach. Many years ago,

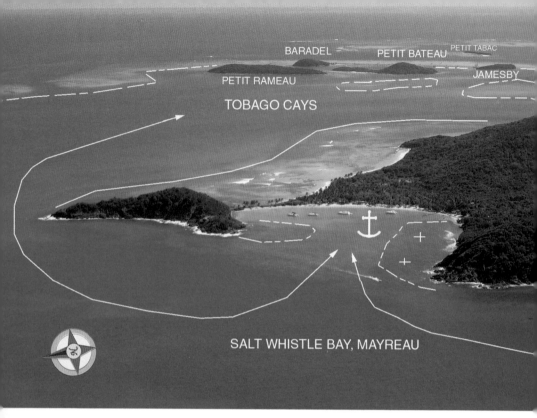

BARADEL — PETIT BATEAU — PETIT TABAC

PETIT RAMEAU

JAMESBY

TOBAGO CAYS

SALT WHISTLE BAY, MAYREAU

Tom and Undine Potter built a little hotel here and did an excellent job of being unobtrusive; it is so well hidden in the trees that people who sail in the bay often question whether it is really there. The rooms have been closed for years now but the restaurant is occasionally active.

Enter right in the middle of the bay, as there are reefs to the north and south. The northern reef is about 6 feet deep and not usually much of a problem. The southern reef is dangerous, because both wind and swells will help drive the inattentive navigator hard onto the coral. Boats often come to grief here, so take care. The holding in the bay is variable; good in sand, not so good in the weed which covers much of it. It is very popular and generally very well protected, but northerly swells occasionally make it rolly. There is a dilapidated and roughly patched dock you can use for your dinghy, but no other yacht services. You can also pull your dinghy up the beach. The Tobago Cay Marine Park offers mooring ($60 a night, less for longer stays). They are not deep, so it is easy for you to check. There is still plenty of room to anchor.

Just to the east, behind the beach, is another beach on the windward side, where shells and driftwood wash ashore. Snorkeling on the reefs and rocks in the bay is fair, but usually murky. A road leads up to the village from near the dock.

Restaurants/Ashore

Eating ashore here is easy and good, with a choice of either tasty local dishes from a string of beach shacks, or more upmarket fancy fare, sometimes at the Salt Whistle Bay Restaurant.

The Salt Whistle Bay Restaurant [$A] has a whimsical, woodland atmosphere: the dining area is set in the open among the trees, and each table is built of stone, with its own thatched roof. It was nicely run last year run by Sonia from France and Justin from Barbados, but I hear they left, so who knows what you will find?

On the south side of the dock, simple local restaurants offer tasty local seafood meals [$B] at a moderate cost. Lobster is available and popular in season, as well as fresh fish and conch, with chicken for the pescaphobes.

Map labels:
MAYREAU & THE TOBAGO CAYS
12° 40'   12° 40'
SCALE IN NAUTICAL MILES
CATHOLIC I. (123')
FL (2) 20S
CATHOLIC
RKS. (77')
DRY SHINGLE POST ONLY
27
CHANNEL RK. (8')
BALEINE RKS. (10')
BREAK RK.
BEST APPROACH
12° 39.5'N 61° 23.0'W WGNS10
12° 39.5'N 61° 22.2'W
N
BLACK & WHITE DAYMARKERS IN LINE AT 142° M
BEST APPROACH
SALT WHISTLE BAY
SEE PLAN
39'   39'
TROISANTS BAY
SEE NOTE 1
WK
MAYREAU
VILLAGE
DENNIS'S HIDEAWAY
FL (9) 10S
GRAND COL PT.
BREAKERS
TOBAGO CAYS (SEE PLAN)
no anchoring
WGNS13
12° 38.0'N 61° 24.5'W
LEAVE CLEAR CHANNEL
SALINE BAY
200'
SMALL CORAL CAYS
POINTS IN LINE LEAD OUT OF SOUTH PASSAGE
PETIT TABAC
NOTE 1: CENTER OF NORTH DOCK ON GRAND COL PT. LEADS OVER THE WRECK OF THE PURINA. 18 FT DEEP, STRONG CURRENTS. NO ANCHORING ON THE WRECK!

These include Mama Jean's, operated by Claude and Jean, who also have a restaurant in the village. The Bar under the Tamarind Tree (a tamarind tree grows right though it) is owned by Rasta Larston. Black Boy and Debbie is a lively place in the middle, Fredericks is close by, and Richard's Last Bar Before the Jungle has the best name. Choose the one that takes your fancy and enjoy!

In the same area you will find many colorful t-shirts and pareos for sale, hung out in the breeze along with local handicraft and sometimes fresh fruit and vegetables.

TROISANT BAY

Troisant Bay lies between Salt Whistle and Saline Bays. It is not as protected as those bays, but still reasonably calm in most conditions. Tribu Resorts are developing this bay as private residences and plan a long dock, beach bar and restaurant at the south-ern end of the bay. The seabed is mainly an excellent grass bed, so wait till they put in moorings, as anchors will tear up the grass.

SALINE BAY

Saline Bay has a lovely, long beach. A large electric-generating plant is on the slope overlooking the bay. It has bright lights that shine over the bay at night but, thankfully, you do not hear it from the anchorage.

As you approach Saline Bay from the north, keep to seaward of the red buoy that marks the long reef off Grand Col Point. It is placed right on the edge of the reef, so do not cut it too fine. If the buoy is not in place, give this reef a very wide berth, as it extends much farther than most people can imagine. The outer part of the reef is 12°38.25'N, 61°24.14'W. Saline Bay has plenty of room to anchor, the holding in sand is good, but avoid the weedy areas. Leave a clear channel for the ferries, with room for them to turn. Try to anchor on patches of sand where the holding is good.

When cruise ships anchor, Saline Bay does a quick imitation of Coney Island. Luckily, the crowds are always gone before nightfall.

St. Vincent & the Grenadines

295

Salt Whistle Bay

Communications/services

Dennis's Hideaway and Combination Cafe both offer internet. Dennis has a desal plant by the main dock and sells water (call 458-8594 to make sure he has some). You can tie your dinghy to one of the two docks.

Ashore

Basic supplies, and sometimes fish, are available in several small groceries. Both Combination Cafe and J & C's have mini markets. First Stop is the newest and probably has the most. A few handicrafts are available in small shops tucked in people's houses. Occasionally, a vendor sets up by the roadside.

Yachting visitors support several Mayreau-owned restaurants and a few handicraft and t-shirt outlets ~ all good for the local economy.

Dennis's Hideaway [VHF: 68, $B] is owned by Dennis, from Mayreau, who used to be a charter skipper. This was the first restaurant here and has the nicest atmosphere, with an open bar and dining area beside a swimming pool and a two-story sunset-view tower.

Late afternoon is the best time to meet other yachting folk. Dennis has a great flair with guests and when he is around you will get excellent local cooking. Dennis's Hideaway also has a modern guesthouse. Dennis has a beach bar down by his desal plant near the main dock and organizes beach barbecues to order.

Almost opposite Dennis is Annie and Alexander's Combination Cafe, and First Stop Supermarket which has a delightful rooftop bar. Stop here and enjoy a drink or cup of coffee, and pick up some of their freshly baked bread. They open for meals from breakfast through dinner. (One reader highly recommends the fish sandwich.) Alexander was a chef in Salt Whistle Bay for many years. Up the hill, Owens Chill Spa is a grill, bar and pizzeria [$B-D], .

Continue uphill for J & C Bar and Restaurant [VHF: 68/16, $B], on your left. It has the best view of the harbor. It is owned by Jean and Claude and is large enough to take a huge group. Jean and Claude are friendly, make a big effort, and their large portions of fish and lambi are excellent value. They have a water taxi and divide their time between here and Salt Whistle Bay.

Robert Lewis "Righteous" is a well-known Rastafarian, and you can groove to Bob Marley and other good sounds and have some good talks with Robert at Righteous & de Youths [VHF: 68, $B]. This is the cool hangout for both locals and visitors. The restaurant is an ongoing art form of construction and decoration and is the character spot on the island. Robert is welcoming and friendly, and serves good local food in his ever-changing restaurant, and someone is always there.

James Alexander has the Island Paradise

BEQUIA

CANOUAN

DRY SHINGLE

SALTWHISTLE BAY

GRAND COL POINT

SALINE BAY, MAYREAU

Restaurant [VHF: 68, $B]. It is well up the hill, with a birds-eye view. This is not a place to come if you are in a hurry, as everything is cooked from scratch, but their Creole fish and curried conch are well worth the wait. They have the biggest sound system on the island, and for those who want to groove to some sounds, they can turn it up after dinner. James also has a taxi and can bring you up.

A little higher, on the righthand side of the road, Jenella's Honey Cone serves good food at a reasonable price.

A walk east from Saline Bay along the salt pond will bring you to a long, pristine beach on the windward side. It is possible to walk north along this beach, almost to the end, then look for the trail, which goes in and out of the bushes. It is unmarked, but easy enough to follow all the way back along the coast to Salt Whistle Bay.

Water sports

Snorkeling on the reef coming out from Grand Col Point is fair.

WINDWARD ANCHORAGE

There is a pretty good anchorage on the eastern side of Mayreau. It is open to the south and can roll, but is excellent in unusual conditions, when northerly or westerly swells make the western anchorages untenable. Approach from the south in good light and identify the reef that extends east off the southeastern part of Mayreau. Follow this reef in. Be careful of the reefs to the east of the anchorage, as some are hard to see.

The Windward anchorage is within the Tobago Cays National Park protection zone, so no fishing is allowed.

The Tobago Cays

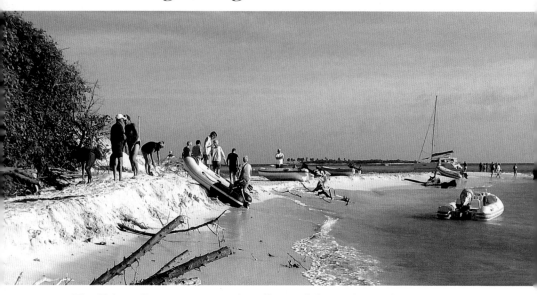

The Tobago Cays are a group of small, uninhabited islands protected from the sea by Horseshoe Reef. The water and reef colors are a kaleidoscope of gold, brown, blue, turquoise, and green. Small beaches of white sand blend into luminous clear water. On cloudless nights, the stars are cast across the sky like wedding confetti thrown in an excessive gesture of bonhomie. Even squalls can be dramatically beautiful as they approach from afar. The anchorage is, however, open to the full force of the ocean winds, which are sometimes strong.

The best approach is between Mayreau and Baleine Rocks, staying south of One Fathom Bank. Black-and-white day markers help you get the approach right. Petit Rameau and Petit Bateau look like one island for most of the approach. Don't cut corners, lest you land on a coral head.

You can anchor just west of Petit Rameau, in the cut between Petit Rameau and Petit Bateau, to the north or south of Baradel, or between Baradel and the other islands. Shallow-draft yachts can anchor to the east of Baradel. Moorings are available in the Cays for $45 EC a night, but are neither compulsory nor always reliable, so check. They mainly surround the turtle-watching area. Do not anchor between the moorings and the turtle-watching area.

There are strong currents in the cut anchorage, so using a mooring is good.

When heading south from the Cays, it is safest to pass round the lee of Mayreau, though the Cays do have a southern channel (South Exit) that is okay for the experienced when the light is good. Avoid using this southern route as an entrance, as it is hard to find, and many charter yachts have gone aground in the attempt.

Regulations

Tobago Cays is a national park. Park fees are currently $10 EC per day per person, which rangers come to collect. Moorings are available for $45 a night. Superyachts should call in advance for advice on where to anchor. While Mayreau is included in the park, no fees are collected in Mayreau anchorages, but diving regulations apply. Yachts are asked to use holding tanks, as this will keep the water clean for swimmers in what can be a crowded area.

This magnificent park offers the most spectacular anchoring in the Eastern Caribbean. Enjoy, and help others to do so, by obeying regulations and being considerate.

A 6-knot speed limit is in effect in the Tobago Cays. This applies to all vessels, dinghies, water taxis, and sailing boats. Please obey it and keep a good look out for swimmers. People swim throughout the anchored yachts to the reef, and to the islands. The speed limit precludes water skiing and many water sports. Sail and kite boarders may exceed the speed limit, but only in the area north of Petit Rameau.

Enjoy snorkeling and looking at the fish and turtles. They are abundant, because this is a conservation area and no fishing is allowed. You may not collect or harm any kind of sea creature, including the corals. Do not take souvenirs of any kind, not even shells or rocks.

A turtle-watching area has been established around the beach in Baradel. It is marked by a series of linked buoys. If you wish to snorkel here, either anchor your dinghy outside or take it directly (and very slowly) into the beach and pull it up on the sand. No anchoring or drifting with your dinghy is allowed, and you should not run your dinghy through this area except to go to and from the beach. Approach turtles slowly, and go no closer than 6 feet. (If you are still and they come closer, that is fine.) Though they look calm and peaceful, they are easily frightened if you chase or try to touch them.

No fires may be made on the beaches, and the vegetation ashore is part of the park and should be left alone.

Do not discharge any oil, chemicals, or other waste into the water or pump your bilges in the park. Avoid using bleach and strong cleaners that get flushed overboard.

Those wishing to scuba dive in the park may only do so with a local dive shop.

Some people get so excited at the beauty of the Tobago Cays that they think the way to complete the experience is to play their favorite music at top volume for the whole

St. Vincent & the Grenadines

anchorage to hear. Cathartic as this might be for them, it may not be what others want. Keep any noise you make on your boat from music, generators, and windmills low enough that your neighbor cannot hear it.

Anchoring is permitted behind Horseshoe Reef and around the islands in sand only. Adventurous and experienced skippers could sail outside Horseshoe Reef (the approach is easiest from the south exit) and find temporary anchorage in Petit Tabac on sand bottom only. This is strictly eyeball navigation and for calm weather. Even so, it is small and rolly. Yachts should not anchor among any of the reefs between Petit Rameau and Mayreau, except in the anchorage we show directly east of Mayreau.

Ashore

Local boat vendors ply the Cays during the season, selling everything from ice, bread, and lobsters to jewelry. They are a friendly bunch and very obliging if you need them to bring you ice or bread the next day. If you want to be left alone, they will do that, too. They offer great beach barbecues and water taxis to places like Baradel.

Rasta Richard Phillips on Jah Live and Larston Browne of Lordag Velocity 2 are among the good barbecuers and they are helpful and have been highly recommended.

Rondel Weeks on Mr. Quality is the only authorized vendor selling the Carriacou Fidel Productions art t-shirts. Each one is a painting by a local artist reproduced on a shirt. Felix-Turtle design by Carriacou artist Felix is the most popular, so popular that one vendor has copied the shirts and pretends to be the artist.

Willie, in Free Willie, is among the good and helpful vendors. Jude has a good water taxi, Bitterz.

Water sports

The snorkeling on Horseshoe Reef is good, though recent hurricanes have damaged some hard corals. The reef near the small boat passage is in the best condition. Fish are plentiful and there are lots of turtles. It can be choppy out there, and anywhere near the small boat passage you will meet current. If you have beginner snorkelers

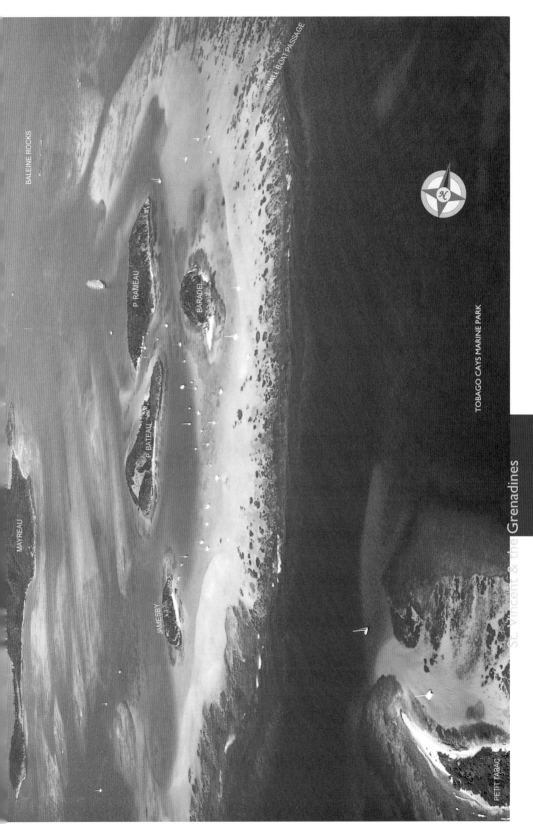

BALEINE ROCKS

P. RAMEAU

BARADEL

P. BATEAU

MAYREAU

JAMESBY

SMALL BOAT PASSAGE

TOBAGO CAYS MARINE PARK

PETIT TABAC

St. Vincent & the Grenadines

on board, the east beach on Petit Bateau (facing Baradel) has some snorkeling that starts in calm, shallow water. The dinghy approach through the reefs is tricky. For turtles, check out the protected turtle area just west of Baradel.

The Tobago Cays are excellent for sailboarding. The designated area for this, when you want to go more than 6 knots, is north of Baradel. Experts can sail out through the small dinghy passage into the ocean.

To go scuba diving, contact Grenadines Dive, who will come and collect you from your yacht. Currents can be very strong and most dives are done as drift dives.

Palm Island

*P*alm Island [VHF:16] was for many years an uninhabited island called Prune Island. John and Mary Caldwell fell in love with it, built a small hotel, and planted palm trees. John was a real character, and his early sailing experiences are outlined in his famous book, *Desperate Voyage*. John had a long and interesting life. After he died, Palm Island was bought by a big hotel group and upgraded to a first-class resort.

The anchorage is off the docks, and holding is fair in 15-20 feet, with a sand bottom. The anchorage can be rolly, so try it for lunch, and if you feel comfortable, stay overnight.

You can use the dock for your dinghy, but use a stern anchor to keep it from riding underneath, where it will be damaged. Leave plenty of room for local boats to come onto the outer end and south side of the dock.

Ashore

Palm Island's Casuarina Beach is one of the most beautiful beaches in the Windwards: a gorgeous expanse of golden sand, lapped by translucent turquoise water ~ the ultimate picture-perfect Grenadine beach. When you step ashore, turn right and you will find a boutique that sells essentials, casual wear, and souvenirs.

The main Royal Palm [VHF: 16, $A] restaurant is open for lunch and dinner daily, and the Sunset Grill beach bar and restaurant is open some nights for dinner. It is all pleasant, but geared to the well-heeled in secluded surroundings.

Patrick Chavailler has an art gallery on Palm Island. He is the Palm Island doctor and helps yachting people in an emergency (458-8829). He does great underwater and boating scenes and undertakes yacht commissions. He also prints his work on tiles (fabulous) and offers limited-edition prints.

Clifton
Grand de Coi
Palm I.

Note the reefs and entrance

Palm to Clifton showing routes

Ask for directions at reception.

Yachts are welcome to enjoy the beach area around the Sunset Beach Bar and the shoreline to the south. You can walk along Casuarina Beach if you stay fairly close to the water's edge. Please respect the privacy of the hotel rooms and facilities. If you think you might want to stay here someday and want to look around, talk with reception; they may be able to arrange a tour.

FTON HARBOUR

Union Island

Union is a great island to visit. It stands out from afar with its dramatically mountainous outline. Clifton, the main harbor, is protected by a reef that shows off its brilliant kaleidoscopic colors and patterns as you sail in. If you anchor or take a mooring out near the reef, the water to the east is an expanse of brilliant green-turquoise; you can jump in the clear, clean water and snorkel on the reef.

Ashore, the main town, Clifton, is charming and colorful, with a picture-perfect market around a green. Union Islanders are welcoming and friendly and there is an excellent choice of restaurants and bars where you can sit outside and watch life in the town. Provisioning is good. The roads and trails offer the best hiking and biking in the Grenadines.

CLIFTON

Clifton is a bustling small port with a cosmopolitan atmosphere, the center of yachting in the southern Grenadines. It has a thriving day-charter industry, with tourists flying into the small airport daily to tour the Grenadines. Those anchored on the reef are treated to great displays of kiteboarding. Union is kept lively and entertaining by various groups of people, and kiteboarding is usually involved. There is no question that Union has become the kiteboarding center of the Windwards.

Jeremie runs the Pro Center Kitesurf, the original shop, which is based in the Anchorage Hotel. They have a great beach bar on the beach by the airport and run the best full moon parties. They also have the Snack Shack in town (see *Restaurants*). Jeremie, his crew, and students are the ones you see doing magnificent displays in the harbor

Happy Kite is run by Lin with Nicolas, and based out of L'Atelier Turquoise, a boutique with a kite and surf shop. The same family owns Captain Gourmet across the road (see *Restaurants*). They do much of their surfing in the big bay by Frigate island.

Will also runs a smaller kitesurfing operation and is probably responsible when you see someone kiting around on foils.

Navigation

When approaching Clifton from the north, it is necessary to sail halfway over to Palm Island to avoid Newlands Reef (keep well outside the three red beacons on its outer edge). When approaching from the south, give Grand de Coi a wide berth.

Clifton Harbour is protected by Newlands Reef, and it has a small reef in the center. The main entrance is just south of this center reef and marked by red and green beacons. It is possible to sail to the east of the center reef and up behind Newlands Reef toward Green Island. Happy Island, a bar, is a landmark on this reef. This area off the outer reef offers a visually great anchorage, but if you prefer to be nearer to the action, anchor anywhere off the town. Leave a wide channel with turning room for the ferries.

The Tobago Cays (485-8191) has put down about 18 numbered moorings for rent, mainly in the shallow water close to the reef. They are marked TCMP and cost $60 a night, less for longer stays. If a local helps you on one, take the ticket he gives you and give it to the ranger when you pay. (You may also tip if you wish.) If those run out, Sail Grenadines (533-2909) has three moorings for their boats, closer to Anchorage Yacht Club, and one may be available.

Regulations

Clifton is St. Vincent's southern port of entry for customs clearance. You can check with customs, then immigration, both in the fishing complex, weekdays from about 0830-1500 (checking in) or 1630 (checking out). You can also clear at the airport; they open from about 0900 and stay open as long as the airport is open, which is often late in the afternoon. They are also open Sundays and holidays. Clear customs as soon as you go ashore. (Overtime is charged after 1600 and on weekends.)

Communications

You can surf the net and make phone calls at Erika's Marine Services [VHF: 68] or the Internet Cafe above Buffalo Trading. Both have good equipment and are helpful, and both have bay-wide wifi. Erika's is agent for UPS; the Internet Cafe is agent for Digicel. Most bars, cafes and restaurants offer free wifi. Both Lime and Digicel have offices on the main street.

General yacht services

Bougainvilla has an excellent little enclosed dinghy lagoon and dock, which you are welcome to use, and at some point you will visit the adjoining L'Aquarium. You can use the Anchorage Hotel or the Grenadines Dive dock. Clifton Beach Hotel and Lambi also have docks, not quite as easy to use.

You can leave garbage in the dumpster on the fishing docks, or give it to Lambi's boat for a small fee. Ice is available at Anchorage Yacht Club, Bougainvilla, Grand Union, Lambi, and many rum shops. Unitech fills cooking gas bottles.

Jean-Marc's Bougainvilla [VHF: 16] is a dock with stern-to berthing for about 20 boats. They sell water (they have a desal plant) and ice. It is the home of the L'Aquarium Restaurant, Mare Blu Boutique, La Cabane sushi and Erika's Marine Services. Wind and Sea charters are based here and do many Grenadines day tours. Air and sea charters are available.

The Anchorage Yacht Club [VHF: 68] has a 12-berth marina where you can tie stern-to a floating dock, and they can supply water, electricity (220 volts), ice (block & cube).

Fresh croissants, ciabatta bread, laundry, and showers are usually available This is the base of Sail Grenadines charter company and sailing school.

When Belgian Freddy sold the Big Sands Hotel, he bought Clifton's gas station. This has a small dock adjoining Lambi's on its south side, and this is a great place to get outboard fuel. It is also the best place to buy diesel as it is good clean fuel, and not something that arrived on a fishing boat from Venezuela. But docking is not too easy. You could drop anchor and come downwind bow-to in 7-8 feet of water. They can also truck to big boats on the main wharf on demand.

Erika's Marine Services [VHF: 68] is in the Anchorage Hotel; speak to Heather or Chille. Their services include laundry (boat collection and delivery), yacht clearance, full provisioning, and an internet station. They are travel agents and can book tickets for you. They are the UPS agent and also rent DVDs, have a good bookswap, and provide water-taxi service. They will even help you out for cash on a credit card if the ATM is broken. They offer full superyacht service, with agents throughout St. Vincent and the Grenadines, and a private plane for emergencies.

Clifton Beach Hotel [VHF: 68, $B-C] has about 9 feet at the end of their dock. You can come in here alongside or stern-to. Ice, laundry and water are sometimes available; ask first.

If you need to fly out, check Joy James at James Travel, Eagle's Travel, or Erika's.

Chandlery

Unitech has a chandlery with mechanical and yacht hardware items, and they now carry such things as second-hand equipment and dinghies. They are agents for Yamaha and can sell you a new one or fix the old. Elodie has a boutique corner with lovely hand-painted, ready-to-go fishing lines, hand-crafted soaps, and special coconut oils. These are also available in L'Ateleier Turquoise, Mare Blu, and several other stores. Unitech also has a bookswap.

Quacy's Marine Tech Services is up a little spiral staircase on main street. He has a good selection of outboard parts along with other accessories. He rents bikes, and fixes outboards and diesels (see *Technical yacht services*).

A fishing store selling tackle is just after the gas station.

Technical yacht services

Need something fixed? Quacy was the maintenance manager of a local charter company, and is now Marine Tech Services. He is also the local maintenance agent for Horizons Yacht Charters. Quacy is good at all boat systems and fixing electrical problems. He will get any make of outboard purring again and keeps many spares. He also repairs Yanmar and Volvo inboard diesel engines. He can also fix general mechanical and plumbing problems. Quacey also rents mountain bikes.

You will fine Laurent at Unitech, just at the beginning of the road to Fort Hill. They repair all kinds of gasoline and diesel motors, including outboards. They weld iron and stainless, and they do fiberglass and electrical repairs. Unitech sells cooking gas and can fill most boat cylinders. If you have torn sails or malfunctioning refrigeration, ask them to point you to the right person.

Almost opposite Unitech, Island Marine Special [VHF: 16] is run by Earl Allen, a good diesel mechanic.

Provisioning

Provisioning in Union is good. The local market is colorful and photogenic. Vendors have an excellent selection of fresh fruits and vegetables in colorful stalls around a green. Don't get so distracted by the market that you forget to look over the road to check out L'Atelier Turquoise (see *Fun shopping*)

Bertram and Signa, at Island Grown grow much of what they sell in their farm up in the hills, so it is always fresh. They always grow their own lettuce and herbs, but also a lot of other vegetables. Some things are kept cool in the fridge, so if you don't see what you want, ask. These days Jennifer and most other vendors keep well-stocked fridges. Another smaller local market is farther down the road towards Grenadines Dive.

Nicolas and Linda's Captain Gourmet [VHF: 08] is on the main street opposite the Clifton Beach Hotel. This great little store has good buys on French wines. They sell fresh French bread and yogurt, frozen shrimps, steak, smoked salmon, and many other meats, along with cheeses and whipping cream for the charter cook. You will also find coffee and many French dry goods. Outside seats make this a pleasant place for a coffee break or lunch. They offer a full provisioning service for yachts and will deliver to your dinghy. Nicolas is a pilot and has a small plane that helps them bring in new stock. Nicolas is also involved with Happy Kite (see *Water sports*).

More small supermarkets will cater to your other shopping needs. Uptown Supermarket is a new, clean, and pleasant mini supermarket. Owner Stephanie stocks cream and cheeses, along with the regular items and a good selection of drinks.

Grand Union sells basics and fresh local chicken. Lambi has wine, packaged food, fresh food, pork and beef from Lambi's farm, and general hardware and household goods.

A tiny path runs alongside Snack Shack

to Yummy Stuff Bakery and Cafe. This is a great little bakery and sometimes sells out fast so go early. They also do rotis and other snacks. Otherwise, for French bread, croissants, and Danish, check out Captain Gourmet, the Anchorage Hotel, and the bakery beside Barracuda. There is also a good little local bakery opposite the market.

Need pet food or a vet? Check the pet people. These include Susie, Heather from Erika's, and Gary from Union. They have the Animal Kindness Charity (SGAK). They get the fur back on strays, food in their bellies, cut down on random animal procreation, and provide animal education in the local schools. Susie is on first-name terms with every dog in the island. They have had a big impact. Those with kids will want to wander along main street to their center, where you will normally find a pen with some dogs that welcome petting. Contributions are always welcome and help pay for vet fees and food, and they welcome anyone who might provide a prospective new home for one of their orphan pets.

Fun shopping

Union is becoming quite the place for boutiques. Robert and Annie-France's L'Atelier Turquoise (Beads and Art gallery) displays original paintings and local handicrafts and souvenirs. These include locally painted calabash art, figures from Haiti and lots more to attract the eye. But the main attraction of the boutique is Annie-France's jewelry hand made from semi-precious stones, including the lovely larimar stone, and beads. Each delightful item is hand

CLIFTON HARBOUR
UNION I.

FORMS SAND ISLANDS

GREEN ISLAND (9')

FORMS SAND ISLANDS

NEWLANDS REEF

HAPPY ISLAND

AIRPORT SECURITY NO PASSING BUOYED LINE

KITE SURFING ACTIVITY BEST NOT TO ANCHOR

TERMINAL BUILDING
CUSTOMS IMMIGRATION

AIRPORT RUNWAY

JT KITESURF & BAR
ANCHORAGE BEACH BAR

GRENADINES SAIL

ANCHORAGE YACHT CLUB

CONCRETE BLOCK & RUINED BEACON

DINGHIES

ANCHORAGE DOCK 25

BOUGAINVILLA DOCK

BOUGAINVILLA
FRESH JUICE & SUSHI
ERIKA'S SERVICES
AQUARIUM
O MARE BLU

DINGHY PORT

CHIC UNIQUE

UPTOWN SUPERMKT

BARRACUDA

CUSTOMS

LEAVE CLEAR CHANNEL

THE LOFT

F.R
FN
ST

L'ATELIER

LAMBI

TURQUOISE

GRENADINES DIVE

FUEL

GRAND UNION

BANK

GIAO PIZZA

MARKET

SNACK SHACK

CAPT. GOURMET

MARINE TECH

LIME

DIGICEL

ANIMAL KINDNESS

PHARMACY

UNITECH

ISLAND MARINE

TO FORT HILL VIEW POINT

TO SAPRROW'S BEACH BAR

1/4

SCALE IN NAUTICAL MILES

0

TO PINNACLE

TO ASHTON

COASTGUARD ST.

N

crafted, special, and sold at affordable prices. This is also the base for Happy Kite kite and surf shop. Ask about equipment, lessons, paddle board rentals and yoga classes.

I have known Charlotte since I first started writing guides, when she ran the Ponton du Bakoua in Martinique. She moved to Union and ran the Anchorage Hotel during its best years. Now she has come out of retirement and opened Mare Blu in Bougainvilla. Charlotte has created a beautiful boutique, using artistic design and lighting, so as you come in you have the feeling of entering Aladdin's treasure trove. It is fun to visit and you will find a little of everything: elegant casual wear, hats, art, carvings, ornaments, fancy bags, jewelry, and books, as well as practical stuff like sunblock and flip flops. This is the place to buy postcards and stamps. You can write them over a coffee in L'Aquarium and bring them back and Mare Blu will mail them for you.

Zoe's Driftwood Boutique is part of, and next to, the Snack Shack, with elegant light clothing, pareos, bathing costumes,

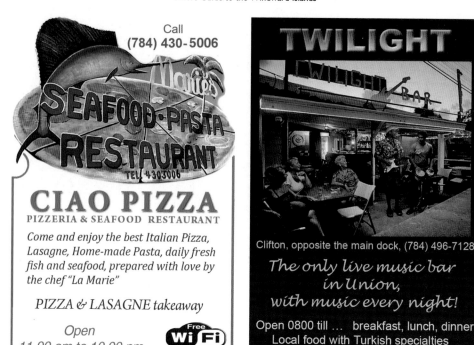
ornaments, and jewelry and essential such as sunblock, and reef walkers.

Cynthia Mills has the Chic Unique right next to Bougainvilla. They are not only a shop but a spa and do massage and other treatments, and if you want an air, sea or land taxi, just ask here.

Juliet's Romeo Boutique is in the market and opens most days. Juliet stocks casual wear, t-shirts, souvenirs, and decorative items, as well as locally made jewelry and metal sculptures. Kazia, from Martinique, has Kazia's Madinina Showroom, with lots of t-shirts and tie-dye items, Felix's sculptures, some applique, and souvenirs. Other shops to check out along the street include Roots and Music Shop Art & Craft. The Clifton Beach Hotel has Sunseekers Shade boutique, with a wide range of casual clothing, souvenirs, and books.

The Grenadines Gift Shop is at the airport. They have batik wall hangings, t-shirts, souvenirs, carvings, film, and hard-to-find camera batteries. You can send your Fedex packages from here.

There are several other small stalls and shops for local handicrafts, and many ladies hang out t-shirts for sale in the fish market buildings.

In Clifton heading south, Kandy Cream is the place for ice cream and cake.

Restaurants

Union has some fine restaurants. For a small island, the selection is excellent.

Barracuda [$B-D] is next to the Bougainvilla complex. It is owned by a very sweet and welcoming Italian couple, Giancarlo and his wife, Tiziana, who is the chef. They are helped by locals: King and sometimes Baby. They offer Italian cooking, including pasta and pizzas, as well as local food such as rotis. It has a nice atmosphere, wonderful background music (at least for me), is not too expensive and the food is tasty and artfully served. They open from about 0830 for breakfast and stay open until after dinner. They serve food at any time of day, so you can have a really early dinner if you want. Save some room for the Italian chocolate cake, which is more like a mousse and is absolutely delicious.

Marie is originally French, but made Union her home so long ago that it was just about when I started writing guides. She has been involved in several good businesses, but Ciao Pizza [$C-D] is the best. She cooks excellent fresh fish and seafood specials, pastas, great gazpacho, and, of course, pizza. She opens daily from 1100-2200. They often have a really good lunchtime smoked fish salad n the menu. Ciao Pizza is right in town, opposite the main dock. You can sit outside and watch the world go by and use the free high speed wifi.

Twilight, next to Marie's, opposite the main dock, is Union's best music spot, as well as a great little restaurant. It is run by Bert, a local musician, and his Turkish wife, Kamile, with their sons, one of whom is a dive master and the other a kiteboard instructor. There is live music every night and when the other bars go to sleep, night owls gravitate here. It opens at 0800 for breakfast and stays open all day till the last one goes and they serve both lunch and dinner. The food is Caribbean with some Turkish dishes. They welcome everyone and it has a friendly family atmosphere.

L'Aquarium [$B-C] has a perfect location in the Bougainvilla complex, open to the harbor and the breeze, with a spectacular saltwater aquarium for decor, and a perfect little dinghy dock lagoon. Gregory Grifith, the owner, is from Martinique and adds a dash of French Creole. They specialize in lobster, seafood and pizzas anytime, while for lunch they also have lighter fare like crepes and pita sandwiches. For dinner you can also have tenderloin, and the fresh tuna tac tac (balsamic caramel and toasted sesame seeds) comes recommended. The standard of food and service is excellent.

Just outside, Jean-Marc's daughter Jade runs La Cabane. It is a tiny colorful shack on the dinghy dock that produces the best sushi, juices (fruit and or vegetable), health drinks and smoothies. They have a nice sitting area around the back, and it is a delight for a fresh juice or light meal.

Bertrand Sailly, brother of Jean-Marc from Bougainvilla, has opened a wonderful hangout called Sparrow's Beach Bar in Richmond Bay by Big Sands, about a mile from Clifton. This is the hot spot in Union right now: everyone loves it. Getting there is easy, just call the free shuttle bus and they will take you, so you get a mini tour when you visit. It opens for lunch and dinner and is delightful any time of day. They have a live lobster tank when lobster is in season and Bertrand cold-smokes his own fish, which is so delicious that he now supplies most of the surrounding hotels. You can ask to buy some to take back on the boat. He prepares delicious raw tuna with a ginger sauce, and it is all served very artistically. They have pastas and salads and lots of fresh seafood, and in the evening they fire up the big barbecue. By day, the energetic will make use of kayaks and water-sports gear, while the more relaxed crowd will go for the loungers, private gazebos, and the great massage/pedicure/manicure shop, run by Sophie. It is romantic on the beach at night, especially with a moon, and they often throw parties with live music, especially on Fridays. Call for details. Some captains like to anchor right off the beach here, and I have seen a huge superyacht anchor for lunch. There is

a blow-up of the bay on my Union chart. The anchorage is weather dependent, best avoided in northerly swells and northeasters, but wonderful on a calm day. You need to be somewhat adept at spotting reefs. If you approach from the northeast and spot the reef in the middle of the bay, you can pass east of it in 70 feet of water and then close the beach slowly, Anchor or pick up one of the two mooring buoys Betrand has put down.

The Snack Shack [$D] is a beach bar right on main street (well, the water is just over the road), bringing beachside relaxing into town and offering a new level of casual chic. Its connection with JT Kitesurf means you will always find a relaxed group chilling out here, along with others intently looking at their computers and I-pads catching up on the world with the free wifi. Panninis, smoothies, cappuccino and ice cream coffee are just a few of the many goodies available from breakfast to dinner. You can arrange your kitesurfing trips here and shop at the attached Driftwood Boutique.

The Loft [$D] adds a touch of sophistication to Clifton. This upstairs bar is indeed

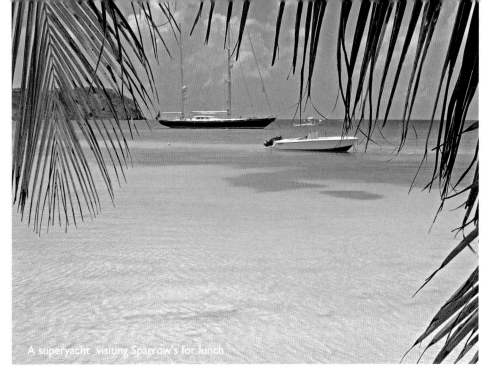
A superyacht visiting Sparrow's for lunch

in a loft, and Jasmine, the owner, has made the most of the roof beams and gable windows with their little balconies to create a relaxing and artistic place to hang out, with great views. In atmosphere it is a wine and tapas bar, but they offer an excellent cocktail selection, smoothies, coffee and fruit punches, along with beer, and Jasmine is working on importing the top microbrewery, draft brews from Grenada. The tasty tapas are great for lunch or dinner if you want to eat light, and they have other bar snacks including homemade dips. They open from 1100 till late, and big screen TV shows the exciting sports events. Happy hour is on Monday, 1900-2000.

The cheapest and fastest food is Teroy Wilson's Big Citi, upstairs opposite the market. He opens all day from about 0700 to 2200. For fast food at local prices, ignore the menu outside, walk upstairs, and choose from the cafeteria-style dishes.

The Anchorage Yacht Club [VHF: 68], owned by the Palm Island group, is pretty, with a delightful view of the harbor. They have a dinghy dock and a pleasant bar for relaxing. They also have a bar on the beach by the kitesurfing. It is hard to know what to say about what you will find, as they seem up in the air about what they are doing. They were talking about closing everything except the dock for the off season, and opening again in the winter. Take a look.

Lambert is smiling these days, and why not? His Lambi emporium [VHF: 68, $B-C], consisting of a supermarket, a waterfront restaurant, and some rental rooms is going well. Each time I come, his building seems to have crept farther out to sea. The conch shell walls give a rough-and-ready atmosphere. The food is reasonably priced and local, as is the entertainment, with lively steel bands many nights in season. Lambert also sells very inexpensive takeaway snacks on the road side.

The Clifton Beach Hotel [VHF: 68, $B-C], run by Marie Adams-Hazell, has a waterfront location and its own dinghy dock. The bar is a popular meeting place. After you have finished shopping, try one of their sandwiches. You can also visit for dinner or the occasional jump-up.

Limelite, open to the main street, is the place to take a break and watch the world go by, and it is the last bar to close at night. Its presence here began the improved look of the main street.

For other good and inexpensive local food, visit T&N [$B-D], which is another pleasant place to watch life go by. Alternatively, walk down the road and check out Evergreen or Jennifer's Restaurant and Bar

Looking south to Frigate Island to Carriacou

[$C-D]. Both serve West Indian food at a reasonable price. Or try out Paula's, opposite the old market.

Glenroy Adams (Grenadines Dive) has a lovely restaurant and his own dinghy dock. As I went to press it was closed and he was looking for a new tenant. Check it out and see what you find.

If you are anchored near the reef, you will notice Janti's Happy Island [$B-D], built on the edge of the reef. Janti is the only man in the Caribbean I know who built his own island by hand. He had a bar in Ashton, but could not find enough customers. He also worked for tourism, trying to clean up the town. One headache was a huge pile of conch shells left by fishermen on the beach. Janti solved both problems by taking the shells from the beach and using them to build Happy Island. It is perfectly placed for snorkeling by day and for taking a sundowner at night. You can tie your dinghy right outside. This is Union's most informal bar; it is fun and has a lovely view as sunset turns to night. Janti is often helped by Andrea.

Transport

Quacy, at Marine Tech Services, rents bikes. These are a great way to see the island, which has little traffic and great views at every turn. He also does biking tours.

Katie, at Sail Grenadines in the Anchorage Hotel, also has a few. She rents by the day or half day.

Water taxis will be happy to take you ashore: $10-20 EC one-way for your group, depending on where you are anchored. Eat with Lambi and he will arrange it for free.

For a taxi, try Rosmund Adams (526-4500 not on Saturday). Ask him about the leatherback turtle-watching. This takes place at night from March to August.

Ashore

Hiking and biking will give you views of the island's beautiful turquoise waters, from Clifton right over to Ashton and Frigate Island and the other Grenadines beyond. The road system enables you to bike all over the island. Two obvious viewpoints for walkers are Fort Hill and the road that leads from opposite the hospital back past the Pinnacle and into Ashton. Farther afield, the roads that rise from Richmond Bay to circle round Bloody Bay and Chatham are beautiful, and the road from Ashton to Mt. Campbell has views to the south. Off-the-road hiking includes the ridge along the western mountain range and, for excellent views, take the well-marked trail to Big Hill, from where the adventurous can rough it up to Mt. Taboi.

The Pinnacle is a tough but sweet climb, with a dramatic, 360-degree, precipitous view at the summit. Looked at from afar, an iguana-like rock lies on the top. The approach is right under the iguana, on the Clifton side of the hill. The best way to do this is to contact Erika's Marine Services and ask them to put you in touch with Bongo, a good local hiking guide, and one of the few who hikes the Pinnacle. Hardy adventurers could try this with a cutlass, after visiting Doyleguides.com for detailed directions.

While in Clifton, visit the Tobago Cays Marine Park interpretation center on the main square. There is not much in here, and the staff don't seem that interested in visitors, but it may improve. They are supposed

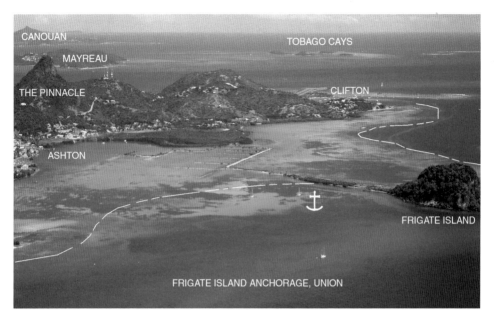

CANOUAN
MAYREAU
THE PINNACLE
ASHTON
TOBAGO CAYS
CLIFTON
FRIGATE ISLAND

FRIGATE ISLAND ANCHORAGE, UNION

to have educational movies about the park and marine matters and a big aquarium.

Water sports

You will find information on the dive shops and some dive sites under the Southern Grenadine diving section. Clifton is the base of Grenadines Dive [VHF: 16/68].

Katie Bingham runs Sail Grenadines out of the Anchorage Hotel. Katie is very friendly and helpful and they offer fully crewed, semi-bareboat, and bareboat charters. They do short term charters to pick you up in one island and drop you off in another. Those who want to advance their skills should ask about their full gamut of practical RYA courses, which you can join as an individual (they offer a free place to locals in these). They also rent kayaks and bikes.

Day-charter boats leave every day to visit the other Grenadines. The main operators of the cats are Land and Sea and Palm Island (Captain Yannis). Then there is Martin's Scaramouche, the lovely Carriacou-built schooner, whose presence enhances the view and is a great addition to any photo of the Tobago Cays.

Union is a major kitesurf center with two first-rate shops. Jeremie runs the Pro Center Kitesurf, which is based in the Anchorage Hotel. They also have the Snack Shack in town, where you can talk kite surfing and book trips. They do a great beach party on full-moon nights, open to all.

Happy Kite is run by Lin with Nicolas, and based out of Captain Gourmet and L'Atelier Turquoise. They do much of their surfing in the big bay by Frigate island.

Both shops are top professionals and they teach at all levels. Many of their customers are sailors who want to learn to kitesurf or become better. If you are anchored on the reef, or in Frigate island, you can enjoy a display of kitesurfing prowess most days. Visit their websites: kitesurfgrenadines.com, happykitegrenadines.com

FRIGATE ISLAND

Frigate Island, although just over a mile from Clifton, is generally quiet and well protected in normal conditions, and exceptionally so in strong northeasterlies. You can anchor in the lee of the island, but enter carefully, as the bottom shelves quickly. Construction started on a large development, including a 300-berth marina, but the company went bankrupt, and the project stopped.

You are within dinghy reach of Ashton, the other town on Union. Ashton is local and delightful, with lower prices

St. Vincent & the Grenadines

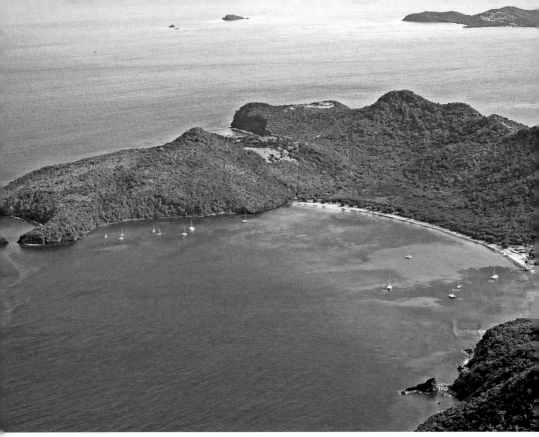

than Clifton. It has a good dock where you can leave your dinghy. You will find small restaurants, friendly rum shops, and several small supermarkets.

Walking ashore is pleasant. Those with a head for heights and a firm grip can scramble high up the hill on Frigate Island for a view. For more ambitious hikes, there are Big Hill and Mt. Taboi. You can find good snorkeling on the reef on the windward side of Frigate. Be careful of the current.

CHATHAM BAY

Chatham Bay, on the lee side of Union, is a large and magnificent anchorage, with a long sandy beach to the east and a steep headland to the north. While you may not have it to yourself, it is often less crowded than most. Anchor anywhere in the north part of the bay. (Just occasionally, you may be asked to move if the fishermen are seine netting.) The wind tends to come over the hills in shrieking gusts. There is a long beach to explore and good snorkeling around the

rocks off Rapid Point. The fish life here is particularly rich and attracts all kinds of birds, including pelicans. A rough road leads to the northern headland, and a path leads to the center ridge, and from these, roads go to Ashton or Clifton. The hiking all around is lovely.

Sunday is often popular with locals, who come over for lunch.

Services/Ashore

If you want to avoid Clifton and have not yet cleared, Seckie will take you by cab and include an island tour for about $120 EC. Sometimes a boat sells fresh bread and ice in the mornings.

At the north end of the beach, several master barbecuers compete to give you an entertaining local-style dinner on the beach. For a full meal, they charge about $65-100 EC depending on whether you want fish, chicken, ribs, or lobster. Sun Beach and Fun also offers snacks so you can go in and drink and then have fish 'n chips or roti or conch fritters. These bars are rough, ready, and lots of fun. Some try a hard sell from their boats.

If you want to avoid that, call up in advance and make arrangements.

Sun, Beach and Eat is run by Seckie and Vanessa and is the pink building with an orange roof, in the middle of the beach. They have a tiny floating dinghy dock and will look after you well; ask about their beach games. They serve fish, chicken, ribs, lobster, and land crabs, and a bonfire is often lit after dark. They arrange for a big drum dance and other entertainment for groups and will organize special events like birthday parties. (If you want a real surprise party, set it up in advance.) They always do a big full-moon party with live music. They are always there in the evening, and sometimes for lunch. For parties of 15 or more they will prepare a full pig roast, and often do smaller pork roasts, with live music when they have enough people. Vanessa hand-makes jewelry for sale; you can ask for a look. They can bring you over from Clifton if you don't make it to Chatham. If you know this is the place you want to go, call in advance and book. It will save you a lot of hassle and high pressure salesmanship from others (who sometimes claim they are closed).

Palm Leaf is at the north end and is owned by Jerry, who recently has had others run it for him. The food was good when I was updating.

Bollhead is next door. His family owns a building in Clifton and he had a bar there. He now does barbecues in Chatham. He will keep you well entertained and fed. It is a happening bar. He has a very quiet generator and plays music so you can dance on the beach in the moonlight. Bollhead's boatkick, Andel, catches fish and lobster early in the morning and sells to yachts.

Shark Attack was the first to offer beach barbecues here. It was hard work, because everything had to come by boat, but he became popular. Eventually, the government put in a rough road. This made life so easy that others saw what he was doing and set up in competition. Shark Attack keeps up his tradition of great barbecues of fish and lobster. He does some carvings.

Pleasure, who has hung out at Chatham even longer than Shark Attack, originally sang for him, and now has Pleasure's Bar, under a big tamarind tree. It is close by the

road and the path that leads to the rest of the island. He and his wife Rosita are very pleasant and will cook you fresh fish or lobster, and he is a little less expensive than the others. Pleasure plays guitar and will provide a little music for your entertainment. He also does fine carvings.

Way down at the south end, Antonio has opened Aqua in two wonderful, open, thatched buildings; a bar and a restaurant that are joined by a swimming pool. This is a completely different experience from the others, a lovely boutique resort, comfortable and elegant, perfect for when you are beach-barbecued out and want somewhere quiet to relax. Manager Lesia is helpful and they are open for a light lunch [$D]: rotis, sandwiches, and grilled fish. Their shrimp and lobster rotis are excellent. They are also open for a gourmet style dinner [$A]. If you come for dinner and need customs clearance, they will do it for you without any extra charge.

Antonio has built an inventive and artistic dinghy dock using giant rocks placed by nature.

St. Vincent & the Grenadines

(PSV) & Petite Martinique

PSV AND PETITE MARTINIQUE

*P*etit St. Vincent (PSV) and Petite Martinique lie just a short sail southeast of Union. PSV is part of St. Vincent, and Petite Martinique is part of Grenada.

PSV

PSV (VHF: 16, closed September/October) was probably the first Caribbean boutique hotel. It is a quiet and exclusive resort, where the guests get pampered in secluded stone cottages. Each cottage has a flagpole that is used to summon the room service, which soon appears in a mini-moke. The hotel does well at top Caribbean rates, probably the Caribbean's most successful small hotel.

It was built by the late Haze Richardson, who operated it from its inception until 2007. The island and resort were purchased in late 2010 by Phil Stephenson and Robin Patterson. The new owners have invested heavily in renovating the entire island and all the cottages. New additions include the yacht-friendly beach restaurant Goaty's Bar, and a new spa complex.

It is managed by husband & wife team Matt & Annie Semark, along with an excellent local crew. The main anchorage is shown on the chart. The current changes with the tide, and if the wind drops, yachts swing about. The reef off the dinghy dock extends farther than some think.

Mopion is a very popular daytime anchorage (see *Water sports*)

Ashore

When you go ashore, keep in mind that this is a very exclusive and luxurious resort, so please be respectful. If we are to continue to be welcome, this is essential. You should only come ashore by the dinghy dock on the leeward side. You are welcome to walk along the shore and use the beach from the hotel dinghy dock to the new beach bar and boutique. All other areas and beaches are private, for in-house residents only, which include the guest cottages and the western

Petit St.Vincent
PRIVATE ISLAND

For reservations or information call 1 (784) 458 8801, VHF:16

end of the beach, past the beach bar. Private areas are clearly sign posted.

You are welcome to visit the main bar and restaurant upstairs, though smart casual attire is expected for this (no bathing costumes by day, or shorts and t-shirts for dinner). Reservations are essential for dinner.

The hotel bar, with a great view of the bay, is open all day, and it is a pleasant place to take a drink ~ especially those frozen daiquiris and fruit specials they are so good at.

Goaty's Beach Bar is more casual and built with visitors in mind, so shorts, t-shirts and even bathing togs are fine, up until sunset when slacks and a sports shirt or similar attire are appropriate. It is open 1030-2200. Their menu includes tapas, salads, sandwiches, burgers, pizza, pasta, and grilled seafood and meat.

On Fridays, the regular menu closes down and they have a beach barbecue with a steel band. Come for the barbecue or just to listen and visit the bar. On Tuesday night Barracuda's band plays great reggae music. On many Mondays, they have a classic movie night, with a big screen set up in the beach bar.

The spa is also open to people visiting on yachts, offering all kinds of massage and beauty or health treatments. Guided island and cottage tours are available on request after 1030. Book by radio, phone, or ask in the bar or office.

If you are longing for a good walk, Petite Martinique is within dinghy range, and if you plan a meal over there, you can get a free ride over and back.

Water sports

The snorkeling on the surrounding reefs is good. Mopion makes an exciting destination for a picnic by dinghy. You can anchor close by as a lunch stop. You can feel your way into anchorages in the reef north of PSV for excellent snorkeling. Pinese makes a fair dive.

PSV is home to Jean-Michel Cousteau Diving. This top-class and upmarket operation is primarily for PSV guests. They may occasionally have room for additional guests.

PETITE MARTINIQUE

Getting tired of all the tourists? Petite Martinique (PM), the last outpost of Grenada, is small and enchantingly authentic. I love to overnight here, take a long walk, and have a meal ashore. It is a good place to take on water and fuel and look for bargains on beer, liquor, and wine. The inhabitants live by boatbuilding and seafaring (and, in days of old, smuggling). Fishing has always been important, and currently, long-line tuna fishing is very successful. Many vessels lie at anchor, and the docks are far busier than the roads. The many fancy new houses are recent, but some of the older wooden, pitched-roof houses are photogenic, especially at the eastern end of the island. PM is a lot larger than it looks. If you turn right from the dock, the road winds round the south side of the island. It is possible to walk all the way round, but the eastern part is a thorny scramble with no real trail. You will find the people here friendly and welcoming, and the island has several shops and a restaurant. For the adventurous explorer and snorkeler, Fota and Petite Dominique

are within range of a seaworthy dinghy.

If you are coming north from Carriacou, you can clear out and visit PM on your way to Union. Many yachts come over directly from PSV or the Grenadines for a quick stop, and it is these yachts that keep the fuel dock and restaurant alive. PM is part of Grenada, but no one is going to sail from PSV to Carriacou to clear in, then sail back to visit PM for a meal or fuel, so many people make an unofficial visit and so far no one has been prosecuted for it. Anchor anywhere off the fuel dock among the other boats. PM can also be visited by seaworthy dinghy from PSV. You can leave your dinghy on the inside part of the fuel dock. Or you can get

St. Vincent & the Grenadines

the Palm Beach Restaurant to bring you over for a meal (see *Shops, restaurants, ashore*).

The holding in PM is in soft mud and not always easy. Use plenty of scope, and if it is blowing hard, use your engine to keep the boat in place to allow the anchor time to sink into the mud before you put strain on it.

The best thing is to eat at the Palm Beach Restaurant. Then you may pick up one of their two free customer moorings off their dock (both marked with their name) .

If you do have a problem, a big, shallow (8- to 12-foot deep) patch of easy anchoring sand is clearly visible about half a mile north and a little east of the docks. It is a fair dinghy ride in, but okay.

Communications

Odinga's Millennium Connection, a pleasant boutique in Matthew's Shopping Center, has high-speed internet access at reasonable rates. They are normally open until about 1800.

Palm Beach Restaurant has free wifi for their customers.

General yacht services

Glenn Clement and Reynold Belmar own B & C Fuels [VHF: 16, Golf Sierra], the best and most convenient fuel dock in the Grenadines. Easy approach and fair prices have made this the main refueling station for large power yachts, charter yachts and bareboats. The dock has 16-18 feet of water alongside and you approach it into the wind. They sell high-quality diesel, gasoline, water, cube ice, and cases of beer or water.

Chandlery & technical yacht services

E&B hardware is on the left as you walk down the main road heading west. It is upstairs, above E&B supermarket, in the same building. Owner Emrol Logan keeps a good supply of resins, cloths, and a little yacht hardware, plus fishing gear, along with general hardware and a lot of plumbing bits. Emrol repairs outboards, so you can bring your broken one here to get it fixed, and he can probably help you with other mechanical problems.

Shops, restaurants, ashore

Replenish your wine, beer, and liquor lockers, and top up on groceries at E & B supermarket or Matthew's Shopping Center at unbeatable prices. Odinga's Millennium Connection is in Matthews and has stacks of clothes, shoes, jewelry, and more. Adjoining is a gift shop with handicrafts.

Palm Beach [VHF: 16, (473) 443-9103, $B-C] is a very pleasant family restaurant managed by Emmanuel. The setting is perfect: a pretty garden shaded by palms, right on the beach. They serve seafood from the local fishing fleet, with chicken or pork for those who don't like fish, lambi, shrimps or lobster. The food is first-rate, the lobster dishes highly recommended, but if you prefer the fish, try the lobster bisque as a starter if it is on the menu. Prices are affordable. Palm Beach has two customer moorings and free wifi. They are happy to come to PSV and pick you up from your yacht in their speedboat for lunch or dinner, and if you want time to hike, shop or wander around before your meal you can arrange this with Emmanuel (not always in service). It is a great way to add PM to your PSV visit. While there is no charge for this service, if you are only one or two people, a gas contribution is greatly appreciated. Palm Beach also has rooms to rent.

Close by, Melodies [VHF: 16, "Tasha P Radio"] is a fancy new guesthouse, built right on the beach. They have a bar/restaurant, but cook meals to advance order only.

If you keep going down the beach, you will come to Francis and Emma's Seaside View. This beachside supermarket makes loading the dinghy easy. They keep a good stock of basics, and for those looking for a room, they have some sweet little self-contained cottages just behind. You can rent scuba gear here (see *Water sports*).

There are several other small super-markets (minimarkets would be a better description), rum shops, and snack shops dotted around the island, along the west-running road. Standing Wave [$D] is a local supermarket, rum shop, and restaurant.

Farther down, M&M is a supermarket. A mobile vendor is often around selling fresh fruits and vegetables.

For a pleasant walk, turn left on the road and follow it round to the east till it ends. For higher views, head up the hill past the church and keep going up till there is a left turn, which takes you up to an aerial with a good view. You can continue to the second aerial. It is not easy to find your way to the highest point (the Piton). A Grenadian called Osbert Felix could take you there in the dry season or give you a cultural road tour any time. He has a one-man charity: he solar-dries roots and vegetables and grates them into flour. He will be your guide for a contribution (535-9192/443-9043).

Water sports

The Seaside View Supermarket fills tanks and rents scuba gear to local fishermen. They are happy to rent to yachts. This is not a sports establishment and has none of the safeguards that go with a dive shop, so satisfy yourself that the gear is in order.

St. Vincent & the Grenadines

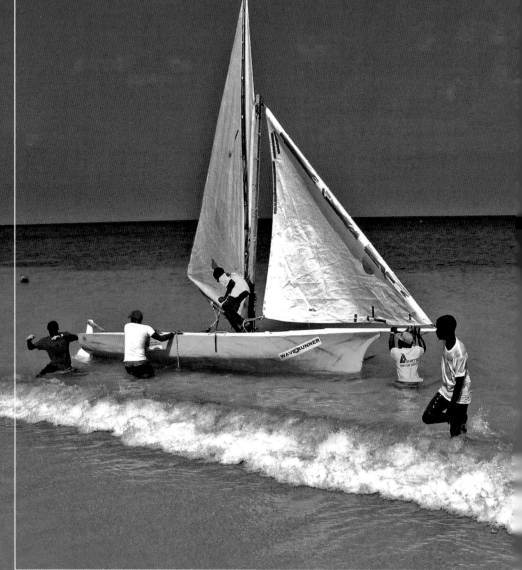

Grenada &
Carriacou

Grand Anse during Grenada Sailing Festival

Carriacou at a glance

Regulations

Carriacou is part of Grenada, and the main customs office for yachts is in Tyrrel Bay at Carriacou Marine, next to the Chandlery/mini mart. They are open 0800-1600 Monday to Friday. They also open 0900-1400 on weekends and holidays, when you will pay a reasonable overtime fee. They are on the Sailclear system and you can use their office computer on those occasions when their internet is actually working. You can also clear in Hillsborough (no Sailclear).

Monthly customs cruising permits are $50 EC not exceeding 40 feet; $75 EC not exceeding 60 feet; $100 EC not exceeding 80 feet; and $150 over 80 feet. You do not pay for months spent in a yard. Crew arriving by plane or from shore pay a $20 EC embarkation fee.

Visitors may not spearfish in Grenada waters and anyone caught doing so will be heavily fined and may be banned from returning to Grenada waters. The water surrounding Sandy Island, the Sisters, and the northern side of Tyrrel Bay is a marine park, The Sandy Island/Oyster Bay Marine Protected Area (SIOBMPA). In these areas, use a park moorings if one is available. The charge for being in the marine park is $10 US or $25 EC per day. Diving in the marine park must be with a local dive shop. Do not fish in the marine park.

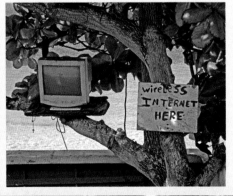

Holidays

See *Grenada*. The Carriacou Regatta usually takes place at the end of July. For details check their website:
carriacouregatta.com

Shopping hours

Shops and offices normally open 0800-1600. Saturday is half-day and most places are closed by noon. Banks open Monday to Thursday 0800-1200 & 1300-1500, Fridays 0800-1200 &1500-1700.

Telephones

The easiest way to call is to buy a cell phone or a local SIM. Lime or Digicel are your options. For overseas calls dial 1 for the USA and NANP countries; 011 plus the country code for other countries (see page 19). For collect and credit-card calls, dial 0, then the whole number. When dialing from overseas, the area code is 473, followed by a 7-digit number.

Transport

There are inexpensive ($1.50-$6 EC) buses running to most villages. Taxis are plentiful. Linky Taxi (VHF: 16) is a good driver, used to working with yachts. Sample taxi rates are:

	$EC
Hillsborough to Tyrrel Bay	35
Tyrrel Bay to airport	40
Island tour (2.5 hours)	200
Mini tour (1.25 hours)	100

Rental cars are available (check our directory). You will need to buy a local license, which costs $60 EC. Drive on the left.

Airport tax for international flights is $50 EC and for flights between Carriacou and Grenada $10 EC. These are usually included in the ticket.

Anse La Roche

Carriacou

his is an island with over a hundred rum shops and only one gasoline station." Frances Kay, Carriacou.

Carriacou is enchanting. The inhabitants live by farming, fishing, and seafaring, and must number among the friendliest in the Caribbean. Just about everywhere in Carriacou is of interest, but Windward should definitely be part of your tour, as should the road running from Windward to the north end of the island. Windward is the traditional center of boatbuilding, and it is here that you can see the fishing fleet arrive under sail. If you cannot afford a taxi, take a bus over to Windward and hike. A destination with a great view is the hospital, which sits high on the mountain overlooking the Hillsborough Bay.

Carriacou has lovely anchorages, pleasant hiking, yacht haul-out facilities, yacht services, dive shops, and entertaining bars, restaurants, and cafes.

Navigation

Carriacou is a Carib word meaning "island surrounded by reefs," but do not worry: the approach down the west coast is simple enough. When sailing from the north, it is safest to pass to the west of Jack a Dan before heading up into Hillsborough. If you take the trickier route east of Jack a Dan, watch out for the reef, which is about 5 feet deep, about one-third of the way between Craigston Point and Jack a Dan. Favor the Jack a Dan side of the channel (but not too close). You can anchor almost anywhere off the town. Hillsborough is a good anchorage, except in bad northerly swells, when you will be better off in Tyrrel Bay.

There is a flashing green light on Jack a Dan and a flashing red light on the buoy east of Sandy Island.

Two anchorages north of Hillsborough are worth a thought. Anse La Roche has a perfect beach, with a big rock on the south side. It is good for temporary anchorage for a swim and beach visit, or even overnight, but northerly swells make it untenable. The snorkeling is excellent. Sparrow Bay is a good anchorage, except during bad northerly swells, but even in moderate swells it will be hard to beach the dinghy. When coming from Hillsborough, pass outside Jack a Dan.

The adventurous might want to poke into Windward and Watering Bay on the northeast coast. You cannot rely on the buoys, but if you eyeball your way in, you will find yourself in a vast, fairly protected lagoon. You can explore right down in this lagoon with a draft of 6 feet, but go carefully as it is all eyeball navigation.

HILLSBOROUGH

Hillsborough is a pleasant town built on a lovely beach. As you walk down the main street, you catch glimpses of the sea through gaps between the buildings. Hillsborough is a good anchorage, with the marine park right nearby. You can also visit by hopping on one of the frequent buses that run between Tyrrel Bay and Hillsborough (fare $3.50). You will find good restaurants and shops, a local market, and you can pop into the tourist office for maps and information, including cultural events.

For pets that need attention, there is a good animal hospital, run by Cathy and Hans, and if you need attention, Carriacou Health Services (CHS) brings in specialists (including a dentist) on various days of the week, and can do tests. They take walk-ins for emergencies but otherwise call ahead. The local hospital has a commanding view of the bay, and Carriacou has a doctor.

Regulations

Hillsborough is a port of clearance and you can clear in Hillsborough. Check with immigration first, then visit customs and port. They are not on the Sailclear.com system.

Yachts wanting an agent to handle their clearance can arrange this though Henry Safari Tours of Grenada. He can also arrange a big beach barbecue complete with band and marquee on Sandy Island.

Communications

Most bars and restaurants have wifi. If you need a computer, Ade's Dream has an internet room in their office at the back. For phone and fax, try Lime (Cable and Wireless) or Ade's Dream.

Transport

Matthew Raymond, aka Linky Taxi [VHF: 16], is a good and reliable cab driver, used to dealing with yachtspeople, and he always carries his phone with him. If you need something done, he can help. Linky also has a select fleet of jeeps available for rent.

Provisioning

Make a beeline for Patty's Deli. Christine, a Carriacou woman who was brought up in England, is charming and helpful and sells all the things the other supermarkets do not in her pleasantly cool air-conditioned shop, Freshly baked French bread, croissants, and other baked goodies come out of her oven around 0900, and you will find cold cuts, yogurts, cheeses, frozen meats and fish, good wines, regular milk, lots of sauces, coffee, and gluten-free foods if you need them, also lots of interesting products in jars and boxes. Sit at a table outside on the pavement and enjoy coffee and baked goodies or a sandwich. Visiting Grenadians ask "Why don't we have a store this good in Grenada?"

Christine will also provision bareboats and yachts with a little notice.

Many supermarkets stock essentials,

though you will have to visit the market or local street side vendors for fresh produce. Liquor prices are good. Check Ade's Dream and Bullens on Main Street. Both of them also stock hardware and Bullens also has a pharmacy. Wander down Church Street to see Kims, A1 Enterprise and the big Mills and Valley Pharmacy.

Fun Shopping

You can find banks, travel agents, and many quaint, small variety stores, each crammed with its owner's ideas of what sells in Carriacou. If you go round to enough of them, you will find a wider selection of products for sale than on many a larger island.

Restaurants

Hillsborough has a great collection of restaurants. Kayak Kafe [$C-D] is bright and cheerful, in a great location, hanging over the beach and looking out to sea. The atmosphere is down-home and friendly. Smoothies and fresh local juice, along with a slice of Carriacou lime pie or banana cake, are always available. The lunch menu includes sandwiches, wraps, soups, salads, and local fish dishes. Closed Tuesdays, otherwise open 0730-1500 for breakfast and lunch. Also for dinner on Thursday, Saturdays, and Mondays until 2100. Dinner includes fresh fish, lambi, lobster in season, and some great pies, including steak and kidney and chicken. In addition, a number of vegetarian options have recently been added to the

Grenada and Carriacou

331

menu. At press time the owner was dealing with some medical problems, but I hope you will find it open.

La Playa [$C-D] is the perfect beach-bar hangout. You can anchor right off and dinghy ashore as long as there are no big swells. La Playa (closed Sundays) is open 1000-1800. This entertaining beach bar is presided over by Kathyanne and owned by the Green Roof people. They offer generous hamburgers, fishburgers, soup and sandwiches anytime they are open. It is a perfect place for that sunset drink or as a daytime hangout; try their homemade ice cream. They sometimes have live music.

Located on the main road just past the entrance to La Playa is Aggie's [$D], a small deli that has baked goods, pizza, and lunch specials. She is open Monday to Saturday from 0800.

Laurena II is cheap, cheerful and serves generous portions of local food. They open around noon and often have live music Saturday nights.

The Mermaid Inn, located on the water just past the fish market, has reopened after many decades of closure, and has taken on new owners who have re-opened its restaurant, Callaloo [$B -C]. Callaloo has a breezy interior and large deck with a spectacular view overlooking the beach. Open daily 0730 - 2200 for breakfast, lunch, and dinner, it boasts a large menu and serves local and international fare alike. Rooms are available.

Eclipse [$C-D] is located across from Ade's Dream. The dining room hangs out over the beach, with the gentle sound of waves brushing the shore. It serves reasonably priced local food and does takeout.

Cuthbert Snagg [VHF: 16] is active in environmental efforts in Carriacou and owns a couple of powerboats to take you on snorkeling trips and expeditions to the offshore islands. He also builds model racing boats. A good place to meet him is at his bar, Snagg's Place, which is on the beach. On occasion, if the group is right, he will organize a lobster bash or fish cookout.

The Green Roof [$B-C] lies about half a mile north of town on the coast. This Swedish establishment is owned and run by Asa and Jonas. It has a nice view and a bar

that is open all day. It serves fresh fruit juice and coffee, along with regular drinks. They open for dinner.

In the other direction, you can walk 10 minutes towards the airport for a good roti at Annie's Roti Shop, just across the road from the beach. She is open from 0730 and does breakfast, lunch, and dinner by reservation. She also rents comfortable wooden beach chairs across the street, perfect for a lazy afternoon on the beach.

Ashore

You can use the low part of the main dock, but you may need to use a stern anchor to stop your dinghy from mashing up in swells. The taxi square is in front of customs. There is a gas station in town and many youths are willing to fetch ice.

The museum is worth the short walk and is open 1000-1600 Monday through Friday, and 1000-1500 Saturdays. It has an eclectic collection, from Arawak pottery to the island's first telephone exchange. For a taste of local life, hang out in the rum shops all around.

Should you arrive towards the end of July or early August, you may witness the famous Carriacou Regatta. The best trading and sailing sloops in the islands are built in Carriacou. Once a year they get together to race on this festive weekend. The boats they build today are unbelievably fast and sweet, and if you are lucky enough to see one sailing into harbor, it is a joy to behold. (They are featured in a great movie: Vanishing Sail).

Carriacou also has an interesting Maroon Festival towards the end of April: carriacoumaroon.com.

Carriacou is one of the last unspoiled islands. One reason for this is that much of the land does not have clear title. However, if you are interested, there are lots available at Craigston Estates, overlooking the sea. Contact Renwick and Thompson or Down Island Realty.

Water sports

Diving is very good, with excellent visibility, and a big marine park. Within the park, you must dive with a dive shop, though you are welcome to snorkel on your own. The Sandy Island / Oyster Bay Marine Protected Area (SIOBMPA) has 15 dive sites that are less than a 10-minute boat ride from either Hillsborough or Tyrrel Bay. New dive sites to the north of Hillsborough are being explored.

Sandy Island has a sheltered shallow site that is a favorite with both divers and snorkelers. Other popular sites include Sharky's (home to several nurse sharks) and Whirlpool (so called for its champagne-like bubbles, which are caused by volcanic activity), both of which are at Mabouya. A reef restoration project and coral nursery has recently been established in the area, and is managed by Deefer Diving. Sisters Rocks features two sites outstanding for their black coral and masses of aquatic life. Within the SIOBMPA, you often see several species of moray eels (green, spotted, chain-link, and chestnut), sea horses, spotted eagle rays, southern stingrays, nurse sharks, angelfish, frogfish, and a multitude of blennies.

Deefer Diving is owned by Austrian/ British couple Alexandra and Gary Ward. They are very welcoming, well qualified instructors who run a good dive shop with enthusiasm and care. Both are experienced PADI IDC staff instructors, and offer a variety of diving courses, from beginner to pro, as well as guided dives for certified divers. Snorkelers accompanying divers are always welcome. In June 2013, Deefer Diving launched their purpose-built catamaran, Bobcat, which is the first of its kind to be built on Carriacou. The dive center retains a PADI 5 Star Centre status and remains one of the most qualified dive centres in the Windwards. Like all dive shops in Carriacou, they prefer to go out with small groups, although large groups can be accommodated by prior arrangement.

They open from 0800 to 1700, although bookings by phone and email can be made at any time, and walk-in business is welcome; scuba and snorkeling gear is on sale, and equipment rental and tank fills are available. A pick-up service from your yacht in Tyrrel Bay or Sandy Island can be arranged. They do frequent lionfish hunts.

Sandy Island, *Lexi Fisher*

SANDY ISLAND AND L'ESTERRE BAY

Sandy Island is nothing but a flawless strip of sand, surrounded by perfect snorkeling and diving reefs. Pelicans and seagulls will be your neighbors in this wonderful spot. Across the bay is Paradise Beach, another idyllic anchorage within walking range of both Tyrrel Bay and Hillsborough.

This area is now part of SIOBMPA, and it costs $25 EC or $10 US per day per yacht to be in the park. Ten Moorings are provided at Sandy Island and six on Paradise Beach. If you need to anchor, it should be to the west and south of the Sandy Island mooring area.

Yachts should use holding tanks.

Sandy Island has changed rapidly in recent times. The beach suffered such degradation that all the trees died, but then a hurricane threw up a coral capping, leaving big tide pools and providing the island some protection. Trees planted by locals have thrived and it is now in fine shape. Respect all beach plants and vegetation: they hold the island together.

You can carry 7 feet quite close to the middle of the island, but watch out for the reefs north and south, and the odd shallower spot. There is not much room to drag, so check your mooring.

L'Esterre Bay, with the long and beautiful Paradise Beach, is right opposite Sandy Island. You can pick up a mooring here in 7 -8 feet of water. Head from Sandy towards the white house with the terra-cotta roof on

334

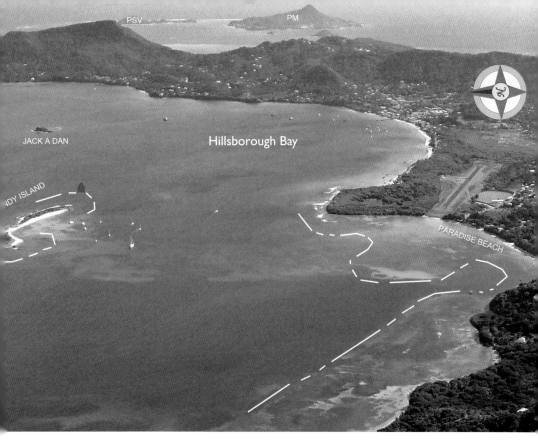

PSV   PM

JACK A DAN

Hillsborough Bay

NDY ISLAND

PARADISE BEACH

the headland west of Paradise Beach. Skirt the really bright green water, then turn east once past it, and you will be in the best spot. You can also dinghy over.

Ashore

The eastern end of Paradise beach is the home of Sandra's Fidel productions. This little container-boutique is unquestionably the best in Carriacou. Everything is locally and artistically made: original calabash art, jewelry, Zaka masks, Putumayo CDs, Art Box, Rasta hats, bamboo and coconut craft, Art Fabrik batik, and original paintings and prints. They have a new line of teas, as well as organic and locally made soaps, creams, and oils that they produce themselves.

They also print art on t-shirts: good-quality reproductions from local artists are sold through their website, fidelproductions. com, or in shops up and down the islands. Treasure in Mustique, Art 'n Beads in Union, and Imagine in Grenada sell them. Mr. Quality sells them in the Tobago Cays. Fidel also produce mojos, each an original, using exotic beads from many materials,

Jump for Joy, Sandy Island

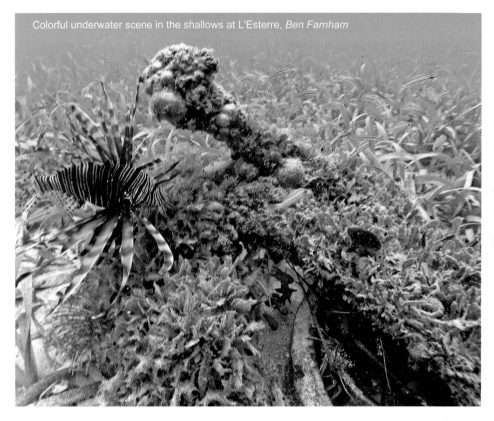

Colorful underwater scene in the shallows at L'Esterre, *Ben Farnham*

often accented with gold and silver.

There are several good little bars here, including Joan's [$D] next to the boutique. Joan does an inexpensive lunch and will cook dinner on order.

Off the Hook [$B-D] is much farther down the beach by the six MPA moorings. Part art, part beach bar, part crazy, Off the Hook, with its upper-level and countless corners seats and hammocks, is entertaining. Curtis Malcolm opens daily, 0900-2300. It is in an open beach area with fishing boats, giving it a pleasant local feel. Curtis cooks fish, lobster, and lambi, serves good pizza, and claims to have the best fries in Carriacou. Come for live music, barbecue and bonfire on Wednesday nights. Men can always get a haircut, as Curtis is a professional barber. Dinner reservations are appreciated. This is a good place to leave your dinghy when you want to take a bus, walk or shop. Tyrrel Bay and Hillsborough are both within walking distance, but you may get your feet wet walking on the beach towards Hillsborough.

TYRREL BAY

Tyrrel Bay is huge, well-protected, and very popular with cruisers. The taking of mangrove oysters is no longer allowed, so do not buy any.

Businesses line the waterfront. A road separates them from the sea. The shore was once thickly wooded with manchineel and seagrapes. Most were cut down to increase the visibility between the boats and the businesses. When Hurricane Lenny threw record-breaking swells into the bay, it devastated the unprotected shoreline and destroyed much of the road, turning several properties into beachfront real estate. The government then built the big seawall that now lines the waterfront. The trees are coming back.

Navigation

Tyrrel Bay is deep and wide and easy to enter. Despite this, a surprising number of people manage to run aground. The buoys are rather confusing. Whatever the original color, they end up Pelican-guano white on top and rusty underneath. Buoys may be added or removed at any time, without notice. There is a reef in the northern part of the bay, towards the center. The deepest channel is to the north of this reef and is marked by three buoys. However, the reef that is most often hit is along the southern shore. There is a small cul-de-sac in this reef called Bareboat Alley, and people manage to go in here and run hard aground. Two large unlit mooring buoys lie in the middle of the southern channel. It is easiest to enter the bay just south of center. You are not in danger of hitting the northern reef until you are more than halfway across the bay. You can pass closely on either side of the big mooring buoys safely, though keep in mind that buoys should not be relied upon. Holding is good if you can find clear sand, but rather poor in the weedy areas.

The northern side of the bay is a marine park, with no anchoring, except in the mangrove swamp during hurricane warnings.

If for some reason you want a mooring, you can call Arawak Dive (443-6960/457-5112), which has two, or you can

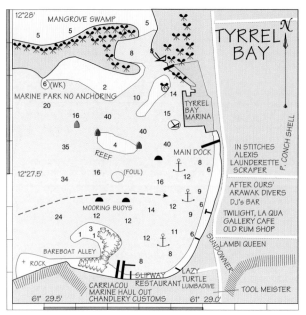

General yacht services

Leave your dinghy at Carriacou Marine, Slipway Restaurant, Lazy Turtle, Gallery Cafe, the main dock, or beach it. Garbage bins are dotted around; try not to overwhelm them.

Carriacou Marine [VHF: 16] is a charming small boatyard and marina. Their fuel dock is open 0800-1730 Monday to Saturday, and 0800-1400 on Sundays. Here you can take on ice, water, and fuel (diesel and gas, both regular and duty-free). If you are after duty-free fuel, this is a good place to buy it.

They have convenient docking, with space for about seven yachts, both on the finger dock and outside of the marine hoist dock.

Yachts are hauled on a 50-ton marine travel-lift. They can take up to 18-foot beam and 8-foot draft. It is one of the more environmentally friendly yards, with a wash-down catchment so that no toxic paint goes into the sea, and they have vacuum systems to suck up the dust. They can take about 17 boats. Normal opening hours are 0800-1600 Monday to Friday and 0800-1200 on Saturdays.

This yard is excellent for general work and for do-it-yourself jobs. They can provide technicians for most things, including carpentry, electrics, and mechanics. For environmental reasons, they are not currently spraying boats, sandblasting, or encouraging major fiberglass repairs, as they lack an enclosed area to contain the fumes and dust.

They have a chandlery, open 0800-2000, with a moderate selection, along with a mini-market. Carriacou Marine has storage rooms for gear and a fair-sized building with a laundry, showers and toilets, a small shop, ice, and rooms for rent for those who prefer to stay ashore. The whole area has wifi.

Jerome McQuilkins and John Walker, have built Tyrrel Bay Marina on the far side of the main dock, the largest development in Tyrrel Bay. There is room for 200 boats ashore to be hoisted by a 150-ton travel lift

ask Carriacou Marine (443-6292), where Dexter, one of their employees, owns one, and they may put down some more. If you accept any other mooring offers, ask anyone else for a mooring, or go to one of the above and then listen to someone telling you "That mooring no good, try mine," you are likely to have problems.

Regulations

Tyrrel Bay is the main customs station for yacht clearance. They open 0800-1600 weekdays and 0900-1400 weekends and holidays. The officers are friendly and Sailclear.com works when they have internet. Their office is in Carriacou Marine. (See also page 327.)

Communications

Carriacou Children's Educational Fund (CCEF), funded by local businesses, and based in the Slipway Restaurant has free baywide wifi. Go in to find out how to link up, and you will be given an opportunity to make a contribution to CCEF. If you have items for the annual yacht auction, take them to the shop at After Ours. The Matterson's very kindly store them, and the auction is held there. Lazy Turtle, Lambi Queen, Gallery Cafe and most other bars have wifi. The Cruiser's wifi signal comes from Lazy Turtle.

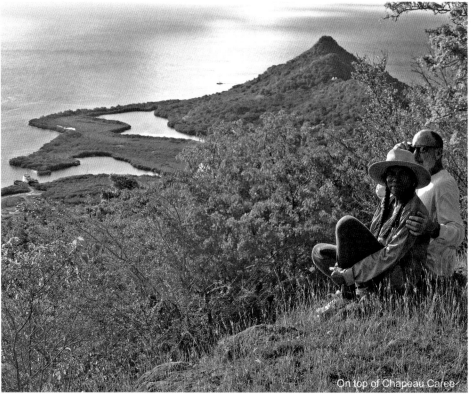

On top of Chapeau Caree

Paradise Beach, *Lexi Fisher*

Grenada and Carriacou

which should be in place before this guide comes out. Right now there is room for a few yachts alongside, but docks are envisaged for about 180 boats.

Gerry owns various tugs and can provide a 24-hour marine emergency service for yachts that go aground or start to sink. He is the right person to contact if you need a hand, as his prices are fair. Call 407-0927 or contact him through Slipway Restaurant.

My Beautiful Launderette, owned by Daniella, is next to the Alexis Supermarket. They will do your wash for you, but if you are obsessive enough to want to do it yourself, you can (the price is the same). They have seats where you can sit while your laundry is washing and a book exchange so you will not be bored if you wait. They open 0700-1300 from Monday to Saturday.

Next to Lambi Queen, Jack's Shorebase Services is a laundry combined with a small supermarket. The laundry opens 0900-1700 weekdays; the supermarket stays open longer.

Chandlery

Carriacou Marine has a good little chandlery, which is linked to Island Water World, and anything they don't have in stock can come on the next ferry.

See also Technical Marine Management in *Technical yacht services.*

Technical yacht services

In Stitches is an excellent canvas and sail repair shop run by Andy and various assistants. Andy lives on his yacht, Yellow Bird, and drives an old BMW bike with a sidecar. You can call him on VHF: 16. The shop is ashore. They are very helpful with all kinds of canvas work, upholstery, sail work (they sell new sails with the Quantum label), and bimini tops. They make very decorative custom flags.

Paul O'Regan, of Technical Marine Management, is in the Gallery Cafe. He used to manage the boatyard and knows most boat systems. He is a good man to contact for rigging problems and general help. He is a knowledgeable Budget Marine agent with access to the large Budget Marine inventory and same or next day delivery from Grenada. He has a hotline to Turbulence Sails in Grenada for rigging hardware.

Tyrrel Bay is first-rate for welding and fabricating, thanks to Dominique [VHF: 16], of Carriacou Aluminum Boats, who does wonders in aluminum, from building a new dinghy to fixing a broken mast. He welds and polishes stainless steel and biminis are one of his specialties. His wife, Genevieve, sews sails and offers therapeutic massage for bad backs and sore necks. You will find him on his trimaraft workshop, not far from the boatyard.

On the mechanical side, check Manny Work Shop in Carriacou Marine or ask for its owner Immanual Clemment. Immanual is from PM and can fix inboards, outboards, and general mechanical, plumbing and electrical problems. He can also do fiberglass and woodwork. He is good at most everything.

Tyrrel Bay has a certified electrician, François Corles, who is also a professional diver. His company is Tall Man Electrics, appropriate for a technician some 2 meters tall. He is French, speaks good English, and is very pleasant to deal with. Look for him on his motor-sailor ketch, Santiago. He can fix any electrical problems, including engines, generators, and other boat systems. If you have a faulty starter or alternator, he can get Al Bernadine in Gouyave to rebuild it. He would be a good person to speak to if you have refrigeration problems.

Transport

Linky Taxi [VHF: 16] is helpful and friendly, and has a good-sized minibus for island tours and shopping trips, backed up by a smaller minibus run by his sister. He is always ready to come. He can rent you one of his modern Jeeps.

Bubbles [VHF: 16] has a fancy, air-conditioned bus with spacious seats.

Provisioning

Several little supermarkets stock a good selection of liquor and beer, along with bread, canned and packaged food, eggs, and chicken. Some also have electronic goods and household supplies. If you don't see what you want, it is worth asking. The Carriacou Marine store is good for liquor and basics. La Qua Supermarket [VHF: 16] is run by La Qua and Diana Augustin. They often have fresh eggs and sometimes block ice on hand and, if not, you can get them to order you a block for the next morning. Alexis Supermarket is run by the Alexis family, who own a fleet of boats, including some of the ferries that run to Grenada. The newest supermarket is After Ours, which sometimes has goodies not found in the others, as does Gallery Cafe, which also has good bread.

Fresh food is sold by Denise in a stall opposite In Stitches. She also has a boutique section. Her sister, Donelyn, has another stall, called Empress Elisha Palace, which sells clothing and produce next door. Rufus has a stall on Saturdays.

Restaurants

The Lazy Turtle [VHF: 16, $B-C] is on the waterfront. Dinghy in, tie to their dock, and walk up the steps to the big decks, where you sit looking out over the bay and enjoy the aromas of good cooking. The owners, Sue and Shayne, run a friendly and informal establishment, They cook excellent thin-crust Italian pizzas, pastas, salads, and a list

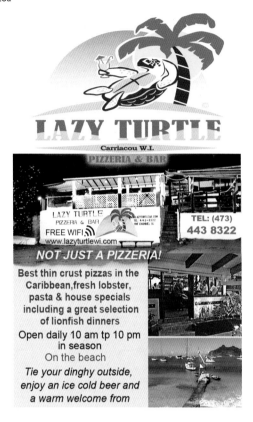

of specials that are posted on a blackboard. These includes reasonably priced fresh lobster in season, shrimps, lionfish (the fish you can feel good about eating) served in about half a dozen different ways, tuna and more. They bring in live entertainment about once a month, and everyone turns up for the party.

Daniella and Kate's Slipway Restaurant [$B-C, VHF:16], next to Carriacou Marine, is excellent. It is in the original Slipway building, complete with a boat in the roof, planers, routers, and other tools, all left standing but artfully converted to form bars, and tables. Daniella greets guest warmly and keeps everyone happy out front, while back in the kitchen Kate cooks like an angel. The menu is posted on a blackboard. The food has a Mediterranean flair, and is very good and reasonably priced with generous portions. They are closed on Mondays and for Sunday dinner (also Thursdays in the summer). Otherwise, they are open 1130-1400 for lunch and 1800-2100 for dinner. Sunday brunch, is popular and runs from

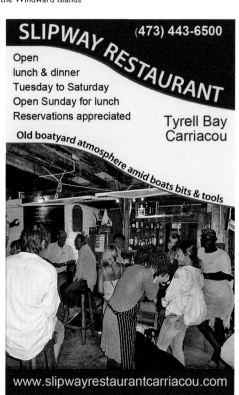
1130 to 1500. Tie up your dinghy on their dock right outside.

Gallery Cafe [closed Sundays] is a lovely, cheerful cafe, local art gallery, and craft shop, which sells fresh baked bread and specialty food items, including gluten-free pasta. They also serve homemade ice cream. It is a friendly place, with free wifi and a bookswap, and Sue will make you feel at home. They open at 0800 for coffee and a snack or a full breakfast. They stay open till 1600. Come for a healthy lunch-time salad, sandwich, or seafood special between 1200 and 1400. Coffee, iced coffee, teas of all kinds, and baked goodies are always available. The handicrafts are artistically made and local. They include leather bags, jewelry, clothes, books, and ornaments.

The Iguana Cafe, at Carriacou Marine [$D], is next to customs. They have pleasant covered outside seating. It is a cafe/restaurant, and boasts authentic stone-fired pizza. You can also get sandwiches, pastries, good fishburgers, and snacks all day long. In the evening they usually fire up the barbecue, so you can get some chicken or fish.

Sundowners, a tiny beachside place between Lambi Queen and Lazy Turtle, is owned by Jeanette and Franky. It opens at around 1630 and stays open, so you can take a sundowner and enjoy dinner. Both Franky and Jeanette are excellent cooks. Some Wednesday nights they host a beach bonfire, starting around 1930. They bake excellent bread that you can order in advance.

The Conch Shell [$D] is just down the street that leads back from Scraper's and is open everyday. Monday to Saturday they serve big local lunch plates for about $15 EC. Ask about dinner.

Lambi Queen [VHF: 16, $C-D] is a cute restaurant with a patio railing made from old barrel planks. The Sylvester family owns it. Edwin goes out fishing, and his son, Sherwin, cooks up the catch in good Carriacou homestyle. Nightly happy hour is 1730-1830. They have a party on Fridays, and you can tie up at their small dinghy dock.

The Twilight Restaurant and Bar [VHF: 16] has a pleasant, intimate atmosphere; the walls are brightly decorated with paintings, many from local artist, Canute Caliste. Owner and chef Diana Augustin cooks spicy West Indian Creole dishes with fresh fish, lobster, lambi, chicken, and pork. Happy hour is 1800-1900. They have two perfect tables across the road hanging over the beach.

Natasha's Bayside Restaurant and Bar [$C-D] sits open to the breeze next door to In Stitches, with one waterfront table across the road. She is often open on Wednesday nights for dominoes. Otherwise, make a reservation.

D Crab Hole is a new local restaurant open every day from 0900, and is located in a building behind the old Baba Supermarket.

The Original Rum Shop [$B-C], run by Casana and Timothy, is a great hangout where you can meet people and play dominoes. They sometimes do meals featuring fresh fish, conch, and lobster, but they need about a half-hour notice to get in gear. The pool table out front is a great way to spend an evening.

After Ours is a handsome building that is a restaurant, nightclub, conference center, shop, and stage. They open from time to time for occasional music, discos, live bands, and other entertainment.

Painted in bright national colors, DJ's [$C] is a newly opened bar and restaurant open 1500-2400 daily and serves reasonably priced local dishes. Happy hour is every Friday from 1700-1900. Music tends to be quite loud. There are several other inexpensive hangouts, including Liz's Place [$D] which is friendly, and where you can get good food.

Ashore

The mangrove swamp in Tyrrel Bay is part of the new marine park and is protected. Switch off the dinghy motor and listen to the peace. (Take insect repellent.) You often see herons, and sometimes iguanas. Yachts are not allowed in except during a hurricane warning. Taking oysters is forbidden.

There are plenty of hiking possibilities, including a pleasant trek up Chapeau Carre, the second highest peak on the island, which offers panoramic views all around. (Hiking instructions are on doyleguides.com.)

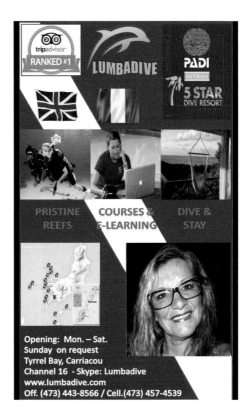

LUMBADIVE
PADI
5 STAR DIVE RESORT
tripadvisor RANKED #1
PRISTINE REEFS · COURSES & E-LEARNING · DIVE & STAY
Opening: Mon. – Sat.
Sunday on request
Tyrrel Bay, Carriacou
Channel 16 - Skype: Lumbadive
www.lumbadive.com
Off. (473) 443-8566 / Cell.(473) 457-4539

Water sports

There is plenty of good diving. All the marine park dive sites are within a 10-minute ride and right off the Sisters is an excellent dive where you find a sloping reef of soft and hard corals, decorated with many sponges. Lots of fish gather here. You are bound to see angelfish and stingrays, and turtles are likely. There are superb dives off Round Island and Kick 'em Jenny, and you can do these on your own, but it is better to go with a dive shop. Here the fish life is outstanding, with sharks, rays, and big pelagic fish. There are 200-foot walls, caves, and many reefs. Since it is a long trip, dive shops do it as a two-tank dive in fair weather only.

Georg Schmitt and Connie Hagen own Arawak Divers [VHF: 16], and they have been in Carriacou longer than all the other dive operators. Georg has lived in Carriacou since 1994, and no one knows the local waters better. Georg does both commercial and pleasure diving. Connie, like Georg, is a PADI instructor. Both of them came from Germany. Their shop is based in the After

Grenada and Carriacou

343

EXPERIENCE THE DIFFERENCE

We put YOU first!
Your enjoyment and safety are our number one priority.

- personalized diving in small groups
- dive as long your air lasts
- diving on the Caribbean & Atlantic side
- pick up service from yachts
- PADI resort / certification courses
- private dive trips & courses on request

ARAWAK DIVERS

located in Tyrrel Bay at After Ours

Phone: (473) 443-6906 or 457-5112
arawakdivers@spiceisle.com
www.arawakdivers.com
VHF CH: 16

Peacock flounder

Ours building and they are happy to pick customers up off their yachts in Tyrrel Bay or Sandy Island. Call them on VHF 16. Their groups are always small and they do private dives. They are good, low-key, and welcoming. They are very much into photography, and their photos are superb. This gives them a keen eye for unusual small critters like flatworms, frogfish, seahorses, batfish and nudibranchs. They know all kinds of small sites where they can find particular creatures.

They have two dive boats: the largest is a 32-footer for the distant sites. They are the Carriacou Trans Ocean base and rent kayaks (a good way to visit the mangrove swamp).

Lumbadive [VHF: 16], in the same building as Lazy Turtle Pizzeria, is run by two Canadians, Diane and Richard, who speak English and French and teach PADI to pro level. They are the only NITROX shop in Carriacou. They have their own dinghy dock and offer VIP service, so boarding is easy and your equipment is already on board. Any surface intervals include water, fruit or Diane's homemade cookies. Their motto is: "You come as a diver, you leave as a friend." and TripAdvisor has rated them the top activity in Carriacou. For those that like to hunt, their Friday afternoon lionfish hunts are popular. They offer Horizon, Sunsail and Moorings customers a 10-20% discount.

They will pick you up from your yacht in most Carriacou anchorages. And Richard may catch you with his GoPro camera underwater or from his drone.

ISLE DE RONDE

STRONG CURRENTS IN THIS AREA

12° 19'N
61° 36'W
WGNS23

SCALE IN N.M.

CARRIACOU

CARRIACOU
TO GRENADA

SCALE IN NAUTICAL MILES

Renwick, Thompson & Co.,
We accept Mastercard & Visa

PASSAGES BETWEEN CARRIACOU & GRENADA

None of the islands between Carriacou and Grenada affords good shelter, though Isle de Ronde is okay in fair weather. The anchorage is in the bay on the northern side of the west coast. Try it for lunch, and in settled weather with no swells, overnighting is possible, though you may have to try a few spots to get good holding sand. Snorkeling is excellent off the sisters (take a dinghy) To explore ashore, I take the dinghy into the northern bay opposite Kick 'em Jenny. About 20 inhabitants live some of the time on the south coast.

Kick 'em Jenny and the Sisters have large nesting-bird populations, and you can see boobies and pelicans, particularly on the Sisters. Beware of the strong currents.

An active volcano that lies about two miles west of Isle de Ronde erupted many times, including; in1988, 1989 and 2001. It, too, has been named Kick 'em Jenny, and you certainly will get a big kick if you happen to be on top when it erupts. To prevent this, the Grenada government has declared a 1.5-km exclusion zone around the volcano at all times (not enforced; it is for your own safety). The exclusion zone increases to 5 km when the volcano is rumbling (For the current status of the volcano, check: uwiseismic.com, or follow the links on doyleguides.com.)

Kick 'em Jenny (the big rock) has the reputation of kicking up a nasty sea as you go north, and this is particularly true if the tide is running east.

When sailing from Grenada to Carriacou, the fastest way is to hug Grenada's lee coast right to the north before heading to Carriacou. Unless the wind is well in the south, take a tack into Sauteurs, as the west-going current is weakest close to the Grenada coast. This will not only get you up faster, but it may keep you outside the 1.5 km volcano exclusion zone.

Regulations

Grenada, Carriacou, and Petite Martinique make up one country, with ports of clearance in Tyrrel Bay, Hillsborough, St. George's, Prickly Bay, Phare Bleu, and St. David's Harbour. Entry is on a single page form. Prickly Bay and Port Louis have sailclear.com. Customs charges you for a monthly cruising permit. It is $50 EC not exceeding 40 feet; $75 EC not exceeding 60 feet; $100 EC not exceeding 80 feet; and $150 over 80 feet. There is no charge for months spent in a yard.

You may clear in and out at the same time for stays up to 3 days (72 hours), but you must do the full clearance both ways.

The port charges an entry fee of $8.10 EC per person, excluding the skipper. You also pay $20 EC per person embarkation tax for those arriving by plane, or who are living ashore. If you want to take a dog ashore, you will need a valid rabies certificate.

Customs hours are 0800-1145 and 1300-1545 on weekdays. At other times you will be charged overtime fees. If you have any questions about yachting, including security, contact MAYAG: (473) 416-7135, mayagadmin@gmail.com.

Visitors may not spearfish in Grenada waters or scuba dive on your own within marine parks. Collecting or damaging coral and buying lobster out of season are strictly forbidden. (Lobstering season is October 31 to April 30.)

Holidays

January 1, New Year's Day
February 7, Independence Day
Easter Friday, Sunday, & Monday, April 14-17, 2017, and March 29-April 2, 2018
Feb. 22, Independence Day
May 1, Labor Day
Whit Monday, June 5, 2017 and May 21, 2018
Corpus Christi, June 15, 2017; May 31, 2018

Emancipation Day, first Monday in August
Carnival, Second Monday and Tuesday in August
October 25, Thanksgiving
December 25, Christmas
December 26, Boxing Day

Shopping hours

Shops and offices normally open 0800-1200 and 1300-1600. Saturday is a half day and most places are closed by noon. Banks normally open weekdays till 1500 and on Fridays till 1700.

Telephones

Cell phones (Lime or Digicel) are the way to go. For overseas calls, dial 1 for the USA and NANP countries dial, 011 plus the country code for other countries (see page 19). For collect and credit-card calls, dial 0, then the whole number. When dialing from overseas, the area code is 473, followed by a 7-digit number.

Transport

Inexpensive ($1.50-$6 EC) buses run to most towns and villages in Grenada. If you are going a long way, check on the time of the last returning bus. Taxis are plentiful. Sample taxi rates (for four, normal hours) are:

	$EC
Prickly Bay to St. George's	50
Airport to St. George's	50
Airport to Prickly Bay	40
Prickly Bay to Grand Anse	30
By the hour	52
Short ride	20

Rental cars are available (see our directory). You will need to buy a local license, which costs $60 EC. Drive on the left.

Airport departure tax is $50 EC, though it is usually included in the ticket.

Nutmeg Princess, Moliniere underwater sculpture park

Grenada

renada, a spectacularly beautiful island, has lush green mountains, crystal waterfalls, golden beaches, and the fragrant spice trees that give the island its epithet "Isle of Spice." Come from late January to early March to get the added bonus of seeing the hills ablaze with hundreds of bright orange, flowering immortelle trees: pure magic.

Grenada's history has been lively, with early wars and revolutions. More recently, things got exciting with the transition to full independence in 1974. Most Grenadians felt this was premature, and instead of jubilant celebrations, the island was on strike and in protest. Nonetheless, independence was thrust upon her, and Grenada came of age under the rule of Sir Eric Gairy, a flamboyant and controversial figure who had a very divisive effect on the population. This resulted in the 1979 left-wing coup by Maurice Bishop, who greatly admired Fidel Castro. Bishop attempted to turn Grenada into a socialist state. He improved medical care and education, but he did so at the cost of freedom: anyone who opposed him was thrown in jail, and all independent newspapers were banned.

However, this didn't insulate him from opposition within his own ranks. Second-in-command Bernard Coard, his wife Phyllis Coard, and members of the army took Bishop prisoner in 1983. After a massive crowd freed him, an army group executed him along with half his cabinet. At this point, the US, along with Grenada's eastern Caribbean neighbors (the Organization of Eastern Caribbean States), launched a "rescue mission" and were welcomed with open arms. Now, many years later, this is old history, and looking back over these last years, Grenada as an independent county has experienced the best, most democratic, and most productive years since it was colonized. Grenadians are a warm and hospitable people, exceptionally so once you get off the main tourist route.

GRENADA

12° 15'N
61° 40'W
WDGA01

12° 02' N
61° 48' W

11° 58' N
61° 46' W

12° 00' N
61° 38' W

SCALE IN NAUTICAL MILES
0   1   2   3   4   5

LONDON BRIDGE

GREEN I.
SANDY I.

HIGH CLIFF PT.
ANTHONY RK. (60')
CONFERENCE RK. (60')
TELESCOPE RK. (60')
SEE PLAN

DAVID PT.
DUQUESNE PT.
SAUTEURS
SUGAR LOAF
LEVERA
HELVELLYN
VICTORIA
GROS PT.
ALMOST PARADISE
LAKE ANTOINE
RIVERS RUM
CHOCOLATE FACTORY
BELMONT ESTATE
MT. ST. CATHERINE 2757'
GOUYAVE
ROSE MOUNT
CLOZIER ROAD
BELVEDERE ROAD
PEARLES
TELESCOPE PT.
GRENVILLE
MARQUIS I.
BLACK BAY PT.
HALIFAX HBR.
CONCORD FALLS
GRAND ETANG
SEVEN FALLS
DRAGON BAY
ANNANDALE FALLS
MOLINIERE PT.
TANKS
GD. MAL.
MT. SINAI 2300'
GT. BACOLET PT.
BACOLET I.
LA TANTE PT.
ST.GEORGE'S
GRAND ANSE
LONG PT. SHOAL
LA SAGESSE
REQUIN PT.
TROU PT.
MARQUIS PT.
PT. BACAYE
ST. DAVID'S HBR.
PT. SALINE
AIRPORT
TRUE BLUE
PRICKLY BAY
HOG I.
MT. HARTMAN B.
TARA I.
CALIVIGNY I.
ST. DAVID'S PT.
WESTERHALL PT.
PT. FORT JEUDY
GLOVER I.
PORPOISES

From a yachting point of view, Grenada has developed rapidly. Haulout facilities are found in St. David's, Prickly Bay, and Clarkes Court Bay. Marina facilities can be found in St. George's, Clarkes Court Bay, Prickly Bay, Phare Bleu Bay, and Mt. Hartman Bay. St. George's has a big state-of-the-art Camper and Nicholson Port Louis marina, as well as a yacht club. Three big chandleries now supply yachting gear, and legislation has been passed that encourages yachting by allowing for low-duty supplies, parts, and chandlery for yachts. The yachting act also allows you to clear out at the same time as you clear in, as long as you are not staying more than three days. However, you do have to fill in all the forms twice.

Grenada is host to a few important yachting events, as well as smaller club races. The Grenada Sailing Festival, a week of racing and social events organized by an independent company, is held in January. All entrants are welcome, from serious racing boats to live-aboards.

The Round Grenada race, a two day event with a stop in Carriacou, is arranged by the Petit Calivigny Yacht Club (PCYC) and normally takes place in August. PCYC also organizes and supplies boats for a match racing every couple of months. Everyone welcome.

The Grenada Yacht Club organizes other races and Grenada has a strong marine trades association called the Marine & Yachting Association of Grenada (MAYAG) (www.mayag.org).

The interior

Few islands are as photogenic as Grenada, with mountains, rivers, rainforest and houses surrounded by flowers. Sometimes when you are hiking along a river amid nutmeg trees, it has an uncanny resemblance to early pictures of the Garden of Eden. A swim in one of the waterfalls will leave you feeling wonderfully refreshed, your hair and skin feeling extra soft. Concord Falls are in beautiful countryside, and anyone with a spark of adventure should hike the extra half-hour to the upper falls. Seven Falls are the best, a lovely one-hour hike. You need a guide if you want to make it to Honeymoon Falls, another half-hour from Seven Falls.

Concord and Seven Falls are on private land, and the owners levy a small charge.

In 2004, Hurricane Ivan did huge damage throughout the island, especially in the rainforest. The island has mostly recovered, and the rainforest is coming back well. The hiking is, in some ways, better than ever: the views are better and the paths drier.

The most beautiful road in Grenada runs from Gouyave to St. Andrew. It has two forks, the Clozier is the prettier, Belvedere the easier. You snake across the heart of Grenada through verdant agricultural land, with lovely mountain views.

Grand Etang is a crater lake, and the Forest Center is close by. You often see monkeys where the buses stop. Trails are laid out so you can wander into the forest. There are wonderful hikes, including one halfway across the island (four hours). The road from St. George's to Grand Etang goes through some lovely forest, and you can include a detour to the Annandale Falls.

Grenada has its own organic chocolate factory, the brain child and passion of Mott, who loved sailing so much that he delivered chocolate to Carriacou in a tiny beach cat. Sadly, Mott died in an accident, but the factory has been marching on. Let the high-octane bars (71, 82, and 100 % cocoa) melt in your mouth for a creamy, chocolate flavor unlike any other commercial brand. Or try the delicious nibulicious or saltilicious bars. They all make perfect gifts. Better still, see where the chocolate comes from at Belmont Estate, a typical and very picturesque country farm, where the cocoa beans grow. Take the tour ($5 US) and watch how cocoa is extracted from the big fruits using the sun and a people-powered dance shuffle. They will show how the Grenada Chocolate Factory takes these beans and processes them, using solar-powered, handmade, and vintage machinery. The Belmont Estate shop sells many kinds of delicious chocolate bonbons laced with local fruits that are only available there. A second factory has followed suit in a lovely old estate, producing Jouvay chocolate, which is competitively priced; their ginger bars are delicious. Grenada has a week-long chocolate festival in May.

Many years ago, I used to keep an eye

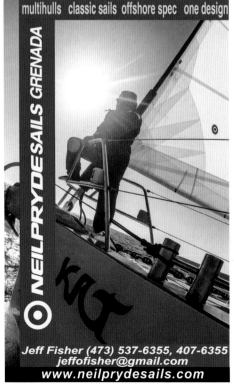
on a coconut plantation for a friend. To get there I passed the River Antoine Rum factory, where they made strong white rum called Rivers. I fell in love with this place, which still runs much as it has since the mid-1800s: a giant water wheel crushes the cane, the dry stalks are burned to heat up the juice, and large wooden scoops manually move the hot juice from one big cast-iron bowl to the next as it gets hotter (they call these bowls "coppers," as the original ones were made of copper). They now open this rum factory to visitors and give tours for $5 EC, which gets you a full explanation and a taste of the rum. (Ask for the strongest rum, drop a bit of ice in the glass, and watch it sink.) They do not fire up the Rum Factory machinery every day, and it is more fun to go when everything is going, so call in advance and ask (442-7109 or 442-4537). The location fits in well with visiting Belmont Estate. Both places serve lunch.

For a great country meal on a day tour, visit Petite Anse [$B-C], which has a delightful location, hanging over its own beach, a five-minute drive west of Sauteurs. Phillip

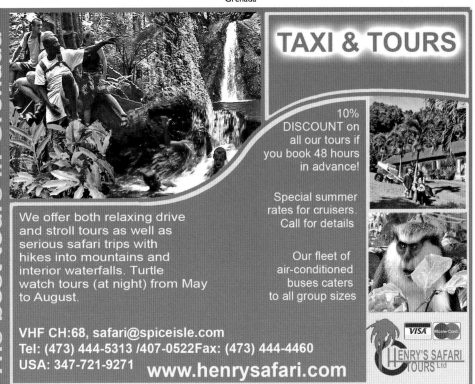

and Annie built this mini-hotel after crossing the Atlantic on the Arc and chartering for four years. You can swim in the pool and walk in the beautiful garden, heading down past cottages tucked amid flowers and trees to the beach.

They serve fruits and vegetables from their own garden, fish and lobster from local fishermen, and much of their meat is from local farmers. Their restaurant, with its wide ranging menu, is popular with both locals and visitors. They offer yachts their local rate for a weekend escape.

Fish Friday in Gouyave is a great event, fun, and inexpensive, with lots of vendors selling different seafoods. Drive, take a taxi, or join a tour. McIntyre does a tour that you can usually join at Prickly Bay or St. George's. They arrive about 1800 and leave about 2100, which gives you plenty of time there.

For hiking, Henry, of Henry's Safari Tours [VHF: 68], is the best man to contact. (Note call sign: Henry Safari Tours.) Henry specializes in hikes and knows the trails well, including Seven Falls. He also does turtle-watching tours from May to August. Most other taxi drivers are reluctant to get their feet muddy, but there are a few exceptions, including Selwyn Taxi, who will hike and keep you happy. (See our section on *Prickly Bay*.)

Keep in mind that all Grenada's anchorages are within an easy taxi ride, so wherever you anchor, read about all the anchorages.

Navigation

There is a major light on Point Saline, visible for 18 miles both to the north and south, flashing (2+1) every 20 seconds. There is a lower-elevation (6+1) flashing light on Glover Island, and another at the western end of the airport runway. The lights have not always proven to be reliable.

Grenada uses the IALA B (red right returning) rule. Unless you draw more than 10 feet, you will not normally have to pay attention to the two big-ship channel buoys outside St. George's or use the leading marks.

The west coast of Grenada is steep-to: a quarter of a mile offshore clears all dangers except Long Point Shoal.

Some people like to sail down Grenada's

Grenada and Carriacou

east coast. It can be rough, but trolling for fish is usually rewarded. It is only advisable in settled weather. Unless visiting Grenville, stay well off Grenada's east coast. Pass either side of Bird Island, but outside all other islands. Keep well away from the Porpoises as you come along the south coast. They can be difficult to see, especially in the afternoon, with the sun in your eyes. Some of the coast lacks landmarks, but you can clearly see Grenada Marine in St. David's Harbour, and look out for the development at Westerhall. Prickly Point has a distinctive saddle shape and a conspicuous house that looks like a lighthouse.

Part of Grenada's west coast is a marine park and has several lovely anchorages, perfect as a last stop for northbound yachts, especially charter yachts that take off after lunch. In the case of northerly swells, Grand Mal and Halifax are the most protected. Snorkel on park moorings to make sure they are in good shape.

The town of Gouyave, about 8 nautical miles north of St. George's, has a very fancy dock, but it is so busy it is not practical to use, except maybe to drop someone off.

Communication

A repeater on channel 66 international connects all Grenada anchorages. It has a morning cruisers' net at 0730, Monday to Saturday.

HALIFAX HARBOUR

Halifax Harbour, a lovely little bay, was turned into a dump, with port authority wrecks on the inside and the island's garbage on its southern side. It was cleaned up, but has backslid, so you sometimes you get flies and smoke. You can anchor in the bay, but you don't have to. The coast outside from Halifax Harbour up to Black Bay Point is perfect for a night stop on your way north or as a destination for a day sail. The snorkeling all around Calypso Island and to its north is excellent.

If you decide to go into Halifax, tuck well in, as the water in the middle is very deep. High-tension cables have been strung across both parts of the bay. On the south side, the lowest wire is about 60 feet above sea level. On the north side, avoid anchoring too close to the low end of the cables. Alternatively, you can anchor anywhere along

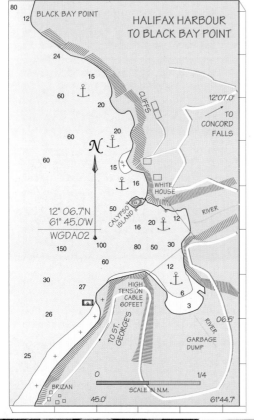

HALIFAX HARBOUR
TO BLACK BAY POINT

BLACK BAY POINT

12°07.0'

TO CONCORD FALLS

WHITE HOUSE

CALYPSO ISLAND

RIVER

12° 06.7'N
61° 45.0'W
WGDA02

HIGH TENSION CABLE 60FEET

TO ST. GEORGE'S

RIVER

06.5'

GARBAGE DUMP

BRIZAN

0   1/4
SCALE IN N.M.

45.0'   61°44.7'

Calypso Island view

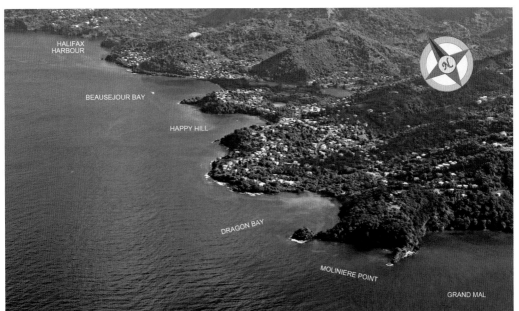

the shore between Calypso Island and Black Bay Point. Make sure you anchor on sand, not coral. There should be a few moorings; check them carefully if you use one.

An added attraction is Calypso Island, developed by Badre and Karen. Intriguing little wooden steps take you from either side of the island to a variety of sitting areas, with an open restaurant area at the top offering views all around. A watchman stays on the island. Calypso Island is available for special groups and by the time you read this, the restaurant should be open. Call 444-3222 to find out what is happening or check out their website: travelgrenadagrenadines.com.

Regulations

A marine park area follows the coast from Beausejour to Grand Mal. You will find white yacht moorings in Dragon Bay, and in Grand Mal Bay, just south of Moliniere Point. The rest are for day charter boats and they have priority. These go back by late afternoon, after which using one will not do any harm. The $10 US charge for taking a boat in the park is sometimes collected; make sure you get a receipt. Snorkel on the mooring to make sure it is in good shape, and if you prefer to anchor do so only in the main part of Grand Mal. Personal watercraft are not allowed.

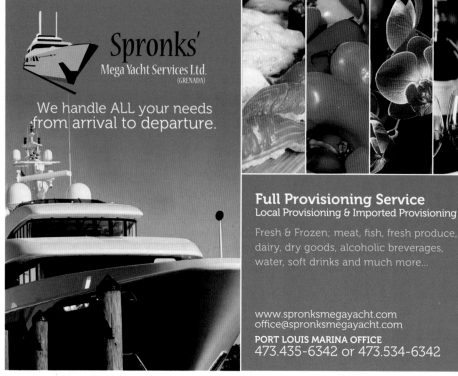
HAPPY HILL

Happy Hill (Flamingo Bay), just north of Dragon Bay, can be very peaceful, and is good except in a bad northerly swell. The narrow beach is backed by a hill, and on the hill is a large, old, silk cotton tree. There is good snorkeling and diving on both sides of the bay around the rocks. Do not anchor, dinghy over from Dragon Bay.

DRAGON BAY

Dragon Bay is delightful, with a palm-lined beach and good snorkeling on both sides around the points. It is usually a good overnight spot. Use the moorings.

You can pick up a dinghy mooring just round the corner in Moliniere Point where you can visit Grenada's world-famous underwater sculpture park created by Jason Decaires Taylor. Snorkel off your boat and look for the statues.

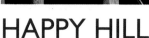

Ashore

Dragon's Hideaway Bar and Grill

[$C-D] is an informal and friendly beach bar owned by Chris Hyacinth and run by Evelyn Dolland when Chris is not around. It is a perfect place to hang out for dinner and a drink on your way north. It is easily accessible from the moorings in the bay or from those south in Grand Mal Bay. It is open every day. The cook starts around 1400, though you can get food before that. You can eat well on the finger foods they serve, but they will also cook good local seafood, if you give them a call. (Evelyn, 404-3918; Chris 533-8077).

GRAND MAL

Grand Mal is genrally a good anchorage. The water is usually clean and the long beach attractive. There are gas storage tanks in Grand Mal and two buoys offshore that are used for unloading tankers. Pipes run out from the small dock to the buoys, so avoid anchoring in this area. Anchor just outside, and a little south of the fishing fleet, or, take a mooring on the north side of the bay. It is fairly well protected in northerly swells.

ST. GEORGE'S

The Carenage, *Lexi Fisher*

St. George's is built on a ridge, with the sea on one side and the protected Carenage on the other. Houses mingle with shrubs and trees, giving splashes of bright color against a background of dark green. From afar, it is as neat and pretty as a picture-book illustration. The historic brick buildings are capped with old "fish scale" tile roofs. The buildings are a reminder of long ago when the profitable journeys were outward bound, laden with rum, spices, and fruit, and returning sailing ships would arrive "in ballast" of bricks.

As you enter the harbor, you see Fort George and the hospital on the left. A little farther in, the channel divides in two: to the left is the Carenage, surrounded by the city of St. George's. To the right is the lagoon and the big new Port Louis Marina. The lagoon is a yachting center, complete with a yacht club, the marina, supermarkets, restaurants, and a chandlery. The eastern side, near the chandlery, has been made into a pleasant park along the water, and you will find convenient dinghy docks to help you explore ashore.

Navigation

A large cruise-ship dock has been built, and considerable land reclaimed off the Esplanade, north of Fort George, facing west out to sea.

The lagoon has two marinas, or you can anchor outside the harbor, south of the channel. You can anchor anywhere along the coast as far as the last headland before Grand Anse. This is usually calm, but occasionally rolly. The holding is not great, and moorings are planned.

Leave the red buoys to starboard and head on into the lagoon. Most of the lagoon has been dredged to over 15 feet deep, with a few corners that are about 10 feet deep.

If you wish to tie up in the Carenage, call the Grenada Port Authority on VHF: 16. Yachts over 200 tons need a pilot to come here or to Port Louis. Seven entries qualifies you to enter on your own.

No town in the Windwards is completely free of theft. Always lock up the boat and dinghy. The marinas have security.

Grenada and **Carriacou**

Regulations

The customs office is in Port Louis. They open weekdays, 0800-1600; weekends and holidays, 0900-1400. They can visit outside these hours by request. If you are paying a quick visit and have a lot to do, consider using the registered agents: Henry's Safari Tours or Spronk's Mega Yacht Services. They are on excellent terms with the officers, can often arrange pre-clearance, and they can clear you from anywhere in the island. For visits of up to three days, they can arrange your inward and outward clearance at the same time. You can hand your passports and papers over and feel free immediately. It is not very expensive.

Communications

Weather and local information are available on a cruiser's net that operates at 0730 on VHF: 66 (except Sunday).

Island Water World has wifi access that covers the lagoon. It is free (charity contributions accepted). Other commercial wifis are often available. The marinas have phones and fax. Port Louis has plug-in internet.

The Fedex office is near Tropicana and DHL is in Renwick and Thompson.

General yacht services

Camper and Nicholson's Port Louis Marina [VHF: 14/16] is a fancy and pleasant marina: very spacious, and beautifully gardened. Customers can relax in the swimming pool overlooking St. George's.

The marina includes 10 berths for yachts up to 300 feet long, 16 berths for yachts up to 120 feet long, and over 140 berths for smaller yachts. To reach the dinghy dock you have

PORT LOUIS

YACHT CLUB

to go right round all the docks, though at low tide you might be able to short-cut under the dock in front of the office.

The berths have electricity, cable TV, plug-in internet, and water. The big boat berths have all kinds of voltages at 50 cycles (60-cycle is planned). High speed fuel (duty-free) is planned.

Port Louis has an excellent team. The professional office staff will make sure you have all the help you need. Docks are for sale, they will be delighted to tell you how this works.

Port Louis is home to Dream Yacht Charters, Sunsail, and The Moorings char-ter companies and Sea Sun Adventures day tours. The Victory Bar is the place to chill out (see *Restaurants*).

The Grenada Yacht Club [VHF: 6/16 "GYC"], includes a modern marina with berthing for about 43 boats and a fuel dock that has both diesel and gasoline. The docks have electricity (110/220-volt, 50-cycle) and water, and the rates are reasonable. The Yacht Club is informal. You can send a fax or get your mail during office hours: 0800-1700 (address mail to Grenada Yacht Club, P.O. Box 117, St. George's, Grenada). Showers, laundry, and garbage disposal are available. Dennis Henry of Henry's Safari Tours picks

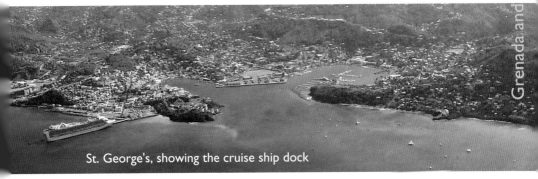

St. George's, showing the cruise ship dock

up empty gas bottles and drops off filled ones on Mondays, Wednesdays and Fridays. Taxis and other services can be arranged. The Yacht Club bar opens at 0900 and stays open till 2200. The restaurant is open every day and is good (see *Restaurants*). The Yacht Club also runs a sailing school program.

The super-yacht agents work well together. Dennis Henry, of Henry's Safari Tours [VHF: 68], is a superyacht agent who also works well with cruisers. He understands that they have different needs and budgets, which has given him an excellent reputation with everyone. He owns the laundry at Port Louis (plus two others), fills everyone's cooking gas cylinders, and has a fleet of taxis, plus Grenada's most colorful service vehicle. He collects and delivers to all Grenada anchorages.

Henry does customs clearance for yachts and their stores and helps superyachts sort out immigration for arriving crew. Other services include arranging dock space, fuel, technicians, travel, and anything ashore. Henry can arrange full provisioning. He loves his job, and having worked with yachts

for some 30 years, he knows just about anything a yachtsperson may want. He learns a few extra tricks each year as new things come along, whether it involves banking, finding a golf partner, or arranging an unusual permit.

Spronk's Mega Yacht Services is run by Roger and Claire Spronk, who own Bananas (see *True Blue*). They have a desk in the Sea Sun Adventure office in Port Louis marina. They are registered yacht agents and clear yachts in and out, arrange visas, fueling, docking, flowers, travel arrangements, taxis, car hire, laundry, crew placement, repairs, flights, and anything else a large yacht could need. The Spronks are also building a private marina in Petit Calivigny Bay (see *Clarkes Court Bay*). This will have easy berthing for the largest of yachts, and make a convenient Grenada base. They are excellent at full superyacht provisioning, which means large yachts can be fully provisioned from scratch in Grenada. Their Gourmet Store in True Blue stocks the best quality frozen fish and cuts of meat, and they own an 8-acre farm for fresh produce. Where possible, they source locally, but for exotic and special items, they

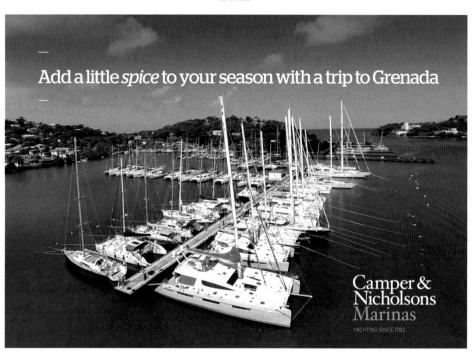

Add a little *spice* to your season with a trip to Grenada

Camper & Nicholsons Marinas
YACHTING SINCE 1782

The 'spice island' of Grenada remains one of the most unspoilt cruising destinations in the Caribbean, and here at Port Louis Marina we are proud of our rare combination of world-class facilities and an authentic Grenadian atmosphere.

Lying just above 12°N, Grenada is also south of the main hurricane belt, which is why growing numbers of yacht owners are staying here during the summer months.

Our well trained staff have unrivalled local knowledge and are dedicated to making your stay as enjoyable and relaxing as possible.

Port Louis Marina provides a safe, secure berth with all the amenities you would expect from a full-service marina run by Camper & Nicholsons.

- Water and electricity
- 24 hour security
- Bar, restaurant and pool
- Excellent air links
- Free broadband
- Berthing assistance
- Haul/technical facilities nearby
- Only 5 miles from the airport

Call us on +1 (473) 435 7431 or email reservations@cnportlouismarina.com
www.cnmarinas.com/plm

port louis marina
GRENADA WEST INDIES

Grenada and Carriacou

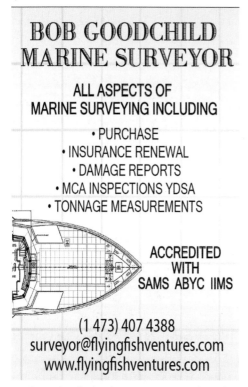
work with all the big international yacht provisioners.

Bob Goodchild owns Flying Fish Ventures. Bob trained as a boatbuilder in the UK and is now a marine surveyor and a member of the International Institute of Marine Surveyors (IIMS) and the Society of Accredited Marine Surveyors (SAMS). He can do tonnage measurements and MCA compliance inspections up to category 2 through his membership in the Yacht Designers and Surveyors Association (YDSA). Bob has been in Grenada for years, is very professional, good, and a great guy to deal with.

Chandlery

Island Water World has a big branch of their huge and very successful Caribbean marine store (50 years old in 2017), in the lagoon, opposite the marina. They have an excellent range of stock at duty-free prices, including batteries, yacht hardware, winches, electronics, outboards, fishing gear, ground tackle, stoves, charts, and cruising guides. If there is anything you need that they do not have, look at their large catalog,

and they can bring catalog items in quickly. On the first Wednesday of the month they run a book/DVD swap coffee morning for charity, and if you want a run-around bike, they will lend you one for free (there is a deposit).

Marine Tech, has a limited stock of electronics and electrical items, including led lights and bulbs, solenoids, regulators for solar and some Raymarine and Garmin electronics. He opens 0900-1700 Monday to Saturday and 1000-1700 Sundays.

Ace Hardware is on the Maurice Bishop Highway (behind *True Blue*). This is Grenada's best general hardware/car parts/household/gardening store. You can get everything here from a dinghy pump to a new tea kettle. They have another branch in St. George's.

Bryden and Minors stationery store is next door to Island Water World, and they may well have ink for your printer. They sell computers and printers.

Marine World, on Melville Street, opposite the fish market, caters to Grenada's fishing fleet. They stock fishing and snorkeling gear and charts, as well as safety gear and some hardware. Spice Island Fish House Tackle Shop, on the Carenage, stocks fishing and snorkeling gear and some electronics, and they sell John Deere diesels.

Technical yacht services

Two business specializing in looking after and fixing boats have offices in Port Louis.

Mark and Anita's Island Dreams, with a fine reputation, long established, has a Port Louis office. Mark and Anita are good people to look after your yacht while you go away, fixing anything that needs doing at the same time, anything from a simple repair to a complete refit. Some jobs they do themselves. For the rest, they bring in the right people. Yard work in any of the boatyards can be arranged through them, but you need to discuss your hauling plan with them before you book. They send regular email work and status reports. They can also store your yacht afloat in Port Louis or any of the marinas, but best discuss that before booking. If you want, they will have your yacht hauled, painted, fueled, launched, and ready to leave when you arrive, and they can

Yacht Guardianage, Maintenance &
Project Management

+ 473 443 3603 | + 473 415 2139
info@islandreamsgrenada.com

islandreamsgrenada.com

book overnight accommodation.

They offer gear storage facilities, which is a big help if the interior is being pulled apart. They represent Little Ships brokers, and are the Cruising Association's Honorary Local Representative.

Horizon Yacht Management is owned by James and Jacqui and this business works well with their charter company, Horizon Yachts, in True Blue. They have a good team of technicians who specialize in maintaining and outfitting yachts while the owners are away. They can repair or install any systems, and can arrange for your haul out and paint job, or oversee any work you may be having done by other contractors. They can also just run a weekly check to make sure everything is okay. Horizon are agents for new Bavaria Yachts, Fontaine Pajot Cats, and Sea Ray and Meridian power boats. They have a full yacht brokerage, so if you need to sell your yacht or buy a new one, check them out.

Brett Fairhead's Underwater Solutions keeps work boats in several harbors, a base in the lagoon, and works all over the island.

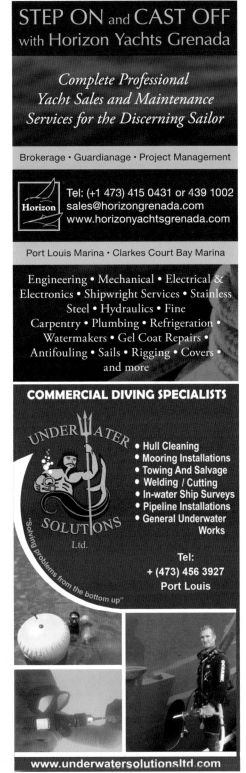
Grenada and Carriacou

They are good enough to get asked to do jobs throughout the Caribbean. Brett is one of the Caribbean's most experienced commercial divers and he has done everything from working under ice to underwater welding in the tropics. He trains and works with a team of Grenadian divers, who clean yacht hulls and props, remove shafts and rudders in the water, and carry out underwater damage survey and repair, including underwater welding, as well as untangling anchors.

They can undertake salvage work and have a small tug to assist in this. They also do bathymetric depth contour surveys and install pipelines, moorings, and channel markers. They do anything underwater, large or small, and maintain most marina moorings. I trust the moorings they maintain. If you visit their shop, check out the lovely coral-encrusted artifacts they have preserved.

Driftwood offers fine yacht woodwork, from fancy joinery to replacing a plank or teak deck. They also have a team that does bottom jobs, antifouling, topside buffing, polishing, gelcoat, and glass repairs. They have a workshop on Lagoon Road and another in Clarkes Court Bay Marina and Boatyard. For full details, see *Clarkes Court Bay*.

Royan Joseph has Royan's the biggest marine metal shop on the island. It is on his own land, conveniently situated so he can reach all the marinas and yards by van quickly. Royan is well used to yachts, having worked with FKG Rigging in St. Martin, and he is used to big boats, having been a welder on cruise ships. He welds and fabricates in aluminum, stainless or steel. He can bend pipe, make fancy arches and bimini frames and do repairs. He has a mobile unit for on board welding in any yard or marina. He is efficient and for small jobs can often do it on the same day. Since he is not in a yard, he offers free pick-up and drop-off from Port Louis and all other marinas and yards. By the time this guide comes out he is hoping to have a full machine shop with a 5-foot lathe and a milling machine. His wife, Valerie, runs the office and is very helpful.

Marine Tech Grenada is run by Stephen Welsh, who is ABYC- and NMEA-certified, and fully insured, with over 25 years of experience. Marine Tech supplies, installs, maintains and repairs marine electrical, electronic and refrigeration equipment.

Stephen and his team are equally at home on superyachts or cruising yachts. The Marine Tech office is on lagoon Road, but Stephen visits nearly all Grenada anchorages by land, and does the electrical and electronic work for some yards. He is willing to work on weekends.

So whether it is a broken GPS, a malfunctioning windlass or generator, a main engine that won't start or charge, a bow thruster that needs attention, or the complete rewiring of your boat, Stephen is your man. He likes sailing, understands boats, and has an excellent reputation for customer service and getting the job done right and on time.

Turbulence Sails has a station in Port Louis. They handle all sail repairs as well as canvas and cushion work. They are Grenada's main riggers and will come sort out your rig and hydraulic problems. They are a first-rate electronics shop and can fix all your instruments (see *Prickly Bay*).

Jeff Fisher is the local Neil Pryde Sails representative. He can measure up and quote for a new sail, and advise on re-using any expensive sail hardware you have. He will fit the sail when it arrives.

Grenada Marine (see *St. David's Harbour*) hauls yachts, repairs all boat systems, and sells and installs electronics, engines, watermakers and more. They have an office in Port Louis.

Other people make boat visits, including Basil St. John, at Lagoon Marine Refrigeration Services, who is good but hard to find, Dexter Hayes (Mr. Cool), at Subzero Air Control, and Michael Cadore (Protech Engineering), who works on fridges, AC, appliances, stoves and any electrical system.

Danny's Nauti Solutions is with Underwater Solutions and Driftwood, on the lagoon. Danny is good at fixing boats. His wife, Lesley, is excellent at general yacht cleaning. Danny spends most of his time these days doing deliveries, but you might catch him there.

If you need a hand to help with some project, be it going up the mast, maintenance, moving a mooring, or havimg someone sail with you, Patrick Andrews is very experienced at looking after yachts and sailing them. He will come to you in Port Louis, at the yacht club, in Prickly Bay or wherever. I have worked with him for years. You can contact him by cell (406-0664/414-1559)

Clarkes Upholstery is run by Vernol Clarke, who does upholstery and is equally good at canvas work for biminis, covers, and awnings, all at competitive prices. Yachts are about half his business and he will come to measure and fit, not only in St. George's, but in any of Grenada's anchorages.

When it comes to boat names, tonnage carvings, and similar things, Panabread, at AJS Enterprises, can do it all. If he is too busy, try one of the sign guys in the Frequente Industrial Park, such as Shield Promotions.

Tan Tan Sam is excellent for hand varnishing, painting, cleaning, and polishing. Call him on his cell: 403-9904. He often works with Sean Thomas (406-4258/419-7454), who also does good work. Ashley (456-9003) is another good professional,

Grenada and Carriacou

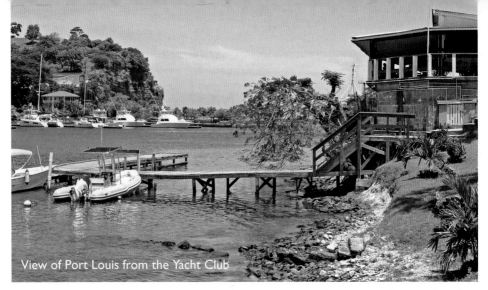

View of Port Louis from the Yacht Club

as is Thadius (410-6224), who often works with Island Dreams. These men will work in any marina.

Al Bernadine in Gouyave (444-8016) is a wizard with alternators, starters, and power tools. He has a small machine shop. If you call him, he can arrange for you to drop off what you want fixed in St. George's.

Also read about the marine services in the south-coast harbors. Most will come to St. George's.

Provisioning

The Merry Baker, owned by Raeanna, is a dreamy home-made bakery just inside the road to the marina. Come here for a wonderful collection of breads, including olive bread, baked goodies, whisky marmalade, preserves and more. Raeanna does excellent inexpensive lunches some days. Wednesday is oildown. This is Grenada's delicious national dish, more of a home food, not often found in restaurants, so try it here. Thursdays she serves rotis, and Friday is the famous $12 EC build-a-burger lunch. All the sides are put out in a buffet and you help yourself. You can also get coffee, soft drinks, beer, etc. Seating room is outside in a prettily painted patio area. Opening hours are weekdays, 0730-1700, Saturdays, 0800-1300.

Hazel Dabreo's The Market Place, in the marina, is a first-rate small deli and convenience store. Buy good meats and cheeses, wines, and cases of beer or water, and as workers have found, this is the cheapest place to buy a cold drink. They do yacht provisioning, big and small, so rather than hustle around the markets, you can put an order in here.

St. George's is a first-rate place to provision, with comfortable, air-conditioned supermarkets. Foodland is in the lagoon, has its own dinghy dock, and is often open quite late at night. Foodland has an excellent selection of regular items and a pleasing delicatessen section. It offers a five percent discount to charter yachts.

You can dinghy from the lagoon over to town. Take this guide with you; our town map will help. St. George's is a busy place, with plenty of traffic, including buses, laden with people, playing loud music, cars, and trucks weighed down with building materials. Sometimes it seems like they are all honking at once. People will shout "taxi!" at you, and vendors may offer fruits from baskets.

Most shops open from 0800 to 1200 and from 1300 to 1600 on weekdays. Banks are open only till 1500, except Friday, when they open to 1700. The post office is open over lunch, but closed all day Saturday. Most shops close Saturday afternoon and Sunday, though you can still shop (see *Grand Anse*). The lovely old financial complex, which used to house the post office, has been restored, creating some of the fanciest government offices in the Windwards.

Those wishing to buy wine or liquor should visit Renwick and Thompson's Best Little Liquor Store in Town [VHF: 16, "Rum Runner Base"]. You can tie your dinghy close

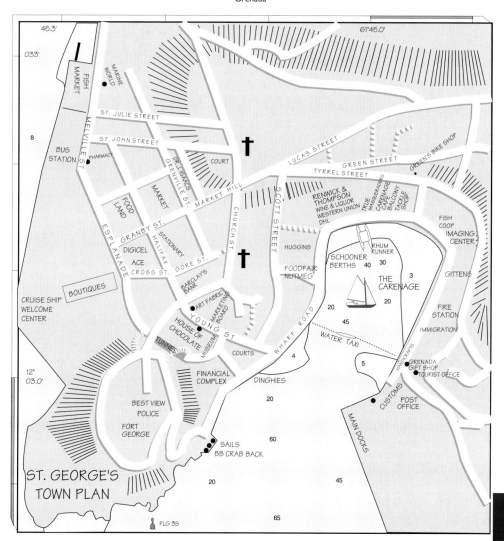

ST. GEORGE'S TOWN PLAN

to the shop. They have a wide selection from all over the world including about 80 different wines from dozens of good houses.

They are very customer friendly, you can mix wines and spirits to make cases for the best deal, and duty-free prices are available with delivery to most marina docks. Allow at least 48 hours for processing. Duty-free has to be delivered after you clear out.

You can transfer money through Renwick and Thompson's Western Union. With increasing bank rates, I often find this to be the most economical way to send money. (They also have a branch in Grand Anse.) You can send many currencies and pay in EC dollars. (It is better not to use US dollars to send US dollars as regulations make them change it to EC first). This is the place to send your DHL packets, and if you are having things shipped in via DHL, Renwick and Thompson offers a full brokerage service to remove any clearance hassle. They provide land and water tours and have an agricultural section where you can find hoses and hose fittings. If you are interested in land in Grenada or Carriacou, they have some of the best for sale.

Food Fair is conveniently close to the water and you can tie up nearby. Food Fair is an excellent supermarket, open weekdays till 1730, except Friday, when they are open till 2045. On Saturdays, they close at 2000.

**Museum-Boutique
Chocolateria-Cafe**

**Grenada Cocoa & Chocolate
at its Best!**

**10 Young Street, St. George's - Grenada
Next to National museum**

**www.houseofchocolategnd.com
info@houseofchocolategnd.com
(473) 440-2310**

They offer charter yachts 5% discount.

Visit the local market, preferably on a Saturday morning. It is a riot of color, where determined ladies under big umbrellas sit amid huge heaps of vegetables. It is one of the most interesting markets in the islands, and you can get fresh produce, spices, and handicrafts. If you need a new watch battery or repair, there is a stall in the market that specializes in this and they can often fix your watch on the spot. The Marketing Board, on Young Street (opposite Tikal), has some of the best prices on fresh produce, although the range is limited.

You can usually get a good selection of fresh fish in the fish market.

Henry B, one of the Port Louis Taxi drivers, has a herb farm and can supply fresh herbs, as well as prepared dried herbs for cooking. These include his own soup herbs, which add flavor to any soup.

Fun shopping

Port Louis has a few boutiques, and more will follow. Fidel Productions sells great art t-shirts, commissioned from Caribbean artists, who receive royalties. They stock hand-painted calabash art, Moho jewelry, decorative items, and souvenirs; all are attractive and of good quality.

Young Street, in town, has several attractions. The House of Chocolate is a special place, part boutique, part cafe, part museum, and all about chocolate. Bright, light, artistic, and interesting, you can see how chocolate is made, from bean to bar, learn about the different kinds of cocoa, and learn about all the benefits of eating chocolate (some will surprise you; one study indicated that eating chocolate gives your skin more protection against the sun). Great coffee, mocha, chocolate brownies, cheesecake, gourmet chocolates, chocolate art and more are on sale. They organize a week-long chocolate festival in May, with trips to chocolate factories, chance to be a farmer for day, chocolate cooking and chocolate massage.

Next door, the museum, in a lovely old building, is well worth a visit for the small entrance fee. They have excellent cultural events at 1730 most Friday nights. Stop by and ask for a program. It includes jazz, good pan, story-telling, and local dance. They have the museum bistro upstairs, which opens at noon and stays open into the evening some nights.

Opposite Tikal and upstairs is Jim Rudin's Art Gallery. Jim is a lovely man who has worked with the arts in Grenada most of his life. He always has a big range of paintings and prints on display, many by local artists. A few steps up the hill is Art Fabric. It is a riot of colorful batik fabrics, clothing, and household items. Batik demonstrations are available on request.

With the advent of the cruise ship dock and land reclamation, the focus of tourist shopping has moved into the cruise-ship area, where there is a mall of bright and cheerful shops selling everything from fresh juice to jewelry, and tons of souvenirs.

St. George's is a lovely town, with plenty of hills to climb to get great views. It is best explored when you have plenty of time and no errands. One of the best and easiest is to climb up to Fort George. Nice steps from either side of the Sendall tunnel take you up, and make an alternative to going though the tunnel (though this is to be experienced).

Restaurants

The Victory Bar and Grill [$A-D] is the all-encompassing restaurant in Port Louis. Open to the breeze, it is big and informal, with a wide-ranging menu to suit everyone from the admiral to the cabin boy, and the food is very good, as you would expect from the owner Uli, who also has the famous Aquarium Restaurant (See *Point Saline to Prickly Bay*). You can dine well here on fresh fish and shrimp or the best steak. Or you can get pizza, pasta, salads, burgers, and sandwiches. They open every day and have a good pizza oven in one section. For a more secluded atmosphere, wander into Yolo, adjoining but with a separate entrance. This has a lounge bar and fine restaurant, specializing in sushi and Thai cuisine.

The Marine View Restaurant [$C-D], in the Yacht Club, is on a big deck overlooking the lagoon. It has a friendly, clubby atmosphere, and is inexpensive and good for lunch or dinner.

Horatio Brizan's Tropicana [$C-D], on the lagoon, is an inexpensive restaurant: cheap enough for any time cooking seems too much of a chore. It is excellent value for lunch or dinner, with a separate and speedy takeout section. If you need a night ashore, they have inexpensive rooms upstairs.

In town, the Nutmeg, overlooking the Carenage, is one of the city's older establishments. You don't really know St. George's

till you have had lunch at the Nutmeg. They also serve dinner.

If you follow the Carenage right round town to the end, you will come to a restaurant corner. You can tie your dinghy right outside, and these restaurants all have an open view of the harbor. Sails [$A-C] has a wonderful, wide deck, open to the view and the breeze. You can tie your dinghy pretty much onto your table leg. The food is good, using good-quality meats and fresh seafood.

Next door Brian and Anna Benjamin's BB's Crab Back [$A-B, closed Sunday] is more upmarket, serving fancy Caribbean food cooked with a European flair. He sometimes teaches a cooking session. You can tie your dinghy to the railing, but it may need a stern anchor.

In the lagoon, The Roof Top is perched at the top of the Mall, near Island Water World. It is a fair spot to hang out,.

Patrick's continues a tradition started by Mama of a giant local feast, featuring a vast array of local dishes, so you can taste everything one time, a real experience.

Transport

The taxi drivers that most often deal with yachts are members of the Marina Taxi Association. They can be found in all Grenada's marinas, including Port Louis, and they set a high standard for reliability and good customer service.

Ashore

Michelle's Spice Isle Retreat Spa is a large and lovely beauty spa in Port Louis, with an area for relaxing between treatments. They offer well over 70 procedures and treatments, from sophisticated hairdressing to facials, nails, pedicure, massage, and more. They have a membership plan where you can get a 30-60% discount, and they often have special offers. They sell hair and beauty products. Michelle and her staff are excellent, and the spa is popular, so it is best to book. Stop by and pick up a brochure.

Been in the sun too long? Dr. Jennifer Isaacs is an excellent dermatologist whose office on Grenville Street overlooks the market. It is best to make an appointment, so you will not be waiting in line for hours.

369

On the path to the fort

St. George's now has the Spice Isle Imaging Center for any medical tests. They do all kinds of blood tests, MRIs, x-rays, and ultra-sound.

If you have a yen for a few hours in a pretty garden 600 feet above St. George's, Sunnyside Gardens is open to the public. It costs $10 US a head. Call 406-1381 for directions and to let them know that you are coming.

GRAND ANSE

Grand Anse is what most people have in mind when they think about the Caribbean: a generous, two-mile sweep of white-gold sand, backed by shady palms and almond trees.

Anchoring is forbidden right off the beach, but the St. George's anchorage comes almost to the beginning of Grand Anse. Moorings are planned for this area and may be laid down during the life of this guide. It is within easy dinghy range of St. George's. The dinghy dock is at the eastern end of the beach, and from here you can walk. Grand Anse contains a wealth of shops and restaurants and is easily visited by bus or taxi from St. George's or Prickly Bay.

Communications

Onsite Software Support, has every-thing for cybernuts: disks, print heads, and ribbons. They offer free stand-up email access for visitors. They repair notebooks, and desktops.

Provisioning

When you get behind the beach, Grand Anse is a big shopping strip lined with malls, from Grand Anse Shopping Center to Excel Mall. Cars and buses hurtle down the main road with little thought for pedestrians. Stay on the sidewalk and take care when crossing the road. Grand Anse is good for Sunday shopping; both Real Value and Value Garden are open mid morning.

The two main supermarkets are Food Fair, in the Shopping Center, and Real Value, in the Spiceland Mall. Food Fair is an excellent supermarket with a big range of products, including fruits and vegetables that are mainly local and refreshed frequently. Charter yachts are offered a 5% discount.

Real Value is like a US supermarket, with the biggest variety, including specialty foods. When a container arrives (usually on Thursdays), you get the widest choice of overseas produce and an excellent deli section. The aisles are wide and everything is attractively displayed in a spacious setting.

Spiceland Mall includes The Wine Shoppe, a good place for retail wines. They open 1000-1900 Monday to Saturday.

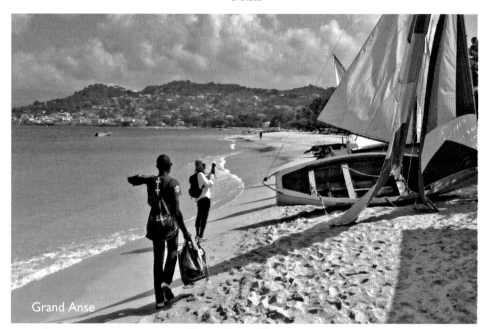
Grand Anse

Almost opposite Marquis Mall, on the far side of the busy road, is a line of businesses in an area known as Wall Street that includes Gittens Drugmart, a pharmacy, with everything from newspapers to prescriptions, a couple of banks that have ATMs for Visa or MasterCard, and Onsite Software Support. If you need to send money, Western Union is in the Grand Anse Shopping Center.

The Marketing Board runs Value Garden in the Excel Mall. They sell a good selection of local products and produce at the best prices. They have a whole area run by Meat and Meet, the butcher from Whisper Cove, who works wonders with local meat, and makes great sausages and other specialty foods.

La Boulangerie (Marquis Mall) sells croissants, baguettes, Italian county bread, quiches, cheese cake and more. Stock up for your next charter, or just drop by for lunch (see *Restaurants*).

When you need fresh flowers, Eleanor Dathorne's Floral Treasures is the place to go. Floral Treasures is on the main road next to Robbie Yearwood's clinic and close to Real Value. She sells mainly local and lovely flowers and she creates stunning and very beautiful flower arrangements. It is probably best to give her a call, and if you can work out what you want she will deliver to other bays.

While shopping and eating, keep an eye out for Sugar and Spice ice cream. It is made in a tiny factory in Prickly Bay, using fresh local ingredients, from the coconut they grate to chocolate from Grenada's Jouvay Factory. Their coffee break is especially delicious, as is their soursop.

Another local product to look for is "Up in Smoke" smoked fish: top-quality fresh local fish cold- or hot-smoked, depending on your preference. Also, don't forget your Grenada chocolate.

Fun shopping

Grand Anse is an easy bus ride from Spice Island Marine Services or St. George's. This is a wonderful shopping area, with three malls, street-side shops, and hotel boutiques.

If you come by dinghy, it is worth checking out the local craft market just behind the beach.

Food Fair is part of Grand Anse Shopping center where you will find Hubbard's Home Center, Mitchell's Pharmacy [open till 2100], Kachi boutique, a hairdressing salon, and Rick's Cafe, [$D], which offers local dishes, fast foods, coffee, and a full range of ice creams. Eat them in the pleasant seating area in the mall square.

Grenada and Carriacou

Spiceland Mall has a host of small shops where you can buy everything from stationery and shoes to clothing and music, I have found nice boat rugs in Linens and Things. You will find a sports clothing and paddle boarding store, a big hardware store, a Lime phone shop, and for refreshment, a fresh food corner, good for fresh-squeezed juice.

Excel Mall has Value Garden, the marketing board shop, now doubled in size, a pharmacy, many small shops, plus three mini-cinemas.

Dr. Mike Radix, a GP who has been treating yachtspeople for years, is upstairs in the Grand Anse Mall. He has Lasic to remove problems from aging skin. Behind Spiceland Mall, over the road, is Ocean House, with surgeon and urologist Robbie Yearwood.

Toothache? Grenada not only has good, highly-recommended dentists, they are easily visited in Grand Anse. Many cruisers have been helped by Dr. Roxanne Nedd at the Sunshine Dental Clinic. Her clinic is next door to Excel Mall, though she has been very busy of late. Two good younger Grenadian dentists, with all the most modern equipment, are at Island Dental Clinic, above Gittens Drug Mart. Dr. Tara Baksh trained in the UK and Dr. Victor Samaan trained in the USA. They can do everything from extractions and root canals to complex crowns. Dr. Yaw, a first-rate dental surgeon, has an office opposite North South Wines in Prickly Bay. These days he is only in Grenada occasionally.

Restaurants

A great little Italian quarter has sprung up in Le Marquis Mall. Michael, an Italian with a taste for fish, has Carib Sushi, a great little Japanese restaurant. On the sushi side, good Oriental chefs use local fish (tuna, dorado, and wahoo), lobster, and lambi, as well as imported salmon, for the best sushi and sashimi. On the cooked side, they offer shrimp, vegetable and fish tempura, beef, tuna tataki (lightly seared), and other Japanese dishes. They open for both lunch and dinner, but are closed in between. Maybe because the food is so healthy, you see some good-looking, healthy people here. Their

takeout can be handy for charter yachts.

Pepeo's La Boulangerie is both a great Italian bakery and a restaurant. They open every day for a breakfast of baked goodies, serve the best coffee, and have pizza, pasta dishes, quiches, and salads for lunch or dinner. They also have tempting desserts, like tiramisu, cheese cake, and many pastries.

Close by, Tortuga, an Italian wine bar, is owned by Marco. They serve a big range of wines by the glass or bottle and appropriate food when you want to make a meal of it.

On Grand Anse Beach, Umbrellas [$D] is a perfect beach hangout, open every day except Monday. It is a longish ride but you can pull your dinghy up on the beach, sit under the umbrellas outside, or up on the roof, or inside. They have an extensive drinks menu and food to go with it. The emphasis is on salads, sandwiches, burgers, fish, and ribs. Save room for some fancy American-style desserts.

Coconut Beach, a French restaurant [$A-B] managed by Scratch, has a superb location on the water's edge on Grand Anse beach. French cuisine has been adapted to local foods.

Lawrence Lambert is a Grenadian who spent some years in Canada and then returned to buy the Flamboyant Hotel and villas, and the Beachside Restaurant [$B-D]. It is at the west end of Grand Anse beach, with a sweeping view to St. George's. I know many yachtsmen who have used the rooms from time to time, and the restaurant has good West Indian and continental food, with a steel band on Wednesday nights in season. Their Owl Sports Bar has two big TVs to keep you on top of the latest games.

The beautiful, but shallow, Morne Rouge Bay is a short ride or healthy walk from Grand Anse. There is a complex here called the Gem Holiday Beach Resort. They run the Fantazia 2001 disco, which is open on Wednesdays for Oldie Goldie night and on Fridays and Saturdays for live music.

Water sports

Grenada has many dive shops, all keenly competitive and happy to take yachtspeople. Many will collect you from the marinas or docks. All dive shops are Padi or Naui establishments with all kinds of courses, including introductory resort courses. We mention just a couple of the Grand Anse dive shops: Aquanauts [VHF: 16] have their main base in True Blue, and a base in Spice Beach Resort. Dive Grenada, run by Phil and Helen, is based at the Flamboyant Hotel. They offer a friendly and flexible service to divers and are a Padi Golden Palm 5-star shop.

Grenada has a variety of good and interesting dives. For sheer drama, you cannot beat the Bianca C, a 600-foot cruise ship that sank and is deep, 100-165 feet. The wreck is vast, and mainly broken, but there are splendid views up at the bow, and the swimming pool is still intact on the deck. Large schools of small snappers, some midnight parrotfish, and a few barracudas get framed by the wreckage. This is an advanced dive, and most dive shops will insist you do one other dive first.

Flamingo Reef starts just outside of the north end of Happy Hill Bay and continues along the coast toward Dragon Bay. This colorful and lively reef offers a changing seascape as you swim along. There is a good balance of healthy hard and soft corals, with a dense, tall forest of waving sea whips, sea rods, and sea fans at the top, on the seaward end. This is the place to look for the flamingo tongue that gives the reef its name. Many grunts, squirrelfish, wrasses, parrotfish, and trumpetfish swim along the sloping reef. Large schools of brown chromis pass by. Deeper on the reef, you have a chance of seeing large groupers. In the sand are mixed schools of spotted and yellow goatfish, probing the bottom with their barbels.

Dragon Bay and Moliniere Point join together and are the easiest dives to get to with your dinghy. Use one of the park moorings. Go out from the little bay in Moliniere Point so you get to see the underwater sculpture park. These dives have a mixture of sand and coral patches, going from shallow water down to about 60 feet. Much of the reef in this shallow area is densely covered with a variety of corals and sponges. When you get to about 30 to 40 feet, you meet a drop-off that goes down another 25-30 feet. Sometimes it is a steep slope, at other times a sheer wall. A few rock outcroppings make

for dramatic valleys, and deep, sand-filled gullies are cut into the drop-off.

Boss Reef starts outside St. George's and continues southwest to Point Saline, a distance of at least two and a half miles. It varies in width from 200 to 500 yards. It is possible to do many dives on this reef. Currents are strong here, and it is best done as a drift dive with a dive shop. A popular dive is the middle section, swimming wherever the current takes you. The depth varies from about 30 to 60 feet. The reef rises from the sand to a somewhat level top that is broken by deep gullies and holes that drop down to sand. This is an exceptionally good dive for coral variety. The top is completely covered in an array of corals, all packed close to each other. There are lots of brightly colored fish, with large schools of blue and yellow Creole wrasses, accompanied by blue and brown chromis. Grazing parrotfish and big schools of doctorfish will pass you by on the reef, and you will see schools of smaller grunts and perhaps a large Spanish grunt. Look under corals and in holes for spotted drums.

Grenada and Carriacou

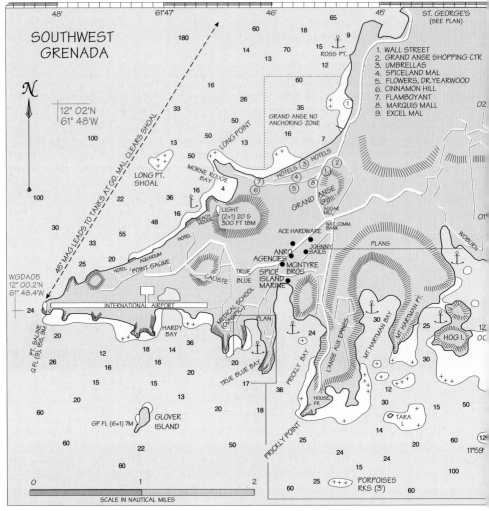

SOUTHWEST
GRENADA

N

12° 02'N
61° 48'W

WGDA05
12° 00.2'N
61° 48.4'W

45° MAG LEADS TO TANKS AT GD MAL CLEARS SHOAL

45° MAG LEADS TO TANKS AT GD MAL CLEARS SHOAL

LONG POINT

LONG PT.
SHOAL

MORNE ROUGE
BAY

GRAND ANSE NO
ANCHORING ZONE

ROSS PT.

1. WALL STREET
2. GRAND ANSE SHOPPING CTR
3. UMBRELLAS
4. SPICELAND MAL
5. FLOWERS, DR. YEARWOOD
6. CINNAMON HILL
7. FLAMBOYANT
8. MARQUIS MALL
9. EXCEL MAL

HOTELS (3) HOTELS

GRAND ANSE

SUGAR
MILL

LIGHT
(2+1) 20 S
300 FT 18M

HOTEL

AQUARIUM

HOTEL / POINT SALINE

CALISTE

ACE HARDWARE

NAT. COMM.
BANK

ANRO
AGENCIES

JOHNNY
SAILS

PLANS

MCINTYRE
BROS

TRUE
BLUE

SPICE
ISLAND
MARINE

WOBURN

MEDICAL SCHOOL
(CONSTRUCT)

INTERNATIONAL AIRPORT

PT. SALINE
Q FL (9), 65, 9M

HARDY
BAY

PLAN

MT HARTMAN BAY

MT HARTMAN PT.

HOG I.

PRICKLY BAY

L'ANSE AUX EPINES

GP FL (6+1) 7M

GLOVER
ISLAND

TRUE BLUE BAY

HOUSE,
FR

TARA
I.

PRICKLY POINT

PORPOISES
RKS (3')

SCALE IN NAUTICAL MILES

PT. SALINE TO PRICKLY BAY

When sailing between St. George's and Point Saline, keep well clear of Long Point Shoal. Head west from St. George's and continue till you are on the line between Point Saline and the tanks at Grand Mal, before heading for Point Saline. Reverse this procedure when you return.

Alternatively, coast hoppers may prefer to explore this shore, which has several pretty beaches. You must, however, be very careful of Long Point Shoal, and only approach when there is good light and you can see the reefs. It is possible to eyeball your way

inside Long Point Shoal, but don't cut too close to Long Point, as shoals come out about 150 feet from shore. As you round Long Point heading west, you will see the beautiful Morne Rouge Bay, which, unfortunately, is only about 4 feet deep (perfect for multihulls). You can sometimes find lunchtime anchorage just outside Morne Rouge Bay.

As you sail round Point Saline and head toward Glover Island, Prickly Point is the farthest headland that you see. When closer, Prickly Bay is easily identified by all the yachts inside and the handsome houses on the hill. There is plenty of water for most yachts to sail inside Glover Island. There is one good anchorage, just before Prickly Bay, called True Blue. St. George's University and Medical School is on the west side of True Blue; it is conspicuous and looks like a town.

Ashore

Two restaurants lie along the north shore leading to Point Saline. Because of their prime beach locations and excellent reputations, many people make the effort to visit them, usually by cab.

Approach Uli's Aquarium Beach Club [$B-D] by taxi or rental car. The setting is spectacular, under some giant rocks that form a headland at the end of an idyllic deserted beach. The architecture has made the most of these features, and the dining room is open to the view on one side and the rocks on the other. They have created interesting corners, with a rock pool and also an open beach bar. The fresh barbecued seafood is excellent, and this is a great place to come for a quiet, romantic, seafood lunch or dinner, or to bring a group and party. The Aquarium Beach Club is popular on Sundays, when people come to swim and snorkel. You get to the Aquarium by driving past the airport terminal, and looking for the sign on your right. They now offer some of the most gorgeous rooms in Grenada, above the restaurant in their Maca Bana villas.

On a calm day, you can anchor off The Beach House [$A-B] in the bay west of Morne Rouge Bay, and get your dinghy ashore to enjoy this elegant beachside restaurant, which is managed by Stanley Minors. Alternatively, take a cab. Come for lunch and enjoy the beach, or make it an evening treat (especially good when the moon is up). The food is first-rate.

Grenada and Carriacou

375

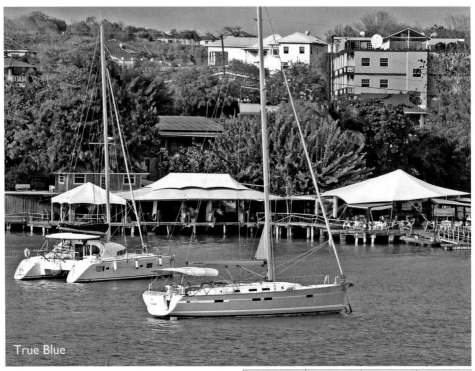

True Blue

TRUE BLUE

True Blue is the bay just west of Prickly Bay. It is a beautiful little bay, colorful and clean, and it makes a lovely anchorage. Russ and Magdalena, owners of True Blue Resort, have spent much time both cruising and working for charter companies, and they love boating customers. A small marina is part of the hotel, and a delightful wooden walkway over the water connects the two.

A distinctive small island is at the entrance. Enter in the middle of the bay between this island and True Blue Point. Go straight up into the bay and anchor inside, take one of the moorings, or tie up at the marina. The water is about 25 feet deep at the entrance to the bay and 13 feet deep up to the outside of the marina. A small surge enters from time to time, when the wind goes south of east. The waves are smaller than in Prickly Bay, but shorter and steeper. This works better for many monohulls, which roll less, but some cats wobble more. If there is a problem, put out a stern anchor to hold you facing out of the bay and into the seas.

That will fix it.

If you are anchored in Prickly Bay, everything in True Blue is easily reached if you dinghy to Spice Island Marine Services and take a short walk.

Communications

True Blue has wifi, you can use the high-speed email station, and the office will send and receive faxes. Bananas has free wifi.

Services

Jacqui and James manage the True Blue Marina and use it as a base to run Horizon Yacht Charters. This is an excellent, owner-run charter company, with bases here and in St. Vincent making one way charters easy. They have a big range of cats and monos.

Their marina takes about 25 boats and, in addition, they have 15 reliable moorings for rent. The mooring fee is $40 EC per night, with less expensive monthly rates. Mooring is optional, as there is plenty of room to anchor. The marina has diesel, water, electricity (110-220 volt, 50 cycles), wifi, showers, and toilets. You can get propane tanks filled and they will get Henry's Safari to come get your laundry. Their office sells ice, cruising guides, and Horizon t-shirts. Jacqui and James will look after you well and help you get any kind of repairs you may need. They look after boats when the owners

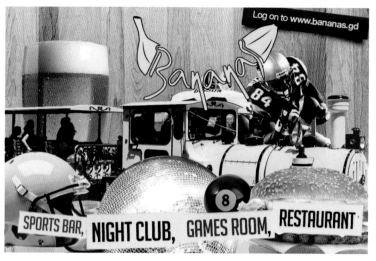

Restaurants

The Dodgy Dock [$B-C], True Blue Hotel's restaurant, is perched over the bay on stilts, with a dinghy dock. The food is very good and blends Mexican, Caribbean, and European flavors, all made from local ingredients. They have snacks, a full menu, children's menus, and daily specials, and in addition to the regular menu, they serve pizzas. They have their own microbrewery (the third largest brewery in Grenada), and their beer is popular. Their nightly happy hour is 1700-1800 with 2-for-1 house drinks, and other drinks discounted.

Monday night is pizza specials. Wednesday night is street food night; select local vendors are invited in to set up stalls and offer you their local specialties. Thursday is Latin night, with Latin music and dancing and Mexican food. Saturday is live-music night in season, with a barbecue. Tuesday night is Caribbean night with local cooking and a steel band. On Sundays, they serve a big brunch. Advance reservations are a good idea, especially for a waterside seat. Russ (from the UK) and Magdalena (from Mexico) and their daughter Marie rank among the most friendly of patrons and are especially welcoming to those on yachts.

Their Blue Haven Spa is open to all with three treatment rooms offering massage and beauty care. Of special note are their herbal soaks, using all local herbs, and their chocolate skin treatments using local chocolate. (Magdalena runs the House of Chocolate Museum in town). They have gentle yoga sessions in their fabulous yoga room (with a view) at 0830 on Wednesday, Friday and Saturday, and at 1745 on Monday, Thursday and Friday.

Rooms are available to yachtspeople at special rates. Other facilities include a

go away and will undertake major project management. They have an office for this in Port Louis. They will also happily arrange a taxi or tour for you.

Spronk's Mega Yacht Services is down the road at Bananas. It is run by Roger and Claire. They provision boats and are superyacht agents. They do customs clearance, arrange docking, find or import parts, organize airline tickets or transportation, and source flowers or anything else (see *St. George's*).

Provisioning/fun shopping

A short walk from True Blue, in the direction of Spice Island Marine Services, is the Bananas complex, run by Roger and Claire Spronk. Downstairs is a pharmacy and minimarket. Go upstairs to the office for the gourmet store. They stock top-quality frozen food, especially fish and other seafood (everything from oysters to black tiger shrimp), and quality meat cuts, as well as burger and sausage. They own an 8-acre farm for produce. This is the place to get your pickled ginger and wasabi powder. They supply many of the local hotels, as well as private homes and all kinds of yachts. Walk in and pick up a list. They also deliver sizeable orders.

Magdalena, at True Blue Resort, runs Truebluetique, which is small, but packed with a tasteful collection of handicrafts, objets d'art, jewelry, souvenirs, and useful items.

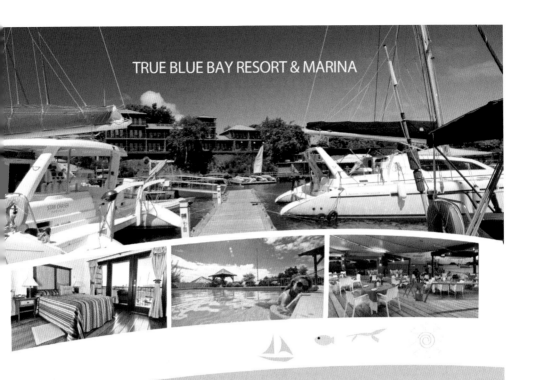

TRUE BLUE BAY RESORT & MARINA

 Full-Service Marina

 Dodgy Dock Restaurant

 Aquanauts Dive Center

 TrueBluetique Shop

 Microbrewery

 Free WIFI

 Accommodation

 Blue Haven Spa

 Sanvic's Car Rental

 Sankalpa Yoga Studio

 Pizza Bar

True Blue Truly Perfect

Walking distance to Spice Isle Marine, Special Sailors
Hotel Rates, Daily Happy Hours.

www.truebluebay.com
windward@truebluebay.com
Phone: (473)-443-8783

TRUE BLUE BAY
BOUTIQUE RESORT
GRENADA

Microbrewery, True Blue

conference room, a small open playground, and a swimming pool.

Esther and Omega run an interactive and entertaining cooking demonstration (including tasting) on Thursdays at 1500 (about $5 US). On Tuesdays at 1750, they have a local rum tasting session. Check the special events on their website, including a kid's Easter treasure hunt and Christmas events.

Imaginative in concept, Bananas [$B-C] was designed by two yachtsmen: Roger, who owns it, and Don, who helped build it. It is a cool restaurant, hangout, and nightspot, with lots of interesting corners and pretty waterways. Bananas has a sports bar with a big TV, and free wifi.

Outside, Carib Cave [$D] is Grenada's first wood-fired pizza oven, for excellent pizzas with cold beer. This is also the place for burgers and snacks. Inside, their restaurant has snacks and excellent meals, with very good and inexpensive lunchtime specials.

Their evening restaurant, Amici Miei [$B-D], is above on a canvas covered deck pleasantly open to the breeze. This is one of Grenada's best and most reasonably priced restaurants. They use all local ingredients and you can taste it. Italian is a big theme, with delicious pastas (I had the fresh tuna with capers and black olives) and pizzas. You can get fresh lobster in season, excellent steak, rack of lamb, fresh fish, and salads and vegetarian dishes. Ask about their changing specials, which may include lobster ravioli and paella on Saturdays, and if you have a gluten problem, they have gluten-free pasta.

Bananas is Grenada's hot spot, with something always going on within the complex for late-night entertainment. They have hosted everything from concerts and magic shows to boxing matches, and their sound-proofed disco and big sports TV screens are a fixture. The easiest way to check out the action is to visit www.bananas.gd.

If you are walking at night from either True Blue or Spice Island Marine Services, take a flashlight, and be cautious on big party nights.

Walk towards the university for more attractions. Options Food Court is a series of small shacks, each selling something different, including the Sushi Shop, pizza and ice cream, and Rumours Vegetarian. Tables have free wifi and power. You can find bikes to rent close by.

Water sports

True Blue is home to Gerlinde and Peter Seupel's Aquanauts Grenada. They are a Padi 5-star Golden Palm Resort and take people diving, do all kinds of courses, fill tanks, and rent diving equipment to those going on charter. They offer nitrox and rebreather dives and training.

Dinghy up to their dock, or they will collect divers from docks in Prickly Bay. Aquanauts has three very large and well-equipped dive boats. Calmer summer weather offers the prospect of exploring special sites off Grenada's south coast, or going up to Isle de Ronde.

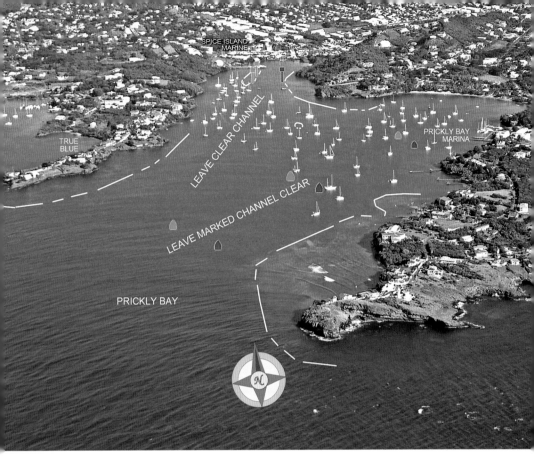

The image contains the following labels: SPICE ISLAND MARINE, LEAVE CLEAR CHANNEL, TRUE BLUE, PRICKLY BAY MARINA, LEAVE MARKED CHANNEL CLEAR, PRICKLY BAY

PRICKLY BAY

(Also known as L'Anse aux Epines, pronounced "Lans O Peen.")

Prickly Bay is pleasant, a well-to-do area of fancy houses, many of which have well-tended flower gardens. At the eastern head of the double-headed bay is a palm-fringed beach. The buildings are overcoming the green areas as people build larger and larger mansions, but you still live with the sound of birds by day and tree frogs by night. St. George's is only 15 minutes away by car, and the airport and Grand Anse are even closer. Spice Island Marine Services is at the western head of the bay, on the True Blue side, and Prickly Bay Marina is in L'Anse aux Epines on the east side of the bay. This makes everywhere from True Blue Bay to Mount Hartman within easy dinghy or walking distance. Buses are plentiful from the True Blue roundabout, at the beginning of the dual carriageway (Maurice Bishop Highway), a short walk from Spice Island Marine Services.

A prominent house at the end of Prickly Point looks just like a lighthouse. This makes it easy to recognize.

Prickly Bay is easy to enter, but don't get careless. There is a reef in the middle, opposite Prickly Bay Marina, that is just deep enough (6 feet) to be hard to see. A second, deeper reef (9 feet) lies a few hundred feet to its west.

Reefs also extend nearly all the way up the eastern shore, and one should give the True Blue headland reasonable clearance. Prickly Bay Marina has put in a marked channel in the middle of the bay. This keeps an entrance channel clear of anchored boats, which can help the big yachts.

Occasional southerly swells can make the bay uncomfortable, though a stern anchor will do much to restore a sense of calm.

Regulations

Prickly Bay is a port of entry, with the customs at Prickly Bay Marina. They normally open every day of the week. Customs officers often have duties on the way in, so they sometimes arrive more like 1000 than 0800. Anchoring is forbidden within 600 feet of the beach, as this area is reserved for swimmers. Small buoys mark the area.

Communications

A cruisers' net operates on VHF: 66 at 0730 weekdays. It includes weather, local information, and coming events. Channel 66 International is a very powerful repeater channel allowed to us courtesy Leroy Baptiste, Grenada's main communications man. It allows you to join in the net or communicate with other boats all over the island.

Prickly Bay Marina has excellent internet with high-speed wifi and special restaurant seats with many computer power supplies. Their wifi covers the docks and the restaurant. If you are farther out in the bay, HotHotHot Spot and Cruisers wifi provide coverage. Hothothot spot has another base in Clarkes Court Bay and many others up island. Cruisers wifi covers several Grenada anchorages, including St. George's and the Clarkes Court Bay, and they have stations in Carriacou and Trinidad.

Spice Island Marine Services has wifi and computers for the use of those on the slip. Other restaurants with wifi include Timbers, Bananas and Dodgy Dock.

General yacht services

Dinghy docks and garbage disposal are available both at Prickly Bay Marina and Spice Island Marine Services. Prickly Bay Marina has fuel, water and ice. You can bring in the boat or use jerry jugs.

Henry's Safari Tours [VHF: 68] has a sub-base in the marina, with on-the-spot laundry and a cooking-gas collection station, collecting and delivering on Mondays, Wednesdays and Fridays. For emergency service, call Henry Safari on the radio [VHF: 68]. Spice Island Marine Services has coin-operated laundry machines.

Prickly Bay Marina [VHF: 16] is a charming, small marina where fresh green lawns are dotted with palms and almond trees. It has an informal atmosphere and docks for about 25 yachts. They have stern-

to docking, showers, electricity (110/220 volt, 50 cycle), diesel, gasoline, water, and ice. Darren, who runs the show, is continually upgrading the yachting facilities. They have an excellent dinghy dock, new toilets, a mini-mart, and a wifi-friendly section of the restaurant, with power outlets.

They also have many moorings out in the bay for rent ($18 a night, less by the month). These have been put down and are maintained by Underwater Solutions so you can be sure they will be in good shape.

Their marina office offers absentee yacht and project management, and they find people to fix any boat problem you may have (see *Technical yacht services*).

This marina houses Henry's Safari Laundry, Essentials Mini-mart, and the Marina Tiki Bar and Restaurant (see *Restaurants*). The owners of this marina have built some very fancy condominiums and plan a bigger marina. Those interested in the condos can ask in the marina or look for Champy Evans.

Spice Island Marine Services [SIM, VHF: 16] is a pleasant, orderly boatyard, with room for 200 boats. It is in the northwestern corner of Prickly Bay, on the True Blue side. It is easy to walk from here to all the places we mention in True Blue Bay. It is a family business and Junior Evans is in charge. Their travel lift can take boats up to 70 tons and 25-foot beam. At present, yachts of up to 10-foot draft can come in at high tide and they have one 12-foot draft boat they manage to drag in. SIM is the first yard in Grenada to go ecofriendly by recycling wash-down water and removing the harmful solids. They will soon have toilet pump out stations. They have full fire-fighting facilities, security cameras and a high perimeter fence.

Sim has a hydraulic stacker and a mast crane with mast racks for those storing their masts off the yacht. They have tie-downs for all boats in the hurricane season, and secure cradle berthing is available. The yard keeps cats separate from monohulls. Demand for storage is so high that you cannot get short storage stays during the summer. Their staff includes a team that washes and chocks, does Awlgrip spray painting, osmosis treatment, hull polishing, and antifouling.

Grenada and Carriacou

PRICKLY BAY TO HOG ISLAND

NOTE: NO ANCHORING BEHIND BUOYED AREA ABOUT
600 FEET FROM PRICKLY BAY BEACH

Their own personnel can do woodworking, electrics, electronics (Raymarine certified) and mechanics (Yanmar agents), mostly with ABYC technicians. They service AB inflatables, and they have a bonded warehouse, so parts arrive almost duty-free.

Sailmaking and rigging are done by Turbulence; welding and fabrication by TechNick. The yard is secure and kept in excellent order.

Yacht crew can do their own work or arrange it through the yard, with their people or, in some cases, outside contractors.

The yard has electricity (110/220 volt, 50 cycle), wifi, and good water pressure. Spice Island Marine Services can look after your yacht while you are away, as well as arrange all the work. While you work, life is made easier with showers, toilets, a coin-operated launderette, email (yard customers only), and a waterfront restaurant (see *Restaurants*). Budget Marine Chandlery is also based at Spice Island Marine Services.

Superyachts can get any help they need in this area from either Henry's Safari Tours or Bananas (see *St. George's*).

Chandlery

Budget Marine has a big, duty-free (to foreign yachts) chandlery at Spice Island Marine Services. You will find a good collection of general and technical chandlery, including everything you need for your haul-out. An efficient special-order service brings goods from the parent store in St. Maarten, or directly from the manufacturer. Monthly containers from St. Maarten and weekly deliveries from various vendors keep things in stock. Budget Marine in Grenada is next to the Spice Island Marine Services Boat Yard. Easily accessible by dinghy from Prickly Bay, it is a short walk from True Blue or the main bus route serving the southwest of the island from St. George's. A knowledgeable Budget Marine agent in Tyrrel Bay, Carriacou (Technical Marine Management) can arrange next-day delivery service from the Grenada store. With 12 locations throughout the region, this chandlery group stocks chandlery that many sailors, fishermen, and pleasure boaters find essential. They currently open weekdays 0800-1700, Saturdays 0900-1200. Bring in your boat papers for the first visit to get the duty-free prices.

Prickly Bay Marina has a small but expanding chandlery section in the marina office building and can bring in anything from the Island Water World catalog.

Ace Hardware, on the east side of the dual carriageway from Spice Island Marine towards town, is good for general hardware.

Technical yacht services

Turbulence Grenada, based in Spice Island Marine Services, has impressive workshops that handle sails, rigging, and electronics. It is owned and run by Richard and Joelle, who are French, but who have lived in English islands almost forever. They are helped by many excellent local employees. Richard is an experienced rigger and sailmaker (and racing helmsman). He used to prepare maxi boats for major races and is well qualified to advise and handle complete new deck layouts. The store is divided into three sections. The rigging

Grenada and Carriacou

shop is long and well equipped to deal with swaging and all rigging problems up to 16-mm wire or up to 10-mm rod rigging. They keep materials to make spinnaker poles on hand and can order whole new rigs through Sparcraft. They stock all the necessary ropes for running rigging and sheets, as well as the blocks and winches (including electric) to help you get them in tight. They repair big boat hydraulics and are agents for Navtec. They stock and install Profurl roller furlers.

The Turbulence sail loft is large, and they work on everything from sailboard sails to massive mainsails from maxi-yachts. They produce sails themselves under the Turbulence logo, or if you prefer, they are agent for Doyle Sails.

They make biminis from scratch and can tackle all other canvas work. Sheldon heads the Turbulence electronics department. They will repair your electronics, whatever the brand, and are agents for NKE, Brookes and Gatehouse, and Ray Marine, and they supply and install these brands of instruments and autopilots. All branches of

Turbulence are also available in Port Louis in St. George's and Grenada Marine in St. David's Harbour, where Louis, from Switzerland, is the manager.

In the same yard, TechNick Yacht Services is run by Nick, who has years of Caribbean experience but originally came from England. TechNick is the place to come for any metal fabrication. Not only does Nick do all the high tech, precision work you need, he used to be the Moorings southern area technical manager, so he understands the broader picture of yacht systems and mechanics and will make sure anything he builds you is going to make sense in the environment in which it is being used. Nick is good: he welds and does metal fabrication in all metals. One of his big specialties is the building of arches and supports for dinghies, biminis, and solar panels. Nick is knowledgeable about all boat systems, and can often give good advice.

On Board Refrigeration (Electrical and Electronics) is run by Oscar Cain. Oscar has a wealth of experience and qualifications in

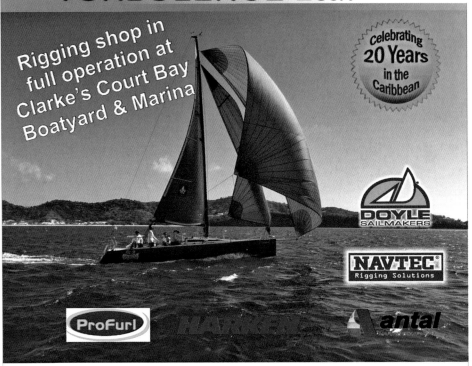
all three fields, plus hydraulics and mechanics, and is an ABYC master technician. He is a qualified Ray Marine technician, has been on the fitting out team of superyachts in Italy and has worked on yachts of all sizes from Antigua to Grenada. You can call him for any electrical/electronic/refrigeration/ hydraulic problem. He covers all the major harbors where yachts hang out, from Port Louis to Woburn. He keeps offices in Spice Island Marine and in Woburn. He sometimes runs an "open workbench". People come with their problems and he solves them and shows them how to fix things. Listen to the net.

Cottle Boat Works is a full marine joinery and carpentry shop. Owner Jim Cottle has been doing marine carpentry since 1972.

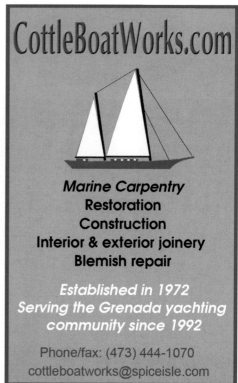
He sailed to Grenada on his yacht, J. Jeffrey, where he has been repairing and building boats since 1992. Jim has a large, modern shop near the Red Crab, full of excellent, top-grade machinery. You get to it by taking the left side road just beyond the Red Crab, and looking on your left. Jim does all his own work, so you can be sure of a good job. He repairs all wood problems and does fine joinery work. Jim can also fix dings, burns, and other blemishes in varnish. He keeps a good supply of teak and other hardwoods on hand. Many of his customers come from the large charter yachts. Jim is happy to work on yachts staying in Prickly Bay, Mount Hartman Bay, or St. George's. He can get booked up, so if you have a big job, discuss it with him as long in advance as possible.

Prickly Bay Marina offers a full repair and caretaking service. They can fix anything that can be done in the water and undertake all kinds of maintenance, and do it quickly. Many technicians are on hand to maintain the apartments, so refrigeration, mechanical and electrical repairs are easily done. They scrub boat bottoms, repair dinghies, paint, polish and service gear. They are efficient and they have an emergency rescue boat to tow you in.

Anro Agencies, run by Robert Miller, is a classy operation. They are agents for BMW and Subaru, as well as Mariner and Mercury outboards, Mercruiser engines and outdrives, Yanmar and Perkins diesels, and Yanmar marine generators. They sell and install new units, do warranty work, repair broken engines, and will make boat visits. New engines can be bought duty-free from their bonded warehouse, and parts may be imported duty-free. They will normally come to any of the Grenada ports to pick up broken outboards. Their shop is a few hundred feet down the road from Spice Island Marine Services, on the Maurice Bishop Highway, the dual carriageway between the roundabouts. They are within easy walking distance of Spice Island Marine Services on the east side of the road. They stock quite a few engine-related accessories in the Quicksilver range, and their prices can be quite competitive.

McIntyre Bros., also on the Maurice Bishop Highway, is within easy walking distance of Spice Island Marine Services, next to the roundabout on the east side of the road. They have qualified diesel mechanics and can fix most engines. They are the sales and service agents for Yamaha outboards and can arrange sales to yachts at duty-free prices. They will pick up your Yamaha for repair from most of the marinas. McIntyre rents cars and do tours (see *Transport*).

Matthew Watton runs Essential Engineering. He lives on a boat and can easily visit yachts in Prickly Bay. He came here eight years ago years ago to work on systems in the Prickly Bay condo complex and now runs his own business and does a good job at a fair rate. He fixes all outboards and inboards, along with gearboxes, sail drives, and the mechanical side of generators. He is also trained in refrigeration, and he can do a simple gas top up, but does not carry equipment for more than that. The easiest contact is to call him 414-7316.

Safe Yachts is a company that looks after yachts and does project management. Owner Denise, lives on a cat in the bay. She has about 10 moorings and will look after yachts in the bay or over in Secret Harbour Marina. Anything she cannot do she subcontracts and supervises. She can also arrange to have a boat hauled and painted in Clarkes Court Bay to be ready for the owner's return. She works with several divers and is a god person to call for a bottom clean. Denise also has a sewing machine and does light sewing. She is active in the local yachting scene and often does the morning net. If you

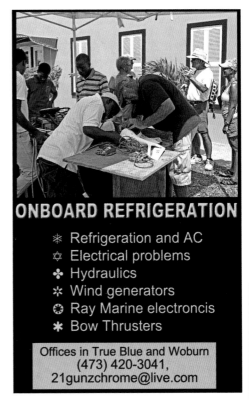

ONBOARD REFRIGERATION

- Refrigeration and AC
- Electrical problems
- Hydraulics
- Wind generators
- Ray Marine electroncis
- Bow Thrusters

Offices in True Blue and Woburn
(473) 420-3041,
21gunzchrome@live.com

are leaving your yacht on a mooring during the hurricane season, ask about hurricane precautions.

Johnny Sails and Canvas [VHF: 16/66] is a sail loft just down the Dusty Highway that leads north from Spice Island Marine Services. Johnny, his son, and the team can do excellent work, from sails to canvas and cushions. Johnny also does inflatable repair.

One-man contractors are available for on-board painting, varnishing, and other work. Glenroy (410-4919/417-9496) and Luxor (414-4383) will scrub bottoms, paint, polish, maintain and look after boats or lend a helping hand. Both are good.

Most technicians based in other yards and bays are willing to visit. This includes Marine Tech and Palm Tree Marine.

For computer repairs and IT you can try Christian and Anand's ModOne by the True Blue roundabout, or Onsite Software Support in the Marquis Mall (see *Grand Anse*).

Transport

There are some excellent taxi drivers around. They have now organized themselves in the Marina Taxi Association which covers all the ports in Grenada. It is easy to call Marina Taxi [VHF: 16]. The Prickly Bay branch has a small office in Prickly Bay Marina. All their drivers are good and one is nearly always available.

If you are renting a car, McIntyre's is close by, will quickly deliver, can provide a local license, and have staff who are used to dealing with yachts. They do excellent hiking and sightseeing tours, including Gouave's Fish Friday, and they arrange weddings.

Provisioning

The Prickly Bay Marina shop, Essentials [VHF: 16] is a convenient mini-market. They are open 0800-1600, Monday to Saturday. They have dry goods, a little fresh produce, frozen fish and and meat, a good selection of wines and liquor, and it is convenient for buying heavy cases of beer and other soft drinks, or gallons of spring water. They also sell ice.

Gilles and Frederique's Le Boucher, a French butcher and delicatessen, is also here. They also stock meat, fine French cheeses, pates, and a variety of wines. They make up sandwiches on fresh French bread, and sometimes they hot-smoke lionfish which makes a great sandwich. Rotisserie chicken is normally available around noon. The meat is all fresh, but they can freeze if you ask.

For more than that, bus or cab to the malls in Grand Anse (buses go from the True Blue roundabout). A little closer is a small local open market by the L'Anse aux

Epines roundabout.

People needing to stock up on their wines will be delighted by North South Wines, a short walk from the boatyard, close by the Calabash. They stock wines from all over the world, including Europe, Australia, South America, and South Africa. You can sit down in a comfortable atmosphere, discuss your needs, and they can recommend wines for different menus. They have a large enough range to satisfy the superyacht owner, as well as those with more modest needs. This is a wholesale outfit, so wines are sold by the case, but they are often willing to mix cases for yachts, and they will deliver to your yacht. If you buy a case of wine and don't want it all at once, they will store it for you in their temperature-controlled rooms. Opening hours are weekdays 0800-1600. They have a retail outlet called the Wine Shoppe in Spiceland Mall (see *Grand Anse*).

Restaurants

The Marina Tiki Bar and Restaurant [$B-D], right in Prickly Bay Marina, is a favorite yachty haunt. You can get great thin-crust Italian pizzas, good meals, and other daily specials that are usually reasonably priced. They have the most popular happy hour in L'Anse aux Epines, from 1700-1800 nightly, except Friday when it runs from 1700-1900. Something happens here every night and it is popular with both yachties and medical students. Monday is half-priced pizzas, Tuesday is trivia night, on Wednesdays they have serious bingo with big prizes, Thursday is two for one pizzas and steel pan music. Friday is the most popular night, with a steel band from 1800, followed by a big music party. Saturday night varies, and Sunday night is movie night. The cruisers net (VHF: 66 international at 0730) gives information about their attractions.

Timbers [$A-C] is the waterfront restaurant at Spice Island Marine. It has a big and convenient dinghy dock. The small bar out at the back is open 24/7, with good free wifi, and it serves drinks, coffee, snacks (good fishburgers) and more. The main restaurant hangs out over the water and serves good meals (lunch and dinner) in a variety of styles.

Local artist Lisa Herrara's Junction [$C-D] is popular with medical students and professors. She opens Wednesday to Saturday. The morning part (till after lunch) is the cafe at the back. This switches to the front from 1700 and continues to 0100. It is quite small, an inside bar with balcony and patio seating that creates cozy and intriguing spaces; there is often live music. She serves tasty burgers and grilled fish. You can ask Lisa about her art; there may be some around.

Next to Junction is The (West Indies Beer Co.) Brewery, a family owned and operated pub and restaurant where Brewmaster Mark produces 12 different beers and ciders. The long wrap-around bar separates the fermentation tanks from the pool table and seating area, where they serve pub-style and local food from 1300 until late. Smokers can rent hookahs, and the bartenders are always happy to pour a taster pallet. When you find the ideal beer, you can buy a growler (resealable bottle) to take home and get it refilled any time.

The Choo Light [$C-D] is run by the Choo family from Hong Kong. The prices are so reasonable that you can eat here any time you don't feel like cooking. The atmosphere is informal and the staff welcoming. They sell takeout.

The Calabash Hotel [$A] has a fine, up-market restaurant in a pleasant atmosphere and with excellent food. They prefer you to be dressed fairly smartly, but this is a great choice when you want somewhere special; reservations are essential.

Ashore

You will find tennis courts at the hotels and a golf club in Golflands. Ask for directions. Everything in True Blue is now easily accessible from Prickly Bay; dinghy to Spice Island Marine Services and take the short walk down the road.

There is a very easy walk between Prickly Bay and Secret Harbour Marina in Mount Hartman Bay. From Prickly, walk from the marina to the road, turn right and take the first left. When you come to a T-junction, turn right, then next left.

Water sports

Scuba Tech is the waterfront dive shop on the Calabash beach, a Padi/Cmas shop. This pleasant shop does all the usual courses, as well as nitrox and rebreathing. They can do annual visual tank inspections and fills, and help repair equipment. They dive with small groups, using a 32-foot pirogue. They visit all Grenada sites including the Bianca C.

If you are after big fish, ask about their wreck sites south of Prickly Bay. San Juan is a small ship 1.5 miles south of Grenada that sank in 27 meters. The 170-foot long Herma 1 was sunk in 2005 and is four miles south and 30 meters deep. The 200-foot long King Mitch is six miles south and 37 meters deep.

These wrecks are in open, rough water, so are weather dependent, challenging, and very exciting. They attract nurse sharks, rays, and spadefish, and turtles often drop by.

Scuba Tech divers usually meet at 0845 to gather equipment for a two-tank dive at 0900. If you have gear, they could pick you up from Prickly Bay on their way out.

Grenada and Carriacou

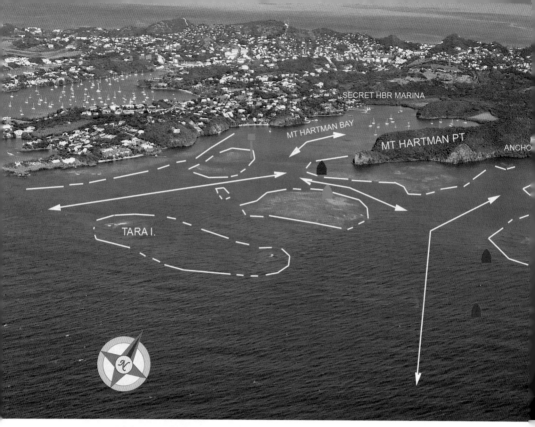

Aerial photograph with labels: SECRET HBR MARINA, MT HARTMAN BAY, MT HARTMAN PT, ANCHO, TARA I.

THE SOUTH COAST BEYOND PRICKLY BAY

(See sketch charts pages 384 and 397.)

The south coast of Grenada has beautiful and protected anchorages, some great restaurants, several marinas, a boatyard, and other facilities. A mass of reefs provides interesting, if somewhat murky, snorkeling. The area should be treated with caution: eyeball navigation is essential. On our charts, we have marked as "too shallow" several areas of relatively shoal water (12-15 feet) that extend well offshore. In normal conditions you can sail over these, but when the going gets rough, seas start breaking on them, and they are best avoided. The Porpoises, about half a mile off Prickly Point, awash and hard to spot, are as nasty a group of rocks as you could find to get wrecked on.

The buoyage system, such as it is, is privately maintained, with a lot of markers placed by individuals for their own purposes.

My sketch charts include the markers I saw when updating. The current buoys are red-right returning into Mt. Hartman, which may confuse a sailor heading to Hog Island.

Buoys come and go and change position. Markers can be extremely unreliable and, when out of place, dangerously misleading. Visit this coast for the first time in good light and rely on your own navigation skills, not on the buoys. When you know the area and know which buoys are in place, they may be helpful on later visits. The exceptions to this are the buoyed channels into Phare Bleu Marina and Grenada Marine in St. David's Harbour, which are well-maintained. The outer yellow buoy for Phare Bleu is steel, unlit, and a long way out; take care.

Entering Mt. Hartman Bay and Hog Island is tricky and demands attention. The main reefs are easy to see in good light. Two shoals, 6 and 9 feet deep, are not as easy to spot. From Prickly Bay, pass about midway between Prickly Point and the Porpoises. Look out for what was Tara Island and is now a shallow breaking spot. Leave Tara to starboard, passing halfway between it and

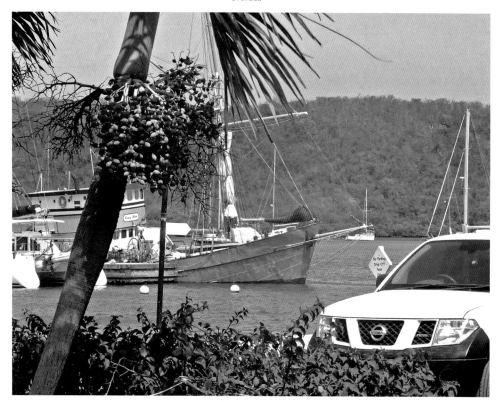

Prickly Point. Head for Mt. Hartman Point, eyeballing your way through the reefs. For Hog Island, follow the inner reef up to Hog Island, leaving the inside red buoys to port. For Mt. Hartman, pass between the red buoy and the green beacon. The channel is buoyed up to the marina. Do not anchor in the channel.

An alternative is a deeper channel south of Hog Island. For this, approach the western tip of Hog Island on a bearing of magnetic north, and eyeball your way around the reefs as you approach Hog. To leave, pass close by the reef just south of Hog Island, and head out on a bearing of 170° magnetic. In both directions, make sure the current is not setting you to the west. A 14-foot bank lies on the west side of the channel, so deep-draft yachts need to be particularly careful. Last time I passed, two red buoys marked part of this channel.

A repeater on channel 66 international connects all Grenada's anchorages and has a morning cruisers' net at 0730. Buses run between the south coast and St. George's.

MOUNT HARTMAN BAY

Mt. Hartman Bay is deep and well protected (see chart *Prickly Bay to Hog Island*, page 384) with a modern marina. This is a suitable area for dinghy sailing or sailboarding, as there is protected water all the way to Phare Bleu Bay. By land, it is a 10-minute walk to Prickly Bay. (From the marina exit, turn right walk up the hill and round the corner; keep going till you come to a crossroads, turn right again, and then take the next small road on the left. When you come to the next main road, turn right again, and the marina is on your left.)

General services

Secret Harbour Marina [VHF: 16], with 53 berths, has a lovely location in a peaceful bay. Fuel, water, ice, showers, telephone, wifi, fax, token launderette, dinghy dock, 24-hour security, and electricity (110/220/380Volt, 50 cycle) are among the marina services.

Grenada and Carriacou

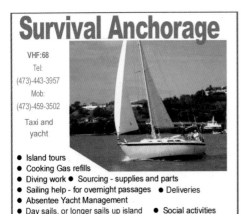

Survival Anchorage

VHF:68
Tel:
(473)-443-3957
Mob:
(473)-459-3502

Taxi and yacht

- Island tours
- Cooking Gas refills
- Diving work ● Sourcing - supplies and parts
- Sailing help - for overnight passages ● Deliveries
- Absentee Yacht Management
- Day sails, or longer sails up island ● Social activities

Duty-free fuel is available. They can take any size yacht from the smallest cruiser up to huge superyachts. The maximum draft on the deepest dock is 20 feet, and a yacht of this depth will have to be careful entering the bay. If you have any questions, call or ask Mitre in the office. They will assist you in docking at the marina, or in finding any services you might need. The marina has a swimming pool, tennis courts a small beach, and lovely self contained cottages along the waterfront to rent. Each is beautifully appointed and has a delightful balcony over the water. (See also *Ashore*)

There is no customs station, so if you want to come straight here, call Secret Harbour Marina and they can arrange for one of the yacht agents to clear you.

Chris and Chrystal's The Multihull Company and LTD Sailing are based here. They are a branch of the Multihull Company brokerage, and they run a sailing school, LTD sailing (LTD sailing.com).

Technical yacht services

George, a taxi driver whose call sign is "Survival Anchorage," refills propane bottles, looks after yachts when owners are away, helps source parts or other things, and can do underwater work, including hull and prop cleaning. He is willing to do overnight passages for those needing an extra hand. He delivers boats in the Windwards, or helps deliver them farther, and he can act as pilot around the reef-strewn south coast. He has his own yacht for day sails or island passages.

Ashore

Secret Harbour Bar, Restaurant, and Pizzeria is open every day from 0730 until the last order. The location is pleasant and the spacious dining room is open, with a view of the bay. Secret Radio (92.7 FM) is in the middle of the restaurant in a transmitting room of its own. Entertainment includes musical jam on Tuesdays, and Movie nights on Thursdays at 1900. On the last Sunday of every month they host a great boat jumble and craft market. Up the hill is the larger Secret Harbour Hotel whose restaurant is open all day every day with live music on Mondays, Fridays, and Saturdays. A new bakery is being built.

George (Survival Anchorage), the taxi driver mentioned in *Services* above, takes people on "Village Life" tours. He will take you to some of the small villages and introduce you to some of his friends to give you an understanding of village life in Grenada.

Mount Hartman Estate Cave House [$A] is an exclusive restaurant within easy walking distance of Secret Harbour. (Go through the main hotel and out the other side up to the road. Turn left to the crossroads, then left again, walk up the hill and down again, and you are there. It is a lovely sculpted building with high ceilings and an open view over Secret Harbour. The food is good; you can eat a la carte, or they offer a two-course meal, which is quite reasonable for such a top-class establishment. It is good for a special night out, but reservations are essential.

HOG ISLAND

North of Hog Island is a huge, protected bay. When you anchor, there will be just a finger of horizon to remind you that the sea is still there. This is one of Grenada's most popular cruising hangouts. Yachties enjoy the peace and Roger's ramshackle shack bar that sprawls along a good chunk of the tiny beach. Access to shore is available at Mt. Hartman Bay and Woburn. On Sundays the cruisers get together for a popular barbecue at Roger's Bar.

See pages 384 and 397 (charts) and page

Aerial view with labels: WOBURN, CCB MARINA, HOG ISLAND, WHISPER COVE, CLARKES COURT BAY, PETITE CALIVIGNY, CALIVIGNY ISLAND, HOG ISLAND TO CALIVIGNY ISLAND

392 for navigation into Hog Island. When you get in, anchor anywhere between Hog Island and the mainland.

A construction company owns Hog Island and Mt. Hartman Estates and development is stalled. So far they have built a bridge to link Hog Island to the shore. (No more sailing yachts through the narrow channel, but you can dinghy through.)

In the land behind Hog, I noticed a lot of grazing horses. I tracked down the owner, Wendell Wilson, who owns Amistad Stables and can take you riding (440-4175/533-8221).

CLARKES COURT BAY

This huge and sheltered bay, with Woburn at its head, has lots of anchoring possibilities: you can explore and find your own spot. It is linked to protected bays to the east and west, offering miles of safe dinghy navigation. This is the home of the huge Clarkes Court Bay boatyard and marina, a well as other marinas and many facilities.

In the old days, big sailing ships would anchor here to take on rum that was brought

Grenada and Carriacou

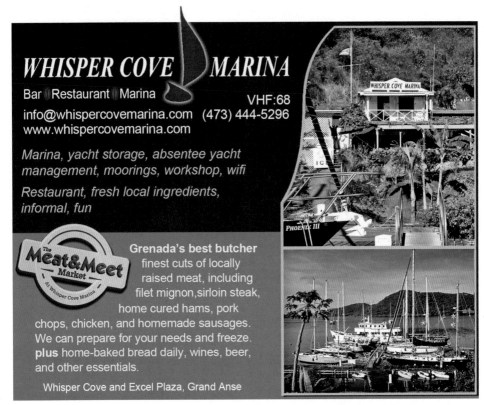
down the river to the head of the bay by small boat. Calivigny Island lies at the entrance to Clarkes Court Bay. It was privately purchased in 2001 and is now a fancey rental resort. As part of this development, the deepest part of the entrance channel has been buoyed. These buoys are privately maintained and have proved unreliable. Check for yourself that they are in position. You need to enter fairly close to Calivigny Island to avoid all the reefs and shoals that extend south of Hog Island. Once inside, you can anchor almost anywhere that takes your fancy.

One popular anchorage is off Calivigny Island just north of the island, off the beach. The bottom shelves steeply, so make sure you are well hooked. Calivigny Island is privately owned and guarded. The beaches, like all Grenada beaches, are public. You should not use the dock, go behind the beach, or use any of the owner's beach huts. But you can pull your dinghy on the beach, have your picnic ashore, and swim. Keep it clean. Guards may check you out, but they know the law. One time when we visited, two big labradors came running out and tried to knock us over with their wagging tails, and then lick us to death. We loved it.

You can find good anchorages almost anywhere in the bay. One delightful little anchorage is in Petite Calivigny Bay, with good snorkeling around Petite Calivigny Point.

Both Calivigny and Hog are dotted with hardy little frangipani trees. Their leaves fall in the dry season, leaving only sweet-smelling, delicate white flowers.

Communications

Clarkes Court Bay Marina has wifi or plug-in, as does Whisper Cove Marina. Bring your own computer. You can probably pull in Cruisers wifi or HotHotHot Spot onboard.

General yacht services

The big new facility in this bay is Clarkes Court Boatyard and Marina. Owned by Kelly it is in the same stable as Blue Lagoon in St. Vincent and Bequia Plantation House. Kelly has made a large investment to create Grenada's newest major player in the marine

HOG I. TO WESTERHALL

SCALE IN NAUTICAL MILES

0   1/2   1

P. BACAYE

WESTERHALL POINT

WESTERHALL BAY

CHEMIN BAY

BREAKS

MANGROVE HIDEAWAY

CALIVIGNY HARBOUR

FORT JEUDY

POINT FORT JEUDY

WGDA13
12° 00.0'
61° 42.1'

WGDA12
11° 59.3'N
61° 42.7W

PORT EGMONT

GARY I.

POINT EGMONT

ADAM I.

PHARE BLEU BAY

WGDAPB
11° 59.3'
61° 42.9'

PETITE CALIVIGNY

PHARE BLEU MARINA

CALIVIGNY I.

WGDA11
11° 59.1N
61° 43.5W

SPRONK'S MARINA

WHISPER COVE MARINA

LITTLE DIPPER MARINA

BENJI BAY

CLARKES COURT BAY

SAGA BAY

WGDA10
11° 59.0N
61° 44.2W

NIMROD ISLAND VIEW

WOBURN

CLARKES COURT BAY MARINA & BOATYARD
PALM TREE MARINE
X-MARINE
ISLAND DREAMS
NORTH YACHT SHOP
TURBULENCE

MT HARTMAN PT.

HOG I.

WHITE BUOYS PRIVATE MAINTAINED

358° M. (178° M)

TARA I.
(0.5ft)

Grenada and Carriacou

397

industry. The yard is operating, with many boats in storage, and is nearly complete.

Hauling is done on a 242-ton travel lift, which lifts up to 37-foot beam with a 13-foot draft. Some smaller boats are hauled on a trailer, which takes 38-tons with a 6-foot draft. There is room for about 300 boats ashore, and tie downs are available. A long work dock is already in use, and this, like the rest of the marina is good for about 12-foot draft. The marina docks are in place, there is be plenty of space for short an long term visitors. The restaurant looks over the docks.

Facilities in the yard include North Yacht Shop Chandlery, Driftwood wood shop, X-Marine glass and composites, and Palm Tree Marine mechanics. You can do your own work, or they will help you arrange it. Arlene, the operations manager, can give you details.

Whisper Cove Marina is a small, pleasant, and friendly docking facility between Petit Calivigny and Woburn, run by Gilles and Mary. It is well protected by a groin. They have 12 berths for boats up to 60 feet and 10-foot draft, with electricity (220 volt, or 110 volt with a transformer); water comes by a long hose, and showers are on the dock. They have hurricane moorings in case of a storm, and these are available for rent outside the hurricane season (or free if you tie up to one for a meal). They have a laundry machine, wifi, dinghy dock, the Meat and Meet shop (see *Shopping*), and a bar and restaurant (see *Restaurants*). They look after their customers well and have a bus for airport runs.

Cruisers love their do-it-yourself workshop with its vice, drill press, and other tools. If you need a hand with very simple welding, Gilles may help. You can drop off propane tanks and laundry for Henry's Safari Tours. Whisper Cove is home to Conservation Kayak (see *Ashore*).

Benji Bay yard is owned by Claire and Roger of Spronk's Yacht Services. This is one of the nicest little bays within Clarkes Court Bay. They have put down moorings available for rent and have a small haul out and typically take just a couple of boats undergoing major projects by the owner. Though they can arrange any work. They also run major full moon parties (see *Ashore*).

The Grenada Yachting Authority, is a private, locally-owned business. They put down moorings (as far as I know, unofficial ones with no water rights; check the quality for yourself) and have a water barge. They are not an official body.

Chandlery

In Clarkes Court haul out, North Yacht Shop is a big new chandlery run by Matt. He carries a lot of the West Marine range and anything in their catalogue, that he does not carry, he can bring in by the next day.

As the shop is in the yard, his primary approach has been to stock products yachts are going to need. This includes a big range of paints and antifoulings (including Sea Hawk), glass for repairs, consumables used in preparation, zincs, pumps, hoses, toilets, plumbing, fasteners and safety gear.

But you will find cool stuff here including portable fridges and freezers, flags, a great selection of LED bulbs, and a lot of general yacht chandlery.

Sherri owns Wholesale Yacht Parts, a

CLARKES COURT

BOATYARD & MARINA
GRENADA W.I.

Tel: 1-473-439-3939,   Fax: 1-473-439-3940,
info@clarkescourtmarina.com   www.clarkescourtmarina.com

Hauling capabilities: Our travel lift "The Hulk" can haul 242 ton, max beam 37ft and max draft 13ft. Submersible Trailer: 32 tons with max beam of 25ft and max draft 7ft.

Long and short-term storage ashore • Marina docks • High Pressure Wash
Chocking • Tie downs • Cradles • Free Wifi • 24hour security

- Divers on every haulout – No additional charge
- No surcharge on subcontractors work
- No surcharge on do-it-yourself work
- No VAT on yacht services
- Restaurant, Apartments, Dinghy Service

On-Site Service Providers
North Yacht Shop-Chandlery
Palm Tree Marine:
  Mechanical-Yanmar Dealer,
  Fuel Cleaning
X Marine: Composites,
  Painting, and Fiberglass
Turbulence:
  Rigging, Sailmaking
Driftwood: Fine woodwork,
  Antifouling
Shipyard Marine Services:
  Air Condition, Refrigeration,
  Abrasive Blasting
Waterfall Marine: Mechanical,
  Electrical, and Hydraulics
Island Dreams: Guardianage
**Selection of Approved
  Subcontractors**

GRENADA'S NEWEST HAUL-OUT AND MARINA

short walk from the dock in Woburn. She can source anything you need from the US, usually at a discounted price, and have it shipped down at a discount off the usual Fedex rates. If you want to ship something of your own from the US, she can help. If you are in another island, she can ship direct to you there. She is in the big four-story building right across the bay from Clarkes Court Bay Marina.

Technical yacht services

X-Marine, in Clarkes Court Boatyard is run by Nicolas and the best place to go for any kind of glass repairs, including major structural repair in glass, composite, or carbon fiber. They fabricate anything in glass or carbon fiber, and have an oven for fixing carbon masts. They spray Awlgrip and gelcoat and can do gelcoat matching. The treat stainless, aluminium and other metals, and plan an anodizer for small parts

Driftwood offers fine yacht woodwork, from fancy joinery to replacing a plank or teak deck. They also have a team that does bottom jobs, antifouling, topside buffing,

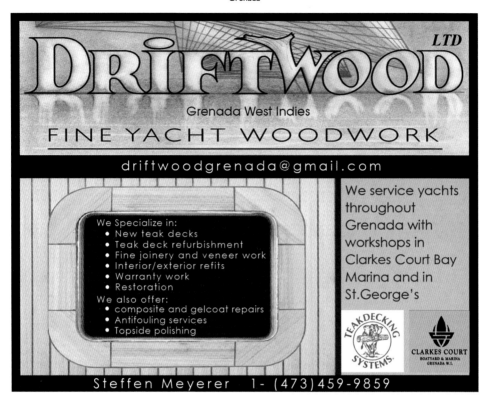

polishing, gelcoat, and glass repairs.

It is owned by Steffen who worked for many years with Chippy in Antigua. He has pulled together a good and reliable team including Judd Tinius, the well known shipwright and owner of the 1899 classic "Galatea". They work on all sizes of boat and any size job, from completely redesigning and building a yacht's interior, to making a new bookshelf. If a woodworking job involves glass or composite work, they have the skills to do that, which considerably simplifies some jobs. The keep a big stock of veneers, including European ones like beech and oak.

They have workshops both in Clarkes Court Bay Marina and haul out and in St. George's (Lagoon Road).

Island Dreams has a branch in Clarkes Court Bay Boatyard, with another office in Port Louis. Owners Mark and Anita look after your yacht while you go away, fixing anything that needs doing at the same time. They do everything from a simple repair to a complete refit. For a more complete description, see *St. George's.*

Mike runs Palm Tree Marine, helped by several Grenadians, including Kevon. This is an excellent place to fix all your mechanical, electrical and refrigeration problems. They work on all brands of inboards, outboards, and generators. They are dealers for Caterpillar, Yanmar, Westerbeke, and Northern Lights, and are equipped for tank cleaning. They are agents for Spectra watermakers and service all makes. They have an efficient mini-machine shop and do steel and stainless welding. Palm Tree Marine has a van for visiting other locations, and their refrigeration department makes boat visits anywhere, but for major mechanical, it is easier to make sure you get them by coming to Clarkes Court Bay Marina.

Mango Projects does surveys and also looks after yachts. Neil Batcheler, the owner, is SAMS accredited surveyor who used to work with Flying Fish (see St. George's) and has now set on his own. He does all kinds of surveys from condition and insurance to damage and valuation. He is also willing to keep an eye on yachts, doing regular checks (but not project management) in Clarkes Court Bay Marina.

Grenada and Carriacou

ing of several people with an outlet right in the marina. Angus coordinates. Ricardo Moultri does refined sandblasting, fixes outboards, fuel injection, and cleans fuel. Dexter Hays (Subzero) does refrigeration and air conditioning. They also have marine contacts in St. Vincent.

Rollin' Stitches canvas and uphol-

Rigging, electronics and sailmaking are taken care of by Turbulence, who are fast, efficient and do a good job at a fair rate. They have shops in all of Grenada's yards, as well as in Port Louis Marina; more details are given under Prickly Bay.

On Board Refrigeration is run by Oscar Cain. Oscar can fix any refrigeration, electrical or electronic problem. He is an ABYC master technician. He keeps an office in the Island View building in Woburn, as well as Prickly Bay. For a full write-up see *Prickly Bay*.

Royan's Welding shop is close by and he charges no extra to come down, give an estimate and pick up your metal work jobs, or work on your boat with a mobile unit (for a full write-up, see *St. George's*)

Marine Tech do refrigeration, electric and electronic repairs and installation; they are willing to come over to do work (for full details, see *St. George's*).

Waterfall Marine, from Trinidad have a branch in Clarkes Court Bay. Waterfall is a company that works with both ships and yachts. It is run by Johan van Druten and Sean Bodden. For yachts they are first-rate at mechanical and electrical engineering, including all prop, shaft and seal work. They can weld most metals, including stainless and aluminum, and can fix hydraulics. They are one of the few companies to do work on marine jet propulsion drives. They do project management, consulting, and survey work on yachts.

Shipyard Marine Services is a group-

stery shop is also in the Island View building and owned and run by Karen. Karen does any kind of canvas work, dinghy chaps, biminis, awnings, bags and covers. She also does upholstery, which most sailmakers do not touch. So for new cushions, and curtains this is the place to come. She keeps a fair stock of Sunbrella, and has a fancy fabric book from which you can choose your interior fabrics. She has a small, informal shop, a pleasant place to pop round and discuss your project.

Shopping

Whisper Cove's Meat and Meet shop is known for the best selection of meat and sausages in Grenada. Gilles is a butcher who buys local animals, which he hangs and processes professionally in his modern facility. The result is that you can buy the best cuts of much finer meat than the imports found in the supermarket. He also makes excellent sausages. They can prepare meat to order, so you can get just what you want by cut or portion, and they can freeze it. Quite a number of charter yachts do their meat provisioning here.

Every day, except Sunday, they bake French bread, which is available from 1030, and sell wines, fresh yogurt and other supplies. Their main shop is in Whisper Cove, but they have an outlet store, the marketing board's Value Garden in the Excel Plaza in Grand Anse.

You can anchor off Woburn or any of the other bays and tie your dinghy to the village dock. Wander up to the road and turn left, and you will find a little corner store called Nimrod and Sons Rum Shop, run by Pat and Sep. You can buy ice here, along with bread, fresh chicken, lettuce, a few canned goods, beer, and rum.

Restaurants

Whisper Cove Marina Restaurant [$B-D] is a fun French bar and restaurant, family-run by Gilles and Mary. They open for breakfast and lunch Tuesday to Saturday Hearty fish sandwiches, excellent burgers, daily specials and fresh salads are often on the menu. Wednesday night is Pizza night, Thursday night is the popular roast chicken and fries night, and dinner on Friday and Saturday features excellent meat, which they butcher themselves ~ melt-in-the-mouth steak, and pork ~ as well as lobster and fresh fish, though they can cater to a vegetarian. They do a popular Sunday brunch buffet starting at 1130, and are often open for special occasions (check the morning cruisers' net). They provide free transport from the other Grenada anchorages for meal guests (call). Bring books for the multi-language book-swap.

Woburn is home to Little Dipper [$D], the cutest restaurant in Grenada. Joan, who owns it with her husband, Rock, the taxi driver, has cooked in several fancy restaurants and serves excellent local food inexpensively, making this a special experience and great value. Enjoy the sweeping view out over Hog Island as you taste fresh seafood with a good variety of local vegetables. You won't find a better deal on lobster, fish, or lambi. They open Monday to Saturday, 1000-2200. They have a small dinghy dock, with a reef in front, so approach carefully along the coast from the north. The dock has a flashing amber light to help you in. It is an adventurous stroll up through mangroves, bananas, and fruit trees to reach the restaurant at the top of their land. Rock can bring you over by taxi from Prickly Bay or Secret Harbour at a special rate.

Taffy's at Island Breeze [$D, closed Monday], owned by Sue and Colin, is a great yachtie hangout right by the dock. It is not a fancy restaurant,. Sue cooks one dish each meal, and she does it well. On Mondays, she cooks fish and chips and on Sundays, she produces a traditional roast lunch. Other days, Sue wanders out in the morning to see what fresh food is available and decides on the dinner dish accordingly. In season, she opens for lunch and dinner with a cruisers lunch for $15 EC. Taffy's is very popular, If you do not reserve for dinner, you may not get in (538-0863).

If you walk down the boardwalk by the dock, you come to Sea Quest, a local bar.

Bob Goodchild, the Surveyor (see *St. George's*), has Mango Cottage, Bamboo House, and several more apartments set in their own private garden, a two-minute walk from Whisper Cove Marina. They are lovely, but usually on long-term leases; you can always ask.

Ashore

Roger's Benji Bay hosts a wild and wonderful full moon party (check the date of the next full moon and put it on your calendar). They have a bar, barbecue, and several good live bands. Their dinghy dock is small, so tie it on a long tether to allow others room.

Jamie and Amber, an energetic young couple from the UK, own and operate Conservation Kayak. Their guided kayak tours give guests an intimate view of the shore, where they learn about mangrove conservation and ecology. Based out of Whisper Cove Marina in lower Woburn, tours range from 2 to 5 hours; no experience is necessary. The longer tours include a stop at an idyllic white sand beach, and include a delicious, locally-sourced organic lunch. The tours have become immensely popular and run most days. You need to book in advance.

Transport

The road running through Woburn looks so rough and rural, with the odd chicken wandering over it, that it seems impossible to imagine a bus hurtling by full of smiling faces and big shopping baskets, but it happens all the time. Whichever way it comes, you can catch it to town if you wait around Nimrod's Rum Shop. On the return run, ask for a bus going to "Lower Woburn." Take it easy on the white rum while you wait, or be prepared to miss the bus.

Grenada and Carriacou

Pirate mast, Phare Bleu

PHARE BLEU BAY

East of Calivigny Island, between Calivigny Island and Point Egmont, is a protected harbor, home to Phare Bleu Marina and Boutique Hotel. Dieter and Jana, the owners, have built a delightful marina and cottage hotel, with a warm and welcoming atmosphere, which has some excellent supporting services.

Entry is down a buoyed channel through the reefs. You have to enter between the shoals that extend south from Adam Island and the shoals that extend east from Calivi-

gny Island. To stay out of trouble, go right up to the outer yellow buoy and follow the markers in from there, red right returning. A couple of boats have tried to cut the corner into the channel and gone aground.

In the channel, there is at least 35 feet of water on your way in. If you are not going into the marina, the best anchorage is in Calivigny Island, a short dinghy ride away.

Petit Calivigny Yacht Club (PCYC) hosts match racing about four times a year at Phare Bleu. They supply the boats, and you can join in. Phare Bleu dinghy concerts have become immensely popular with cruisers, who attend in their hundreds. They run about five a year from a barge in the bay. The concert lasts about an hour and is in the late afternoon. The band is on the barge (as is a bar), and dinghies gather all around. Usually Phare Bleu has a barbecue afterwards.

Phare Bleu also organizes an excellent music festival in the spring.

Regulations

Le Phare Bleu is a port of clearance.

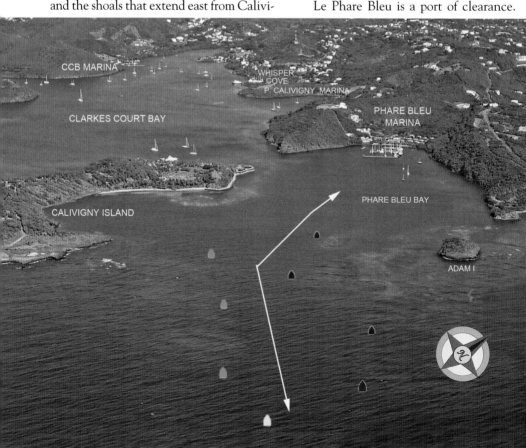

CCB MARINA

WHISPER COVE

P. CALIVIGNY MARINA

PHARE BLEU MARINA

CLARKES COURT BAY

CALIVIGNY ISLAND

PHARE BLEU BAY

ADAM I

Le Phare Bleu
Boutique Hotel & Marina

Calivigny Bay, St. George's, Grenada, W.I. POS 12°00 11N / 61° 43 29W

- 60 Slip Marina able to accommodate boats up to 120 ft. and 15 ft. draft
- 230/110v (50hz) electricity, Water Supply, Fuel Dock & 24 hr. Security
- Grenada Port of Entry with Customs & Immigration Office
- Island Dreams Yacht Services, Grenada Chiropractic Clinic & Henry Safari Laundry Services
- Approved Hurricane Moorings
- Complimentary WiFi, Restaurants & Bar, Live Music Night, Mini Market, Beach & Pool
- Accommodations: One & Two Bedroom Villas and Apartments available on property

Phone: 1-473-444-2400   **Email:** hotel@lepharebleu.com   **Website:** www.lepharebleu.com

Customs are open from 0800-1600, but they sometimes have to leave early. On weekends, they start later and end earlier.

General yacht services

Le Phare Bleu is a 50-berth marina (for yachts up to 100 feet), using mainly heavy floating docks. There is water and electricity (110/220-volt, 50-cycle), gasoline, and diesel available on the docks. Henry Safari has a laundry ashore and fills gas bottles (open 0900-1600). Wifi is free to customers (ask for the password). Phare Bleu has a good tug, which can help out for rescue and recovery. Phare Bleu recycles glass, cans, juice, boxes, and plastic bottles; please separate. They also have oil disposal.

Restaurants

Phare Bleu's The Deck Restaurant ($B-C), is in a big high-roofed building open to the breeze. You sit almost on the beach. The pool and lounging area make it a great hangout, they offer a wide-ranging menu, and the food is very good. Happy hour is 1700-1830 nightly, a favorite being a six-pack of Carib on ice for $24.50 EC.

They have music a couple of nights a week; listen in on the morning cruiser's net (VHF: 66 international, at 0730)) for details.

Phare Bleu's Lightship ($B-D) is in a lovely, old Swedish lightship alongside the dock. It is a wonderful, casual space with nautical museum overtones (ask to see the engine, built in 1925, maybe one of the oldest boat engines still in active use). They open Tuesday to Saturday, 1500-2300, and offer bar food: pizzas, burgers, and salads, plus a big beer and wine selection to wash it down.

The snorkeling off Adam Island and on all the surrounding reefs is fair.

Ashore

Ashore you will find a good little mini-market that sells fresh bread daily, baked by the restaurant, as well as fresh produce, some good frozen meat, and sometimes fresh herbs from the garden

Next door is a car rental agency and Gary Adams, a chiropractor, sailor, and good blues musician (aka Doc Adams).

Grenada and Carriacou

Petit Bacaye

PORT EGMONT

Port Egmont is a completely enclosed lagoon, surrounded for the most part by mangroves. It is quite pretty and makes a first-class hurricane hole. Enter the outer inlet fairly close to Fort Jeudy, keeping an eye out for the reefs that lie near the shore. Fort Jeudy is developed, and there are several prosperous-looking houses on the hill. Anchor anywhere in the inner harbor. Or you can anchor outside, off the little beach at the inner end of Fort Jeudy, but keep an eye out for the shoal off the northern end of the inlet.

The southwest shore of Port Egmont, from the inner harbor all the way out to Point Egmont, is currently being developed. The inner harbor is Grenada's best hurricane hole. The main people behind this development, Andrew Bierzynski and Geoffrey Thompson, are both local, and, as developers go, have concern for the environment. They have done a magnificent job to this point,

with a new bridge over the mangroves and well-laid-out roads that afford lovely views of the bay. If you sail in and fall in love with the place and want to build, contact Renwick and Thompson.

CALIVIGNY HARBOUR

Calivigny Harbour, sometimes called Old Harbour (not to be confused with Calivigny Island), is another enclosed harbor with a fine, palm-shaded beach. It makes an acceptable hurricane hole, though heavy rains can create currents that cause boats to lie sideways to the wind from time to time. The entrance to the outer harbor is between Fort Jeudy and Westerhall Point. You must have good enough visibility to see the reefs off Fort Jeudy. The shoals coming out from Westerhall Point are deeper and harder to see, though they often cause breaking seas. Stay with the devil you can see. Find the reef off Fort Jeudy and follow it into the outer harbor. This entrance can be hairy in heavy winds and large swells, and I would only recommend it to sailors with a lot of experience in reef navigation. When passing into the inner harbor, favor the Fort Jeudy side, as a shoal extends out from the sand spit. Anchor anywhere in the inner harbor.

In the deepest recesses of the bay, Mangrove Hide-Away [$C-D], run by Rhoda Benoit, is a largish informal restaurant and bar with wifi, TV, pool, and table tennis. Use their dock for your dinghy, but take care; it is due for a rebuild. They keep some macaws,

PHARE BLEU BAY
PORT EGMONT
CALIVIGNY HARBOUR
FORT JEUDY
WESTERH

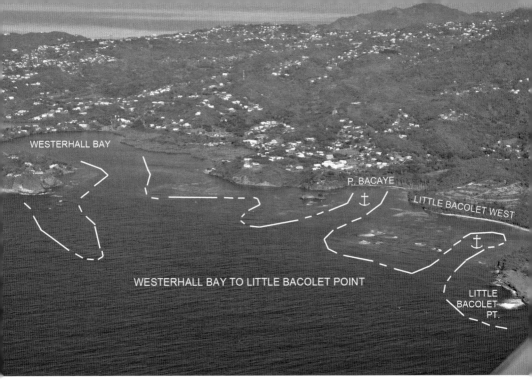

WESTERHALL BAY

P. BACAYE

LITTLE BACOLET WEST

WESTERHALL BAY TO LITTLE BACOLET POINT

LITTLE BACOLET PT.

and wild tortoises, iguanas, and other birds roam freely. They open every day from 0800 and serve pizza and a choice of good daily specials. Thursday nights is coconut bakes and saltfish souce, Saturday is soup day, with a choice of good local soups. Try the mannish water if you dare, but don't ask about the ingredients till you have finished.

Aubrey's is a bar/restaurant/shop right at the entrance to Westerhall Estate, where you can catch a bus to town. If you turn right at the main road and walk a while, you come to the Coop supermarket. See also *Petit Bacaye*, which is a fair walk away.

WESTERHALL POINT

Westerhall Point is an attractive housing development, with well-tended grounds, easily seen by walking up from Calivigny Harbour. Westerhall Bay is a protected anchorage if you tuck up in the southeast corner of the bay, behind the mangroves. In rough conditions the entrance is tricky and the exit heads straight into wind and sea. I would suggest anchoring in Calivigny Harbour and walking over to take a look

before you attempt this.

Theresa has some nice, very reasonably priced apartments overlooking Westerhall Bay, good for those in Phare Bleu or anywhere on the south coast. Call 443-5779.

PETIT BACAYE

Petit Bacaye and Little Bacolet West are two great little anchorages, so small that four boats in either would be a crowd. Space in both is limited enough that I recommend dropping the main before you enter. Petit Bacaye is an idyllic little bay, full of flowers and palm trees, with a little island you can swim to. It has a micro-hotel of the same name [$B-D, often closed], with a few thatch-roofed rooms, a small bar and restaurant, and a tree top platform in the lovely gardens. If it opens it does so from 1100 to 1800 for lunch and snacks. Take a book, swim, and laze away a day. Entering is strictly eyeball navigation. A visible rock on the western reef helps.

The entrance to Little Bacolet West is narrow: follow Little Bacolet Point and stay just outside the fringing reef. Development has just begun here. This is generally a calm hideaway.

Grenada and Carriacou

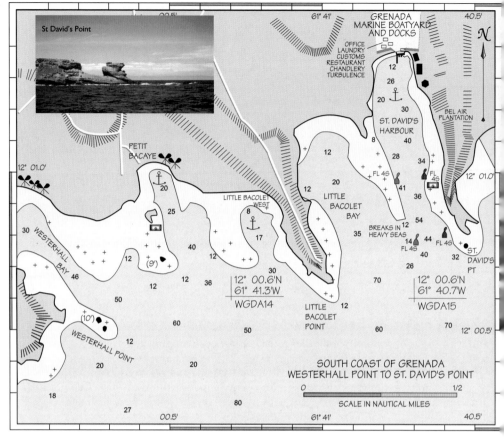

ST. DAVID'S HARBOUR

St. David's Harbour lies 1.2 miles east of Westerhall Point. Many years ago, sailing ships would sail in here to load up on spices and produce bound for Europe. Although never the site of a town, it was an important harbor. It is deeply indented enough to be well protected, and the reefs at the entrance reduce the swells when the trades turn south of east. It can rock a little, in which case a stern anchor to face you out of the bay is a good fix. Wind and current can switch around, so leave far more room between anchored boats than you would expect. St. David's Harbour is a lovely bay with a narrow sandy beach, palm trees, and jungly vegetation crowding down to the waterfront. A pleasant breeze keeps things cool.

Grenada Marine is a haul-out operation for those who want the pleasingly rural atmosphere of Grenada. It is the kind of yard where you can swim right off the beach after work. They must do something right, as about 60 percent of their customers return. Owners Jason and Laura Fletcher have 10 acres at the head of the bay and can take up to 250 boats.

The entrance is easy if you approach in good light, provided you have correctly identified the bay. The reef dividing St. David's from Little Bacolet is much harder to see than the one off St. David's Point, so favor the St. David's Point side of the channel, staying in deep water. Part of the channel is buoyed with red and green markers. They flash about every four seconds. St. David's is well situated if you come down the east coast of Grenada, and it is an easy downwind sail from here to the other south-coast anchorages.

408

Regulations

St. David's Harbour is a port of entry, with customs and immigration. Customs is there every Monday to Thursday from 0800 to 1600. Immigration will come anytime.

Communications

Grenada Marine has free wifi. If you don't have a computer, ask in the office.

General yacht services

Grenada Marine [VHF: 16] is a work and storage yard with room for 250 boats. They use a 70-ton Travelift, which is specially designed at 32 feet wide to haul catamarans as well as monohulls. Yachts of up to 12-foot draft can be hauled. After hauling, a hydraulic stacking trailer puts yachts close together. Early booking is advisable, as the yard fills up in the summer. Jason manages the yard, and his wife, Laura, the restaurant. The yard is equipped with hurricane tie-downs for every boat, and secure cradles are available for those who want them. Masts are often lifted for hurricane security and they have a state-of-the-art mast storage rack outside the rigging shop. Diesel and water are available on the outside of the hauling pier. A 300 foot work dock comes out into the bay, dockage is available and they offer reliable moorings in the bay.

As more people are doing major refits here, they are building a series of storage lockers where you can take everything off the boat and store it. They have two huge paint sheds, so your boat can be sprayed in ideal conditions.

The office staff are very helpful and will make your hauling arrangements, put you at ease, find you a rental car, or help with sending a fax or making a phone call. You can do your own work or use the yard. Since they can handle all jobs, they aim to have a kind of turnkey service where you can tie your yacht to the dock, give them the keys, and come back months later to find it has been hauled, all the work has been done, and it is on the dock waiting of you.

You can do your own laundry in the machines or send it out to be done with Henry's Safari Tours. He will also fill your cooking gas bottles.

409

ST. DAVID'S HARBOUR
GRENADA

Chandlery

Island Water World has a branch of their chandlery here. This comprehensive and first-rate store carries everything you need and tempts you into buying things you just want. If you don't find it here, ask, as it may be in stock in their larger branch in St. George's. They have a catalog, and anything can be brought in at short notice.

Technical yacht services

The yard has about 90 employees including a good team of technicians (many ABYC) who work in glass, spray Awlgrip, and re-gelcoat finishes. They do proper osmosis treatment. The atmosphere is reasonably dry and they use a heat and vacuum system to dry out the hull completely before recoating. They can apply airless-spray antifouling. Owner Jason, and his assistant Andre, aided by a state-of-the-art computer program, keep track of, and oversee, all the work. The head of the metal department, Dietmar Zuber, is one of the best in the islands. Ben Jeffries who heads the woodwork, is also excellent. They have an office in Port Louis and can do some in-the-water installation or work there.

Their rigging and sailmaking are run jointly with Turbulence and managed by Louis (rigging) and Martin (sails). Masts are stored in custom-made racks, so you can remove yours for extra hurricane security. They can check out your rig while you go away and do any kind of rigging repair, including a whole new rig. (They share a rod-rigging machine with their larger shop in True Blue). The sail department does sail construction, repair, and canvas work.

Grenada Marine's mechanical shop can handle all mechanical repairs, and they are agents for Yanmar, Perkins, Volvo, Northern Lights, and ZF drives, along with some watermakers. You can buy these systems though them. They have a full electronics shop (agents for Raymarine), as well as a complete woodwork shop.

Owners and their crew are welcome to do simple jobs like antifouling, brush painting, and removing shafts and underwater systems.

Ashore

The Galley Bar at Grenada Marine [$D] is a restaurant and hangout for technicians, crew, and owners. It is cheap, cheerful, and

410

right on the waterfront. They do tasty and hearty food, serve lunch and dinner daily, and are open 0800-2100. They sometimes have live music, usually on Fridays.

Just a bay to the east is La Sagesse Hotel and Restaurant, a 12-room hotel owned by Mike and Nancy. It is set in lovely gardens on a gorgeous bay, with one of the longest and broadest palm-backed beaches in Grenada. The handsome main building was put up by the infamous Lord Peregrine Brownlow, who closed beach access to locals, which resulted in a "people's reopening" sponsored by revolutionary leader Maurice Bishop.

The garden, beach, and peace make La Sagesse a perfect antidote to boat work. The room prices are reasonable, especially in the off-season, and, if things are quiet, they offer yachtspeople 30 percent discount. Lots of cruisers take advantage of it, in part because Mike and Nancy offer a generous free transport service between La Sagesse and Grenada Marine. If you are staying, they will run you over and back whenever you want, and if you are not staying they will happily collect you and bring you over for lunch or dinner.

Their beachfront restaurant is open all day from 0800 till 2200, with informal lunches and romantic fine dining at night. They use fresh ingredients and offer some of Grenada's best seafood. This is a great escape from the boatyard and work. If you have time, you can walk over the hill for lunch.

When you get tired of work and want a little trip to the country, consider visiting the Laura Herb and Spice Garden, which is a few miles down the road. It is part of an herb and spice marketing cooperative that sells Grenadian herbs and spices worldwide. They have about eight acres under cultivation in the garden, with well-laid-out trails and signposted plants. The atmosphere is peaceful, with birds singing in the trees and plenty of shady areas. You pay a $5 EC entry fee and if you ask (you should), they will give you a tour of the garden and explain the plants to you.

Grenada and Carriacou

St. David's Harbour

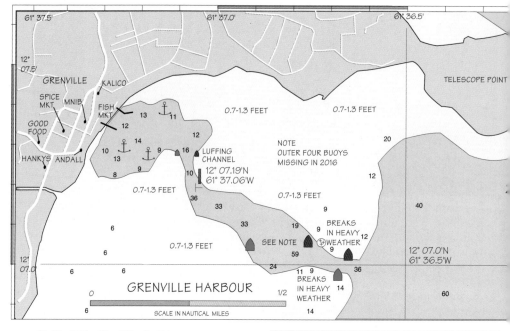

GRENVILLE HARBOUR

SCALE IN NAUTICAL MILES

GRENVILLE

Grenville is Grenada's second largest town and serves most country folk well away from the tourist areas. Most basic services are easily found, grocery stores are well stocked, and restaurants serve up hefty portions of local fare. It lies on the east coast of Grenada, a good harbor for skilled reef navigators who want to go somewhere really local. It is not for charterers on a one-week vacation. It is a port of clearance (by the police station).

Navigation

Grenville is a harbor protected by reefs with wind and sea pushing you in. It is an entrance where you can really get in trouble, should something go wrong. If you are coming from the north you can pass inside or outside Telescope Rock.

Approach only n the morning with the sun behind. The entrance is a narrow passage between two reefs that are shallow enough to get you in trouble, but deep enough you cannot easily see them. If the buoys are in place it is simple, but they are sometimes missing. Leaving Grenville is best in the afternoon with the sun behind.

The alignment of the church over the buildings below can be helpful; the photo

was taken at the outer entrance. You see the road coming down in front of the church. The channel is over 30 feet deep and the reefs at the entrance are 8-14 feet, breaking in heavy weather, A shallow reef patch lies on the north side, just inside.

Once in the channel, the shallow water is more visible and you should be able to spot the rather nondescript beacon well ahead that marks the beginning of the luffing channel. The beacon is on the shoal, not in deep water. Round it turning to starboard. You should be able to eyeball the shallows here, but with luck the inner buoys will be in place. Both are red, but one has a green top. Pass between them and anchor in the basin leaving plenty of room for any vessels using the main docks.

Pool near Mt. Carmel falls

Boats of yore sailed in and out of this harbor (a few sloops still do), so it can be done, but I don't advise it till you know it well. There is no dinghy dock, and the fishing dock is busy, though fine for a drop off or quick stop. If you want to lock up and leave your dinghy, beaching it north of the fishing dock and locking it to whatever is convenient would be a good option.

Communications

Computer Visioneers is air conditioned and offers sit-down internet access, printing, faxing, and scanning. Find them on the second story of the Grenlec building, on the street north of the Spice Market. The FedEx office is in Rhamdanny & Co, next to Good Food. Most bars and restaurants provide free Wifi for patrons.

Provisioning

There are a few fair-sized grocery stores in town. Kalico, at the north end, just before the main roads merge, carries a good selection of groceries, toiletries, some hardware and appliances. They are open from 0800 until 2000 Monday-Thursday, and until 2100 on Friday-Saturday, and until 1300 on Sundays. If you're doing early-morning provisioning, Andall's, at the opposite end of town, carries similar stock and opens at 0700 daily. Besides street-side vendors, fresh produce and spices can be found in the main building of the Spice & Craft Market in the middle of town. The Marketing Board (MNIB) also sells produce, both local and imported, liquor, and frozen meats and fish. The counter at the back provides baked goods and ready-made breakfast and lunch. They open 0730 -1900 Monday to Saturday, and Sundays from 0900-1300. Across from MNIB you'll find the Meat Market. Visit the fish market vendors every day from 0800 until 1700; 1800 on Fridays and Saturdays. For tools and hardware, visit L.L. Ramdanny & Co., located beside the pharmacy.

Restaurants

Moore's is a sweet little sit down open-air bar and restaurant above Kalico groceries. Newly opened, they serve made-to-order breakfast, lunch, and dinner every day from 0700. The breakfast menu includes sandwiches, wraps, and a local favorite, salt fish and bakes. Lunch and dinner include more of a variety, from pizza to barbecue chicken, rice, pasta, and salad. The Melting Pot, above Andall's, at the opposite end of town, serves up hefty portions of ready-made local fare in addition to baked goods and local juices. They are open from 0800 every day but Sunday

Ashore

Take a bus heading south to Munich and ask to be put off at the Mt. Carmel falls (a 10-minute ride). From the main road, the trail entrance is under the green Mt. Carmel sign and down the concrete steps. This is private land, and you may be asked to pay a small fee. An easy 15-minute hike brings you to a delightful series of pools and falls, great for an afternoon picnic or refreshing swim.

Once at the river, the path splits at a patch of bamboo, where you keep left to get to an impressively vertical wall face of rushing water. Return to the bamboo, cross the river, turn right and follow the path for another few minutes. You will come to a lovely pool beneath a cascading slope, great for swimming and sitting under the falls for a vigorous all-natural back and shoulder massage.

If calling a Martinique regular phone from a foreign country dial + 596 596 + 6 digits
If calling a Martinique mobile phone from a foreign country dial + 596 696 + 6 digits

MARTINIQUE EMERGENCY

Ambulance, (0596) 75 15 75

Cosma (Lifeboat) (0596) 70 92 92 VHF: 16

Dr Monique Roussi, Marin (0596) 58 90 16, mroiussi@wanadoo.fr

Dr Deloge, Marin (0596) 74 98 24

Nurse Stephanie Eustache, (0696) 68 39 58/(0696) 27 94 75

Hospital, (0596) 50 15 15

Medical emergency (emergency doctors), (0596) 63 33 33/60 60 44

Police Emergency, 17

Police headquarters, (0596) 63 00 00

Pompiers (fire department) **18**

MARTINIQUE AIRLINES

Air France, (0820) 820 820, (0596) 55 33 00/33, (0596) 55 33 08

Air Caraibes, (0820) 835 835

Air Canada, (0825) 880 881

American Airlines, (0596) 42 19 19

LIAT, (0596) 42 21 11

MARTINIQUE CHANDLERY FISHING GEAR

Accastiallage Diffusion, 0596) 74 62 12

Akwaba, (0596) 66 67 88, akwaba972@ orange.fr, fishing gear

Caraibes Marine, (0596) 74 80 33, 98, (0696) 27 66 05 contact@caraibesgreement.fr

Carene Shop, (0596) 74 74 80, carene.shop @wanadoo.fr

Clippers Ship, (0596) 71 41 61, clippersship@ wanadoo.fr

Coopemar, (0596) 73 37 54, coopemar @ sasi.fr

Intersport, (0596) 63 39 89

Le Grenier du Marin Marin, (0596) 67 98 50, legrenierdumarin@ gmail.com

Le Ship, (0596) 74 87 55, le-ship-martinique@ wanadoo.fr

Littoral, (0596) 70 28 70,

Mer & Sport, (0596) 50 2 75/50 67 59,

Polymar, (0596) 70 62 88, polymar@ orange. fr, Baie de Tourelles,

Sea Services, (0596) 70 26 69, seaservices972@orange.fr

W.I.N.D, (0596) 68 21 28, wind@wind-flag. com

MARTINIQUE COMMUNICATIONS

Cyber Base, Customs computer, Les Anses D'Arlet, 0596-68-62-84

Cyber Deli, (0596) 78 71 43

Cyber Base, St. Pierre, (0596) 62-52-31

Marin Yacht Harbour, Blvd Allegre, Le Marin, 97290, Martinique, (0596) 74 83 83, VHF: 09

MARTINIQUE GENERAL YACHT SERVICES

A&C Yacht brokers, (0596) 74 94 02, 0696 73 70 27, acybmichel @wanadoo.fr

Antilles Nautism, (0696) 43 70 11, Power boat brokers

Bichik Fuel dock, Marin, (0596) 74 70 94, fuel, laundry, car rent

Blanc Marine Marin, 0696 82 65 63, blancmarine1@gmail.com, laundry

Carbbean Yachts (0596) 74 16 70/ (0696) 23 43 38, stephanie.dupland@ caribbean-yachts.com, brokers

CarenAntilles, Fort de France, (0596) 63 76 74, VHF: 16, carenfdf @wanadoo.fr, haul-out

CarenAntilles, Marin, (0596) 74 77 70, VHF: 73, M. De Lucy (0696) 55 77 03, carenantilles.marin@wanadoo. fr, haul out

DCML, Quai de Tourelles, (0596) 71 74 64, (0696) 91 60 48, dcml.sarl@wanadoo. fr, fuel

Dock Cleaner Ecologique, (0696)-92 62 47, dry dock

DYT Yacht Transport, (0596)-74-15-07, 0696 22 88 13 nadine@ yacht-transport.com

Douglas Yacht Services, (0696) 45 89 75, (0596) 52 14 28, VHF: 09, douglas@yachtservices.fr, super-yacht agent

Eva Yachting, (0696) 29 71 14, evayachting@orange.fr, brokers

Kay Zaza, Grand Anse D'Arlet, (0596) 68 74 22, kayzaza972@ yahoo.fr, laundry

Laverie Prolaunet, Anse Mitan (0596) 66 07 79, laundry.

Marin Marina, (0596) 74 83 83, VHF: 09, port.marin@wanadoo. fr

Martinique Dry Dock, (0596) 72 69 40/72 67 48

Pressing du Port, (0596) 74 62 66, Fax: (0596)-74-04-72 lysev@netcourier.com

Surveyor, (Jacques Scharwatt, (0596) 74 02 14, emcscharwatt @wandoo.fr

Somatras Marina, (0596) 66 07 74, VHF: 09, marina3ilets@wanadoo.fr, Anse Mitan, marina

Z'Abricots Marina, (0596) 75 11 57, contact.zabricots@ marinov.fr

MARTINIQUE MISCELLANEOUS

Centre de Decouverte des Sciences de la Terre, (0596) 52 82 42, cdst@cg972.fr

Eau de Tiare, (0696) 37 47 50, (0596) 74 33 57

Fedex, (0596) 42 41 00

Martinique Yachting Association, (0596) 45 89 75, contact@ martiniqueyachtingassociation.fr

Pre Colombian Museum, (0596) 71 57 05

Tourist Department, (0596)-60-27-73

Zoo Martinique, 0596 52 76 08, info@ zoomartinique.com

MARTINIQUE SAILMAKERS CANVAS CUSHIONS

Manu Voiles, (0596) 63 10 61, (0696) 90 76 33, manuvoiles@ wanadoo.fr

North Sails (Sud Voilerie), (0596) 58 24 69/ (0690) 67 89 98, gavin.dove@north-sails.com

Martinik Voilerie, (0696) 32-70-99, martinkvoilerie@gmail. com wanadoo.fr

Incidences, Marin, (0596) 74 77 47, VHF: 16, incidences.cara-ibes@wanadoo.fr

Sellerie Marine, (0696) 16 92 35, contact@sellerie-marine-cj.com

Voilerie du Marin, (0696) 25 94 01, dan. karner@wanadoo.fr

MARTINIQUE TECHNICAL YACHT SERVICES

Alize Composites, glass, gelcoat, paint specialist, (0696)-00-12-34/07 30 75, clippers-ship@wana-doo.fr

Altec Marine, (0696) 28 44 78 machine shop

Antilles Greement, (0696) 50 97 07/29 16 64, antilles-gree-ment@ hotmail.fr

Atelier Sylvestre, (0596) 50 58 91/45 45 56, hydraulics

Azur Spirit, (0696) 50-96-44, Jimy.bouvrais@ azur-spirit.com, Boat sales, charters, repair and guardianage

Caraibes Greement, (0596) 74 80 33, cgmar@wanadoo.fr, rigging, electircs

Caraibes Menuise-rie (0596) 74 80 33, contact@caraibes-menuiserie.fr

Chalmessin, (0596) 60 03 75/60 03 79, welding & fabrication cooking stoves

Continental Marine, (0596) 29-51-11, Yamaha agent

Debrouilla Marine, (0696) 45 92 20, marine electrics

Diginav, (0596) 74 76 62, diginav@wanadoo. fr, electronics

EM Composites., (0596) 62 91 95, (0696) 23 24 57, glass work and painting

Equniox, (0696) 41-33-33, equinoxalu@ gmail.com, welding fabrication.

Caraibes Refrigera-tion, (0696) 82 24 04, patrice@caraibes-refrigeration.com, refrigeration, air-conditioning

Inboard Diesel, (0596) 78 71 96, (0696) 45 95 93, Marin: (0696) 37 35 81 frank@inboarddiesel. com, info@inboarddie-sel.com mechanics

Infologeek, (0596) 67 30 53, 0696 71 79 77, contact@infologeek. com

La Survy, (0596) 74 63 63, (0696) 43 07 53, la.survy@wana-doo.fr, inflatables

Madiana Diesel, (0596) 51 16 13, injec-tor pumps & injectors

Maxi Marine, (0596) 63 75 49, Marin (0596) 74 62 12, info@ maximarinefwi.com, Mercury, Cummins

Mecanique Plai-sance, (0596) 74 68 74, Workshop, (0596) 74 72 72, pc.mecaplai @wanadoo.fr, me-chanics

Meca Boats, Marin, (0696) 03 74 41, vanille-st@hotmail. com, inboard/outboard repair

Moderne Marine, (0696) 82 40 72, Mercruiser engines

Nautic Froid, (0696) 22 71 13, nauticfroid97290@ hotmail.com

Nautic Services, (0696) 45 61 60, nau-tic.services@hotmail.fr Marin, sandblasting & antifouling

Pochon, (0596) 38-33-45 (0696) 13 91 22, martinique @pochon. com.fr

Propeller Caraibe Services (0596) 63 13 64/(0696) 34 64 10, prop.car.serv@gmail. com

Proto Meca, (0596) 97 15 18, (0696) 26 09 26, protomeca@ hotmail.fr, metal fabri-cation

RM Service, (0696) 72 25 44, repairs, maintenance, remser-vicesnautique@live.fr.

Renovboats, (0596) 57 7928, (0696) 25 01 92 Fort de France, renovboatfwi@gmail. com fiberglass and painting, electrics.

Sarl A2M, (0696) 70 66 25, (0596) 53 74 85, 2m972@orange. frmetal fabrication

Sea Services, (0596) 70 26 69, rigging

SMS, (0596) 71 09 31/ (0696) 22 48 70, plein-sud972@wanadoo.fr, boat signs

Tilikum, (0696) 22 79 89/ (0596) 74 67 03, VHF: 16 tilikum@wa-nadoo.fr, refrigeration

Tony Crater, (0596) 74 66 60, welding and fabrication

Tony Boats, (0696) 26 55 65 outboards

Yes, (0596) 65 05 24, (0696) 45 29 87, yescaraibes@hotmail. com, electrical

MARTINIQUE TRANSPORT

GD location, (0596) 58 27 89, (0696) 30 09 90, gd location@ orange.fr

Europcar, Central, (0596) 42 42 44, Fort de France, (0596)

Madin-Loc,(0596) 74 05 54, madin-loc @ wanadoo.fr

Nad in Car, (0596) 61 14 00, (0596) 61 25 88

Jumbo Car, (0596)-74-71 77, (0696) 90 10 67

Velo Club Aosa Cap 110 (0696) 25 34 18, JVLH@orange.fr

Vincent Thomas (0696) 07 54 37, taxi. norden.vincent@gmail. com. English speak-ing, good taxi

MARTINIQUE PROVISIONING

Appro Zagaya, (0596) 74 39 75, (0696) 07 16 29, cathy@appro-zagaya. fr

Champion at Centre Annette, (0596) 74 85 85

Eden Bio, (0596) 74 77 77, bioma-rine.972@orange.fr

Le Millesime, (0596) 38-74-12/0696 26 33 65, cavemillesime@ orange.fr

Martinique - St. Lucia

Port-Apporte, (0696) 25 82 94, contact@port-apporte.fr

Simply (0596) 59 17 13

Vatier, (0596) 70 11 39, impex.vatier@wanadoo.fr

MARTINIQUE FUN SHOPPING

Levalois Racing, (0596) 73 11 96, CS-gas, personal protection

Ozar, (0596) 38 44 07, (0696) 29 80 99

Sea Services, (0596) 70 26 69, fine casual clothing including *Saint James*

MARTINIQUE BANKING

Change Caraibes, (0596) 60 28 40/73 06 16

Martinique Change, (0596) 66 04 44

MARTINIQUE RESTAURANTS

Antonio Beach,(0596) 78 17 36, $B-C

Aux Poisson D'Or, (0596) 66 01 80,$C

Beach Grill, (0596) 78 34 02 $B-C

La Baie, (0596) 42 20 38 $B-C

L'Alsace a Kay, $C-D, (0596) 67 53 65, (0696) 77 68 67, phm.glaciere@hotmail.fr

Le Black Pearl, (0696) 56 01 82 $A-C

Le Littoral, (0596) 71 58 98/0696-44-20-61, $B-C

Le Mayday, (0596) 78 75 24, (0696) 34 50 95, $B-D

Le Petibonum, (0596) 78 04 34 $B

Le Reservoir, $C-D, (0696) 41 83 50/98 71 42

Bidjoul, (0596) 68 65 28, $D

Copacabana, (0596) 66 08 92, $B-C

Delices Caraibes, (0596) 76-96-39, (0696) 81 97 29, delicescaraibes@yahoo.fr $B-C

Fleur de Sel, (0596) 68 42 11, food.atomic7@gmail.com, $A-B

Kano, (0596) 78 40 33, $B-C

KokoaRum, (0596) 48-02-21, $B-C

La Manureva, (0596) 66 16 45, $A-B,

l'Annexe (0596) 38-84-77, $B-C

L'Escapade Marine, (0596)-69 64 26, $D

La Cave a Vin, (0596) 70 33 02, $A

La Dunnette (0596) 76 73 90, $C

Le Coco Neg (0596) 76 94 82, coco-neg@wanadoo.fr $C

Le Mahot (0596) 65 24 38 evelyne.murat@orange.fr $C

Le Tamaya, (0596) 78 29 09, $C

Lina's, (0596) 71 91 92, $D

Mango Bay, (0596) 74 60 89, $D, mangobay@wanadoo.fr

Numero 20 (0596) 66-02-84, $B-C, numero20.martinique@Yohoo.fr

The Yellow, $A-B, (0596) 75 03 59. Theyellow@orange.fr

O Ble Noir (0596) 48 12 01, $D

Sextant (0596) 63 41 24, $D

Ti Payot, (0596) 68 71 78. $C

Ti Toques, (0596) 74 72 32, $B-D

The Crew, (0596) 73 04 14, $B-C

MARTINIQUE CHARTER

Autremer Concept, (0596) 74 79 11/ (0696) 43 55 33 info@autremerconcept.com cats, cruisers, racers

Corail Caraibes, (0596) 74 10 76, corail.mart@wanadoo.fr, cat FP

Dream Yacht Caribbean, (0596) 74 81 68, martinique@dreamyachtcharter.com, cats and monos

France-Escales, (0696) 61 17 37, contact@escales-grenadines.com (charter by the cabin)

Punch Croisieres, (0696) 18 14 00, technique@punch-croisieres.com, all charter

Regis Guillemot Charter, (0596) 74 78 59, (0696) 17 27 37, contact@regisguillemot.com, catamaran charter

Star Voyage, (0596) 74 70 92, lemarin@starvoyage.com, all kinds of charter

VPM, Port de Plaisance, Marin, 97290, Martinique, (0596) 74 70 10, martinique@vpm-bestsail.com, all kinds of charter

MARTINIQUE SCUBA DIVING

Alpha plongee, (0596) 48 30 34

Anthinea, (0596) 66 05 26

Case Pilote Diving Club, (0596) 78 73 75/61 60 01

Corail Club Caraibes, (0596) 68 36 36, corail@fr.st

Calypso Plongee, (0696) 45 05 25

Attitude Plongee, (0596) 66 28 73, (0696) 72 59 28

Immersion Caraibes, (0596) 53 15 43/(0696) 33 40 95, chrisreynier@gmail.com

Kalinargo, (0596) 76 92 98, kalinargo2@wanadoo.fr,

Lychee Plongee, (0596) 66 05 26,

Localize, (0596) 68 64 78, (0596) 68 68 88

Mada Plongee, (0696), 51 60 70, madaplongee@hotmail.fr

Marin Plongee, (0596), 74 05 31, (0696), 83 13 51, marinplongee@wanadoo.fr

Natiyabel, (0596) 36 63 01

Nautica Antilles, (0596) 57 15 15, F: (0596) 51 85 56

Paradise Plongee, (0696) 34 56 16

Planete Bleue, (0596) 66 08 79, planbleu@ais.mq

Papa D'Lo, (0596) 78 12 06

ST. LUCIA

ST. LUCIA EMERGENCY OFFICIAL

Customs, Castries, (758) 458-4846, 24-hour; (758) 468-4859

Customs, Marigot, (758) 458-3318

Customs, Rodney Bay, (758) 452-0235

Customs, Soufriere, (758) 459-5656

Customs, Vieux Fort, (758) 468-4933/4

M-Car Medical Center, (758) 453-2552/452-9032, drnega@member-clinic.com

St. Lucia

Rodney Bay Medical Center, (758) 452-8621 docb@candw.lc, (multi services)

Tapion Hospital, (758) 459-2000 (multi services)

Kent Glace, (758) 458-0167, glaceassociates@gmail.com-com, dental surgeon

Police Marine, (758) 452-2595, VHF: 16

Marine Emergency, HELP (4357) VHF:16

ST. LUCIA AIRLINES

Air Caraibes, (758) 453-0357

Air Jamaica, (758) 453-6111, 800-538-2942

American Airlines, (758) 454-6777/6779,

American Eagle, (758) 452-1820/453-6019, **BWIA,** (758) 452-3778

LIAT, (758) 452-3051-3

Travel World, (758) 451-7443/453-7521, travelworldslu@hotmail.com, travel agent, car rental, tours

Virgin Atlantic (758) 434-7236

ST. LUCIA CHANDLERY FISHING GEAR

Johnsons Marine Hardware, (758) 452-0299, chandlery, fishing gear

International Inflatables, (758) 450-8622, 715-9671, info@internationalinflatablesltd.com

Island Water World, (758) 452-1222 IWWSLIAN@candwlc, major chanderly

NAPA, (758) 542-5034, chandlery, auto parts

ST. LUCIA COMMUNICATIONS

IGY Rodney Bay Marina, (758) 572-7200

Lime, (758) 453-9055/6/7

Marina at Marigot (758) 451-4275, marina@ marigotbay.com

ST. LUCIA GENERAL YACHT SERVICES

Ben's Yacht Services, (758) 459-5457, VHF: 16, Cell: (758) 714-8217/484-0708/721-8500, saltibusb @ slucia.com, bensyachtservices@hotmail.com, yacht agent

Fletcher's Vieux Fort Laundry. 758 454 5936; fletcherdrycleaning@live.com

Harmony Yacht Services, (758) 267-4261/518-0081/ 519-7416 VHF: 16, info@ harmonyyachtservices.com, yacht agent

Ian Dusauzay (Reliant Brokerage), (758) 484-3782/484-3782, rbsbroker@gmail.com

Capella Marigot Resort and Marina, (758) 451-4275/728-9948/9, contact. manager@marigotbaymarina.com, if that does not work: (contact.marinaslu@capellahotels.com)

Kessel Marine, (758) 450-0651/ 484-3547/ 720-0100, F; 758 450 0241,kessellc@candw.lc, surveys

Kessel Lisa, (758) 484-0555, Customs brokerage

IGY Rodney Bay Marina, (758) 572-7200, VHF: 16, rbmreservtions@igymarinas.com

Sud's Laundry (758) 486-0718

St. Lucia Yacht Services (758) 452-5057, VHF: 16, fuel

Chateau Mygo has Marigot docks see *Restaurants.*

ST. LUCIA MISCELLANEOUS

Cocao St. Lucie, chocolate factory (758) 728-3131/459-4401, cocoasaintelucie@gmail.com

Face to Face Day Spa, (758) 452-0394/721-9250, facetofaceconsulting@gmail.com

Forestry Department, (758) 457-1427, forest hikes

Home Services, (758) 452-0450, homeservices@candw.lc, real estate

National Trust, (758) 452-5005, E: natrust@candw.lc, hikes

Morne Courbaril, (758) 459- 7340/712-5808

Soufriere Marine Management Assn., (758) 459- 5500, Head Ranger cell: 718-1196, 724-6333, manager cell:719-0579, VHF: 16, smma@candw.lc,

St. Lucia Golf and Country Club, (758) 450-8522/3, golf@candw.lc

St. Lucia Marine Terminals, (758) 454-8739/42, port authority

St. Lucia Tourist Board, (758) 452-4094, slutour @candw.lc

Tropical Discoveries, (758) 458-9656, sales@tropicaldiscoveries.net

ST. LUCIA SAILMAKERS CANVAS CUSHIONS

Lubeco, (758) 454-6025, allain@candw.lc, Castries branch, (758) 452-3912, fitted sheets and matresses

Rodney Bay Sails, (758) 452-8648, (758) 584-0291, rodneybaysails@hotmail.com Full sail loft

ST. LUCIA TECHNICAL YACHT SERVICES

Chinaman, (758) 518-1234, metalwork

Cox Enterprises, (758) 384-2269, glass & paint

Complete Marine Services, (758) 458-3188/485-1141, info@cms-sl.com, yacht/project mangement

Destination St. Lucia (758) 452-8531, Call us on VHF: 72 "DSL" ulrich@dsl-yachting.com, absentee yacht management and repair, all systems

Island Marine Supplies, (758) 450-9879/584-9441, outboard repair, Mariner & Mercury agent.

KL Marine (758) 450-5565, Yamaha

Liferaft & Inflatable Center, (758) 715 9671, 452-8306, 452-8306, info@liferaftandinflatble.com

Mac's Marine, (758) 452-8061/485-1530, macsmarine@gmail.coom, echotec, Mapi outboards

MarinTek, (758) 484-6031/450-0552, marintek@gmail.com electrical, watermakers, Volvo dealer

TECHNICAL YACHT SERVICES (cont)

Mermaid Marine (Elvis), (758) 488-5291, glass/paint

Pride, (758) 284-7948, woodwork

Prudent Repairs, (758) 459-4334, cell: (758) 384-0825, refrigeration

Quick and Reliable, (758) 520-5544/584-6544, QRMS44@gmail.com diesel mechanic

Quick Fix Refrigeration, (758) 484-9016

Remy, (758) 450-2000 woodworking, fixing TVs, cds, etc

Regis Electronics, (758) 452-0205, VHF: 09, stlucia@regiselectronics.com

Ryte Weld Enterprises, (758) 450-8019, metal work

Scribble, (758) 718-0224/572-0224, Jo@scribbledesign.com, boat names, brochures

Tyson, (758) 452-5794/487-5641, cecilgirard@candw.lc woodwork

Tony's Engineering, (758) 715-8719/452-8575, tonysengineering@hotmail.com mechanics

Yacht Services, (758) 718-3888/2781/520-6400, gardiana22@hotmail.com

ST. LUCIA TRANSPORT

Ben's Taxi Service, (758) 459-5457, VHF: 16, Cell: (758) 714-8217/484-0708/721-8500, saltibusb@slucia.com, bensyachtservices@hotmail.com, yacht agent

C.J. Taxi Service, Rodney Bay, St. Lucia, (758) 450-5981/458-4283, Cell: (785) 584-3530, VHF: 16,

Mystic Man Tours, (758) 459-7783/455-9634, info@myticmantours.com

Soufriere Water Taxi Assn., (758) 459-7239/5500, VHF: 16, richie@candw.lc

Theresa Taxi., (758) 384-9197/458-4444 (Vigie)

Taxi Service Marigot, (758) 451-4406, VHF: 16

Sixt RMB, (758) 452-9404, car rental.

Winson Edward Taxi, (758) 584-1183/520-5231, Vieux Fort

ST. LUCIA BANKING

CITS, (758) 452-1529, American Express agent

Royal Bank of Canada, (758) 452-9921,

ST. LUCIA PROVISIONING

Chateau Mygo (Marigot Bay), (785) 451-4772/724-7335, VHF: 16, info@chateaumygo.com

Crown Foods Ltd, (758) 452-0531/285-4197, kevincrownfoods@candw.lc

Glace Supermarket, 758 452-8814/0514/8179, Cell: 484-1415, glaceg@candw.lc

BBs (The), (758) 452-0647, carmenftaylor@gmail.com

Eroline Foods, (758) 459-7125/5299, F: (758) 459-7882

Flower Shack, (758) 452-0555, mail@flowershack.net

MariGourmet, (758) 451-4031, marigourmet@candw.lc

Super J Supermarkets, (758) 457-2000

ST. LUCIA FUN SHOPPING

Bagshaw's, (758) 452-6039

Caribbean Perfumes, (758) 453-7249, caribperfumes@candw.lc

Handicraft Center, (758) 459-3226

La Place Carenage (758) 452-7318, slaspa@candw.lc

Sea Island Cotton Shop, (758) 452-3674

Sunshine Bookstore, (758) 452-2322, sunbooks@candw.lc

The Art Boutique, (758) 452-8071, caribbeanart@candw.lc

Zaka Art Cafe, (758) 457-1504/384-2925/384-5859, zakaart@yahoo.com

ST. LUCIA RESTAURANTS & ACCOMMODATION

Anse Chastanet, (758) 459-7000, $A-C

BB's (The), (758) 452-0647, $B-D

Big Bamboo (758) 455-9171/724-8681, $C-D

Big Chef Steak House (758) 450-0210, bigchefsteakhouse@gmail.com $A-B

Blue Olive, (758) 458-2433/, $A-B,

Buzz, (758) 458-0450/718-0392, $A-B

Cafe Ole, Boardwalk Bar, (758) 452-8726, $D

Capella Marigot Bay, (758) 458-5300, res.marigotbay@capellahotels.com

Chateau Mygo, (785) 451-4772/724-7335, VHF: 16, info@chateaumygo.com, $B-D

Coal Pot, (758) 452-5566, xavier@cand.lc, $B

Delirius, (758) 451-3354, info@deliriusstlucia.com

Doolittles, (758) 451-4974, $B-C

Elena's (758)-458-0576, $C-D

Fire Grill (758) 451-4745, firegrillstlucia@gmail.com

Harmony Beach Restaurant, (758) 459-5050/287-4261, harmonyiii@hotmail.com, $C D

Hummingbird Resort, (758) 459-7232/721-7995/717-3503, VHF 16, Fax: (758) 459-7033, hbr@candw.lc, $A-B

Jacques (758) 453-7249, $B cathy@jacquesrestaurant.com,

Jambe de Bois, (758) 452-0321, VHF:16, $C-D, btipson@candw.lc

JJ's Restaurant & Bar, (785) 451-4076, VHF: 16, $B-C

Kimatrai, (758) 454-6328, $C-D, info@kimatraihotel.com

La Haut, (758) 459-7008, Lahaut@candw.lc, $C-D

Ladera Resort (Dasheen), (758) 459-6623, dasheen@ladera.com.$A-B

Landings Beach Club, (758) 458-7375, $B-C

Mango Bay, (758) 4485-1621/458-3188, judith@marigotbay.com, accommodation

Fond Doux, (758) 459-7545/8/7790, fonddoux@cqndw.lc, $B-C

Old Plantation Yard, (758) 454-6040, oldplant@hotmail.com, $D

Orlando's, (758) 459-5955, $A-B

Pink Plantation House, (758) 452-5422, $B-C

Pirate Bay, (758) 727-9898, ulrich_augustin@hotmail.com, $B

Pizza Pizza, (758) 452-8282, $D

Rainforest Hideaway, (758) 286-0511/ 451-4485, judith@marigotbay.com.$A

Razmataz, (758) 452-9800, $B-C, razmataz@ candw.lc,

Rituals Sushi, (758) 458-4334, $B-D

Spice of India, (758) 458-4234/716-0820, info@spiceofindiastlucia.com, $B-C

St. Lucia Yacht Club, (758) 452-8350, VHF: 16, $D

Still Estate (The), (758) 459-5179, (758) 459-7301, duboulayd@ candw.lc, $B-D,

Stonefield Estate, (758) 453-3483, 453-0394, $B-C

Sugar Beach Resort, (758) 456-8000, viceroyhotelsandresorts.com/sugarbeach@thejalousieplantation.com, $A.

Tapas on the bay, (758) 451-2433, $C-D

Ti Kaye, (758) 456-8101/03, Ti Manje, (758) 456-8118, info@tikaye.com

Villa des Pitons, (758) 459-7797, $C-D

Winsdjammer Landing, (758) 452-0913

Zaika, (758) 459-2452/ 45-zaika, (758) 488-2777, zaikathetaste.slu@gmail.com, $B-C

Zaka Cafe, (758) 457-1504/384-2925/384-5859

Zoe's, (758) 455-9411, $C-D

ST. LUCIA CHARTER

Bateau Mygo, (758)-458-3947, VHF: 16, kiteboarding cruises, bareboat, day, skippered

BBC Yachting, (758) 716-7610/ 458-4643, bbcyachting@ live.com, bareboat, skippered, day charters

Destination St. Lucia Box 2091, Gros Islet, St. lucia, W.I. Call us on VHF: 72 "DSL" Telephone: (758) 452-8531, Fax: (758) 452-0183, destsll@ candw.lc, all charter

Caribbean Yachting, (758) 458-4430 Fax: (758) 452-0742, Ben@candw.lc

Cats, 450-8651, day-charters

Saltwater Services, (758) 451-5965/716-4300. saltwaterservicesltd@gmail.com

The Moorings, 758-451-4357, mooring@candw.lc, all kinds of charter

ST. LUCIA SCUBA DIVING/WATERSPORTS

Action Adventure Divers (AA) (758) 459-5599, 485-1317

Dive Saint Lucia, (758)-451-3483, info@divesaintlucia.com

Buddies Scuba, (758) 450-8406

Island Divers, (758) 456-8101, diving @ tikaye.com

Iyanola Dive

Adventures, (758) 584-5642/720-2017, scuba@ianoladiveadventures.com

Scuba St. lucia, (758) 459-7000, VHF: 16

Windward Island Gases, (758) 452-1514/1339

ST. VINCENT

ST. VINCENT EMERGENCY

Customs Kingstown, (784) 456-1083

Customs Chateaubelair, (784) 485-7907

Customs Blue Lagoon, no number

Emergency, 999 - fire, police, medical

Maryfield Hospital, (784) 457-8991/1300, private hospital

Police, (784) 456-1185

Police Chateaubelair, (784) 458-2229

During Marine Emergencies call St. Vincent Signal Station on VHF: 16 for an appropirate relay.

ST. VINCENT AIRLINES

American Eagle, (784) 456-5000,

Air Martinique, (784) 458-4528/456-4711,

LIAT, (784) 457-1821,

SVG Air, (784) 457 5124, svgair@ vincysurf.com, air charters

ST. VINCENT CHANDLERY FISHING GEAR

KP Marine, (784) 457-1806, kpmarine @ vincysurf.com

ST. VINCENT COMMUNICATIONS

Computec, (784) 456-2691, sales@computecsvg.com

see also Barefoot and Lagoon marina under General yacht Services, Cumberland Bay has bay wide free wifi.

ST. VINCENT GENERAL YACHT SERVICES

Bay Central, (784) 527-3298, 431-1899, water, washing machines

Barefoot Yacht Sails, (784) 456-9526, VHF: 68, barebum@vicysurf.com, sailmake, moorings

Blue Lagoon Marina and Hotel, (784) 458-4308, VHF: 16/68, Bluelagoon@kgroup.vc

Charlie Tango, (784) 458-4720/493-2186/593-1882, info@charlietangotaxi.com, moorings

Ottley Hall, VHF: 68, haul out

Sam Taxi Tours, (784) 456-4338/ 528-3340, F: (784) 456-4233, VHF: 68/16, sam-taxitours @vincysurf.com, Bequia, 458-3686 Sam, Union, 494-4339, shipping, customs clearance

St. Vincent Yacht Club, (784) 457-2827, stvincentyachtclub.com

TMM, Blue Lagoon, T: (784) 456-9608, VHF: 68, moorings

Wallilabou Anchorage, (784) 458-7270, VHF: 68, $C-D, water

MISCELLANEOUS

Dept of Tourism, (784) 457-1502/1957,

Cumberland tour guides, Suzanne, (784) 454-9236, Marsden, (784) 497-3516, Abbey, (784) 531-0237

St. Vincent - Bequia

ST. VINCENT GENERAL YACHT SERVICES continued

Montreal Gardens, (784) 432-6840

Richmond Vale Academy, (784) 492-4058, info@richmondvale.org

ST. VINCENT TECHNICAL YACHT SERVICES

Barefoot Marine Center, (784) 456-9334/9526, VHF: 68, barebum@ vincysurfsurf.com, sail loft, diesel repair. Electronics dept, electronics@ barefootyachts.com

Howard's Marine, (784) 457-4328, VHF: 68, mechanics, inboard and outboard, haul-out

Nichol's Marine, (784) 456-4118, VHF: 68, starter motors and alternators

Oscar's Machine Shop, (784) 456-4390

TRANSPORT

Fantasea Tours, (784) 457-4477/5555, fantasea @ vincysurf.com

HazEco Tours, (784) 457-8634, hazeco@ vincysurf.com

Ivan Oliver Taxi, (784) 529-1222/458-4303, VHF: 68,

Harold Taxi, (784) 493-3779, VHF: 68,

Sam Taxi & Tours, (784) 456-4338, VHF: 68/16, sam-taxi-tours@ vincysurf.com,

ST. VINCENT BANKING

Caribbean Banking Corp., (784) 456-1501,

CITS, (784) 457-1841, Amex agent

ST. VINCENT PROVISIONING

Gonsalves Liquor, (784) 45-1881, F: (784) 456-2645, gonliq@vincysurf.com

Gourmet Food, 456-2987/2983/528-3188, charm_dev@ yahoo.com

Greaves C. K., Kingstown (784) 457 1074, Fax: (784) 456-2679, Arnos Vale, (784) 458-4602, ckgreaves@ vincysurf.com

ST. VINCENT RESTAURANTS & ACCOMMODATION

Beachcombers, (784) 458-4283, F: (784) 458-4385, beachcombers @ vincysurf.com, $B-C

Beach Front Restaurant, (784) 458-2853, VHF: 68/16, $B-C

Beni, (784) 434-9328, VHF: 16, benett@ vincysurf. com, $C

Black Baron, (784) 485-7904, VHF: 16, $B

Driftwood, (784) 456-8999, $B-C

Flow Wine Bar (784) 457-0809, cell: 494-0869, & **Flowt Beach Bar** (784) 456-8435, $C-D, andrewwilliams@flowwinebar.com

Grand View Grill, (784) 457-5487, $C-D

High Tide, (784) 456-6777, hightide@ vincysurf.com, $B-D

Mareyna Bar and Grill, (784) 457-5233, $C-D

Mariner's Hotel, (784) 457-4000 French Vrnda Restaurant(784) 453-1111, $A-B

Marsy Beach Bar, (784) 458-2879/ 430-8437, VHF:16, $C-D

Mojito, (784) 530-2791/496-6352, $C

Oleander, (784) 456-1989, info@oleander-corner.com

Paradise Beach Hotel, (784) 457-4795,info @ paradisesvg.com

Pirate Grill, (784) 495-5758, $D

Rock Side Cafe, (784) 456-0815/430-2208, $C, rosimorgan@ vincysurf.com

Surfside Restaurant, (784) 457-5362, $B-C

The Loft, (784) 458-4308, $A-C

Wallilabou Anchorage, (784) 458-7270, wallanch@vincysurf.com, VHF: 68, $B-C wallanch@gmail.com

Wilkie's Restaurant, (784) 458-4811, $A-B, grandview @vincysurf.com

Young Island Resort, (784) 458-4826, VHF: 68, $A

ST. VINCENT CHARTER

Barefoot Yacht Charters, (784) 456-9334/9526, VHF: 68, Email:barebum @ vincysurfsurf.com, all kinds of charter boats.

Dream Yacht Charters, Blue Lagoon, (784) 451-1525/494-4321, mtaylor@ dreamyachtcharters.com, all kinds of charter

Horizon Yacht Charters, (473) 439-1002, Info@horizonstvincent.com, all kinds of charte

ST. VINCENT SCUBA DIVING

Dive St. Vincent, (784) 457-4714, VHF: 68

Indigo Dive, (784) 493-9494, info@ indigodive.com

Serenity Dive, (784) 528-8030, serenity-dive@hotmail.com

BEQUIA EMERGENCY

Police, (784) 458-3211,

Customs, (784) 457-3044, VHF: 16

Imperial Pharmacy, (784) 458-3373,

Bequia Hospital, (784) 458-3294, VHF: 74

BEQUIA CHANDLERY FISHING GEAR

Dockside Marine, (784) 458-3360, bequiaexpress@ vincysurf.com

Grenadine Yacht Equipment,(784) 458-3347,VHF: 16 gye-bequia@ vincysurf.com

Lulley's Tackle Shop, (784) 458-3420, lulley@ vincysurf.com

Piper Marine, (784) 457-3856/495-2272. VHF: 68

BEQUIA COMMUNICATIONS

ACS, (784) 458-3967/454-9519, DHL and computer store

Bequia Technology Center, (784) 458-3045, info@bequiatech.com

Fedex, Solana's, (784) 458-3554,

Maria's Cafe, (784) 458-3116, mitchell1@ vincysurf.com

RMS, (784) 458-3556, VHF: 16/68/10, rms@ vincysurf.com

BEQUIA MISCELLANEOUS

A Caribbean Wedding, (784) 457-3209/528-7444

Bequia Land & Home, (784) 458-3116/533-0677, bequialandandhome @vincysurf.com

Caribbean Compass, (784) 457-3409

Caribbean Woods, (784) 457-3000,caribwoods@vincysurf.com

Grenadines Island Villas, (784) 529-8046/455-0696, island-villas@ mac.com

Kenmore Henville, (784) 457-3212, Cell: (784) 529-5005, VHF: 77, marine photographer

Old Hegg Turtle Sanctuary, (784) 458-3245/3596, oldhegg@ vincysurf.com

Serenity Day Spa, (784) 532-2559, serenity_dayspa@yahoo. com

BEQUIA GENERAL YACHT SERVICES

African, (784) 593- 3986,VHF: 68, yacht management, deliveries, moorings, provisioning

Bequia Marina, (784) 495-0235/431-8418, capt.waterdog@gmail. com VHF: 68, docking, water

Daffodil Marine, (784) 458-3942, VHF: 67,daffodil-harris@ yahoo.com, water, fuel, laundry

Lighthouse Laundry, (784) 458-3084,VHF: 68, laundry

Miranda's Laundry, (784) 530-6865,VHF: 68, laundry

Papa Mitch, (784) (784) 458-3116, laundry

BEQUIA SAILMAKERS CANVAS CUSHIONS

Allick Sails, (784) 457-3040/458-3992, VHF: 68

Bequia Canvas, (784) 457-3291, VHF: 68, beqcan@vincysurf. com

Grenadine Sails, (784) 457-3507/3527, VHF: 16/68, gsails@ vincysurf.com

BEQUIA TECHNICAL YACHT SERVICES

Caribbean Diesel, (784) 457-3114/ 593-6333, VHF: 68, mechanics, fuel polishing

KMS Marine Services, (784) 530-8123/570-7612

Piper Marine, (784) 457-3856/495-2272. VHF: 68, rigging

Simpson Engineering, (784) 457-3692/526-6729, dee. williams @hotmail. com, VHF: 68, mechanics

Winfield Sargeant, (784) 458-3058/526-0882, VHF: 68, friendshipside2@ yahoo. com, varnishing etc.

BEQUIA TRANSPORT

Admiralty Transport, (784) 458-3348, admiraltrans@ vincysurf. com

Challenger Taxi Service, (784) 458-3811, VHF: 68, challenger-taxi@ yahoo.com

De Best, (784) 458-3349/530-4747, VHF: 68, friendshipgapt @ vincysurf.com

Gideon Taxi, (784) 458-3760/527-2092, VHF: 68, gideontaxi@ vincysurf.com, taxi, rentals

Handy Andy, (784) 458-3722, VHF: 68, rentals

BEQUIA FUN SHOPPING

Bequia Bookshop, (784) 458-3905, bequiabookshop@ hotmail.com

Claude Victorine, (784) 458-3150, claudevictorine @ vincysurf.com

Local Color, (784) 458-3202, chappell@ vincysurf.com

Oasis Gallery, (784) 497-7670, bequiaboathouse @vincysurf.com

Solana's, (784) 458-3554, solanas@ vincysurf.com

Whaleboner, (784) 458-3233,VHF: 68

BEQUIA PROVISIONING

Bequia Foodstore (784) 457-3928

Doris Fresh Foods, (784) 458-3625, VHF: 68

Knights Trading (784) 458-3218, knightstrad @ yahoo.com

Linas, (784) 457-3388

Nature Zone, (784) 458-3793

Mama's, (784) 457-3443

Maranne's Ice Cream, (784) 458-3041

Select Wines, (784) 457-3482

BEQUIA RESTAURANTS & ACCOMODATION

Bequia Beach Hotel, (784) 458-1600, info@ bequiabeach.com

Black Pearl at Gingerbread, (784) 456-9868, VHF: 68, $A-C

Coco's Place, (784) 458-3463, VHF: 68, $B-D

Colombo's, (784) 457-3881, $B-D

Daffodil, (784) 458-3942, VHF: 67, $B-D

Dawn's Cafe, (784) 492-6508, $D

De Reef, (784) 458-3412/3484, $D

Devil's Table, (784) 458-3900/3222 VHF: 68, $A-D

Fig Tree, (784) 457-3008, figtree@ vincysurf.com, $B-D

Firefly Hotel Bequia, (784) 488-8414/458-3414, VHF:10, liz@ fireflybequia.com, $A

Frangipani, (784) 458-3255, VHF: 68, $B, info@ frangipanibequia.com

Gingerbread Hotel, (784) 458-3800, $D, info@gingerbreadhotel.com

Kingsville Apartments, (784) 458-3404/3932, kingsville @ vincysurf.com

L'Auberge des Grenadines, (784) 457-3555, VHF: 68, $A, auberge@ caribrestaurant.com

La Plage, (784) 458-3361, $B-C

Mac's Pizzeria, (784) 458-3474, VHF: 68, $C-D, beqvilla @ vincysurf.com

Maria's Cafe, (784) 458-3116, mitchell1@ vincysurf.com, $D

Papa's, (784) 457-3443, $B-D

Porthole, (784) 458-3458, $C-D

Sugar Reef, (784) 458-3400, info@sugar-reefbequia.com

Tantie Pearle's, (784) 457-3160, $B-C

BEQUIA RESTAURANTS & ACCOMODATION-Continued

The Yacht Club at Bequia Marina, (784) 529-6074/457-3361, VHF: 68, info@bequia-marina.com, $B-D

Tommy Cantina, (784) 457-3779. $C

Whaleboner Inn, (784) 458-3233, VHF: 68, whalebonerbequia @ hotmail.com $C-D

BEQUIA CHARTER

Island Time Holidays, grenadines@ vincy-surf.com

Sail Grenadines, (784) 533 2909, 530-8399, info@sailgrena-dines.com

Sail Relax Explore, (784) 457-3888/495-0886/9

Tradewinds Cruise Club, (784) 457-3407, info@ tradewind-scruiseclub. com

BEQUIA SCUBA DIVING

Bequia Dive Adventure, (784) 458 3826, VHF: 68, adventures@ vincysurf.com, dive shop

Dive Bequia, (784) 458-3504/ 495-9929, VHF: 68,16, cathy@ divebequia.com, dive shop

MUSTIQUE MISCELLANEOUS

Mustique Moorings, (784) 488-8363,VHF: 16/68

Horse riding, (784) 488-8316

Berris Little (Slick) (784) 527-9043

Mustique Company, (784) 488-8000,

Airport, (784) 488-8336

Doctor,(784) 488-8353

MUSTIQUE SHOPPING

Coreas, (784) 488-8479

The Purple House, (784)- 528-8788 boutique, elegant wear

MUSTIQUE RESTAURANTS & ACCOMMODATION

Basil's Bar,(784) 488-8350,VHF: 68, $A-B

Cotton House, (784) 456-4777, VHF: 68, cottonhouse@ vincy-surf.com $A

Firefly Mustique, (784) 488-8414, (784) 488-8514, VHF: 10, stan@ fireflymustique.com, $A-B

The View, (784) 488-8807/532-2421, $C-D

MUSTIQUE SCUBA DIVING

Mustique Watersports, (784) 488-8486, VHF: 16/68

CANOUAN COMMUNICATIONS

Tamarind Bay Hotel, (784) 458-8044

CANOUAN GENERAL YACHT SRVICES

John's Marine Services VHF: 16, cell: (784) 593-0875, moorings, water, fuel, ice

Marcus Marine Services VHF: 16, (784) 492-3230/458-8375, moorings, water, fuel, ice

CANOUAN TECHNICAL YACHT SERVICES

Gazimo Marine Service (784) 491-1177, gazimo.marine@ gmail.com

CANOUAN TRANSPORT

Gazimo Mule Rental (784) 491-1177, gazimo.marine@ gmail.com

Phyllis Taxi, (784) 593-4190

CANOUAN HOTELS/ RESTAURANTS

Phyllis, (784) 593-4190, $C-D

Pink Sands Club, (784) 458-8000, $A

Sea Grape, (784) 482-7601/492-7601/494-2050, $C-D

Tamarind Bay Hotel, (784) 458-8044,VHF: 16, info@tamarind.us, $A

The Mangrove, (784) 482-0761/593-3364, VHF:16/68, $C-D

CANOUAN SCUBA DIVING

Canouan Dive Center, VHF: 16, (784) 528-8073, info@can-ouandivecenter.com

MAYREAU RESTAURANTS & ACCOMODATION

Dennis's Hideaway, (784) 458-8594, VHF: 16/68, $B-C

J & C Restaurant, (784) 458-8558, VHF: 16/68, $B-C

Island Paradise, (784) 458-8941/8068, VHF: 68, $B-C

Righteous & de Youths, (784) 458-8203, VHF: 68, $B-C

Salt Whistle Bay Restaurant, (784) 430-4088, 458-8005, $A

PALM ISLAND

Palm Island VHF: 16, Tel: (784) 458-8824, Fax: (784) 458-8804

Patrick Chavailler, Palm island doctor and artist, (784) 458-8829, palmdoc@vicysurf.com

UNION ISLAND EMERGENCY

Customs, (784) 458-8360

Health Center, (784) 458-8339

UNION AIRLINES

Eagle Travel, (784) 458-8179, eagtrav@ vincysurf.com, VHF: 68

UNION COMMUNICATIONS

Erika's Marine Services, (784) 485-8335/ 494-1212, F: (784) 485-8336 VHF: 68, info@ erikamarine.com

Internet Cafe, (784) 485-8326,

UNION MISCELLANEOUS

Happy Kite, (784) 430-8604/458-8734, happykitegrenadines@ gmail.com

Pro Center Kitesurf (784) 432-8821/434-0764, info@ kitesurf-grenadines.com

Tobago Cays Marine Park, (784) 485-8191, info@tobagocays.com

Southern Grenadines Animal Kindness (784) 485-8287

UNION GENERAL YACHT SERVICES

Anchorage Yacht Club, (784) 458-8221, VHF: 16/68, stay@ unionanchorage.com, docking, laundry

Bougainvilla, (784) 458 8878/8678, laquarium@ vincysurf.com, VHF: 16, docking

Erika's Marine Services (784) 485-8335, VHF: 68, info@ erikamarine.com

Unigas (784) 485-8969/526-4206, naert@gmail.com

UNION TECHNICAL YACHT SERVICES

Island Marine Special, (784) 458-8039, VHF: 16, mechanics

Marine Tech Services, (784) 526-8510/432-4208, VHF: 16, marinetechsev@gmail.com, all yacht systems, mechanical and electrical

Unitech Marine Services, (784) 458-8002/530-5915, unitech@vincysurf.com, VHF: 16, mechanics & glass work

UNION TRANSPORT

Marine Tech Services, (784) 526-8510/432-4208, VHF: 16, marinetechsev@gmail.com, Bike rental and tours

Sail Grenadines Bike Rental, (784) 533 2909, katie@sailgrenadines.com

UNION RESTAURANTS & ACOMMODATION

Anchorage Yacht Club, (784) 458-8221, VHF: 16/68, $A-B

Barracuda, (784) 458-8571/527-5163, giancarlotiezzi@gmail.com

Big Citi, (784) 458-8960/494-8424, $D

Bollhead Bar & Restaurant, (784) 593-1660, $C

Ciao Pizza, (784) 430-5006,$C

Clifton Beach Hotel, (784) 458-8235, VHF: 68, $B-C

Janti's, (784) 455-3611, happyisland@unionisland.com $D

L'Aquarium, (784) 430-4088/458-8678, caribbeadelicacy@yahoo.com, $B-C

La Cabane, (784)434-6704, $C-D

Lambi, (784) 458-8549, VHF: 68, $B-C

Limelite Bar, (784) 485-8486, $D

Shark Attack, (784) 527-2694/2691, sharkattack2006@hotmail.com, $C

Sparrow Beach Bar, (784)-458-8195/593-1713, free shuttle, 454-1888, info@grenadinesislandestates $B-D

Sun, Beach & Eat, (784) 531-6965/530-5913, VHF: 16, njide12@hotmail.com, seckietours@gmail.com, $C

The Loft, (784) 532-8687, $C-D

The Snack Shack, (784) 434-0764, $C-D

UNION FUN SHOPPING

Clifton Boutique, (784) 458-8235

Driftwood Boutique, (784) 434-0764

L'Atelier Turquoise, (784) 458-8734, anniefrance@vincysurf.com

Mare Blu, (784) 494-8880

UNION PROVISIONING

Captain Gourmet, (784) 458-8918, VHF: 08 (USA) capgourmet@vincysurf.com

Island Grown, (784) 532-2914/529 0935

UNION CHARTER

Sail Grenadines, (784) 533 2909, In UK, 800-321-3801, katie@sailgrenadines.com

Wind and Sea, Union I., Bougainvilla, T: (784) 458-8678/8678, windandsea@ vincysurf.com

UNION SCUBA DIVING

Grenadines Dive, (784) 458-8138/455-3822, VHF: 16/68, E: gdive@ vincysurf.com

PSV RESTAURANTS & ACCOMODATION

Petit St. Vincent Resort VHF: 16, (784) 458-8801, $A-B, Jean-Michel Cousteau Diving, 784-458-8984

GRENADA, CARRIACOU & PM

PETITE MARTINIQUE GENERAL YACHT SERVICES

B&C Fuels, (473) 443-9110, Fax: (473) 443-9075,BandCfuels@gmail.com, VHF: 16, "Golf Sierra" fuel, water

PM COMMUNICATIONS

Millenium Connection, (473) 443-9243, ieshodinga @yahoo.co.uk

PM CHANDLERY TECHNICAL SERVICES

E&B Hardware, 473-443-9086

PM RESTAURANTS & ACCOMMODATION

Palm Beach, (473) 443-9103, VHF: 16, emmanuel.palmbeach@ygmail.com, $C-D

Melodie's Guest House, (743) 443-9052/9093/9108,

Seaside View, (473) 443-9007,

PM SHOPPING

Matthew Shoppng Center, (473) 443-9194

Millenium Boutique, (473) 443-9243,

CARRIACOU EMERGENCY

Customs, Tyrrel B. 443-9379/6100 Hills. (473) 443-7659

Hospital emergency, 774

CHS, (473) 443-8247, chscarriacou@gmail.com

Carriacou Animal Hospital, (473) 443-7177

CARRIACOU AIRLINES

LIAT, (473) 443-7362

Bullen, (473) 443-7468/7469, Fax: 443 8194, travel agent

CARRIACOU GENERAL YACHT SERVICES

Bullen, (473) 443-7468/7469, Fax: 443 8194 vbs@spiceisle.com, duty free fuel

My Beautiful Launderette, (473) 403-0164/405-1148

Shorebase Services, 443-6449

Carriacou Marine, (473) 443-6292/6940/533-8927, info@carriacoumarine.com

CARRIACOU SAILMAKERS CANVAS CUSHIONS

In Stitches, (473) 443-8878/406-4117, VHF: 16, asmelt@gmaill.com

Sling's Uphostery, (473) 403-4416

CARRIACOU TECHNICAL YACHT SERVICES

Dominique Wer (473) 407-1151, VHF: 16, aluminum & stainless (Genevieve's therapeutic massage)

Hezron Wilson Refrigeration, (473) 443-6212

Manny Workship (473) 416-1169/406-9460

Paul O Regan, (473) 416-5491, rigging, chandlery, general help, T.M.M.carriacou@ gmail.com

Tall Man Electrics, (473) 403-6505

Tool Meister, (473) 445-8178, tmmachine @spiceisle.com, machine shop, mechanics

CARRIACOU TRANSPORT

Ade's Dream, (473) 443-7317, adesdea@ spiceisle.com, car rentals

Bubbles Turtle Dove Taxi, VHF:16, (473) 407-1029/443-7194

Cuthbert Snagg, (473) 443-8293, bikes, marine eco-tours

Linky Taxi Service, Tel: (473) 443-7566, Cell: (473) 406-2457/416-5358, VHF: 16,

Lambi Queen Cycles, (473) 443-8162, VHF: 16

CARRIACOU RESTAURANTS & ACCOMMODATION

Ade's Dream, (473) 443-7317, $D

After Ours', (473) 443-6159, $C

Bayside Bar and Restaurant (473) 443-8008, $C-D,

Gallery Cafe, (473) 443-7069, gallerycafe@outlook.com, $D

Iguana Cafe, (473) 443-6292, VHF: 16, carriyacht@ spiceisle. com, $D

Kayak Kafe, (473) 406-2151, sallyandjinger@yahoo.co.uk, $C-D

La Playa, (473) 410-4216, $C-D

Lambi Queen, (473) 443-8162, VHF: 16

Lazy Turtle, 473-443-8322, VHF: 16 lazyturtlewi@gmail. com $B-D

Le Petit Conch Shell, (473) 443-6174/7233 $C-D

Off the Hook, 473-533-4242, $C-D

Slipway Restaurant, (473) 443-6500, info@ slipwayrestaurant.com, $B-C

Sundowners (473) 533 3430, $C-D

Swampy Jo, 473-443-8831/8760, $D

The Green Roof, (473) 443-6399, greenroof@ spiceisle. com

Twilight, (473) 443-8530, VHF: 16, $C

CARRIACOU FUN SHOPPING

Fidel Productions, (473) 435-8866/415-0710, 443-6185, 443-7366

CARRIACOU PROVISIONING

Ade's Dream, (473) 443-7317, F: (473) 443-8435, adesdea@ spiceisle.com

After Ours', (473) 443-6159, $C

Alexis Supermarket, (473) 443-8530

Bullen, (473) 443-7468/9, VHF: 16 vbs@ spiceisle.com

Patty's Deli (473) 443-6258, shop@pattysdeli.com

Twilight, (473) 443-8530, VHF: 16

CARRIACOU DIVING

Arawak Divers (473) 443-6906/457-5112, VHF: 16, arawakdivers@spiceisle.com

Deefer Diving, (473) 443-7882, VHF: 16, info@deeferdiving.com

Lumbadive Ltd., (473) 443-8566, cell: (473) 457-4539, VHF: 16, dive@ lumbadive. com

GRENADA EMERGENCY/ OFFICIAL

Emergency: police/ coastguard 911

Customs, Prickly Bay, (473) 444-4509,

Customs, St. George's, (473) 440-2239/2240

Customs, Phare Bleu Marina, (473) 443-3236

Coastguard, 399

Dr. Mike Radix, (473) 444-4855/443-4379, emergency: 443-5330

Dr. Jennifer Isaacs (dermatology), Grenville St. St. George's, (473) 440-3963, jenniferjapalisaacs@ gmail.com

Robbie Yearwood (surgeon), Ocean House, Grand Anse (afternoon) (473) 444-1178, ho: (473) 444-5624, rosbrad@ spiceisle.com

Hospital, (473) 440-2051

Police, 911,

Port Authority, (473) 444-7447, VHF: 16, port

St. George's School of Medicine, (473) 444-4271

Spice Isle Imaging Center, (473) 444-7679/415-2754/405-4557, images@ spiceisle.com

True Blue Pharmacy, (473) 444-3784

St. Augustin Medical Clinic, (473) 440-6173-5, staugms@ spiceisle.com, private hospital.

Sunsmile Dental Clinic, (473) 444-2273

Island Dental Care, (473) 437-4000, islanddentalcare @ yahoo.com

GRENADA AIRLINES

American Airlines, (473) 442-2222

British Airways, (800) 744-2997 (local 800)

BWIA, (473) 444-1221-2/4134

LIAT, (473) 440-2796-8,

GRENADA CHANDLERY FISHING GEAR

Budget Marine, 473-439-1983, budmargd@ spiceisle.com

Marine World, (473) 440-1748

Island Water World, (473) 435-2150, (473) 435-2152, sales@ islandwaterworld.com

North Yachts Shop, (473) 432-1201, info@ northyachtshop.com

Wholesale Yacht Parts, (473) 458-6306/ 763-8387/ Miami: (305) 454-2971, sherri@wholesale yachtparts.com

Grenada

Spice Island Fish House Tackle Shop, (473) 435-0189

GRENADA COMMUNICATIONS

Grenada Yacht Club, St. George's, Grenada, (473) 440-3050, VHF: 16

Fedex, (473) 440-2206

Onsite Software Support, Marquis Mall, (473) 444-3653

Renwick & Thompson, (473) 440-2198/2625, renthom@spiceisle.com, Western Union & DHL agent

Spice Island Marine Services, P.O. Box 449, St. George's, Grenada, (473) 444-4257/4342, VHF: 16, info@ spicislandmarine.com

Carenage Cafe, St george's, (473) 440-8701

GRENADA GENERAL YACHT SERVICES

Bob Goodchild Surveys, (473) 443 5784/407 4388, surveyor@flyingfishventures.com

Clarkes Court Haul out and Marina, (473) 439-3939/405-2739, info@clarkescourtmarina.com

Grenada Marine, (473) 443-1667, Port Louis, (473) 444-1667, info @grenadamarine.com, haul out

Grenada Yacht Club, (473) 440-3050, VHF: 16, gyc@spiceisle.com, marina, fuel

Henry's Safari Tours, (473) 444-5313/407-0522 F: (473) 444-4460, safari@ spiceisle.com, VHF: 68, laundry, yacht agent

Horizon Yacht Management, 473-439-1000/535-0328, info@horizongrenada.com. marina, moorings

Island Dreams, (473) 443-3603/ 415-2139, VHF: 74, info@ islandreamsgrenada.com, absentee yacht project management

Le Phare Bleu Marina & Resort, (473) 444-2400/ 409-7187 contact@ lepharebleu.com

Secret Harbour Marina (473) 444-4449, VHF: 16,71, secretharbour@spiceisle.com, marina, fuel

Prickly Bay Marina, (473) 439-5265, info@pricklybaymarina.com, VHF: 16, marina, fuel

Port Louis Marina, (473) 435-7431/2, dockmaster (24-hour) (473) 415-0820, VHF: 14, reservations@ cnportlouismarina .com

Rock Taxi, (473) 444-5136, VHF: 16, absentee yacht management

Spice Island Marine, (473) 444-4257/3442, Cell: (473) 407-4439, simco@spiceisle.com, haul-out

Spronk mega yacht Services, (473) 444-4662/407-3688/439-4369/ 443-5663, claire@ spronksprovisioning .com

Survival Anchorage, (473) 443-3957/459-3502, VHF: 16, gas refills

The Multihull Co, (473) 440-1668

Whisper Cove Marina, (473) 444-5296, $A-D, info@whispercovemarina.com.

GRENADA MISCELLANEOUS

Conservation Kayak, (473) 449-5248, info@ conservationkayak.com

Jouvay Chocolate, (473) 437-1839

Grenada Board of Tourism, (473) 440-2279, (473) 440-6637, gbt@spiceisle.com

Grenada Chocolate Factory, (473) 442-0050, info@ grenada-chocolate.com

Grenada Golf Club, (473) 444-4128

Mayag, (473) 443-1667, mayagadmin@gmail.com

Peter Evans, (473) 444-3636, cell: (473) 441-7864, real estate & yacht broker

River Antoine Rum factory, (473) 442-7109/442-4537

Sunnyside Gardens, (473) 440 1588/456-5096/406-1381

Spice Island Retreat Spa, (473) 231-6167, info@spiceisland retreat.com

GRENADA SAILMAKERS CANVAS CUSHIONS

Clarke's Upholstery, (473) 414-1827, v-clark-upholstery@hotmail.com

Johnny Sails & Canvas, (473) 444-1108/9619,

Neil Pryde Sails, (473) 537-5355

Rollin' Stitches, (473) 420-6010/534-7290, rollinstitches@ gmail.com

Turbulence, Grenada (473) 439-4495, turbsail@spiceisle.com

GRENADA TECHNICAL YACHT SERVICES

Anro Agencies, (473) 444-2220/1/444-4269, info@anroagencies.com, Yanmar, Mariner, Mercruiser

AJS Enterprises, (473) 440-0192, yacht names

Albert Lucas, (473) 440-1281, machine shop

Cottle Boat Works, (473) 444-1070, cottleboatworks@ spiceisle.com, shipwright

Dave's Gas Service, (473) 444 5571,davidbenoit@ spiceisle.com, stoves

Driftwood, (473) 459-9859, driftwood-grenada@gmail.com, woodwork

Essential Engineering, 473-414-7316, essentialengineeringgrenada@gmail.com, VHF: 68, All engines, outboartd and inboard.

Horizon Yacht Management, 473-439-1000/535-0328, info@ horizongrenada.com

Lagoon Marine, (473) 440-3381, refrigeration

Marine Tech Grenada, (473) 406-1800, marinetechgnd@gmail.com

ModOne, (473) 439-6631/405-6631/415-2417, computers, wifi

McIntyre Bros, (473) 444-3944/5, (473) 444-2899, macford@spiceisle.com, mechanics inboard an outboard

Nauti Solutions, (473) 416-7127/7537, svmagnum@hotmail.com, mechanics

425

On Board Refrigeration Electrics and Electronics, (473) 420-3041, 21gunz-chrome@live.com

Palm Tree Marine, (473) 443-7256/407 2783, info@ palmtreemarine.com, mechanics

Protech Engineering Services, (473) 403-6371/538-3080, mncadore@gmail.com

Royan's, (473) 443-3868, 406-0894, VHF: 68, royanwelding@ hotmail.com, royanjoseph44@gmail.com, metalwork

Safe Yachts, (473) 410-0241, VHF: 68, denise@safeyachts. com, absentee yacht/ project management, sewing, cleaning.

Sipyard Marine Services, (473) 405-4767/ 444-4767/ 407-2727, smsgrenada@gmail. com

Subzero Air Control, (473) 440-4072/409-9376, refridge/ac

TechNick, (473) 536-1560/405-1560, tech-nick@ spiceisle.com, welding, fabrication

Tan Tan Sam, 1-473-403-9904/444-5190, varnish, paint, polish.

Turbulence, Grenada (473) 439-4495, St. David's: (473) 443-2517, turbsail@ spiceisle.com, rigging, electronics

Ultimate Filtration, (473) 440-6887, Cell: (473) 407-4989, outboards, fuel tank cleaning

Underwater Solutions, (473) 456-3927, brettfairhead@ yahoo. com

Waterfall Marine, info@waterfallmarine. com

X-Marine, (473) 420-2421/415-0180, info@ xmarine.info

GRENADA TRANSPORT

Marina Taxi Association, (473) 444-1703, VHF: 16, taxi

K&J Taxi (473) 409-9621/ 440-4227, VHF: 16, kjtours@ genada-explorer.com

Grenada Adventure, 473-444-5337/ 473-535-1379, adventure@ spiceisle.com

Henry's Safari Tours, (473) 444-5313, F: (473) 444-4460, safari@ spiceisle.com, VHF: 68

Maxwell Adventure Tours, (473) 444-1653, cell: (473) 406 4980, VHF: 68

McIntyre Bros, (473) 444-3944/5, (473) 444-2899, macford@ spiceisle.com

Rock Taxi, (473) 444-5136, VHF: 16/10

Survival Anchorage, (473) 443-3957/459-3502

Telfor Bedeau (473) 442-6200, hiking guide

Y&R Car Rentals, (473) 444-4448, Y&R@ spiceisle.com

GRENADA BANKING

CITS, (473) 440-2945, AmEx agent

National Commercial Bank (The), (473) 444-2265, (473) 444-5501, ncbgnd@ spiceisle.com

GRENADA FUN SHOPPING

Ace Hardware/Napa, (473) 440-5090

Arawak Islands, (473) 444-3577, F (473) 444-3577

Fidel Productions, (473) 435-8866

Tikal, (473) 440-2310, fisher@spiceisle.com

Yellow Poui Art, 473-440-3001, yellow-poui@ spiceisle.com

GRENADA PROVISIONING

Best Little Liquor Store in Town, (473) 440-2198/3422, VHF: 16 "Rhum Runner base", renthom @ spiceisle.com

Essentials, (473) 444-4662

Food Fair, (473) 440-2573, hubbards @ spiceisle.com

Floral Treasures, (473) 444-2832, floral-treasuresgrenada@ gmail.cm

Le Boucher, (473) 456-3232, leboucher. inc@gmail.com

North South Trading, (473) 444-1182, nst. wines@spiceisle.com

Merry Baker, (473) 435-6464, themerry-baker1@gmail.com

Spronk's Provisioning, (473) 407-3688/444-4662, F: (473) 444-4677

The Wine Shoppe, (473) 444-1182, nst. wines@ spiceisle.com

Phare Bleu Mini Mart, (473) 443-4232

See also Spronk Megayacht Services and Henry Safari Tours in General Yacht Services

See also Spronk Megayacht Services and Henry Safari Tours in General Yacht Services

GRENADA RESTAURANTS & ACCOMMODATION

Amici Miei, (473) 444-4662, $B-C

Aquarium, (473) 444-1410, aquarium@ spiceisle.com, $B-D

Bananas, (473) 439-4662, (473), F: (473) 444-4677, $B-D,

BB's Crab Back, (473) 435-7058, bbscrabback@ hotmail .com $B-C

Beachside Terrace, (473) 444-4247, F (473) 444-1234, $B-D, flambo@spiceisle.com

Calabash, (473) 444-4334, $A

Carib Sushi, (473) 439-5640, $B, caribsu-shi@ spiceisle.com

Choo Light, (473) 444-2196, $D,

Coconut Beach, (473) 444-4644, $A-B

Dodgy Dock, True Blue, 473-439-1377, $A-D

Dragon Bay Hideaway, 473-533-8077/231-0808, $D kelelectric@hotmail. com

Edge, Grand Anse, $B-C

Grenada Yacht Club, (473) 440-3050, VHF: 16, $D

Helvellyn House, (473)-442-9252/418-6405, sark@spiceisle. com

Taffy's, (473) 538-0863, VHF: 16, SD

Junction, (473) 420-1086, $C

La Boulangerie, (473) 444-1131, $D papaya@ spiceisle. com

La Sagesse, (473) 444 6458, LSnature@ spiceisle.com

Little Dipper, (473) 444-5136, VHF: 10/16, $D

Mango Cottage, (473) 407-4388, mangocottagegrenada@gmail.com, accommodation

Mangrove Hide-Away, (473) 443-2782, 405-0244, $B-C

Mount hartman Estate, (473) 407-4504, reservations@ mount hartmanbay.com, $A

Museum Bistro, (473) 416-7266, $D, tapas

Nutmeg, (473) 440-3654, ($C-D)

Patrick's, (473) 440 0364/ 449 7243, $B-C

Petit Anse, (473) 442-5252, info@ petite-anse.com, $B-D

Petit Bacaye, (473) 443-2902, $B

Red Crab, (The), (473) 444-4424, crab @ spiceisle.com, $A-B

Rose Mount, (473) 444-8069, $D

The Beach House, (473) 444-4455, beachhouse @spiceisle.com, $B

Sails, (473) 440 9747, $B-D

Timbers, (473) 439-4401, $A-B

Tropicana Inn, (473) 440-1586, $C-D

True Blue Bay, (473) 443 8783, windward@ truebluebay.com, VHF: 16, $A-C

Umbrellas, (473) 439-9149, $D

Victory Bar/restaurant, (473) 435-7263, $A-D

Yolo, (473) 435-7263, $A-B

GRENADA DIVING

Aquanauts, (473) 444 1126, VHF: 16, aquanautsGDA@gmail.com

Dive Grenada, (473) 444 1092, info@ divegrenada.com

First Impressions, Whale watching, 473-440-3678, cell:407-1147, starwindsailing@ spiceisle.com

Scuba Tech, (473) 439-4346, info@scubatech-grenada.com

GRENADA CHARTER

Dream Yacht Charters, Port Louis, (473) 4440-8800/536-1187, cats monos, skippered bare.

Horizon Yacht Charters, True Blue, (473) 439-1000, toll free: 1-866 463-7254, info@ horizongrenada.com, all kinds of charter

Footloose Charters, (473) 440-7949, (473) 440-6680, footloos@ spiceisle.com, VHF: 16, yacht agent

John Clement, (473) 406-2064, johnclement80 @hotmail. com johnclement08 @ yahoo.com

TUI Marine (The Moorings and Sunsail), (473) 6661/2/ 405-8633,

OTHER BUSINESSES OF INTEREST

AB Inflatables, see Budget Marine, Grenada

Doyle Sailmakers, 6 Crossroads, St. Philip, Barbados, (246) 423-4600,

Floatinator, www.floatinator.com

Power Boats, (868) 634-4303, VHF: 72 pbmfl @ powerboats.co.tt

Peake Marine, (868) 634-4427/3

Seajet 038 Taisho, The new ecofriendly antifouling that works.

See WIND, Martinique

INTERNATIONAL CHARTER

Ed Hamilton, (207) 549 7855, all kinds of charter

The Moorings, (888)952-8420, sales@moorings.com

INTERNATIONAL YACHT SALES

Multihull Co, +1-215-508-2704, Info@multihullcompany.com 207)

General Index

Anchoring, 45-46
Admiralty Bay, 249-273
Anse a L'Ane, 104-105
Anse Chastanet, 188
Anse Cochon, 181-184
Anse de Canaries, 184-185
Anse D'Arlet (Les), 109-110
Anse Dufour, 105-106
Anse Figuiers, 113
Anse la Raye, 179-181
Anse Meunier, 114
Anse Mitan, 100-104
Anse Noir, 105-106

Baggage (luggage), 18
Baie des Anglais, 136, 137-139
Baie des Tourelles, 65,86,88-89
Baie du Marigot, 111-112
Barrouallie, 221
Bequia, 244-274
Blue Lagoon, 229-240
Boat vendors,
Bois de Nave Falls, 131
Botanical Gardens, 77-78, 93,
   212-225, 238, 370,
Britannia Bay, 275-281
Buccament Bay, 222-223
Bugs, 23-24
Buoyage (beacons), 42

Calivigny Harbour, 406-407
Calivigny Island, 404
Canouan, 282-287
Cap Estate, 165-166
Caribs, 71, 219, 220, 28, see
   also Kalinargo
Carriacou, 326-346
Cas-en-bas, 163-164
Case Pilote, 79-81
Castries, 167-170
Charlestown Bay, 282-287
Chartering, 51-53
Charts, 42-44
Chatham Bay, 318-319
Chateaubelair, 213-215
Chocolate, 16, 22, 142, 164-
   185, 194, 196, 197, 351, 368,
   371, 378
Clarkes Court Bay, 395-403
Clifton, 304-317
CAMMA, 179,186
Cohé de Lamentin, 90
Corbay, (see L'Anse Guyac)
Communications,
 - (see also our directory),
   19-20,
   Martinique, 63, 86, 98, 101,
   114, 119

St. Lucia, 141, 148, 168, 174,
   189, 192, 204
St. Vincent, 209, 219, 226, 233
Bequia, 241, 246-247, 269
Mustique, 275, 279
Canouan, 284
Mayreau, 296
Union Island, 306
Petite Martinique, 324
Carriacou, 237, 329-330, 338
Grenada, 347, 358, 370, 377,
   382, 396, 409, 413

Concord Falls, 351
Cul de Sac Marin (see Marin)
Cumberland Bay, 215-217
Currency (change), 18
Currents, 42
Customs, see also regulations,
   44-45

Dangers, 23-24
Darkview Falls, 214
Diamond Rock, 68-70,
Diving & Snorkeling, 57-59
   Martinique, 104, 15, 106, 109,
   110, 117, 136-137
   St. Lucia, 164, 179, 183, 188,
   190, 196, 199, 202
   St. Vincent, 214, 220, 222-223,
   224, 238-240
   Bequia, 271-272, 274
   Mustique, 281
   Grenadines, 287, 297, 300-
   302, 317
   PSV, 322
   Petite Martinique, 325
   Carriacou, 332, 343
   Grenada, 356, 372-373, 380,
   391
Dogs, 44
Dragon Bay, 356
Drugs, 18

East coast of Martinique, 137-
   138
Email - see Communications
Environment, 34-39

Falls of Baleine, 208
Fish poisoning, 32
Fishing, 30-32, 34
Flag illustrations, shown in
   Islands at a Glance, 63, 141,
   209, 347
Food, 404-412
Fort de France, 83-93

Friendship Bay, Bequia, 273-274
Friendship Bay, Canouan, 287
Frigate Island, 317-318

Garbage, 36-38,
Grand Anse, 370-373
Grand Anse D'Arlet, 107-109
Grand Anse des Salines, 114
Grand Cai, 282-283
Grand de Coi, 290, 292, 304
Grand Etang, 351
Grand Mal, 356
Green Flash, 32
Greetings, 20
Grenada, 347-371
Grenada's East Coast, 353-354,
   412-413
Grenada's South Coast, 374-411
Grenadines, 244-346
Grenville, 412-413
Gros Islet, 146, 147, 163, 164, 16
GPS, 44
tables, 48-49
GSM phones, see Communica-
   tions

Halifax Harbour, 354-355
Happy Hill, 356
Happy Island, 304, 316
Hawaiian sling, 30
Hillsborough, 329-333
Hog Island, 394-395
Holding tanks, 38, 298, 334
Holidays, 33-34
   Martinique, 63
   St. Lucia, 141
   St. Vincent & the Grenadines,
   209
   Grenada & Carriacou, 347
Hummingbird anchorage, 189-19
Hurricanes, see Weather

IATA codes, 22
Immigration, 44, see also regula-
   tions,
Industry, 261
Isle de Ronde, 346
Industrial Zones, 93-98
Jet ski, 20
Kalinargo, 14-15, 210, 225
Keartons Bay, 218-220
Kick'em Jenny, 346
Kingstown, 225-228
Laborie, 200-202
L'Anse Aux Epines (see Prickly
   Bay)
L'Anse Guyac, 283

L'Esterre Bay, 334-336
Le Carbet, 79
Lobster, buying, 32, 39, 254, 279, 300
   regulations, 32, 34, 39, 141 209, 347
Lower Bay Bequia, 248-250, 258
Mail drop (see Communications in the directory)
Malgretout, 197-199
Manchineel, 23-24
Marigot Bay, 172-179
Marin, 118-136
Market (local), 22, 74, 75, 81, 90, 92, 99, 110, 115, 134, 157, 167, 169, 176, 201, 227 258, 279, 286, 303, 397, 308, 331, 368, 390, 413
Martinique, 62-139
Mayreau, 293-297
Medical care, 29-30
Mega-Yachts, see Professional Yachts
Mesopotamia Valley, 212, 238
Mileage table, 43
Mobile phones, see Communications
Montreal Gardens, 212, 238
Montezuma Shoal, 277-278, 281
Moonhole, 273
Mooring, 46, 246
Mount Hartman Bay, 393-395
Mount Pleasant, 254, 269, 270
Museum, 73, 75, 76, 78, 79, 93, 100, 220, 269, 270, 274, 281, 332, 368
Mustique, 275-281
Newlands Reef, 290, 292, 304
Old Hegg Turtle Sanctuary, 269
Ottley Hall, 224
Palm Island, 302-303
Passages
   Carriacou to Grenada, 345-346
   Martinique to St. Lucia, 139
   Northern Grenadines, 240-243
   Southern Grenadines, 288-292
   St. Lucia to St. Vincent, 207
Peggy's Rock, 270
Petit Bacaye, 407
Petit Bateau, 289, 298, 299, 302
Petit Byahaut, 223-224
Petite Anse, 352-353
Petite Martinique, 323-325
Petit Nevis, 274
Petit Rameau, 299. 300
Petit St. Vincent, 320-322
Pigeon Island, Bequia, 272
Pigeon Island, St. Lucia, 145-147, 164

Pinnacle, 292, 310
Phare Bleu Bay, 404-405
Photography, 29
Pitons, The, 199-200
Pointe Borgnesse, 113
Pointe du Bout, 98, 100-104
Point Saline, 374-375
Port Egmont, 406
Prickly Bay, 381-391
Professional Yachts (mega-yachts superyachts), 54-56, 120-121, 128, 129, 134, 148, 150, 156, 172, 192, 193, 225, 253, 274, 298, 306, 314, 360, 364, 384, 390, 394
Quai Ouest, 86
Radio (AM SSB FM), 40
Rameau Bay, 283, 287
Reduit Beach, 146-147
Regatta, 33-34, 270, 327, 332
Regulations, see also customs, 44-45
   Martinique, 63, 73, 79, 85, 101, 107, 110, 114, 119, 137
   St. Lucia, 141, 147, 167-168, 172, 179, 186, 204
   St. Vincent, 209, 213, 215, 218-219, 225, 230
   Bequia, 244, 250-251
   Mustique, 275, 278
   Canouan, 283, 284, 287
   Tobago Cays, 298-299
   Union, 306
   Carriacou, 327, 329, 338
   Grenada, 347, 355, 358, 381-382, 404-405, 409
River Rock Falls, 179-181
Rivière Pilote, 113
Rivière Salée, 96-99
Rodney Bay, 145-165

Saline Bay, 295-297
Salt Whistle Bay, 293-295
Sandy Island, 334-336
Sapphire Falls, 196-197
Schoelcher, 82-83
Seven Falls, 255,351,
Sisters, Carriacou, 327, 333, 327
Sisters, Isle de Ronde, 346
SIOBMPA, 327, 329, 332, 337, 343
SMMA, 179, 181, 185, 186, 188, 190, 192, 202
Snorkeling, see Diving & Snorkeling
Soufriere, 185-200
South coast of Martinique, 111-138
South coast of St. Vincent, 228-240

South Glossy Bay, 287
Spearfishing, 30
Special events, 32-34
Ste. Anne, 114-117
St. David's Harbour, 408-411
St. George's, 357-370
St. Lucia, 140-205
St. Pierre, 71-78
St. Vincent, 208-240
Star charts, 12-13
Suntan, 20
Superyachts, see Professional Yachts

Telephones, see Communications
Thieves, 28
Tides, 42
Tobago Cays, 298-302
Transport, 22
   Martinique, 63, 93, 133-134
   St. Lucia, 141, 156, 165-166, 168, 176, 193
   St. Vincent, 208, 238
   Bequia, 224, 268-269
   Mustique, 275
   Canouan, 286-287
   Union Island, 316
   Carriacou, 326, 330, 341
   Grenada, 347, 369, 390, 403
Trinity Fallls, 214
Trois Ilets, 98-100
Troisant Bay, 295
Trou au Diable, 188
Trou Etienne, 100
Trou l'Oranger, 179
Troumakar Bay, 215
True Blue, 376-380
Tyrrel Bay, 337-344

Union Island, 303-319
Vermont Nature Trails, 219, 220
Vieux Fort, 203-205
Vigie, 167, 170-171
Volcano, 71, 193, 196, 197, 207, 210-212, 213, 214, 219, 220, 229, 238
   underwater, 346

Wallilabou, 218-221
Water Skiing, 20
Weather, 39-42
Westerhall Point, 407
Windjammer Landings, 166
Windward Anchorage, Mayreau, 297
Woburn, 387, 394, 395, 398, 400, 402, 403
Young Island Cut, 229-240

CRUISING GUIDE TO THE VIRGIN ISLANDS

*By Nancy &
Simon Scott
18th Edition,
2017-2018*
ISBN 978-0-9978540-0-8
6 x 9, 350 pp. **$34.95**

Completely re-designed and updated style, with more Virgin Island photography and full color detailed anchorage charts, these guides have been indispensable companions for sailors and visitors to these islands since 1982. Includes a free 17 x 27 color planning chart, with aerial photos of some of the anchorages. Covers the Virgin Islands including all the U.S. and British Virgin Islands!

- GPS co-ordinates for every anchorage
- Anchoring and mooring information and fees
- Customs, immigration and National Park regulations
- Particulars on marina facilities and the amenities they offer
- Water sports-where to go and where to rent equipment
- Shore-side facilities, restaurants, beach bars, shops, provisions, internet connections

Everything you will need to help make your vacation an enjoyable and memorable experience in a concise easy-to-use format.

VIRGIN ANCHORAGES

*By Nancy & Simon Scott
2012 Edition*
ISBN 978-0-944428-84-9
8.5 x 11, 96 pp. **$29.95**

Virgin Anchorages features stunning color aerial photography of 46 of the most popular anchorages in the Virgin Islands. Graphic overlays aid in navigating to safe anchorages. This is an excellent companion to Cruising Guide to the Virgin Islands.

LEEWARD ANCHORAGES

By Chris Doyle
ISBN 0-944428-82-7
8.5 x 11, 91 pp **$29.95**

Leeward Anchorages shows aerial photographs of all the favorite anchorages from Anguilla through Dominica with graphic overlays to illustrate dangerous and safe passages from a bird's eye view. Carefully researched and recorded by Chris Doyle, safe passages, markers, buoys and hazards are all marked to guide you to safe, enjoyable anchorages. This is a companion book to use with The Cruising Guide to the Leeward Islands.

THE CRUISING GUIDE TO THE NORTHERN LEEWARD ISLAND

*Chris Doyle
2016-2017*
ISBN 978-0-9914550-5-8
6 x 9, 288 pp **$29.95**

This fourteenth edition has been split into two guides. The Cruising Guide to the Northern Leeward Islands covers the islands of Anguilla, St. Martin, St. Barts, Saba, Statia, St. Kitts, Nevis, Redonda, and Montserrat. This guide is an essential tool for all cruisers sailing this region. Chris Doyle spends months sailing these islands to update each edition. Included are over one hundred up-to-date color sketch charts, full color aerial photos of most anchorages, island pictures, and detailed shore-side information covering services, restaurants, provisioning, travel basics and island history. Information is linked to the author's website where you can download the GPS waypoints given in the sketch charts, learn of essential updates, print town maps, and obtain links to local weather, news, and businesses. A free 17 x 27 inch waterproof planning chart of the northern and southern Leeward Islands is now included in each edition!

THE CRUISING GUIDE TO THE SOUTHERN LEEWARD ISLANDS

*Chris Doyle
2016-2017*
ISBN 978-0-9914550-6-5
6 x 9, 324 pp **$29.95**

This fourteenth edition has been split into two guides. The Cruising Guide to the Southern Leeward Islands covers the islands of Antigua, Barbuda, Guadeloupe, Marie Galante, the Saintes, and Dominica. This guide is an essential tool for all cruisers sailing this region. Chris Doyle spends months sailing these islands to update each edition. Included are over one hundred up-to-date color sketch charts, full color aerial photos of most anchorages, island pictures, and detailed shore-side information covering services, restaurants, provisioning, travel basics and island history. Information is linked to the author's website where you can download the GPS waypoints given in the sketch charts, learn of essential updates, print town maps, and obtain links to local weather, news, and businesses. A free 17 x 27 inch waterproof planning chart of the northern and southern Leeward Islands is now included in each edition!

Advertisers Index

AB Inflatables, 21
Admiralty Transport, 268
Animal Kindness, 313
Anro Agencies, 388
Aquarium, Grenada, 375
Aquarium, Union, 309
Arawak Dive, 344
Atelier Turquoise, 311

B & C Fuels, 325
Barefoot Yacht Charters, 27
Barefoot Sails and Services, 233
Barracuda, 313
Basils Bar, 280
Ben's Yacht Services, 147, 192
Bequia Bookshop, 258
Bequia Canvas, 254
Bequia Marina Yacht Club, 245
Big Chef steak house, 161
Black Pearl, 261
Bleu des Isles, 74
Blue Lagoon Hotel & Marina, 231
Bob Goodchild, surveyor, 362
Bougainvilla, 309
Bread Basket, 159
Budget Marine, 349

Cacem, 94
Cafe Ole, 159
Café Soliel, 235
Cap Gourmet, 311
Caraibes Marine, 125
Carenne Shop, 127
Carib Sushi, 373
Chamelion Café, 262-263
Chateau Mygo, 173
Chris Joseph, 157
CK Greaves. 227
Clarkes Court Bay Marina, 399
Clippers Ship, 123
Cottle Boatworks, 388

Daffodil Marine, 252
De Reef, 266
Deefer Diving, 333
Diginav, 129
Dive Bequia, IFC, 1, 271
Dive St. Lucia, 165
Dockside Marine, 255
Doris Fresh Food, 257

Douglas Yacht Services, 120
Doyle Offshore Sails, OBC
Driftwood, 401
DSL, 152
Ed Hamilton, 53
Erikas Marine Services, 240, 308 ,252

Fidel Productions, 300, 336
Fidel, 368
Fig tree, 262
Floatinator, 21
Flower shack, 157

Gallery Café, 342
Gazimo, 287
Gideon Taxi Services, 268
Gingerbread, 261
Grand View, 236
Grenada Marine, 409
Grenada Yacht Club, 360
Grenadines Dive, 300

Happy Kite, 311
Henry Safari, 352-353, 395
Home Services, 150
Horizon Yacht Services, 363,
Horizon Yacht Charters, 234, 377
House of Chocolate, 368
Hummingbird, 191

In Stitches, 340
Inboard Diesel Services, 80
Incidences, 128
Island Dreams, 363, 400
Island Water World, OC flap

Jacques/Caribbean Perfumes, 163
Jambe de Bois, 145
Johnson's hardware, 151
JT Pro Center, 304

Kayak Café, 331
Kent Glace & Associates, 150

La Cabane, 309

La Phare Bleu, 405
la Sagesse, 411
Ladera Resort, 195
L'Alsace a Kay, 74
Lazy Turtle, 341
Le Kano, 70, 102
Le Ship, 122
Life Raft & Inflatables, 154, 155
Linky's Taxi, 331
Lubin taxi, 269
Lumba Dive, 343

Mango Bay, 135
Mango Projects, 400
Mare Blu, 309
Maria's Café, 264
Marie's Restaurant, 312
Marine tech Grenada, 365
Marine Tech Services, 307
Marintek, 153
Martinique Yachting Assn., 111, 121
McIntyre Bros, 389
Mecanique Plaisance, 131
Multihull Co, IC flap

Neil Pryde Sails, 352
North Sails, 127
North South Trading, 391

On Board Refrigeration, 389
Orlando's, 189

Palm Beach Restaurant, 325
Palm Tree Marine, 400
Papas, 263
Paradise in Black and White, 176
Pattys Deli, 329
Peak Yacht Services, 41
Piper Marine, 253
Plantation House, 260
Polymar, 88
Port Louis Marina, 361
Porthole, 256
Power Boats, 206
Prickly Bay Marina, 385
PSV, 322

Rainforest Hideaway, 177
Razmataz, 160

Regis Electronics, 153
Relais du Parc Naturel St. Pierre, 76
Renwick & Thompson, 346
Rockside Café, 219
Rodney Bay Marina, 143
Rodney Bay Sails, 152
Royons Welding, 365

Sail Grenadines, 251, 304
Sam Taxi, 230
Sea Services, 86,87, 118,119
Seckies, 319
Slipway Restaurant, 342
SMMA, 185
Sparrows, 314
Spice Island Marine, 383
Spronk Limited, 356, 378, 402
St Lucia Yacht Club, 162
St. Lucia Tourist Board, 171
Sugar Reef, 266
Survival Anchorage, 394

Tamarind Beach Hotel, 285
Tamaya, 75
Technick Yacht Services, 386
The Moorings, 35
Travel World, 166
True Blue Bay, 379
Turbulence, 387
Twilight Bar, 312

Underwater Solutions, 363
Unigas, 307
Unitech, 307

Ville de Case Pilote, 81
Ville de Sainte Pierre, 64-67
Whisper Marina, 396

Wilkies, 236
WIND, 95, IBC

X-Marine, 398